NIAGARA 1814

NIAGARA 1814

America Invades Canada

Richard V. Barbuto

University Press of Kansas

Published by the University Press of Kansas (Lawrence, Kansas 66049), which
was organized by the Kansas Board of Regents and is operated and funded by
Emporia State University, Fort Hays State University, Kansas State University,
Pittsburg State University, the University of Kansas, and Wichita State
University

Library of Congress Cataloging-in-Publication Data

Barbuto, Richard V.
  Niagara 1814 : American invades Canada / Richard V. Barbuto.
    p. cm.—(Modern war studies)
Includes bibliographical references and index.
  ISBN 0-7006-1052-9 (alk. paper)
  1. Niagara Frontier (N.Y.)—History—War of 1812—Campaigns. 2.
Lundy's Lane, Battle of, 1814 3. Fort Erie (Ont.)—History—Siege,
1814. 4. Chippewa, Battle of, 1814. 5. United States—History—War
of 1812–Campaigns. I. Title. II. Series.
  E355.6.B37 2000
  973.5'23—dc21   00-008820

British Library Cataloguing in Publication Data is available.

Printed in the United States of America

10 9 8 7 6 5 4 3 2 1

The paper used in this publication meets the minimum requirements of the
American National Standard for Permanence of Paper for Printed Library
Materials Z39.48-1984.

To Joseph V. Damiano, uncle and mentor,
whose character and love of history are burned indelibly
into my soul.

CONTENTS

Photo section follows text page 162.

PREFACE

My interest in the War of 1812 began during indoctrination training at West Point in the summer of 1967. We new cadets were told that our gray uniforms were in recognition of Winfield Scott's brigade at the Battle of Chippawa. It seems that the British commander mistook the gray-clad soldiers for Buffalo militia such as those his troops had easily beaten before. As the Americans came on steadily through shot and shell, maneuvering smartly and firing with telling effect, this same commander was said to have exclaimed, "Those are regulars, by God." His mistaken identification in the opening stage of the battle was believed to have contributed to the British defeat that day. After two years of tactical failure, the U.S. Army could once again experience the pride it had felt at Yorktown.

The Chippawa battlefield on the Niagara River was within fifty miles of my hometown. I had always envied my Virginian classmates their many battlefields. Now I had my own. Its magical lure would bring me back many times. On these excursions along the Niagara, I discovered Forts George, Niagara, and Erie, as well as Queenston Heights and Lundy's Lane. The more I walked the battlefields and the more I read about the battles, the more fascinated I became with this last campaign to invade Canada. I wondered why Jacob Brown's army, arguably the best trained, best led, and best supplied of any to be fielded during the war, had failed in its bid to sever Upper Canada from the British Empire. It is in pursuit of an answer to this question that I wrote this volume.

I thank my adviser, Professor Theodore A. Wilson, for his advice and criticism, but mostly for his support. Donald E. Graves, William B. Skelton, and Roger J. Spiller reviewed early drafts of the manuscript, and their professional advice was most helpful in advancing this project. I acknowledge a debt of gratitude to my many friends and colleagues from the Combat Studies Institute of the U.S. Army Command and General Staff College. Their insights, shared over many years, directed my inquiry and sharpened my judgment. I thank the librarians of the Combat Arms Research Library at Fort Leavenworth, the Canadian Forces Command and Staff College Library in Toronto, and the Buffalo and Erie County Historical Society archives. Time and again these people went the extra mile in securing sources critical to this investigation. My mapmaker, Barbara Baeuchle, earns high marks for adding clarity to this story. My wife, Ann, served for the past seven years as chief editor, coach, and cheerleader. To her goes my enduring appreciation and love.

INTRODUCTION

The historiography of the 1814 campaign in the Niagara Valley is somewhat thin. The subject is treated superficially in general military histories of the war. However, the major battles that make up the 1814 campaign—Chippawa (spelled Chippewa in American reports and in most American-produced histories; I use the British spelling), Lundy's Lane, and the siege of Fort Erie—have enjoyed scholarly investigation. The excellent work of Jeffrey Kimball, Donald E. Graves, Joseph Whitehorne, and John C. Fredriksen informs this attempt to deal with the campaign comprehensively and to link it firmly to British and American strategic and diplomatic frameworks. Why is campaign analysis important?

In 1975 an American colonel was speaking to his North Vietnamese counterpart during a round of negotiations in Hanoi. "You know you never defeated us on the battlefield," boasted the American. After pondering a moment, the North Vietnamese replied, "That may be so, but it is also irrelevant." The profound implications of this exchange prompt an examination of the conceptual links between battlefield success or failure and the ultimate realization of strategic success. A model of warfare divided into three levels—tactical, operational, and strategic—serves to identify the vital links between activity on the battlefield and the accomplishment of national goals. Armed with the several tools this model provides, it becomes obvious why the military histories of the 1814 campaign and its constituent battles are often unsatisfying. Previous writers have not clearly traced the linkages between the national goals of the belligerents and the guidance and resources provided to the commanders in the theaters of operations and to the commanders on the fields of battle.

The methodology of this study links military activity at the tactical level to the accomplishment of national aims. The national aims are derived from, and sometimes expressed as, the causes of the war. American historians have created for themselves a veritable cottage industry in their attempts to discern the causes of the War of 1812. An understanding of the causes of this conflict can lead to an understanding of how an invasion of Canada might address the national goals of the American republic in its early childhood. Historians have pointed to myriad causes, either singly or in combination: impressment, orders in council, and the desire to seize Canadian land, suppress the Indians, redress insults to the national honor, and even advance republican ideology.

Historians have reached no consensus on the causes of the war. Nor was there consensus among Republicans on the hierarchy of the various national goals or how the possession of Canada would attain those goals. If security of an expanding frontier was the issue, then annexation of Canada was the solution. However, would the occupation of Canada resolve maritime issues? Would it affirm republicanism at the expense of the Federalists?

Although disagreement remains on the causes of the war and on the rank ordering of war goals, the competing American and British strategies can be discerned fairly clearly from the historical record. It is from these competing strategies that I derive a methodology of three components.

First, I treat the campaign as an integral part of a larger strategy directed by the heads of government of the belligerents. Britain was fighting a global war against Napoleonic France, a war of survival in which the defense of British North America was clearly a sideshow. Likewise, the United States was involved not only in invading Canada but also in suppressing the Indians and defending an extensive coastline from the world's premier naval power.

Second, my study is comparative and balanced among the participants. Too many of the previous histories failed to portray the Indians as key players. Often the Indians' role was depicted as one of pointless savagery. The Americans, the Canadians, and the British were not fighting for their survival. The Indians were.

Third, this study is broadly based. It gives nearly equal analysis of the preparatory phase of the campaign as of its execution. It examines in sufficient depth the political, diplomatic, economic, and social aspects of America's last attempt to conquer its northern neighbor and now closest ally.

In spite of considerable improvement within the American military and naval forces since the start of the war, the American 1814 campaign came to nothing. Failure stemmed from several sources. The federal government did not concentrate sufficient military force in the critical theater. Strategic confusion permeated the American military establishment from the commander in chief down to the commanders in the field. These strategic failures were nearly redeemed in execution by a few aggressive and determined commanders who led well-trained, hard-fighting soldiers. However, the American army and navy commanders in the theater of operations made enough poor decisions to tip the balance in favor of the British.

The British ultimately succeeded not only because of American mistakes but also because of the flexibility of their defense. The defenders maintained their freedom of action because neither side could decisively control the waters of Lake Ontario. Nonetheless, British aggressiveness, entirely appropriate in 1812 and 1813, put the success of their defensive efforts at serious risk in 1814.

All told, the four-month-long campaign was marked by the valor and sacrifice of its participants, the thousands of Americans, British, Canadians, and natives who struggled for possession of the Niagara Peninsula. What follows is their story.

NIAGARA 1814

CHAPTER ONE

The Road to War

If War is declared before we have a force raised sufficient to subdue Canada, we shall have war upon our northern frontier, and perhaps it will be pushed into our territory. This will be particularly alarming and distressing to the inhabitants on the Canada line; and your militia will be called out from their usual business and avocations of life into the field, as soldiers for the protection of the frontier settlements, and you will have all the expense of a regular campaign without any of its benefits.
—Senator Obadiah German, 3 June 1812

In the very early hours of 19 December 1813, a body of British soldiers armed with axes, scaling ladders, and unloaded muskets forced its way through a poorly guarded gate and over the ramparts of Fort Niagara. Mindful of Lieutenant General Gordon Drummond's order that "the bayonet is the weapon on which the success of the attack must depend," they went about the grisly work of quelling the sporadic resistance offered by the aroused defenders.[1] The sick in the hospital put up the stoutest fight; they, as well as others, were bayoneted even as they begged for quarter.[2] This well-executed surprise attack yielded 65 American dead from the 400-man garrison. It was also the precursor of a devastating assault on the communities on the American side of the Niagara River.

On the evening of 29 December, the British followed up their success at Fort Niagara by crossing the river near its mouth on Lake Erie and attacking the village of Black Rock. Alarmed by the loss of Fort Niagara, over 2,000 American militia and a handful of Iroquois Indians and Canadian Volunteers rallied to defend Black Rock and nearby Buffalo. The untrained and largely inexperienced militia was no match for Major General Phineas Riall's regulars and Indians; after feeble resistance, it broke and fled. The following morning the village trustees of Buffalo implored Dr. Cyrenius Chapin, a sometime leader of irregular raiders, to negotiate a surrender. Over the next two days, nearly every structure along the

1

thirty-seven-mile course of the river except for Fort Niagara itself was burned by soldiers and Indians, the contents stolen or destroyed. A few of Riall's Indian allies killed and scalped about a dozen civilians. Nearly the entire population fled eastward into the snowy forests, fugitives in what had become a cruel war.[3]

Riall was not a dishonorable man; it was arguable that by the end of 1813 there were no private dwellings along the Niagara. Thousands of American regulars and militia had been quartered in virtually every structure on the Niagara Frontier. The citizens understood that this invited destruction. As recently as 20 December, the Committee of Public Safety of Buffalo had met with General George McClure, New York militia commander, to protest the use of private homes for military purposes. The committee was very concerned because just ten days earlier McClure had ordered the burning of Newark (modern name, Niagara-on-the-Lake), a peaceful village outside of Fort George on the Canadian side of the river opposite Fort Niagara. This despicable act, with no military justification, had resulted in Canadian women, children, and elderly men being forced from their homes with no prior warning of the destruction to come.

Riall justified his act not as retaliation for Newark, however. He and his superior, Drummond, had long ago understood that if the opportunity presented itself, they must destroy the shelter of the thousands of American troops that were stationed on that frontier, ready to invade Upper Canada. Riall also noted that Chapin, with whom he had signed the agreement, was not in command. In fact, he was not even mustered into state or federal service. Thus he was not competent to negotiate a surrender instrument.

General Lewis Cass wrote to Secretary of War John Armstrong: "I passed this day the ruins of Buffalo. It exhibits a scene of distress and destruction such as I have never before witnessed."[4] War advocate and governor of New York Daniel D. Tompkins wrote to Armstrong of the Indian brutality and the depopulated frontier. He issued a stark warning that the British might continue their attack to Erie, Pennsylvania, and destroy the fleet there, which, under Oliver Hazard Perry, had gloriously won control of Lake Erie only months before.[5]

The Niagara Frontier, area of natural splendor and starting point for the invasions of Canada fourteen months earlier, was now depopulated, burned, and occupied by Canada's would-be defenders. How had things come to this? How could this war launched so confidently to reassert American sovereignty result in such staggering defeats and disgrace with only a few consoling victories? The answer begins with the transfer of political power from the Federalists to the Jeffersonians.

When the Republicans took office in 1801, they began dismantling Federalist programs. They cut taxes and cut spending. Republican military policy rested on two inexpensive pillars: the militia and privateers. Congress cut the standing army, always a political threat to civil liberty, by 28 percent and reduced the navy to seven frigates.

Meanwhile, in Europe, the warring parties wielded their economic clout to force their opponents into submission. As the world's major neutral shipper, the United States enjoyed nearly constant growth in exports and carrying trade by picking up much of the business forfeited by the belligerents. However, changing interpretations in British admiralty courts, seizure of vessels and cargoes, and impressment of American sailors were attacks on American sovereignty. Even more galling to American sensitivities was the location of these incidents of vessel seizure and impressment. The Royal Navy regularly violated the U.S. three-mile limit in order to stop vessels and impress sailors as they exited American ports, regardless of their destination.

On 22 June 1807, the captain of HMS *Leopard* hailed the USS *Chesapeake*, a frigate, and demanded the return of four British deserters allegedly serving on its crew. When the commander of the *Chesapeake* refused, the *Leopard* fired on the frigate, killing three and wounding eighteen. This act violated Britain's own previous policy that exempted neutral warships from search. The public was outraged. Jefferson, with a good understanding of his limited options in the matter, temporized and hoped that the British would declare their error and make restitution. Eventually they did so, in 1811, but the harm was done. As far as most Americans were concerned, Britain had demonstrated an unconscionable arrogance and disregard for U.S. sovereignty.

Federalist foreign policy had been backed up by a willingness, if scant ability, to use the sword. Republicans, recognizing that U.S. military potential was limited, perceived that U.S. economic power was not. According to Republican strategists, Europe wanted the American trade, and European avarice would eventually win out over this mutually destructive economic war between Britain and France. The deft use of American economic power, that is, incremental economic sanctions inflicted at timely intervals, would bring the warring parties to their senses. Unfortunately for the nation, if not for the Republicans, the strategists overestimated the lethality of the economic weapon, at least when it was used incrementally. Jefferson's embargo had precisely the desired effect in Britain: it kept American traders out of European markets. British Tories were convinced that their hard-line policies were correct and that fears of the United States declaring war were largely unfounded. America, they reasoned, had given no evidence that it would go to war over maritime issues. However sound this reasoning may have been, London failed to calculate the weight given in Washington to the issue of security along the frontier.[6]

Following the *Chesapeake* affair, Sir James Craig, governor in chief of British North America, understood full well that in the event of war, the Americans would seek resolution in the Canadas. He therefore took clandestine measures to align the western tribes with Britain. Of course, this was a delicate maneuver, for he did not want to start a war; Upper Canada was too vulnerable. But in the event of war, he wanted Indian allies. His intentions were transmitted by Indian agents who influenced the tribes by persuasion and by gifts given at annual gatherings. These kinds of machinations could not long escape detection by the Americans. Starting in 1808, congressmen began calling for the expulsion of Britain from the Canadas.[7] Soon this exhortation became the nearly unanimous prescription of the war hawks of the Twelfth Congress.

The British were mistaken if they believed that they could decisively influence Indian activity. Tecumseh had his own agenda and was not so sanguine about the possibility or desirability of preventing war. The articulate, even charismatic Tecumseh and his brother, the Prophet, had been putting together an Indian confederation to resist continued white expansion westward. In November 1810, Tecumseh informed Captain Matthew Elliott, superintendent of Indian affairs in Upper Canada, that the Indians would soon be ready for war. Craig understood that he would be blamed if the Indians started a war on the American frontier. He therefore ordered his agents to dissuade the Indians and convince them that Britain would not aid them in the event of war. However, Tecumseh's movement toward Indian unity had built up a momentum of its own, certainly beyond British desires. Craig reversed himself again, and his agents continued their efforts to put together a wartime alliance.

By 1811, events in the West were hurtling toward open warfare. Governor William Henry Harrison of Indiana Territory wrote in February to the secretary of war that "If the intentions of the British government are pacific, the Indian Department of Upper Canada have not been made acquainted with them: for they have lately said every thing to the Indians, who visited then, to excite them against us."[8] While Tecumseh was in the South negotiating with tribal leaders to join his confederacy, Harrison marched on Tecumseh's capital city, Prophetstown, in a show of force to discourage Indian raids and depredations. The Prophet urged his followers to resist and prompted a night attack on Harrison's camp. After a short but sharp exchange, the Indians drew off. Harrison burned Prophetstown, declared victory at Tippecanoe, and returned home. Nonetheless, fear drove many settlers off their farms and into forts or back east. As for Tecumseh, he returned north to find his capital in ruins and his confederation badly shaken. He went to Amherstburg in Upper Canada, opposite Detroit, in May 1812 and pledged his loyalty to George III.

Westerners believed that the British had armed the Indians and had provoked the attacks on them. In Ohio and Kentucky in particular, a consensus was forming that the only sure way of stopping the Indians from attacking was to eject the British from North America.[9] The Canadians, as might be expected, saw these events in a different light. A typical view appeared in the *Quebec Gazette* before news of the Battle of Tippecanoe reached that city. "They [the United States] will not yield up the smallest portion of their interest on the ocean to England even in a case wherein she considers her existence as a nation at stake, but they extract of the Indians that they should deliver up their country and their means of subsistence, in subserviency to the interests of the United States. The cant of the American Government about justice, meekness, moderation, and humanity ought not deceive anyone."[10] Canadians were perhaps wise to be wary of Americans. There were signs that some of their neighbors to the south coveted their lands.

When the Twelfth Congress convened on 4 November 1811, the Republicans controlled 75 percent of the House seats and 82 percent of the Senate. Addressing Congress on 5 November, President James Madison noted that the orders in council were tantamount to economic warfare and asked Congress to prepare the nation for military conflict. The House Foreign Relations Committee issued its report focusing on the maritime grievances and recommending measures to strengthen both the army and the navy and to permit the arming of merchant vessels. The war measures passed by Congress were not entirely what the administration wanted and reflected a lack of consensus on how a war might be fought. Congress raised the top strength of the regular army from 10,000 to 35,000 and raised the recruiting bonus and further sweetened it by adding 160 acres of land. The increased bonus recognized that the army strength was little more than half of the old authorization, and incentives were necessary if the army was to expand to nearly seven times its current strength. Congress authorized the president to raise 50,000 one-year volunteers. Presumably, volunteers would be easier to raise because of the one-year rather than five-year term of service. Congress also gave the president authorization to call up 100,000 militia for up to six months. Finally, Congress voted a modest sum for expanding coastal defenses and upgrading existing frigates, but there would be no increase in the number of frigates and no ships of the line.

This congressional action, before war was declared, determined in large measure how the war was to be fought. Refusal to expand the navy was a recognition that no amount of funding could produce a force strong enough to successfully challenge the Royal Navy. Since the militia could not be required to serve outside the territory of the United States, Congress intended the larger portion of the authorized troops to defend the nation from invasion or raids on the coast or frontier. The regulars and volunteers were the only arm that provided a potentially decisive offensive weapon. Congressional action directed that the war was to be conducted on land and not on the high seas. Thus, by implication, the decisive theaters of operations encompassed Britain's Indian allies and Canada.

During the six months preceding the war, the British made several moves to defuse the crisis. The attack on the *Chesapeake* was disavowed, and Royal Navy ships' captains were ordered to avoid provoking American vessels at sea. Finally, in mid-June, the ministry suspended the orders in council. This left only impressment as an outstanding maritime grievance. But news of this latest concession reached the American shore after Congress had declared war. In a virtual replay of the American Revolution, British public policy marched one step behind American public opinion. Had the orders in council been withdrawn six months earlier, perhaps conflict would have been averted. But in 1812, unlike in 1776, Britain was locked in a protracted war of immense proportions. Events in North America were marginal to this effort and drew a correspondingly small share of Britain's attention.

Unaware of the softening of the British position, Madison sent a secret message to Congress on 1 June.[11] He cited the orders in council, impressment, violations of coastal waters, subversion, and malicious influence over the western Indians as evidence of warlike acts. The House Foreign Relations Committee studied the president's message and rendered a report calling for war. The congressional vote was decisive: seventy-nine to forty-nine in the House, and nineteen to thirteen in the Senate. The vote correlated both regionally and by party. Votes for war came largely from the West and South; those against from the North and East. Frontier districts were pro-war. Only 23 of 121 Republicans voted against the war; they were joined by all 39 Federalists.

As a group, Republicans had come to realize the limitations of economic power in resolving their problems with Britain and France. They were suspicious of British motives and were quick to perceive slights to the national honor. It had become increasingly clear to them that Britain was unwilling under present circumstances to accord the United States full sovereignty as they defined that term. Since economic sanctions had failed, perhaps war would succeed.

Nowhere did Madison or Congress articulate a set of national goals. The act declaring war was a short statement that a state of war existed and that the president was authorized to prosecute the war and issue letters of marque.[12] A likely set of national goals might be derived from the five grievances cited by Madison in his war message. If so, then the national goals would be accomplished when Great Britain stopped impressment; stopped illegal seizure of merchant vessels, particularly in U.S. waters; stopped sending agents into U.S. territory; and stopped provoking the Indians to warfare. Revocation of the orders in council had already defused a major grievance. Since the charge of subversion had evolved from an isolated incident, presumably the issue of subversive agents was a minor one. That left impressment and provocation of the Indians as the outstanding issues.

Whatever Madison understood the national goals to be, one of his first acts of war was to order a large-scale invasion of Canada. How did Canada fit into the nation's war goals? Was the possession of Canada an end in itself, or was it a means to an end? The answer to this question, if Madison had given an explicit answer, should have guided the actions of the military commanders charged with the task of seizing Canada. Madison was assailed on all sides by those who coveted these northern lands and those who saw grave dangers in annexation. He was clearly on the horns of a dilemma. Without a large navy, the United States could strike at Great Britain only through Canada. If Madison declared his intention to annex Canada, then he could not exchange it for concessions on the maritime issues. However, if he stated that Canada would be occupied only until a satisfactory peace were negotiated, then support for invasion, particularly from the pro-war West, would dry up, rendering a successful invasion unlikely. Madison refused to address the question directly, and only toward the end did he tilt toward trading Canada away. In any event, Madison would not be compelled to answer until Canada was in American hands, and that never happened.

Of course, in 1812 there was no country named Canada. The term was an imprecise geographic expression referring to all of British North America or to just two of the provinces considered as a unity. British North America was reorganized in 1791 to consist of four provinces: Nova Scotia, New Brunswick, Lower Canada, and Upper Canada. The majority of francophones lived in Lower Canada, and the term *Quebec* technically referred only to the city of that name. The governor in chief of British North America resided in Lower Canada. He supervised that province directly and the other three through lieutenant governors. Upper Canada and Lower Canada taken together were referred to as "the Canadas," or frequently just as "Canada." American desire to possess Canada, and the desire of some Canadians to be possessed, originated in the earliest days of the Revolution.[13]

After France was expelled from mainland North America in 1763, the British were faced with the task of grafting a large francophone community onto their empire. The habitants of what had been New France differed from their conquerors in language, religion, law, and social structure. Sir Guy Carleton, the far-sighted governor of the colony, lobbied hard for the Quebec Act of 1774. By this act, Parliament protected the language and customs of these French-speaking citizens of the British Empire. Carleton was motivated both by a sense of justice and by his desire to ensure the loyalty of French Canadians in any future Anglo-French conflict. In the years following the French and Indian War, anglophones moved into this new province called Quebec. Many were merchants from the thirteen colonies, and they settled in the cities of Quebec and Montreal and maintained trading connections southward. As the winds of rebellion blew from New England into Quebec, the revolutionary message struck a resonant chord with many of the anglophones and not a few of the habitants, who suffered under the social and political domination of churchmen and seigneurs.

In October 1774, Congress addressed a letter to the people of Canada inviting them to join in the struggle to force Britain to respect colonial rights. The anglophone minority was divided in its allegiance, and so was the francophone majority. The Roman Catholic clergy and the landholding seigneurs threw in their lot with the British authorities. The lower-class French Canadians, legally strapped with tithes and feudal obligations, looked hard at American propaganda; to them, this talk of liberty was appealing.

The rebels conducted a two-pronged attack to seize Montreal and Quebec City. Carleton had difficulty mobilizing the militia; the habitants' loyalty to their seigneurs was not strong enough to compel them to enlist. Former British officer Richard Montgomery attacked north from Ticonderoga, while Benedict Arnold took a difficult overland route far to the east. On 13 November, Montreal surrendered to Montgomery. Quebec could not be brought into the revolution until the fortress of Quebec City at the narrows of the St. Lawrence was in rebel hands. On 3 December, the two small forces linked up outside of Quebec City. The combined army numbered about 1,000 poorly clothed, underfed, inadequately armed volunteers, including over 200 Canadians. The army's greatest assets were its commanders, Montgomery and Arnold, whose leadership and force of will nearly added a fourteenth star to the new flag.

Unable to cut the city off from resupply by the river, and without guns large enough to batter down Quebec's solid walls, the Americans were compelled to assault. Montgomery and Arnold were betting that in the final moment the francophone militia would not assist the British regulars in defending the city. They lost this desperate gamble, and brave Montgomery lost his life. The assault collapsed with 461 casualties, most of them captured. Attacking with Arnold was one Captain Henry Dearborn, who would figure prominently in the next war.

Carleton's forces outmaneuvered and outfought the Americans in several engagements as Arnold fell back into New York. With Arnold was Captain James Wilkinson, who displayed both energy and initiative in the final stages of the campaign. As a senior commander in the next war, Wilkinson would never get as close to Montreal as he had in 1776, despite making two attempts to do so. The United States would not invade Canada again during the Revolution due to a lack of ability, not a lack of desire. In 1778, George Washington wrote of Canada: "If that country is not with us, it will, from its proximity to the eastern States, its intercourse and connexion with the numerous tribes of western Indians, its communion with them by water and other local advantages, be at least a troublesome if not dangerous neighbor to us; and ought, at all events, to be in the same interests and politics, of the other States."[14]

The invasion of Canada was a near-run affair, or at least that is how it was perceived in America. Several other notions could not fail to take hold as a result of the 1775–1776 campaign. First, a future invasion could expect some support from the Canadians, particularly if they were handled with respect. Their allegiance to Britain was based on self-interest and therefore was brittle. Second, if a ragtag army took Montreal and nearly seized the fortress of Quebec, then a large, well-supplied army could reasonably expect victory. It would not be clear in 1812 that only fierce determination and uncommon audacity on the parts of Arnold and Montgomery had brought American forces to the gates of Quebec. And in the final analysis, even these were insufficient to take the fortress. Both Dearborn and Wilkinson, witnesses to the drama but without a hint of the force of character required, would fail when their turn came.

After the American Revolution, the proportion of anglophones in British North America increased as Tories in the United States emigrated northward as United Empire Loyalists. Many of these persons had been dispossessed by their rebel neighbors; they had neither affection nor respect for the democratic chaos in their erstwhile native land. These people, and their descendants, would form the hard kernel of resistance in the upcoming war.

After the firing upon the *Chesapeake,* there was a palpable threat of war felt throughout British North America. Canadians understood, largely from U.S. newspapers, that they would bear the brunt of American anger. The stark inconsistency was not lost on Canadians any more than it was on the Federalists: how would an invasion of Canada resolve disputes over maritime issues?

Henry Clay, perhaps the leading war hawk, saw the connection between Canada and maritime grievances clearly. In an oft-quoted speech to the Eleventh Congress, he said: "The conquest of Canada is in your power. I trust I shall not be deemed presumptuous when I state that I verily believe that the militia of Kentucky are alone competent to place Montreal and Upper Canada at your feet. Is it nothing to the British nation; is it nothing to the pride of her Monarch, to have the last of the immense North American possessions held by him in the commencement of his reign wrested from his dominion?"[15]

Clay was foursquare behind taking Canada and retaining it. In 1813, after two invasions had been turned back, he wrote to a colleague that "It has ever been my opinion that if Canada is conquered it ought never be surrendered if it can possibly be retained."[16] However, in 1810 Clay had eloquently and effectively persuaded a number of rising Republicans that seizing Canada would be not only worthwhile but also easy.

The war hawks, in the early days of the Twelfth Congress, argued that seizing Canada would be worth both the effort and the risk and hinted strongly that possession would be permanent. For example, Peter B. Porter of western New York argued that Canada was "almost indispensable to the existence of Great Britain," providing as it did the ship timber so necessary to its fleets. He did not mean to trade Canada back; possession of Canada would compensate the United States for any losses suffered at sea.[17] Invoking the sanction of the Deity, Kentuckian Richard M. Johnson noted the geographic proximity of the lands drained by the St. Lawrence and those drained by the Mississippi. He declared that "the Great

Disposer of Human Events intended those two rivers should belong to the same people."[18]

The expansionist imperative that would later be called Manifest Destiny laced the rhetoric of the war hawks. Jefferson himself held some of the assumptions that drove the war effort. Shortly after the declaration of war, he wrote to William Duane, Republican editor of the influential *Philadelphia Aurora*, that "the acquisition of Canada this year, as far as the neighborhood of Quebec, will be a mere matter of marching; & will give us experience for the attack of Halifax the next, & the final expulsion of England from the American continent."[19] Expansionism would fail in 1812, in part because of military policies introduced by Jefferson. War hawks Peter B. Porter and Richard M. Johnson would both take to the field later as unit commanders, and both would serve competently, even brilliantly. However, their efforts would not result in moving the frontier even a mile northward. Expansionism made a false start this time; later it would run its race to the west and south.

Madison would not declare himself on the issue of the annexation of Canada. This strategic indecision, however politic at the national level, had repercussions at lower levels. Two commanders charged with invading Canada in 1812, William Hull and Alexander Smyth, both political appointees, issued proclamations to the Canadians hinting at annexation. These proclamations muddied the waters during peace negotiations, and ultimately Madison was compelled to deny that these documents had his approval or that the United States had any intent of retaining Canada.[20] Madison's ambivalence on this issue is evidence of the strategic confusion that permeated down to his military commanders throughout the war.

The analysis of events leading to war reveals much about the war goals of the three belligerents. The Franco–British economic war trounced on Americans' understanding of neutral rights, as well as on the United States' nationalistic sensibilities as a new republic. Americans went to war to preserve their rights and their honor and to secure their frontiers. Some, no doubt, made war to push those frontiers both north and south. The British and many, but certainly not all, of their Canadian subjects fought to defend the sovereignty of this part of the empire. In attempting to maintain an alliance with the Indians, British agents may have unwittingly helped to provoke the war they were trying to prevent. The Indians, many of whom had subordinated tribal goals to those of an emerging confederation, went to war to retain their lands and maintain their way of life in the face of relentless westward migration of whites.

Canada, where much of the war was fought, was an ambiguous objective. Neither the president nor his congressional party had declared whether that northern land was an end in itself or a means to an end. That declaration could wait until after the conquest. As had been shown in 1775, conquest clearly appeared to be within the national capability. And what could Britain do to the United States in retribution for the invasion of its North American colonies? Caught in a protracted economic and military war against Napoleon on the Continent, Britain could spare few resources to defend Canada. Acting with skill and boldness, American armies might have accomplished much in a single campaign season. But that was not to be.

CHAPTER TWO

The Disappointing War

America may with some reasonable prospect of success, contend about the establishment
of a boundary line, or the navigation of a small river in the vicinity of her territory; but
to attempt to coerce Great Britain on the Ocean, is quite as preposterous, as if a bear
were to leave his native element, in order to drown a shark, or prey upon a sword fish.
                                                          —*Montreal Gazette*, 17 August 1807

Madison signed into law the Declaration of War against the British Empire on
18 June 1812. Was it, as the writer in the *Montreal Gazette* stated, like a bear
doing battle with a shark? The two belligerents were quite incongruous in their
sources of national power and in their ability to project that power into North
America, the primary theater of war. A comparative analysis of some of the elements of national power (geographic, economic, demographic, political, and military) and an investigation of how these elements were harnessed can provide
some insight into the strategies adopted by both parties.

The United States and British North America were separated by a land
boundary in the east and a water boundary in the west. The border between
New England and part of New York in the south and New Brunswick and
Lower Canada in the north ran through densely forested hills with very few
roads, all of poor quality. Arnold, in 1775, brought a very small force through
this wilderness en route to Quebec. The inherent difficulty in doing so discouraged the United States from attempting a similar feat in 1812. There was
one break in this part of the international boundary: the Richelieu-Champlain-
Hudson Valley, the traditional north-south invasion route. Along this axis, relatively large bodies of troops could move without great difficulty if they
controlled the waterways. This route was the scene of much of the military
activity during the war.

The boundary between New York, Pennsylvania, Ohio, and the Michigan

Territory in the south and Upper Canada in the north ran along the Great Lakes and their connecting rivers. Military operations across these rivers and lakes were not difficult for the side controlling the water. Military movement into the interiors of either country could be conducted only along those rivers that drained into the boundary waters—the Thames in Upper Canada and the Maumee in Ohio, for example. Roads were few and abysmal, generally precluding large-scale supply efforts by land.

The problems presented by geography were staggering to both sides, but particularly to the British. Virtually every item of war used by the British and Canadian forces came across the ocean from Britain and then up the St. Lawrence River and into the Great Lakes. This line ran along the border for much of its distance and was therefore vulnerable to attack. The distance between Britain and Fort Malden on the Detroit River was 6,500 kilometers. The Royal Navy ensured that cargo originating in Britain would arrive at Quebec in about eight weeks unless picked off en route by American privateers. The cargo was then transloaded to schooner for its trip to Montreal and transloaded once again to bateaux for movement to Kingston at the foot of Lake Ontario. Along this last stretch of the St. Lawrence were three sets of rapids, and depending on weight and water conditions, the cargo might be moved around the rapids by wagon. Movement across Lake Ontario by schooner was easy as long as the U.S. Navy stayed in port. The trip up the Niagara River was interrupted by the portage around the falls. Once on Lake Erie, the final leg of the trip to Fort Malden was direct. Transportation was further complicated by winter ice, which closed down nearly all water transport west of Quebec for about three months. The British commander in chief had to anticipate his needs well in advance, for it took between four and six months from the time his staff ordered an item until it appeared on the fighting front.

The implications of geography on the war were several. The British line of communication was extremely vulnerable, and transportation of supplies was labor-intensive in teamsters and boat crews. The Americans would reap a large payoff—perhaps even a decisive one—if they could cut the British line of communication. The British, in contrast, were compelled to allocate a large proportion of their limited manpower to secure their line of communication as well as move supplies along it. Both sides fought for control of the waterways—the Americans in order to cut off British supplies, and the British to prevent that occurrence.

The deterministic character of the geography of the theater of war in North America suggests a further subdivision into theaters of operation. *Theater of operations* is a twentieth-century term that identifies a geographic area characterized by political or operational unity. Theaters of operations are often both physically and conceptually separated from neighboring theaters. Often the strategic commander delegates responsibility for military operations to a single joint commander or to a land and a naval commander. The term *theater of operations* suggests an area large enough to warrant military operations on the order of major campaigns—sequences of related battles.

Sir George Prevost, governor-general of the four British provinces, and Madison delegated their military command authority along political boundaries, either state or provincial. However, in retrospect, the military operations of the War of 1812 cry out for an analytical model that corresponds to geographic factors rather than political ones, because the former virtually determined where military activity might translate into strategic success.

The North American theater of war was subdivided into four theaters of operations. The Atlantic Theater included the waters of the western Atlantic and the coastal waters from Nova Scotia to Spanish Florida that drained into the ocean. This was the scene of naval warfare and amphibious raids inland. The Southern Theater was the setting of fighting for control of the American hinterland and America's access to the Gulf of Mexico. This theater was marked on the north by the Ohio River and included the Gulf of Mexico in the south. The Western Theater encompassed the United States north of the Ohio River and that part of Upper Canada that drains into Lake Erie and the upper Great Lakes. The Central Theater, the scene of the largest operations, generally included the land drained by the St. Lawrence River up to the southern mouth of the Niagara River. The precise borders of the analytical construct are blurred, but they enclose the area of military activity as played out during the war.

Both the British Empire and the United States were self-sufficient in agricultural and industrial production; problems arose in the transportation of food and implements of war from the site of production to the fighting front. Of these two general classes of supply, food was the heaviest and bulkiest. If Britain could feed its troops from Canadian production, then more ships would be available to move guns, powder, anchors, cable, and other items required by the army and navy.

Canadian agriculture was not much above the subsistence level. In a good year, Canada produced enough wheat and meat to feed itself with a small residue for export. But agricultural production from year to year was unpredictable. The government usually imported some foodstuffs to feed the 5,600-man peacetime garrison. With the declaration of war, large numbers of militiamen were mobilized to man boat and wagon crews and to guard the lines of communication. This was a double liability. It not only took laborers out of the field but also shifted responsibility for feeding them to the government. Militiamen exerted nearly constant pressure on the government to return them to their fields quickly. The British also mobilized their Indian allies, who

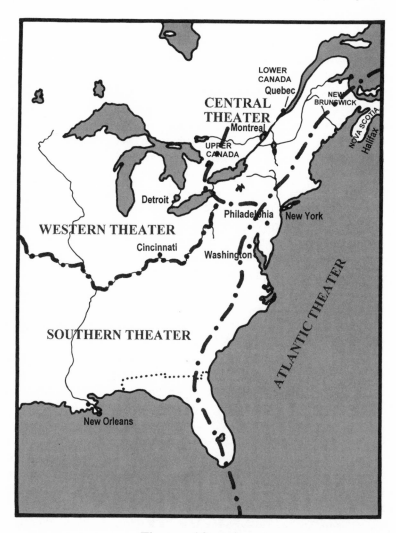

Theaters of Operation

moved with their families to rendezvous points such as Fort Malden, where the government assumed responsibility for feeding them. Some relief came from an unexpected source: large numbers of cattle were driven by their New England owners through the forests of Vermont to be sold in Lower Canada. A large portion of the meat in the diets of British and Canadian soldiers was American in origin.[1]

The Americans had a decided advantage in agricultural and industrial production. America was an exporter of foodstuffs even in the worst of times. Congress prohibited trade with Canada and with British Empire ports from the outset, but it made a conscious decision to allow merchants to carry American grain in American ships to feed British soldiers fighting Napoleon's armies in Spain. The British were a party to this, issuing special licenses to facilitate this trade. In theory, American farmers and merchants could still turn a profit during the war without influencing Britain's ability to conduct war in North America. Thousands of Britain's peninsular veterans who had been well fed on American grain would descend on Washington and burn its public buildings in 1814, a telling comment on congressional shortsightedness.

American industry was far beyond what it had been during the Revolution, when the continental army depended on French largesse for every commodity of weapon and equipment. In 1812, the United States produced everything required to build and outfit a warship or an army, and in sufficient quantity. Perry's fleet was built from the waterline up from Pennsylvania timber, canvas from Philadelphia, guns from Washington, ammunition from Pittsburgh, and fittings cast in Erie.

Large quantities of small arms were fabricated in arsenals at Springfield, Massachusetts, and Harpers Ferry, Virginia.[2] The two arsenals were augmented by extensive civilian contract production for cannon. Over 530 furnaces and forges were contracted for artillery production in 1811 alone. Throughout the war, field commanders had sufficient small arms and artillery for their forces.

Demographic data further typify the incongruent nature of this war. Great Britain, with a population approaching 10 million, had nearly 350,000 of its citizens in the army or navy in 1812. Newly raised troops hardly replaced losses. When native troops were raised, they were most often kept to defend their home colonies. The population could hardly support an expansion of the military to fight in Canada. Also, the Royal Navy got priority for manpower, as did industry. Because Parliament refused to enact conscription, the army remained limited in size. Any troops sent to British North America would come from other theaters. The approximate white population of British North America is shown here.

Province	Estimated Population (Year)	Potential Militia
New Brunswick	25,000 (1803)	4,000
Nova Scotia	65,000 (1805)	11,000
Upper Canada	77,000 (1811)	11,000
Lower Canada	335,000 (1814)	60,000

The population of the United States, including slaves but excluding Indians, was approximately 6 million. Over 700,000 men were on the rolls of the militia, and the regular army consisted of 6,686 officers and men. There was considerable room for expansion.

Great Britain had been at war with revolutionary France since 1793, with a short break in 1802. Britain was committed to what it perceived to be a life-or-death struggle. Congress was fully aware that it was declaring war at a time when its adversary was otherwise occupied. Britain would have to extend itself to take on the United States. It appeared to the war hawks that if they rapidly mobilized the people, they could strike a decisive blow before Britain could bring its immense strength to bear in North America. Thus, circumstances of demographics were decidedly in the favor of the United States in a short war but would tip gradually toward Britain as war dragged on.

As a further advantage to the United States, a large proportion of the inhabitants of Upper Canada were native-born Americans who had moved north for a variety of reasons. Some were the residue of Revolutionary War Tories, but most had probably come for cheap land. This group was the source of considerable disaffection in that province during the war. February 1812 saw Major General Isaac Brock beginning to prepare Upper Canada for war. He asked the legislature to suspend habeas corpus and to demand a loyalty oath from militiamen. The legislature refused his request. Brock attributed this to the large number of settlers from the United States and the fear they inspired in loyal citizens, but there is no evidence that American emissaries spread propaganda in Upper Canada in 1812, as they had in Quebec in 1775. There was no need. A large part of Upper Canada's population was disposed to support the United States or at least remain neutral in the upcoming war.[3]

There was also active opposition to the war south of the border from the Federalist Party. The Federalist power base was shrinking, but it remained strong in the mercantile and financial sectors along the Atlantic coast. To the Federalist elite, it seemed that any expansion of territory northward would only increase the numbers of Republican voters, perhaps rendering the decline of their party permanent. Thus the two-party system represented sectional differences: the frontier and agricultural interests opposed by the commercial centers in the East.[4]

Thus both the British authorities in Canada and the Madison administration had lively opposition. The lieutenant governor of Upper Canada was never certain of the numbers or reliability of the militia, which he was forced to mobilize from time to time. Madison was more secure. Unless he had badly miscalculated, the Republicans would retain a majority in both houses, and he would win nomination and election for another term. So far, the elements of power were tipped in America's favor, but an analysis of the land and naval forces in existence at the start of the war redresses the imbalance.

On the high seas, the Royal Navy enjoyed an insurmountable advantage over the U.S. Navy. With 120 ships of the line, 116 frigates, and 350 lesser vessels, the Royal Navy had been conducting a most effective maritime campaign against France.[5] To counter this, the U.S. Navy had 7 frigates, 10 sloops of war, and 62 gunboats for coastal defense. The Americans held a decided advantage in their capacity to outfit and put to sea hundreds of privateers. Whereas the U.S. Navy captured 165 enemy merchantmen, 526 American privateer vessels captured or destroyed 1,334. The Royal Navy had trouble protecting the merchant marine, because most privateers could outrun war vessels. Duty as a privateer seaman held little risk and the possibility of sharing in enormous prize money. Navy recruiters could hardly compete with privateers for experienced seamen.

The massive preponderance of Royal Navy numbers could not be brought to bear on Lake Champlain or the Great Lakes, where the greater part of the fighting would occur.[6] Vessels larger than bateaux could not negotiate the rapids of the St. Lawrence, so fleets for use on the inland lakes had to be built on those bodies of water. Likewise, Niagara Falls precluded vessels built on Lake Ontario from operating in the upper lakes. Although most Lake Erie vessels could negotiate the Detroit and St. Clair Rivers to reach the three uppermost lakes, they had to pass the guns of Fort Malden on the Canadian shore and Fort Detroit on the American shore. Thus control of either of those forts secured the lakes above or below them. The impact of geography was such that the naval war was broken up into five discreet areas of operation: the Atlantic and Caribbean, Lake Champlain, Lake Ontario, Lake Erie, and the three upper lakes.

How, then, could naval power on the ocean be brought to bear on the inland lakes? The answer: with the skill of shipbuilders and seamen. Both Britain and the United States sent officers and crewmen and a host of artisans from the seacoast inland to build the fleets necessary to gain and maintain control of the Great Lakes and Lake Champlain.

At the start of the war, British vessels on the Great Lakes were part of the Provincial Marine, which was autonomous from the Royal Navy. The Provincial Marine, with fewer than 100 sailors, conducted government business and transported troops and supplies under orders from the army. There were naval yards at Kingston on Lake Ontario and at Amherstburg on the Detroit River. In April 1813, the Provincial Marine came under Royal Navy control as the British committed themselves to disputing control of the Great Lakes. But at the outset of the war, the British had only seven war vessels on Lake Ontario, ranging from schooners with eight guns to the *Royal George* with twenty-two guns. These few vessels dominated the single American vessel, the sixteen-gun *Oneida*, but the U.S. Navy quickly added six purchased schooners to restore balance. On Lake Erie, the Provincial Marine had three vessels ranging from six to sixteen guns, and the Americans had a six-gun brig. The inland lakes were the scene of feverish shipbuilding efforts and two decisive naval engagements.

The ground forces of the belligerents demonstrated a disparity similar to that of the navies. At the beginning of the war, the British army consisted of over 200,000 soldiers. Half of these were stationed in the West Indies, Ceylon, India, and a multitude of minor stations. The infantry was organized into more than 100 regiments of foot, which consisted of anywhere from one to five battalions. A vast gulf existed between the social position of officers and that of their men, but it was becoming increasingly common for gentlemen officers to share the privations of common soldiers and to lead by example.

Britain maintained a little over 10,000 regulars and fencibles in British North America: approximately 5,800 in Nova Scotia, 4,000 in Lower Canada, and 1,200 in Upper Canada. This stationing arrangement was consistent with the relative importance of Halifax and Quebec to the defense of British North America and the increasing difficulty of supplying troops the farther west they were located. A fencible regiment differed from a regiment of the line in that fencibles were raised in North America and were not to be deployed outside of that continent. Also, fencible units were named rather than numbered (e.g., the Royal Newfoundland Fencibles). As the threat of war approached, the fencible regiments energetically recruited with good success.

There were about 86,000 men available for militia duty in British North America. Prevost persuaded the legislature in early 1812 to call out 2,000 militia for three months. This term of service would be extended to one year in the event of invasion. Unlike in 1775, Lower Canada had no intention of being Americanized, and the lawmakers generally worked well with Prevost.[7]

The tale was different in Upper Canada. The Upper Canada Militia Act of 1808 authorized the use of militia outside the borders under certain conditions, one of which allowed preemptive attacks on the United States.[8] However, there was considerable difference between what the law allowed and what the people would do. Only three weeks after the declaration of war, General Brock complained to Prevost that his militiamen were already clamoring to return to their farms. He was apprehensive that many would desert at harvesttime, because he could impose only a twenty-pound fine. Brock had just enough weapons to arm those militiamen he had actually called out—not enough to arm everyone, if that became necessary. "The militia assembled in a wretched state in regard to clothing," he complained, and "many were without shoes, an article which can scarcely be provided in the Country."[9]

In the beginning of 1812, the U.S. Army consisted of nearly 7,000 soldiers scattered in small posts along the frontier and the coast. The greatest concentration of force was at New Orleans. The officers were a mixture of Revolutionary War veterans and other gentlemen who were connected with political sponsors. The military academy at West Point, founded only ten years prior, had graduated only seventy-one officers, most of whom were quite junior in rank. In preparation for the war, Congress voted to expand the authorized strength of the regular army from 10,000 to 35,000, all enlisted for five years. To spur recruiting, Congress steadily shortened the term of service and increased the bounty. It is uncertain how many new soldiers came forward prior to the declaration of war; recruiting records, such as were made, arrived at the War Department late or not at all.[10]

Few of the recruits served with the old established regiments. Unlike men recruited into the well-established British army, most of these new American soldiers were met by newly commissioned officers, and together they built their companies and regiments from the ground up. There were myriad problems involved in expanding the army sevenfold over two and a half years, not the least of which was finding a common tactical doctrine. The regular army had adopted Steuben's system of discipline in 1779. However, this tactical doctrine did not account for the changes in tactics brought about by the war of the French Revolution. Early in 1812, the War Department required the regular army to follow an adaptation of the French regulations of 1791 translated and edited by Alexander Smyth. This system was not widely accepted by the officers, who were slow to implement it. To further complicate matters, William Duane, editor of the Republican paper the *Aurora*, published his own tactical manual and submitted it to Congress for consideration for adoption.[11] Thus, in the first year of the war, newly commissioned officers were using any one of four doctrinal manuals: Steuben, Smyth, Duane, or the French regulations. The militia was still using Steuben, if anything at all.

The Militia Act of 1792 required the enrollment of all able-bodied white males between the ages of eighteen and forty-five. States were slow to send their strength reports to the War Department, but certainly over 730,000 were enrolled during the war years.[12] The state and the federal government made extensive use of the militia during the war; the total number of tours of duty has been variously estimated between 326,011 and 471,622.[13] This gives only a vague sense of the dependence on the militia. A tour of duty might be for a few days or as long as six months. This does not mean, however, that these two estimates represent the number of men who actually served under federal control; the number was far less. Many individuals and militia units served multiple tours of duty. This was particularly true on the seacoast. As an example, some militia units in Maryland in 1813 were called for up to ten short tours of duty due to repeated coastal raids.[14]

Much has been written about the poor performance of the militia during the war, as exemplified by its poor training, ill discipline, and refusal to cross international boundaries.[15] This was generally true in 1812, but by 1814, at least on the Niagara Frontier, the militiamen fully redeemed themselves. This has largely escaped the notice of historians. By 1813, the militia was fairly well armed, unlike its Canadian counterpart. Militia formations nationwide controlled 416 pieces of ordnance ranging from three-pound guns to brass twelve-pounders. State arsenals sheltered over 291,000 shoulder-fired weapons (muskets and rifles), 89,761 bayonets, and 56,763 knapsacks.[16] Training was generally poor except in the various volunteer companies that uniformed and armed themselves. An account of muster day in Goshen, New York, in June 1811 is perhaps illustrative of the general militia. Henry Leavitt Ellsworth, a recent Yale graduate and future mayor of Hartford, Connecticut, passed through Goshen and made a biting appraisal. He saw a group of thirty militiamen gathered for muster. Every weapon was rusty, and only one bayonet was visible; no uniforms were in evidence, and he witnessed numerous instances of indiscipline. Needless to say, no training was apparent.[17] These are the same yeoman warriors who underpinned Jeffersonian military policy, an exceedingly thin reed in 1812.

The War of 1812 was an Indian war, at least for a large minority of the native population. Decades of penetration by or close contact with white settlers had made many native communities uneasy. In the thirteen original colonies and the maritime provinces of British North America, native communities had been destroyed, displaced westward, or relegated to truncated parcels of land. Tribal foreign policy had been guided by astute self-interest. Alliances with other Indian tribes or with the French, British, or Americans were made to protect long-range tribal interests. At best, tribal foreign policies had only delayed the time when the tribe would be surrounded by white communities whose agricultural and individualist-based cultures overpowered hunting and communal-based native cultures too weak to resist.[18]

By 1810, tribal foreign policy was affected by two contradictory impulses. First, tribal organization was such that tribal leaders did not command the obedience of all members. Tribal political elites could not, therefore, speak for the entire tribe or enforce tribal agreements on the entire community. Second, a centripetal force acted among the tribes, pulling them toward one another in the face of a relentless westward white migration. This force was represented by Tecumseh's confederacy in the American Northwest and echoed by similar movements in the American South.

The result of these contradictions was that tribal unity was fractured, and the Indians entered the War of 1812 more as individuals than as members of a unified tribe guided by an integrated foreign policy. For example, the Iroquois Confederacy was entirely fractured by 1812, with pieces in Lower and Upper Canada and New York. Iroquois communities, officially neutral much of the time, provided warriors to both sides. The Creek War in Alabama never maintained the active support of the majority of Creeks, who were anxious to avoid American reprisals when the uprising ultimately failed. Only in the fur-trading

regions of Upper Canada and the American Northwest was the native population generally pro-British and willing to fight the Americans. The effect on the
battlefield of even a few Indians could be decisive. Time and again, American
forces were terrorized by war whoops and shrieks, surrendering or fleeing rather
than risk massacre. The British used the threat of relinquishing control of their
Indian allies to advantage on many occasions. The 1812 version of psychological warfare often proved decisive in blunting American invasion attempts.

The British Empire and the United States differed widely in their abilities
to harness the components of national power and direct them in pursuit of their
respective national goals. Britain, already at war for nearly two decades, held an
enormous advantage. Failures in previous campaigns had led to positive adjustments in organization and command and control. However, Parliament was
unwilling to loosen its control over the military, and therefore several safeguards
were in place that tended to decrease efficiency. Within the cabinet, the war was
directed by the secretary of state for war and colonies, Lord Henry Bathurst.
Bathurst managed to integrate the political and military aspects of the war in
British North America to a large degree.

The army, however, was not under unified command. The infantry and cavalry were under the commander in chief, whose headquarters was the Horse
Guards. Artillery and engineers were the responsibility of the Board of Ordnance,
and another board supervised medical activities. Supply functions were in the
hands of the Commissary, which was a branch of the Treasury. Sometimes this led
to administrative chaos in the theater of operations. In British North America, the
worst aspects of inefficient organization at the strategic level were ameliorated.
Prevost, the governor in chief, was a soldier; military and political powers were
united in his hands. The lieutenant governor of Upper Canada, Francis Gore, was
on leave in England for the duration of the war. His powers were delegated to the
president of the council and administrator of that province, who enjoyed nearly
dictatorial powers once the war began and the legislative assembly was prorogued.
The four men who successively directed the war effort in Upper Canada (Brock,
Sheaffe, de Rottenburg, and Drummond) were all soldiers and could unify the
political and military aspects of the war. Indeed, these men were sometimes in the
field personally directing the fight. In Brock's case, it cost him his life. Nearly as
important, these four were commanders in chief and as such directed both land
and naval operations in the primary theater of operations.

In stark contrast to Britain, the United States was quite new at the game of
making war on a modern European power and quite unprepared. The Madison
administration failed to understand the depth of the problem, and Congress was
unwilling to give the administration a blank check to address the issues. At the
heart of unpreparedness was the widely held view of the war hawks that Canada
would fall easily. An example is John C. Calhoun's unbridled confidence in a

speech on 6 May 1812. "So far from being unprepared, sir, I believe that, in four weeks from the time that a declaration of war is heard on our frontier, the whole of Upper and a part of Lower Canada will be in our possession."[19]

The Federalists, of course, were caught in an ideological trap. Traditionally in favor of a strong military establishment, they were unwilling to support a military controlled by the Republicans. Unable to stop the move toward war, Federalists and their antiwar Republican allies did water down some of the administration's preparedness measures.

Congress rejected the administration's plan to finance the war in favor of a loan of $11 million. By the declaration of war, only a little more than $6 million of the loan had been subscribed to. As for creating an army to invade Canada, Congress had gone only halfway. It authorized a larger force and issued incentives to man the force but otherwise had done little to mobilize the necessary manpower.

The war also called into question the power relationship between the federal and state levels. Authorized by Congress to call up the militia, Madison did so upon the declaration of war. The governors of Massachusetts, Connecticut, and Rhode Island refused to support the call-up on the grounds that there was no evidence of foreign invasion. Some of the militiamen who answered the call maintained their constitutional right not to serve outside the borders.

Within the administration, the tasks of waging war were divided between the Departments of War and Navy. Prior to 1812, the secretary of war was also the quartermaster general, commissary general, master of ordnance, Indian commissioner, commissioner of pensions, and commissioner of public lands. He was also, in effect, the army commander, because no single general was authorized by Congress to command the entire army lest he be tempted to provoke a coup. However, supplying the armed forces was a Treasury Department function. Although this organization seemed to concentrate sufficient power to wage war on land in the hands of one civilian, the opposite was true. Denied a sufficient staff and of decidedly limited managerial ability and energy, Secretary of War William Eustis could not transform the army from a small constabulary force into an offensive weapon. Eustis's shortcomings were public knowledge, and Congress acted to expand the secretary's staff and to rationalize the functions of his office. Despite Congress's efforts, the War Department frequently failed to provide adequate logistical support to the armies in the field.[20]

In 1812, Congress established the Quartermaster, Ordnance, and Commissary Departments. Immediate problems arose that prevented these departments from coming to grips with the logistical requirements of an expanded army and an offensive war. First, Congress had drawn up their functions so vaguely that department heads were entirely unsure of their responsibilities or their relationships with the others. Second, these new departments were staffed slowly and with people of mixed competencies.[21]

A nineteenth-century army traveled on its stomach, and it was in this area that failure was most vexing. Food was provided by private contractors, with one contractor responsible for feeding all troops in each of sixteen geographical districts. There was no provision to provide food outside of U.S. territory. Furthermore, the contractor, his agents, and his wagon crews were all civilians not subject to military discipline. When contractors failed to feed the army, which was often, local commanders were authorized emergency powers. They could direct their quartermasters to obligate funds to feed the troops, but if the contractor could not locate food in a region at a good price, it was unlikely that a deputy quartermaster would be able to either. The army limped though the war fed by the contractor system. When the troops were stationary, they were generally sufficiently fed. On the march, getting fed regularly was much more difficult.

Later in the war, the War Department divided the territory of the United States into nine, and eventually ten, military districts. Each was headed by a commanding general with a staff that included representatives of the Quartermaster, Commissary, and Ordnance Departments. This went a long way toward rationalizing the logistics system. After considerable growing pains, it eventually became standard procedure that the commissaries made the purchases and the quartermasters received, transported, and issued them. The entire system was nearly crippled by poor record keeping. The failures of the logistics system needlessly limited the ability of field commanders to accomplish all that the size of their armies suggested was possible.

The young republic was experiencing growing pains as its various political elites—the president and Congress, state governors and legislatures—maneuvered around the several constitutional issues involved. This lengthy process was complicated because the nation did not enter the war of one mind or with clearly stated goals. This strategic confusion prevented the United States from capitalizing on the many inherent advantages it enjoyed. It also tainted the formulation of strategic plans for the conduct of the war. In this the British, with a clearer understanding of what had to be done to defend Canada, were at a decided advantage.

The British government understood full well that while Britain was engaged in an economic and military war with France, British North America was vulnerable to American attack. However, what form that attack would take and the means to defeat it were the source of some debate. This controversy centered around the question of whether Britain could successfully hold all its territory. If the answer were no, then what portion of British North America should be defended with a prospect of success?

If Upper Canada were to be defended, then troops had to be stationed at vital points in the upper province as well as along the supply line. Troops positioned there could not defend the two vital points of British North America: Quebec, the gateway to the Great Lakes, and Halifax, one of the finest natural harbors in the New World and home port of the Atlantic squadron. Likewise, the British could not control Upper Canada for long if the American navy gained control of Lake Ontario for even a few months.

Writing to Lord Liverpool in 1812, Prevost elevated the defense of Quebec above all other concerns. As long as the British held Quebec, Prevost reasoned, they had a foothold on the continent from which to begin the reconquest of the upper and lower provinces. "I have considered the preservation of Quebec," wrote Sir George, "as the first object, and to which all others must be subordinate."[22] As soon as he learned of the declaration of war, Prevost deployed a large body of troops under Major General Francis de Rottenburg to block the Richelieu Valley and prevent the Americans from using the traditional invasion route north to Montreal and Quebec.[23]

A component of the British strategy was to widen the breach between Federalists and Republicans by keeping the war out of New England, the stronghold of the Federalist Party. The Royal Navy did not blockade New England ports until the last year of the war. New England responded to Britain's blandishment of sparing the lash by withholding support for the war. Furthermore, New Englanders invested heavily in British treasury notes while refusing to subscribe to federal loans. Trade between New England and British North America, particularly in meat and other foodstuffs, reached scandalous proportions. If Lower Canada was spared somewhat by New England's general reluctance to support the war, Upper Canada was less fortunate.[24]

Brock prepared Upper Canada to defend itself; he understood that little assistance would be forthcoming from Lower Canada. His strategy included alliance with the Indians as a key element. By going on the offensive early and striking successfully at Forts Detroit and Michilimackinac, which guarded the strait between Lakes Huron and Michigan, Brock was confident of inspiring the Indians with British determination to press the fight.[25] Once even a few Indians joined the British, Tecumseh might give the signal to his confederacy to begin the long-awaited attack to drive the Americans east across the mountains. When war began, Brock implemented his strategy with stunning success.

British defensive strategy was somewhat of a compromise. The governor in chief subordinated all other efforts to the defense of Halifax and Quebec yet did not pull back troops allocated to the defense of Upper Canada from the outset. Prevost allowed Brock and subsequent commanders in chief to attempt to hold on to the West, as long as they did not draw on forces guarding Quebec. The

Americans, contradicting the assumption of British strategic thought, did not appear to be focused on Quebec or Halifax but instead concentrated their attacks on Montreal and points west.

Congress's first concern, however, was for the defense of the United States, and it directed the secretary of war to estimate the resources required to safeguard the seacoast and the western frontier. Eustis replied that it would require nearly 30,000 infantry and artillerists to man the coastal fortifications alone. Eustis presumed that it was not Congress's intent to man all the fortifications at maximum strength "but to provide such a force as may be sufficient to meet probable emergencies, and to defend the most exposed and important posts."[26] Eustis offered his opinion that it was "impracticable" to give a definite reply to the question of how many troops were required to defend the existing fortifications, since the nature of the attacking force would determine the number and type of defensive troops.[27] Eustis's reply could not have been particularly enlightening to Congress, which was searching for a professional judgment of the force structure required to carry out Congress's responsibility to defend the country. However, there was no shortage of opinions on how to carry the war to the enemy.

As early as February 1812, war hawk Peter B. Porter outlined a plan to attack Canada. Porter assumed that the British would leave a large garrison at Quebec in recognition of the vital nature of that city to the defense of British North America. Considering the 20,000 Canadian militia that might be mobilized to be inferior to Americans in arms, discipline, and national spirit, Porter argued in favor of a quick attack by volunteers. Volunteers, a grade of soldier between regular and militia, could not hide behind the militia's right not to leave U.S. territory. Also, because their term of enlistment was for only one year, they could be raised faster and in larger numbers than regulars. These volunteers would cut the St. Lawrence River between Montreal and Quebec and then lay siege to Quebec while a regular army was recruited and trained in the United States. Since it would take months for a relieving force to arrive from Europe, the American regulars would take over the siege lines before the British reinforcements arrived. Porter's plan was perceptive, in that he understood that speed in assuming the offensive would minimize the risk of failure. He also understood, as did the British strategists, the importance of the fortress of Quebec and of the St. Lawrence as the vital artery into Upper Canada.[28]

General Henry Dearborn expanded on Porter's concept. While echoing the requirement for a decisive attack north from Lake Champlain to cut the St. Lawrence at Montreal, he added supporting attacks originating from Detroit, the Niagara Frontier, and Sacketts Harbor on Lake Ontario.[29] However, the western war hawks clamored for an attack from Detroit to neutralize Fort Malden, thus eliminating much of the Indian problem. Many noted the strategic inefficiency of this course of action. Among them was Senator Obadiah German, who argued that to attack Malden and then move eastward would only force the enemy back on its own supply lines. "But let your army be enabled by its strength to first possess itself of Montreal, and all the upper country must fall of course."[30] Madison saw the dilemma. An attack on Montreal made the most military sense, but he well understood the political issue: the westerners would be the first to raise an army of volunteers but would not move to attack Montreal, since it would mean leaving the frontier open to Indian attack.[31] Madison approved Dearborn's plan for a multipronged attack against Canada. America's offensive was to be piecemeal across the extensive frontier, none of the forces in supporting distance of the others. Still, each attacking force would enjoy numerical superiority if the attacks were made simultaneously, thus preventing the British from crushing each one in turn.

Jefferson articulated perhaps the most visionary of the American strategies. Assuming that the Americans would take Quebec in 1812 and Halifax the following year, Jefferson anticipated a British naval response. "Their fleet will annihilate our public force on the water but our privateers will eat out the vitals of their commerce. Perhaps they may burn New York or Boston. If they do we must burn the city of London, not by expensive fleets or Congreve rockets but by employing an hundred or two Jack the painters, whom nakedness, famine, desperation & hardened vice will abundantly furnish from among themselves."[32] Jefferson presented a glimpse of a farsighted strategy of military, economic, and sociopolitical dimensions. Of course, after two years of struggle, no American army seriously threatened Quebec or Halifax.

A quick review of the war in 1812 and 1813 paints a picture of a competent British strategy staving off repeated American offensives. The few American successes were operationally stillborn; that is, the tactical success achieved could not be extended to further strategic advantage.

Shortly before the outbreak of the war, the United States was divided into three parts for military operations. Henry Dearborn, the senior major general, commanded the Northern Department consisting of New England and the Middle Atlantic states. His main army, referred to as the Northern Army, was concentrated on the Hudson-Champlain Valley, anticipating the main attack toward Montreal. Subordinate forces gathered along the Niagara Frontier. Major General Thomas Pinckney commanded the Southern Department. His responsibility was the defense of the Gulf and Atlantic coasts forming the outer perimeter of his department. The Northwest Department encompassed Ohio and the territories carved out of the Northwest Territory. Commanding this department was William Hull, governor of the Michigan Territory and recently commissioned brigadier general. His main force, the Army of the Northwest, was to attack Upper Canada from Detroit. The creation of three commands subordinate to the Department of War was not without confusion. For example, for the first few weeks of the war, Dearborn did not realize that he commanded the forces along the Niagara and at Sacketts Harbor and that he was charged with the defense of those vital posts.[33]

In Lower Canada, the legislature immediately ordered all Americans to leave the province in two weeks. The dilatory nature of Dearborn's preparations allowed the time needed to get Lower Canada into a defensive posture. In Upper Canada, Brock did not enjoy the support of his citizens as Prevost did in Quebec; yet he possessed a genius for war that made up for the lack of spirit in the populace. While Dearborn raised his army in the Central Theater of operations, fighting began in the Western Theater. In Dayton, Hull collected an army of enthusiastic Ohio volunteers stiffened by a regiment of regulars. With an untrained and poorly equipped volunteer force, the Army of the Northwest marched north through the wilds of Ohio to Detroit and into Upper Canada. Hull's line of communication ran hundreds of miles through forest and swamp and then for sixty miles along the shore of Lake Erie and the Detroit River, where it was threatened by the Provincial Marine on the water and Tecumseh's warriors on land.[34]

No sooner had the Americans invaded Canada than Brock appeared at Fort Malden. His first act was to order a successful attack on Fort Michilimackinac on Mackinac Island, which guarded the narrows connecting Lakes Michigan and Huron. The Indians of the upper lakes, encouraged by British boldness and apparent commitment to fight the Americans, flocked to Tecumseh. These native warriors multiplied the combat power of Brock's slender force of regulars, giving it power beyond its numbers.

Hull, meanwhile, issued a proclamation to the Canadian people and distributed it widely throughout the region, hoping to profit by the popular lack of fervor for the British cause. He promised to protect the "peaceable unoffending inhabitant" while reminding them of their lack of voice in the decisions made in Britain concerning them. Hull warned those Canadians choosing to fight with the British that they would "be considered and treated as enemies" and, if found fighting alongside the Indians, faced "instant destruction." He concluded his address with a stark choice: "The United States offer you Peace, Liberty, and Security—your choice lies between these and war, slavery, and destruction." Although not openly promising the annexation of Canada, that notion was implicit in his language.[35]

The effect was immediate if not decisive. Hundreds of Canadian militiamen voluntarily gave Hull their parole and returned to their farms, thus removing themselves from military obligation until officially exchanged. Others volunteered to act as scouts. Brock attributed these acts of treason to a general belief among the populace that American victory was a virtual certainty. Brock's decisive action would soon disabuse them of this view, but first he issued a proclamation of his own.

Declaring that the American invasion was unprovoked, he went on to remind civilians that the prosperity they enjoyed was the result of British naval superiority, which guaranteed Canadians access to world markets. Brock was blunt about the consequences of an American victory: "It is but too obvious that once exchanged from the powerful protection of the United Kingdom you must be reannexed to the dominion of France." Addressing Hull's vow to summarily execute Canadians found fighting alongside Indians, Brock promised retribution "in every quarter of the Globe" for what he termed the "deliberate murder" that Hull threatened.[36] It is difficult to say what effect Brock's words may have had on the people of the upper province, followed as closely as they were by his audacious military action.

Hull withdrew from Upper Canada because he could not keep his army supplied. Without control of Lake Erie, the Army of the Northwest depended on its land line of communication. Few wagons, teams, or pack animals were available, and on the occasion when resupply columns were ordered to Detroit, they were ambushed by Indians. Most of Hull's army was in Detroit when Brock and his force crossed the river and opened siege on 15 August. Hull was paralyzed with fear lest Tecumseh's Indians slaughter the families under his protection. Although outnumbering Brock's army, even augmented as it was by Indians, Hull surrendered the soldiers with him and 500 more who were guarding his supply route south of Detroit.

After he was exchanged, Hull was convicted by court-martial for neglect of duty and sentenced to death but received a presidential reprieve. The results of this first invasion of Canada were a far cry from those predicted by the war hawks. Instead of victory, hundreds of volunteers and regulars were captured, and numerous Indians threw in their lot with Tecumseh.

Madison eventually gave Hull's command to William Henry Harrison, a major general of the Kentucky militia as well as governor of the Indiana Territory. Harrison ordered multiple punitive expeditions to destroy Indian villages and foodstuffs found there. These raids were effective in quieting the natives while Harrison struggled to raise, equip, and train a new army. Madison was slowly becoming educated in the strategic issues involved. In a letter to Dearborn, he approved Harrison's heavy-handed tactics with the natives in order to "stamp deep on the Indian mind, the little security they have in British protection." Madison also came to appreciate the decisive importance of permanent naval control of the Great Lakes.[37]

Dearborn prosecuted the war in the Central Theater of Operations with as little success as Hull enjoyed. He initially occupied himself with preparing the defenses of New England and New York City. On 7 August, Dearborn wrote to Eustis to request that New York State militia Major General Stephen Van Rennselaer take command of all troops on that front, both regulars and militia. Rennselaer's poorly equipped and virtually untrained force became known as the Army of the Center.[38] Disaster befell that force on 13 October 1812 at Queenston Heights. The militiamen who made up the bulk of Rennselaer's army refused to cross the border, thus squandering the success of the initial assault. Although victorious in repelling the American invasion, disaster of another kind struck the British that day. While leading a desperate attack, the brilliant and heroic Brock was killed in action. These same American militiamen who showed more constitutional awareness than courage at Queenston Heights reasserted their right not to serve outside the territory of the United States six weeks later, forcing regular Brigadier General Alexander Smyth to cancel two attempts to invade Canada.

The secretary of war had charged Dearborn with the responsibility of leading the main attack into Canada by way of the Champlain-Richelieu Valleys. Dearborn seemed stymied by the requirement to defend the coastline while conducting an attack several hundred miles inland. He was plagued by slow recruiting, and the governors of Massachusetts and Connecticut refused to answer the president's call for militia. In the last half of November, Dearborn's Northern Army lurched into Canada and at the La Colle River was stopped in its tracks by a small, mixed force of Canadian fencibles, Indians, and militia. Suffering only a handful of casualties, Dearborn's force meekly withdrew to Plattsburg.

What little success the United States enjoyed was found on the water. In September, the Navy Department gave Isaac Chauncey command of all naval forces on the Great Lakes. Luring a few hundred seamen from the Atlantic coast to Sacketts Harbor with promises of prize money, Chauncey began building a fleet on Lake Ontario. Cruising in November with a flotilla led by the newly launched *Madison,* he captured three merchant vessels and chased the largest British vessel, the *Royal George,* into Kingston Harbor. None of this had lasting significance, but the naval arms race begun by Chauncey on Lake Ontario had an unforeseen and unfortunate effect on the 1814 campaign.[39] Eclipsing events on Lake Ontario, the U.S. Navy won repeated victories on the high seas of the Atlantic Theater during 1812. In that year, the navy captured forty-six merchantmen. However, it was in ship-to-ship combat that the navy and its fighting captains won justifiable glory. On 19 August, Isaac Hull (nephew of the disgraced general) led the crew of the USS *Constitution* to a decisive victory over Richard Dacre's frigate HMS *Guerriere.* A month later, the sloop of war USS *Wasp* met HMS *Frolic.* In a ferocious fight, the *Frolic* yielded after suffering 84 percent casualties among its crew.

On 25 October, the fifty-four-gun *United States* met the *Macedonian,* carrying forty-eight guns. Stephen Decatur's ship and crew mauled the British frigate and brought *Macedonian* into Newport, Rhode Island; this was the only time a captured British frigate was brought into an American port. Near the end of the year, *Constitution* (now commanded by William Bainbridge) met HMS *Java* in the South Atlantic and overpowered it. These victories were largely the result of superior gunnery skills of American crews. The performance of the navy restored some pride in a nation humiliated by the deplorable showing of its several armies.

The federal government took half measures to address some of the worst deficiencies revealed in the previous campaign season. Madison fired Eustis, which was an act of mercy for a man so obviously out of his depth. Congress increased the authorized strength of the army to over 57,000 and allowed one-year enlistments. Officers were commissioned, but the regiments filled slowly; only one-third of the authorized strength was attained. The war dragged into 1813 with some tactical victories on the ground for the Americans but scant gains in achieving the national goals.

As the new year opened, the war seemed to be following the pattern of disasters established in 1812. In the Western Theater of Operations, a force of about 1,000 Kentucky volunteers and regulars occupied Frenchtown on the River Raisin. On 21 January, the American force was mauled, and over half were captured. In the aftermath of the battle, some Indians, well fortified with whiskey, slaughtered a large number of wounded prisoners of war. Kentucky was inflamed with rage and prosecuted the war with the same fervor that possessed Henry Clay.

In Washington, strategic direction of the ground war was given to John Armstrong, the new secretary of war, on 13 January. Armstrong had more energy, political savvy, and strategic sense than his predecessor. However, he also brought with him a well-deserved reputation as an intriguer and would feud with Monroe to the detriment of the war effort. What Madison needed was a secretary of war who would push the generals to act aggressively, and it appeared that Armstrong was the man.[40] While Armstrong understood that only operations against Montreal, Quebec, and Halifax would be decisive in achieving the nation's war aims, it was in the Western Theater that the only permanent gains of 1813 were made, and these by a general and commodore who required no prodding from Washington.

In May, Lieutenant Colonel Henry Procter followed up his victory at the River Raisin with a siege of Fort Meigs on the Maumee River. Procter eventually broke off the siege so that his militiamen could return to Upper Canada to plant their crops, but not before an American relief force met catastrophe, losing about 650 killed or captured within a short distance of their objective. Major General Francis de Rottenburg, the new commander in Upper Canada, warned Procter that if the Americans won control of Lake Ontario, de Rottenburg would withdraw all forces from the West as far back as Kingston. This reflected a sound understanding that tactical victories in the West would be irrelevant if the line of communication was cut anywhere to the east. Procter wanted to destroy Perry's fleet being built at Presque-Isle at the eastern end of Lake Erie, but Tecumseh would cooperate only in a second attempt to take Fort Meigs. The garrison of Fort Meigs withstood a second siege in late July without difficulty. Procter turned his attention to Fort Stephenson on the Sandusky River in early August. The British and Indian assault was bloodily repulsed by the defenders—160 regulars under Major George Croghan.

The stage was now set for the most decisive battle of the Western Theater of Operations, the Battle of Lake Erie.[41] The opposing commanders, Robert Barclay at Amherstburg and Oliver Hazard Perry at Presque-Isle, were at the western ends of long lines of communication. Perry had the advantage in building his fleet, in that the material he required was available in the United States. Much of what Barclay required, except ship timber itself, had to come from Europe. The epic proportions of the shipbuilding effort on both sides enhanced the magnitude of the American victory. Neither Barclay nor Perry received much assistance from their superiors—Sir James Yeo at Kingston, and Chauncey at Sacketts Harbor. Commodore Perry's dramatic victory over his hard-fighting foe on 10 September earned decisive results only because of the extremely good cooperation Perry enjoyed with Harrison. The ground commander timed his preparations to coincide with those of the aggressive Perry. Within two weeks of the lake battle, Perry disembarked Harrison's well-trained army of 5,000 Kentucky volunteers and regulars three miles from Amherstburg.

The loss of Lake Erie proved catastrophic for Tecumseh and Procter. The British at Amherstburg could not be supplied by land from Burlington Heights at the western end of Lake Ontario. Procter took the only action he could to save his army: he withdrew eastward up the Thames River Valley. Of course, this enraged Tecumseh, who saw his dream of an Indian confederation collapsing with the loss of British support. The tragedy of the western Indian was played to its conclusion at the Battle of the Thames, in which Harrison destroyed the British-Indian force. Tecumseh was killed, fighting to the bitter end.[42]

Although the twin victories of Lake Erie and the Thames buoyed American spirits and chastised the Indians in the Old Northwest, they had little effect on securing American war aims. Harrison could not support an advance further eastward to Lake Ontario. He returned his army to Detroit, where it could be fed. Armstrong offered Harrison a command in Cincinnati, far from the action. Harrison, the only general who was winning battles, resigned in disgust. The United States retained a toehold in western Upper Canada that might be useful at the peace negotiations. However, success in the subordinate Western Theater was to be counterbalanced by ultimate defeat in the strategic Central Theater.

Even before taking office, Armstrong had understood that only operations against Montreal, Quebec, and Halifax would be decisive. In February 1813, Armstrong analyzed the military situation and was forced to conclude that Dearborn's army in northern New York was just too weak to capture Montreal before the ice on the St. Lawrence broke up and the British could reinforce Montreal from Quebec. He turned his attention to and saw real possibilities along Lake Ontario. "It then remains to choose between a course of entire inaction, because incompetent to the main attack, or one having a secondary, but still an important object."[43] Timing was important; Dearborn would have to start his offensive well before May, when the ice on the St. Lawrence broke up. Control of the lake was critical, and Chauncey persuaded Dearborn and Armstrong that a raid on York (modern name, Toronto) to destroy a ship being built there would go far in tipping the naval balance in the Americans' favor. Thus at the beginning of 1813, the focus of American offensive action was diverted from the decisive objective of cutting the British line of communication to lesser objectives toward the west, prizes that would have fallen of their own weight had Montreal been taken.[44] A detailed account and analysis of the military operations in the Central Theater are found in subsequent chapters. The following is an abbreviated description.

Dearborn and Chauncey led the raid on York on 27 April 1813, which resulted in the destruction of the British warship and the unfortunate death of an aggressive American commander, western explorer Zebulon Pike. They followed up their victory with a successful attack on Fort George at the mouth of the Niagara River late in May. Brigadier General John Vincent, who evacuated his force from Fort George rather than risk its destruction, withdrew toward Burlington Heights.

Sir James Yeo raided Sacketts Harbor while Chauncey was away supporting Dearborn's operations. Successfully commanding the defenders of the largest American shipbuilding base on the Great Lakes was militia Brigadier General Jacob Brown. Brown displayed spirit and skill that would serve the American cause well in subsequent campaigns. Although a tactical failure, Yeo's raid served to draw Chauncey back to his base and to make him more reluctant in the future to support the army if it meant risking his fleet or his base. Dearborn tried to force Vincent into decisive combat but was rewarded for his efforts with twin defeats at Stoney Creek on 6 June and Beaver Dams on 24 June. This was too much for Armstrong, who assigned Dearborn to a quiet sector ostensibly for health reasons and appointed James Wilkinson to command the Northern Army.

In July, Armstrong was forced to return to the conclusion of the cold strategic logic of the war: decisive results would follow only with the cutting of the British line of communication—the farther east the cut, the more decisive the result. Unfortunately, Armstrong's strategic insights were not enough to make up for the shortcomings of the commanders charged with winning the battles.

Armstrong planned a two-pronged offensive. Starting from Sacketts Harbor, Wilkinson would feint toward Kingston and then dash down the St. Lawrence toward Montreal. Meanwhile, Major General Wade Hampton, also a veteran of the Revolution, would advance north from Lake Champlain. The two forces would link up and together reduce Montreal. Hampton and 4,000 regulars were defeated on 25 October by Lieutenant Colonel Charles-Michel de Salaberry, a veteran of the Napoleonic Wars, and his small force of fencibles and Lower Canada militia. Wilkinson fared no better. He chose to retreat after a setback at Crysler's Farm on 11 November. Hampton and Wilkinson were pale shadows of Richard Montgomery and Benedict Arnold. Armstrong's strategy to win in 1813 in the decisive theater of war lay in ruins.

In the Atlantic Theater of Operations, the U.S. Navy's impressive string of ship-on-ship victories ended on 24 February, when James Lawrence's sloop of war *Hornet* destroyed HMS *Peacock*. In June, while in command of USS *Chesapeake*, Lawrence died fighting unsuccessfully against Philip Broke's *Shannon* outside of Boston Harbor. By this time, the British blockade was firmly in place, although from time to time small U.S. Navy vessels slipped through the cordon to conduct nuisance raids. None of the frigates launched in 1813 made it to the open seas. The blockade drove import duties from a prewar high of $413 million to just $2 million. American exports shrank 80 percent from prewar figures. Coastal shipping was dramatically reduced, but land transportation could not pick up the slack. Retail prices rose. To top it off, the Royal Navy under Admiral Sir George Cockburn brought the war to the coastal communities along the Chesapeake, destroying private homes along with public property, warehouses, ferryboats, and mills. One is forced to conclude that the Republicans' short-sighted—indeed, naïve—naval policy was the primary cause of America's inability to break the blockade or to defend its coast.

The war also exploded in an unforeseen area: the Southern Theater of Operations. The Creek War, fought largely in Alabama, was an uprising sympathetic to Tecumseh's war in the Western Theater. The Creek Nation in 1813 was in a similar position in relation to the United States as the United States was to Britain. Its 24,000 people had grievances that could not be resolved by negotiation. Creek national pride was stung by the refusal of American authorities to stop settlement in Creek lands. While the United States was fully occupied in a faltering war effort, some Creeks (generally known as Red Sticks) decided to strike. On 30 August, about 1,000 Red Sticks massacred over 500 adults and children at Fort Mims. The governor of Tennessee directed Andrew Jackson, major general of militia, to punish the anti-American Creeks.

The war was brutal in the extreme, with atrocities perpetrated by both sides. Militia and volunteers from surrounding states joined in the war effort, but it was Jackson's iron will that won the decisive campaign. On 27 March 1814, at the Battle of Horseshoe Bend, Jackson's volunteers and a regiment of regulars crushed the major Red Stick fighting force. The war was devastating for the Creek Nation. Besides suffering large loss of life, the Creeks ceded 20 million acres of their land to the United States. In some measure, the United States was achieving its goal of securing its frontier from Indian attack not only by eliminating British influence in the Old Northwest but also by physically destroying the anti-American factions among the tribes.

The failure of the 1813 campaign to seize the Canadas or to drive Britain to make maritime concessions encouraged the antiwar faction in Congress. They articulated the strategic dilemma of the administration: forces used to attack Canada were unavailable for the defense of the coast.[45] To emphasize their apprehension, the Maryland House of Delegates sent a memorial to the president and Congress in February 1814, decrying the "awful condition of national affairs, and the exposed and defenseless situation in which the State of Maryland had been hitherto left by the General Government, under the impending calamities of war."[46]

Under political pressure to stop British attacks on the Atlantic coast, the administration equivocated on the future of Canada. As early as June 1813, Monroe sent secret instructions to his team of peace negotiators that he believed it "proper" to reestablish the boundary with British North America northward, so as to give the United States control over the Great Lakes. He did not, however, require the expulsion of Britain from mainland North America. This gave his negotiators some room to conclude a peace quickly.[47]

At the beginning of 1814, the British could look to the previous eighteen months with a sense of satisfaction. They had beaten back repeated attempts to seize Canada, and the pro-American faction had proved to be not much more than a nuisance. The British counteroffensive of 1814 was planned in London and consisted of two components.[48]

The first took a form most feared by the Maryland House of Delegates: naval raids on the coast. A second offensive, aimed at eastern Maine, attempted to secure the land line of communication between Halifax and Quebec. To make matters worse for the Americans, Napoleon's strategic retreat in Europe released thousands of veterans of the fighting in Spain for operations in North America. Many of these troops joined Admiral Alexander Cochrane's campaign on the Atlantic coast, and the remainder were eventually directed at New Orleans by sea and New York by way of the Champlain-Hudson invasion route.[49]

The first few months of 1814 saw a serious reassessment of strategy by the administration. Month after month, the signs became unmistakable that Britain was moving to seize the military initiative that so far had been enjoyed by the Americans. That Napoleon's defeat at the Battle of Leipzig meant the release of tens of thousands of British soldiers was not lost on Congress or the administration. Recruiting for American regular soldiers was at a virtual standstill, and conscription was rejected because it would be politically damaging to the Republicans.

Early in January, Washington learned of the loss of Fort Niagara and the destruction of settlements on the Niagara Frontier. Governor Tompkins, New York's strong supporter of the war, wrote to Armstrong that the British, "if left unmolested . . . will inevitably go to Erie to destroy the vessels there & will besides take Detroit." Tompkins was adamant that militia alone could not salvage the situation. He proposed a joint counteroffensive. If Armstrong would send 2,500 regulars, Tompkins would provide 5,000 militiamen. Tompkins was strategist enough to understand that the British line of communication was vital to keeping the British at Niagara. He proposed an immediate attack on Prescott, Upper Canada, across from Ogdensburg, New York, to cut off supplies to Kingston and points west.[50] The Niagara campaign of 1814 grew out of Tompkins's proposal, but that strategy evolved slowly and in a twisted fashion.

February brought news that had both negative and positive implications. The American government learned that Napoleon's armies had largely withdrawn into France, and Wellington had crossed north of the Pyrenees. Although the defeat of France released British forces, it also removed Britain's requirement for impressment. With the orders in council already revoked and the Indian uprisings being quelled, many of the tangible reasons for war were disappearing.

The war hawks saw the writing on the wall. They had been unable to win the war in 1812 or 1813. Victory in Canada would be unlikely, and devastation of American cities possible, if Britain deployed its immense combat power to the Western Hemisphere. A window of opportunity (an interval of unknown length) existed in which Canada might still be seized before it was strongly reinforced. It was to this end that the Madison administration directed its strategic thought. There might be time and resources for one more attempt. The strategic imperative, disregarded so often in the past, mandated that the decisive campaign be directed at cutting the line of communication that sustained British North America. The last chance to win the war, to capture Canada, to assert national honor would be played out in the Central Theater. Standing in the way was a slender force of British regulars, Canadian fencibles and militia, and those few Indians in whose minds still flickered the brave dream of confederation.

CHAPTER THREE

The Central Theater of Operations

But it seems this is to be a holiday campaign—there is to be no expense of blood, or treasure, on our part—Canada is to conquer herself—she is to be subdued by the principles of fraternity. The people of that country are first to be seduced from their allegiance, and converted into traitors as preparatory to the making them good citizens.
—Congressman John Randolph, 10 December 1811

The principal theater of operations was clearly the Central Theater, for it was there that the belligerents expected to decide the war. By 1812, the region was peopled by the progeny of those who had so desperately disputed the land in the previous centuries: the scattered remnants of a once powerful Iroquois Nation, unenthusiastic French-speaking subjects of George III, descendants of those British loyalists who chose to emigrate rather than accept American republicanism, and finally, the confident children of the American rebels.

The course of the war in the Central Theater of Operations revealed stark contrasts and unexpected consequences. This expanse of thick forests divided by two wide rivers and an inland sea had witnessed the greatest American efforts and their most decisive and humiliating defeats. The war in this theater exposed the bankruptcy of U.S. strategy and flaunted the corresponding success of desperate British defensive measures. The conflict marked the ruin and manifested the rise of the reputations of warriors on all sides. Episodes of extreme physical courage in combat were matched by incidents of moral cowardice away from the battlefield. Fighting that had been characterized in the beginning by patriotic motivation and chivalrous conduct had become increasingly marked by treasonous self-interest and brutish violence against former neighbors. It was in this context that the belligerents planned and conducted the Niagara campaign of 1814. To understand this last American invasion of

37

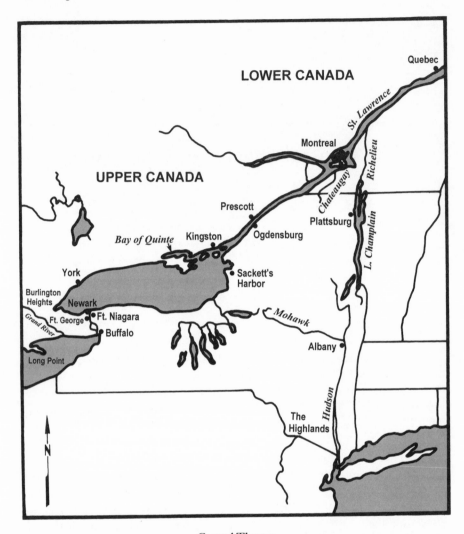

Central Theater

Canada, some sense must be made of the geographic, demographic, and political realities of the time and region.

In 1812, the secretary of war decided that military operations on such a vast scale could not be managed directly from Washington. Eustis divided the country into three areas, each the responsibility of an army commander. The area that Americans of the time referred to as the Northern Frontier generally corresponds to the Central Theater. Eustis's scheme proved unmanageable for two of the army commanders—Hull and Dearborn. Early in 1813, the United States was divided into nine, later ten, military districts delineated generally along state boundaries.[1] The American portion of the Central Theater was designated the Ninth Military District and included all of Vermont, New York north of the Highlands, and much of western Pennsylvania.[2] The U.S. Navy, subdividing its forces differently, gave Chauncey command of all forces on the Great Lakes and Lake Champlain. Thus the naval command spanned both the Ninth Military District and the Eighth, which was composed of the states of Ohio and Kentucky and the territories of Indiana, Illinois, Michigan, and Missouri. The Eighth District corresponded generally to the American portion of the Western Theater of Operations.

The British delegated military and naval command within provincial boundaries. Governor-General Sir George Prevost was commander in chief of all army and navy forces in British North America. The governor-general delegated command of the army and navy in Upper Canada, New Brunswick, and Nova Scotia to the lieutenant governors of those provinces while retaining direct military command in Lower Canada. The British enjoyed an enormous advantage by vesting both land and naval commands in a single person at the provincial level, whereas in the United States, army and navy commands came together only in the person of the president himself in his role as commander in chief.

The provinces of Upper and Lower Canada were divided politically into districts and further subdivided into counties. Militia units were raised along county lines; for example, the Second Lincoln Militia was raised in Lincoln County of the Niagara District of Upper Canada. This was also generally true in the American militia, although some regiments drew men from several counties but always from the same state. However, British regular units were organized along other lines. In Upper Canada, for example, the lieutenant governor subdivided his command into divisions that were primarily administrative headquarters but could also serve as tactical headquarters. The three divisions were the Right Division in the western part of the province, the Center Division encompassing the Niagara Peninsula and York, and the Left Division centered on Kingston. The term *division* in this usage is unlike the European meaning of that time: a level of organization between an army corps and a brigade. These divisions had no set boundaries, and units were interchanged among them freely as the military situation demanded.

Within the Ninth Military District, regular and volunteer units were often found in three concentrations: along the Niagara River, at Sacketts Harbor, and straddling Lake Champlain at Plattsburg and Burlington. These concentrations were grouped into brigades, and the brigades (along with separate units such as cavalry and artillery companies) collected into divisions. As in the British construct, American divisions had no fixed organization.

The geography of the Central Theater sharply limited the range of options open to the opposing commanders. The primary waterways, which were the principal highways in this undeveloped land, did not provide secure lines of communication to the fighting front but rather defined the fighting front. Except for the short stretch of land border between Lower Canada and New York, major waterways defined the political border between the belligerents. In the case of the British, the political border was also the primary line of communication connecting Quebec with nearly all the Canadian settlements. Since the roads throughout the Central Theater were fair at best and often unusable in wet weather, the waterways carried the vast bulk of cargo traffic. On average, water travel was six times faster than land travel and correspondingly less expensive except when icebound.[3] An examination of these waterways reveals much about the parameters and imperatives of strategy in the Central Theater.

Starting at Quebec and moving upriver, the St. Lawrence was readily navigable to Montreal. Entirely within British territory, this stretch of river was also fairly easy to secure and was paralleled by a road of good quality. However, between Montreal and Kingston at the foot of Lake Ontario, river traffic was impeded by three sets of rapids. These rapids were best negotiated by bateaux, which had to be towed from the shore in some places. During the war, convoys of bateaux were escorted by gunboats for protection. This security measure slowed down travel, and convoys typically took eight days to move from Montreal to Kingston.[4] A road of uneven quality, often not much more than a trail, paralleled this portion of the river. From Kingston, cargoes were transloaded to larger vessels and sailed up the first of the Great Lakes. The St. Lawrence becomes icebound in January and is not completely open to navigation until mid-May. Thus, winter cargoes were moved by sleigh on frozen roads or, more likely, remained under cover until spring.

Geography also limited American transportation from the base at New York City northward into the theater of operations. The Hudson River–Lake Champlain–Richelieu River corridor pointed like a sword to Montreal. Three small steamboats plied the Hudson and in thirty-six hours could move mail, passengers, and small cargoes upriver from New York to Albany.[5] From Albany, cargo was moved by water and short stretches overland to Plattsburg on Lake Champlain. Plattsburg was the American base of operations for thrusts down the Richelieu, which emptied into the St. Lawrence about fifty miles downriver from Montreal.

The American line of communication to Sacketts Harbor, the major American base on Lake Ontario, also passed through Albany. Cargo was brought up the Mohawk River to Rome, then by combinations of road and water to the mouth of the Oswego River, and finally by boat eastward to the home base of the American Ontario squadron. The Oswego River was interrupted by Oswego Falls, actually a stretch of rapids rather than a falls. Oswego Falls was a major bottleneck in the line of communication to Sacketts Harbor, and immense quantities of supplies were usually stockpiled at the southern end of the rapids awaiting shipment.[6]

The road from Rome directly to Sacketts Harbor was of such poor quality that heavy loads such as cannon had to be sent by water. Plattsburg and Sacketts Harbor were connected by the St. Lawrence turnpike, a poor-quality dirt road that passed through Malone in Franklin County. Virtually all the roads in northern New York were poor at the best of times. For example, a stagecoach leaving New York City required five days to reach the St. Lawrence. The roads were most useful when frozen.[7]

Lake Ontario bisected the Central Theater, separating its two invasion routes: an eastern route along the Richelieu Valley, and a western route across the Niagara Peninsula. The lake itself was a broad waterborne avenue of invasion. Depending on the weather, a fleet could move an army the length of the lake in three days or cross it in one. That same army would take eighteen days or longer to march around the northern shore of the lake. Thus command of the water yielded a decided—indeed, potentially decisive—advantage. When neither side commanded the lake, the attacker would enjoy a short-lived advantage, as the defender would have to march troops some distance to meet the invader. This advantage usually fell to the Americans, who typically kept troops at three jumping-off points (Plattsburg, Buffalo, and Sacketts Harbor), thus threatening to cross the St. Lawrence, the Niagara, Lake Ontario, or all three. This forced the British to maintain a balanced but weak defense across the entire front.[8]

The shape of Lake Ontario favored the British. They enjoyed two excellent harbors: Kingston and York. The British determined that Kingston would be the major base, as it was closer to Montreal and therefore more easily supported. Additionally, the British controlled Burlington Bay and the Bay of Quinte, which served as refuges for British vessels chased by the American fleet. In contrast, the Americans had only Sacketts Harbor. The mouth of the Niagara River was adequate as a sheltered haven, although vessels might have to wait out rough waters before landing their cargoes. However, the river mouth was useless for this purpose unless both Forts George and Niagara were in friendly hands. This was the case for seven months of 1813, when its shores were in American hands, and for all of 1814, when the British controlled both sides of the river's mouth.[9] Lake Ontario was generally ice-free by early April, six weeks before the St. Lawrence was open completely. Thus the Americans could begin operations west of Kingston in earnest well before the British could bring reinforcements from Montreal or Quebec.[10]

The thirty-seven-mile Niagara River is actually a strait connecting Lakes Erie and Ontario. The Niagara, flowing from south to north, would be unremarkable except for its magnificent fall over a 200-foot-high ledge that runs for nearly

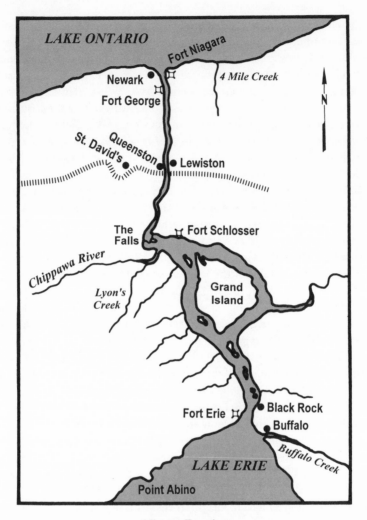

Niagara Frontier

eighty miles perpendicular to the river. Through the millennia, the Niagara cut a deep gorge from the edge of this escarpment eight miles to the lip of the falls. The effects of the escarpment define the trafficability of the river.

Starting at the mouth of the river at the eastern end of Lake Erie, the Niagara is nearly level with the land on both sides, rendering access to the river and crossing it fairly easy by human- or sail-powered vessels. About five miles north of its start, the river bifurcates, only to unite again seven miles downstream. The resulting landform, Grand Island, is low and flat and in 1812 was wooded, as was most of the Niagara region. From Grand Island, the river flows westward for a few miles and then turns sharply north. Here begin the rapids, entirely uncrossable, which lead in short order to the precipice. From the falls, the river wends its way through the steep and deep gorge that makes access to the river impossible. Once past the edge of the escarpment, the Niagara flows seven more miles into Lake Ontario. This last segment is easily crossed, as the river is once again just a few feet below ground level on either shore. Dozens of small creeks feed the Niagara along its course. The largest, the Chippawa River, enters the Niagara at a turn in the river just above the falls. Few of these streams were fordable at their mouths, although all could be waded by men and horses at some distance from the Niagara. In 1812, the mouths of the streams were crossed by wooden bridges, and these bridges connected by two rough roads, one on each side of the river and parallel to it.

The Niagara River forms the eastern edge of the Niagara Peninsula. This landform is bounded on the north by Lake Ontario and on the south by Lake Erie. The land is generally level, divided into two unequal pieces by the escarpment. North of the escarpment, a dozen creeks flow northward into Lake Ontario and are generally named by their distance from the northern mouth of the Niagara. These creeks are unfordable at their mouths, but most can be crossed upstream.

At the northwestern corner of the peninsula is Burlington Bay, a large body of water protected from the worst of the lake storms by a spit of low land nearly closing off the mouth of the bay. In 1812, the major road network was an east-west dirt road north of the escarpment that connected the Niagara River to Burlington Bay and bridged the many intervening streams. At the time of the war, the Niagara Peninsula was checkered with tracts of cleared and cultivated land, most of them near the Niagara or Lake Ontario. However, most of the generally flat land was densely wooded, cut by numerous streams and shallow ravines, and marked at intervals by small swamps.

The terrain of the Niagara Peninsula largely determined the location of military operations. Large bodies of troops with artillery, wagons, and horses could cross the Niagara only south of the rapids or north of the escarpment. The escarpment itself, fairly steep and wooded in most places, was not easily crossed by artillery or supply wagons. Thus any large-scale advance over the peninsula was effectively restricted to the very narrow corridor of land north of the escarpment. An invading army would require sustenance while moving and fighting across the peninsula and therefore would want to remain in proximity to Lake Erie or Lake Ontario or to the Niagara River in order to be resupplied by a combination of boat and wagon convoy. Small raiding parties of mounted men, foraging as they might, could operate in the interior away from the lakes; large bodies of infantry could not.

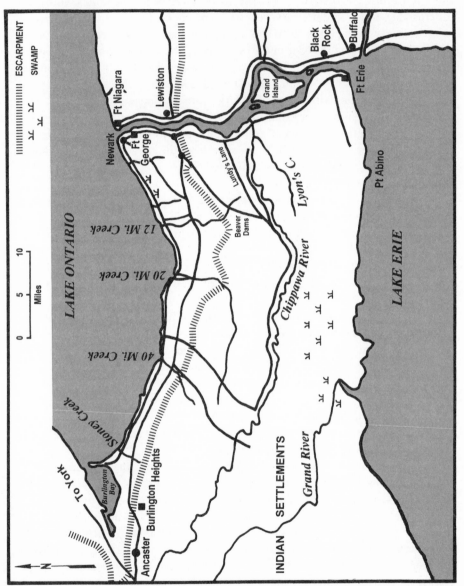

Niagara Peninsula

The Central Theater of Operations   45

Lake Erie separated the Central Theater from its neighboring Western Theater of Operations, which the Americans called the Northwest. Military activity seemed to divide naturally along this fault line, largely because of the lack of harbors on Lake Erie from which to support operations and the appalling lack of trafficable roads. American forces in the Central Theater were supported logistically through New York City, and those in the Northwest drew their support largely from Philadelphia through Pittsburgh or Cincinnati. The road between Philadelphia and Pittsburgh was quite good, and Pittsburgh was connected by water to Lake Erie, except for a short portage.

The Americans recognized this natural division of theaters of operations from the beginning, forming separate commands to fight loosely related campaigns. Later, the formation of military districts perpetuated the distinction, with the Eighth District in the Western Theater and the Ninth in the Central Theater. To the British, the distinction was not quite so sharp. Whereas the Americans enjoyed several secure lines of communication running generally perpendicular to the fighting front, the British had one long unsecured line of communication that in many places defined the political border as well as the fighting front. The British could do little if their line of communication were cut. In 1813, when the Niagara was in American hands, the British supported forces west of the Niagara by opening an overland supply route from Burlington westward to Long Point. Obviously, this method used wagons and animals in great numbers and was slower and less cost-effective than the water routes. Both sides were sensitive to the vulnerability of the British line of communication, and much of the fighting centered around efforts to cut or defend this slender lifeline.

While the terrain delineated natural avenues for the conduct of military operations and logistics, the overlay of settlements further determined where the fighting would take place. Lower Canada, with over 300,000 white inhabitants, was by far the most populous province of British North America; it had four times the population of Upper Canada. About 85 percent of the white population was francophone, and approximately 15 percent lived in cities, with Quebec and Montreal being by far the largest. The rural population occupied the river valleys, particularly the shores of the St. Lawrence between Montreal and Quebec.[11]

Those natives who participated in the fighting came from the "Seven Nations of Canada." Mostly Iroquois, these natives were descended from persons who had attached themselves to seven French mission settlements in the seventeenth and eighteenth centuries. By the time of the war, most of these Indians were settled in the St. Lawrence Valley. The two most important settlements were at Caughnawaga (modern spelling, Kahnawake) near Montreal and the St. Regis (modern name, Akwasasne) Reservation, which straddled the border with New York near the St. Lawrence River.[12]

Like Lower Canada, that part of the upper province within the Central Theater was also settled in fairly distinct strata. The Huron homeland was located
between Lake Ontario and Georgian Bay, and the Huron conducted intermittent warfare with the Iroquois from south of Lake Ontario. Venturing into the
region during the period of French colonization were a handful of explorers,
missionaries, and trappers, but few settlers. The first wave of English-speaking
settlers arrived after the American Revolution as a direct result of that conflict.

During the Revolution, Tories were frequently deprived of their civil liberties
and often dispossessed by the local patriots. Following the war, thousands were
evacuated to Nova Scotia and the present province of New Brunswick. It proved
difficult to absorb these newcomers, many from the large urban centers of the
East Coast, into what was still a wilderness province. In 1784, Governor-General
Sir Frederick Haldiman opened up the area west of the Ottawa River to white
settlement. Many loyalists, nearly 5,000 in 1784 alone, chose to migrate once
more. They brought with them bitter memories of their treatment by their erstwhile neighbors and hatred for everything for which the republic to the south
stood. These United Empire loyalists formed the hard core of civil support for
the British defensive efforts. In 1791, the province of Upper Canada was created, with John Graves Simcoe as lieutenant governor.[13]

Two streams of immigrants entered the new province over the next twenty
years. The smaller flow came directly from Great Britain and by 1812 perhaps
equaled the loyalists in number. By far the greatest flow came directly from the
United States. Land-hungry Americans sometimes passed themselves off as victims of republican persecution in order to claim loyalist status and qualify for
grants of land. The required oath of allegiance was tolerated as the price to pay
for otherwise free land. This is not to argue that the newcomers were ardent
American nationalists; many were the disaffected residue of the Whiskey Rebellion in Pennsylvania and came north presumably to escape taxation. Many were
Quakers and Mennonites, proscribed from bearing arms by their faith. In any
case, it is clear that regardless of their motivation to migrate north, they entertained no deep loyalty to Britain.[14]

By 1812, these layers of migrants had formed an irregular but discernible
pattern of settlement. Of the 77,000 white inhabitants, approximately one-third
were loyalists, immigrants directly from Great Britain, or the descendants of
both groups. The remainder recently had been Americans. The loyalists and
British immigrants were most densely settled in the Niagara District, near
Kingston and the Bay of Quinte in the Midland District, and in the Eastern District, closest to Lower Canada. Considerable numbers of Americans were in
these and the intervening districts, but Americans made up the overwhelming
proportion of the population west of the Grand River. In those settlements with
large numbers of loyalists, the loyalists clearly made up the social, political, and

economic elites. The Americans, as newcomers of questionable loyalty, enjoyed lesser status.[15]

Although the majority of residents lived as yeoman farmers on small plots along the lakes and the major rivers, the settlements of Upper Canada were often the objectives of American attack. Along the upper St. Lawrence was Prescott, directly across the river from Ogdensburg, New York. Prescott was the site of Fort Wellington, a small earthwork and timber fortification whose guns could fire at any vessel passing. Beyond the western end of the St. Lawrence stood Kingston, the home of the Ontario squadron of the Provincial Marine and later the Royal Navy.

Proceeding westward was the Bay of Quinte, which formed a natural harbor but in 1812 was underdeveloped as a base of operations. Farther up Lake Ontario was York, situated on another natural harbor. The seat of the provincial government, York had between 600 and 800 residents in 1812, and although the social elites were loyalists, there was a large number of recently arrived Americans. With only a minor shipyard and a small garrison, York was nonetheless an important stop along the British line of communication westward.[16]

The Niagara District consisted of the single county of Lincoln and was the most densely populated region of Upper Canada. By 1812, Lincoln County had approximately 12,000 inhabitants, about one-third of them recent arrivals from America.[17] The strong loyalist component ensured that the five regiments of Lincoln militia retained a hard core of steadfast fighters throughout the war.

In 1812, the rural population of the Niagara Peninsula occupied the eastern margin from the Niagara River westward to a depth of about twenty miles inland and the east-west corridor at the base of the escarpment. The largest settlement was Newark (modern name, Niagara-on-the-Lake), with about 1,500 people before the war.[18] Large numbers of citizens left Newark at the beginning of the war when it became obvious that the city and nearby Fort George would be primary objectives of American attack. Some of these people returned to the United States, but most moved inland. During the war, the population was about 600 women, children, and older men.

Adjacent to Newark and south of it was Fort George, built between 1796 and 1799 as a counter to Fort Niagara. Fort George consisted of six bastions connected by an earthen wall topped by a wooden palisade, about twelve feet high in all. A shallow ditch surrounded the fort, which enclosed two large wooden blockhouses, a stone magazine, and assorted smaller wood frame buildings.[19] Fort George was on slightly higher ground than Fort Niagara, a circumstance that gave the British guns a distinct advantage during the intermittent artillery duels.[20] South of Fort George and at the base of the escarpment sat Queenston, with about 300 people living in nearly 100 houses. Farther south was the village at Chippawa, with perhaps twenty houses. Queenston and Chippawa were terminals of the portage that bypassed the falls on the Canadian side. At the southeast corner of the peninsula was Fort Erie. The still unfinished fort consisted of two masonry bastions and a redan enclosing two stone barracks.[21] In 1814, this small fortification endured the longest siege of the war.

Along with the white loyalist immigration following the Revolution came an influx of Indian loyalists. The Iroquois chief Thayendanega, whose English name was Joseph Brant, brought hundreds of his followers into Upper Canada to escape a decidedly vindictive American government. Settling on a grant of land straddling the Grand River just west of the Niagara Peninsula, Brant's settlement was home to Iroquois, Delaware, and others who gave up their longhouses in favor of rough-hewn log cabins. Blacks, whites, and Indians chose to live there for a variety of reasons, and by 1812, the Grand River settlement was home to 1,800, including about 300 warriors.[22] The shore of Lake Erie between the Grand River and Long Point was very sparsely settled by individual families. A small settlement that figured in the 1814 campaign was Port Dover on the shore of Lake Erie.

On the American side of the Central Theater, the population was denser. Lake Champlain separated two towns of note: Burlington on the Vermont shore, and Plattsburg on the New York side. Both became American army and naval bases in support of operations aimed north on the Richelieu Valley corridor. Ogdensburg, across from Prescott on the St. Lawrence, was the largest settlement on that river in New York State. Ogdensburg was notorious for flouting the trade embargo against the British Empire and for consorting with its Canadian neighbors.

Before the war, Sacketts Harbor had only twenty-four residences. After the U.S. Navy made Sacketts Harbor its primary naval base for the Lake Ontario squadron, the village became a boomtown, sheltering thousands of soldiers, sailors, shipbuilders, and contractors. South of Sacketts Harbor and on the supply line between Albany and that naval base sat Oswego on the shores of stormy Lake Erie. Oswego, at the mouth of a river of the same name, had 500 inhabitants and had been a robust commercial village even before the war, when it was the primary port for trade with York and Kingston.[23]

America's Niagara Frontier was about as populous as Upper Canada's Niagara District. Buffalo and its neighbor Black Rock were growing frontier towns of about 700 people before the war. Even after the depopulation of the frontier in the winter of 1813–1814, Buffalo refused to die. By May 1814, Buffalo had nineteen taverns and shops and twenty-three houses and many more under construction. The rebuilding of the Niagara Frontier was financed by army money spent to feed and shelter the troops preparing for the next campaign.[24]

The Niagara Frontier was also home to large numbers of the Iroquois Nation. The Tuscarora village on the escarpment overlooking the village of Lewiston was destroyed by Riall's troops, along with the rest of the settlements on the frontier.

However, the largest concentration of Iroquois, the Seneca reservation along Buffalo Creek, survived. Nearly 600 warriors lived there and in surrounding villages. These New York Iroquois had adopted many white ways, particularly in cultivation and animal husbandry. Fortunately for the Americans, they still retained the warrior spirit, and they provided a valuable component of Jacob Brown's invasion force.[25]

Fort Niagara, although not a center of American settlement, was important as the oldest, strongest fortification along the border. By 1812, Fort Niagara consisted of a large masonry building and two masonry redoubts surrounded by Vauban-style bastions and palisaded earthworks. After it was taken in 1813 by stratagem, neither side was willing to storm or lay siege to this most formidable defensive work.[26]

As a region that was essentially just behind the frontier of white settlement and still largely wilderness, the Central Theater could not support large-scale military operations without considerable assistance from outside. However, the troops were fed, sheltered, and supplied to some degree by resources within the theater of operations. Food production in Upper Canada was barely above subsistence level even in the best of years. Mobilizing the militia distorted the patterns of agriculture and often resulted in shortfalls in production. For example, on the Niagara Peninsula, the 1812 crop of corn, peas, and buckwheat was very good, but much of the buckwheat was not gathered, because the militia had been called up for the Battle of Queenston. It is estimated that fewer than half the farmers sowed their winter grain in the first year of the war. The government took measures to conserve the province's food supply. In 1813, the assembly even prohibited the distillation of liquor in order to save grain. It did not take this action, however, until a sufficient supply of whiskey had been bought for issuance to the troops.[27]

Complicating the food situation was the lack of salt. Prior to the war, Upper Canada's salt came from New York, shipped from Oswego. Salt, of course, was used to extend the suitability of meat for human consumption. Despite small loads smuggled into the province and additional imports from outside British North America, Upper Canada was in a salt deficit throughout the war.[28]

As requirements for food in Upper Canada increased, pressure on the line of communication grew correspondingly. Wagons and teams were never sufficient in Upper Canada once the war began. As more teams were required, the need for forage along the supply routes increased. Providing forage was always difficult and became increasingly expensive.

The bateaux service between Montreal and Kingston continued to demand increasing numbers of boats and men to move supplies. These boatmen were called-up militiamen taken from their farms, thus putting food production in Lower Canada at risk. The convoy service on the upper St. Lawrence required over 4,000 laborers to keep the full fleet of bateaux and Durham boats in maximum service. The militiamen of Lower Canada grew increasingly tired of the call-ups, which affected virtually every family between Montreal and Kingston.[29]

Heavy reinforcements from Europe arriving in the spring and summer of 1814 compounded the problem. Lower Canada never had enough manpower to keep agricultural production up and keep the supply lines working at full capacity. Writing to Lord Bathurst in February 1814, the Duke of Wellington noted that even with naval control of the lakes, operations would be limited to the coast of the Great Lakes and the shores of navigable rivers, because the problems of supporting a large land force by road were difficult to overcome. He concluded that the number of troops earmarked for deployment to North America was probably as large as could be militarily useful because of the difficulties of supplying them at any great distance from the water.[30]

The food and transportation situation prompted three problems for the British in the Central Theater, but especially in Upper Canada. First, the military commanders could never generate the amount of manpower that the militia rolls suggested was possible. Each militiaman mobilized represented not only an additional mouth to feed but also one less person working the fields. Bringing in additional regulars solved part of the problem, but every regular sent into the upper province was one less to defend Quebec City, the most vital point in Canada. The arrival of thousands of peninsular veterans at Quebec City in 1814 exacerbated the logistical difficulties besetting the British.

A second problem concerned the vulnerable supply lines. As more regulars were sent west, more food had to be shipped from Lower Canada, and Lower Canada militiamen had to be mobilized to keep the convoys of supply boats moving to Kingston. Upper Canada became increasingly dependent on the lines of supply. Thus as the war went on, the war effort in Upper Canada became increasingly sensitive to even temporary breaks in the line of communication.

A third problem involved mills used to convert grain to usable flour. The Americans understood that destroying a mill had a longer detrimental effect on food production than the seizure of grain itself or of wagons and boats used to transport it. Thus, the mills became primary targets of raids. Even though mills were private property and therefore not legally subject to destruction, both sides burned them whenever possible. The British faced a virtually impossible task: the militia normally defended the mills and thus was unavailable for other missions.

The war also disrupted commercial patterns of the Central Theater, since northern New York and Vermont were tied into the Canadian commercial network. Settlers in northern New York burned wood to produce potash, which was shipped to Montreal for the production of soft soap. Potash was the major cash crop in the area, and even Jacob Brown cut a road from his settlement to Lake Ontario in order to smuggle potash during Jefferson's embargo. The British collected no import duties on either potash or lumber, and therefore trade with the Canadas was more profitable than trade with New York City for northern New Yorkers. While salt, lumber, and potash went north, the Americans received finished goods from Montreal in exchange. Travel between Ogdensburg and Montreal was open year-round either by boat or by sleigh. Mail between these cities took three or four days, whereas a letter from Philadelphia might take three or four weeks to reach Ogdensburg.[31]

The war officially ended this commerce, but many Americans continued trading openly and illegally. Support for the war was generally lukewarm at best in northern New York, and local commanders were forced to allocate some of their manpower to curb flagrant smuggling. Customs collectors and soldiers sent to assist them were ostracized by much of the population. Militiamen tasked to stop illegal trade often ignored violations by their neighbors.[32]

Upper Canada and the Niagara Peninsula in particular experienced an initial shock to commerce with the declaration of war. Trade came to almost a complete standstill, as people were anxious to hold on to their hard money. Debts could not be collected, nor was credit extended. What trade existed took the form of barter, a throwback to primitive frontier days. However, government spending accelerated trade, and no doubt Brock's victories restored confidence in the economy.[33] Nonetheless, the British were very sensitive to any activity, enemy or their own, that might distort or break the economy.

In any war, but certainly in a conflict that relied so heavily on the militia and volunteer soldiers, an understanding of the political climate is essential to comprehend the course of military operations. The French Canadians of Lower Canada were much more willing to support the British cause in 1812 than they had been in 1775, when some habitants had joined Richard Montgomery's army. To some extent, national pride was a factor. The francophones had long suffered the bigotry of some anglophones, and military service was a demonstration of civic virtue. Much of the francophone community was royalist in sentiment and unfavorably disposed to the republicanism of its southern neighbor. When the war began, the francophone social elite eagerly sought commissions in the militia and various volunteer corps. The depressed economy left a large pool of unemployed who sought military service in the ranks for income. Although recruiting into volunteer units was fairly brisk, involuntary conscription into full-time militia units provoked some initial resistance. In anticipation of war, the assembly of Lower Canada authorized the governor-general to conscript militiamen for one or two years to form five battalions called Select Embodied Militia. As the units lost people, they would be replaced by further drafts.[34]

Although Lower Canada was explicitly threatened by conquest, the population of the province widely (if weakly) supported the British government. This support was never seriously challenged, as the Americans could never make good on their threats. The militia of Lower Canada made a major contribution to the war effort. Whether on the battlefield, in garrison duty, or working the supply convoys on the St. Lawrence, they performed loyally and well.

The situation in Upper Canada was much more precarious. In the years immediately preceding the war, the political scene was enlivened by a vocal minority espousing republican values. These malcontents were centered at York and, to a lesser extent, at Newark. Joseph Willcocks, one of their leaders, had come from Ireland and settled in York in 1800. He managed to be appointed sheriff of York County and later was elected to represent York in the legislative assembly. Dismissed from office for his outspoken antagonism to the government, Willcocks moved to Newark, where he published an opposition newspaper. Later in the war, Willcocks would lead the Canadian Volunteers (made up of some of the disaffected of Upper Canada) as part of the U.S. Army.[35]

Early in the war, Brock became aware that the population of the Niagara Peninsula had already coalesced into opposing camps. Writing from Fort George in July 1812, he noted, "There can be no doubt that a large portion of the population in this neighborhood are sincere in their professions to defend the country, but it appears likewise evident to me that the greater part are either indifferent to what is passing, or so completely American as to rejoice in the prospects of a change of Governments."[36] However, for the most part, the loyalists on the Niagara Peninsula held the upper hand over the disaffected, although the Niagara Valley was the scene of a low-intensity civil war in 1812 and 1813.[37] In 1812, the disaffected of Upper Canada represented a potential source of strength to the American cause in the western half of the Central Theater. That they did not reach this full potential in the opening months of the war was largely due to Brock's victories, which cowed the opposition and encouraged the loyalists to reassert their status as the political and social elite of the province.

The war in the Central Theater displayed two facets: a military war for the capture or defense of territory, and a political war for the hearts and minds of the people. The native population was an objective in this second war, as well as warriors in the first. The Indians of the Central Theater depended for their survival on the government's gifts of cloth, food, and iron tools and weapons. Their settlements, now permanent, were in areas long overhunted. Despite decades of setback, Iroquois self-confidence was intact.[38]

Both sides understood that the service of native warriors could be useful. In their own mode of fighting—the ambush—the Indians were unsurpassed. Previous wars had established their value in terrorizing the enemy to withdraw or surrender. However, the Iroquois had no consensus regarding with which camp their interests lay. Iroquois history was replete with bad experiences and broken promises. The Iroquois Confederacy, which had reached its height of power in the seventeenth century with the subjugation of all neighboring tribes, was clearly in a slow but steady decline by 1812. The confederacy was physically split when Joseph Brant led many supporters of the British, nursing feelings of betrayal by their allies, to the Grand River settlement.[39]

Despite many setbacks, the Iroquois Confederacy had never been conquered. Although Britain and the United States might claim sovereignty over the land, it was clear to the Iroquois that they were an independent nation that would fight, if at all, as an independent ally under their own war chiefs. The British, short of manpower from the outset, viewed Indian participation as potentially decisive. Upon the declaration of war, Prevost sent an Indian agent to St. Regis to enlist active support for the British cause. About eighty warriors immediately joined the British forces. As many as half of the 770 warriors of Lower Canada participated in the fighting at one time or another and were particularly successful at Beaver Dams in the upper province in 1813.[40]

In Upper Canada in May 1812, Isaac Brock addressed a council of Grand River Indians to solicit their active allegiance in the impending conflict. John Norton, the acknowledged leader of the Grand River settlement, gave strong support to Brock. However, no general consensus to aid the British emerged.[41] Little Billy, a chief of the New York Iroquois, visited the Grand River settlement in June to plead with his brothers to maintain a unified position of neutrality. He argued that the British had abandoned them in the American Revolution and that the Iroquois should not risk their lives aiding inconstant allies. But the Grand River Indians remained divided. The result of the June council was that the neutrality of the New York Iroquois would be respected, but the Grand River Indians reserved the right to support the British. Norton and a handful of followers would exercise this right in short order. In no event, agreed the delegates, would Iroquois fight Iroquois.[42]

Fissures within the Iroquois Nation appeared almost immediately. In August, rumors spread that the British had occupied Grand Island in the Niagara River. This was Iroquois land, and the Seneca leader Red Jacket proposed dropping his nation's stance of neutrality and mounting an attack to take back the land. He was well aware that if the island remained in British hands at the end of the war, the Americans might surrender sovereignty to the British. Although the rumors proved false, this episode demonstrated to the Seneca at least that neutrality was not entirely consistent with their best interests.[43]

The New York Iroquois and a few other tribes met in early September near Buffalo to forge a consensus. A common theme among the speakers was the lack of success, over several years, in trying to persuade their fellow Indians north of the border to remain neutral. Many spokesmen, particularly those representing the younger men, were anxious to fight. Erastus Granger, the head agent to the Indians of western New York, read a letter from William Eustis asking the Indians to remain neutral. Some were offended that the federal government would not accept them into the army. Eustis, who had anticipated his inability to preclude Indian involvement, had taken steps to gain some measure of control. Confidentially, he had given Granger authority to organize those Indians who were determined to participate.[44]

In October, the New York Iroquois once again tried to persuade their Grand River brothers not to fight. Even as Rensselaer was preparing to invade Upper Canada, the Iroquois held a small council at Queenston. The New York Indians used a new argument: if the Canadian Iroquois fought for the British, then the Americans would require the New York Iroquois to fight also, refusing to supply them if they balked. However, acceptance of an American ultimatum of this sort would certainly result in Iroquois fighting Iroquois. Thus, for a part of the confederacy to remain neutral, it was necessary that all Iroquois refuse to fight. However, for those few Grand River Indians gathered on the Niagara to defend Upper Canada, the hard choice had already been made. They clearly saw that the best interests of the Grand River Iroquois were served by actively defending the frontier and, therefore, their homes.[45]

The Iroquois concept of warfare was so foreign to European patterns of fighting that it provoked the scorn of many white officers and men. Sergeant Commins of the Eighth Regiment of Foot saw quite a bit of active campaigning, often alongside Indian allies. On 21 August 1815 he wrote: "So far from being those brave warriors and have such a contempt of death as you may have heard before, I conceive them to be the most cowardly despicable characters I ever saw (except scalloping a defenceless man or plundering the wretched inhabitants be an act of bravery) their cruelty exceeds everything I have ever seen among enemies."[46] Clearly, Indian concepts of bravery and cruelty were measured against a different yardstick than those of European regulars.

Because the native economy was organized and conducted at a near subsistence level, the death of a warrior was a calamity for his extended family, and the loss of large numbers of adult males could prove disastrous for the tribe or community. Therefore, although the warrior fought to prove his courage, he saw no point in dying. He might give evidence of his bravery in a single encounter and therefore not be compelled to continue through the duration of a long campaign. Thus the native warrior, faithful to the logic of his own world, appeared both fierce and ill disciplined to his European or American ally.[47]

Although death was considered a tragedy, those Indians who were chosen or aspired to be war chiefs were motivated toward conspicuous bravery verging on recklessness. The traditional Indian scalp lock was a taunt to foes, a dare for them to try to take it. Also embedded in Iroquois values was the imperative to avenge a death, which could lead to an ever-increasing cycle of murder and subsequent revenge killings. A band of natives might join a white expedition motivated by the requirement to seek revenge for a prior killing. Once vengeance had been exacted, the party would return to its village, much to the dismay of the white commander, who adhered to European concepts of war fighting and wanted to continue the operation beyond the opening battle.[48]

By 1812, the Indians had adopted European-style firearms and adhered to a few of the conventions of "civilized" warfare. Europeans and their North American descendants likewise learned from the natives, subsuming many techniques of woodland fighting into what was still recognizable as a European style of warfare. Those whites most closely associated with the natives tended, unlike Sergeant Commins, to assume Indian attitudes as well as behavior. It has been noted that British Indian agents "were no more shocked by the burning of a prisoner than a regular army officer was shocked by the flogging to death of a soldier for a military offense."[49]

The amalgamation of native war parties into western military forces, even temporarily, was fraught with risks. Although there is no denying the Indians' contribution to victory on the battlefield, excesses committed after the battles excited the passions of the American public and the army to punish both the Indians and their British "masters."[50]

The geography, economy, and political climate of the Central Theater blended into an environment that imposed its own logic on military operations. The lack of roads dictated that military activity conform to the pattern of the waterways. Military decision could flow only from a successful contest for control of the water. The unorthodox location of the British line of communication, along the front rather than at a right angle to it, introduced a strategic principle: that a cut in the British supply line would yield decisive results west of the cut.

The British economy within the Central Theater imposed major constraints on the ability of the political leadership to harness resources in the prosecution of the war. British authorities had to carefully balance the allocation of manpower to the production of food, the transportation of supplies, and the fielding of fighting units. The Americans, who had a much more robust agricultural and industrial economy, enjoyed considerable latitude in this regard.

The heterogeneous political demography compelled its own logic. People were widely divided in both the direction and the magnitude of their loyalties. Patriots, neutrals, and traitors could be found in all populations—Canadian, American, and Indian. Their mixed aspirations, coupled with the real need to mobilize as many people as possible in support of the war effort, meant that the contest would be as much for hearts and minds as for waterways and cities. Into this complex matrix of geographic, economic, and political imperatives strode the military leaders of 1812.

CHAPTER FOUR

Startling Victories, Unexpected Defeats

*First we will take Canada. Be it so. It is however more easily said than done. The
Canadians are a bold and hardy race of men, probably love their government and
their country as we love ours, and would defend it as bravely.*
—Extract from the *Connecticut Courant*, reprinted in the *Nova Scotia Royal Gazette*,
6 November 1811

In the Central Theater in the fall of 1812, three American forces, each great in
numbers if not in military skill, had stood poised to conquer Canada. By the end
of November, each had been turned back from the border in humbling circumstances. Stephen Van Rensselaer, who commanded the failed attack on Queenston, retired from the militia before he could be relieved. Alexander Smyth, who
could not bring himself to issue the order to cross the Niagara, was quietly
dropped from the rolls of general officers. Henry Dearborn, Van Rensselaer's
and Smyth's superior, managed to hang on to the command of the Northern
Department until successive failures led to his transfer to a quiet sector. The
British and the white and native Canadians, despite overwhelming odds, had
defended their sovereignty and their line of communication to Great Britain,
and the Iroquois Indians of New York had maintained their precarious neutrality. However, the Madison administration, particularly the War Department,
was in great confusion as it ended the year trying to understand what went
wrong and what would be necessary to accomplish the war goals in 1813.

On 24 June 1812, as word of the declaration of war reached the Central Theater, both sides made hasty preparations to join battle. In Upper Canada, many
settlers born in the United States who refused to take an oath of allegiance were
issued passports for safe emigration south. A steady if thin stream of expatriates

entered the United States throughout 1812, many crossing Lake Erie on the ice during the winter months.[1] Isaac Brock asked the legislature for the power to require an oath of allegiance and to suspend habeas corpus. When it refused him these powers, he prorogued that body and assumed nearly dictatorial powers. Immediately, the process of oath taking separated some of the most recalcitrant citizens from those who were more loyal or at least neutral. Brock mustered the militia from these remaining citizens and ordered intensive training for those he could arm. That the task of removing or quieting the disloyal element was only partially successful would become clear to the British in 1813.

South of the border, the business of raising, equipping, and training armies of invasion began at once and quickly ran into difficulties. The War Department had called up 100,000 militiamen in April. New York's share was 13,500. In June, Governor Daniel O. Tompkins quickly raised twenty-two regiments largely from volunteers and sent them to the borders and to the defense of New York City. Brigadier General James Wadsworth took command of the five regiments of militia allocated to the Niagara Frontier. On 28 June he wrote to Governor Tompkins: "My knowledge of the military art is limited; indeed, I foresee numberless difficulties and occurrences which will present themselves to which I feel totally inadequate. . . . I confess myself ignorant of even the minor details of the duty you have assigned me, and I am apprehensive that I may not only expose myself but my government."[2]

Wadsworth's first task would be difficult for even a professional soldier. No arms, ammunition, or camp equipment were available to the militiamen who were mustering at their various rendezvous points. These necessities came from Boston, New York, and Philadelphia and arrived in insufficient quantities.[3] More fundamental than issues of arming and equipping the militia was the issue of defining responsibilities for the conduct of military operations. The War Department gave command of the Northern Department to Dearborn in February. He occupied himself with the defense of New England and the raising and equipping of troops for that purpose. He had an incorrect understanding of the extent of his authority and responsibility, and it was not until August that Dearborn was made to understand that his command extended from the Niagara Frontier east and north and included all the border with Upper Canada.[4] That the man responsible for one of the two invasions of Canada was not aware of his charter is indicative of the profound confusion and inefficiency surrounding the American war effort.

Nonetheless, Dearborn moved to correct the situation. He requested Major General Van Rensselaer, commander of the New York militia, to assume control of all forces (both militia and regular) on the Niagara Frontier and to invade Canada. Meanwhile, the War Department sent the newly promoted Brigadier

General John P. Boyd to assume command, subordinate to Dearborn, in New England, thus allowing Dearborn to focus on offensive rather than defensive operations.[5] Van Rensselaer arrived on the Niagara Frontier in August, only to find about 1,000 militiamen ill equipped, unpaid, without tents, and generally without discipline. Because the roads were so poor, his line of communication extended from Fort Niagara along the shore of Lake Ontario to Oswego and was therefore, like that of his enemy, subject to being cut by naval forces.[6]

Over the next few weeks, additional forces straggled onto the Niagara Frontier to join what was being called the Army of the Center. Militia strength grew to 2,650, and over 3,500 regulars, most of them nearly as untrained as the militia, were spread along the riverfront. About 1,650 of the regulars were under the command of Brigadier General Alexander Smyth at Buffalo. Smyth refused to subordinate himself to Van Rensselaer, with disastrous results for both men. Meanwhile, Brock had gathered only 1,600 regulars and militia and several hundred Indians.[7]

Like the army, the U.S. Navy started its buildup on the waters of the Central Theater from a very modest foundation. Outnumbered seven to one in war vessels on Lake Ontario at the outset, the Americans purchased six schooners to redress the deficiency. In September, the Navy Department ordered Isaac Chauncey from command of the New York Navy Yard to command all naval forces on the Great Lakes. There were few seamen on Lake Ontario, so Chauncey lured more of them from the Atlantic coast with bounties and promises of prize money. Most seamen preferred to stay on the Atlantic because the privateering business seemed more promising. Nonetheless, Chauncey sent over 800 sailors, carpenters, and marines, as well as over 100 cannon to Sacketts Harbor. The commodore himself arrived in October and energized the shipbuilding program.[8]

Chauncey's subordinate on Lake Erie was Lieutenant Jesse D. Elliott. Elliott's single brig was opposed by three vessels of the Provincial Marine. Personally brave and eager to establish his reputation, Elliott led a small party in early October to cut out two vessels from under the guns of Fort Erie. Accompanying Elliott's raiders were Captain Nathan Towson of the Second Artillery and Dr. Cyrenius Chapin of the Buffalo militia, both of whom would play prominent roles in the fighting on this frontier. Elliott's success was small compensation for Brock's decisive victory at Detroit in August but served to buoy American morale.

After his capture of Detroit and the surrender of Hull's Army of the Northwest, Brock moved quickly to defend the Niagara River line. The unequivocal and unexpected victory at Detroit had a steadying effect on the loyal citizens of Upper Canada and also served to quiet the disaffected and encourage even more Grand River Indians to throw in their lot with the British. Given this respite, Brock still faced formidable odds. The Niagara River was crossable north of Queenston and south of Chippawa—a considerable distance to defend, considering the paucity of forces available. Brock's best chances of victory hinged on detecting the crossing early enough to oppose it before the entire force had crossed.

Having won the respect of the regular, militia, and Indian alike, Brock found full range for his energy to set up procedures and forces to react quickly to any incursion along the river line. John Norton's Indians, swollen to over 500 eager warriors, ventured across the river in small scouting parties to gather information about Van Rensselaer's preparations. They discovered that the Americans were making little progress.[9] In late September, Dearborn made clear to Van Rensselaer that both forces—Dearborn's gathering at Greenbush, New York, and Van Rensselaer's—would invade Canada. "At all events we must calculate on possessing Upper Canada before winter sets in," he wrote.[10] However, Van Rensselaer was doubtful of his ability to defend the Niagara Frontier, much less attack. Besides feeding, sheltering, arming, training, and organizing a growing mass of militiamen, Van Rensselaer faced the tasks of not only planning a river crossing that would likely be opposed but also reducing one or more formidable fortifications. He called on Major General Amos Hall of the New York militia as well as Brigadier General Smyth to plan a two-pronged attack to clear the British and Canadians from the river line. The insubordinate Smyth refused to attend the planning conference. Van Rensselaer, forgoing any help from Smyth, believed that he had no recourse but to conduct a single crossing.

Without Smyth's brigade of regulars at Buffalo and various other detachments manning Fort Niagara and gun batteries along the river, Van Rensselaer still had a large body of men with which to force a crossing. Five regiments of New York militia, called into federal service in April, were under his command. These militiamen were augmented and to a certain extent stiffened by several companies of regulars.

Whereas American tactical doctrine envisaged infantry regiments of ten companies operating together in line of battle, the reality was quite different in 1812–1813. The original seven regiments, all in existence by 1808 and manned by long service veterans, started the war with their companies scattered in fortifications along the frontier. Authorized in January and June 1812, the new regiments were recruited slowly, and their companies were sent to the front one or two at a time as they were filled with recruits. Van Rensselaer had the services of two companies of the Sixth Infantry, a veteran regiment. He also had two companies of the Thirteenth Infantry, a regiment authorized the previous January, and three companies of the Twenty-third Infantry, raised since June. Formed in

1808, the Regiment of Light Artillery provided forty men who fought as infantry; two companies of the Second Artillery, recruited in January, manned the batteries on the New York shore. The vast bulk of the officers, generally political appointees, were as new to military service as their recruits. The few exceptions were the field-grade officers who transferred from the veteran regiments with a promotion in order to speed up the training of the new regiments.[11]

An example was Winfield Scott, who came into the army in 1808 as a captain in the Regiment of Artillerists. Upon the declaration of war, Scott was promoted to lieutenant colonel and transferred to the Second Artillery as second in command under Colonel George Izard. The regiment was organized near Philadelphia, and as soon as two companies were formed, Scott took them directly to Buffalo to join Smyth's regular brigade there. On the eve of battle, Scott received Smyth's permission to support Van Rensselaer's attack. After reporting to Van Rensselaer, Scott left his artillery under the company commanders and crossed over with the assaulting infantry.

In 1812, the qualitative difference between regulars and militiamen was not so pronounced as it would be later in the war. Most of the regular regiments were filled with raw recruits as well as officers new to the service. In their favor, they enjoyed priority for the issue of uniforms and equipment. They were volunteers, which presumably spoke to greater motivation than their counterparts in the militia. Finally, if the regiments were commanded by experienced, energetic officers such as Scott, there was the promise that they would mature into a satisfactory fighting force. However, these units did not exist in October 1812, and the American invasion suffered by their absence.

The Battle of Queenston was marked by episodes of personal bravery and cowardice, tactical brilliance and incompetence. The battle was fought in two phases: the first marking a limited American victory, and the second a decisive British triumph. Before dawn on 13 October, twelve boats—all that could be found—carried a few hundred regulars and militiamen to the Canadian shore at the base of the escarpment and the edge of the village of Queenston. Shore batteries as well as one heavy gun halfway up the escarpment opened fire, their noise alerting Brock at Fort George. As Brock rushed reinforcements to the crossing site, Captain John E. Wool led a band of regulars undetected up the side of the Niagara Gorge to the top of the escarpment and down the face of that cliff to capture the gun that was playing havoc on the crossing bateaux. As Brock arrived on the battlefield, he found the Americans on the heights overlooking Queenston Village. Brock, whose physical courage and charismatic leadership were unsurpassed, led a counterattack to regain the heights and with them the initiative over the invaders. At the front of his men, he was shot and killed, as was his adjutant, who attempted to maintain the momentum of the counterattack. With Brock's heroic death the first phase of the battle ended; the Americans perched precariously atop Queenston Heights.[12]

Despite the initial success of the attack, Van Rensselaer faced problems beyond his ability to solve. The task before him was to push more people across the river in order to expand the bridgehead in expectation of another British counterattack, which might materialize at any time. The militiamen who had not yet crossed had seen the desperate nature of the fighting and the horribly wounded being evacuated back to the American side. Ignoring exhortations from their militia officers, the men refused to get into the boats. They claimed that the Constitution proscribed service outside of the national borders without their consent. Van Rensselaer could do nothing to support the regulars and militiamen who had already crossed.

On the heights, militia Brigadier General Wadsworth wisely and graciously yielded tactical command to Winfield Scott. Together these officers did all they could to prepare a defense against the expected counterattack, but many of the Americans were slinking away to hide in the woods and craggy rocks of the heights and the steep side of the gorge. The courage of the Americans, regular and militia alike, was being drained away by the activities of a handful of Indians under Norton's leadership and that of Ah-you-wa-eghs (Christian name John), the eighteen-year-old son of Joseph Brant. Norton and Brant and their warriors fired from behind cover while Scott was organizing a defensive line, part of which was in the open. Their nerves shattered by the Indian yells and the mounting casualties, the Americans were no match for the British counterattack.[13]

Phase two of the battle was a frontal assault that pushed the Americans against the edge of the gorge. Major General Roger Hale Sheaffe, a Boston-born Tory, gathered up all available forces during the morning and early afternoon and led them on a wide, flanking march up the escarpment. His forces consisted of British regulars, assorted flank companies of militia, a volunteer company of blacks, and the Iroquois, all of whom were in a mood to avenge the heroic Brock. Sheaffe's assault collapsed the American defense in minutes. Scott displayed conspicuous bravery in negotiating a surrender and protecting his men from the Indians, who were disinclined to observe the customary protection of prisoners. Nearly 300 Americans were killed or wounded in the battle, and nearly 900 were captured. The British and their Iroquois allies suffered just over 100 casualties. The British released most of the militiamen, who were thus free to return to their homes, having given their parole not to take up arms until exchanged. The regulars were marched as prisoners of war to Quebec.

The Battle of Queenston was a decisive and humiliating defeat for the American cause. Like Detroit two months earlier, an invading American army was taken prisoner by a smaller force. Over 1,000 soldiers and militiamen were lost.

Van Rensselaer, their tragic commander, resigned in partial atonement for his failure. The craven behavior of the New York militiamen mortified their commanders and Governor Tompkins and sent a powerful message to officers of the regular army that militiamen were unworthy to bear arms.

At least one regular army officer, however, disputed the conventional wisdom. This anonymous soldier in a letter to *Niles' Register* opined that "such of the militia as could be kept from returning [to New York] fought well. It is not courage they want, but habits of discipline."[14] The events of 1814 along the Niagara would prove this officer correct.

To the British, the battle was a success, qualified only by the calamitous loss of the irreplaceable Brock. The line of communication remained secure from Quebec to Michilimackinac. Loyal citizens were again encouraged, and the disaffected were cowered. There appeared among the citizenry a feeling that ultimate victory was indeed possible; this was a reversal of earlier notions of defeatism. This sense of self-confidence was the product of healthy contempt for American fighting abilities that had been fairly earned by Van Rensselaer's army. The only redeeming factors were the flashes of leadership among some of the officers, among whom Scott and Wool were prominent.

The American failure at Queenston was followed by the defeat of the next two attempts by American invading armies. Only on Lake Ontario was some measure of success secured, and that by the navy. Chauncey aggressively put to sea in November and destroyed one schooner of the Provincial Marine and captured three merchant vessels. He also chased his most powerful rival, the *Royal George,* into Kingston Harbor. By the end of the month, Chauncey's building program bore its first fruit as the *Madison* was launched. This vessel was the largest on the Great Lakes and assured the Americans superiority until the lateness of the season forced both squadrons into port.[15]

Dearborn had responsibility for the main invasion of 1812. Forming at Greenbush near Albany, his Army of the North would attack directly toward Montreal. Dearborn suffered the same kinds of problems experienced by Hull, Smyth, and Van Rensselaer. His regular troops trickled into camp in company-sized packets as they were recruited in the major cities of New England and the Middle Atlantic states. Only in Greenbush did they begin serious training. In September, Dearborn started moving regiments north to Plattsburg, closer to Canada yet still along a water route, which made supplying them relatively easy.

At Plattsburg, Dearborn collected seven regiments of regular infantry and one of regular artillery, none of them up to full strength. A detachment of the Sixth Infantry was the only unit of long-term soldiers. Five regiments—the Ninth, Eleventh, Fifteenth, and Sixteenth Infantry and the Third Artillery—had been authorized in January and recruited since then. Two regiments, the Twenty-first and Twenty-fifth Infantry, were authorized in June. As with Van Rensselaer's army, a few field-grade officers were professional soldiers. A conspicuous example was Zebulon Pike, a major in the First Infantry in 1802 and now the colonel of the Fifteenth. Dearborn organized his regulars into two brigades: the First under Brigadier General Joseph Bloomfield, former governor of New Jersey, and the Second commanded by Brigadier General John Chandler, former congressman from the Maine District of Massachusetts.

The British were likewise active. Paralleling Brock's actions in Upper Canada, Prevost also took drastic steps to remove potential spies and traitors. On 19 September he proclaimed that all those who claimed to be subjects of the United States or who had not signed a loyalty oath must leave Lower Canada by 15 October or be treated as prisoners of war.[16] Additionally, Prevost moved thousands of troops into the Richelieu Valley to block a thrust on Montreal. These troops were covered by a small advance guard of light infantry and Indians who would warn Prevost of the size and direction of the expected invasion.

Dearborn's Army of the North amounted to little more than 3,000 regulars, nearly all raw recruits, and approximately 5,000 militiamen and volunteers, even greener that the regulars. The Vermont militia, the entire number that had been requested by the War Department, joined Dearborn at Plattsburg. The troops there had an opportunity to witness military justice firsthand. On 15 October, William Henmann of Pike's Fifteenth Infantry was executed for deserting with intent to pass over to the enemy. The serious nature of this business was becoming apparent to regular recruit, volunteer, and militiaman alike.[17]

A month after Van Rensselaer's defeat, Dearborn moved north with 5,000 troops. On 20 November his advance guard, commanded by Pike, crossed the international border. In confused circumstances, Pike's regulars mistakenly opened fire on a unit of New York militia, which returned the compliment. After this mistake had been discovered and corrected, the British advance guard attacked. This party consisted of the Canadian Voltigeurs and their commander, Lieutenant Colonel Charles Michel de Salaberry, and about 300 Mohawks.

In some ways, the Voltigeurs was like the new American regiments. Authorized in April as a body of light infantry, the Canadian Voltigeurs was a fencible regiment whose ranks were filled by volunteers from Lower Canada. However, several of the officers, like de Salaberry himself, were professional soldiers who helped the regiment reach a fairly high standard of efficiency more quickly than most American units. The Voltigeurs displayed a remarkable degree of multicultural composition. Three-quarters of the men were francophones; the remainder spoke English. A handful of blacks had been recruited into the ranks, and the regiment habitually operated alongside Captain Lamothe's company of Lower Canadian Mohawks. The Voltigeurs made its military debut against Dearborn's advance guard and would be represented in several of the key battles in the Central Theater.[18]

The skirmish between advance guards was not particularly hot, nor were the Americans defeated. Yet this brush with the enemy was enough to convince Dearborn to return south with his army. Dearborn had not made contact with the British main force, approximately 5,000 regulars and militia under Major General Francis de Rothenburg, which blocked the route to Montreal. Instead, Dearborn put his army into winter quarters at Camp Saranac near Plattsburg and wrote his reports.[19]

Because the main armies were never decisively engaged, no conclusion can be drawn as to the relative quality of the forces. However, this campaign, if it can be called such, speaks eloquently to the character of the major general in whom the president reposed his special trust. Dearborn's abortive invasion of the Canadas mocked the desperate campaign of Montgomery and Arnold. What was transpiring at nearly the same time at Buffalo, however, approached burlesque.

Alexander Smyth was a political appointee in 1808 when he came into the army as a colonel and was given command of the elite Rifle Regiment. The president promoted him to brigadier general in March 1812, and he moved to the Niagara Frontier to command some of the regulars gathering there. Without a doubt, his refusal to cooperate with Van Rensselaer contributed to the failure at Queenston. Three days after that battle, the defeated general yielded command of the Niagara Frontier to Smyth. The new commander of the Army of the Center, as the force on the Niagara called itself, immediately wrote to the secretary of war of his intentions to invade Canada if Eustis would provide him with 8,000 men and twenty guns. "Give me here," Smyth wrote, "a clear stage, men and money, and I will retrieve your affairs or perish."[20] In an attempt to coordinate the various invasion forces, Smyth suggested to Dearborn that all three armies—Smyth's, Harrison's, and Dearborn's—"should strike on the same day. If not, the command of the Lakes will enable the enemy to beat us in detail."[21] Certainly Smyth's grasp of strategy was adequate. A coordinated and determined three-pronged invasion that threatened the British line of communication simultaneously would present Prevost with near insoluble problems, given the slender British resources. Fortunately for the defenders, the Americans were not able to coordinate the advance of multiple forces.

Smyth also learned from Van Rensselaer's mistakes. The former commander on the Niagara did not have enough boats to cross more than 600 soldiers at one time. The necessity of crossing the force in shifts gave Van Rensselaer's militiamen—those who remained in New York while the first wave crossed—time to contemplate the degree of risk they would accept by entering a boat.

No doubt Smyth saw the lack of boats as contributing to the collapse of the militia's morale. Smyth contracted to build enough boats and scows to cross nearly 4,000 in one impulse. He expected these to be ready by 20 November.

Smyth's major problem, however, was to gather enough troops willing to cross over into Canada. Van Rensselaer had managed to get nearly 1,200 across, but this was not enough to defeat the British, Canadian, and Indian defenders. Dearborn suggested—Smyth would later say "ordered"—that the crossing be made by 3,000 soldiers in a single wave.[22] However, over 900 Americans had been captured at Queenston, and many of those remaining with the Army of the Center were those militiamen and volunteers who had refused to cross with Van Rensselaer. Even after Smyth gathered 3,000 or more who were willing to cross, he still needed to keep enough on the American side to protect his fortifications and line of communication while the crossing force dealt with Forts Erie and George and the force at Chippawa.

Among the regulars were pieces of ten infantry regiments. Three of these were old regiments, four had been formed since January, and three since June. One regiment, the Twenty-second Infantry, was garrisoning Fort Niagara. All the regiments were of poor quality. Most were unpaid; in fact, Smyth reported to Dearborn that two regiments had mutinied because of no pay.[23] Eventually the officers restored order, but they could not adequately address other problems.

Perhaps typical of the regulars, the Fourteenth Infantry demonstrated a host of inadequacies. On 5 October, Captain William King inspected the Fourteenth, which was then under the command of Colonel William H. Winder. King reported to the War Department that although the field-grade officers appeared to be trying to learn their duties, the company officers were "almost as ignorant of their duty as when they entered the service." The enlisted men were "generally only tolerably good recruits." The muskets were "in infamously bad order," and a considerable amount of the ammunition was "very bad; some of the cartridges are said to have been made up in 1794." King found the tentage inadequate and the troops still in their linen summer uniforms; the wool ones had not yet arrived for issue. In summary, King pronounced of these regulars that "they are militia, and if possible even worse, and if taken into action in their present state will prove more dangerous to themselves than to their enemy." King found the situation in Colonel Thomas Parker's Twelfth Infantry almost as bleak.[24]

The volunteers and militiamen were in no better shape than the regulars were. Several companies of six-month volunteers had mustered throughout New York, Pennsylvania, and Maryland and marched to the Niagara Frontier, where they were consolidated into three small regiments. Francis McClure's regiment, for example, was composed of eleven companies representing all three states. The militia consisted of three brigades. Two were the remnants of New York militia that had refused to cross with Van Rensselaer, and the third was Adamson Tannehill's brigade of 2,000 Pennsylvanians who arrived at Buffalo on 8 November. Smyth ordered an inspection of one of the New York brigades. On 4 November, he received the report. The inspecting officer concluded that "the brigade is such as to be little better than an undisciplined rabble, and it may be a question whether they are not of more disservice than of use."[25] He noted that "on Saturday evening one hundred deserted, and no measures taken to bring them back; a spirit of mutiny seems to pervade the camp." Events would prove the Pennsylvanians no more committed to the war effort than their New York counterparts.

As starved for manpower as he was, Smyth declined to accept the services of the Iroquois. "It is the desire of your Great Father the President," Smyth told them, "that you should take no part in the war between the United States and Great Britain, but remain at peace and take care of your wives and children." However, Smyth did agree to accept their assistance if Indians from Canada invaded the United States.[26]

It was clear to General Smyth, if not to Madison, that the purpose of invasion was to annex the Canadas. As the time for his assault drew closer, Smyth issued a proclamation to his army. He exhorted the men to remember that the Canadian people were not the enemy. They would soon become American citizens. It was against the British that they were to make war. What propaganda effect his proclamation might have had on the disaffected of Upper Canada is unknown, since no American army landed in force to claim their allegiance.[27]

Smyth initially ordered the attack for the evening of 25–26 November, but Colonel Winder convinced him that preparations would not be completed by then. Smyth next ordered the crossing to be made on 28 November, preceded by a raid to spike the guns of three batteries that swept the crossing site and to destroy a bridge the British reinforcements from Chippawa would cross to challenge the landing. The raid, made before dawn, was a partial success. Over 400 regulars and sailors succeeded in spiking several guns but only damaged, not destroyed, the bridge over Frenchman's Creek. The defenders and attackers lost evenly in the several skirmishes that made up the raid, about 100 casualties or prisoners on each side.

Meanwhile, embarkation proceeded slowly while British regulars and Canadian militiamen gathered on the far shore. Midafternoon, Smyth ordered a general disembarkation and further ordered the men to return to their respective camps to eat. Smyth later claimed that only 1,200 soldiers had managed to enter the boats and that he reached his decision only after consulting several of his officers.[28] Brigadier General Peter B. Porter, the senior New York militiaman at Buffalo who was not consulted by Smyth, recalled that between 2,000 and 2,600 men were in boats, and about 2,000 more were on the shore waiting to climb into the many empty boats. The Americans had been sitting in the boats or standing on the shore in the wind and snow since early morning. There was widespread disappointment among Smyth's command. Porter claimed that Smyth's order "produced among the officers and men generally great discontent and murmuring."[29] Another participant recalled the "mortification" produced by Smyth's decision.[30]

Smyth ordered a crossing for the next day regardless of the weather conditions, but the British managed to get some guns back into position. General Porter and Colonel Winder persuaded Smyth to postpone the crossing until 1 December so that more preparations might be made. While Smyth wrestled with the inability of the army to meet what he understood to be Dearborn's minimal requirements to cross, sickness was decimating the ranks of his regulars. Several companies reported as many as one-third of their number ill. In the hospital tent of the Thirteenth Infantry, five dead had remained lying with the sick overnight because no coffins were available. It was a credit to the regulars that many of the ill had embarked with their companies on the first attempt to cross.[31]

Having lost whatever surprise he may have enjoyed on his first attempt, Smyth changed his plan. Smyth's scheme envisioned that his men would climb into their boats in the early-morning hours of 1 December. Then, two hours before daylight, the flotilla would move five miles downriver to a landing spot closer to Chippawa. This nighttime operation might regain some element of surprise.

At the appointed hour and amidst a layer of new-fallen snow, the loading began, but by one hour after daylight, fewer than 1,500 men by Smyth's count had managed to load into the boats. Many of them were too sick to march or fight. Perhaps as many as 150 refused to enter the vessels; thousands, apparently, had not marched to the crossing site but had remained in their camps. Smyth gathered several of his regular officers, and this council agreed unanimously that no attempt to cross should be made. Smyth again ordered a general disembarkation, but this time he pronounced that no further attempt would be made until the army was reinforced.

Ill disposed toward the militia even before the crossing attempts, Smyth blamed the failure on the nonregulars. "The affair at Queenston is a caution against relying on crowds who go to the bank of the Niagara to look on a battle as on a theatrical exhibit; who if they are disappointed of the sights, break their muskets: or if they are without rations for a day desert."[32]

Some of the men broke their muskets upon learning of their commander's decision, but not before firing them wildly or in Smyth's direction to express their rage. The officers made no concerted attempts to control them. Porter was outraged. He had been viewing the loading from his boat in the river and therefore was unaware of the council of officers. He estimated that over 4,000 were in boats or waiting to cross. Porter publicly ascribed the debacle "to the cowardice of General Smyth."[33] Porter withdrew this charge only after he and Smyth exchanged shots in a duel seven days later.

Porter was far from alone in blaming Smyth. Besides being shot at, Smyth was refused lodging by several local tavern keepers. The *Ontario Messenger,* a Republican paper, was typical of popular opinion. "With grief and shame do we record that Smyth, who promised so much, who . . . was to convince the American people that all their generals were not base, cowardly and treacherous, even Smyth must be added to the catalogue of infamy which begun with the name of Hull."[34] To characterize Smyth as treacherous conveniently absolves the hundreds of militiamen and volunteers who refused to enter the boats. Fewer than one-quarter of Tannehill's Pennsylvania Brigade agreed to cross into Canada. Tannehill was mortified that hundreds of his men were joined by many of their officers in deserting in the days following the failed crossing.[35]

Smyth's deficiencies in leadership and organizational skills were no doubt largely responsible for the failure of his offensive. However, the obstacles to success were immense, and few if any American leaders were up to the challenge. His heterogeneous force of regulars, volunteers, and militiamen was similar only in its low degree of training. Clearly, his force lacked officers and noncommissioned officers who could convert his orders into action. His mercurial militia could not be relied on to cross, and even militia officers could not get their men to enter the boats. Sickness, measles most notably, was continuing to increase among those who had been in camp for several weeks, largely the regulars. Additionally, rations were insufficient in amount and deficient in quality. Most soldiers were owed pay. A Benedict Arnold or Richard Montgomery might have overcome such obstacles. It was clear that neither Smyth nor his subordinates, nor even Porter, could rise to the occasion and provide the iron will necessary to succeed.

Smyth could not effectively answer the accusations made against him. In his report to Dearborn he wrote: "I am sorry the situation of the force under my command, had not been such as to make the propriety of a forward movement obvious to all. Circumstanced as we were, I have thought it my duty to follow the cautious counsels of experience, and not precipitation, to add to the list of our defeats."[36] America's requirement to blame a single commander rather than the collective failure of its military institutions could not, however, be denied. Smyth left his command on the Niagara and in March of the following year was quietly dropped from the rolls of the officer corps without the spectacle of a court-martial.

The year ended in the Central Theater with the British having succeeded at defending Canada from invasion. Although they were never seriously challenged, the British, Canadians, and Indians proved equal to the task. Only on Lake Ontario did the American effort show promise of future success. The lines of the naval war were taking shape: a naval arms race with sorties at those times when one squadron or the other judged that it enjoyed an advantage. On the

American side, there was no indication that the naval and land campaigns would be coordinated either in Washington or in the theater of operations.

Both armies were inadequately trained and equipped. Man for man, the American regulars were equal to their British counterparts; they obeyed orders and fought hard in small-unit actions. The Americans had not taken opportunities to challenge the British in linear firefights, an arena in which the British could expect to enjoy a considerable advantage until American officers learned how to drill their men. Logistical inadequacies aside, the fundamental problem with the American regulars was that too few officers knew their duties well enough to develop tough, competent companies and regiments. Of the American commanding generals, only the militiaman Van Rensselaer had the personal courage to decide to attack and then to press the fight. Dearborn and Smyth, the regulars, were deficient in this regard.

Among the militia, the Canadians did all that was asked of them. The flank companies in particular fought resolutely under their steady militia officers. On the American side, of course, the legacy of the first year of the war, and indeed of the whole war in popular memory, is one of militiamen refusing to cross the border into Canada. Although refusal to invade Canada was certainly widespread, a sizable minority of militiamen did put their lives on the line to accompany the regulars, fighting and dying beside them. This number would increase throughout the war in the Central Theater as the volunteers and militia would grow like their regular counterparts in skill, confidence, and dedication to their cause.

Britain's Indian allies did their share of defending the Canadas. At Queenston Heights in particular, the fear of Indian atrocity was key to the American defeat. By the end of 1812 came signs that the uneasy agreement within the Iroquois Nation was dissolving. Many warriors in New York were willing to fight the British for reasons far removed from protecting neutral trading rights.

The fighting in 1813 in the Central Theater of Operations was no more decisive in advancing the American war aims than that during the previous season. As the American army—that polyglot mixture of regulars, volunteers, and militia—grew in skill, the British and Indian forces found it more difficult to defend their wide frontier. Fortunately for the British, American strategic confusion served to dull the potential sharpness of the two major land thrusts. On the Great Lakes, the major naval battle was decisive only in the Western Theater, and its impact on the fighting east of the Grand River was minimal. To the Americans' credit, the land and sea forces cooperated to the degree necessary to win key battles, even if in the end they could not make common cause long enough to win campaigns.

The two major campaigns in 1813 were Dearborn's attempt to clear the Niagara Peninsula and Wilkinson's and Hampton's joint attempt to seize Montreal.

In addition to beating back both invasions, the British raided the American shore at Sacketts Harbor, which might have completely unhinged the American war effort in this theater had it been successful. However, the first activities of the new year were a pair of raids on the St. Lawrence.

That portion of the St. Lawrence River that forms the international boundary was defended in early 1813 on both sides by small and scattered detachments of militia stiffened with regulars. Two of the regular units would distinguish themselves repeatedly during the war for their skills in raids and skirmishes, which made up much of the fighting. The Glengarry Light Infantry Fencible Regiment was formed in 1812 from among the Highland Scots who had settled in Upper Canada. They were opposed on the American shore by a battalion of the Rifle Regiment.[37]

On 6 February, newly promoted Major Benjamin Forsyth of the Rifle Regiment led a raid on Elizabethtown, Upper Canada (modern name, Brockville), which succeeded in freeing a number of prisoners of war held there. His informants warned Forsyth that the British would soon retaliate. Charged with the defense of Ogdensburg, Forsyth asked Dearborn for reinforcements. Dearborn advised Forsyth to avoid further "small partisan warfare," as it could lead to the retaliation that the commander of the riflemen feared. Dearborn refused to send more men but granted Forsyth the authority to abandon Ogdensburg if he judged it necessary.[38]

Forsyth exercised that option, but not until it was forced on him by a skillfully executed attack across the ice against Ogdensburg on 22 February. Major "Red George" MacDonnell and 800 Glengarries and militiamen caught the 300 Americans at breakfast and amidst bitter fighting pried them from the town. Accompanying the riflemen out of town were many of the citizens of Ogdensburg. Despite British attempts to prevent it, these temporarily abandoned homes were looted by local Indians and by citizens of Prescott (immediately across the river in Upper Canada). The returning people of Ogdensburg were quite vocal in expressing their desire that Dearborn not station troops in Ogdensburg, thus making it a military target. For the remainder of the war, Ogdensburg was in effect a neutral city. A large amount of contraband, particularly cattle, entered Upper Canada through this city during the remainder of the war.[39]

On the American side, the months of February and March were spent formulating an invasion plan. This process was complicated by two important factors. First, the planners were widely separated, located at various times in Washington, Plattsburg, Albany, and Sacketts Harbor. Second, the concentration of sufficient combat power to achieve decisive results could occur only by leaving a vital post denuded of troops and therefore vulnerable to countermeasures. The result, unfortunately for the Americans, was that the upcoming campaign yielded tactical successes that could not be converted into a decisive victory.

On 8 February, Armstrong presented his strategic analysis to the cabinet. He argued that Montreal was too well defended to be captured by the regulars stationed on Lake Champlain. However, he estimated that no more than 2,100 regulars were defending Upper Canada between Fort Erie and Prescott. Armstrong proposed sending 6,000 Americans against Kingston. A successful attack there would be followed by attacks on York and Forts George and Erie. "It remains then," wrote Armstrong, "to choose between a course of entire inaction, because incompetent to the main attack, or one having a secondary, but still an important object." Armstrong was confident of success if Dearborn could launch the offensive by 1 April, since Prevost could not move reinforcements west from Quebec until the St. Lawrence thawed in mid-May.[40]

The president approved Armstrong's proposal, and in turn, the secretary of war ordered Dearborn to gather 4,000 soldiers at Sacketts Harbor, stripping the Lake Champlain garrisons if necessary. In cooperation with the navy, Dearborn would then attack Kingston first, followed by York. Once these posts fell, Dearborn was to clear the Niagara Peninsula, aided by 3,000 troops at Buffalo. Dearborn, then in Albany, agreed to carry out the campaign as proposed but voiced concern that the British would read the American intentions and shift forces from Montreal to Kingston. It appears that Dearborn did not understand that Prevost would not risk Montreal to save Upper Canada.[41]

Dearborn moved to Sacketts Harbor, where he received an alarming report that Prevost was at Kingston with 6,000 to 8,000 troops preparing to cross the ice and attack Sacketts Harbor. For the next two weeks, while the ice was still crossable by an army on foot, Dearborn prepared to receive the British assault. With only 3,000 troops, Dearborn was not confident of success. When the attack did not materialize (for Prevost had less than one-quarter of the forces ascribed to him), Dearborn nonetheless told Armstrong that Kingston was too heavily defended and that the plan sent to him was therefore unfeasible.[42] That Dearborn was so easily deterred by an exaggerated report speaks to his lack of aggressive spirit.

Dearborn, Chauncey, and their principal officers met to hammer out a workable strategy to replace that of the secretary of war. The resultant plan envisaged a joint attack on York for the purpose of destroying the two war vessels there. This joint army-navy force would continue on to seize Fort George and link up with the force from Buffalo, which had in the meantime cleared the western shore of the Niagara River. The final phase was to be an attack on Kingston. "After the most mature deliberation, the above was considered by Commodore Chauncey and myself as the most certain of ultimate success," wrote Dearborn to the secretary of war.[43] The plan displayed a serious shortcoming. Unless the British squadron was eliminated as a threat by being either bottled up in port or destroyed in combat, it could do irreparable harm to the war effort on Lake Ontario. First, the troop transports would be vulnerable to attack, even by a numerically inferior fleet. Second, the only American naval base on Lake Ontario—Sacketts Harbor—would be vulnerable to attack from Kingston while Chauncey and Dearborn were away with the bulk of American forces.

Armstrong approved the plan but cautioned Dearborn to concentrate as many men as he could for the venture. "If our first step in the campaign . . . should fail, the disgrace of our arms will be complete." Armstrong continued, "The public will lose all confidence in us, and we shall even cease to have any in ourselves." He wrote, in an uncharacteristic lapse of strategic sense, "When the fleet and army are gone, we have nothing at Sacketts Harbor to guard nor will the place present an object to the enemy. How then would it read that we lost our object on the Niagara, while we had another brigade at Sacketts Harbor doing nothing?"[44] One can only imagine Chauncey's reaction had he read this letter. If the supplies and the shipyard at Sacketts Harbor were destroyed in a raid, the Ontario squadron would be so enfeebled that it could probably not stand up to the British in a fleet-on-fleet action. With the destruction of the American fleet, land operations could be only defensive in nature.

On 19 April and after consulting with Madison, Armstrong sent further guidance to Dearborn. Armstrong correctly surmised that Prevost's strategy included the option of pulling his forces in the west back to Kingston if they were seriously threatened with capture or destruction. A further withdrawal to Montreal was also possible and, from the British point of view, preferable to having the line of communication cut between Kingston and Montreal. Therefore, Armstrong directed Dearborn to plan for two eventualities. If Prevost withdrew from his western posts to Kingston, Dearborn and Chauncey should cut the British supply line between Kingston and Montreal and then jointly attack Kingston. If Prevost were to withdraw all the way to Montreal, then Dearborn should attack that city.[45] Considering his faulty notion of the numbers facing him, these branches of the plan presented Dearborn with unjustifiable risks. In the event, Prevost never believed his forces to be so threatened as to justify the abandonment of Upper Canada west of Kingston.

The raid on York succeeded in accomplishing the American goals at an acceptable cost. Major General Sheaffe, victor of Queenston and Brock's successor as president-administrator of Upper Canada, took personal command of the weak defenses of his provincial capital. Sheaffe commanded about 800 defenders, the usual mixture of regulars, militiamen, and Indians. Expecting a two-pronged attack that could cut off his forces from retreat, Sheaffe put regulars, supplemented by militia and Indians, on both the eastern and western edges of the city and kept the bulk of militia in the city proper to respond to threats in either direction.[46]

At dawn on 27 April, Chauncey's fleet carrying Dearborn and 1,700 soldiers appeared. Landing only west of York, the army under Brigadier General Zebulon Pike pushed the outnumbered defenders back into the city. As the British regulars withdrew in good order, the militiamen lost heart, many of them leaving the battle. Sheaffe, who demonstrated inspirational leadership during the fighting, ordered the main magazine exploded in order to deprive the enemy of powder. The explosion rattled windows as far away as Fort Niagara and killed or wounded 232 Americans. Among the dead was Pike, who lived long enough to accept the British flag presented to him by his men after the surrender.

Canadian militia officers negotiated the surrender after Sheaffe withdrew his regulars toward Kingston. The Americans, no doubt infuriated by the loss of so many of their number to the explosion, were overzealous in victory. Bands of soldiers not only destroyed public buildings and property but also vandalized homes. The soldiers were assisted in these violations by a sizable number of pro-American citizens of York. Dearborn, crippled by the loss of his second in command, could not impose control over his ill-disciplined troops.[47]

Sheaffe lost York because his forces, expecting attacks from both flanks, could not concentrate to stop Pike's men on the single landing beach. His militia chose to remain in the protection of the city rather than to run the gauntlet of Chauncey's guns. Prevost replaced Sheaffe for his unsuccessful defense of York, prodded by those same militia leaders who could not motivate their men to fight. Reluctant militiamen existed in considerable numbers on both sides of the border.

The Americans remained until 8 May. They captured one of the ships at York; the other was destroyed by Sheaffe's men. Chauncey managed to carry off considerable naval supplies that were intended for Barclay's flotilla on Lake Erie, thus assisting Perry's decisive victory in September. The raid on York was an important step in the naval arms race on Lake Ontario. Both sides pulled out all the stops in attempting to outbuild each other, and they could speed up the process by inflicting incremental losses on their opponent's fleet. Chauncey won this round.

The army and navy cooperated well at York. Chauncey's naval gunfire intimidated the Canadian militia, although it could not prevent the escape of Sheaffe's regulars. Dearborn held Chauncey's support in high regard. He wrote to Armstrong that he was "under the greatest obligations to Commodore Chauncey for his able and indefatigable exertions in every possible manner that could give facility and effect to the expedition." He went on to note, "The Government could not have made a more fortunate selection for the important trust he holds."[48] This model of joint operations was the result of a convergence of army and navy goals. Jacob Brown would curse Chauncey the following year when service objectives widely diverged.

The raid on York also demonstrated to the British the extent of disaffection in Upper Canada. Many of the pro-American citizenry assisted the raiders as well as exacting vengeance on their loyal neighbors for the harassment suffered since the beginning of the war. Significant numbers tendered their parole to Dearborn's officers; thus, by the rules of war, they could legally evade service in the militia and public projects connected with the war effort. The loyalists of York were demoralized by the defeat, the plundering, and the despair of ever trying or convicting those parolees who evaded militia service.[49]

After York, Prevost went to Upper Canada himself and sent more troops westward as well. This signified a slight shift in his strategy of defending Quebec at all cost, even the loss of the upper province. Prevost hoped to spell the hard-pressed militiamen, who needed time to seed their fields and also to intimidate the disloyal.[50] Perhaps encouraged by the general trends of the war thus far, Prevost may have entertained the idea that Upper Canada could indeed be defended. In September, Prevost announced his intention of deporting those who gave parole from disloyal intentions.

Chauncey and Dearborn returned to Sacketts Harbor, where the fleet was replenished and the army greatly reinforced for the second phase of the campaign: the attack on Fort George. Chauncey landed Dearborn's force at Four Mile Creek east of Fort Niagara while final preparations were made. Two of America's shining lights, Oliver Hazard Perry and Winfield Scott, planned this amphibious operation, which was every bit as successful as the joint attack on York.

On the other side of the river, Brigadier General John Vincent, who commanded on the Niagara Peninsula, prepared for the inevitable attack. He had between 1,800 and 1,900 regulars, fencibles, and volunteers to defend the entire peninsula. These were backed up by perhaps an equal number of militiamen from the five Lincoln regiments. However, the militia was demoralized. Vincent reported, "Every exertion has been used and every expedient resorted to, to bring them forward and unite their efforts to those of His Majesty's troops but with little effect, and the desertion beyond all conception continues to mark their indifference to the important cause in which we are now engaged."[51] Even severe court-martial sentences could not stanch the flow of militiamen from their military duties.

The operation to seize Fort George began on 25 May with an artillery bombardment from Fort Niagara. The numerical superiority of the American artillery was telling, and within hours, every building inside Fort George was in flames. As the gunners ceased fire in order to conserve ammunition, the navy sent in boats to reconnoiter the water, taking depth readings and placing buoys to mark where the large vessels should station themselves to provide covering fire without endangering the landing boats.[52]

The next day, on exceptionally calm waters, 134 boats carrying from thirty to fifty soldiers each landed in waves west of Fort George. Gunfire from Chauncey's large vessels was quite effective in suppressing the defenders positioned near the landing beach until the advance guard, under Scott's command, hit the shore. For several critical minutes, the determined British defenders kept Scott's men pinned down at the water's edge. The next wave brought a preponderance of American firepower. In an unequal firefight, the British sustained horrific losses before being forced to retire. Vincent ordered Fort George evacuated and his army to withdraw from the line of the Niagara River into the interior, stopping to regroup at Forty Mile Creek.[53]

Scott, always at the head of the army, was the first into Fort George as the British were vacating, and he personally hauled down the British flag. He gathered the available troops and pursued the fleeing British for several miles until he obeyed the third order he received to cease the chase and return to the fort. Dearborn justified this decision in his report to Armstrong. "Our light troops pursued them several miles," he wrote. "The troops having been under arms from one o'clock in the morning were too much exhausted for any further pursuit."[54] Certainly the British were every bit as exhausted. Scott, who was developing a pattern of audacity nearly to the point of recklessness, believed that the pursuit could and should have been continued.[55]

For his part, Vincent was determined to defend Burlington Heights. By withdrawing from Forts George and Erie and the entire river line in between, he had allowed the water line of communication between Kingston and Amherstburg to be severed. However, Burlington guarded the land route between those two places, and Vincent had by no means abandoned hope. Nonetheless, the evacuation of Fort Erie had decisive results elsewhere. Five American vessels—two schooners, one sloop, and two gunboats—had been trapped in the navy yard at Black Rock, prevented from entering the upper Great Lakes by the British guns at Fort Erie. Now the way was clear, and teams of oxen hauled the vessels upriver against the three-knot current. Once in Lake Erie, these craft were a welcomed and needed augmentation to Perry's fleet being built at Erie.[56]

Dearborn was again most complimentary to Chauncey for naval support. He wrote to Armstrong that "the army is under the greatest obligation to that able naval commander for his indefatigable exertions, in cooperation in all its important movements, and especially in its operations this day."[57] Chauncey and the fleet, however, quit the campaign abruptly when word arrived that while Dearborn was adjusting his laurels at Fort George, Sir James Lucas Yeo and Prevost raided Sacketts Harbor and came within measurable distance of destroying that vital base.[58]

Commodore Yeo arrived on Lake Ontario on 15 May to take command of all naval forces, Royal Navy and Provincial Marine, on the Great Lakes. His instructions put him squarely under the command of Prevost. The Admiralty ordered Yeo not to undertake "any operation without the full concurrence and approbation of him [Prevost] or his commanders of the forces employed under him."[59] Yeo and Prevost quickly took advantage of the absence of the American squadron and sailed for Sacketts Harbor.

In the absence of Dearborn and his regular army generals, the ranking soldier in the vicinity of Sacketts Harbor was militia Brigadier General Jacob Brown. Brown, who made his living as a gentleman farmer and smuggler, was active in Republican politics, and Governor Tompkins had appointed him a general officer in 1811. Early in 1813, Armstrong offered Brown a regular commission as colonel of a newly formed regiment of infantry. Brown refused the demotion. Jacob Brown's actions in the defense of Sacketts Harbor would bring him national attention.[60]

Yeo's squadron landed 750 experienced troops who easily brushed aside the 400 local militiamen Brown had positioned to oppose the assault. The British then attacked 600 regulars, mostly new recruits or those too sick to accompany the force attacking Fort George, who stood between them and the shipyard. Brown managed to bring some of the militia back into the battle to fire on the flank of the British attack. Losing one-third of their numbers, the British broke off the attack, but not before a misinformed naval officer started the preplanned destruction of the partially finished ship and the stores. Brown stopped the unnecessary fires, but not soon enough to save half a million dollars' worth of supplies and the sails of the *General Pike*.[61]

Brown, whose tactical plan and inspirational leadership were the catalysts of victory, was sorely disappointed by the performance of the militia. "Your Excellency as Commander in Chief may think that I bear hard upon the militia," he wrote to Governor Tompkins. "I do them justice sir. . . . The noble men . . . of the Regular Army & some few, precious few Citizen Soldiers who nobly resisted the Shock of the foe . . . are the men who merit the honor of this Victory & Sir they must have it."[62] Besides serving to point out the risks inherent in depending on untrained militia, the raid on Sacketts Harbor had other effects on operations in the Central Theater of Operations.

Brown displayed two vital qualities in addition to physical courage. He was an inspirational leader who persuaded some of the militiamen to return to the battle after their initial flight, and he kept his head in confusing circumstances. In August, Brown received his reward: appointment as brigadier general in the regular army.

Chauncey sailed away from Dearborn's operation on the Niagara Peninsula. The near loss of his base dampened any enthusiasm Chauncey had for joint operations or for taking calculated risks.[63] Support for land operations receded in priority as the commander of naval operations on the Great Lakes focused his efforts on winning the naval arms race with Yeo. The defensive works surrounding Sacketts Harbor were extensively expanded, and both Tompkins and Armstrong were increasingly sensitive to its security.

The failure at Sacketts Harbor did not curb Yeo's aggressiveness. While Chauncey returned to his base to protect it, Yeo led his squadron to the head of the lake, where his presence was probably critical to the British decision to limit Dearborn's gains to the environs of Fort George itself. Without Chauncey's assistance, Dearborn could hardly outflank Vincent, nor could his forces be certain of resupply by water at any distance from Fort George.[64] Yeo's timely assistance contributed directly to two stunning British victories on the Niagara Peninsula that put an end to American hopes in that quarter for the remainder of the year.

Vincent withdrew his depleted force to his earthworks on Burlington Heights, the part of the escarpment that overlooks Burlington Bay and guards the road between York and Amherstburg. Dearborn, who had called off Scott's pursuit earlier, changed his mind when he heard reports that Brigadier General Henry Procter in western Upper Canada was marching to aid Vincent in an attempt to recapture Fort George. This possibility was entirely consistent with Prevost's strategy. Dearborn dispatched newly promoted Brigadier General William Winder to attack Vincent before Procter could arrive.

Winder's force marched west along the narrow corridor bounded on the south by the escarpment and on the north by the shore of Lake Ontario. This avenue of advance was cut at frequent intervals by creeks running north from the steep-sided hill line into the lake. Supply vessels traveled a parallel course along the lakeshore. Arriving in front of Vincent's position, Winder discovered that his force was too small to ensure success, so he sent back to Dearborn for instructions. Dearborn dispatched reinforcements under Brigadier General John Chandler, who, like Winder, was a political appointee. The combined American force bivouacked west of Stoney Creek and forty-six miles from Fort George.

Vincent pondered his options. He could withdraw to York rather than risk destruction of his force. However, this would leave Procter, still out west, subject to attack from two directions and would amount to abandonment of the

Grand River Indians and the loyalists of western Upper Canada. Vincent could defend his field fortifications on the heights, but failure in battle would not only leave Procter, Norton's Indians, and the loyalists stranded but also add more battle losses to those already suffered defending Fort George. The last option, a night attack, might garner results well worth the risk.

Night attacks were notoriously subject to chance, because the commanders could exercise only loose control over their troops and because the terrors of the darkness compounded the fear associated with mortal combat. Conversely, the darkness could hide inferior numbers and perhaps multiply the effects of surprise. A careful reconnaissance of the American camp revealed defects in the positioning of their forces. For their part, the Americans were apprehensive of a night attack but had not planned or rehearsed their actions if one materialized. Vincent gave the order to Lieutenant Colonel John Harvey to attack. Failure might still allow the British to defend Burlington Heights, but success would go a long way toward redressing the loss of Fort George. Harvey's attack one hour before dawn on 6 June resulted in moderate losses on both sides, but most importantly, both Winder and Chandler were captured in the confused fighting.[65]

The Americans had quickly recovered and fought back hard. Without their generals, however, they were at a loss as to what to do when the sun came up and the British had withdrawn. Command devolved to Colonel James Burn of the Second Dragoons. Burn ordered his men to fall back on their supply vessels at Forty Mile Creek. The Americans were demoralized; they did not bury their dead, and they abandoned large amounts of tentage and camp equipment. At the mouth of Forty Mile Creek, Burn's command was joined by Generals John Boyd and Morgan Lewis. Lewis took command, but now the Americans faced new and potentially mortal threats. Norton's handful of Indians surrounded the camp on land, and Yeo's squadron fired on the Americans from offshore. The American supply vessels were no match for the British schooners, and without hope that Chauncey might arrive to drive off the Royal Navy, Lewis believed that he was left with little choice but to return to Fort George.

Vincent followed at a safe distance and closed in on Fort George in a loose ring. His smaller force had kept the Americans from exploiting their initial advantage. Dearborn, perhaps unwilling to acknowledge that no offensive could succeed until command of the lake had been wrested from the British, blamed his subordinates instead. In his initial report to Armstrong, Dearborn tried to explain why his men had withdrawn from a battlefield they had retained after a night attack. "If either of the general officers had remained in command, the enemy would have been pursued and cut up, or if Colonel Burn had been an officer of infantry," rationalized the disappointed general.[66] Dearborn's campaign, off to a promising start, was coming unraveled.

Encouraged by his success at Stoney Creek, Vincent drew in closer to Fort George. Reinforced by Indians and regulars, his division could now challenge American foragers and patrols leaving the security of Fort George, although it was still too weak to conduct a close siege. Dearborn took ill, and command of the forces in Fort George devolved temporarily upon General John P. Boyd. Boyd was a professional soldier who had commanded large numbers of natives on the Indian subcontinent; after returning to America, he commanded the Fourth Infantry at Tippecanoe. Boyd understood that to get the campaign moving forward again, he must defeat Vincent's command in the field or somehow maneuver it off the Niagara Peninsula. To that end, he planned a raid to surprise and capture or destroy one of Vincent's strong points maintaining the loose encirclement. Chosen to command the raid was Colonel Charles G. Boerstler.

Boerstler's force of 700 included cavalry and artillery and was built around his own regiment, the Fourteenth Infantry. Although Boerstler himself had some combat experience, his regiment had few officers or soldiers who had seen serious fighting. The previous November, Boerstler had led 200 of his men on a raid across the Niagara in support of Smyth's operations, but since then, the Fourteenth had seen no action. On 23 June, Boerstler led his inexperienced command out of Fort George and along the muddy roads toward the British outpost at Beaver Dams.

The Americans made slight progress the first day; on the second day, they entered a densely wooded area. Constricted to a narrow path, Boerstler's men formed a long, thin column. It was then, when most vulnerable, that the Americans were surrounded by fewer than 500 Indians. Most were Iroquois from Lower Canada, but a handful were from Norton's Grand River Indians and tribes farther west. Less than fifty men died on either side in the fighting, which lasted three hours. Boerstler was wounded early in the fight, and the Americans had a difficult time trying to move to a more defensible position while bringing their wounded with them. Although outnumbering their foe, the Americans were terrorized by the prospects of a massacre. For their part, the Indians had neither the inclination nor the skill to negotiate an end to the fighting.[67]

That role was expertly played by Lieutenant James FitzGibbon, who commanded an independent company of the Forty-ninth Foot. By playing on the Americans' fear, FitzGibbon convinced Boerstler to surrender his command. Denied some of the plunder by the terms of the agreement, the Indians of Lower Canada left in disgust, but they were guilty of no atrocities. On the British side, the fight was entirely carried on by native warriors, and it was clearly the terror they inspired that convinced Boerstler to surrender rather than risk destruction during a retreat back to Fort George.[68]

The British were not scrupulous about keeping their side of the agreement. Having consented to release the American militiamen rather than march them off to captivity along with the regulars, FitzGibbon reneged when he discovered that among Boerstler's command was Dr. Cyrenius Chapin. Chapin had led a partisan force from Buffalo that was notorious for its raids on the Niagara Peninsula and its running fights with the Lincoln militia and volunteer dragoons. Notably, Chapin escaped en route and returned to his home in Buffalo.

The military results of the action at Beaver Dams were predictable. The British and Canadians and their Indian allies, greatly encouraged, closed in even further on Fort George and thereby stopped Dearborn's campaign in its tracks. Congress, Armstrong, and Madison came to realize that their faith in Dearborn was misplaced. Although he could still make a contribution to the war effort, it was not as the commander of the main army. Armstrong directed Dearborn to relinquish command, ostensibly to regain his health. Boyd retained command on the Niagara, but he would be under James Wilkinson, who would take over the Ninth Military District from Dearborn. Armstrong, referring to the previous commander, warned Boyd, "There is no excuse for a general who permits a beaten army to escape and to rally."[69] As it was dawning on the secretary of war that high-quality leadership from his senior general was absolutely essential to success, he was also growing disenchanted with the naval situation on the Great Lakes. "I am afraid," he had written to Dearborn in early July, "that we have all along acted on the belief, very pleasing but ill founded, viz: that we were ahead of the enemy as to naval means and naval preparation on the lakes."[70]

Time remained for another major operation in the Central Theater, and Armstrong had to decide whether to reinforce failure on the Niagara or to start anew in a different quarter. Whatever he decided, he could not count on control of Lake Ontario. It would be late fall before the next campaign set off, and the intervening months saw some action of significance.

Activity around Fort George was limited to raids by both sides on patrols and pickets. In mid-July, an American picket was attacked by a group of about 150 western Indians, who scalped and mutilated the dead, including some apparently killed after they had surrendered. Even though both sides disputed the circumstances, the Americans expected the British to ensure that their native allies adhered to European standards of conduct. In any event, the Indians were effectively keeping Boyd's men from venturing too far from the fort. "The enemy has lately kept his Indians so constantly scouring the woods of our vicinity," Boyd wrote to Armstrong, "that we gain no deserters nor intelligence of his movements."[71] Boyd was becoming increasingly inclined to accept the active assistance of the New York Iroquois.

The British were not only keeping Boyd holed up in Fort George but also raiding across the Niagara. On 11 July, Lieutenant Colonel Cecil Bisshop led an attack on the naval yard at Black Rock, which burned a small schooner and captured a large amount of supplies, including 123 barrels of precious salt. Peter B. Porter organized a force of regulars, militiamen, and Seneca to drive off the raiders. The British made good their escape, but Bisshop was mortally wounded. Bisshop's loss was demoralizing to the British. Formerly an aide to Arthur Wellesley in Portugal, Bisshop was particularly successful in leading mixed forces of regulars, militiamen, and Indians. Also wounded was Young King, chief of the Seneca.

The Seneca were about to scalp the British dead but were prevented from doing so by Porter. This was the first time that the New York Iroquois fought alongside the Americans. Without authorization from Governor Tompkins or the War Department, Porter organized about 140 Indians into a volunteer company under the Seneca war chief Farmer's Brother. The Iroquois warriors were paid $8 monthly, and their officers greater amounts. Farmer's Brother received $40 each month. Meanwhile, the New York Iroquois declared war on Lower and Upper Canada, although their intent was defensive only; they would defend American territory. In this unprecedented adaptation of European and U.S. custom, the Iroquois produced a document that urged the war chiefs to "call forth immediately their warriors under them and put them in motion to protect their rights and liberties which our brethren the Americans are now defending."[72]

Farmer's Brother and his company, as U.S. volunteers, were not bound by the defensive aspect of the Iroquois declaration of war. On 17 August, they saw action when Porter led an attack on a British picket outside of Fort George. This action pitted Grand River Iroquois against their New York tribesmen. Norton recalled that this action "spread no small dismay among the warriors attached to the British Army."[73] The uneasy peace among the Iroquois was shattered, and the fratricide would continue for nearly a year before both sides were sufficiently sickened by the bloodshed to focus on preserving their mutual nation.

Earlier in July occurred the Americans' last serious attempt to relieve the pressure on Fort George. Satisfied for the time being that his base at Sacketts Harbor was secure, Chauncey picked up Scott and 500 soldiers and headed for Burlington Heights. Destruction of the supplies there might convince Major General Francis de Rottenburg, who had recently replaced the unfortunate Sheaffe, to call off the siege at the mouth of the Niagara. Arriving at Burlington Bay, which was under the protection of earthen fortifications on the escarpment, Scott and Chauncey assessed the odds and found them stacked against them. Refusing to sail back to Fort George with nothing to show for their efforts, the Americans sailed east again and on 31 July raided York once again. York was nearly defenseless, for most of the British were on the peninsula holding Boyd in check. Scott's raiders captured over 400 barrels of food, burned down barracks and warehouses, and freed many of Boerstler's men in captivity there.[74] The success of this raid demonstrated not only the advantages of even temporary naval control of the lake but also the diffused nature of British defenses west of Kingston. De Rottenburg's men were spread thinly. In order to limit American gains to Fort George and its immediate environs, the British accepted risk elsewhere.

The Americans spent the rest of the year penned into a tiny corner of the Niagara Peninsula as the focus of the war shifted toward the St. Lawrence River. However, new patterns of fighting had emerged that to some extent would condition the fighting in 1814. It was clear that neither side had a monopoly on courage, initiative, leadership, or tactical skill. The Americans demonstrated that they were not the inept warriors of the previous year and, in fact, had nearly closed the gap between themselves and the British and Canadians in many important ways. Their victories, particularly the first attack on York and the Battle of Fort George, pointed to the improvements.

These two battles demonstrated a high level of cooperation between the army and navy. The respective ground and sea commanders found a coincidence of goals, and the strengths of each complemented the other. The amphibious assaults were executed flawlessly, and naval gunfire helped to weaken the enemy defending on the beaches. As laudable as this sophisticated level of cooperation was, victory seemed to be the product of two other factors: the Americans attacked on each occasion in overwhelming numbers and without reliance on the militia.

The two stunning British and Indian victories, Stoney Creek and Beaver Dams, also demonstrated similarities. In both cases, despite numerical superiority, the defenders seized the initiative and delivered surprise attacks. British victory was not the result of superior fighting abilities. In each case, all participants showed high levels of fighting skill, and neither side shrank from close combat. In both cases, the American command was degraded, either by the capture of Chandler and Winder at Stoney Creek or by the wounding of Boerstler at Beaver Dams. British victory was the result of the perception by the American commanders, both Burn and Boerstler, that their force was isolated and at grave risk of destruction. Burn chose to retreat, Boerstler to surrender.

The combat activity on the Niagara Peninsula in 1813 pointed to an improved American army. Officers and men were better trained and more aggressive. However, the army was still brittle; it could be damaged by a sharp blow. For their part, the British were rewarded for their willingness to seize the initiative and to attack against larger numbers. As a result, British commanders grew bolder, more confident, and would seek opportunities to counterattack despite the numerical odds. This tactic continued to win battles in 1813 against frangible American forces but would be singularly unsuccessful in 1814 against a combat-toughened foe.

As the land fighting on the Niagara Peninsula died down, naval activities on the Great Lakes developed in a way to shape the competing strategies for the remainder of the war. Although Perry's victory in September was decisive to fighting in the Western Theater, the activity on Lake Ontario from July through October was more indicative of the dynamics that would shape the 1814 campaign. Throughout these months, the arms race proceeded feverishly, and the two fleets postured and sparred but managed to avoid the kind of all-out battle that Barclay and Perry sought. In fairness to both naval commanders, Chauncey and Yeo, the asymmetry of their ordnance argued against the mutual consent required by the arms-race mentality. The American ships were armed with a greater proportion of long-range guns, whereas those of the Royal Navy had an advantage in the short-range carronades. Thus Chauncey preferred a long-range gun duel, while Yeo constrained himself to exchanging horrific blows at very short range. Circumstances of wind and position were never right to convince either commodore that he enjoyed enough advantage to justify the risk. And the risk of failure was heavy. Both Yeo and Chauncey understood that the loss of Lake Ontario meant losing the ground war not only on the margin of that lake but also on all the Great Lakes and in the upper Mississippi Valley.

It was fairly easy for either squadron to refuse battle, as Yeo did in late September when he fled into Burlington Bay with Chauncey at his heels. And of course, Chauncey had a protected refuge at Sacketts Harbor should he be caught at a disadvantage. Each commander understood that the arms race would have no logical conclusion unless the fleets joined in decisive battle, and battle could be avoided as long as safe havens existed. Yeo, on the strategic defensive, could accept inconclusive results; Chauncey could not. To the end, Chauncey hoped that Yeo would accept a fight even when the British bases were not eliminated. The havens could not be successfully attacked without large ground forces. Thus Chauncey's cooperation with the army early in 1813 is understandable in the logic of the arms race. This same logic argued against Chauncey's supporting Brown in 1814.[75]

While Yeo and Chauncey danced at a distance on Lake Ontario, Barclay and Perry willingly embraced in a dance of death on Lake Erie. This extraordinarily violent naval clash had profound repercussions on the war in the Western Theater. Barclay, with refuges for his squadron at either end of the lake and mindful of the same asymmetry of ordnance that confounded Yeo, chose to fight Perry. Was it wise to do so when so much was at risk?

Barclay and Perry were in an arms race on their lake every bit as frantic, if on a smaller scale, as that on Lake Ontario. However, Barclay was at a serious logistical disadvantage and would eventually be outnumbered and outgunned. Both Yeo and Chauncey were ungenerous in their support of their subordinates, in both men and material. Their stinginess arose from a cold analysis that victory out west was, by the nature of the geography, limited in value, whereas the course of the entire war might ride on victory or defeat on Lake Ontario. Barclay was not rash in seeking to bring Perry to battle while the Royal Navy had a fighting chance. He was temperamentally inclined to do so, having lost an arm at Trafalgar, perhaps the most decisive fleet-on-fleet battle in the nineteenth century.[76]

Shortly after Perry's victory on 10 September, Armstrong wrote to Harrison directing him, after the capture of Fort Malden, to attack into the Niagara Peninsula, forcing the British to break the loose siege of Fort George. "By giving this new direction to your operations," wrote the secretary of war, "you will readily perceive of how much more importance it is, in the opinion of the Executive, to be able to expel the enemy from the country lying between the two lakes, Erie and Ontario, than to pursue the Indians into their woody and distant recesses."[77] While logistical problems kept Harrison's Army of the Northwest from relieving Fort George, the future president managed to bring Procter's regulars and Tecumseh's Indians to battle on the Thames River and destroy them. This battle, unthinkable without Perry's victory, had several far-reaching results. With Tecumseh's death, many Indians withdrew from active support of the British. The loss of Procter's force and Barclay's fleet greatly reduced the requirements for British supplies west of Burlington Bay. While Harrison's many volunteers returned to their homes, his regulars were freed up for operations in the East. More naval supplies were now available to both Lake Ontario squadrons, since the arms race on Lake Erie was effectively finished. However, the British did not give up on western Upper Canada. They opened a road from York north to Georgian Bay on Lake Huron and, by extraordinary efforts, continued to defend their holdings on the upper Great Lakes. The Americans conducted intermittent raids on the loyal settlers on the north shore of Lake Erie, aided by a considerable pro-American faction. The war there smoldered throughout 1814.

American offensive operations in the Central Theater for 1813 ended with the twin disasters at Chateauguay and Crysler's Farm. The seed for these defeats was planted in early March, when Armstrong ordered James Wilkinson, newly promoted to major general, to depart his command in New Orleans and report to Dearborn's headquarters. Wilkinson did not arrive in Washington until 31 July, at which time he was given command of the Ninth Military District, Dearborn having been relegated to a quiet command in New York City. Armstrong erred in appointing Wilkinson, an inveterate intriguer, to this crucial command.

Wilkinson did not enjoy the confidence of all his officers, and the mutual loathing he shared with Major General Wade Hampton was no secret in the army. Hampton, a legitimate hero of the Revolution, commanded the forces on Lake Champlain and would be expected to cooperate with Wilkinson to some degree in any operations that Armstrong devised.

The inability of Dearborn to parlay the capture of Fort George into gains of strategic dimension caused Armstrong to rethink his strategy. Once again, and correctly, Armstrong concluded that severing the British line of communication between Kingston and Montreal would be decisive to the war effort. On 23 July, Armstrong gave his new commander a choice of two courses of action. First, he proposed a main attack against Kingston, with a secondary attack against Montreal. This might provoke Prevost to withdraw troops from Kingston to defend Montreal. The second option was a two-pronged attack on Montreal, with one force originating at Plattsburg and the other from Sacketts Harbor. This would cut the supply lines to Kingston in short order. Wilkinson replied with a counterproposal that essentially would reinforce the army on the Niagara Frontier and move on York and then Kingston. Armstrong responded that such a strategy would serve only to "wound the tail of the lion. . . . Kingston . . . presents the first and great object of the campaign." Wilkinson could attack Kingston directly, or he could do so indirectly by moving on Montreal.[78]

Armstrong joined Wilkinson at Sacketts Harbor, and with Chauncey they tried repeatedly to hammer out a plan. Armstrong had a secondary mission of coordinating the efforts of Hampton, who had offered his resignation rather than serve under Wilkinson. Hampton was sufficiently appeased by Armstrong to remain in command until after the campaign ended, and by late September, his army of inexperienced recruits was poised on the border waiting for the signal to advance on Montreal. Early in October, Wilkinson ordered most of the regulars defending Fort George to move to Sacketts Harbor; on 17 October, Wilkinson issued orders for the army to move to Grenadier Island, where Lake Ontario tapers into the St. Lawrence River. His subordinate commanders were still unsure, as was perhaps Wilkinson himself, whether they were moving on Kingston or Montreal.[79]

Having received orders to move from Armstrong, Hampton advanced down the Chateauguay River on 21 October with 4,000 troops and Brigadier General George Izard as his second in command. Nearly all of the 1,400 New York militiamen with him had refused to cross the border. A month earlier, Prevost had called out 8,000 Lower Canada militiamen to block the path to Montreal. The militiamen, mostly francophone, had responded quite well. They were drilled in the rudiments of soldiering and adequately armed.

On 25 October, Hampton drew up to a series of barricades and abatis blocking his way. Defending the works were the Voltigeurs, numerous militiamen, and a sprinkling of Indians, about 1,700 in all, led by their veteran commander Lieutenant Colonel Charles de Salaberry. Hampton ordered a night flanking movement as a prelude to his main attack to be delivered frontally the next morning. The flanking movement miscarried, but perhaps more critically, Hampton received word that Armstrong had ordered winter quarters to be built not in Montreal but south of the border. It was apparent to Hampton that the secretary of war himself was pessimistic about their prospects.[80]

The following day, Hampton ordered an attack that did not amount to much more than a two-hour-long firefight in front of the first barricade. After losing fifty men, Hampton called off the attack and the campaign and returned to the United States. He refused Wilkinson's order to continue the advance by citing a lack of supplies and sickness among the troops. "The force is dropping off by fatigue and sickness to a most alarming extent," wrote Hampton, "and, what is more discouraging, the officers, with a few exceptions, are sunk as low as the soldiers, and endure hardship and privation as badly. . . . Fatigue and suffering from the weather have deprived them of that spirit which constituted my best hopes."[81] Hampton resigned in disgust in March of the following year. One prong of the American offensive was defeated by stalwart Canadians, to be sure, but also by confusion and mistrust in the mind of the commander, induced not by enemy action but by the intrigue and incompetence of superiors.

Wilkinson was unaware of Hampton's fate until after his own force had been tested in battle at Crysler's Farm. However, things began going wrong for the Sacketts Harbor force soon after they embarked. The Americans rowed or sailed in hundreds of bateaux through fierce rain and sleet storms all the way to Grenadier Island, losing dozens of boats and scores of men en route. The survivors, many in summer uniforms and without overcoats, suffered miserably while the army concentrated prior to pushing down the St. Lawrence. Chauncey failed in his mission of keeping the Royal Navy bottled up in Kingston Harbor. Captain William H. Mulcaster led a small flotilla that followed the Americans, harassing them as best it could. Another force from Kingston, consisting of two understrength regiments, was led by Lieutenant Colonel Joseph Morrison. Morrison tailed the nearly 8,000 Americans, keeping just out of reach with his 800 men. The British were certainly audacious, a trait growing from the frequent experience of beating larger numbers of Americans in battle.

The greatest impediment to Wilkinson's movement downriver was not the numerous snipers and several gun batteries firing from the shore, nor was it Mulcaster's gunboats or Morrison's infantry; it was the Long Sault rapids, which stretched for eight miles. The Americans would march by land while the lightened boats navigated the rough water. Ably assisted by Winfield Scott, Jacob Brown commanded the advance guard, which successfully cleared out all foe en route to the far end of the rapids. It was while the main army, camped near John

Crysler's farm, was preparing to follow Brown's force that Morrison drew a little too close.[82]

Wilkinson was too sick to take to the field, so the American main body was commanded by Brigadier General John P. Boyd, an officer of considerable combat experience. Boyd attacked Morrison's slender force piecemeal with four brigades. The British fired and moved like the well-trained and disciplined soldiers they were, driving back each American attack. Although the Americans assaulted with spirit, they could neither fire nor maneuver as quickly as their foe. Even a cavalry attack was stopped by heavy fire before the dragoons could close with saber and pistol.[83]

An analysis of combat experience of the infantry of the opposing sides does not explain the British success. True, the oldest and most experienced American regiments were with Brown in the advance guard and did not participate in the battle. Of the ten infantry regiments with Boyd, six had not seen combat or had only minimal combat experience. Of the remaining four, each of which had been represented in two or three battles prior to Crysler's Farm, only two had participated in victories. The most experienced regiment to fight under Boyd was the Sixteenth Infantry, which had fought at York, Fort George, and Stoney Creek.

Of the two British regiments, the largest was Morrison's own Eighty-ninth Regiment of Foot. Since arriving in British North America in October 1812, only the light company had seen any action at all, and this company missed the battle, being on the Niagara Peninsula at the time. Brock's old regiment, the Forty-ninth, had participated in many of the battles of the war—Queenston, Fort George, Stoney Creek—but only about 200 of the "Green Tigers" were with Morrison that day. Perhaps Wilkinson's assessment to Armstrong explains the poor American showing: "Since the action of 11th [*sic*], British officers have acknowledged our dauntless courage, but observed we were undisciplined and fought without order, and indeed the scenes of that day justify these observations."[84]

Having failed to destroy Morrison's pursuing force on 11 November, Wilkinson might have tried again had he not received the report that Hampton was returning to the United States. A hastily convened council of war agreed with Wilkinson's inclination to go into winter quarters at French Mills, just inside the New York border. Wilkinson lost no time in blaming his personal enemy. Writing that same day, he stated that Hampton's refusal to unite with Wilkinson's army "defeats the grand objects of the campaign in this quarter, which, before the receipt of your letter were thought to be completely within our power."[85] Armstrong, in turn, criticized Wilkinson directly. On 18 November he wrote, "Because it is quite incredible that, finding in your rear a heavy corps capable of disturbing the main action of the campaign, you should not have taken effectual measures to beat and destroy it. If 1,600 men were not sufficient for this purpose, 6,000 were so; and the garrisons of Kingston and Prescott destroyed (though we failed of getting Montreal) the upper province was won."[86]

Where does the blame lie? Although Hampton complained repeatedly of the poor training of his soldiers, he had taken considerable effort at Plattsburg to improve their drill.[87] His plan of attack at Chateauguay was sound and was defeated only when the flanking force lost its way in the wilderness. True, he did not press his attack vigorously, but the defenses were immensely strong against a frontal assault, and his decision to break off the attack certainly saved lives on both sides. Hampton is guilty of breaking off the campaign; even a stalemate on the Chateauguay River would have served to divert defenders away from Montreal.

For his part, Wilkinson contributed much to the failure. He took his time reporting for duty. His lengthy negotiations with Armstrong over strategy appeared to be efforts to escape blame rather than to devise the best chance for success. He wasted considerable time at Sacketts Harbor, which pushed the operation into worsening weather. Finally, after the setback at Crysler's Farm, Wilkinson did not turn with his full force on Morrison. Had he destroyed Morrison in the field, Kingston's defenses would have been less formidable and perhaps would have fallen to a land-based siege and naval blockade.

Armstrong, who had abandoned direction of the entire war from Washington in order to participate personally in the major campaign of the Central Theater, certainly earns the greatest share of the blame. He cooperated with Wilkinson by unnecessarily protracting the planning phase; as Wilkinson's superior, he could have ended the discussion by issuing orders rather than offering Wilkinson choices. He knowingly vested command of the forces to two elderly Revolutionary War veterans who were personal enemies. After promising to coordinate their efforts, Armstrong left Sacketts Harbor for Albany and effectively coordinated nothing. Armstrong was a competent strategist, but his lack of will and sense of personal responsibility contributed to the failures of 1813.[88]

After Wilkinson's force moved to French Mills, all the generals left except Brown. Many of the regimental officers took this opportunity to leave their units until spring. The weather was severe. Most of the troops lived in tents while they worked for weeks to build huts. Food, blankets, and medicine were all scarce. At one time, half the army was on the sick list. Could Valley Forge have been much worse? British agents circulated surrender notices, offering the men five months' wages to turn themselves in to British outposts. Few soldiers took up the offer.

While Lieutenant Colonels de Salaberry and Morrison were earning laurels in the defense of British North America, events back on the Niagara Peninsula were unfolding in a way that would end tragically for hundreds of civilians on both sides of the border. Early in October, Wilkinson ordered the majority of the regulars at Fort George to move to Sacketts Harbor in preparation for the attack on Montreal. He left Scott in command of the garrison, about 800 regulars, 700 militiamen, and 350 Indians. Brigadier Generals Peter B. Porter and George McClure of the New York militia were leading volunteers, militiamen, and Indians as far west as Forty Mile Creek, keeping the British away from the now weakly defended post. Scott, on his own initiative but within the parameters established by Wilkinson, departed Fort George with his regulars in order to join the campaign being organized at Sacketts Harbor.[89]

On 24 October, William Henry Harrison arrived at Buffalo with over 1,000 combat-experienced infantrymen and dragoons. He and McClure were planning an attack on Burlington Heights when Harrison received orders to sail to Sacketts Harbor to defend that critical base while Wilkinson attacked Montreal. Ever anxious to protect his shipyard, Chauncey moved Harrison's regulars to the naval base in mid-November. Harrison himself took leave of his veterans and went on a triumphal visit to New York City and Washington.

McClure was left with no regulars, and the term of service for his militia expired on 9 December. He wrote of his predicament to Armstrong, who in turn asked Governor Tompkins to call up 1,000 militiamen to replace those expected to depart Fort George. McClure, who had his men repairing the fort rather than building shelters for themselves, was under no illusions that he could induce any of the men to extend their enlistment for even a day. "The circumstances of their having to live in tents at this inclement season," he wrote to Tompkins, "had produced all the bad effects that can be imagined." To Armstrong he complained of his inability to pay his men all that the government owed them. "The best and most subordinate militia that have yet been on this frontier, finding that their wages were not ready for them, became, with some meritorious exceptions, a disaffected and ungovernable multitude." Between 7 and 10 December, virtually all of his militiamen crossed the Niagara back into the United States.[90]

A large British reconnaissance party was slowly approaching, and McClure, with only 100 men left, decided to abandon the nearly defenseless fort. The Americans blew up the main magazine but left seven cannon, large stores of tentage, ammunition, and camp equipment to fall into British hands.[91] This was an unfortunate end to the campaign that had started so promisingly with the capture of Fort George in May. However, McClure's next act brought well-deserved disgrace upon American arms.

McClure roused the inhabitants of Newark from their homes and into a snow flurry. His Canadian Volunteers torched the 130 or so houses, leaving about 400 women, children, and elderly men to fend for themselves. He justified this barbarous act by claiming that he was depriving the British soldiers of winter quarters. If that was so, why had he left several buildings and numerous tents standing inside the fort? As further justification, McClure produced a letter from Armstrong dated 4 October. "Understanding that the defence of the post committed to your charge may render it proper to destroy the town of Newark," wrote Armstrong, "you are hereby directed to apprise its inhabitants of this circumstance, and to invite them to remove themselves and their effects to some place of greater safety."[92] Newark was about a mile from the fort, across an open field. If the British used its buildings as cover, the Americans would be justified in firing on them. However, McClure's actions clearly exceeded the intent of Armstrong's guidance.

That McClure would commit such a provocation when this frontier was so vulnerable defies logic. The militia called up by Tompkins would take some time to appear, and McClure had only about 250 militiamen and volunteers under his command along the entire river line. McClure was under no misapprehension that the British would refrain from retaliating. He warned Captain Leonard, in command of the regulars at Fort Niagara, to expect an attack soon. Moving from town to town in western New York, the hapless general tried to raise volunteers to repel the attack he expected momentarily. Wherever he went, he experienced the justifiable scorn of the citizenry, who well understood that they would bear the brunt of a British quid pro quo.[93]

The account of the capture of Fort Niagara from a negligent garrison and the de-housing of virtually every American in the Niagara Valley has been told in chapter 1. This swift, efficient series of actions was accomplished by fresh blood. Arriving on the Niagara Frontier almost as soon as McClure left was Lieutenant General Sir Gordon Drummond, replacing de Rottenburg, who returned to Lower Canada. Drummond brought with him Major General Phineas Riall, who replaced the ill Vincent. The Canadian-born Drummond wasted no time in ordering the night attack on Fort Niagara and directing the follow-up operations to clear the eastern shore of all Americans, military and civilian.

Besides securing their front line for many months to come, the British captured immense stores in Fort Niagara. Drummond reported seizing twenty-seven guns, over 4,000 muskets and rifles, thousands of pairs of shoes, thousands of blankets and greatcoats, and enormous stores of food and camp equipment. Drummond could not occupy the American side of the river, but he was determined to keep the fort. He brought in six heavy guns to augment those already inside. He also positioned the batteries of Fort George to sweep the southern approaches to Fort Niagara. Drummond now had a secure haven for lake vessels in the mouth of the river and a strong toehold in America.[94]

In his first few weeks in office, the new president of the council and administrator of Upper Canada demonstrated traits that would stand him in good stead in the bitter campaigning of the last year of the war. Drummond exercised his authority with boldness and decision. His instructions to his subordinates reflected a determination to operate within the constraints of civilized warfare. He would tolerate no scalp taking from his native allies nor plundering from his white troops. Finally, he displayed a fondness for cold steel as a weapon of choice. For his part, Riall established a reputation for competence and gallantry.[95]

Having earned the disdain of his fellow citizen soldiers, McClure was replaced by militia Major General Amos Hall. Hall's first experience was to preside over the utter collapse of his militia organization under the onslaught of fewer than 700 British regulars, Canadian militiamen, and allied Indians. General Lewis Cass unofficially investigated the futile defense of Black Rock and Buffalo and reported to Armstrong on the misconduct of the 2,500 to 3,000 militiamen involved. "All except very few of them," he wrote, "behaved in the most cowardly manner. They fled without discharging a musket."[96]

As the war entered a new year, the military situation in the Central Theater appeared not to have changed much since the end of 1812. The British and Canadians and their Indian allies had not only thrown back every invasion but also occupied a secure toehold in the United States. True, the war had taken a decided turn for the worse in western Upper Canada, but this had not yet spilled over into the Central Theater of Operations. British commanders at all levels were confident in their supposition that to challenge larger numbers of American regulars was not a particularly risky undertaking. Boldness worked.

From the American perspective, several trends emerged. Although Armstrong's grasp of the strategic imperatives was sharpened, he still did not demonstrate the strength of character to impress his will upon his subordinates. The army in the field, both the individuals and the regiments, gained valuable combat experience. Weak generals were weeded out, and strong leaders were identified to command regiments, brigades, and districts. The army had shown bursts of competence, such as the raid on York and the capture of Fort George. These two battles demonstrated a high level of army-navy cooperation not to be seen again until the siege of Vera Cruz. Even in defeat, the Americans in 1813 did not plumb the depths of incompetence as had Smyth the year before. Wilkinson ultimately failed, but he mobilized, deployed, and sustained a force on a scale and for a duration far beyond the proficiency of any American commander in 1812. Growing American competence was on a collision course with British overconfidence. The impact would not occur until July.

As for the Indians, their tenuous truce completely unraveled. Iroquois from both sides of the border had fought against one another with no sign of moderation. The fratricide within the Iroquois Nation would also culminate in July.

CHAPTER FIVE

Polarizing Attitudes, Stagnating Strategies

You will enter a country that is to be one of the United States. You will arrive among a people who are to become your fellow citizens. It is not against them that we come to make war. It is against the government which holds them as vassals.
—Alexander Smyth, 17 November 1812

The wisdom of Smyth's words was lost on his countrymen—soldiers and civilians alike. His pleas for benign treatment of Canadians was overcome by the strong passions unleashed by war. In 1812, all sides displayed intentions to fight within recognized parameters of accepted behavior. However, eighteen months of war witnessed increasing harshness and incidents of savagery. Brutality in war seems to pursue a logic of escalation despite the best intentions of commanders to act humanely. A few instances of ruthless policy and brutal behavior drove the polarization of attitudes among the civil populations on both sides of the border.

Almost from the beginning of the war, British policy took measures that Americans could only view as hostage taking among legitimate prisoners of war. Following the Battle of Queenston, twenty-three American captives identified as Irishmen by their accents were put in irons and sent to Britain to face charges of treason. The British were invoking the same legal principle that justified impressment: one could not expatriate oneself. When Fort George was taken in 1813, an equal number of British prisoners were held in close confinement, and Prevost was notified that they could expect the same fate as the allegedly Irish-born Americans. The prince regent ordered Prevost to double the ante. In October 1813, Prevost announced that forty-six American officers and noncommissioned officers would be held in close confinement for the safety of those British officers held hostage. Madison retaliated in November by ordering forty-six British officers held hostage. Clearly, Madison saw this as an issue of sovereignty and therefore basic to his war aims. In January 1814, Prevost took the first step to defuse the issue, and after considerable negotiation the surviving hostages on both sides were released.[1]

The escalating hostage taking added to the slow ferment of American attitudes. In direct distinction, native acts in the West, the Raisin River Massacre key among them, provoked immediate and sustained calls for retribution, particularly among settlers in Kentucky, Tennessee, and the Old Northwest. These feelings spilled over into the regulars. Captain Daniel McFarland of the Twenty-second Infantry perhaps is typical of his fellow officers. In February 1813, he wrote to his brother:

> The acc[oun]t given by the Prisoners of the conduct of the savages and their more savage allies the British is too fearful for an American to recount. Yes Brother the wounded and a number of Prisoners were KILLED IN COOL BLOOD after they had surrendered, far be it from me to wish a war of extermination, but with a nation whose honour is violated faith, whose humanity is savage ferocity I ask no quarter not will I give it, the sword of Vengeance is Drawn and I trust in God it will not be sheathed till it is glutted.[2]

McFarland lived and died these sentiments, perhaps passing them on to his soldiers. He was killed in action leading his regiment at Lundy's Lane.

In Upper Canada, the war had come to display aspects of a civil as well as an international war. After the Battle of the Thames, the war degenerated into nearly continuous raiding. This region, with its particularly high proportion of American-born settlers and its near subsistence-level economy, was too poor in food and fodder to support large bodies of troops. American raiders, guided and reinforced by pro-American settlers and under the loosest control of their district commanders, moved with impunity intimidating loyalists and destroying public property and private mills. The losses of mills, food stores, and farm animals crippled the economy and caused untold hardship. The pro-American settlers used the raids as cover to settle private scores, capturing militia leaders who tended to be the social elite and sending them to Detroit and captivity. When the militia managed to strike back, the pro-Americans who fell into the hands of their erstwhile countrymen were branded traitors and sent east for trial. It was clear to the loyal settlers what life would be like in an American Canada.[3]

Similar incidents occurred in eastern Upper Canada. The otherwise successful raid on York was marred by charges of American soldiers and pro-American Canadians plundering unoccupied homes in direct violation of military convention and specific orders. Following the fall of Fort George, Dr. Cyrenius Chapin of Buffalo led a small body of mounted New York volunteers on frequent raids up and down the Niagara Valley. His band became known as the "forty thieves" for its scant regard of the customs of civilized warfare. The destruction of Newark and the treatment of its civilians by McClure were barbarous. The British infantrymen who took Fort Niagara were accused of bayoneting Americans begging to surrender. Finally, the western Indians who accompanied Drummond's forces scourging the American side of the Niagara killed men, women, and children, maiming their dead bodies. The war that began as a fight between gentlemen had sunk into a horror of needless death and destruction.[4]

Certainly military and civilian leaders took steps to stop the worst excesses. In July 1813, de Rottenburg ordered William Claus, his head Indian agent in Upper Canada, to notify the natives that once an American surrendered, he was to be protected from harm. De Rottenburg ordered that any Indian bringing in an unwounded prisoner was to be paid $5. The Indian captor of a wounded foe received $2.50. Prevost himself tried to stop the cycle of retaliation. In January 1814, he issued a proclamation stating that it was not his intention "to pursue further a system of warfare so revolting to his own feelings and so little congenial to the British character unless the future measures of the enemy could compel him again to resort to it."[5]

The issue of interpreting the rules of warfare was complicated by the very nature of the military organizations in North America. The militiaman, when called up into state or federal or provincial service, was a de facto combatant. But what was his status when not mustered into service? Both sides frequently offered protection to noncombatants, but the distinction was not crystal clear. For example, what was the status of a member of the local militia who, although not officially called into service, was seen armed and patrolling his own land? Could militia officers not called into service be captured? Were they prisoners of war? Raiders into Upper Canada frequently returned with militiamen as prisoners. Chapin's surrender of Buffalo was considered invalid by Drummond, since Chapin was not technically in American service. That did not prevent Chapin from being taken to Fort Erie as a prisoner.

What about the pro–American Canadians? Many were expatriate Americans who by British policy presumably could not give up their American citizenship. Nonetheless, British magistrates had accepted their oaths of loyalty to the king in exchange for the right to own land. Scores later joined the American army and therefore, as far as the Americans were concerned, enjoyed the same protection as American citizens in the regulars, volunteers, or called-up militia. The British treated them as traitors, as they did their citizens accused of aiding the enemy. As far as British authorities were concerned, their disloyal citizens had abused the system of giving parole in exchange for protection from imprisonment, seeking instead to release themselves from requirements to serve with the militia. This confusion in legal status resulting from the blurring of lines among regulars, volunteers, and militiamen was the source of much personal hardship and hard feelings.

The hardships and the increasing brutality of the war in the Central Theater polarized the populations on both sides of the border and the Iroquois Nation, which straddled the border. In Upper Canada, of course, with its high proportion of American-born, the polarization into loyalist and disaffected camps was most pronounced and greatly complicated the British response to American aggression. The government had to repel the Americans without encouraging its own people to withdraw their support for the war or to actively support the enemy. Ultimately successful, the British effort was not without its critical episodes.

Soon after the declaration of war, Brock sought to identify the disaffected. Persons refusing to make an oath of allegiance were detained or given forty-eight hours to leave the province. Within a few months, over 300 disaffected citizens were in jails on the Niagara Frontier. Hundreds more of military age fled into the wilderness. These shirkers emerged from time to time to raid the homes of the loyalists. However, for the most part, the British were moderate in their treatment of the disaffected. Persons who had committed no violent act and whose only crime was to claim American citizenship were given their passports to leave the province. To some degree, the ejection of the Tories from the newly independent United States was now avenged.[6]

The British victory at Queenston went a long way toward intimidating the disaffected and encouraging the loyal. The militia rounded up the shirkers, and they were dealt with by the magistrates, who displayed a new confidence in the province's chances of success. The two raids on York in 1813 illustrated quite well that the British had only temporarily cowed their estranged citizens. In April, Dearborn's troops freed eighteen or twenty pro-Americans from the York jail. These men had refused to take an oath of allegiance and had spent the previous winter in caves near Lake Simcoe until they had been captured. Perhaps as many as 300 disaffected were in hiding in the wilds north of York at one time or another. These and others volunteered information to the American raiders and joined in the general plundering of loyalist homes. When Scott returned to York in July, pro-Americans again emerged in numbers to provide information.

The Executive Council of Upper Canada confessed great difficulty in stamping out dissent. Juries could not be depended on to convict accused traitors; too many with pro-American sentiments might be hidden in the jury itself. By early 1814, however, the worst crisis was over. The legislative assembly by then was controlled by a loyalist majority. The assembly voted to confiscate the property of known traitors and made the prosecution of suspected traitors easier. Drummond confessed to Bathurst that the "greater part of the inhabitants are well disposed."[7]

This turnabout resulted not only from coercion but also from blandishments. The British power elite ran both official and unofficial propaganda organs. Prevost and his lieutenant governors published proclamations to counter those the American generals made to the people of Upper Canada. The target population of this official propaganda was the same. Both the Americans and the British were competing for the support of the Canadian people. More pervasive perhaps were the newspapers, which featured patriotic speeches, sermons, and letters with the goal of strengthening the will of the loyalists. Many editors published extracts from the American press. Canadian editors were not beyond distorting articles from the Republican newspapers, portraying them in their worst light. Perhaps the most powerful propaganda were the printed extracts from the *Federalist Papers*, which criticized the Madison administration for its conduct of an ill-considered war.[8]

Besides propaganda, the loyalist elite also offered tangible aid to ameliorate the worst of the suffering. John Strachan of York founded the Loyal and Patriotic Society of Upper Canada, which provided aid to families of killed, disabled, and imprisoned militiamen. Members of the society were also active in identifying and reporting on the activities of the disaffected. Representing the conservative social elite, the society worked hand in hand with the lieutenant governor. While Strachan's society represented the most loyal segment of Upper Canadian society, the opposite extreme of a polarized population went over to the enemy.

The history of the Canadian Volunteers begins with its leader Joseph Willcocks. Emigrating from Ireland in 1800, Willcocks was sheriff of the Home District of Upper Canada from 1803 to 1807 and served in the legislative assembly from 1808 to 1812. During these years, Willcocks was critical of the provincial government and a gadfly to the lieutenant governor. Following the capture of Fort George, Willcocks offered to raise a volunteer corps of Upper Canadians who would fight as part of the American army. Dearborn accepted the offer and armed those volunteering to fight in this renegade band. By September, Willcocks had about 130 pro-Americans in his force. The Canadian Volunteers roamed the Niagara Peninsula scouting for the Americans, plundering the homes of loyalists, and capturing their leaders. In November, Willcocks was joined by a party from western Upper Canada under Benajah Mallory. Mallory had fought on the American side during the Revolution and at one time held a commission in the Upper Canada militia. As the regulars left Fort George to join Wilkinson's advance on Montreal, George McClure's command consisted of Willcocks's men and an ever-decreasing number of reluctant New York militiamen. It is unclear how much influence Willcocks exerted over McClure in his decision to burn Newark. However, witnesses testified that it was Willcocks who personally directed the burnings.

The status of the Canadian Volunteers was somewhat ambiguous. They were not paid by the federal government, nor were the commissions of the officers granted from the president. Willcocks, for example, was commissioned by Dearborn. Peter B. Porter interceded on behalf of the Volunteers; in April 1814, Armstrong legitimized the corps and the commissions of its officers by declaring the unit as Volunteers of the United States. However, the unit could recruit only men who had been British subjects at the declaration of war. Later on, this was redefined to preclude the enlistment of British deserters. Vilified by Canadian loyalists, the Canadian Volunteers performed well for their American commanders.[9]

On the American side of the border, there was no counterpart to the Canadian Volunteers. Nonetheless, the war further polarized the two political parties and their supporters. At the national level, the Federalists pointed to the Madison administration's utter inability to gain its war goals and to the increasing danger in which Americans would find themselves as the war continued. Within New York, the polarization of the populace continued. In the spring of 1813, Governor Tompkins beat off a challenge for his position by Federalist General Van Rensselaer, although the Federalists gained a majority in the state assembly.

It seemed that economics, as much as ideology, played a role in the widening gap between diverging opinions. Nowhere was this more apparent than in the open city of Ogdensburg, which U.S. troops vacated early in 1813, ostensibly because Dearborn could not guarantee its security. Ogdensburg was home to millionaire entrepreneur David Parish. He and his Federalist commercial allies increased their wealth by trading openly with Canada. Calling the conflict "Mr. Madison's War," Parish and his many agents did all in their power to maintain cordial relations with British officials. Often Parish entertained British officers in his home, and Canadians frequently crossed the St. Lawrence to shop in Ogdensburg.[10]

Military operations worked their corrosive effect on the unity of the Iroquois Nation. Prevost, sensitive to American charges that the British were condoning native atrocities, prohibited taking Indians on raids into American territory during 1813. The turning point in relations among the Six Nations Indians came in the summer of that year, when New York Iroquois resisted the raid on Black Rock in which Lieutenant Colonel Cecil Bisshop was killed. Bisshop had been much admired by the Grand River natives, who met in council in August to consider what to do about the actions of the New York tribesmen, which they considered to be breaking the covenant of neutrality. The council decided that the intervention of the New York tribes released the Canadian Iroquois from their promise not to harm them. Now it was official policy on both sides to accept the possibility of intertribal warfare.[11]

While the Indian agents in western New York actively organized companies of tribesmen under their own officers and on the U.S. payroll, the Tuscarora met with the Grand River Indians to repledge neutrality in return for security from attack. However, when the British captured Fort Niagara, several Tuscarora actively aided the Americans. In consequence of the actions of a few, the Indians Drummond unleashed on the Niagara Frontier razed the Tuscarora village near Lewiston. Few natives were now untouched by hostilities, and the Iroquois Nation was in full civil war. An incident in the summer of 1814 in the streets of Buffalo illustrates the extent to which this internecine conflict had deteriorated. A Canadian Indian visiting that village let slip, apparently under the influence of drink, that he had taken both white and Indian scalps. Farmer's Brother murdered the accused in cold blood. Other Seneca disposed of the body. No official notice was taken; apparently, white authorities considered it an internal Indian matter.[12]

Besides the readily perceived disadvantages of inciting atrocity or leaving the campaign prematurely, native participation had less obvious drawbacks. The Indians did not fight for free, any more than the militia did. Norton warned Brock early in the conflict that the overriding concern of the Grand River Indians was the welfare of their families. A major irritant throughout the war was the slowness with which the British provided tribesmen with promised goods and food or monetary compensation for their casualties or for American prisoners turned over to the British. The natives had always suspected the British of accepting their assistance without fully intending to fulfill their commitments in return.[13]

Another unforeseen result of a wider participation of natives in the war was to discourage the raising of volunteers and to reduce the effectiveness of mustering the local militia. White settlers on both sides of the border were loath to leave their homes undefended while they were in the field with their companies. It is impossible to tell whether white commanders fully understood what they were giving up when they accepted native allies.[14]

Despite differences in dress, custom, and military effectiveness, the natives and the white militiamen shared a pivotal value: the welfare of family. This, more than ideological principle or sense of nationalism, set the limits of the risks they were willing to bear and the timing and duration of their absences from home. For example, when York had fallen to the Americans, John Norton tried to raise a force of Grand River Indians to defend along the Niagara River. Most refused to join him, largely because they saw that the white militia was reluctant to mobilize. As the gulf between supporters of the war and their opponents widened among the American, Canadian, and native populations, a small number of persons—both patriots and traitors—assumed perhaps the greatest risk of all: the risk of execution, fully sustained by the laws of war in Britain and the United States and by tribal custom.

In a theater rife with disaffection and in which English speakers of both nationalities could readily pass for each other, espionage was extensive. Governor-General Prevost put in place a network of spies directed by Edward Doyle in Prescott and Leon Lalanne in Montreal. These agents granted licenses to trade in Canada to American merchants in exchange for information. The informants, who traveled to and from Canada, were also given bits of information to pass on to American authorities so that their illegal trading activities would be overlooked.[15]

American authorities well understood that their own countrymen were in the pay of Great Britain. On 1 July 1813, Commodore Chauncey caught Samuel Stacey, an American from the St. Lawrence Valley, and charged him with spying. It seems that Chauncey had been tipped off by one of his own spies to have Stacey watched. Surveillance discovered that Stacey left his home near Ogdensburg ostensibly on a business trip to Utica. Instead, he appeared in Sacketts Harbor asking specific questions about the navy's operations there. Chauncey was certain that it was Stacey who informed the British that the troops and fleet had departed Sacketts Harbor for an attack on Fort George, thus prompting the British raid on Chauncey's nearly undefended base.[16]

The Americans, in like manner, capitalized on disaffection in Upper Canada. Many American sympathizers came forward to offer their services. Willing individuals were asked to travel through Canada to report on troop strength and readiness, the condition of the fleet, and the progress of the British shipbuilding program. The letters of Dearborn and Wilkinson are laced with references to unnamed spies and the results of their missions.

The tale of David Kilbourn may be typical of the lot of these accessories to war. Kilbourn was a native of the United States who moved to Upper Canada after the Revolution. He professed never to have lost his attachment to his native land. In 1813, he was asked to report on the numbers and locations of the troops in the province, which he did through one of General Wilkinson's agents. Kilbourn was caught and threatened with the universal fate of apprehended traitors. Escaping, he made his way to Wilkinson's headquarters at French Mills. Kilbourn received some compensation from the United States, but not enough to make up for his house and property in Upper Canada, which was seized and sold by provincial authorities.[17]

The Staceys and Kilbournes were essential to the war effort as each belligerent prepared for the 1814 campaign season. Each side was building up its naval and land forces, and information concerning its opponent was essential in developing a feasible operational concept. The forces immediately available and in reserve at the beginning of the new year were vastly superior to those of June 1812 in both quantity and quality. The naval forces in the Central Theater in particular, though orders of magnitude larger than just two years earlier, were still in rough balance. Yet the fleets on Lake Ontario never fought a battle to the finish, as had occurred on Lake Erie in 1813 and on Lake Champlain in 1814, although both commanders professed a willingness to do so. Naval activity on that lake followed a logic of its own, divorced by mid-1813 from that of ground operations. For the Americans, this would lead directly to the failure of the 1814 campaign. For the British, the result was the successful defense of Upper Canada.[18]

In order for the Americans to win the war, it was necessary to seize and then hold both Lower and Upper Canada. This land could then be annexed outright or traded for a guarantee of neutral rights. However, the primitive condition of land transportation meant that the Americans required the permanent control of Lake Ontario in order to supply an invading or occupying force. This could only follow the destruction of the Royal Navy on that lake.

The British fleet could be destroyed by four means: a storm, the capture of all British-controlled ports, the cutting of supply lines to the fleet, or a decisive naval battle. American strategic planners imperfectly understood this logic, and the resulting campaign plans rarely integrated land and water forces in a joint venture aimed at decisive objectives. Part of the problem, of course, was organizational; the only person who commanded both land and naval forces was the president himself. Yet cooperation among commanders in the field could overcome this strategic flaw, and the raids on York and the capture of Fort George are exemplary. However, the near loss of Chauncey's base in 1813 while he was cooperating with Dearborn at the mouth of the Niagara resulted in a fundamental change in the way he viewed his responsibilities as commander of all naval forces on the Great Lakes. He became much more focused on the destruction of Yeo's squadron in a decisive fleet-on-fleet action than in cooperation with the army to seize Kingston or to cut the St. Lawrence line of supply. Yet despite this focus, Chauncey failed to bring Yeo to battle as Perry had done Barclay. Instead, he settled into a mutually agreeable arms race with his counterpart, an arms race that could yield victory to the Americans only if it culminated in a decisive battle. For the British, however, a protracted arms race and the avoidance of battle would contribute to strategic victory. Chauncey never could solve the problem of forcing Yeo to fight. His failure is wrapped up in the complexities of fleet building and fighting on Lake Ontario.

In theory, the purpose of an arms race is to bring a fleet into battle that is more powerful than that of the enemy. The naval commander would avoid dividing his fleet, thereby risking defeat in detail. He would be unwilling to take on tasks that might result in the fighting of a major battle under unfavorable circumstances. Both Yeo and Chauncey were reluctant to escort supply and troop transport vessels with combat craft. They were reluctant to stray too far from their major bases, lest this invite attack. Priority in shipbuilding was given to the rapid construction of fighting ships rather than of transport craft or the gunboats required to guard them on their supply runs. To the mind of a naval commander fully committed to an arms race, the purpose of the army is to defend the shipbuilding facilities and to guard the supply routes carrying naval stores, ordnance, and sailors en route to the fleet.

Both commanders understood that victory in the decisive battle culminating the arms race would not necessarily go to the fleet that appeared to be stronger on paper. Each side knew the precise weight of metal it could send at its enemy with each broadside. This was a generally recognized standard of comparison. Each commander, through his network of spies, had a reasonable estimate of the same capability of his enemy. The many unquantifiable factors, however, might tip the balance to the ostensibly weaker squadron. Circumstances such as visibility, wind direction and speed, and surface condition of the water could combine to affect the fight in ways that could not be predicted. Unmeasurables such as crew training, the skill of the officers, morale, and, most elusive of all, chance made the prediction of outcomes highly speculative. Can Yeo and Chauncey be blamed for not seeking battle until those factors that were measurable demonstrated overwhelming preponderance? In the final analysis, decisive victory on Lake Ontario would very likely decide the war, and either commander could win or lose the war in an afternoon.

Each commander wanted to achieve a greater advantage in the weight of the fleet broadside, and each wanted this advantage on a small number of large vessels rather than a greater number of smaller craft. This would serve to concentrate firepower, conserve manpower, and ease the burden of controlling the fleet in battle. The escalation in the size of vessels became an imperative. In at least one instance, a plan for a ship was enlarged when it was discovered that the original plan would result in a craft smaller than was being built concurrently by the enemy. In requesting that the plan be enlarged, Yeo wrote to Prevost: "The Enemy I have no doubt will build another Ship capable of carrying heavy Metal, if they do, I have only to assure your Excellency that had I any number of Brigs, they would not be of the smallest service against Ships mounting such Metal."[19] Each side raced to build bigger ships faster than the enemy did. Despite Herculean construction efforts, however, the design characteristics of the two squadrons conspired to thwart the occurrence of a fleet-on-fleet battle.

Chauncey's vessels were relatively strong in long-range guns, whereas the Royal Navy's advantage was its short-range carronades. "The great advantage which the enemy have over us from their long twenty-four pounders almost precludes the possibility of success," wrote Yeo to Prevost, "unless we force them to close action, which they have ever avoided with the most studied circumspection."[20] This presented the U.S. Navy with a dilemma. In order to gain the greatest probability of battle success, the fleet would seek to conduct the fight at extended range. Yet this allowed the Royal Navy a greater opportunity to break contact and escape if the fight appeared to be going badly.

Furthermore, the British vessels were easier to handle in battle, as Chauncey's numerous schooners, essentially civilian craft adapted for war, had difficulty keeping up with his warships, particularly on rough water. Therefore, Yeo was at an advantage fighting at short range and in difficult water, and Chauncey was reluctant to offer battle except at greater distances and on smooth seas. With the consequences of a single naval battle so clearly linked to strategic victory or defeat, the opposing commanders were understandably reluctant to accept battle except under the most advantageous circumstances. And these circumstances were mutually exclusive.[21]

Despite the many circumstances that ultimately precluded decisive battle, the arms race continued until the end of the war. Yeo was served by a fine group of subordinates; many of his senior officers were veterans of Nelson's fleet or of combat action on Lake Ontario. As the U.S. Navy's Atlantic Squadron was increasingly blockaded in port, a growing number of experienced officers joined Chauncey at Sacketts Harbor. However well-off the navies were in officers, they were short of sailors to man the ever-growing fleets. Both commanders were ungenerous in sending scarce sailors to their subordinate squadrons on the upper lakes, which was further recognition of the decisive nature of Lake Ontario to the war effort.[22]

Sailors, although a scarce resource, were nonetheless military members subject to orders and thus relatively easy to transfer from locale to locale. The labor force that built the ships was a civilian force, subject to laws of supply and demand rather than military law. The arms race required more shipwrights and carpenters than sailors, and neither Kingston nor Sacketts Harbor had enough at the beginning of the war to support such a massive effort. Slowly the labor force was attracted to the work, and by war's end, each base was temporary home to over 1,200 skilled craftsmen and common laborers.

The feverish activity in Kingston and Sacketts Harbor paid off. At the start of the war, the Provincial Marine's largest vessel was the *Royal George,* armed with twenty-two guns. In April 1814, the *Prince Regent* with fifty-eight guns led the Royal Navy squadron of eight warships, with a total of 222 naval guns. In June 1812, the largest American vessel on Lake Ontario was the *Oneida,* armed with sixteen guns. In April, the frigate *Superior* with sixty-two guns led the American fleet to rough parity with the British. In June, the launching of the forty-two-gun *Mohawk* gave the advantage in tonnage and armament to Chauncey, an ascendancy he would enjoy until mid-September, when the *St. Lawrence* with 102 guns hit the water at Kingston.

The naval arms race on Lake Ontario in 1814 pursued a logic of its own that was leading, unless Yeo accepted battle, to a successful defense of the Canadas. For numerous reasons, Chauncey could not force the Royal Navy to fight. The British were blessed with several safe havens—the Bay of Quinte, York, Burlington Bay, the mouth of the Niagara—into which detachments of ships could slip in order to evade battle. It was never clear to Chauncey that his chosen plan of campaign was leading to a strategic dead end. Perhaps he hoped that Yeo would, like Barclay before him, risk all on one throw of the dice. Quite possibly, Yeo had learned well from Barclay's defeat. In any event, cooperation between the American land and water forces would not again attain that high level experienced at the seizure of Fort George.

While the navies were fighting a building war, an American army was again humiliated in Lower Canada. In mid-February, Wilkinson broke up winter quarters at French Mills. He sent part of the force under Jacob Brown, about 2,000 men, to Sacketts Harbor and took the remainder with himself to Plattsburg. Completely disillusioned with Wilkinson, Armstrong opened a dialogue with Brown on the planning of the upcoming campaign. Wilkinson, still in command of the district and Brown's division, read reports that Brown was dispatching troops westward. Unaware of the secretary of war's intentions, Wilkinson nevertheless decided on a limited offensive that might serve as a diversion for Brown's activities. Wilkinson was perceptive enough to understand that he might soon undergo a court-martial inquiring into his responsibility for the failure at Crysler's Farm. A victory, however small, might temper the proceedings. With 4,000 men, he crossed the border on 30 March.[23]

Wilkinson's division was not supplied for a march on Montreal. However, by following the Richelieu River north, he would threaten the Royal Navy shipyard at Isle Aux Noix. Victory here would help secure American control over Lake Champlain. Drawing up to the La Colle River, the Americans were confronted by a mill defended by about 200 British regulars and Canadian militiamen. The mill was solidly constructed of stone reinforced by heavy timbers. For several hours, the Americans blasted away ineffectively at the mill, their twelve-pound guns hardly denting the walls. For their part, the British valorously charged the Americans three times, hardly denting the ranks of infantry. Wilkinson broke off the offensive and returned to New York, perhaps recognizing that the cost in lives to assault the mill would be high.

Wilkinson's lack of tactical skill and will was glaring. There were other ways of getting past the mill on the La Colle that would not require a costly assault. Even an assault, if successful, might accomplish something positive for the Americans, such as perhaps misleading Prevost as to the focus of American efforts in the coming campaign season. Once back in Plattsburg, Wilkinson discovered that Armstrong had removed him from district command and had ordered an inquiry of the 1813 campaign. The last of the Revolutionary War fossils was gone.

La Colle Mill had been a false start for the American campaign, and it is not known how Prevost interpreted that strange foray across the border into Lower Canada. He was very much concerned with the numbers of troops at his disposal and had repeatedly requested more. Troops from the maritime provinces or Europe could not arrive at Quebec by water until May. Anxious for reinforcements earlier than that, Prevost ordered the Second Battalion of the Eighth Foot to march to Quebec from New Brunswick. This battalion completed its long trek on snowshoes in March, and before July it was joined by three more battalions of infantry. Even before fresh troops arrived in Quebec, Prevost shuttled many of those already in that city toward the border. Welcome additions were two battalions of Royal Marines who wintered in Quebec and in the spring were distributed among the ships of the Ontario and Richelieu River squadrons. Prevost husbanded his forces carefully in the early months of 1814. He did not know then that by August the trickle of reinforcements would turn into a flood. Between July and September, seventeen veteran battalions would arrive at Halifax or Quebec, and then Prevost would go on the offensive. But that spring, he was more concerned with defending Canada through the summer.

In Upper Canada, Drummond's share of the troops released from the defense of Quebec was the 103d Regiment of Foot and the Second Battalion Royal Marines. This reinforcement hardly made up for combat losses from the previous year. Drummond was forced to place great reliance on the fighting strength of his militia; in this regard, he was better off than Brock two years earlier. Whereas Brock had been uncertain about the loyalty of his militia, by now the five regiments of Lincoln militia defending the Niagara District had been largely purged of American sympathizers. These regiments, however, were seriously understrength, totaling perhaps 1,500 in all. Besides these, Drummond's regulars on the Niagara Peninsula were backed up by the Grand River Indians under their war chiefs Norton, Brant, Blackbird, and Oneida Joseph. Although lack of troops was a serious problem, of more immediate concern was lack of money. So many government debts had gone unpaid that Drummond's agents were having trouble purchasing supplies anywhere west of York. Compounding the problem were the homeless natives and settlers who had fled western Upper Canada with Procter. Besides feeding his troops on the Niagara Peninsula, Drummond was also feeding over 3,000 natives and civilians. The drain on resources was debilitating.[24]

On the American side, perhaps the single most important preparation for the upcoming year was a near-complete changeover in military leadership. Following the twin defeats at Chateauguay and Crysler's Farm, Revolutionary War veterans Wade Hampton and Morgan Lewis left the service voluntarily. In December 1813, Armstrong recommended George Izard and Thomas Flournoy for promotions to major general. Armstrong passed over Andrew Jackson and

Jacob Brown, two brigadiers with arguably the best fighting records. Izard had been with Hampton at Chateauguay but prior to that had commanded the defenses of New York City. Flournoy had spent much of 1813 commanding in New Orleans, Wilkinson's old command. It is quite likely that Armstrong's intention was to eliminate his competition for the rank he cherished for himself— lieutenant general. In January, Madison sent his nominations to Congress: Izard and Brown.[25]

Within a few months, a constellation of stars fell on a deserving group of colonels: Alexander Macomb, Thomas Smith, Daniel Bissell, Edmund P. Gaines, Winfield Scott, and Eleazar Ripley. The average age of the general officers at the outbreak of the war was sixty. These new brigadiers averaged thirty-three years of age. Armstrong and Madison had exchanged Revolutionary War experience and the wisdom of age for energy and tactical skill. Armstrong's nominations recognized merit, and Madison kept intrigue out of the selection process. An unfortunate loss was Harrison, who resigned in May when it became obvious to him that Armstrong was shunting him off to a quiet sector.

The regular army itself saw some modest expansion in the first half of the new year. In January, there were about 20,000 regulars. About 6,000 were in the Ninth Military District, although only about 100 of these were west of Sacketts Harbor. Another 8,000 were guarding the Atlantic and Gulf coasts, and the rest were in the interior or at Detroit. Congress raised the recruiting bounty on 27 January, and nearly 14,000 recruits enlisted between then and the end of September. Congress also authorized the raising of three additional rifle regiments, which was recognition of the yeoman service rendered by the one rifle regiment on the regular establishment. Unfortunately, the colonels of the new rifle regiments persuaded only 1,006 men to enlist in these elite units. This was only one-third of their authorized strength.[26] Since the regular army was authorized 62,274 soldiers but only about 35,000 would be on the rolls by October 1814, most regiments were understrength in enlisted men. During the war, some regiments were consolidated, but in a manner that led to a major disagreement between Madison and Armstrong.[27]

While new recruits were entering the American service, Prevost and Drummond were hammering out a defensive strategy to keep these enthusiastic young men on their own side of the border. Drummond had grown overconfident with the seemingly easy victory on the Niagara Frontier in December and January. Following the seizure of Fort Niagara, he proposed to regain all that Procter had lost. "I am convinced that Detroit and the whole of the Western Country might be reoccupied by us at any moment without difficulty provided we had it in our power to detach a force for that purpose." Drummond confessed to an ulterior motive in suggesting an attack on Detroit. He wanted to rid the Niagara region of the thousands of western Indians who would soon become an "intolerable burthen." Drummond proposed marching a force westward along the Thames while supplies moved by sleigh on the iced-over river. If Detroit fell, Drummond proposed to follow up with an attack over the ice on Lake Erie to capture the American squadron. He was forced to call off the scheme when an early thaw rendered the route unusable.[28]

At first glance, Drummond's proposal seems inconsistent with Prevost's strategy to retain Quebec at all costs, even the loss of Upper Canada. However conservative his approach, Prevost entertained thoughts of aggressive action if the risk was minimal and the gain contributed ultimately to the defensive effort. By way of analogy, the garrison of a besieged fort, although outnumbered, might sortie when the opportunity presented itself in order to upset the besieger's timetable. Along these lines, Prevost ordered Drummond in January to resupply the small British garrison on Mackinac Island. To do this, Drummond opened a road from York to the well-protected bay at Penetanguishene on Lake Huron, where he established a small naval yard. This was an economy-of-force measure; just enough supplies and men were allocated to resupply Mackinac for the year. If successful, the venture would encourage the western natives to stay in the war and perhaps lead to the recapture of Amherstburg from the rear. The new water route would outflank the American squadron on Lake Erie at very little risk to the British.

While Drummond explored opportunities to hurt the Americans, he took action to improve his defenses. He strengthened the garrison and armament at Burlington Heights and built Fort Mississauga at the mouth of the Niagara, overlooking the beach where Dearborn's troops had landed the previous year. A small star-shaped earthwork, Fort Mississauga was reinforced by stone and brick recovered from the ruins of Newark. Armed with twin twenty-four-pound guns, it could reach out to an invasion fleet. Drummond also improved the defenses of Fort Niagara by adding timber pickets taken from Fort George. In addition, he ordered a small fortification built atop Queenston Heights that would be permanently manned by a small garrison.

Drummond put one regiment of regulars at York, three on the Niagara Peninsula, and the rest at Kingston and east to guard the line of communication to Montreal. The regulars on the Niagara Peninsula were organized as the Right Division and were under the immediate command of Major General Phineas Riall. Riall had his regulars, the Lincoln militia, Norton's natives, and assorted volunteer companies. He put one battalion of regulars in Fort Niagara and spread the other two along the river line and at Burlington Heights. His militia, volunteers, and natives would respond as necessary.[29]

Clearly, Drummond had too much border to defend; he could not be strong everywhere. He hoped to anticipate the point of the Americans' attack, hold their territorial gains to a minimum, and concentrate enough forces from everywhere in the province to counterattack. Even if outnumbered, he was confident that his well-trained regulars could win in an open fight.

In March, Drummond sent Riall general guidance for the defense of the Niagara Peninsula. Although he had no accurate information on American intentions, he believed that the most likely offensive would be an attack to regain Fort Niagara. This operation, wrote Drummond, might very well be supported by an invasion landing somewhere along the shore of Lake Erie between Long Point and Fort Erie. If this was the American plan, Riall was directed to leave the garrisons of Forts George and Niagara to defend themselves while he withdrew to Burlington to concentrate his forces for a counterattack. Presumably Drummond would send him reinforcements there.

Drummond expected that the American force coming from the west would be under the command of Harrison, whom Drummond characterized as a cautious commander. Drummond expected Riall to defeat the Americans who would be occupied in laying siege to Fort Niagara. Earlier, Riall had introduced the possibility of reducing his garrison at Fort Niagara. Drummond responded that "5 or 600 men of your division, cannot be better occupied, than in occupying, as they in all probability will, at least ten times their numbers, and that is confidently hoped for no inconsiderable period." Drummond was guilty of making his plans based on his assessment of American intentions rather than capabilities. Nonetheless, he believed that Riall was capable of taking care of the Niagara District. As late as 7 April, there were no indications of any American regulars on the Niagara. Drummond therefore turned his attentions to the American fleet and force at Sacketts Harbor.[30]

With the launching of two new frigates on 14 April, Yeo had gained the edge on Chauncey. He reported that he had "no doubt" of his squadron's ability to gain and maintain ascendancy on Lake Ontario and even boasted of his confidence in bringing Chauncey to "decisive action." Alarmed by a report of 7,000 American troops seen on the Niagara Frontier in late April, Drummond and Yeo explored the possibility of raiding and destroying the American shipyard.

On 25 April, Drummond wrote to Prevost proposing an immediate attack on Sacketts Harbor to preempt the invasion he foresaw across the Niagara River. Without the American fleet to transport supplies, an invasion force could not advance too far into the province. Yeo and Drummond agreed that they could seize the American naval base with 4,000 troops. The several new fortifications built by the Americans since the previous year justified this large number. Drummond did not have 4,000 regulars and fencibles, even if he called up the militia to free every regular in the province. Furthermore, he was not sure he could supply a force laying siege to Sacketts Harbor. Another problem he and Yeo identified was that the Americans might attack across the Niagara in light of the thinner defenses there.

Prevost responded that Drummond would need to concentrate 1,000 men at Kingston to secure that base while 4,000 troops attacked the Americans across the lake. Prevost rejected Drummond's proposal on principle. Drummond was having great difficulties feeding the troops currently in his province, and transferring more troops in would leave the defense of Lower Canada to the provincials and militia. "The views of His Majesty's Government respecting the mode of conducting the War with America, do not justify my exposing too much on one stake. It is by wary measures and occasional daring enterprizes with apparently disproportionate means, that the character of the War has been sustained, and from that policy I am not disposed to depart."[31] Prevost certainly understood that the loss of Sacketts Harbor would cripple the American war effort against Upper Canada yet not necessarily contribute to the security of Lower Canada. Hampton—and Montgomery and Arnold before him—had approached from a different quarter. Prevost would not approve such a risky venture, yet he left the door open for operations that would not endanger the defense of the lower province, even if unsuccessful. The raid on Oswego in May followed from this line of strategic reasoning.

The American campaign strategy for the campaign in the Central Theater ignited from the embers of a burned Buffalo. In January, Governor Tompkins sounded the alarm with Madison and Armstrong that the British would surely follow up their attacks on the Niagara Frontier with a campaign to regain all they had lost in the West the previous year. This was not hyperbole. Drummond shared the same thought, at least until the warm weather dashed his plans to cross the lake on the ice. Tompkins proposed offenses aimed at Kingston and Burlington and promised 5,000 New York volunteers to accompany the regulars. Such a pledge seems implausible in consideration of the repeated failures of militia, even volunteer militia, to cross the border.[32]

Nonetheless, the seed for the upcoming campaign was planted and took root in Armstrong's mind. Wilkinson was thoroughly discredited by his failure on the St. Lawrence. Armstrong therefore looked to Brown at Sacketts Harbor to lead the coming offensive. Mindful that Napoleon's troubles in Europe would likely result in numerous British troops transferred to North America, the secretary of war lost no time in proposing a course of action to his new commander. Unfortunately, Armstrong was too clever by half, and what transpired next left Brown bewildered and his troops footsore.

On 28 February, Armstrong sent Brown two letters. Repeating Tompkins's assessment, Armstrong noted that it was probably Prevost's "intention to re-establish himself on Lake Erie during the coming months."[33] In order to do so, reasoned Armstrong, Prevost would have to weaken his garrison at Kingston. If Brown discovered that this was the case, he should attack Kingston across the ice in a "coup de main" if several conditions were met: the weather and the

condition of the roads were adequate, the force at Kingston was degraded considerably, and Chauncey promised "full and hearty co-operation." If he decided
to attack Kingston, continued Armstrong, Brown should consider using the
second letter "to mask [Brown's] objective."

The second letter, marked number sixteen, informed Brown that Scott had
been ordered to the Niagara Frontier to command a force of 400 Indians and
4,000 volunteer militiamen for the purpose of retaking Fort Niagara. "The truth
is," wrote Armstrong, "that public opinion will no longer tolerate us in permitting the enemy to keep quiet possession of Fort Niagara." Brown was ordered to
move his brigade from Sacketts Harbor westward to Batavia and there to receive
further orders. As for the British, Armstrong claimed that "no intention exists of
attacking [Sacketts] harbor." If the British had other plans, Wilkinson would act.[34]

Armstrong's intention was straightforward, but both Brown and Chauncey
misinterpreted his plan; for this the secretary of war cannot be blamed. Armstrong was not proposing a campaign plan for the upcoming season. He was
merely encouraging Brown and Chauncey to seize Kingston if the conditions
warranted the risk. The loss of Kingston would so disturb the balance of power
that Prevost would very likely draw his regular forces eastward to protect Montreal and Quebec, abandoning all to the west. Clearly, Armstrong's intention was
to suggest that his newly appointed major general be alert to a window of opportunity that might open for a short period and that Brown not waste time asking
Armstrong's permission to act but seize the opportunity immediately.

Armstrong might be gently criticized. He did not offer Brown any options
should the conditions he stipulated for the attack on Kingston not be met. Nor
did he explicitly state when Brown might receive guidance for the upcoming
campaign season if the attack on the British naval base was unsuccessful or not
attempted. His cover letter could be interpreted as a second course of action, to
be chosen if the cross-ice attack was unworkable. The stratagem of a cover letter surely would be disquieting to Brown and Chauncey. It presupposed that
they could get the letter into British hands. There is no evidence that Brown or
Chauncey had ever attempted such a deception before; why would Armstrong
assume that they could pull it off? The contents of the letter itself might back-
fire. Assuming that Drummond received the information and believed that
Brown was vacating Sacketts Harbor, might he not take that opportunity to
attack that post across the ice himself?

The secretary of war's plot deceived his commander in the field rather than the
enemy. Brown dutifully met with Chauncey and determined that the cross-ice raid
was not practical. Among other reasons, Brown had only about 2,000 regulars fit
for service after the ordeal at French Mills. Now what should the new major general do? Chauncey convinced him that it was Brown's duty to march his brigade to
Batavia, that the second letter became operative if the first was not acted on.

In a matter of days, Brown got his men on the roads heading west. His brigade consisted of the Ninth, Eleventh, Twenty-first, and Twenty-fifth Infantries, eight companies of the Third Artillery acting as infantry, and Nathan Towson's battery of the Second Artillery. Divided into four groups that marched at one-day intervals, the men were sheltered each night of the march in the villages along the route. Averaging about twenty miles each day, the march was almost leisurely until toward the end, when the thawing roads meant that the troops were marching through ankle-deep mud.[35]

At Geneva (about 110 miles into the march), Brigadier General Gaines persuaded his commander that they had misunderstood Armstrong's purpose. In a decision that could not have inspired confidence in his leadership, Brown ordered the brigade to reverse course while he sped back to Sacketts Harbor for further consultations with Chauncey. Once there, Brown was again convinced by Chauncey that the first interpretation was correct, that Armstrong wanted Brown and his men at Batavia. Reversing himself once more, the bewildered general directed his men to Batavia, where they closed at the end of March and would remain for four weeks. Brown put Gaines in charge of the army forces remaining at Sacketts Harbor while Brown was at Batavia on 31 March.

Not until 8 April did Brown receive Armstrong's letter (written on 20 March) that made clear his intentions. The secretary of war wrote that the letter "was intended merely as a mask for the operation against Kingston, had that been thought advisable. If you hazard anything by this mistake, correct it promptly by returning to your post. If on the other hand you left the Harbor with a competent force for its defense, go on & prosper. Good consequences are sometimes the result of mistakes."[36] Recognizing that his ploy had misfired, Armstrong was content to leave the choice of the objective of the critical campaign of the war to chance. Armstrong fully realized that the seizure of Kingston or Montreal would yield greater results than the recapture of Fort Niagara or even the destruction of British forces on the Niagara Peninsula. Nonetheless, he lacked the will to refocus Brown toward objectives that might yet win the war before Wellington's veterans arrived on American shores.

Armstrong relieved Wilkinson of his duties on 12 April, the day after Napoleon abdicated his throne. He chose not to appoint a successor to command the Ninth District. Instead, he left his two major generals, Izard and Brown, to work out their own command arrangements. Although both Izard and Brown were promoted to major general on the same day, Izard appeared first on the order and therefore outranked Brown. However, Armstrong treated the two generals as independent commanders, sending orders directly to Brown rather than through Izard. Neither Izard nor Brown was sure whether his command was a body of troops or a geographic area.

When Izard posed this question to the War Department, Armstrong responded that "territorial limits of command are found inconvenient. The corps assigned to your division, and all officers belonging to these unless specially designated for other duty, will form your command. Where two or more divisions unite; the senior officer will necessarily command. The quartermaster general, the apothecary general, and the ordnance department, at Albany will obey your requisitions."[37] This solution is a stunning demonstration of mismanagement on Armstrong's part. Armstrong left Brown and Izard to compete for limited resources, and only the War Department had the authority to resolve disputes. Both generals had authority to call out militia in an emergency, but without territorial limits, they might inadvertently impose authority over the same units while leaving others idle. Without a common understanding of their defensive responsibilities, the British could attack between them and perhaps enjoy some success while the two Americans decided who would respond. There was no unity of command in the Ninth Military District.

Armstrong handled the command situation in nearly the same muddled manner as he had the previous fall. Wilkinson and Hampton did not have a mutual understanding of their command relationship, nor did Armstrong impose one. Whereas in 1813 the secretary of war had traveled north to plan the campaign, in 1814 he remained in Washington. Armstrong expected Brown and Izard to coordinate their activities, but he never communicated this expectation to them. Armstrong's failure to impose unity over the upcoming campaign prevented the Americans from taking advantage of several operational opportunities.

Not having heard from Armstrong since 20 March, Brown on 17 April sent a letter to the secretary of war that revealed much about Brown's understanding of the situation. Brown began by confessing that he was "anxiously expecting" to receive guidance from the secretary. Then he hoped Armstrong would "excuse the liberties" Brown took as he outlined two courses of action. First, he discussed the attack on Kingston. "I take it for granted," penned Brown, "that this, the first and greatest object, will not be attempted, untill, we have command of the Lower Lake, such appearing to be the will of the Gov't, from the Vessels authorized to be built on Sackett's Harbor."[38] Perhaps pessimistic that Chauncey could force Yeo into battle and thus win control of Lake Ontario, Brown offered an alternative plan. The squadron on Lake Erie could move Brown's force, which Armstrong would increase from 2,000 to 4,500, to the south shore of the Niagara Peninsula. From there, Brown would move on Burlington Heights and eventually clear the rest of the peninsula. If Armstrong saw fit to expand his force to a division of two brigades, Brown asked that New York militia Brigadier General John Swift, a fifty-two-year-old veteran of the Revolution, be given command of the Second Brigade. Scott would command the First. Brown noted that although Armstrong had not explicitly given him responsibility for the defense of Sacketts Harbor, he nonetheless assumed that task and left Gaines there for that purpose. Hardly had the ink dried on Brown's proposal when he received an alarming note from Gaines at Sacketts Harbor.

On 11 April, Chauncey wrote to Secretary of the Navy William Jones that an attack on Sacketts Harbor was imminent. Although the British might wait for the American fleet to depart the harbor as it had the previous year, Chauncey was gravely concerned that they might "be determined to make the attack at all hazards, as the object of them is of immense importance." A spy had reported to Chauncey that 3,000 British troops were embarking at Kingston for a raid on the American shipyard. Gaines, arriving the next day, immediately notified Brown of Chauncey's apprehension and asked for reinforcements. Brown, occupied with planning the upcoming offensive, had every right to feel confused, since Chauncey had twice hurried him and his brigade to Batavia. He responded with a handful of troops and encouragement. "Victory in such a contest," wrote Brown, "will cover you with immortal honors, and I feel that your chances are enviable should the enemy presume to attack your post." He chided Chauncey: "You never intimated to me a doubt of your ability to face the Enemy at any moment after the ice was out, and I must confess, that I was so confident of your strength by water that I did not expect there would be any alarm for that post." Brown remained near Lewiston for two days before deciding to return to Sacketts Harbor to see to its defense himself.[39]

Before he left, Brown directed Scott to gather information useful in planning an offensive into the Niagara Peninsula. Brown wanted to know the state of the naval squadron on Lake Erie and the disposition of American troops in and around Detroit. He also directed Scott, "by all the means in your power," to learn of the British forces and their movements. En route to Gaines, Brown hastily wrote a letter to Scott. "By this mail I have received a letter from the Sec[retary] which allows me to act very much as circumstances dictate but makes me responsible for everything. This is . . . precisely what I like & my only regret is that such a letter did not reach me before I left for Sackett's Harbour." Upon his arrival at the naval base, Brown found that Chauncey's and Gaines's concerns had been exaggerated. Calculating that the defenders would inflict serious losses on a British attacking force, Brown reported to Armstrong "that an attack is more to be desired than apprehended." Brown, concerned with the defense of the naval supplies at Oswego, remained in Sacketts Harbor until 25 May. Perceiving that Armstrong had given him broad discretionary powers to plan a campaign, Brown focused his efforts on the operational possibilities on the Niagara Peninsula and in gathering a force adequate to his goals. Armstrong, persuaded that he could not count on friendly control of Lake Ontario, recommended Brown's concept to Madison on 30 April. Madison, convinced that he must retake Mackinac in order to secure the West from native attack, sent Armstrong's note to the secretary of the navy for study. However, it was not until a cabinet meeting on 7 June that Madison approved a coordinated plan in the Western and Central Theaters of Operations.[40]

Madison's plan reflected muddled strategic thinking and a virtual surrender of control to events, to local commanders, and to chance. The plan removed the Erie squadron from supporting Brown and sent it instead to retake Mackinac. During May and June, while Madison and his cabinet thought, man-of-action Brown prepared his forces for the upcoming campaign on the Niagara Peninsula. Brown's concept consisted of several phases. In the preparatory phase, the American commander had to raise, equip, and train a sizable force, perhaps double the number then under him. He must gather supplies and information about the enemy. In the deployment phase, the navy would move Brown's division across Lake Erie to some suitable point on the south shore of the Niagara Peninsula. In the employment phase, the army would fight its way north across the Grand River and take Burlington. The final phase, the exploitation, would see the reduction of British holdings: Forts Erie, George, and Niagara. While all this was happening, Brown was required to defend Sacketts Harbor and Oswego.

This plan was feasible, although many issues were out of Brown's control. Could sufficient quantities of supplies, troops, and transportation be found? Would the Lake Erie squadron cooperate in moving the troops and then continue moving supplies throughout the campaign? Would not the Grand River Indians resist any attempt to cross their lands? If Brown managed to take Burlington Heights and protect his long line of communication, how could he then pry the British out of their forts? If Chauncey won his big battle, the British might evacuate the forts before Brown could trap them. If Yeo won, Brown's army would be exceedingly vulnerable, as would Sacketts Harbor itself. If no naval battle took place, Brown might be forced to lay siege to the forts, a chancy business at best. The final question concerns strategic ends. Even if Brown succeeded in clearing the Niagara Peninsula of British and native forces, how would that contribute to Madison's war goals?

During May and June, Brown wrestled with these weighty issues. It is clear that the administration exercised control over many of the factors that complicated Brown's efforts. Madison, for his part, temporized unnecessarily about forging a coordinated strategic plan. He was not forceful in reconciling the goals of the army and navy and allowed a costly arms race to continue unquestioned. Armstrong should not be forgiven for effectively splitting command within the Ninth Military District. His attempt to coordinate the activities of Izard's and Brown's forces himself from Washington resulted in inefficiencies and confusion. Despite the many unknowns and the U.S. government's self-inflicted wounds, Brown's army would give Britain its most serious challenge to the sovereignty of Upper Canada. That was to come in the summer. During the spring of 1814, both sides scrambled to prepare for the impending campaign.

CHAPTER SIX

Final Preparations

But the weakness of our enemy . . . will make our first errors innocent & the seed of genius which nature sows with even hand through every age & country & which need only soil and season to germinate, will develop themselves among our military men. Some of them will become prominent and, seconded by the native energy of our citizens, will soon, I hope, to our force, add the benefits of skill.

—Jefferson to William Duane, 4 August 1812

As if in response to President Jefferson's prophesy, a "seed of genius" had indeed germinated within the American army in the Central Theater. Jacob Brown, who had won his laurels by displays of tactical skill and bold leadership in battle, now faced perhaps the most difficult challenge of a general officer: the planning and execution of a campaign. Assisting him were a trio of new brigadiers, all of whom would face difficulties in the upcoming months that would test their character as well as their physical courage and military skill.

Winfield Scott, tall, vain, aggressive to the point of foolhardiness, had placed himself at the forefront of battle numerous times and escaped death as often. Captured while leading the desperate defense of Queenston Heights, he found revenge as the first American to enter Fort George the following year. Under Brown in the advance guard of Wilkinson's invasion, he had opportunities to study the art of command in both success and failure. On 9 March 1814, at the age of twenty-seven, Scott became a brigadier and traveled from Albany to Buffalo to join Brown's Left Division. In the upcoming months, his military genius would find expression in organizational and training achievements of the highest order.[1]

Edmund Pendleton Gaines, Virginia-born like Scott, had moved to Tennessee at age thirteen. He entered the army in 1809 and spent the first part of the war in the Army of the Northwest. Gaines was Harrison's adjutant general for the Thames campaign, although he missed that culminating battle because of illness. The War Department then ordered Gaines east. He commanded the Twenty-fifth Infantry with skill at Crysler's Farm. Like Scott, Gaines could not bear the incompetence of senior leadership in the campaign and must have rejoiced as the Revolutionary War veterans were eased out. Promoted to brigadier the same day as Scott, Gaines shared other characteristics: he too was tall, with polished manners, and somewhat vain. Brown entrusted Scott with the training of the invasion force; he charged Gaines with the defense of Sacketts Harbor, the most important post in his command.[2]

Rounding out the triumvirate of Brown's principal subordinates was Eleazar Wheelock Ripley. Unlike Scott and Gaines, Ripley was not a professional soldier but had been a successful lawyer and politician. He had risen to the presidency of the Massachusetts legislature before the war. In March 1812, the War Department commissioned Ripley a lieutenant colonel in the Twenty-first Infantry and promoted him to colonel in the same regiment the following March. Ripley saw action at the raid on York, the capture of Fort George, and Crysler's Farm. But Ripley was apparently tired of soldiering. On 29 March 1814, he wrote to the president requesting that he be considered for appointment to the position of district attorney in the district of Maine. He could not have known that Madison would sign his promotion order two weeks later. Ripley was intelligent, reserved, and an effective trainer, and he initially enjoyed the professional respect of both Scott and Brown. Not as impetuous as Scott or as aggressive as Brown, Ripley proved to be a bit of a misfit when the three crossed the Niagara in July.[3]

Armstrong had given Brown three fine subordinate generals; however, the number of regular soldiers allocated to the Left Division was woefully short for the task of conducting the main attack into Canada. Brown departed winter quarters at French Mills with about 2,000 men, leaving Izard's Right Division with about 6,000. In mid-April, Brown wrote to the secretary of war that he would need at least 4,000 regulars to clear the Niagara Peninsula, and these troops were to be supplemented by native warriors and militiamen.[4] Armstrong's efforts to bolster the numbers in the Left Division proved paltry—a failure for which he bore full responsibility. Apparently, Armstrong had been depending on a vigorous recruiting effort to fill Brown's army, but the results were insufficient.

The War Department never solved the problem of raising manpower in its regular formations or even accurately counting those under arms. This stemmed from a continuing inability to measure the success or failure of recruiting or to account for the number of soldiers who chose discharge rather than reenlistment. These difficulties grew out of the decentralized nature of recruiting. Each infantry and rifle regiment recruited from an assigned geographic area, but dragoon and artillery drew their new blood from the country at large. Typically, the colonel or his lieutenant colonel and about 30 percent of the other officers were performing recruiting duties at any time. The senior officer superintending recruiting for the regiment was obligated to report to the War Department monthly, but these reports often arrived late, if at all.

Further complicating the matter of computing force strengths was the circumstance that every regiment operated in at least two locations: in the field and at the recruiting rendezvous. Many regiments had troops at three, four, and even more locations or en route between posts. General officers in the field frequently consolidated detachments of regiments in order to effectively train and fight. Often, however, regimental identity was lost when it came time to submit strength reports. Thus, War Department clerks could calculate regimental strength accurately only if all detachments reported in a timely manner and in such a way as not to obscure regimental affiliation. This occurred infrequently.

In the early months of 1814, recruiting was proceeding poorly. By the War Department's best estimate, only 9,421 soldiers enlisted or reenlisted between January and June. Of these, 2,801 belonged to the fifteen regiments whose recruiting stations were in the Eighth or Ninth Military Districts, the districts from which Armstrong was presumably going to fill Brown's force. Many experienced soldiers came up for reenlistment in early 1814—those five-year enlistments that started when the army expanded in 1808–1809, and the many twelve- and eighteen-month enlistments from 1813. In the first half of 1814, so few of these soldiers reenlisted that recruiting did not make up for losses. The total strength of the regular army actually declined until about August, when the numbers stabilized and then rebounded. Unfortunately, raw recruits were replacing experienced soldiers. The secretary of war, forced to deal with incomplete information, did not understand until too late that his confidence in a rush of patriotic recruits to fill Brown's ranks was entirely misplaced.[5]

In April 1814, Brown's division consisted of five infantry regiments, a battalion of riflemen, a troop of dragoons, and several companies of artillerists, some serving as infantry. Most had wintered with Brown at French Mills, and Brown was confident in their fighting abilities.[6] A unit-by-unit review reveals an army of experience and with the potential to meet the best Drummond could throw at them. The Ninth Infantry was authorized by Congress in January 1812 and recruited in Massachusetts. The regiment marched north into Lower Canada with Dearborn in November but saw no action. A detachment of about 100 fought well under its major, Thomas Aspinwall, in the successful defense of Sacketts Harbor the following May, at which time Aspinwall came to Brown's attention. Aspinwall received a brevet promotion for gallantry in that action. Later he led the entire regiment at Crysler's Farm, but in the spring, these men marched under Major Henry Leavenworth. Like Aspinwall, Leavenworth had practiced law until 1812. He had been commissioned a captain in the Twenty-fifth Infantry, and his promotion brought a transfer to the Ninth. At thirty years of age, Leavenworth enjoyed the respect of both his men and the many officers in the army. He left a small detachment back at Sacketts Harbor, but about 200 of the Ninth Infantry were with him at Batavia in March.[7]

The Eleventh Infantry recruited in Vermont and New Hampshire in the spring of 1812. Like the Ninth Infantry, the Eleventh marched into Canada with Dearborn but returned without seeing the enemy. Six companies of the regiment were with Wilkinson at Crysler's Farm, while the other four accompanied Hampton's invasion force down the Chateauguay. Nearly 500 men were at Batavia, having marched there under the command of Lieutenant Colonel Moody Bedel, a veteran of Benedict Arnold's expedition against Montreal. The elderly Bedel returned to Vermont to recruit more men; the regiment trained for the upcoming campaign under Major John McNeil, a six-foot-two giant of considerable military talent.[8]

The Twenty-first Infantry was ordered into existence in June 1812 and drew recruits from both Massachusetts and New Hampshire. Also a participant in Dearborn's short-lived invasion of Lower Canada, the Twenty-first saw no action as a regiment until Crysler's Farm. When Eleazar Ripley, who had been with the regiment from the beginning, was promoted, command went to Colonel James Miller. A practicing lawyer, Miller had joined the Fourth Infantry in 1808. In Hull's otherwise abortive campaign, Lieutenant Colonel Miller led his regiment to victory at the skirmish at Maguaga. Captured with the rest of Hull's force, Miller spent a short time as a prisoner of war. He commanded the Sixth Infantry as part of Brown's advance guard in Wilkinson's invasion. Cool under fire and possessing a store of natural leadership, Miller was a worthy successor to Ripley.[9]

Authorized by Congress in June 1812, the Twenty-fifth Infantry drew its soldiers from Connecticut. As had the other infantry regiments, the Twenty-fifth saw its first campaign but no action with Dearborn in November. The following year, the regiment fought well at Stoney Creek and Crysler's Farm. At winter quarters at French Mills, so many officers found reasons to leave the army in the field that the regimental commander, Edmund Gaines, ordered every regimental officer to join the unit. Colonel Gaines's promotion left a hole in the leadership of the regiment. The regimental major, Charles Gardner, assumed command for a short time before Brown appointed him adjutant general of the division, with duties that kept him away from his unit. Major Thomas Jesup, formerly of the Seventh Infantry, joined the regiment in mid-April, and Scott designated him to command on 16 May. A career soldier, Jesup was Hull's brigade major and was surrendered with Hull's army. After his exchange, he proved to be a valuable officer for Harrison.[10]

Also part of Brown's Left Division was the hard-used Twenty-third Infantry. This regiment was recruited from upstate New York, and its separate companies were sent to the front as quickly as they were formed. As a result, small detachments of the Twenty-third represented the regiment on many battlefields: Queenston, Fort George, Sacketts Harbor, Stoney Creek, Beaver Dams, and La Colle Mill. In the spring of 1814, bits and pieces of the regiment were scattered at posts throughout the district. Lieutenant Colonel James Mullany remained at Utica to recruit; command of the detachments in the field fell to Majors Daniel McFarland and George Mercer Brooke. McFarland, a Pennsylvanian, had been commissioned in the Twenty-second Infantry but moved to the Twenty-third in August 1813, following his promotion to major. Brooke, who had entered the army and the Fifth Infantry from his native Virginia in 1808, transferred into the Twenty-third upon his promotion in May 1814.[11]

Brown also enjoyed the services of a battalion of the First Rifle Regiment, the workhorse of the war effort. Detachments of the Rifles were represented on more battlefields and at more skirmishes than any other regiment in the army. Raised in 1808, the regiment's first colonel was Alexander Smyth. When the war began, the regiment was scattered in detachments in northern New York, along Georgia's border with Spanish Florida, and throughout the Ohio and Mississippi Valleys. By 1814, the regiment was consolidated into three detachments: the First Battalion of about 300 riflemen under Major Ludowick Morgan at Sacketts Harbor, the Second Battalion of about 223 effectives under Lieutenant Colonel Benjamin Forsyth with Izard's Right Division, and a company of fewer than 100 serving in Georgia. A highly competent officer, Morgan entered the regiment in 1808 from Maryland. He was well served by his second in command, Major Daniel Appling, a Georgian, who also was commissioned a lieutenant of riflemen in 1808. The First Rifles was an experienced, hard-fighting formation, particularly skilled in woodland and skirmish warfare. It was equal to the best of the British army in North America. Of the three new rifle regiments ordered by Congress in February, the Fourth Rifle Regiment was busy recruiting in New York and Pennsylvania, and these partially trained men joined the Left Division and saw combat before the end of the campaign.[12]

Brown's requirement for mounted soldiers was satisfied to a small extent by Samuel Harris's company of fewer than 100 troopers from the Second Light Dragoons. Captain Harris fought gallantly at Crysler's Farm and was temperamentally well suited for independent command. Harris was both aggressive and talented, but despite his eagerness for mounted combat, Brown depended on him more to keep up an efficient express message service among his detachments and with Albany, where the military messengers connected with the regular postal service. Those dragoons not acting as couriers spent their days patrolling around Sacketts Harbor to guard against surprise attack from the land approaches.[13]

Nearly 700 artillerists were assigned to Brown's division: one company of the Light Artillery, and several each of the Second and Third Artillery. While many of these men manned the fixed guns at Sacketts Harbor and other posts, others served the mobile guns equipped with limbers, caissons, and full teams of horses. At least four companies of the Third Artillery served as infantry, there not being enough guns, fixed or mobile, to go around. Three officers deserve particular note. Lieutenant Colonel George Mitchell of the Third Artillery was the senior artillery officer. Second in seniority was Major Jacob Hindman, who had been commissioned into the infantry in 1808 but transferred to the Second Artillery just prior to the war. Captain Nathan Towson, who had commanded a company of Maryland volunteer artillery before the war, now led a mobile company of the Second Artillery. This trio proved their courage and leadership many times in the Niagara campaign, although Towson set a standard hard to duplicate. Just prior to the Battle of Queenston, Towson assisted navy Lieutenant Jesse Elliott in cutting out the brig *Caledonia* from under the guns of Fort Erie. Later captured at Stoney Creek, Towson escaped from the British and returned to American lines. All three artillerymen were particularly competent and trained their soldiers to high standards.[14]

Except for the First Rifles and the Twenty-third Infantry, most of Brown's foot soldiers had seen little combat, and what they had experienced was mostly defeat. But by 1814, they were inured to the rigors of campaign, and the weak officers had left the regiments (an officer could resign his commission and leave the service pretty much at his desire). Most of the field-grade officers had several years' service prior to the war. Both they and the junior officers were experienced, brave, eager to meet the enemy, and now served under generals equally brave and eager. But their numbers were few, and without help from the volunteer militia, they could not hope to prevail.[15]

Governor Tompkins was squarely behind the effort to supplement Brown's invasion force with militia. In the panic following the devastation of the Niagara Frontier, Tompkins promised Armstrong 5,000 militiamen if the War Department provided 2,500 regulars. In the months that followed, when there were virtually no regulars in New York west of Sacketts Harbor, Tompkins ordered ninety-day levies to defend what was left of Lewiston, Buffalo, and Black Rock. Now, as Brown's small division was closing on Batavia, Tompkins ordered a second levy of militia for another ninety days to relieve those whose tours of duty were drawing to an end.[16]

In theory, New York could support the invasion by drafting even larger numbers of militiamen for three-month terms. Of course, the operational and political drawbacks were many. First, the militiamen could refuse to cross the border. Second, most of them could be depended on to leave the colors when their time was up, regardless of where they were or the state of the campaign. Third, the militia of the western counties had been called up repeatedly to defend the frontier; the burden of militia service was being borne unevenly. Yet militiamen drafted from areas far from the frontier had less at stake than their frontier cousins and presumably would be less likely to risk their lives in defense of the border regions. Fourth, there remained strong Federalist sentiments in New York; a heavy reliance on the draft for offensive operations might cost Tompkins and his party a heavy price, particularly if the invasion was as unsuccessful as all those prior.

Governor Tompkins understood the issues and chose an alternative. On 13 March, he issued a general order that authorized the raising of about 2,700 volunteers for six months of service. He nominated Peter B. Porter as the commander of this contingent, and he promised the volunteers the same pay and allowances as federal troops. Tompkins's choice of Porter as commander was notably fortunate. Though unschooled in the technical aspects of military operations, Porter was well respected, intelligent, and, like Brown and Scott, whom he would eventually join, aggressive and brave. Porter also had a personal stake in the outcome. As a war hawk, his efforts had helped bring about the war. As a resident of Black Rock, his home overlooking the Niagara River had been consumed by fire with the rest of that village. Porter's brigade was competing for recruits from the same pool as the Twenty-third Infantry and the Fourth Rifles. Although service in the regulars promised a plot of land upon mustering out, it also carried a twelve-month tour of duty. More New Yorkers chose the opportunity to serve for a shorter period under officers selected democratically.[17]

Other sources of manpower existed. Since the British raid on Black Rock in July 1813, the New York Iroquois, particularly the Seneca on the Niagara Frontier, were willing to defend their lands, even if this meant fighting their Grand River cousins. The Seneca chief was Sa go ye wat ha ("he keeps them awake"), but he was known in the white community as Red Jacket. He earned that name for the scarlet coat the British had given him late in the Revolution for services to the Crown. Now in his sixty-fourth year and a fervent nationalist, Red Jacket believed that Iroquois interests would best be served if Indian lands remained within American boundaries. Red Jacket was an eloquent speaker. He was complemented by the war chief, Ho na ye wuo (also known as Farmer's Brother). Now in his eighties, Farmer's Brother had been present at Braddock's defeat in 1755. In 1813, he led about thirty Seneca to chase off the Black Rock raiders. In the spring of 1814, he was anxious to lend at least his moral support to the Seneca effort. Other key players in bringing the Iroquois into the war in an organized way were Erastus Granger, chief Indian agent to the Seneca, and his assistant, Jasper Parrish. Granger held a militia commission as a lieutenant colonel, and he served for a while as postmaster at Buffalo. Like Porter, Granger had also lost his home to the British winter raid. He spared no efforts in ensuring a strong native contingent to support Brown's impending invasion.[18]

Not to be forgotten was the small contingent of Canadian Volunteers under Lieutenant Colonel Joseph Willcocks and his two majors, Benajah Mallory and

Abraham Markle. Although the Volunteers fought bravely and well in the defense of Buffalo and Black Rock, militia Brigadier General Amos Hall tried to disband them in the months following. Perhaps Hall hoped to appease Drummond and defuse the cycle of retaliation. Meanwhile, Willcocks was in Washington lobbying for federal recognition and succeeded with Porter's help. He returned to the Niagara Frontier on 1 May to find his battalion shrunk to about sixty men present for duty. Dozens of those who had enlisted in 1813 were now absent without leave. Markle brought a small group of Volunteers to Erie and, using a network of American sympathizers in western Upper Canada, circulated spies for several months prior to the invasion. Because they were familiar with the territory, the Canadian Volunteers would be valuable as scouts. Of course, the men were somewhat desperate. Capture while in Upper Canada would lead directly to trial for treason, for the British would not give them prisoner of war status and its traditional protections.[19]

At the end of March 1814, Brown's division was concentrated in two locations. Gaines commanded the regulars at Sacketts Harbor: the Twenty-third Infantry, First Rifles, Harris's dragoons, and a few companies of artillerists, about 1,000 men in all. The rest, four regiments of infantry and nine companies of artillerists without guns, were with Brown at Batavia. After a few days' rest, Brown issued orders to march to the Niagara Frontier. He ordered the Twenty-fifth Infantry to the vicinity of Lewiston. There it could keep an eye on the British in Fort Niagara, as well as watch the crossing sites north of the escarpment. The artillery companies remained at Batavia, not only to wait for guns to equip four companies but also to serve as a central reserve between Oswego and the Niagara Frontier. The remaining three infantry regiments, the Ninth, Eleventh, and Twenty-first, were organized as a brigade under Scott and ordered to Williamsville, about eight miles northeast of Buffalo. Williamsville had not been burned by the British, so the troops would have some shelter while awaiting their tentage. Brown ordered Scott to bring the troops to a "high state of discipline." Discipline in this context referred not to law and order or immediate obedience to command, but instead was the common term for battlefield drill, both individual and as a unit.[20]

Scott was to use this charter to create a legend in the U.S. Army—the gray-clad regulars who met and bested their British foe on the plains of Chippawa. But legendary exploits lay several months in the future; Scott had much work ahead of him, and he wasted no time. Upon assuming brigade command, Scott published his first order, meant to inspire confidence in the troops. Scott, the order read, was "happy to find it [the brigade] composed of regiments with whom high character for discipline, patience under fatigue and conduct in times of danger, he is well acquainted." Scott extended his command by appointing two aides-de-camp whom, Scott advised the brigade, were to be obeyed and respected as speaking for the general himself.[21]

Within a few days, Scott's brigade closed on Williamsville, and the men busied themselves with putting up huts and inspecting and repairing their tentage. They had arrived none too soon, as Brigadier General Hall had already begun dismissing the militiamen who had completed their ninety-day tours of duty. Brown, who collocated his headquarters in Williamsville with Scott, requested that Hall keep the militia on duty to guard supplies so that the regulars could train. Hall refused. Among other reasons, he had no money to pay his men for the three months they had already served. On 14 April, Brown ordered Scott's brigade to Buffalo. Nine inches of snow fell that evening, delaying the move for five days.[22]

The brigade marched to Buffalo and occupied the angle between the Buffalo River and the lakeshore, just south of the village. Scott ordered his quartermaster to provide floorboards and straw for the tents. He also ordered Henry Leavenworth to establish pickets around the remains of the town and the inhabitants who had returned to rebuild. Jarvis Frary Hanks, a drummer in the brigade, wrote in his journal: "When we came there & saw the smoldering ruins, it gave us feelings of deep sympathy for the desolate and plundered inhabitants; and sharpened up our courage to prepare for effectual retaliation when we should enter Canada upon the anticipated campaign." Viewing the handiwork of Drummond's troops probably did more than any exhortation to steel Scott's men for the arduous training ahead.[23]

Scott's brigade had hardly set up camp in Buffalo when Brown was compelled to return to Sacketts Harbor to ensure the security of that most important post. Brown gave Scott command of all troops on the Niagara Frontier, not only his brigade but also the Twenty-fifth Infantry near Lewiston. The several companies of artillery at Batavia remained Brown's reserve and were under the immediate command of Lieutenant Colonel George Mitchell. In anticipation of the coming invasion, Brown directed Scott to gather information about the American troops around Detroit who might be available to assist the effort. He also told Scott to seek information on the Lake Erie squadron that would transport the division into Canada.[24] Brown had total confidence in Scott's abilities. That confidence was shared by many of the officers of the division. While marching westward toward Batavia, Captain Rufus McIntire of the Third Artillery, who had served under Scott during the Crysler's Farm campaign, penned the following comments: "Brig[adie]r Gen[era]l Scott so distinguished as a fighting character (and in my opinion the best officer in the whole army of any grade) has joined us and is the only brigadier present. If it be possible to meet the enemy I know Scott will manage to meet him if he can do it on anything like equal ground."[25]

Scott needed their confidence, for the task of preparing his men to carry the war once more into Canada was daunting. He had to clothe his soldiers, many of whom were in rags. They must be armed and trained to meet a competent, brave enemy. While the brigade conducted rigorous training, Scott had to maintain the men's motivation and discipline at a high standard. In Brown's absence, Scott was now responsible for setting up a logistical base to support the invasion and to gather information on friend and foe alike—duties that normally would have fallen to the division commander. Prior to 1814, Scott had not enjoyed what now amounted to an independent command and the opportunity to give full range to his abilities, at least until Brown's return. Scott began work with a passion that spread to his officers.

Getting uniforms for the men was one of Scott's top priorities. The job was not accomplished until the last hour and required the intercession of the secretary of war. Most of the troops were in the same coats and trousers they had worn during Wilkinson's campaign and the frozen winter at French Mills. Before Brown left Williamsville, he directed Gaines to forward clothing from Sacketts Harbor; once at the harbor, he received the same requests from Scott. But there was little to be had. It seems that Wilkinson, in a remarkable display of pettiness, gave strict orders to the deputy commissary general in Albany to send all clothing, including that earmarked for Brown's regiments, to the Right Division at Plattsburg. What little clothing and shoes could be found were sent to Buffalo, but as late as 17 May, Scott complained to Brown that two of his regiments were "now almost in a state of perfect nakedness."[26]

Scott ordered Sunday inspections of the serviceability of the men's personal weapons and equipment. Shortages were put on requisition. Weekly inspections reminded the men that they must be ready to march at a moment's notice. Since Scott could not inspect all his men himself, he appointed an assistant inspector general. The foremost duty of this officer was to ensure that the spirit and letter of Scott's orders were obeyed. He observed drill during the week and oversaw inspections on Sunday. Scott even stipulated the acceptable contents of the men's packs and ordered that "the soldier on the march shall not be encumbered with scraps and shreds of old clothing." He ordered regimental commanders to ensure that every man had a haversack (a suspended cloth pouch carried on the left side) large enough to hold three days' rations. If necessary, Scott ordered, haversacks were to be made from unserviceable tents. He made the presence of haversacks an item of inspection, and in June he ordered all enlisted men to carry their haversacks at all times. Scott even ordered the men to get their hair cut so that no hair hung out from under the leather cap in the front or over the collar in the back. Over time, Scott's men began to look like soldiers, not rabble, and their pride must have grown with the transformation.[27]

While the brigade was slowly being clothed and equipped, Scott set about the business of drilling the men. His first decision was to standardize the drill manual to be used throughout the brigade. This was necessary because at least three systems of drill were prevalent in the army, and Scott saw this as incompatible with military efficiency. In his memoirs, Scott related that he chose the "French system" as his standard. He made the astounding claim that he possessed the only copy in French and that throughout his command only a single other copy existed, and this was a "bad translation" into English. A discussion of tactical doctrine illustrates why Scott's claim stretches credibility.[28]

On 22 April, Scott directed that "the French regulations or the system of discipline laid down by Smythe—which are the same will govern the Infantry." Six days later, he further directed that "commanders at all levels are ordered to study Steuben's regulations and to read appropriate sections to their soldiers."[29] Steuben's regulations, known throughout the army as the *Blue Book,* got the American army through the Revolution. However, since Valley Forge, tactical doctrine had evolved. The French regulations of 1791, with their balance between line and column formations, lent both greater speed and flexibility, and ultimately greater firepower, to the armies of revolutionary France. Congress retained the *Blue Book* for the militia for its ease of learning but looked for something more up-to-date for the regular army.

Two texts aspired for official sanction. In 1812, Alexander Smyth (who gained infamy on the Niagara Frontier) and William Duane (editor of the Republican newspaper *Aurora*) published competing drill manuals that purported to take advantage of the latest advances in tactical drill. Smyth's *Regulations for the Field Exercises, Manoeuvre and Conduct of the Infantry* was fundamentally an abridgment of the French regulations. Smyth covered drill from the individual soldier through all levels of command to brigade. Smyth's manual borrowed material from Steuben and added new material dealing with diverse subjects such as march order, reviews, salutes, and weapons maintenance. For its time, Smyth's manual was comprehensive, concise, and useful. The War Department adopted Smyth's *Regulations* at the beginning of the war, and 1,000 copies of the first edition were printed and available before the war began. Perhaps because they were so complicated for the hundreds of new officers appointed by the president, or perhaps because they became discredited with their author, Smyth's *Regulations* lost official sanction in March 1813, to be replaced by Duane's *Handbook for Infantry.* The *Handbook* was also an abridgment of the French regulations of 1791, but Duane cut too deeply. He failed to address adequately the tactical movements of brigades and larger formations.[30]

For whatever reason, Scott rejected Duane's *Handbook* and chose the French regulations or Smyth's abridgment of that compilation. With hundreds of copies of Smyth's *Regulations* in circulation, it is unthinkable that only one officer of the dozens at Buffalo had Smyth's text with him. Certainly the officers who by this time had two years of hard service under their belts were familiar with Steuben's, Duane's, and Smyth's systems. Scott's order to his officers to read passages from Steuben to the troops presumes that there were adequate numbers of the *Blue Book* available in camp or that Scott would allow the reading of text from Smyth, which paraphrased Steuben. While Scott drilled the French system, Izard prescribed the *Blue Book* for the Right Division. These systems had different formations and different commands, and therefore the regiments in each division of the Ninth District were not easily interoperable.[31]

For years, the legend of Scott's training camp at Buffalo rested on Scott's claims in his memoirs and went unchallenged. Scott, who recorded his memoirs in the third person, wrote:

> He began by forming the officers of all grades, indiscriminately into squads, and personally instructed them in the schools of the soldier and company. They then were allowed to instruct squads and companies of their own men—a whole field of them under the eye of the general at once, who, in passing, took successively many companies in hand, each for a time. So, too, on the formation of battalions; he instructed each an hour or two a day for many days, and afterward carefully superintended their instruction by the respective field officers. There was not an old officer in the two brigades of infantry. Still if the new appointments had been furnished with a textbook, the savings of time and labor would have been immense.[32]

It is difficult to judge whether Scott's portrayal reflected bad memory or if he was intentionally building his legend. If Scott considered himself an "old officer," then there were several like him: Ripley, Miller, and Jesup, for example. Nonetheless, what Scott accomplished on the drill field at Buffalo proved the key to success later that summer.

The importance of drill, given the weapons of the day, cannot be overstated. The smoothbore musket was slow and troublesome to load and, if fired at an individual target, quite inaccurate. But when fired by the hundreds, one volley every twenty-five seconds or so, it was a proven killing machine. A hit anywhere on the body was enough to knock a man down and, if he survived, discourage him from continuing the fight. Even the untouched soldier, eyeing the horrible wounds of those next to him and hearing the screams of the fallen all about, might lose his nerve. A unit might receive only three or four volleys before it broke and ran. If fire alone was insufficient to break the enemy, a disciplined unit would fix bayonets and charge, perhaps with a yell to steel its own nerve and break that of the enemy. Rarely would regiments cross bayonets; one almost always lost its collective courage and withdrew before contact was made.

The keys to success were drill, discipline, and motivation. The unit must be trained in all the formations and how to change from one to another. The unit must be willing and able to respond immediately to the orders of superior officers. Finally, the men of the unit must be convinced that despite the consequences to personal safety, they would prevail and not falter before the fire of the enemy. Drill, discipline, and motivation were the focus of Scott's training program.

Drill was the means by which a unit could inflict physical damage on the enemy. All things being equal, the unit that could inflict the greater number of casualties once the firefight began had the better chance of causing the other side to break first. The purpose of formations was to put the greatest number of weapons in range of the enemy in the smallest amount of time. The elegance of the French system was the use of column formations to move the regiment quickly to a point just out of range of the enemy, followed by transformation to a line formation to bring the greatest number of weapons to bear as the unit moved into lethal range. Both formations required men to move in dense masses and yet be flexible enough to change from column to line quickly, thus the requirement for marching in step. The imperative of putting as many muskets into action as possible required the men to space themselves closely, in two or three ranks, and yet have room to load the cumbersome weapons. All this required months of intensive training, starting with the individual soldier loading and firing his weapon in the prescribed manner and ending with a brigade of several regiments moving and firing in concert.

In his memoirs, Scott claimed to have formed squads of officers and then personally to have trained these officers in individual and group drill before allowing them to train their units. Other than Scott's memory, there is no evidence that these officer squads existed; there is no mention of this methodology in Scott's published orders, nor do any of his subordinates offer corroboration.[33] Yet it is possible, even likely, that Scott chose this somewhat unorthodox method. Presumably he did this to ensure that all units would be trained to the same standard, particularly if some regiments had been trained according to Steuben and others to Duane or Smyth. And there was a precedent. At Valley Forge, Steuben had gathered about him a small cadre of each regiment, which he personally trained to a uniform standard. These men returned to their regiments as drillmasters to transmit the new drill to the entire force. In this way, Steuben extended his influence. Scott perhaps did the same, meeting with his officers, watching them go through the motions, ensuring uniformity of movement and command, and then releasing them to train their companies and battalions. This would save valuable time and lessen the chance that Scott would feel the need to correct officers in front of their men. If these sessions with the officers were short and perhaps conducted informally, Scott might not have seen a need to formally order the gatherings. Likewise, such sessions might have been so episodic as not to have merited a sentence in the journals and letters of the officers involved.

Scott ordered drill to begin on 22 April. He ordered company drill in the morning. Presumably, this included individual drill in loading and firing, as well as company formations and movement. At three o'clock, the regimental commanders drilled their battalions for two to three hours. Scott himself, from time to time, drilled each battalion. After this, Scott gathered two or more battalions together to drill them as a brigade. Scott's methodology is remarkable in several respects. By drilling each battalion himself, he ensured uniformity. This also gave him the opportunity to correct errors or personal interpretations of the regulations. Whether intended or not, Scott probably introduced a level of competition. Certainly if Scott himself drilled every battalion, the men could expect to be compared with those of other regiments.[34]

Scott chose not to conduct sequential training—that is, individuals and units demonstrating skill at each lower level before attempting the next higher level. Instead, starting on the first day, he warned his troops that they could expect him to maneuver the entire brigade. By emphasizing drill each day at all levels, individual through brigade, he let his troops know where they were going: each piece fit into a succession of larger pieces and ultimately into a brigade acting as a coherent whole. Scott was not aware of how much time he had, probably suspecting action in as few as five weeks. By training at all levels each day, he ensured that his brigade would have some level of expertise regardless of how long the training program lasted.

As training proceeded, he picked up the pace and intensity. He ordered paymasters and quartermasters to drill; apparently, they had used training time to pursue their other duties. In battle, these officers might very well be required to take over their companies and battalions from fallen commanders, and they needed the skill as much as anyone else. Scott ordered four hours for morning drill, an enormously long time at one spell for the arduous labor of carrying weapons and equipment. Scott canceled training only for heavy snowfall or rain and the Sunday inspection. By and large, the intensity and single-mindedness of the brigade commander won the approbation of his subordinates. Captain George Howard of the Twenty-fifth Infantry wrote to his spouse in May: "General Scott is in command at present. He is a fine man—a severe disciplinarian—a perfect *Frederick*." He continued: "We drill 7 hours of the day and he is determined to open this campaign at the head of troops who know how and wish to fight."[35]

Weeks of grinding drill were not sufficient to prepare the men for battle, because drill could not replicate to the necessary degree the sights, sounds, and feelings that would confuse the men and create fear in their ranks. Indeed, in some ways it obscured the realities of battle. To understand this contradiction, one must return to the musket. To save cartridges and flints for battle, the men learned to load and fire by "dry firing." A soldier probably dry-fired hundreds of times in training for each round fired in anger. Since a flint was good for only twenty or so shots, soldiers substituted wooden flints called "snappers." They pretended to bite paper cartridges and load them. Dry firing went a long way in developing the skill to fire two, sometimes three, rounds a minute for sustained periods. But dry firing eliminated much of the reality of live firing.[36]

The raw recruit, perhaps firing live rounds for the first time in battle, experienced much that was dangerous and frightening. The discharge of hundreds of weapons created a deafening roar and clouds of impenetrable smoke. After two volleys, the musketeer probably could not see his target and perhaps feared that the enemy was even then attacking with the bayonet. Before long, his eyes burned, and he began to gag on the smoke. Splinters from flints breaking against frizzens and bits of burning powder hit unprotected faces. The kick of the musket was similar to that of the twelve-gauge shotgun of today. The barrel grew hot to the touch. Biting into cartridges with their heavy content of saltpeter for any length of time caused great thirst and swollen, cracked lips. Men dropping, perhaps good friends, caused fear, and fear led to mistakes and the inability to detect a malfunction. The smoothbore musket was unforgiving of error.

Perhaps the greatest danger to the musketeer after the enemy's weapons was his own. Misfires, undetected by fear or inexperience, could seriously injure the firer or take his life and those of nearby comrades. A misfire occurred when the powder in the chamber failed to burn, and therefore the powder and ball remained inside the weapon. Subsequent loadings and misfires might result in a large amount of powder in the barrel. If the powder were eventually ignited, the explosion of the weapon could be lethal. A broken flint resulted in misfire, and amid the noise and smoke, a soldier might not notice that there was no flash in his powder pan nor any kick when he pulled the trigger. Likewise, a vent plugged with the residue of burned powder would keep the flash in the pan from being transmitted to the chamber. Either case produced a potentially dangerous situation.

Other problems arose if the soldier forgot to remove his ramrod and unintentionally fired it across the battlefield. He would need a substitute rammer, or he would be useless in the firefight. Confusion might cause a soldier to forget where he was in the firing sequence, and he might inadvertently jostle his neighbor, upsetting his drill. With hot barrels and ramrods flying about, the men could easily interfere with their comrades.

A partial solution was the use of blank cartridges—rounds containing powder only—for training. This replicated the kick, noise, smoke, heat, and potentially the misfires. Although the use of blanks in training cut into the powder supply, it went a long way toward approaching the realism of a pitched firefight. Of course, no amount of realistic drill could simulate fear; this was the product of actual combat. Most of Scott's men had seen some fighting, and except for the recruits, these soldiers understood the necessity of long hours of repetitive drill.

Although Scott's training accomplishment should not be downplayed, he ignored much that might have been useful. Past operations in the Central Theater encompassed much more than battlefield maneuver on open ground by bodies of troops in close formation. The nature of much of the terrain dictated that many engagements would be fought by loose bodies of soldiers maneuvering over broken ground and in or on the margins of forest. To get to the fight, the army marched in secure formations through these same broken and forested lands. There was an art in forming and moving a large body of men, horses, guns, and wagons so that they would be secure from ambush. Likewise, deploying solders into the fight from movement formations required considerable skill—skill attained only by practice. Much of the early fighting in this war was to capture or defend fortifications. There is no evidence that Scott (or any other American commander in the Central Theater) exercised his men in moving or fighting over broken, wooded ground or in storming fortifications, yet it could not have escaped him that this would be required of his army in Canada.

While training occupied the troops' time, Scott also piled on other duties. He maintained outposts, guards, and night patrols. He emphasized military courtesy, calling such rules "the indispensable outworks of subordination." He ordered a salute fired on 30 April in honor of Andrew Jackson's victory at Horseshoe Bend. Perhaps this was to suggest to the troops that the war was now moving in their favor and that victory was achievable.[37] Scott was generally pleased with the progress of training. On 23 May, he wrote to Brown, "The troops here are getting into a state of very tolerable organization, police & discipline. No exertions of mine have or shall be spared to perfect them in those essentials."[38] To his friend General Winder, he displayed pride: "I have a handsome little army of about 1700. . . . The men are healthy, sober, cheerful, and docile. The field officers highly respectable, and many of the platoon officers are decent and emulous of improvement. If, of such materials, I do not make the best army now in service, by the 1st of June, I will agree to be dismissed from the service."[39]

On 19 May, Scott organized his forces into two brigades. He commanded the First Brigade consisting of the Ninth, Eleventh, and Twenty-fifth Regiments. Ripley commanded the Second Brigade—built upon the Twenty-first Infantry, his old regiment. Ripley had been with the Twenty-first since it had been raised, and he knew all the officers and many of the men. They could be expected to drill and fight well rather than embarrass their former commander. To the Second Brigade eventually was added a company of each of the Seventeenth and Ninteenth Infantry Regiments and a battalion of the Twenty-third Infantry.

While Brown was at Sacketts Harbor, Scott continued to command all troops on the Niagara Frontier, as well as the First Brigade. And he continued to place his indelible stamp on them. He created a small section of pioneers in each regiment. A pioneer was a strong, bright soldier equipped with a tool as well as his weapon. Armed with ax, shovel, or saw, the pioneer was at the front of his company while on the march to clear the route; in retreat, he created obstacles to slow down the enemy. Usually the company pioneers worked as a team under the direction of a corporal. When putting up fieldworks or building bridges, the pioneers (under guidance of engineer officers) led work parties of soldiers.[40]

Scott virtually eliminated sickness in his command. In a published order, he made himself clear. "Discipline," he admonished, "is but the *Second* object in the Brigade. The first is the health of the troops." He insisted on camp sanitation. He ordered tents struck and bedstraw changed after each rain. He ordered the men to bathe in the lake, not in streams. Scott made his officers sample all meals before the men ate. He controlled liquor by forcing sutlers to gain the permission of the regimental commanders before selling to the men. The results were men physically capable of enduring the hardship of the training regimen.[41]

Instilling discipline, the willingness to obey orders instantly without regard for personal safety, was a challenge for Scott and his regimental commanders. Soldiers were recruited overwhelmingly from rural areas in which individual freedom with minimal societal or legal restraints was highly regarded. Turning such individuals into soldiers who could conduct, under fire, the complex drills required to bring the heavy weight of fire against the enemy was no easy matter. Rewards such as promotion were restricted by the number of spaces available, and only promotion brought economic gain. The most powerful motivators, then, were negative. Soldiers were disciplined by peer pressure; the informal group enforced its own standards of conduct. Noncommissioned officers punished slow or recalcitrant soldiers with menial tasks or sometimes physical punishment. Being singled out for the corporal's attention also drew the derision of one's peers. Woe be it to the malefactor who gained the attention of an officer. Courts-martial had a wide range of penalties from which to choose: imprisonment, hard labor, paddling, branding, cropping (maiming the ears), dunking, and execution by firing squad or hanging.[42]

Although officers suffered their share of courts-martial, they also enjoyed an escape mechanism unavailable to enlisted soldiers. An enlisted man was required to serve out his term of enlistment, but an officer could resign at any time, provided his commander was willing to accept his resignation. Thus an officer whose conduct was approaching the limits of acceptability might be persuaded by peers or superiors to avail himself of an honorable escape. Any plausible reason might be given for this decision. Lieutenant John Clarke of the Twenty-second Infantry, for example, requested to resign on 26 May, just five weeks prior to the invasion. He gave his reason as "pecuniary circumstances and the duty he owed his family." Although this reason was likely enough, it might have masked a more sinister set of circumstances. In any event, his regimental commander, Colonel Hugh Brady, accepted Clarke's plea on 3 June and deprived the regiment of the services of an officer at a particularly critical juncture.[43]

Scott certainly held his officers to high standards of conduct, starting with military courtesy. In order to build unit pride and respect between the men and their officers, Scott ordered his soldiers "in very specific and forceful language, to render salutes at all times." An officer, it seems, had walked by a sentry who rendered a snappy salute with his musket. The officer failed to return the courtesy. The incident came to the attention of Scott, who sent an aide to the errant officer to direct him past the sentry once again and correct his oversight or receive trial by court-martial. This affair helped set the tone for conduct in the brigade.[44]

Scott impressed upon his men that the record of their conduct would follow them after they completed their enlistment. He ordered company commanders to ensure that discharge certificates included a statement whether the soldier had "faithfully performed his duties while in service." After the first two weeks of rigorous training, Scott bragged to Brown that he had not yet had the need to establish a provost guard, a body of military policemen, to enforce his regulations.[45] However, by the end of May, serious breaches of discipline threatened all that the brigade had accomplished up to that time.

Payday was traditionally a dangerous time for the discipline of the U.S. Army, and Scott's command illustrated this tradition. Paid for the first time in many months, tired by the hard drill, and burdened by the memories of the bitter winter at French Mills, some of Scott's men grabbed the chance to blow off steam. Others, more deeply impressed by the suffering and perhaps rebellious of exacting discipline, saw their pay as a means of escape. Unwilling to let his efforts be wasted, Scott reacted with determination. In a general order, he noted that "the Provost Guard is now filled with deserters and other criminals and the streets and shops with drunkards and rioters." He charged each soldier "to remember that the honor of the army is his own." Scott prohibited gambling and ordered his officers to conduct roll calls more frequently to identify those who deserted. Deserters were to be chased down and "slain on the spot" if they resisted apprehension. A handful of deserters were caught, and Scott made an example of them to preserve the spirit of discipline in the rest of the command.[46]

A court-martial convicted six soldiers charged with deserting between 15 April and 20 May 1814. Major Jesup, president of the court, sentenced five to be shot and one to have his head shaved and ears cropped and to be branded and drummed out of service. The next day, the unfortunate five were marched into a square formed on three sides by the men of the brigade. Officers passed out weapons to five firing squads as the convicted were blindfolded and positioned next to their coffins and freshly dug graves. The sentence was read, the order to fire given, and the five ill-fated felled. Then one stirred. Because of his extreme youth, Private William Fairchild of the Eleventh Infantry had been, without his knowledge, pardoned by Scott. The brigade commander returned the dazed Fairchild to his company. The drama had the desired effect. Acts of ill discipline were few as preparations for the invasion continued. The garrison at Sacketts Harbor saw similar acts of military justice. A court-martial convened in mid-May ordered one officer cashiered for being drunk on guard. The same court sentenced several to be shot for desertion and one to be hung for allowing two British officers to escape from confinement. The serious nature of their business should not have escaped the attention of any soldier of Brown's division.[47]

While Brown and Scott were readying the Left Division, Congress ordered the reorganization of the artillery and cavalry. In May, Congress consolidated the three artillery regiments into the Corps of Artillery. The Regiment of Light Artillery was unaffected by the consolidation. Within the Left Division, the four companies of the Second Artillery, Scott's old regiment, were given guns and organized as a battalion under Major Jacob Hindman. Four companies of the Third Artillery formed a battalion under Lieutenant Colonel George Mitchell and served as infantry. At Buffalo, Scott organized an armory, laboratory, and workshop to support the requirements of Hindman's battalion.

At the same time, the two regiments of light dragoons were consolidated into the Regiment of Light Dragoons under the command of Colonel James Burn, who formerly commanded the Second Light Dragoons. This consolidation recognized the cold fact that the Department of War could not keep the twenty companies on the establishment manned, mounted, or equipped at anything approaching full strength. The new regiment was authorized eight companies. Harris's company suffered nothing more than a name change.

In addition to drilling, disciplining, and motivating his men, Scott wrestled with the problems of supporting them once they landed on the Canadian shore. Brown designated Rome as the main supply depot and Batavia as a forward depot. Supplies slowly accumulated at these points awaiting movement to the Niagara Frontier. The American line of communication, far inland, was much safer than that of the British, exposed as it was along a shared border. Unfortunately, inland waterways covered only a fraction of the route from Rome to Buffalo, and most supplies traveled considerable distances by wagon and at great expense.[48]

At Buffalo, most of Scott's supplies were stockpiled along Ridge Road, which started on Lake Erie just south of Buffalo and ran eastward toward Batavia. Because the current supply points were vulnerable to British raids, Scott ordered many of his supplies moved ten miles farther inland. He believed that this would discourage raids, but it also strained his ability to feed his men while they were in training.[49]

The invasion required huge amounts of powder, shot, tools, tentage, camp equipment, medical supplies, wagons, teams, forges, horseshoes, spare weapons, baking ovens, and food—food for thousands of men and animals for several weeks. This posed a major problem, since the usual method of feeding the troops was to contract for that service. Both Brown and Scott opposed the contractor system of feeding soldiers. Brown remembered that at French Mills there had been no food when the tired, cold, and hungry troops arrived after the Battle of Crysler's Farm, and it had been forty days before the contractor could comply adequately with the terms of his contract. Scott firmly held that the contractor system was an unalloyed evil. The contracting agent, not subject to military law, had the power to bring a campaign to a halt by failing to make a delivery, supplying faulty goods, or treacherously passing information to the enemy.[50]

Scott took measures to break the stranglehold of the contract system. He set his bakeries to producing tens of thousands of rations of hard bread. Hard bread, which Civil War armies would call hardtack, was simply flour and water mixed without leaven or salt and baked. The resulting flat square, when completely dried, could be preserved for months in a barrel. Scott knew that a soldier could carry five or six days' rations of bread in his haversack, and even without meat, he could march "more than one hundred miles independent of ovens, wagons, or contractors."[51]

Brown had directed Scott to gather information on the enemy, and in this regard, their efforts resulted in a nearly perfect order of battle of Drummond's forces. Both Brown and Scott conducted espionage operations. Brown had hardly departed Williamsville for Sacketts Harbor when Scott sent his first spy into western Upper Canada. It is probable that the spy operator was Abraham Markle of the Canadian Volunteers working out of Erie. Commodore Sinclair transported the spies to the Canadian shore west of Long Point, where it was unlikely that roving patrols of militia or the Nineteenth Light Dragoons would catch them as they landed. Moving from safe house to safe house, the undercover men compiled information from American sympathizers as to the strength, whereabouts, and intentions of enemy forces.[52]

Returning to Erie, Markle forwarded his findings to Scott's inspector general, Major Azor Orne, who, when he was not busy inspecting the troops, sifted through the bits of information gathered by Markle's spies and obtained from other sources: deserters, traveling civilians, even the British themselves. Early in May, Orne interviewed three persons who had recently landed in Buffalo from Upper Canada. One was an American civilian, another an imprisoned American soldier who had escaped, and the third an American-born Canadian who, for whatever reason, was able to travel freely throughout Upper Canada. From these three sources, Orne was able to locate every regiment then in Upper Canada. Some information came to the Americans serendipitously. An American captain, under flag of truce, accompanied a paroled officer, Captain Chalmers of the Forty-first Regiment, across the Niagara. As they disembarked, Chalmers, anxious to return to his unit, asked the British officer who met them the whereabouts of the Forty-first. Without hesitation, and without thinking, the man blurted out, "at York." This up-to-date information corroborated that which Orne had gathered from other sources. Orne fed his reports to Brown's headquarters in Sacketts Harbor, where they were integrated with those compiled by Brown's staff. The result was a fairly accurate picture of the strength and positions of Drummond's forces.[53]

While Scott was preparing his and Ripley's brigades of regulars for the invasion, the nonregular forces of militiamen and native warriors were also gathering and preparing. Scott himself held militia forces in low regard and had no qualms about sharing this opinion. In October 1813, while in command of Fort George, for example, Scott reported to Wilkinson of a raid led by Porter and McClure of 1,000 volunteers, militiamen, and natives to find and fight the enemy west of the fort. "There is no danger of their coming up with the enemy or they would be in great danger of a total annihilation," he stated. Later, Scott described a skirmish between Cyrenius Chapin's band and a British picket guard. "After a great waste of ammunition the parties retired to their respective camps with little loss on either side," he noted with scorn. Porter, the quartermaster general of New York's militia force, was aware of Scott's opinions, and relations between the two general officers would remain professional yet cool throughout the summer.[54]

For his part, Porter was optimistic that he would command a sizable force into Canada. Early in April, he asked the Iroquois for their support and was confident that hundreds of warriors would accompany his brigade as auxiliaries. As for the state militia, Porter expected well over a thousand volunteers to sign up to join the brigade of six-month volunteers authorized by Governor Tompkins in March. Although most would come from the regions close to the war, he expected company-size contingents from the counties of the more secure interior.[55]

The notional brigade organization proposed by the governor was more advanced than the hodgepodge of units that had reported to Van Rensselaer in the fall of 1812. Porter's brigade, assuming Tompkins's model was followed, would consist of two regiments of infantry and a separate battalion of light troops. The infantry regiments would be virtually identical to their regular counterparts. Each would consist of ten companies of 108 men each. With the addition of regimental headquarters, the regiment at full strength would number 1,100 troops. The separate battalion consisted of four companies: one of riflemen, two of light infantry, and the last of mounted riflemen.[56]

In some regards, Tompkins's brigade organization was well matched to the requirements of warfare in the Central Theater. The bulk of the brigade, twenty companies, comprised musket-firing infantry. These would form a line of battle and presumably stand up to their counterparts, the Canadian militia, or, if need be, to British regulars. But little of an army's time is spent in battle. Much more time is spent marching, and if all went well, this brigade would do most of its marching in enemy territory. The separate battalion with its four specialized companies would provide security for the force until it entered into the fight. The mounted riflemen could patrol at a distance while the riflemen and light infantry guarded the front and flanks of the marching column or the bivouac. These elite units would keep the enemy skirmishers and natives away from the bulk of the brigade, leaving it free to march quickly or rest securely. What Tompkins did not include was artillery integral to the brigade. For this, Porter had to depend on the regular artillery of the Left Division. Tompkins also authorized only one type of mounted soldier—the rifleman. These troops could be highly effective in providing security at a distance or reacting quickly to changing requirements, but their use on the battlefield was somewhat limited. Mounted riflemen, unlike the saber- and pistol-wielding dragoons, were not well suited for mounted attacks. Although the infantry arm of Porter's brigade would be secure in its movements and capable of delivering a large volume of small-arms fire, it would still be dependent on the regulars for artillery and battlefield cavalry.

Tompkins's order stipulated that the officers were to be selected by the volunteers of each company. The elected company officers would then meet to choose the regiment's field-grade officers. Tompkins emphasized that ability, not current rank, should be the criterion for selection. By 1814, the better candidates for commissions among the militia had probably been identified on battlefields at Queenston, Fort George, and Sacketts Harbor. Tompkins was so optimistic as to the outcome of the campaign that he included in the order the statement that there was "every reason to believe" that the brigade would be mustered out of service before six months had elapsed.

Tompkins's hopes collapsed because of lack of equipment. While volunteers collected in their various counties and selected their officers, Porter refused to order a muster at the brigade rendezvous at Canandaigua until there were sufficient quantities of tents, cooking kettles, cartridge boxes, knapsacks, blankets, axes, and other tools. The federal and state supply depots in the Ninth District had been virtually emptied after two years of war. Porter postponed the 1 May rendezvous until 20 May, and then again into June. Recruiting slowed down as word got out that there was insufficient equipment for those who had already come forward. Porter informed Brown that the company of mounted riflemen was ready but that the organization of the infantry was at a standstill. He appealed to Brown for assistance in the form of money and equipment.[57]

Brown sent $500 immediately. Porter replied that this sum was "totally inadequate" to support a brigade of 1,000 men in a march to Buffalo from central New York. Taking this admonishment in stride, Brown forwarded $1,500 more and assured Porter that he should consider his command "on the same footing with the regulars as to all expense." Brown requested Armstrong's assistance, and the secretary of war had his staff start the necessary equipment toward New York, but not without advising Brown of the great quantities of federal equipment that had already been issued and apparently wasted by the militia of New York. Brown, who had gained national prominence as a general of the New York militia, offered no opinion about Armstrong's statement. As camp equipment trickled in, Porter decided on 8 June to order his volunteers to Canandaigua.[58]

By mid-June, Porter's brigade of volunteer militia consisted of the company of mounted riflemen and a single regiment of eight companies of infantry under Colonel Philetus Swift. This was far short of Tompkins's vision of a 2,700-man brigade. Swift's second in command was Lieutenant Colonel Hugh Dobbin, who had commanded a regiment of detached militia under Van Rensselaer at Queenston Heights. On 23 June, Brown ordered Porter to send his volunteers and native warriors to Buffalo immediately, ready or not. Porter rode with his mounted company while Swift's regiment slowly marched behind. More companies continued to muster in the interior of the state, but these would miss the opening battles. Largely because of the delay in receiving their equipment, Porter's men were neither trained nor disciplined to the level achieved by the regulars.

Porter was disappointed at the amount of time it took to raise these 1,000 volunteers. He was more disappointed at having to deal with the regulars, Scott and Ripley. To Tompkins, Porter revealed that if he had known how things would turn out, he never would have undertaken the task of raising the volunteer brigade. Porter's animus toward Scott was returned. Scott was convinced that Porter and Tompkins were conspiring to replace him as the commander of the invasion force. Scott wrote to Brown that Porter was concealing a militia commission of major general or perhaps even lieutenant general. Porter, thought Scott, would someday reveal this commission and assume control of the invasion force that Scott had trained. Scott's suspicion proved unfounded.[59]

Contrary to his opinion of militia, Scott called the Iroquois "powerful auxiliaries," and he was pleased to have native warriors with him on the campaign. He ordered 500 rifles sent to Buffalo to arm the Indians who mustered there. Gathering a force of natives went smoothly for Porter. He, Erastus Granger, and Joseph Parrish had met with Red Jacket in early May, and the Seneca chief had assured them that 500 warriors would volunteer to serve. In the event, over 600 joined from among the Onondaga, Oneida, Tuscarora, and Seneca tribes. Many were motivated by a desire to avenge the burning of the Tuscarora village near Lewiston by the Grand River Iroquois the previous winter. The natives were given unofficial ranks by the Indian agents and pay ranging from $8 a month for warriors to $40 for their native captains. About half were armed with their own firearms, some used bows, and all carried tomahawks and knives. Although some wore pieces of uniforms, most were in native dress. Captains were distinguished by sashes worn over the right shoulder and tied at the left hip. Some wore their hair in the traditional "Mohawk" cut, and others wore small skullcaps with clusters of feathers falling down and a single eagle feather standing at the crown. Warriors might wear untucked shirts or go bare chested, but nearly all were in leggings and moccasins; Iroquois believed that moccasined feet helped the dead find their way to heaven. Several women carried weapons and would fight alongside their men. By mid-June, Porter's native contingent was gathered at Buffalo waiting for the signal to cross the Niagara.[60]

Although Porter's New York volunteers were undersubscribed, additional manpower appeared from an unexpected source. In March at Gettysburg, hundreds of volunteers mustered into Colonel James Fenton's Regiment of Pennsylvania Volunteers. As companies formed, they marched off to Erie. Once there, the Pennsylvanians, over 900 of them, began their training. Fenton wrote to Scott on 3 May revealing that the governor of Pennsylvania had ordered the regiment to report to the Left Division. Scott was surprised, for he was unaware of any militia reinforcements coming from that state. Certainly he was disappointed; Fenton noted that his men were without ammunition and in danger of starving. Scott did not hide the disdain he held for the Pennsylvanians. He wrote to Brown: "Col. Fenton and his militia are already in march for this place. I am sorry for this circumstance, for I had rather be without that species of force, than have the whole population of New York & Pennsylvania at my heels. I now give it as my opinion that we shall be disgraced if we admit a militia force either into our camp or order of battle."[61]

Several hundred volunteers from Fenton's command raided into Upper Canada in May. Shortly thereafter, Fenton ordered his men to march to Buffalo. The order was met by seething discontent from a large minority of the enlisted men who were hungry and without pay, and many of whom were shoeless. Some of the officers, apparently without Fenton's orders, arrested a few ringleaders. A regular officer assisted by ordering his cannon, loaded with grapeshot, turned on the masses. The incipient mutiny collapsed, and the men marched off. As they arrived at Buffalo starting on 14 June, Brown issued them two months' pay and integrated the regiment into Scott's training program. When the invasion began, Porter's brigade would be composed of the mounted riflemen, the Iroquois warriors, and Fenton's Pennsylvanians.[62]

While Scott was feverishly building a striking force at Buffalo and Brown was finalizing plans on how to use it, General Drummond was preparing to thwart the Americans. His natural inclination to seize the initiative by aggressive maneuver was now tempered by a more complete understanding of Prevost's strategic vision. Prevost, it will be remembered, was not opposed to offensive action on a small scale and with limited objectives, as long as such forays did not put at risk the defense of the fortress at Quebec, the center of gravity of British Canada. Prevost was willing to yield pieces of Upper Canada in order to preserve the defensive integrity of the lower province—willing, but not eager. He directed Drummond to retain Fort Niagara unless the Americans gained control of Lake Ontario. In that event, Drummond should consider abandoning the post and destroying it. The memory was still clear in Prevost's mind of how quickly the destruction of Procter's force and Tecumseh's revolution had followed the defeat of the Royal Navy flotilla on Lake Erie.[63]

For his part, Drummond believed that the focus of the American effort on the Niagara Frontier would be the retaking of Fort Niagara. This task, in Drummond's estimation, might be supported by a landing on the north shore of Lake Erie. Once there, the Americans would move on Burlington Heights or Fort George in order to cut off resupply to the garrison in Fort Niagara. Drummond had two general options to defeat the American plans. First, he could keep his mobile forces concentrated, perhaps at Burlington Heights, and attack once the enemy's intentions became known. This approach gave Drummond the choice of attacking the Americans while their forces were divided, one part besieging Niagara, the other moving across the Niagara Peninsula. The second option saw the British spread thinly along the Niagara River with small concentrations at Forts Niagara, George, and Erie and at Burlington Heights. This plan, which risked defeat in detail if the Americans struck fast and hard, would allow the British to size up the situation more quickly, and it offered opportunities to slow down the Americans at key points. Drummond, whose estimation of his opponent's abilities was low, did not shrink from the riskier option.

To put the defensive plan into motion, Drummond ordered Riall in March to maintain a thin screen of forces along the Niagara and to defend Fort Erie with a strong company and some artillery. Drummond believed Fort Erie to be "in perfect security against anything short of an invasion in force." He further ordered that the defenses on the Chippawa River be "strongly occupied." This river, the deepest and longest flowing into the Niagara on the Canadian side, was a natural defensive position, and a small force there might very well slow down or stop a large force trying to cross. The defenses referred to by Drummond were the blockhouses and earthworks near the village of Chippawa on the north side of the river. However, Riall was advised to consider this force at Chippawa an offensive as well as a defensive weapon. Drummond directed Riall that "a rapid movement should be made from Chippawa to support the Detachments on the Right [west and south], and to oppose any descent made from above [south of] Chippawa." Lest the aggressive nature of Drummond's intentions be lost on his subordinate, Drummond emphasized that Riall was free to pull the force at Chippawa out from behind its defenses to confront an invasion south of the Chippawa River. As for Fort George, its guns would threaten the southern approaches to Fort Niagara, and its garrison was available to move to confront the invasion, wherever that occurred.[64]

Aggressive by nature, Drummond saw the value of seizing the initiative, and his instructions to the commander of the Right Division bear this out. Drummond directed Riall to occupy positions that gave flexibility to the defensive operation. Flexibility was essential, since Drummond admitted in March that he had "no accurate information" about American plans. His picture of the American order of battle improved somewhat in April because of the testimony of one Constant Bacon, a civilian sutler serving Scott's brigade. To escape his debts, Bacon turned himself in to the British at Fort Niagara. He paid for protection with treason. As a sutler, Bacon had moved freely throughout the American defenses on the Niagara Frontier and picked up much information in casual conversation, which he passed to the British. He described troop camps and supply depots. Fortunately for his countrymen, Bacon estimated American strength at 7,000, over twice the number of regulars and militiamen then present. This testimony painted a picture of a grand offensive, perhaps the major operation of the season, aimed at the Niagara Peninsula.[65]

Drummond's forces were allocated accordingly. Riall's Right Division consisted of six regular and fencible infantry regiments—four on the Niagara Peninsula and two at York. The Left Division was under Drummond's immediate control and was composed of four infantry regiments that defended Kingston and the line of communication eastward to the border with Lower Canada. The defense of Kingston, of course, was supplemented by hundreds of Royal Marines and Royal Navy seamen. Drummond's infantry force was complemented by appropriate numbers of artillerymen and a slender force of dragoons. These full-time troops were backed up by the entire militia organization of Upper Canada and hundreds of native warriors.

Riall's Right Division had about 3,300 hundred regulars and fencibles in April, and reinforcements sent by Drummond brought that number to about 4,100 by the time Brown struck in July. The mainstay of Riall's division was the infantry. Leading the corps of infantry was the First Battalion of the First Regiment of Foot, the Royal Scots. The Royal Scots had arrived at Quebec from Europe in August 1812 and were transferred to Upper Canada in detachments starting in May 1813. The Royal Scots participated in the raid on Sacketts Harbor, and the grenadier company attacked Fort Niagara. About half the battalion scourged the Niagara Frontier under Riall, and in June, nearly 800 Royal Scots were at Fort George under Lieutenant Colonel John Gordon.[66]

The Eighth, or King's, Regiment of Foot had defended Canada during the

Revolution, helping push Arnold back from Quebec. The First Battalion returned to British North America in 1809. Detachments of the regiment fought at Ogdensburg, Fort George, York, Sacketts Harbor, Stoney Creek, Black Rock, and Buffalo. The regiment was ordered to garrison dreary Fort Niagara in January, and its morale collapsed over the next two months. Toiling to repair the defensive works in the bitter cold, the men deserted in ones and twos. Replaced by the 100th Regiment in April, the 600 men of the Eighth manned the Niagara River line between Fort Erie and Chippawa.[67]

The First Battalion of the Forty-first Regiment of Foot had arrived in British North America in 1799 and was thinly spread throughout the Canadas in small detachments. By the beginning of the war, the Forty-first was in western Upper Canada and fought at Maguaga and Frenchtown and participated in the unsuccessful sieges of Forts Meigs and Stephenson. About 150 of the regiment fought with Barclay's fleet as marines, and 119 of these were captured. Smashed by Richard M. Johnson's mounted Kentucky riflemen at the Battle of the Thames, much of the regiment surrendered to Harrison. The Second Battalion arrived at Quebec in May 1813, participated in the raid on Black Rock in July, and was later amalgamated with the remnants of the First Battalion. With a strength of about 600, the Forty-first was at York in the spring of 1814.

The 100th Regiment of Foot was also known as the Prince Regent's County of Dublin Regiment. Raised in Ireland in 1805, the regiment transferred to British North America the same year. The 100th had little battle experience. Its grenadier company participated in the raid on Sacketts Harbor, but the majority of the regiment did not see combat until the night attack on Fort Niagara and the devastation of the Niagara Frontier. The regiment garrisoned Fort Niagara until it was relieved by the Eighth. When morale collapsed in the Eighth, Riall sent the 100th back in. In June, about 650 officers and men of the 100th were in the fort awaiting the expected siege.

Raised in 1806 as the Ninth Garrison Battalion, the 103d Regiment of Foot received its designation in the regiments of the line in 1809. Arriving at Quebec in 1812, the 103d soon earned Prevost's opinion that it was the worst regiment in Canada. The regiment's only combat experience was gained at the raid on Plattsburg in 1813. In the spring of 1814, Prevost transferred the 103d to Drummond's command, and by June, the last company arrived at Burlington Heights. During the march west from Quebec, a detachment of the 103d suffered a breakdown in discipline, resulting in the murder of a civilian. The bulk of the regiment remained under its commander, Colonel Hercules Scott, at Burlington Heights as Riall's reserve, but two companies were sent forward toward Long Point to watch for the invasion.[68]

The last unit of full-time infantry was the Volunteer Battalion of Incorporated Militia of Upper Canada. The legislative assembly authorized this battalion of Canadians in March 1813 and lured volunteers with a promise of land. Company-size detachments saw action at York and Fort Niagara and at the burning of Black Rock and Buffalo. In March, Drummond ordered the 400 men of the battalion consolidated at York, where they underwent training to prepare for the upcoming campaign. Clothed in scarlet, the Canadians were hardly distinguishable from their British counterparts. Their commander was Lieutenant Colonel William Robinson, a brevet major from the King's Regiment.

Rounding out the field of regulars were the artillerymen and dragoons. There were enough gunners from both the Royal Artillery and the Royal Marine Artillery to man Drummond's mobile and stationary batteries, and nearly 250 gunners were assigned to Riall's division. Unlike their American counterparts, British artillerymen did not fight as infantry. Drummond's mounted arm was slender. Three squadrons of the Nineteenth Light Dragoons arrived in Quebec in May 1813, and Prevost sent one squadron to Upper Canada. Occupied continuously in patrolling, escorting, and delivering messages, there were never enough dragoons to do all that was required. Riall enjoyed the services of about 135 dragoons who patrolled the border from Long Point to Fort George. These were backed up by about forty Provincial Light Dragoons, a full-time volunteer troop.

The militia organization that backed up Riall's regulars, fencibles, and volunteers had been largely purged of American sympathizers by 1814. Its fighting power was still largely in the flank companies, two per regiment, although some of the fittest men had joined the Volunteer Incorporated Militia. The seven regiments of the London and Western Districts were occupied in defending their homes from American raids, and Riall could not reasonably expect their services in the upcoming campaign. On the Niagara Peninsula were the five regiments of Lincoln militia, and further east were the three regiments of York militia in the Home District. A company of militia artillerymen and another of blacks, Captain Runchey's Company of Negroes, backed up the Lincoln militia. These militiamen had been repeatedly called up over the past two years, and many had seen action in battle and skirmish. Like their American counterparts, they were not combat hardened, but neither were they as likely to run as they might have been in 1812.

Riall also could draw upon the services of a considerable number of natives. Nearly 300 Grand River Indians under John Norton were camped near Niagara Falls. This did not represent the full warrior strength of the Canadian Iroquois, as many at the Grand River settlement resolutely rejected Norton as their leader, claiming that he was a divisive force within the Iroquois community. About 500 or 600 western Indian warriors were organized under Lieutenant Colonel William Caldwell, Sr., who had served in the Revolution with Butler's Rangers. These western Indians were refugees from Tecumseh's confederation, and that leader's brother, the Prophet, was now their spokesman. In exchange for food, the Prophet pledged that even "their smallest boys capable of bearing arms shall be ready to march at a moment's notice."[69]

The services of the western Indians came at a steep price. Over 3,000 natives, mostly women and children, had sought refuge near Burlington Heights after Tecumseh's death the previous September. The fighting in western Upper Canada had so interfered with their harvest that these refugees had no alternative but to depend on British rations—rations that Drummond desperately needed to feed his own soldiers. By April, Riall was issuing the natives 1,200 barrels of flour monthly, more than was consumed by his soldiers on the Niagara Peninsula. Food was hard to come by in Upper Canada. The 1813 harvest was poor, and salt to preserve meat was in short supply. The mild winter resulted in soft roads and therefore a slowdown in moving food from farm to settlement. Finally, British buyers had all but destroyed their credit because of a severe shortage of specie with which to pay even their oldest debts. Farmers were reluctant to sell to a government that might very well be overthrown by American invaders before it paid its just debts.[70]

Drummond took several measures that led, by summertime, to a solution to the food shortage. He repeatedly prevailed upon Prevost to send food. "Should not the most ample supplies of Provisions, particularly flour, be sent from the Lower Province, I feel strongly apprehensive that the Right Division will not be able to hold its ground even though the entire resources of the Country should be at our command," he noted. Drummond took decisive steps to squeeze the farmers of Upper Canada hard for their food. Sensitive that the legislative assembly would not grant him the authority he needed, he proclaimed martial law, compelling farmers to sell food and forage to his buyers at prices set by the district magistrates. Farmers received a fair price in promissory notes. The assembly agreed to continue the ban on distilling grain. Drummond's efforts, and those of his supply officers, paid off. By June, Riall's division had enough meat to last until early September and enough flour to make it to October. The Right Division was issuing 8,700 rations each day, a healthy share to noncombatants. A six-month supply was needed at Fort Niagara, for the British expected a long siege of that post. Drummond's force at Kingston paid part of the price; there was enough food for only thirty days there. Of course, Kingston was closer to rations procured in Lower Canada. Drummond had to be careful in calling out the militia, for once the men were mobilized, responsibility for feeding them fell to the government.[71]

Having taken sharp measures to fight famine, Drummond took extreme steps to combat disaffection. In February, Drummond asked for and received from the assembly expanded powers to deal with treasonous citizens such as Willcocks and Markle. The acting attorney general for the province indicted more than seventy persons, nineteen of whom were in custody, on charges of high treason. Most of the accused were recent immigrants from the United States who had joined or actively supported American raiders in the western part of Upper Canada. A few were accused of spying. On 23 May, trials began in Ancaster, near Burlington Heights. Of the nineteen in custody, the jury acquitted only four. Eight were sentenced to death, and the judge recommended leniency to the prince regent for the remaining seven. On 20 July, the condemned were, according to the ancient ritual for those convicted of high treason, hung, their bodies decapitated, and the severed heads put on public display. Of those awaiting the will of the prince regent, three died in prison, one escaped, and the rest were eventually forced to leave the country. The jury outlawed most of the accused not in custody; their lands and property became forfeit.[72]

Aside from quelling dissent in his own backyard, Drummond was also responsible for coordinating both land and sea operations. In this regard, he held an inestimable advantage over Brown, for Yeo was required by his orders to subordinate his command to that of Drummond. Fortunately for the British, Drummond's and Yeo's objectives were congruent and complementary. The grand objective was the preservation of a British power at Quebec and, in support of that, control over as much of Upper Canada as possible for as long as possible. Yeo was committed to an arms race and, like Prevost, was willing to conduct low-risk raids that contributed to that end. He explored any opportunity to slow down the American shipbuilding effort. In June, for example, Yeo and Drummond toyed with the idea of firing rockets at the American fleet at anchor in Sacketts Harbor. The Congreve rocket was an incendiary weapon, and the flotilla presented a target large enough to offset the inherent inaccuracy of the missile. Yeo went so far as to divert the shipbuilding effort a bit in order to build rocket-firing craft. Luckily for the U.S. Navy, Yeo had too few gunboats to protect the rocket craft and he was, in the final analysis, unwilling to risk larger vessels for that purpose. Drummond also investigated the idea of issuing a new challenge to the U.S. fleet on Lake Erie. Once Yeo's fleet enjoyed superiority on Lake Ontario, Drummond proposed building a new Erie squadron at Turkey Point.[73]

Persuaded that they were in danger of losing the naval arms race and too weak to attack Sacketts Harbor, Yeo and Drummond decided on 27 April to attack Chauncey's exposed line of communication at Oswego on the shore of Lake Ontario. At Oswego, supplies and equipment that came downriver were transloaded to lake vessels for the trip to Sacketts Harbor. Heavy loads, such as guns and cables, came by this route, as they were too heavy to travel easily by road. Farther upriver, about eight miles, were the rapids at Oswego Falls; the vast bulk of Chauncey's supplies were at this bottleneck awaiting skilled crews to negotiate the natural obstacle.

As he became aware of the danger, Chauncey asked Brown to defend the supplies, particularly the numerous guns needed to arm the ships then approaching completion in the shipyard. Brown ordered Lieutenant Colonel Mitchell, at Batavia with his artillerymen, to "occupy and defend the old fort at the mouth of the river . . . so long as would be consistent with the more important duty of covering the naval stores collected at the falls." After a forced march of 150 miles, Mitchell and nearly 400 of his men arrived on 30 April to be greeted by an unsatisfying sight. The remains of a fortification stood on a rise about sixty feet above the level of the lake. Such wooden pickets as remained were rotten, and the few guns were unmounted. Hard work resulted in some improvements, but the Royal Navy arrived offshore on 5 May and cut short further preparations.[74]

After a long cannonade, Yeo landed about 550 infantry and Royal Marines and 200 sailors armed with pikes and edged weapons. After a short but stalwart defense, Mitchell ordered his men to fall back to Oswego Falls. He understood well that his mission was to defend naval guns, not a dilapidated fort. The Americans lost about sixty prisoners, half of them wounded. British casualties approached ninety. As the American artillerymen set up their defense upriver, the British chose not to pursue but rather to load 2,400 barrels of food and salt onto three captured schooners. After burning the public buildings, Yeo and Drummond returned to Kingston and congratulated their men and themselves for their "compleat success." Brown, too, praised the defenders for a resolute defense.[75]

Both sides enjoyed mixed success in this encounter and perhaps can be forgiven for claiming the laurels. Brown overstated the number of attackers in his report to Armstrong, which served to magnify Mitchell's honors. The fact remains, however, that the vital guns and cable had been safeguarded. Brown was criticized in naval circles for not sending more troops to defend Oswego. Without knowing for certain the target of the raid, Brown would have been open for justifiable censure had he sent troops away from Sacketts Harbor just prior to an attack there. Once he was certain that Oswego was under attack, Brown hurried dragoons and riflemen westward to support Mitchell. The unsuccessful defense of Fort Oswego was the result of the rotted state of the fortification and the insufficient number of guns and, in a larger sense, the rotted state of defense and the insufficient number of troops under the Jeffersonians.

For their part, the British captured enough food to meet their needs for two weeks and enough salt to preserve thousands of barrels of meat. They conducted a very skillful joint operation in the face of a determined foe and at a low cost. Also, they slowed down the American shipbuilding effort for vital weeks by forcing Chauncey and Brown to go to extreme measures to move guns and cable to Sacketts Harbor. Could Drummond have pushed his 1,000 ground troops to Oswego Falls? Perhaps, but they would have moved into the interior without the assistance of the Royal Navy and its supporting gunfire. Drummond, mindful of the risk involved, satisfied himself with important, if not decisive, gains. He and Yeo would try later to keep the guns from reaching Sacketts Harbor. For the time being, Drummond's defensive strategy was proceeding according to plan.

For the most part, Prevost and his subordinates in Upper Canada, Drummond and Yeo, enjoyed a common understanding of the strategic goals and the ways in which their military capacity could, with minimal risk, contribute to those goals. Such an understanding did not exist among Madison and his secretaries of the navy and of war, nor among Brown, Izard, and Chauncey in the Central Theater. Perhaps persuaded by Governor Tompkins and Secretary Jones, Madison feared a British resurgence in the Northwest and was inclined to use the troops at Detroit and the Erie squadron to retake Mackinac Island. Armstrong saw merit in Brown's ideas for a major offensive to clear the Niagara Peninsula. Brown, though anxious to attack targets on the Niagara Peninsula, was, for the time being at least, fully occupied in defending Sacketts Harbor and the exposed line of communication between that base and Oswego. Writing to Scott on 28 April, four days after arriving there, Brown declared Sacketts Harbor to be of "national importance and as the Sec[retary] considers me responsible for the safety of this post I dare not leave it until this new ship is completed and Com[modore] Chauncey can face Yeo."[76]

Brown must have been perplexed and perhaps frustrated while at Sacketts Harbor. There were two major impediments, neither of which was under his control, to be overcome before he could send an invasion force into Canada with confidence. First, Chauncey would have to win control of the lake, and second, Armstrong would have to reinforce his division with thousands more trained, equipped troops. On 29 April, he wrote to Armstrong about his concerns. Reminding the secretary that he had only 3,500 men in his command with which to secure Chauncey's base and to invade Canada, Brown asked whether "with such limited means, could I be justified in again putting to hazard the honor of the Army and Country by commencing offensive operations?" He rejected Armstrong's suggestion to lay siege to Fort Niagara and revealed his intention to remain at Sacketts Harbor until Armstrong sent orders.[77]

Armstrong understood Brown's problem and saw Madison's insistence on a campaign to the upper lakes as the biggest obstacle to a victorious thrust in the Niagara region. An expedition to Mackinac would divert transports desperately needed by Brown. Armstrong wrote to Madison on 30 April, hoping to persuade the commander in chief to call off the expedition. He argued logically, although ultimately unsuccessfully, that Brown's offensive against Burlington would result in securing the American Northwest by cutting off British supplies from those western Indians still inclined to carry on the war. Armstrong envisioned a force of 5,000 regulars and 3,000 volunteers operating against the British in the Niagara region. Madison, who was at Montpelier resting, retorted that an offensive aimed at Burlington would be vulnerable unless Chauncey controlled the lake. Nevertheless, Madison passed Armstrong's plan on to Jones for the secretary of the navy's consideration. "I cannot do better than to leave it in the hands of yourself," wrote Madison, "and the Secretary of War, whose interchange of information and sentiments, promises the soundest result." Upon receiving the president's reply that he would yield in favor of a plan agreed to by his two military secretaries, Armstrong sent orders to Brown to concentrate his forces, including a siege train, as soon as possible in order to cross Lake Erie and drive on Burlington Heights. Armstrong included his letter of 30 April to the president and passed off this document as a plan approved by Madison. Brown should expect the cooperation of the Erie squadron, wrote Armstrong, and he could expect his 8,000 men by 10 June. In neither letter—from Armstrong to Madison or from Armstrong to Brown—did the secretary of war identify a requirement that Chauncey control Lake Ontario.[78]

Brown was elated when he received this order from Washington. Earlier, he had complained to Scott that if he must wait for a naval battle, it would be "very possible that nothing will be done this season." He had already warned Scott that the Erie squadron might be unavailable to transport the army to Canada. Brown was also concerned—and Armstrong's order did nothing to address the issue— that no one with authority was close enough to coordinate the efforts within the Ninth Military District. He admitted to Scott: "I observe the great embarrassment under which we are laboring for the want of a military chief whose headquarters would be Albany to supply and command the divisions of the army in this district as the public interest should require." Brown hit the nail squarely on the head. Armstrong had moved to Sacketts Harbor and later to Albany to coordinate the pincer attack by Wilkinson and Hampton the previous fall, and it probably occurred to Brown that the invasion had come unraveled only after Armstrong returned to Washington. Brown might have gone on to complain that no one was directing the cooperation of his troops with Chauncey's fleet or with the Lake Erie squadron.[79]

Early in May, Scott opened up a dialog with the naval commander at Erie, Captain Arthur Sinclair. Sinclair had commanded the *Argus* in the Atlantic squadron until the Navy Department assigned him to Sacketts Harbor in mid-1813. In April, Chauncey gave him command of the flotilla on the upper lakes, and with it the mission to retake Mackinac Island. Sinclair professed that his transports were sufficient to carry only 1,000 men, the number he expected to take with him into Lake Huron. However, he pledged to Scott that he would leave enough naval strength at Erie to retain control of that lake and would order the senior naval officer there to help Scott in any way within his power. Clearly, even if Madison agreed to call off the expedition to Mackinac, the available transport would be hard-pressed to carry and supply 8,000 troops across Lake Erie. Scott, conscientious in so many ways, apparently took no steps to address this major shortfall in transport vessels, other than informing Brown.[80]

By the end of May, Brown was ready to depart Sacketts Harbor and return to Buffalo to take command of the invasion force, which he hoped would materialize by 10 June. Leaving 1,500 troops with Gaines to defend Chauncey's base, he directed the riflemen at Oswego Falls to guard the guns and cable that were to move secretly eastward along the lakeshore to Sacketts Harbor. Brown ordered Hindman's artillery battalion, as well as the Twenty-third Infantry, westward to Buffalo. To conceal his intentions, Brown ordered Mitchell at Oswego Falls to let slip that these reinforcements for Buffalo were actually replacements for Mitchell's artillerymen who were nearing the end of their enlistment. However, once the guns and cable to complete Chauncey's last ship departed Oswego Falls, there was nothing left of such importance to merit a garrison. Perhaps to ensure the discipline of the troops remaining with Gaines, Brown ordered the execution of deserters by firing squad and the hanging of a nineteen-year-old who, while on guard duty, had helped two British officers escape from prison. Fifteen of Brown's officers signed a letter requesting that Brown spare the errant guard. At the time of his offense, he had been in the army only two or three months and deserved clemency, they wrote. Without answering the petition, Brown formed his command at Sacketts Harbor, about 2,500 men, to witness the youth's death and unceremonious burial under the scaffold.[81]

When Scott learned that Brown was returning to Buffalo to command the invasion, he was both surprised and disappointed, for he fully expected that honor himself, and he believed that it was Armstrong's intention that he do so. Although his ego may have predisposed him to that opinion, there was evidence to support his view. When Brown left Buffalo, he wrote to Armstrong that Scott would be in command until Brown's return. Brown expected to stay at Sacketts Harbor only until he was satisfied that it was secure from attack. Once in place, he told Armstrong: "I do not intend to leave this post again until I receive orders from you." Armstrong, who chose to deal with two independent commanders in the Ninth Military District, Brown and Izard, then began treating Scott as a third commander by sending him information directly rather than through Brown. Once Brown left, Scott took steps to assert his independence. He informed Brown that he was going to forward strength reports directly to the War Department rather than through Brown at Sacketts Harbor. Thus, Armstrong inferred that Brown was willing to relinquish tight control over Scott. By mid-May, Brown was complaining that he had received no campaign guidance from Armstrong since 7 April, but Scott told his superior that he was in receipt of instructions from the secretary. Scott hinted to Brown that he aspired to command the invasion. Relating his understanding, which Brown shared, that Sacketts Harbor was of greater strategic importance than the Niagara, Scott presumed that Brown would "prefer" to retain personal command of army forces at the naval base. Perhaps the picture was becoming clearer for Jacob Brown. Writing to Armstrong to inform him of his intention to return to Buffalo, Brown noted that "you have not ordered me there, but I suppose you consider me as having the necessary authority." En route westward, Brown made his motivation clear to the secretary. Relating to Armstrong in a private letter that Scott assumed that the War Department intended to have him command the invasion, Brown wrote that he would "certainly despise" himself if he did not command his division in person.[82]

Brown assumed command on the Niagara Frontier on 6 June. On 14 June, he received new guidance from Armstrong that was written before the secretary knew that Brown was determined to lead the Left Division from the front. Armstrong directed Brown not to weaken the garrison at Sacketts Harbor until Chauncey's fleet was stronger than that of Yeo. He then asked Brown, in consultation with Chauncey, to answer the question: "If Scott can make his way to Burlington or York with what force, naval and military from Sackett's Harbour can you join him & when?" Armstrong's intention became clear only when Brown read a letter to Scott written the same day. Armstrong warned Scott not to expect any reinforcements from Detroit because the twelve-month enlistees were leaving the service and those who remained in uniform were ordered to retake Mackinac. All Scott would receive were the Pennsylvania militia and regular garrison at Erie. Armstrong directed Scott to strongly consider marching directly on Burlington Heights to cut the land line of communication with Forts George and Niagara. Although it would be preferable to wait for Chauncey to seize control of the lake, Scott might have to attack earlier. However, if Chauncey were beaten in battle or blockaded in port, Scott was to return to the shore of Lake Erie.

These letters, taken together, introduced remarkable changes in the plans and provided insight into the secretary of war's professional weaknesses. First, Armstrong's endorsement of Scott as making the main attack was clear. Perhaps the secretary did not want Brown to gain more laurels. Second, Armstrong tacitly admitted that he could not make 8,000 men available. Scott would have about half that number in his striking force. Third, Armstrong now accepted Madison's concern that an American army on the Canadian shore of Lake Ontario was at risk unless Chauncey controlled the water. Armstrong was now willing to abort the major invasion of Canada based on a naval battle that might never take place, much less be won. Fourth, by failing to send Brown a copy of his letter to Scott, Armstrong was guilty of unforgivable incompetence. How could Brown support his subordinate if he was unaware of what Scott had been ordered to do?[83]

As soon as Brown received this latest round of instructions, he penned a response that revealed a remarkably clear understanding of the flaw that bedeviled the American planning effort. Lest his chief suffer from any delusions as to the state of affairs in the Central Theater, Brown replied that Chauncey would not willingly transport Brown's men to Burlington until control of the water was wrested from Yeo. Asked Brown rhetorically, "Will Yeo give the Commodore a chance for beating him?" The logic of this arms race was that no battle would be fought. Insisting that Sacketts Harbor was safe, Brown reiterated his ambition to lead the invasion himself. It must have been evident to Brown that his government in Washington was unable to provide the support he had been led to believe would be available. Having wasted weeks waiting for help, Brown was determined to press on by his own efforts. On 19 June, he informed Armstrong that he would cross into Canada as soon as he could gather a force of 3,000 regulars.[84]

Brown wrote these comments before he received final instructions from the secretary of war. On 7 June, Madison met with the cabinet to determine an overall strategy for the Western and Central Theaters. The two military secretaries reported the strength and locations of their respective forces. Armstrong reported that 8,000 regulars guarded the American coast and 2,100 were in the Western Theater. Fully 8,000 were in the Ninth Military District; of these, Izard had 5,000 and Brown the rest. Armstrong believed that over 7,000 recruits were at rendezvous points throughout the country and available for commitment. Unfortunately, Armstrong's hopes to convince Madison to cancel the expedition into the upper lakes were dashed. Madison approved a strategic plan of four components. On 9 June, Armstrong sent Brown the results of that session, which reached Brown on 21 June. First, 1,000 troops and the bulk of the Lake Erie squadron would clear the British from the upper Great Lakes. Second, the boatwrights at Sacketts Harbor would construct fifteen gunboats, each seventy-five feet long. These boats would be sailed into the St. Lawrence and cut the river line of communication between Montreal and Kingston. Izard would build and garrison a fortification on the river to secure the gunboats. Third, Izard would make a demonstration toward Montreal to divert British attention from Brown's operation. Fourth, Brown was to make the main attack and seize Burlington Heights. If Chauncey defeated Yeo, Brown, in cooperation with Chauncey, would continue the attack eastward to York and perhaps Kingston.[85]

The actual wording of the record was somewhat ambiguous as to whether Brown was cleared to act immediately to take Burlington Heights without waiting for the results of a naval battle. Armstrong, in detailed instructions to Brown, discussed the issue. Making a rough calculation of supply requirements and the considerable problem of moving food and equipment from Lake Erie to Burlington Heights, he advised Brown, "though the Expedition be *approved,* its execution must be *suspended* 'till Chauncey shall have gained the command of the Lake." According to Armstrong, this would allow time for reinforcements to reach Buffalo. Secretary Jones told Armstrong that Chauncey was expected on the lake no later than 15 July. Apparently as an afterthought, Armstrong introduced a new idea—a concept that probably had not been discussed at the cabinet meeting two days earlier. "To give immediate occupation to your troops and to prevent their blood from stagnating," Armstrong suggested that Brown consider an attack on Fort Erie, perhaps followed up by clearing the west bank of the Niagara River all the way to Fort George. To an aggressive soldier like Brown, impatient at the foot-dragging of his superiors and their staffs, this was all the authority he needed. A few days before receiving these instructions, Brown had despaired of receiving the active assistance of the residue of the Lake Erie squadron, and he decided to cross the river near Fort Erie instead. Armstrong's afterthought matched perfectly with the plan developing in Brown's mind. In a letter to the quartermaster at Albany in which he requested that equipment be hurried to Buffalo, Brown wrote: "I have this day received a letter from him [Armstrong] permitting me to be governed by *circumstances*. Circumstances it appears to me render it proper that I should cross and it is my intention to take possession of the opposite shore of the streight [*sic*] before the 4th of July."[86]

Madison's strategic plan was open to considerable criticism. First, Madison articulated his overarching plan so late in the season that he was constrained by the current position of the forces. Had he promulgated a strategy three months earlier, the troops could have moved to their jump-off positions and still have had time for adequate training. The president's tardiness was inexcusable, considering that it was common knowledge that Napoleon's defeat would release thousands of British veterans and the Americans would have to strike fast before these reinforcements arrived in strength. Second, Madison allocated to the main attack only a fraction of the forces available. Brown had fewer than 4,000 regulars, and he was required to defend Sacketts Harbor as well as to seize Burlington Heights. Madison gave Izard a secondary mission, although he had more men than Brown. Third, Madison did not order Chauncey to leave port and seek decisive battle with Yeo or to support Brown. Apparently, he satisfied himself with Jones's assertion of Chauncey's willingness to do so. The day prior to the cabinet meeting, Jones wrote to the president that "the Naval Force is at all times, ready to cooperate with the Military, and, I presume, there can be no doubt of a cheerful reciprocation." Lulled with these words, Madison failed to give positive orders to his naval commander. Fourth, Madison erroneously approved the campaign to clear the British from the upper Great Lakes in spite of Armstrong's well-reasoned counterargument that the seizure of Burlington Heights and York would have the same result. Madison's decision deprived

Brown's invasion of 1,000 troops and the Erie squadron. Madison never grasped the key strategic principle that severing the line of communication would slowly but surely result in the capture of everything west of the cut. Sending gunboats east of Kingston was a step in the right direction, but the summer offensive would likely run its course before this slender gunboat flotilla achieved decisive results. A century afterward, J. W. Fortescue, historian of the British army, examined Madison's decision to make the main attack on the Niagara and a decidedly secondary effort to stop traffic on the St. Lawrence. He pronounced: "Thus the object which should have been primary was made secondary, and that which should have been secondary was made primary, according to the approved practice of the amateur strategist." Fortescue's judgment was, if anything, too gentle; the commander in chief and his secretary of war had designated the main invasion effort and, through neglect, had neither given it sufficient resources nor supported it.[87]

What Madison and his cabinet failed to do at the national level was left for Brown and Chauncey to make up on the spot. Brown and Scott and, to a lesser degree, Porter made tremendous efforts to gather and prepare a land force, and no one can doubt Chauncey's single-minded efforts to outbuild Yeo. The problem was to coordinate the land and naval effort. Chauncey and Dearborn cooperated in 1813 in the raid on York and the attack on Fort George, but after the near loss of his base, Chauncey was reluctant to pursue further joint operations. Brown, of course, was instrumental in saving Sacketts Harbor in May 1813. However, Brown was irritated the following April when Chauncey sought his help to defend the base from an attack that never came. The army defended the naval guns at Oswego, and Brown, before he departed Sacketts Harbor, allocated his most experienced regiment, the riflemen, to ensure that the guns reached Chauncey's shipyard. Upon his return to Buffalo in June, Brown sent a confidential note to Armstrong in which he complained of the one-sided nature of this relationship. He believed that the Ontario fleet was "under great obligations to the Army for its preservation and support." However, he had "not seen in this navy, a magnanimous expression of the obligation." Brown concluded by professing his personal friendship for Chauncey and his continued support for the navy. In June, Brown's worry was whether Chauncey would appear at the head of the lake when Brown approached from the south.[88]

Throughout June, Chauncey proclaimed his willingness to sail by 1 July if he had sufficient numbers of sailors to crew his fleet. The secretary of the navy assured Madison and Armstrong that seamen were on the way. Brown analyzed the strengths of the competing fleets and was satisfied that Chauncey's fleet was stronger and that Yeo would refuse to accept battle. What Brown lacked was Chauncey's promise to meet him with his fleet. Brown confessed this uncertainty to Gaines, probably hoping that his subordinate might coax a commitment from the commodore. "I do not know that I am to be supported by the Fleet of either Lake but I intend to enter the Enemy's Country about the first of July and shall hope not to be disgraced. If Commodore Chauncey can meet me between Burlington and Fort George by the 15th of July I do not doubt but that with the assistance he can give, Fort George and Niagara will be in our power."[89]

Now it was Brown's turn to irritate Chauncey. On the day Brown wrote to Gaines, he also sent a note to the commodore. He chided Chauncey for not writing for nearly four weeks. He stated categorically that Yeo would not dare to accept a decisive battle. There is no record of Chauncey's thoughts as he read the former militia general's analysis of the naval situation. Then Brown asked the key question: "Upon receipt of this, will you have the goodness to let me know by Express, when you will be out and if I may expect you in the neighborhood of Fort George by the 10th of July? or what day?" He concluded with the hope that Chauncey would bring with him a pair of eighteen-pound guns.[90]

Chauncey penned a reply on 25 June. It probably arrived just as Brown ordered his men into Canada. Chauncey explicitly communicated to Brown the conditions under which Brown might expect to see him. Chauncey expected to sail on 10 July, "but I shall not leave this vicinity," he wrote, "unless the Enemy's fleet leads me up the Lake." Chauncey warned Brown that if Yeo refused battle and remained in port, Chauncey would "be obliged to watch his movements, to prevent his doing mischief." Chauncey acknowledged a slight superiority in guns but countered that Yeo's fleet had more sailing time that year than the American fleet and was therefore better trained. Chauncey's real fear was that the large number of troops arriving from Europe would be used to attack Sacketts Harbor while Chauncey was away. Dreading a possible attack, Chauncey refused to send the pair of big guns to Brown. This stark warning should have made clear to Brown that he probably would not see the fleet. After all, he himself had told Chauncey that Yeo would likely stay in port rather than risk battle. For reasons that are unknown, Brown continued to profess an expectation that the fleet would join him in mid-July. When the fleet failed to show up, Brown's campaign took a new and unforeseen direction.[91]

Without the active cooperation of the Lake Ontario fleet, neither Armstrong nor Brown expected America's main attack to get beyond Burlington Heights. Brown did expect the cooperation of the Lake Erie squadron to help him cross either that lake or the Niagara River. On 18 June, Brown wrote to Sinclair asking for the number of transports or smaller vessels that might be available and when he might expect them at Buffalo. The following day, Sinclair departed on the expedition to Lake Huron, but the officer he left at Erie replied to Brown's query that he had four schooners and a barge capable of carrying up to 100 men. This paltry flotilla, and Chauncey's virtual refusal to sail toward Fort George, was the real demonstration of Jones's spirit of cooperation articulated to Madison in early

June. Brown must have seen the irony of the situation while reading the reply from Erie and thinking back to Armstrong's earlier intention to transport and supply 8,000 men across Lake Erie. Brown confirmed his decision to cross the river directly into the face of the enemy, as Smyth had attempted in 1812, and he gave the order to build new boats and to repair all that could be found. Madison's grand plan was coming unraveled.[92]

Although Brown was disappointed by the dearth of support from the Departments of War and Navy, there was much that pleased him at Buffalo. He positively beamed with the high levels of training, drill, and discipline achieved by Scott and his officers. Brown took action quickly to assert authority over the troops who had been toiling under Scott since April. His first act was to order a salute fired to celebrate the action at Sandy Creek, in which the riflemen had stymied a British attempt to prevent the guns at Oswego Falls from reaching Sacketts Harbor. He ordered the men to bathe in the lake three times each week, to fire twenty blank cartridges at drill weekly, and to parade and maneuver as a division each Sunday. He accepted the resignation of a major, suspended a captain for conduct unbecoming an officer, and appointed three sergeants to be acting ensigns in anticipation of commissions from the president.[93]

Other tasks required his intervention. Brown had not depended entirely on Chauncey to acquire those heavy guns he expected to need to batter down the several fortifications he would likely encounter. He wrote to the officer commanding at Detroit to send all the eighteen- and twenty-four-pound guns and ammunition he could spare. He told this officer that the heavy guns were "indispensable" to the upcoming campaign. Of course, Detroit was in the Eighth Military District, and Brown had no command authority in that region. Brown needed current information on the enemy, so he dispatched his engineer, the talented Major Eleazar Wood, a graduate of West Point's class of 1806, to lead a reconnaissance party. Escorted by thirty men, Wood discovered Fort Drummond, a newly erected earthwork on Queenston Heights. He noted the repairs to Fort George and reported on the progress of Fort Mississauga opposite Fort Niagara. Brown's efforts to acquire boats paid off, and by the end of June he boasted enough vessels to carry 800 soldiers at once. Now all Brown needed were additional soldiers to flesh out the splendid but thin brigades trained by Scott and Ripley.[94]

Although Brown was never sure how many troops he would command or if there would be enough to achieve decisive results, the War Department was confident that enough troops were indeed in the Ninth Military District or en route there. As of 1 July, Armstrong's clerks calculated that nearly 15,000 troops, over half the effective strength of the regular army, were physically under Brown's or Izard's command or under orders to join them. Although these numbers seem sufficient to gain important results, by 1 July, these troops were not concentrated with either of the two divisions. Izard's Right Division, whose mission was largely defensive and secondary, had 4,908 men according to War Department estimates. The divisional strength would be bolstered to about 9,600 when all troops reported in, but there was no telling when that might occur. In Brown's Left Division, which would strike the major blow of the campaign as well as defend the fleet at Sacketts Harbor, the picture was less sanguine. Armstrong believed that Brown had 3,041 regulars already, and he had ordered 2,317 more to join Brown. Thus Armstrong hoped that Brown might soon have 5,358 regulars. Armstrong apparently was willing to allow Brown to strike the main blow of the war with about one-third of the regular soldiers available in the Ninth District.[95]

Between the efforts of Brown and the War Department, troops started to trickle in to Buffalo during June. Brown asked Gaines for the rifle battalion if it could be spared, but Gaines replied to his superior that this elite infantry unit was one of the "main pillars of defence" of Sacketts Harbor. However, between 14 June, when the main body of Fenton's Pennsylvania volunteer militia arrived, and 3 July, when the Left Division invaded Canada, over 1,100 regulars turned up in time to cross the Niagara. Much of the regular garrison at Erie—several companies of the Eleventh, Seventeenth, and Nineteenth Infantry Regiments— marched into camp on the heels of the Pennsylvanians.[96]

In May, Armstrong ordered the Twenty-second Infantry, with detachments at Sacketts Harbor, Philadelphia, Erie, and several towns in Pennsylvania, to concentrate on the Niagara Frontier. By 30 June, just three days before the invasion, four companies of this regiment appeared. The Twenty-second, a Pennsylvania regiment, was not new to the Niagara Frontier. Early in the war, several companies had been with Smyth, and during the first winter, they had garrisoned Fort Niagara, where over fifty of them succumbed to disease. The regiment had been in the first wave of the attack on Fort George and later that year fought under Brown as part of the advance guard of Wilkinson's failed attempt to seize Montreal. But these veterans, or the few who survived, were with Izard, not Brown. The portion of the Twenty-second that materialized at Buffalo was a battalion made up largely of new recruits. The regimental commander, forty-six-year-old Colonel Hugh Brady, had been an ensign with Mad Anthony Wayne in the Fallen Timbers campaign. Brady had resigned in 1795 but in 1812 rejoined the colors. Because Brady was still en route to Buffalo, Scott temporarily consolidated Brady's command with Leavenworth's Ninth Infantry.[97]

The largest reinforcement to join Brown was the Twenty-third Infantry, which had been actively recruiting in central New York State. Early in June, Brown ordered the senior major, Daniel McFarland, to gather up his companies of veterans and new recruits and march them to Buffalo. On 26 June, about 400 men of the Twenty-third appeared there. These June reinforcements were a

Effective Strengths, 30 June 1814

mixed blessing. None of the volunteers or regulars had more than a few days' benefit of Scott's training program, and the difference between them and the veterans of ten weeks' drill must have been stark. Brown reorganized his two brigades of regulars to even out the quality. Scott's brigade consisted of the Ninth, Eleventh, Twenty-second, and Twenty-fifth Infantry Regiments. Scott attached the Twenty-second to the Ninth for operations so that his brigade comprised three maneuver elements. Ripley received the Seventeenth, Nineteenth, Twenty-first, and Twenty-third Infantry Regiments. He attached the two companies of the Nineteenth and single company of the Seventeenth to James Miller's Twenty-first Infantry. His brigade, therefore, consisted of two maneuver elements. Porter, arriving in camp at the eleventh hour, took command of a brigade made up of Pennsylvania infantry, New York mounted volunteers, and the Iroquois contingent. While Brown and his subordinate generals had undertaken, over the past months, to assemble, train, and supply this small army that now gathered at the southern end of the Niagara River, other events in the Central Theater and elsewhere had occurred that would all influence, in varying degrees, the impending offensive.[98]

In May, Colonel John B. Campbell of the Nineteenth Infantry and commander of army troops at Erie undertook, on his own authority, a raid across the lake. Abraham Markle of the Canadian Volunteers accompanied Campbell and probably assisted in planning the operation. Several hundred of Fenton's Pennsylvanians joined about 150 regulars and a detachment of volunteer sailors on the expedition to destroy several mills at Port Dover. Although they were private property, the mills were of considerable military value, as they were indispensable in converting wheat to usable flour. On 15 May, Campbell's mixed band of raiders burned three flour mills, sawmills, distilleries, twenty to thirty private homes, and a dozen barns. They shot livestock, leaving carcasses to rot. Campbell reportedly told the village women that his men's actions were retribution for British depredations at Buffalo, Lewiston, and Havre de Grace. This latest step on the spiraling staircase of retaliation provoked an inquiry from Riall whether the U.S. government had authorized this destruction. Campbell replied that the raid had derived from his orders and that he had planned and conducted the raid on his own responsibility. To his credit, Armstrong immediately ordered an inquiry, and Scott, who presided over the board, exonerated Campbell for the destruction of the mills and distilleries but censured him for the rest. Brown gave Campbell command of the Eleventh Infantry, which John McNeil had so diligently trained. The government's efforts to conduct the war along recognized rules of behavior had once more been foiled by a renegade officer.[99]

After Brown departed Sacketts Harbor in late May, Drummond ordered still another raid against the exposed line of communication between Oswego and the American naval base. Drummond had been quite pleased at the success of the earlier raid on Oswego, but within a week his spy at Sacketts Harbor informed him that the raiders had missed the most important targets—the heavy guns and cable. The spy noted that Chauncey could not complete his large vessel without these items and that the guns were too heavy to travel on the poor roads. The spy's message presented the British with yet another opportunity to get ahead in the arms race at comparatively little risk.

At dusk on 28 May, nineteen bateaux loaded with thirty-five guns and ten large cables departed Oswego under command of Master Commandant Melancthon Woolsey. One hundred fifty riflemen under Major Daniel Appling defended the valuable cargo, and about an equal number of Oneida Indians moved by land adjacent to the small flotilla to assist if needed. Before too many hours had passed, a British squadron of gunboats fell into pursuit. At noon the next day, the Americans pulled into Big Sandy Creek with the intention of moving the last several miles to Sacketts Harbor when it became safe to do so. A British force of three gunboats and four other vessels led by Commander Stephen Popham entered the creek searching for the prized ordnance. Instead, they found an ambush. In a matter of minutes, those British who were not dead surrendered. The guns and cable made it safely to Chauncey's boatyard.[100]

In his initial report of the victory to Secretary Jones, Chauncey apparently forgot to mention the army's role in the affair. Although Woolsey was in charge, clearly it was Appling's skillful ambush that led to the one-sided victory. Brown, upon arriving at Buffalo, caught wind of Chauncey's report and wrote confidentially to Armstrong to warn him that the navy appeared to be trying to claim the credit for saving the guns, a move that Brown said he would resist to the utmost. The circumstances of the skirmish at Sandy Creek became too well known for the navy to claim more than its fair share of the glory, but Brown never lost the perception that there was a sinister side to Chauncey and that army-navy cooperation on Lake Ontario was increasingly one-sided. The material result of the failed British raid was that Chauncey had all the guns and cable he needed to complete his fleet, and Yeo had 200 fewer sailors and marines to man his.[101]

While Brown and his subordinates were working at a feverish pace to prepare for the main campaign of the year, Izard's force, which was larger by far than Brown's, was sitting idly along the shores of Lake Champlain. George Izard of South Carolina was one of the few American generals prepared academically for his profession. Before accepting his commission in 1794, Izard had been educated in military schools in Britain, France, and Hesse-Cassel. He resigned in 1803, but with the prospect of war in early 1812, he won commission as the colonel of the Second Artillery. In March of the following year, Madison elevated Izard to the rank of brigadier general; with the promotion came command of the Third Military District and the defense of New York City. Displaced by

Dearborn when Armstrong eased that elderly gentleman from active campaigning, Izard joined Hampton's march to Chateauguay and acceded to command of that force when Hampton resigned his commission in the spring of 1814. Izard wrote to Armstrong on 7 May so that there would be no doubt in the secretary's mind as to the quality of the soldiers who marched out of those dreadful winter quarters at French Mills. Izard reported that his men were wretchedly clothed and equipped. The dragoons had weapons that were largely unserviceable. Drill was poor. Most of the men had been unpaid for months, the riflemen for over a year. Enlistments for the large number of one-year men were due to run out. To top it off, Izard expressed his concern that Armstrong had not defined the extent of Izard's command, and as a result, Izard hesitated to give orders to officers on detached service. Of course, circumstances in Brown's division were similar, but whereas Brown and Scott set about the job of building a fighting force with energy and passion, Izard was content to conduct business as usual. Izard failed to provide vision or motivation to his four brigadiers: William Winder, Alexander Macomb, Thomas Smith, and Daniel Bissell, a foursome of uneven talent. For his part, Armstrong relegated Izard's division to a subordinate role while awaiting the results of recruiting efforts.[102]

According to Madison's strategy for 1814, Izard was expected to build and man fortifications on the south bank of the St. Lawrence to protect the gunboats intended to challenge British control of that river. He was also to make a demonstration toward Montreal to divert attention from Brown's offensive. In response to Izard's pessimistic assessment of the troops under his command, Armstrong wrote: "If the regiments assigned to your division can be filled by even the first day of August next the campaign may be a good one." With this letter, Armstrong had given Izard a start date of 1 August. Armstrong knew that Brown would invade Canada weeks earlier. Thus, the secretary of war limited the potential value of Izard's demonstration by allowing it to begin well after Brown needed to divert Prevost's attention elsewhere.[103]

Armstrong expected Izard to defend the American portion of the Richelieu-Champlain corridor. Implied in this mission was the task of protecting Captain Thomas McDonough's small fleet, which was opposed by a similarly small squadron of the Royal Navy commanded by Captain Daniel Pring and based at Isle aux Noix. Pring ventured into American waters early in May but returned after an unsuccessful attempt to corner McDonough. Anticipating such British forays, Armstrong ordered Izard to seize and fortify Rouse's Point, which was just inside the American border and overlooked a very narrow channel of Lake Champlain. A battery placed here, expounded Armstrong, could fire across the lake, thus interdicting Pring's squadron from entering American waters. This would effectively stop a large-scale British incursion, because supplies to support a major force must of necessity be moved on the lake. Other than a strong garrison to protect the batteries there, the balance of Izard's force would be free for other assignments. In June, Armstrong repeated his preemptory order to Izard to establish a strong blocking position at the narrows. Izard demurred. Citing an inability to protect a battery at Rouse's Point, Izard told the secretary that he would, instead, fortify Cumberland Head. These batteries, though giving some protection to McDonough's flotilla in Plattsburg Bay, could not cover the width of the lake with fire and therefore could not interdict British vessels. Izard's chief engineer later testified that his commander's reservations concerning Rouse's Point were without foundation. Izard's muddled thinking thus defeated Armstrong's purpose. Armstrong chose to believe that Izard's "extraordinary" refusal to obey precise orders originated in unfounded fear. Whatever the reason for Izard's disobedience, there were no guns at Rouse's Point in September when a Royal Navy squadron sailed past carrying supplies for 14,000 British regulars marching toward Albany.[104]

That large invasion force was the direct result of the fall of Napoleon. As Scott trained his slender brigade, Madison's worst nightmare was coming to pass. Tens of thousands of British soldiers and sailors, released from two decades of war with France, were now available for operations elsewhere. In May, while Madison rested at his country home, Armstrong warned his superior of reports appearing in British papers outlining a counteroffensive against America's coastal cities. In order to defend their lengthy coast, the Americans would be obliged to pull troops back from the Canadian border. Thus, according to the logic of the British press, Britain could defend Canada by attacking Boston, New York, Baltimore, or New Orleans. On 26 June, Madison received a 6 May dispatch from Gallatin and Bayard, his negotiators in London. Public opinion in London called for a vigorous prosecution of the war against America. Petitions were being circulated that urged the ministry to limit American fishing rights, clear American shipping from the Great Lakes, and adjust the border southward. Madison and Armstrong took several steps to strengthen the coast. The first of these was to create a new military district. Previously, the commander of the Fifth District was charged with the heavy responsibility of defending all of Maryland, Virginia, and the District of Columbia. On 2 July, Armstrong allocated responsibility for the defense of Maryland, the District of Columbia, and a slice of Virginia across from Washington to a new commander. Armstrong plucked William Winder from Izard's division and gave him command of the Tenth Military District and direct responsibility for the security of the national capital. Madison's concern for the safety of the Atlantic coast was enhanced by a growing disillusionment with the man charged with the conduct of the war on land. Apparently impelled by suspicions of his incompetence, the president ordered Armstrong to turn over to him much of the War Department's correspondence—including the letters between Armstrong and Generals Brown, Izard, and Gaines. Madison sifted through this mass while Brown crossed the Niagara, and the results of his personal investigation contributed to Armstrong's downfall. But along the Niagara River on those hot days at the end of June, the men in Riall's and Brown's divisions waited for the signal that would end their long months of preparation and begin the bloodiest campaign of the war.[105]

Congress and the administration gave ample evidence that the new republic had not mastered the process of conducting war outside its boundaries. Short enlistments in both the regulars and the volunteers ensured that commanders in the field devoted much of their energy to raising and training armies each year rather than enjoying an early start to the campaign season. Madison could not competently wield national power in pursuit of the goals of state. The failure to arrive at an integrated strategic plan until June, even in the face of a growing body of evidence that Britain was about to land hammer blows on a largely unprotected coast, must be laid at the feet of the chief executive. The plan was flawed, though not fatally. The diversion of resources to retake Mackinac robbed Brown of the Erie squadron and about 1,000 troops. The cabinet's attempt to cut the line of communication to the Great Lakes with a paltry force of gunboats rather than the combined might of Brown and Izard speaks to a painful misunderstanding of the lessons of the previous two years of war.

Interservice problems within the Central Theater, largely attributable to the secretaries of war and navy, diluted American strength. Neither Armstrong nor Jones understood that the logic of the naval arms race precluded long-term cooperation between Brown and Chauncey. Armstrong, who possessed the best strategic sense within the administration, nonetheless perpetrated inexcusable failures within the theater of operations. Despite complaints from his two division commanders in the Ninth District, he never defined the extent of their responsibilities or authority, and one might readily attribute this to a conscious and nefarious decision on his part. One of the unanticipated results of Armstrong's failure to unify command within the district was that supply accountability was lost. Thousands of New York volunteers who appeared ready to take the war into Canada were left at their rendezvous points awaiting tentage and cooking pots. The litany of Armstrong's failures continues. There is no evidence that he tried to resolve strategic differences with the secretary of the navy. He failed to coordinate the activities of his two division commanders; Izard was never fully aware of what Brown was doing or of his own role in assisting the main attack. Armstrong's failure to provide resources to Brown, to the main effort of the national strategy, reveals staggering incompetence. His belated efforts to march raw recruits to the Niagara Frontier mocked the serious nature of the daunting task facing Brown. Armstrong knew that Brown's reputation had been established by fighting, not by any demonstration of strategic skill. Yet Armstrong left his new major general to flounder in the development of a campaign plan. His advice to his subordinate was sound, but it was direction, not advice, that Brown wanted early in the year. Fortunately for the Americans, Brown soon realized that he had to take charge himself and not depend on his superior.

Take charge Brown did. His efforts at Sacketts Harbor resulted in the security of that base and the safety of the guns needed to complete Chauncey's fleet. Other than its basic flaw—not striking the British line of communication well to the east—Brown's campaign plan was quite competent. It represented a rational balance of ways, means, and ends. Brown had a sound understanding of the capabilities of his army and of his officers. His decision to give Scott full rein at Buffalo paid handsome dividends during the summer. Scott ensured that the Left Division was, man for man, equal to anything Drummond could throw at the invaders. The men's appearance matched their prowess. In the last days of June, 2,000 new gray uniforms arrived in camp.[105]

In comparison, British efforts during the preparatory phase of the campaign were chiefly successful, for Prevost and his subordinates shared a common understanding of strategic goals and methods. Unity of command of land and sea forces in Upper Canada was vested in Drummond, and he and Yeo worked well together. By judicious use of his political and military powers, Drummond had made prodigious progress in harnessing the slender resources of his province. Prudent application of martial law enabled Drummond's quartermaster officers not only to avert an ominous famine but also to deepen the logistical resources of the army and gain the allegiance of the refugee western Indians. Disaffection was quelled, if not eliminated. Drummond's only failure was his faulty appreciation of the enemy. He based his campaign plan on two assumptions that eventually proved false. First, Drummond expected the Americans to focus their efforts on the recapture of Fort Niagara. Second, Drummond expected the Americans in 1814 to exhibit the same brittleness on the battlefield that they had demonstrated at Queenston Heights, Chateauguay, Crysler's Farm, and Buffalo. This led Drummond to take unjustified risks; he spread his forces too thinly, and he encouraged an unwarranted audacity among his subordinates. The opening battles would determine whether Drummond's flaws would prove fatal or whether they would be offset by the deep-rooted deficiencies within the American military system.

President James Madison by Thomas Sully after Gilbert Stuart. (Courtesy of the
Virginia Historical Society and the Naval Historical Foundation [NH-48047])

Above: Secretary of War John Armstrong by John Wesley Jarvis. (Courtesy of the National Portrait Gallery, Smithsonian Institution [acc. no. NPG.72.12])

Facing page: Major General Jacob Brown by James Herring after John Wesley Jarvis. (Collection of the New-York Historical Society [acc. no. 1923.3, neg. 6384])

Commodore Isaac Chauncey by David Edwin after Joseph Wood. (Courtesy Toronto Reference Library [T-15206])

Major General George Izard. (Courtesy Arkansas History Commission)

MAJOR GEN. WINFIELD SCOTT.
Of the United States Army

Brigadier General Winfield Scott. (Courtesy National Portrait Gallery, Smithsonian Institution [neg. 07910])

Facing page: Brigadier General Eleazar Ripley. (Courtesy Hood Museum of Art, Dartmouth College, Hanover, N.H.; gift of Mrs. A. W. Roberts)

Brigadier General Peter B. Porter. (Courtesy Buffalo and Erie
County Historical Society)

Brigadier General Edmund P. Gaines by Rembrandt Peale. (Courtesy Historical Society of Pennsylvania [acc. no. 1869.2])

Lieutenant General Sir Gordon Drummond by Mrs.
Malcolm Drummond. (Courtesy McCord Museum of
Canadian History, Montreal [M400])

Commodore Sir James Yeo by Henry Cook after Adam Buck. (Courtesy Toronto Reference Library [T-15241])

Lieutenant General Sir George Prevost. (Courtesy Musee du Chateau Ramezay, Montreal)

Fort Niagara as seen from Fort George. (Courtesy National Archives of Canada [C-099561])

Fort George as seen from Fort Niagara. (Courtesy National Archives of Canada [C-000026])

Sacketts Harbor. (Courtesy Naval Historical Foundation [NH-1696])

CHAPTER SEVEN

The Opening Battles

War was a new game to the Americans as they had not seen an hostile engagement in the country these forty years, except with the Indians, but I can assure you they improved by experience and before peace was concluded begun to be a formidable enemy.
—Sergeant James Commins, Eighth Foot, 28 August 1815

On the morning of 2 July 1814, General Jacob Brown, accompanied by Winfield Scott and Peter B. Porter, carefully examined Fort Erie and the far shore where Lake Erie abruptly narrowed into the Niagara River. He returned to his headquarters and met with his brigade commanders and senior engineers to develop a detailed crossing plan. Brown determined that his first objective was the elimination of the British garrison in Fort Erie. With most of the Lake Erie squadron en route to Mackinac in accordance with Madison's ill-conceived plan to retake that distant post, Brown was left with only enough transport to move less than half of his command at a time. Accordingly, he ordered Scott, with the bulk of his brigade, to cross the Niagara and land at about dawn north of Fort Erie; Ripley, with as many men as could be carried in two schooners and two smaller vessels, was to cross the lake and land southwest of the British fort. The schooners would remain offshore, protecting the landing force, while all the other vessels returned to start ferrying the remainder of the division. Meanwhile, Ripley and Scott were to surround the fort to prevent any British from escaping while the artillery blasted them into submission.[1]

As the brigade commanders issued orders, the officers and men made known their eagerness to begin the long-awaited invasion. Brown had kept his intentions secret. He had even accepted an invitation to a Fourth of July dinner hosted by his staff, knowing full well that the dinner, if served at all, would be served in Canada. Riding into Buffalo at about this time was Captain Harris and his troop of dragoons. Just five days earlier, the cavalrymen had been patrolling around

163

Sacketts Harbor, their young commander frustrated at being left out of the action. Upon receipt of orders to join Brown, the jubilant Harris force-marched his men 250 miles, arriving in time to secure space on the transport craft.[2]

That evening, Ripley met with Brown and asked for additional boats so that he might land a larger force in the first wave. He had seen, he told his superior, signs of the enemy near his intended landing beach, and he expected to have to fight his way ashore. Brown would not reallocate vessels so close to loading time. Any additional vessels could come only from Scott, and moving the vessels along the shore might alert the British. In any event, changing the plan at this late hour would delay execution. Ripley resigned on the spot, but Brown refused to accept the proffered resignation, and Ripley relented. Perhaps Ripley had developed cold feet. In any event, this confrontation marked the beginning of Brown's loss of confidence in the commander of the Second Brigade.[3]

At about midnight, the troops assigned to the first wave started climbing into their boats. Scott's men loaded at a beach about halfway between Buffalo and Black Rock, while Ripley loaded his boats in the mouth of Buffalo Creek. As Scott pushed off from shore, Brown, who had been with the First Brigade, ordered his boat to move south toward Ripley's point of embarkation. Only a portion of Ripley's men had boarded the vessels, and their commander was nowhere in sight. An irate Brown left orders for Ripley to depart the shore as soon as possible. Brown then entered the lake, and his oarsmen pulled for Scott's landing beach about a mile and a half away.[4]

The first of Scott's units to land was Jesup's Twenty-fifth Infantry. As they approached shore in the dark and fog, a picket guard from the Nineteenth Light Dragoons fired a volley and withdrew to Fort Erie to sound the alarm. Brown landed shortly after daybreak and found Scott and his first wave formed up and ready for action; the boats were en route to Black Rock to pick up the next wave consisting of the remainder of both Scott's and Ripley's men. Brown ordered Scott to send a battalion forward toward the fort to keep the garrison from fleeing. Off marched Jesup's men and Brown's engineers, McRee and Wood, to reconnoiter the British defenses. Brown, ignorant of Ripley's whereabouts, had a staff officer remain on the beach to gather up Ripley's second wave as it arrived and lead them southwest around Fort Erie to the lakeshore. Thus the British garrison would be caught between the two brigades. Meanwhile, Ripley's pilots had lost their way in the dense fog on the lake and arrived offshore well after dawn. Ripley brought with him some Indians and volunteers, as well as his regulars.[5]

For the next several hours, Brown's troops moved into position. Ripley united both parts of his brigade—those who had sailed with him and those who had landed on Scott's beach—and positioned them near Snake Hill, a sandy rise near the shore and about half a mile south of the fort. While marching his battalion

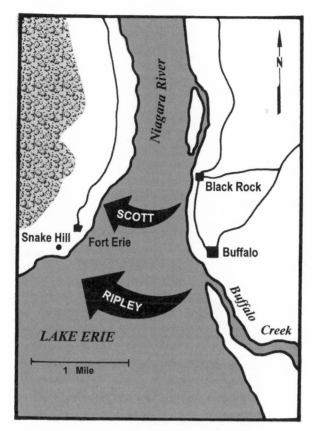

3 July 1814

through the woods, Jesup encountered a local citizen and "by threats and promises" persuaded him to guide the Americans to the fort. As Jesup formed his men in the open and within sight of the fort, a Royal Artillery gun belched fire and thunder. The shrapnel round exploded over the color guard of the Twenty-fifth, wounding four of the six color corporals, whose names became the first on what would become an exceedingly long roster of casualties. Jesup pulled his regiment back into the cover of a wood line.[6]

Major Thomas Buck of the Eighth Foot commanded the garrison of 137 soldiers, mostly infantrymen of the 100th Foot. At his disposal were three guns, none of which fired rounds larger than twelve pounds. Buck believed that he could not hold the fort for very long, for the Americans were certain to have artillery that outranged his field pieces. He consulted with some of his officers and soon decided that it would be better to march his men out as prisoners of war than to see them die in a valiant yet futile effort. As his intentions became apparent to his men, many clamored to defend the fort to the last. Their remonstrances were in vain. Buck sent out a party to discuss terms. They could not have missed the American guns moving into position to open a bombardment. Negotiations proceeded quickly, and at five o'clock a company of the Twenty-fifth Infantry marched into the fort, hauled down the British flag, and posted the regimental colors on the ramparts. Brown transported Buck and his unfortunate command to Buffalo. The Left Division had won a nearly bloodless victory.[7]

Brown's soldiers spent the evening consolidating their toehold in Canada. Brown placed a small garrison in the fort under artillery Lieutenant Patrick McDonough, with the mission of improving and extending the fort's defenses. Brown asked Captain Kennedy to station his schooners off Fort Erie to protect both the fort and the ferrying operations. Throughout the night and into the next day, the river vessels and their oarsmen strained to transfer men, animals, guns, wagons, and supplies to the Canadian shore. Brown ordered Scott to march the following day with his brigade, Towson's company, and Harris's dragoons to capture the bridge over the Chippawa River before the British arrived there in strength. Meanwhile, Porter remained in Buffalo with his brigade (Fenton's Pennsylvanians and Red Jacket's Iroquois), waiting to cross over. Swift's regiment of New York volunteers had begun the march from Batavia, but they were still short of bayonets, sabers, and blankets. Porter was annoyed that it had taken the secretary of war far too long to send equipment "or even [to take] any notice of the existence of such a corps."[8]

The British reaction came quickly. Lieutenant Colonel Thomas Pearson commanded at Chippawa, and as soon as he learned of the American landings, he sent word to Riall at Fort George. Pearson headed south with the flank companies of the 100th Foot, some militiamen, and a handful of Norton's Grand River Indians to size up the invasion force. He found Scott's brigade north of the fort, opposite Black Rock. Pearson remained out of contact, fearful that any Americans landing north of him would cut off his retreat. Pearson was unaware that Buck had surrendered. Riall pushed five companies of Royal Scots south to Chippawa and ordered the Eighth Foot at York to move immediately to Fort George and then on to Chippawa. Riall considered attacking the Americans that night while they were most vulnerable but decided to wait for the arrival of the Eighth Foot. The troops got what little rest they could.[9]

The next morning was Independence Day. Scott's reinforced brigade, the advance guard of the division, marched north toward Chippawa following a single narrow road that hugged the river line. Pearson's mixed battalion, reinforced with the light company of the Royal Scots and a detachment of the Nineteenth Light Dragoons, was determined to slow the American advance and buy time for Riall to strengthen the position at Chippawa. Pearson's troops drove off cattle and horses and burned bridges over the numerous creeks. Unfortunately for the British, the water levels were so low that these streams were readily fordable by men and horses. Scott's foresight in forming sections of pioneers in each regiment now paid dividends. Work parties, supervised by the pioneers, repaired the bridges so that the supply wagons with the main body of the division could cross without delay.

As Scott approached Black Creek, Pearson's men were visible on the far side, prepared to dispute the crossing. Scott ordered Towson's guns to the front to engage the British, Canadians, and Indians. He also ordered Captain Crooker of the Ninth Infantry to take his company on a wide flank march across the creek and to hit Pearson on the right of his line. Under Towson's fire, Pearson withdrew his men, but not before they had removed all the planking from the bridge. Crooker appeared across the stream and in front of Scott, too late to trap Pearson's men. Out in the open and isolated, the company of infantrymen was surprised and charged by Pearson's dragoons. Scott feared the worst; his guns could not be brought to bear on the fast-riding cavalrymen. The quick-thinking Crooker withdrew his men to the cover of a house, and their fire drove off the attackers. Scott was impressed, later writing: "I have witnessed nothing more gallant in partizan war than was the conduct of Captain Crooker and his company." Scott pushed his brigade across the creek and forged ahead.[10]

Pearson made his last attempt to slow down Scott on the open plain south of the Chippawa River. In a brief skirmish, Scott's lead battalion easily brushed aside the defenders. But as Scott rode in sight of Chippawa bridge, he observed a formidable defense. In addition to the entrenchments and blockhouses north of the river, there was a sizable *tête-de-pont* earthwork defended by Royal Artillery guns and flanked by nine companies of the Second Lincoln Militia. British guns opened fire with grape and canister, persuading Scott not to assault but to gather up his men strung out along the road and encamp them south of Street's Creek. Rain began to fall as Scott's men opened their bivouac.[11]

Affairs proceeded at a more leisurely pace for the rest of the American regulars. Not until late in the afternoon did Brown get Ripley's brigade and Hindman's artillery battalion on the route north. For his part, Riall hurried more men to Chippawa, and this force included the main body of Norton's Grand River warriors who were then at Niagara Falls. They arrived in camp after the skirmish and took position in the woods at the extreme west of the British defensive line. The British withdrew north of the river after burning some buildings south of the river that otherwise might have provided cover and concealment to the Americans. As they crossed, the last British removed the planking from the bridge over the Chippawa.[12]

Brown with the main body of the Left Division joined the advance guard at 11 P.M. and immediately encamped south of Scott's men. Brown had written to

Gaines earlier that day to send three eighteen-pound guns with Chauncey's fleet. Brown anticipated augmenting his heavy artillery if it became necessary to bombard Fort George or other defensive works in his way. Brown had earlier requested the commander at Detroit to send heavy artillery, but he had not heard from him, nor would it be easy to move heavy guns from Buffalo if and when they arrived. As Brown received Scott's report and contemplated his options, he formed a plan to attack Riall on 6 July, after Porter's brigade closed on the division. Porter was irritated that Brown had the Third Brigade bringing up the rear; however, he hid it well. All day long and into the night, his men, wagons, and equipment crossed the Niagara. Over 100 of Fenton's Pennsylvanians refused to traverse the border, but almost five times that number followed their officers into Canada. Porter bedded down his men, determined he would march early on the fifth.[13]

Riall, back at Chippawa, pondered his alternatives. He could remain behind the naturally strong river line, backed up by a dozen or more guns. Thus situated, he could easily repel a direct assault and would probably be successful in thwarting a thrust toward his open west flank. But this option did not sit well with the intent of Drummond's instructions; nor did it appeal to Riall's pugnacious spirit. Captain Merritt of the Provincial Light Dragoons described Riall as short, stout, nearsighted, and also "very brave." Riall "is thought by some rather rash, which, by the by, is a good fault in a General officer," remarked the volunteer cavalryman.

Riall decided to attack. He would wait for the Eighth Foot, which was then disembarking at the mouth of the Niagara River and forming up for an all-night march of fourteen miles. Riall ordered the planking to be relaid on the bridge so that he could quickly deploy men and guns onto the plain. He gave orders to Pearson, Norton, and his militia commanders to prepare to occupy the woods and fields between Chippawa and Street's Creek and to harass the American pickets the following morning. Riall expected to stop this invasion in its tracks and throw the Americans back across the Niagara with one determined attack, much like Brock and Sheaffe before him. At least one of his subordinates was not so hopeful. Colonel Hercules Scott, commanding at Burlington Heights, considered "it probable that an attack may soon be made on this post." Upon hearing of Brown's landing, Colonel Scott mobilized his regulars and militia in a crash program to improve the defenses of his important base. Working feverishly, they widened the ditches, repaired picketing, built gun platforms, and emplaced abatis along the natural approaches to the earthworks. As it turned out, neither British officer—not the optimistic general nor the pessimistic colonel—got it right.[14]

The Battle of Chippawa was fought on flat ground between the Chippawa River and Street's Creek. The shore of the Niagara between the mouths of these two lesser streams describes a gentle convex arc, almost two miles long. The

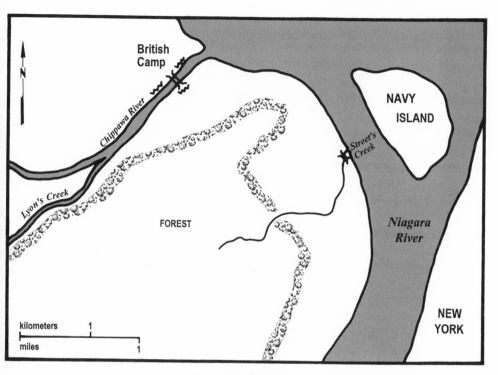

Chippawa Battlefield

ground closest to the Niagara was meadowland, covered in waist-high grasses and partitioned by rail fences. About three-quarters of a mile from the river line lay a primeval woods, dense and cluttered with fallen trees. A tongue of these woods, perhaps 300 or 400 yards wide, stretched to within a quarter mile of the Niagara, thus forming a natural defile in the middle of the otherwise open ground. This tongue of woods also blocked the view between the Chippawa and Street's Creek. About a mile upriver from the mouth of the Chippawa, Lyon's Creek emptied into its much larger brother, their confluence forming a sharp angle. A river-line road connected the wooden bridges across the Chippawa and Street's Creek. North of the Chippawa, in addition to defensive works, were some private dwellings, barracks, and warehouses. South of the river and guarding the bridge was the *tête-de-pont*, an earthen parapet perhaps ten feet high and less than fifty yards long. A few hundred yards west of the mouth of Street's Creek was Samuel Street's farmhouse. The wood line continued south of Street's Creek, and Brown's camp was between this forest and the Niagara.[15]

American operations during the first two days had proceeded satisfactorily. It is a tribute to Brown and Scott that the regulars were mentally and materially prepared to embark on this major operation with only hours of warning. Brown deserves criticism for waiting until the morning of 2 July to plan the details of the river crossing and the reduction of Fort Erie. An opportunity existed for more thorough planning, and such a course of action might have given Ripley greater confidence and forestalled his sour confrontation with Brown.

Buck's surrender of Fort Erie was a mistake, and the major was deservedly court-martialed for his error. He might have evacuated the fort as soon as his dragoons reported the invasion. This would have kept Buck's men out of prisoner stockade but would have forfeited an opportunity to slow the American advance. Despite being outnumbered, Buck might have withstood the bombardment and perhaps thrown back an assault. Depending on how quickly Brown launched an attack, it is not inconceivable that Riall might have arrived to raise the siege. The worst-case scenario (short of surrender) would be that Brown launched an assault quickly, perhaps on 4 July, that overran the defenses. Even this event would have bought time for Riall. One must wonder whether Riall had articulated his defensive plans in sufficient detail to Buck so that the major understood that surrender without a fight was unacceptable.[16]

Lieutenant Colonel Pearson did well in his delaying action. Despite being outnumbered, he forced Scott to stop and maneuver. By the time Scott arrived at the Chippawa River, there were enough forces there to contest a direct assault. Pearson had an opportunity to use his militia and natives even more aggressively in firing from the woods onto Scott's march columns. This annoying measure might have provoked a time-consuming reaction from Scott. But the companies of Pearson's mixed battalion had not worked together before, and such loose tactics might have been beyond his ability to control.

Brown hoped that Scott would seize a crossing over the most difficult natural obstacle between him and Fort George. This would be possible only if Riall offered battle and was defeated south of the river. Riall was inclined to do so if he had the Eighth Foot with him. In the event, Scott did not know the size of the force sitting behind earthen walls at Chippawa, and he was wise to resist any urge to launch an immediate assault.

Early in the morning of 5 July, a party of Grand River Iroquois supported by some militiamen of the Second Lincoln crossed the Chippawa, entered the woods, and moved directly south toward the American camp. Their mission was to harass the enemy pickets and to spy on the Americans. Riall wanted to know the strength of the opposition before him. These Indians and Canadians crossed Street's Creek and worked their way closer to the American camp. At intervals in the forest were American pickets, groups of soldiers whose mission it was to keep the enemy out of musket range of the camp and to sound the alarm in the event of a major attack. Secure behind this screening picket line, Brown met with Scott and Ripley to plan their attack for the next day. Brown was searching for ways to turn Riall's naturally strong position behind the river.[17]

Some Canadians and Indians passed around the pickets and fired their muskets from the wood line toward the encampment hundreds of yards away. This long-range fire was more irritating than effective. However, a body of skirmishers came upon a picket of a few dozen men of the Twenty-first Infantry guarding a forest trail leading toward the camp. The Indians and militiamen fired, surprising the Americans and wounding one of them. The regulars returned fire and fled; their officer, Captain Joseph Treat, ran after them, vainly trying to rally his startled troops. The wounded soldier lay where he was shot. Captain Thomas Biddle was with his battery guarding a corner of the campsite when he heard the nearby fire and saw the gray-jacketed infantrymen running out of the wood line. Without hesitation, he rode straight for the panicked platoon. As he and Treat regrouped the soldiers, up galloped General Brown. Quickly surmising the situation and learning that Treat's men had abandoned a comrade, Brown dismissed Treat from the army on the spot. Biddle led the chastened infantrymen back to their position.[18]

"Anxious that no officer shall remain under my command during this campaign that can be suspected of cowardice," Brown acted without ascertaining the facts. Treat was no coward, although he had lost control of his men for the moment. To his great credit, he refused to leave the army but chose instead to fight as a private for the remainder of the campaign. At the price of one officer's reputation, Brown served notice to the soldiers of the Left Division that he expected them to stand and fight.[19]

Riall received reports from Indians and militiamen, who had climbed trees to get a better view of the American camp, that there were no more than 2,000 Americans in front of him. He inferred that the remainder of Brown's division was still laying siege to Fort Erie, for no report of the fall of that post had reached him. Actually, Brown had about 2,750 men in camp. His bivouac site was squeezed into the narrow corridor between the woods and the Niagara, and it appeared to contain fewer soldiers than it did. Nor was Riall aware that Porter's brigade was even then approaching. As the tired men of the Eighth Foot tramped into Chippawa, General Riall delayed his attack until after these reinforcements had had a few hours' rest. He believed that the Eighth Foot raised his strength to 1,500 regulars and 300 militiamen and natives. Actually, there were more than 2,100 British, Canadians, and Indians under Riall's immediate control. Riall set the attack for 4 P.M. To maintain control of the woods, he sent more native warriors and militiamen into its depths.[20]

After the Treat incident, General Brown, riding south out of camp for three miles, met Porter at the head of his column. As they rode, Brown briefed Porter and ordered him to use his Iroquois, "aided if necessary by the volunteers," to scour the woods and eliminate all enemy south of the Chippawa River. Brown needed the forest secured if he was to move through it the following day in an attempt to turn Riall's flank. Brown expected Porter's men to make a sweeping envelopment through the woods and across Street's Creek, herding the enemy out into the open and toward the Niagara. Brown would assist Porter's movement by having his pickets north of Street's Creek fall back, perhaps luring the enemy closer to the American camp and drawing their attention from their rear. Porter's men moved into an open field south of Ripley's brigade to rest and eat what little food was available, two pieces of hard bread per man. Porter had his men marching at sunrise, and they had not eaten yet that day. Brown rode across Street's Creek bridge to issue his orders to his picket line.[21]

While Fenton's men ate, Red Jacket's Iroquois put on war paint. To distinguish themselves from their enemy, the natives painted red lines on their foreheads and black vertical stripes on their cheeks. They topped off this "uniform" with white headbands. When asked to accompany the native warriors into the forest, the tired and hungry Pennsylvanians balked. To inspire their men, several of Fenton's officers took off their swords, picked up muskets, and volunteered to enter the woods as privates. Three hundred militiamen volunteered to fight, taking off their hats to distinguish themselves from the Canadians. The 200 who chose not to come forward were kept under arms and remained in camp.[22]

Porter had about 850 men to make his sweep. In the open area south of the American camp, he formed the Indians and militiamen into a single file perpendicular to the Niagara. The Iroquois were on the west flank and the Pennsylvanians on the east. Red Jacket was at the front of the slender column, and Porter positioned himself between his two battalions. With Porter was Captain Pollard, the senior war chief after Red Jacket, and Major Wood, the engineer. The line extended for three-quarters of a mile. South of Porter was a company of regulars who would act as a reserve. On command, Porter's thin column walked quietly westward until the Iroquois were in the forest and the Pennsylvanians remained in the open. The men faced right (north), each one close enough to hold hands with the individuals on his flanks. Indian chiefs moved forward about twenty paces, and Indian scouts advanced even farther. About 4 P.M., the long line paced forward slowly and quietly. The scouts found Riall's skirmishers, a body of nearly 100 western Indians, behind the thick bushes along Street's Creek. The signal was passed back to stop. Porter's men prepared to meet the enemy.[23]

Within minutes, the signal to attack was given, and Porter's line surged forward. The western Indians fired first, and many withdrew as the Iroquois and Pennsylvanians waded the creek, emerged on the opposite shore, and gave chase. The fight was confused and fierce as only combat in dense woods can be. War

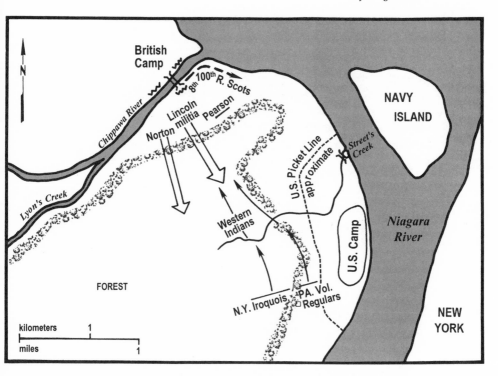

Battle of Chippawa: Forest Fight, 5 July 1814

cries and heavy musket fire pierced the air. Porter's Iroquois line disintegrated into smaller parties moving rapidly northward, bowling over Britain's native allies, scores of whom fought to the end rather than surrender. The Pennsylvanians were drawn into the woods and did their best to keep up with the New York Indians in a running fight. Brown had pulled his picket guards back to Street's farmhouse, only to hear the noise of the fight move northward toward the Chippawa rather than eastward into the open fields. It was then that Brown saw a column of dust rising into the summer sky above the tongue of woods blocking his view of Chippawa bridge. A large number of men were approaching. Unable to recall Porter, who was probably unaware of the new threat, Brown galloped into camp, heading directly for Scott's tent.[24]

Riall started his division crossing the Chippawa bridge at about 4 P.M. His advance guard was Pearson's ad hoc battalion composed of the light companies of the three regular regiments and Lieutenant Colonel Dickson's Second Lincolns. Also out front were about 200 of Norton's Grand River Iroquois. Behind them marched the regulars and two batteries of Royal Artillery, each with three guns. When he heard the musketry and war whoops from Porter's attack, Riall responded by pushing Dickson's militiamen directly into the woods and sending Norton on a wide envelopment west of where the fighting was going on. Pearson's light battalion remained in the open area between the tongue of woods and the bridge. Riall was careful to protect the right flank of his column of regulars as they marched, one battalion at a time, through the defile formed by the tongue of woods and the Niagara.[25]

Brown found Scott's brigade formed up in camp. Scott was about to march his men across Street's Creek and drill them in the open area beyond. Brown ordered Scott to fight the British, whom he believed were en route to attack the American camp. Scott could not believe that Riall would come out from his strong defensive line and accept battle. Nonetheless, he directed his brigade and Towson's company forward across the narrow bridge. Leavenworth's combined battalion of the Ninth and Twenty-second Infantry Regiments led the way, followed by Campbell's Eleventh and Jesup's Twenty-fifth. As the Americans moved steadily over the bridge, shot and grape flew over their heads and landed in the Niagara. In moments the Royal Artillery would get the range right. Brown rode on to alert Ripley to ready his brigade for action.[26]

Porter's Indians and militiamen met Dickson's militia in the forest and, amid hand-to-hand combat, momentarily forced the Canadians back out of the woods and through Pearson's regulars. As some of the New York Iroquois emerged on the far side of the forest, they were met with a volley from Pearson's regulars. This was enough to prompt their retreat. Porter, still in the woods with the Pennsylvanians, rallied those Iroquois he could and led them all to the wood line. Now it was their turn to face the concentrated firepower of Pearson's light infantrymen. Pearson's men fired one volley and then attacked. Porter ordered a retreat. That proved an unnecessary gesture; those still with him broke and fled, pursued by Canadians and Indians.[27]

Porter lost control of his brigade. It disintegrated, although his men had suffered only light casualties. Porter later reported twelve dead among his command. The casualties on the British side were calamitous; the New York Iroquois searching the woods the next day found the bodies of eighty-seven Canadian Indians and eighteen militiamen. Lieutenant Colonel Dickson had entered the forest fight with 110 militiamen in four companies. He reported forty-seven casualties, including three of his company commanders killed in action. The loyalists on the Niagara Peninsula and their Indian allies paid a heavy price that day to repel American aggression. The result of the forest fight, however, was that as the regulars formed up in battle line, the British had two secure flanks, but Brown still had to take measures to protect his forest flank.[28]

When the Royal Scots and the 100th Foot cleared the defile, they came abreast of one another, the Royal Scots closer to the river. The Royal Scots was under the command of Lieutenant Colonel John Gordon; George Hay, the Marquis of Tweeddale, commanded the 100th. Tweeddale, who had considerable combat experience in the Peninsular War, had joined his new command only days earlier. These two battalions moved forward, with their companies still in column, to make room for the Eighth Foot bringing up the rear. The Eighth was commanded by Major Thomas Evans. The battery firing on Street's Creek bridge was positioned on the river road by Captain Mackonochie, Riall's senior artilleryman. This battery consisted of heavy guns: two twenty-four-pounders and a five-and-a-half-inch howitzer. Riall sent his second battery, consisting of three six-pounders, to the right or west of his line. With the Eighth Foot in reserve, Riall presented a balanced attack to the Americans. As they drew nearer, the Royal Scots and the 100th deployed into a two-rank-deep line formation.[29]

Captain Towson, Scott's artillery commander, set up his battery of two six-pounders and a howitzer immediately across the bridge between the river road and the Niagara. He returned the fire of the heavier British guns while Major Leavenworth brought his battalion onto the line with its right anchored to the road. Next across the bridge was Colonel Campbell, who brought the Eleventh Infantry up on line on the left of Leavenworth's troops. Campbell suddenly collapsed of a severe knee wound. As Campbell was evacuated to the rear, Major John McNeil assumed command. Towson's guns were in danger of being masked by Leavenworth's battalion, which had moved beyond the battery. Towson quickly displaced his guns forward and alongside Leavenworth. Riall, seeing the gray uniforms of the First Brigade, remarked optimistically to Tweeddale that he should have no trouble defeating what were obviously militiamen. As Scott's men marched steadily, smartly onto line, heedless of the shots and shells screaming into their ranks, Riall amended his earlier pronouncement. "Damn," he blurted out to the twenty-seven-year-old marquis, "these are regulars!" Last to cross the bridge and deploy was Jesup's Twenty-fifth. Scott, seeing a stream of friendly natives and Pennsylvanians withdrawing along the margin of the forest, sent Jesup to the far left and into the wood line to guard the brigade flank and to envelop the British battle line. With Jesup operating independently, Scott focused his attention on McNeil's and Leavenworth's men. At this point, the two battle lines were formed, and Scott and Riall moved their men into musket range.[30]

Both sides had some room to maneuver. By most accounts, the open meadow was approximately 1,300 yards across, from the woods to the river. The Royal Scots and the 100th, in lines only two men deep and with their light companies detached, occupied about 225 and 200 yards of front, respectively. Leavenworth's men, three deep, took up only 190 yards; McNeil's, likewise three deep, about 140 yards. Jesup's men were at least partially in the woods, and the artillery batteries probably presented a frontage of 40 yards each. Not including the

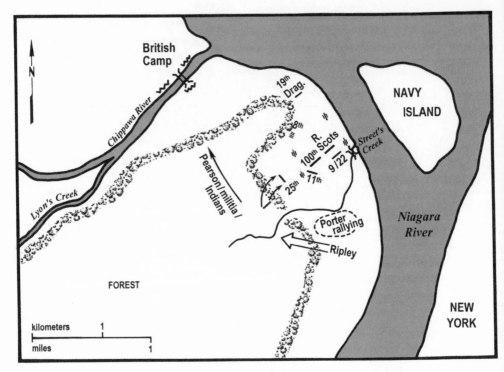

Battle of Chippawa: Climax

Eighth Foot (450 muskets), which was held in reserve, Riall brought six guns and about 950 muskets into the fight, while Scott had three cannon and 1,000 muskets. Jesup added about 350 muskets, although he seems initially to have fought Pearson's men (perhaps 150 still in the fight) in the woods. When Brown brought up four more guns, the sides were quite evenly matched.

The Royal Scots and the 100th Foot had only a short gap between them as they advanced alongside each other. However, Riall did not coordinate their movement, and Evans and Tweeddale moved their battalions independently. As they marched forward, they left the supporting artillery behind. These guns were never more than 500 yards from Scott's brigade, and they kept up a brisk and effective fire. The battery near the Niagara directed its fire at Leavenworth's men and Towson's guns, disabling one cannon early in the fight. In Leavenworth's battalion, a shot nearly severed Captain Harrison's leg. Harrison refused any assistance until after the battle. Scott reported that "so glorious a display of fortitude had the happiest effect." The American officers were determined to win, and they transmitted this notion to the men.[31]

Scott had left a wide gap between Leavenworth's and McNeil's battalions.

As the British advanced, they were overlapped by the Americans, who were also moving forward. Seeing potential in this juxtaposition, Scott ordered NcNeil to move even farther to the west, increasing the distance between him and Leavenworth. As the lines closed to musket distance, they opened fire. Scott ordered NcNeil to throw forward his left flank, thus forming a funnel into which the British marched. Scott's aides rode behind the two battalions transmitting McNeil's and Leavenworth's orders, the noise being so great that the battalion commanders' voices were drowned out. Now aware that Porter's brigade was effectively out of action, Brown sent Captain Harris to rally the fugitives with his dragoons and form them up behind Street's Creek. With Porter's men gone, Jesup was stranded on the left. Brown sent word to Ripley to bring his brigade forward inside the wood line, so as not to be seen by the British. Attacking out of the woods, Ripley might trap the British. When he received the order, Ripley promptly led his men forward. Brown noticed Captain John Ritchie's artillery company crossing the bridge, and he ordered the four guns into action on McNeil's left.[32]

The firefight was fierce, with neither side willing to give an inch. Tweeddale and Gordon led their regiments on horseback but dismounted as the musketry began. Gordon was an early casualty, shot through the mouth and unable to give commands. As Tweeddale's 100th moved further, its right flank was much closer to McNeil's oblique battalion than the rest of the regiment and consequently in greater danger of envelopment. Riall ordered Evans's Eighth Foot to come up on Tweeddale's right, but the battle reached its climax before Evans could get there. Both sides loaded and fired furiously, the American fire—musket balls accompanied by three buckshot—causing greater destruction. A lucky shot from one of Towson's guns exploded an ammunition wagon, momentarily distracting the British artillerists. Then Towson turned his gunfire toward the left flank of the Royal Scots. In the woods, Pearson's battalion kept up a galling fire on Jesup's Twenty-fifth. Jesup ordered an attack that threw back the outnumbered and tired light infantrymen. He sent a company to pursue the withdrawing British. Jesup now entered the main arena. He moved completely out of the woods and wheeled his line to the east. Ordering his men to "support arms," he marched forward toward the 100th and the Eighth Foot. The Twenty-fifth halted, fired three volleys, and charged. So did McNeil, followed by Leavenworth. This was too much for the British infantrymen, who faltered and fell back despite the efforts of their officers to keep them in the fight. Tweeddale moved to his grenadier company, only to see its commander fall. The other two company officers were also down. Then it was Tweeddale's turn; a bullet severed his Achilles tendon. Placed on his horse, he watched helplessly as his battalion pulled back in the face of overwhelming fire delivered to its front and flank. The Royal Scots fell back with them.[33]

Riall tried to rally his men. He and his aide rode between the two lines in a brave but vain attempt to encourage the troops. An American musket ball seriously wounded the aide, and Riall, who judged his forces heavily outnumbered, decided that it would be best to impose control over the withdrawal. Between the British and safety were two narrow points: the defile between the woods and the Niagara River, and the bridge over the Chippawa. His command was in danger of complete destruction if the Americans pursued with any vigor. The Nineteenth Dragoons charged forward and covered the withdrawal of the Royal Artillery battery, which was closest to the river. Pearson's hard-used battalion reappeared and, along with the Eighth Foot, formed a screen behind which the officers of the other two battalions re-formed their men. Once re-formed, they quickly marched around the *tête-de-pont* battery and across the Chippawa to safety.[34]

Various American participants claimed that Brown quickly launched a pursuit, but these claims fall to the evidence. When the British line faltered, the Americans were as close as eighty yards away, McNeil's men perhaps even closer. Jesup's Twenty-fifth was nearly behind the 100th Foot. Riall got his men away because neither Brown nor Scott ordered an immediate charge, one that could not have failed to catch up with the British as they fell back through the defile or tried to move around the *tête-de-pont* battery and over the bridge. Riall had at least 1,200 unwounded regulars, scores of walking wounded, and six guns under his command south of the Chippawa when he acknowledged that he must withdraw or lose them all. Many of his soldiers were carrying their wounded comrades with them. Even at a run, it would have taken several minutes for this mass of men, horses, and limbers to cross the Chippawa bridge.[35]

Eventually, Scott moved his brigade through the defile and into view of the *tête-de-pont* battery. The British guns opened fire as soon as the withdrawing infantry cleared their field of fire. Porter brought up about 200 of his men on Scott's left, and Ripley's brigade arrived also. Hindman brought up nearly all his guns, and Brown's first inclination was to storm the *tête-de-pont* and seize the bridge. Scott and Major Wood, the engineer, convinced Brown that the price would be too steep. Brown, who had planned to turn the British position the next day anyway, ordered his division back to camp as the sun was setting.[36]

In an oft-quoted passage, Henry Adams wrote: "The Battle of Chippawa was the only occasion during the war when equal bodies of regular troops met face to face, in extended lines on an open plain in broad daylight, without advantage of position; and never again after that combat was an army of American regulars beaten by British troops. Small as the affair was, and unimportant in military results, it gave to the United States army a character and pride it had never before possessed."[37] J. W. Fortescue pronounced that "it was evident that the experience of two campaigns had at last turned the Americans into soldiers who were not to be trifled with."[38] Although these conclusions are superficially satisfying, the Battle of Chippawa deserves a more thorough analysis, perhaps by investigating its principals.

Riall offered battle in keeping with Drummond's instructions. Riall correctly read his chief when he inferred that he should not shrink from taking any judicious opportunity to attack the Americans. Their well-established reputation for brittle troops and cautious commanders reduced the risks. Riall believed that he was confronting only an advance guard of 2,000, most of which appeared to be militiamen. He assumed that the main body of Americans, perhaps as many as 8,000, was still besieging Fort Erie, because no one had told him otherwise. He might be gently criticized for not verifying that information, perhaps by interrogating prisoners or scouting out the fort itself. Norton's Indians were equal to either task.[39]

A British victory would go a long way toward stopping the American advance and might lead to raising the alleged siege at Fort Erie. Presumably, Riall planned a direct assault south across the creek and into the American camp. There is no hard evidence that documents Riall's attack plan. There is no reason to believe that Riall expected to meet Brown north of Street's Creek; after all, Riall came out of his camp first. When he began to cross the Chippawa, the forest was in British hands; thus, he could anticipate secure flanks all the way to the American lines. Even if this maneuver were successful, however, the Americans had an open escape route back to Fort Erie and numerous positions from which to delay their pursuers. Although he might knock it back, there was little chance that Riall could destroy an advance guard. As well, Riall might have considered attacking from the west and pushing the Americans into the Niagara. Scouts could lead his regulars through the woods to positions opposite the American camp. Given the supposed brittleness of the foe, such a venture should render decisive results. Certainly, Riall could have infiltrated a body of Indians and light infantry through the forest to a blocking position south of the American camp. If Riall's direct assault from the north was successful, the Americans, trapped, might very well surrender. As it was, Riall's decision to attack was bold, but his plan lacked imagination and would probably not be decisive.

On the battlefield, Riall's generalship was unexceptional. He did not coordinate the movements of his two lead battalions. He committed his reserve, the Eighth Foot, too late to matter and thus lost the effect of hundreds of muskets. As a result, the 100th marched bravely into a firestorm. There is no evidence that Riall maneuvered his two batteries once they were in position. For this he can probably be forgiven, since their fire would cease while they displaced forward. Riall performed well during the withdrawal, saving his division from likely destruction. But he was aided more by Brown's hesitancy than by any action on his part.

Brown's handling of his division was adequate, but not without room for criticism. Planning to turn Riall's position on the sixth, Brown was surprised that the British came out from behind their naturally strong position to offer battle. He made the correct decision to accept battle before Riall had a chance to reconsider. Brown must have wondered why Riall would attack with obstacles on three sides, since retreat would be potentially devastating. An American victory on the Chippawa would open the road all the way to Queenston Heights and bring Brown closer to Chauncey. Brown could have settled for throwing back Riall's attack. To do this, he merely had to form Scott's men on the south bank of Street's Creek. Without hesitating, however, Brown threw Scott onto the open plain beyond the creek. This ensured that Scott was in a better position to support Porter, and victory on the plain had the potential for being decisive.

During the battle, Brown left Scott to fight his brigade while Brown tried to bring the rest of the division into action. He failed in this. Most of Hindman's artillery battalion never got into the fight. His idea to envelop the British with Ripley's brigade was inspired, as it would lead to a decisive victory. Controversy surrounds this event. Brown recalled ordering the envelopment within minutes of spying the dust rise above the Chippawa bridge. Other observers noted that Brown's first order to Ripley was to prepare for battle, guard the artillery park, and await further orders. The order to move through the woods undetected and to fall on Riall's flank probably came later. There is no evidence that Brown and Scott talked once battle was joined, and Scott probably did not understand that the decisive blow would be delivered by Ripley. Had he understood his role, Scott might have held the British in position rather than maneuver McNeil to hasten their collapse and withdrawal. The precipitous British retreat eliminated any chance that Ripley's men, moving in column through the woods, could catch up with the flow of battle.[40]

Scott stands out as the person most closely associated with the American victory, not only for his inspirational leadership and direction of his brigade on the battlefield but also for his work at Buffalo in preparing the regulars of the Left Division for the campaign. Brown stated nothing less than the truth when he penned this assessment to Armstrong: "Brig[adier] Gen[era]l Scott is entitled to the highest honors our country can bestow to him, more than to any other man, am I indebted for the victory of the fifth of July."[41] Scott handled his three battalions and Towson's battery with precision, issuing clear orders appropriately timed for best effect. There can be no doubt that the long days of drill in Buffalo paid big dividends. The brigade formed quickly under fire and maneuvered skillfully. The days of floundering on the battlefield, of which Crysler's Farm was an example, were over.

Scott's error was in not continuing his attack on the British as they withdrew. By allowing Riall to successfully break contact, Scott forfeited all that a prompt pursuit might have yielded. Brown, as division commander, shares some of the responsibility for this failing. His last order to Harris was to round up the fugitives from Porter's brigade. A more useful mission would have been to ride down the fleeing British. Nonetheless, the greater share of responsibility falls to Scott, for he was closest to the action, and the forces that were positioned to make the pursuit were his. The failure to destroy Riall's division in the open haunted the American campaign for the next several weeks.

Porter did well, considering that his Iroquois and militiamen had not trained together. Given the mission to clear the enemy from the deep and dense woods, Porter chose an appropriate formation and moved with a sense of urgency. He probably knew that he would lose control once heavy contact was made, but that is the nature of forest warfare. Porter had second thoughts on his handling of the brigade as it came to the northern edge of the woods and ran into Pearson's light infantry. He wrote to Governor Tompkins: "I rallied and led a scattered line, (formed to scour the woods and not to fight a regular force,) exhausted by the fatigue of pursuit a second time, against a compact line of British regular troops perfectly fresh . . . by which I lost several valuable officers."[42] Porter was probably concerned for the reputations of both his brigade and himself. In the glorious victory, Porter's men played what would appear to many to be an inglorious part. They had not left Brown's flank secure, and many saw Red Jacket's Indians and Fenton's volunteers fleeing the battlefield.

The regulars uncovered evidence of the ferocity of the forest fight and the fighting prowess of Porter's men in the days following the battle, as scores of enemy bodies were removed from the woods. In his official report to Armstrong, Brown wrote that Porter's conduct was "gallant." Brown, who had a good understanding of the brittleness of inadequately trained militiamen, was neither surprised nor disturbed that Porter's brigade had broken when confronted by regulars. He continued to give his Third Brigade missions consistent with their capabilities. To Porter's continued dismay, this often meant guarding prisoners and supplies.[43]

One might expect that the battle toll would fall unevenly across the units in proximity to the fighting, and a quick glance reveals that such was the case. The following table illustrates the distribution of American casualties among all the units with Brown in his Street's Creek camp.

	Troops Present in Camp	*Casualties*	*Percent*
Scott's brigade	1,380	262	19.0
Ripley's brigade	1,029	8	.8
Porter's brigade	1,250	35	2.8
Hindman's artillery	317	20	6.3
Harris's dragoons	60	0	0.0
Total	4,036	325	8.0

Of course, these units were involved in the fight in varying degrees—Ripley's men, for example, hardly making contact at all. Also, some units had everyone in battle (e.g., First Brigade), whereas others had some proportion of their soldiers left out of battle. By identifying troops in heavy contact, American casualties look like this:

	Troops in Heavy Contact	*Percent Casualties*
Scott's brigade	1,380	19
Porter's brigade	636	6
Towson's company	89	22
Total	2,105	15

Casualties fell severely among Scott's and Towson's men. Every fifth man was dead or wounded seriously enough to be treated and perhaps evacuated. Other units might break under such stress, being unable to meet the enemy again. Scott's and Towson's troops performed admirably at Lundy's Lane and during the long siege of Fort Erie. The training at Buffalo and the quality of leadership combined to keep these men in the fight in spite of severe casualties at Chippawa.

An analysis of British casualties is likewise revealing. It is difficult to say how many troops participated in Riall's attack, but it seems likely that this number exceeded that which Riall reported to Drummond. In his official report, Riall claimed that he crossed the Chippawa River with 1,500 regulars and 300 militiamen and Indians. The following chart uses figures consistent with the bulk of the documentary evidence.

	Troops in the Attack	*Casualties*	*Percent*
Royal Scots	500	128	25
Eighth Foot	480	27	6
100th Foot	450	204	45
Other regulars	100–150	13	9–13
(staff officers, gunners, artillery drivers, and dragoons)			
Lincoln militia	300	43	14
Native warriors	300–400	70–100	25
Total	2,130–2,280	485–515	20 +/-

The number of casualties had to be Riall's best estimate, since the Americans were left in possession of the battlefield. When the British sent an officer under a flag of truce to ask to recover their dead, Brown reportedly responded: "Tell General Riall that I can bury all the men I can kill."[44] Although this version of events is perhaps apocryphal, it appears that Riall compiled his estimate from roll calls conducted by the units shortly after battle.

Casualties were highest among the 100th Foot, which was caught in a firestorm delivered from both front and flank. This regiment was mauled, and the Royal Scots was severely damaged. That these two battalions endured such heavy punishment before withdrawing speaks to the famous steadfastness of the British infantryman and the example of his officers.

A curious inference derives from an examination of the types of casualties reported by the British infantry.

	Killed	*Wounded*	*Missing*
Royal Scots	63	35	30
Eighth Foot	3	24	—
100th Foot	69	134	1

The Royal Scots reported a large proportion of soldiers missing in action. Presumably, these were soldiers left dead, wounded, captured, or deserted south of the Chippawa. The 100th, which suffered the lion's share of casualties, reported only one man unaccounted for. Perhaps the 100th Foot was a more cohesive unit than the Royal Scots, its soldiers bringing back as many wounded as possible during the withdrawal. Considering that the 100th was savaged in the firefight, a more likely inference is that the surviving officers were too battle shocked or too busy to compute their losses correctly and chose to designate all unknowns as killed or wounded. The wounded Tweeddale, when he got his men safely into camp after the battle, reported turning command over to "the only subaltern who was slightly wounded."[45]

Riall spent the next day writing his reports and getting his little army into shape to fight again. He was determined to hold the Americans south of the Chippawa for as long as he could while waiting for reinforcements. The Lincoln militia had been hard hit, and some militiamen departed to look after their families.[46] Likewise, many of the western and Grand River Indians, disillusioned by the heavy casualties suffered the previous day, disappeared from camp. Riall was convinced that he was greatly outnumbered and feared that Brown would try to outflank the British base by crossing the Chippawa farther upstream. That was exactly Brown's intent.

The Left Division spent much of 6 and 7 July moving the wounded, both friends and enemies, to Buffalo and burying the dead. The Americans scoured the battlefield collecting weapons and equipment. About twenty Iroquois chiefs visited Porter with the scalps taken during and after battle, expecting the brigade commander to pay a bounty. When Porter refused to meet their demands, the natives destroyed the scalps by burning them or throwing them into the Niagara. Porter did agree, however, to pay for nearly twenty prisoners taken in the forest fight. The Iroquois then returned to the scene of their fight to recover the bodies of their comrades. Porter later recalled that upon their return from the woods, the Indians told him of finding three wounded enemy Indians. Red Jacket's men slit the throats of two of them but recognized the third as one of their own who had moved to the Grand River. This former comrade was given a canteen of water and left alone to die. The sight of so many dead natives, many of them Iroquois, left a powerful impression on Red Jacket and his war chiefs.[47]

Elation over a grand victory was tempered by the notion that the American campaign plan was no further along than it had been on the morning of 5 July, but now Brown's battle-tested army was engaged in cleaning up the battlefield and preparing for the next move. Brown wrote to Armstrong: "I will advance, not doubting but the gallant and accomplished soldiers that I have the honor to command, will break down all opposition, to the Shores of Ontario north of Fort George when, if Commodore Chauncey *can* meet us, it is well, if he *cannot*, this Army will trust in the smiles of Providence upon our just and honorable cause, and endeavor not to be disgraced."[48] Brown understood that his victory over Riall had not been decisive, and without Chauncey, his gains might be limited to operations within supporting distance of his supply depots on the American side of the border. But his immediate problem was how to pry Riall out of his strong position on the Chippawa. There were two bridges over the river obstacle. The first, at its mouth, was guarded by the British base, and they had removed the planking. The second bridge over the Chippawa was about sixteen miles upriver at a place coincidentally called Brown's, but the roads leading there were poor. Jacob Brown needed something closer, and as if in response to his letter to Armstrong, Providence smiled upon the Left Division. On the evening of 6 July, a local citizen offered the information of "an old timber road" that led from the battlefield to the confluence of Lyon's Creek and the Chippawa.[49]

At dawn on 7 July, Jesup and Wood scouted out the unused and overgrown road and reported its condition to Brown. The division commander decided to look for himself, and Wood led Brown, Porter, and McRee along the trail. Brown liked what he saw and ordered Ripley to open the road and force a crossing of the Chippawa with his brigade and two companies of Hindman's artillery. Brown ordered Scott to maintain a threatening presence south of the British camp to distract Riall's attention from Ripley's activities upstream.[50]

For the remainder of the day, Brown's engineer officers, McRee and Wood, directed work parties to clear the trail sufficiently for artillery and wagons to pass. On the next day, Ripley brought his men and cannon one and a half miles

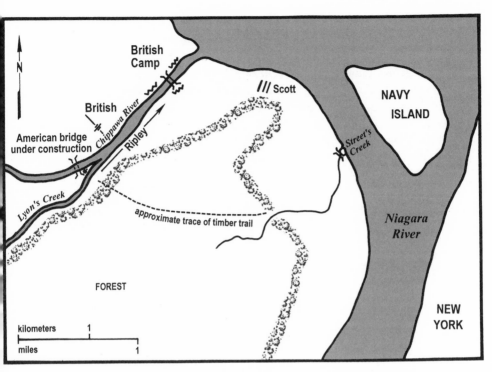

8 July 1814

from camp to the soft, wet ground where Lyon's Creek entered the Chippawa. Ripley had with him wagons loaded with small boats and planking with which to build the bridge. Fording Lyon's Creek, Hindman set up his guns on a rise of land in the angle formed between the two bodies of water. He covered the infantrymen as they built a bridge over the wide Chippawa. Concerned that Ripley might not push the project as energetically as he might, Brown rode out to take charge personally.

Riall, learning of the Americans threatening his flank, sent 400 men and three guns to oppose their crossing. This was not enough, and the American artillery drove off the British. Believing his force to be greatly outnumbered, Riall reasoned that he could not prevent Brown's attempt to outflank him. Choosing to save his army from another costly defeat, Riall gave the order to abandon the camp on the Chippawa and to withdraw as quickly as possible to the safety of Fort George.[51]

Scott discovered the British moving out and sent word to Brown, who ordered Ripley's men to stop work on the bridge, now halfway across the river. Instead, Brown ordered the Second Brigade to march along a trail on the south bank of the Chippawa to unite with the First Brigade. Riall's force at Chippawa quickly dwindled down to a rear guard of dragoons and some guns. Harris tried to get his company across the river to pursue, but his horses refused to swim across. Brown came upon the scene, and Captain Harris asked permission to swim his men across, leaving their mounts on the southern shore. Brown agreed. Into the water plunged the intrepid cavalrymen. Reaching the opposite shore, Harris confirmed that the British had indeed evacuated their camp. To honor Harris, Brown ordered the Left Division to use his name as the countersign that evening. Brown ordered boats brought up, and all through the night the regulars ferried themselves across.[52]

While Riall was pressing his men northward as fast as they could march, Lieutenant General Drummond, in Kingston, was reading Riall's initial report of the costly setback on 5 July. Drummond was unwilling to give up the Niagara Peninsula after one battle, and he took immediate steps to reinforce Riall. Drummond pushed the troops in his province up Lake Ontario, while depending on Prevost to backfill these with units from Lower Canada. The Volunteer Battalion of Incorporated Militia had already joined Riall from York. Drummond ordered the Glengarry Light Infantry Fencibles to Burlington from York, where they were replaced by the Eighty-ninth Foot. That battalion, under its aggressive commander Lieutenant Colonel Joseph Morrison, had gained renown for its tactical skills displayed at Crysler's Farm. Drummond decided to keep two battalions at Kingston, the 104th Foot and De Watteville's, at least until Prevost could replace them from the lower province. Since Chauncey had not yet sailed from Sacketts Harbor, Drummond felt secure about sending reinforcements for the Right Division by water. To do so, he had to divert bateaux from the supply convoys to carry the soldiers. Drummond feared that he could not feed a large army west of York, particularly if the U.S. Navy appeared, but that concern did not stop him from deploying enough combat power to challenge Brown.[53]

Drummond's decision to waste no time in reinforcing Riall was fortunate, because the British were about to lose hundreds of their native allies. Once the passion of battle subsided, Red Jacket and his subordinate chiefs assessed the carnage of the forest fight. Although many of the bodies removed from the woods were those of western Indians, most were Iroquois. The New York Iroquois recognized friends and relatives among the slain. Red Jacket, with Brown's approval, quietly sent emissaries to Norton's camp at Burlington to sound out the Grand River Indians on a proposal to mutually withdraw from the war. Meanwhile, the western Indians at Chippawa reported to the Prophet near Burlington their suspicion that the British were giving up the struggle on the Niagara. Always distrustful of British intentions, particularly after Major General Henry Procter had withdrawn from the fight in the West the previous fall, the Prophet sent a delegation to ask Norton if the British were once again aban-

doning their Indian allies. Before Norton could answer the Prophet, the circumstantial evidence, long columns of redcoats streaming north toward Fort
George, persuaded the last of Tecumseh's followers that no good would be
accomplished by remaining in the field. Although a handful stayed on with Norton, most of the western warriors withdrew from the campaign.[54]

Meanwhile, Red Jacket's emissaries met with their fellow Iroquois in council near Burlington. Many natives saw that the Iroquois Nation was being
ground up in this dispute between white men, a pattern that had been repeated
since the wars between France and Britain. As was the Indian way, the decision
to continue the fight or to withdraw was left up to each individual. The majority of Grand River Indians agreed to honor Red Jacket's proposal of mutual
neutrality and waited for word that the New York Iroquois had returned home.
Norton, John Brant, and a handful of their followers would fight for the cause
they held in common with Great Britain at Lundy's Lane and Fort Erie, but
within days, large-scale Iroquois participation in the War of 1812 would be at
an end. Red Jacket the nationalist had won; he got the Iroquois out of the war
with honor.[55]

On the evening of 8 July, the main body of Riall's division marched to Fort
George while Brown's division was crossing the Chippawa. The two forces were
still quite evenly matched. On the following morning, most of the Left Division
was across the Chippawa. Brown sent his cavalry, now reinforced by 150 New
York mounted volunteers under Captain Boughton, to pick up Riall's trail and
secure the routes northward. A party of Red Jacket's warriors also scouted the
woods north of the river. Brown wanted to destroy Riall's division before it was
reinforced. If Chauncey showed up to cut the British supply lines into the Niagara Peninsula and prevent Riall from escaping by water, Brown believed that
he would be able to accomplish his goal. Even if Riall holed up in Fort George,
Chauncey's large guns would batter down those timber walls. Brown was skeptical that Chauncey would appear, and without the navy, Brown's task was much
more difficult. The American commander was confident, however, that his army
could defeat Riall again in a stand-up fight with anything like even odds. Brown
hoped and believed that the British commander would halt his flight at the
earthen fortification on Queenston Heights. Therefore, he made his plans to
attack him there.[56]

Brown ordered the men of his two brigades of regulars to carry three days'
rations in their haversacks. At noon they would march north from Chippawa
toward Queenston Heights. He ordered Porter to remain at Chippawa guarding
the baggage, supplies, and battering train (four eighteen-pound guns). Brown
did not have enough wagons and teams to bring his supplies with him on the
march, and the rapids leading to Niagara Falls began at Chippawa, so river traffic north was impossible. A captain of Fenton's volunteers refused to cross the

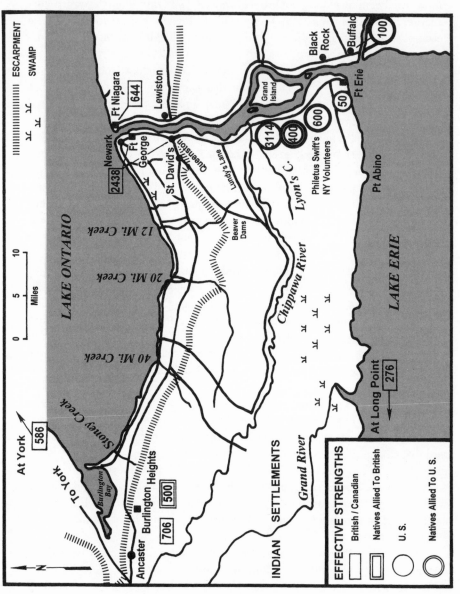

Effective Strengths, 8 July 1814

Chippawa and tried to convince his men not to cross. Brown ordered the recalcitrant officer and other malcontents back to Fort Erie to work on the improvements being made there. At 1 P.M. on 9 July, the Left Division began its march to Queenston Heights.[57]

Along the route of march, Red Jacket's Iroquois roved the woods and harassed the farm families still in their homes. They also found and seized several score barrels of wine and brandy, which Brown ordered confiscated, to the general disappointment of the native warriors. Marching past the magnificent falls without stopping, Brown's regulars arrived at Queenston Heights at 5 P.M. To Brown's great disappointment, Riall had not accepted battle but had blown up parts of the fortification and abandoned the heights and Queenston village below. Riall's men left large quantities of entrenching tools and supplies in the earthworks as evidence of their haste or, more likely, lack of wagons and teams. Brown sent out scouts in all directions, but no British were found, and all signs indicated that Riall had marched north to Fort George. Riall had indeed gotten his men into the relative safety of the fort, and he sent the last of his wounded to York by schooner. Brown decided to bring the remainder of his division and his supplies to Queenston and wait for Chauncey.[58]

As Brown consolidated the Left Division at Queenston on 10 July, he was pleased to receive into camp two groups of reinforcements. Lieutenant Colonel Philetus Swift's regiment of New York volunteers, about 600 strong, joined Porter's brigade. This made up for the loss of those Pennsylvanians who, refusing to continue, had remained in Buffalo or had been sent back to Fort Erie. Also marching into camp was a company of bombardiers, sappers, and miners under Lieutenants Douglass and Story. This unique unit, with both artillery and field engineering skills, had been a demonstration company at West Point when it received orders to join the Left Division. Brown assigned the unit to Hindman's artillery, and Hindman gave engineer Lieutenant David Douglass command of half of his battering train—two heavy eighteen-pound guns, each pulled by six horses.[59]

Brown set up an extended camp with Porter and most of the artillery atop the heights and the regulars in a broad semicircle around the village of Queenston. Refusing to depend entirely on Chauncey's arrival for the success of the campaign, Brown sent an order to Gaines to load five eighteen-pound guns and the rifle regiment in boats and move them along the shore of Lake Ontario to the mouth of the Genesee. There they were to await further orders. In the near future, Brown might have to decide whether to lay siege to Fort George without naval assistance or to bypass it and move on Burlington. Brown apparently feared that his few heavy guns would not be sufficient to batter down the walls of Fort George.[60]

Riall was not sanguine about the capability of Fort George's walls to withstand the American guns. He wrote to Drummond that the fort would likely fall if subjected to a bombardment. With the initiative clearly in American hands and Brown at Queenston, Riall and Drummond pondered their next move. Drummond was gravely disappointed that Major Buck at Fort Erie had failed to keep the Americans in check for several days, and he wrote of his dissatisfaction to Prevost. In seven days, Brown had cleared the British presence from the Niagara River, except for the garrisons in Forts George and Niagara. The American army was less brittle than it had been in the two previous campaign seasons, and the soldiers were apparently better trained. Although Drummond was satisfied with the performance of his regulars and militiamen, he declared that the "Indian allies, as usual, proved of little service." In this he was mistaken, but he drew this inference from the paucity of information provided by Riall concerning the natives' role in the forest fight and Riall's report that the Indians had abandoned his force at Chippawa. Drummond did not seriously consider a move against Sacketts Harbor; his intelligence sources led him to believe that the American naval base was so well protected that it would take 7,000 troops to seize it. Assembling such a force at that time was entirely out of the question. While he shuttled troops up the lake to reinforce Riall, Drummond also considered going there himself to take command.[61]

As the Americans were settling into their camp at Queenston on 10 July, Scott displayed characteristic ambition. Scott sent his aide, Lieutenant William Jenkins Worth, to Brown with a private note. Scott complained that his brigade's accomplishment at Chippawa had received too little notice from Brown. "I do not learn," he complained, "that the officers of my brigade have been noticed in any manner whatever." As a consequence, Scott believed himself honor bound to offer his resignation. Brown replied in a conciliatory manner. "No man can more highly appreciate the gallant conduct of the 1st Brigade . . . than I do," read Brown's response. "All that could be expected from the most accomplished soldiers, was performed by this Brigade." The division commander went on to remind his subordinate that the official report of the battle, already submitted, was privileged correspondence unless and until the secretary of war chose to release it to the public. Scott accepted Brown's reply and later confided to Brown that his action had been "hasty."[62]

Scott's action prompted Brown to fire off a confidential note to Armstrong recommending brevet promotions for Scott, his three battalion commanders, the intrepid Captain Crooker, and Brown's and Scott's aides. Armstrong lost no time in recognizing the valor of these deserving officers, and on 9 August, the Left Division received word that all, except Scott, had been brevetted one rank. By then, Scott had been put in for a brevet promotion to major general for gallantry at Lundy's Lane, a promotion that was approved later that year. Brown handled this tiff well. It was hardly likely that Scott would resign his commission over the matter. Brown's overriding concern was to keep the peace among his subordinate brigadiers. He was already losing faith in the cautious Ripley and must have detected Porter's distrust of the regular army generals and his suspicion that the accomplishments of his volunteers would not receive recognition. Had Scott's complaints become public knowledge within the division, the results for morale might have been debilitating. Brown needed his little army to maintain its esprit and its focus on a campaign that had just begun.[63]

Brown decided, reluctantly, to be sure, that his best course of action was to remain at Queenston while awaiting the fleet. He was unwilling to lay siege to Fort George until his few heavy guns could be augmented. From Queenston he could move quickly to either Burlington or Fort George, but he was unwilling to telegraph his intentions to the British until he was assured of resupply from Chauncey's fleet. Brown hoped that Riall would leave the security of his fortifications and offer battle. Whatever the future held, the Left Division would be prepared. Brown ordered a divisionwide inspection for the afternoon of 11 July. He also sent his mounted troops (Harris's dragoons, Willcocks's Canadians, and Boughton's mounted volunteers) ranging through the forests and fields to scout the enemy. If Riall made a move, Brown needed to know immediately.[64]

While Brown waited for Chauncey to sail, so did Drummond. Drummond wanted to eject the Americans from the Niagara Peninsula, but he was concerned for the safety of Kingston. Drummond believed that Chauncey would take with him a sizable land force, which might be used to attack Burlington and thereby isolate Riall, or which might attack Kingston directly. Drummond wrote to Prevost on 11 July that Kingston was in a "very defenseless state," and he pressed his superior for more reinforcements to replace those that Drummond was shuttling westward. Drummond called up the local militia to garrison Kingston, but this measure could hardly guarantee the security of the British naval base. Both Drummond and Brown, it seemed, were relying on the American commodore's actions to help them decide their strategy.[65]

For his part, Chauncey was quite direct with Brown. Writing to the land commander on 8 July, Chauncey related that he expected to sail "in a few days" to a position that would bottle up the Royal Navy in Kingston. However, he continued, if Yeo sailed up the lake, Chauncey would follow him and offer battle. On 12 July, Gaines wrote to his superior that the American squadron at Sacketts Harbor was not ready to sail. "Nor am I sure," he warned Brown, that "the Commodore will feel at liberty to co-operate with you at the head of the lake when he does sail." Gaines also alerted his chief that British reinforcements were on the move westward from Montreal to York. With his campaign plan coming unraveled, Brown reconsidered his options.[66]

Riall, too, had to think through the emerging situation. He had troops in the three forts at the mouth of the Niagara: George and Mississauga on the west bank, and Niagara on the east. He also had Colonel Hercules Scott and a large garrison guarding supplies at Burlington Heights. Opposing him, he believed Brown to command between 5,000 and 6,000 troops, and Chauncey might appear at any moment with thousands more. Riall consulted with his engineer and artillery officers and asked their collective opinion regarding the state of defense of the forts at the mouth of the Niagara. The British officers concluded that Fort George was "in a very bad state," capable of "little or no resistance" to American heavy artillery. Even an infantry assault not supported by heavy artillery could seize Fort George. The guns of Fort George swept the approaches to Fort Niagara, and with George captured, the Americans could lay siege to Niagara, but it "would be some time before they could oblige it to surrender." Mississauga, on Lake Ontario, could resist assault but had little overhead cover for its garrison. A heavy bombardment would eventually compel its fall. This consensus drove Riall's next move. He was unwilling to abandon the Niagara, but he understood that to stay risked defeat of his division. Riall also understood that by remaining behind the walls of his forts he was surrendering the initiative to the Americans. Therefore, he decided to create a sizable maneuver force that could threaten the Americans besieging either Fort George or Mississauga. To do this, he pulled 900 men out of Fort George and ordered Colonel Scott's 103d Foot to unite with them behind the Forty Mile Creek. He also ordered the militia and Indians to operate against Brown's supply lines to Buffalo. Riall did not intend to come out from behind the creek unless Brown moved on the forts. If Brown wanted to take Fort George, he would have to contend with a significant regular force on his flank and irregulars and Indians at his rear. This plan did not guard against all eventualities; if Chauncey successfully attacked Burlington, all might be lost. Yet if enough reinforcements arrived, Riall would be well postured to go over onto the offensive. Given what Riall understood of the situation, his plan was a judicious and bold attempt to defend the Niagara Peninsula.[67]

While they decided what to do next, both sides contested the forests and fields between their respective camps—the Americans to learn more about the British defenses, and the British to prevent them from doing so. After Chippawa, Porter was joined by militia Brigadier General John Swift. Swift was a veteran of the Revolution and was still an active man at age fifty-two. On 12 July, Porter sent Swift and 120 New Yorkers to reconnoiter Fort George. Within a mile of that post, Swift and his small battalion surprised and overwhelmed a patrol of five or six soldiers of the Eighth Foot. In the process of surrendering, one of the British soldiers shot the general. The sound of gunfire alerted Major Thomas Evans of the Eighth and his Light Company, which were also on patrol. The two forces collided, but numbers told, and the British retired into the fort. Swift, to the grief of the New Yorkers, died in camp the following morning. He was buried that evening, and Porter's brigade paraded at the funeral, rendering a final salute to the hero.[68]

The days of 13 and 14 July were quiet as each side garnered strength. Riall decided to position his maneuver force on the heights behind Twenty Mile Creek. From this protected site astride a road network leading to the falls, Queenston, Burlington Heights, or Fort George, Riall was well positioned to attack or withdraw as circumstances warranted. He sent orders for Colonel Scott and the 500 men of the 103d at Burlington Heights to meet him there. As the 103d departed camp, the Glengarry Light Infantry Fencibles arrived from York. Riall left the battered 100th in Fort George and marched part of the Eighth Foot westward. He posted the First Lincoln Militia at Twelve Mile Creek, where it could more easily strike at Brown's supply lines. Riall learned shortly thereafter that Drummond had decided on 13 July to take command on the Niagara Peninsula himself. Drummond, taking a big risk that Chauncey might visit York or Kingston in his absence, decided nonetheless to hurry troops westward and eject the Americans from Upper Canada.[69]

The Americans received a welcome reinforcement on 13 July. Colonel Hugh Brady marched into camp with several companies of the Twenty-second Infantry. A veteran of Mad Anthony Wayne's Indian campaign, Brady had been colonel of the Twenty-second since the beginning of the war. During the Crysler's Farm campaign, Brady and his regiment had fought under Brown in the advance guard. The companies with him were merged with the three companies that had fought at Chippawa with Henry Leavenworth's Ninth Infantry. The reunited regiment remained in Scott's First Brigade. There had been other visitors to the American camp. Apparently concerned that the locals were spying on his division, Brown forbade women to enter the campsite without his permission. Brown also completed shifting supply arrangements. Supplies now would be sent to Lewiston and then rowed across the Niagara to the safety of the camp at Queenston.[70]

Neither reinforcements nor spies nor supplies were his greatest concern. In a last desperate attempt to persuade Chauncey to sail toward the Niagara, Brown wrote a letter in which he implored his naval counterpart for help. "There is not a doubt resting in my mind but that we have between us the command of sufficient means to conquer Upper Canada within two months if there is prompt and zealous cooperation and a vigorous application of these means; now is our time before the enemy can be greatly reinforced."[71] Brown suggested that if Chauncey would carry the supplies, the Left Division could march on Burlington Heights and then York and even Kingston in succession. The forts at the mouth of the Niagara would wither away when the supply lines to Kingston were cut. Brown's tone betrayed intense frustration. "For God's sake let me see you," he penned. To address Chauncey's greatest concern, he added emphatically: "Sir James will not fight."[72]

Brown's operational vision was expansive. He promised to end the war on the Great Lakes and in Upper Canada in a matter of weeks. Was this venture feasible? Brown did not need Chauncey's fleet; he wanted only some heavy guns and transports to carry supplies along the lakeshore. Chauncey's plan was to blockade Kingston in any event. He could threaten Yeo with his combat vessels and still send transports to aid Brown. Would Drummond send Yeo to fight Chauncey if Brown's army captured Burlington Heights and threatened York? What if York fell and Brown marched on Kingston? Chauncey had it in his power to force Yeo to fight or to scuttle the Lake Ontario squadron in Kingston Harbor. Brown, for his part, was proposing to accept tremendous risk. His army performed surprisingly well at Chippawa, but there would be several battles ahead as Riall defended behind every creek, contested every foot, in a long, slow withdrawal to York. Then there was the matter of numbers. The British out-numbered Brown's army, and without assistance from Izard on Lake Champlain, Brown's division might win an impressive number of Pyrrhic victories en route to Kingston. Too, there were peninsular veterans and the troops in Lower Canada. Unless stopped by Izard, large numbers might march to Kingston before Brown arrived. Brown set the correct parameters for success—prompt and zealous cooperation. Unfortunately, communication links were extremely slow. It would take nearly a week for Brown's proposal to reach Chauncey, and a few more before he received a reply. In the interim, events on the Niagara rendered Brown's proposition stillborn.

In the early hours of 15 July, Porter led his brigade and a company of regular artillery out of the American camp, through the village of St. David's, and to the shores of Lake Ontario, about a mile west of Fort Mississauga. Ripley brought his brigade northward also but positioned it along the Niagara and south of Fort George. Brown had ordered Porter and Ripley the evening prior to conduct a careful reconnaissance of the two forts. Porter took with him the capable Major Wood of the engineers, who would scrutinize the British defenses. On their march, Porter's troops saw numerous women who watched from their houses as the Americans passed. General Porter left small pickets of mounted men along his route of advance to give warning of enemy activity. When he arrived at the shore of the lake, Wood examined, as best he could, Forts Mississauga and Niagara; the latter was about two miles distant. After leaving a body of troops to watch Mississauga, Porter turned his brigade toward Fort George.

Porter's men pushed back the British pickets until the Americans were about a mile from Fort George. Then Porter sent Wood, protected by several hundred volunteers and Indians, into a copse of trees only a few hundred yards from the timber walls and bastions of Fort George. After Wood completed his study of the fort, Porter ordered the brigade to join Ripley's men, and the two brigades returned to camp. As the Americans were departing, British guns positioned out-side of the forts fired on them, wounding two men. One of Porter's patrols—

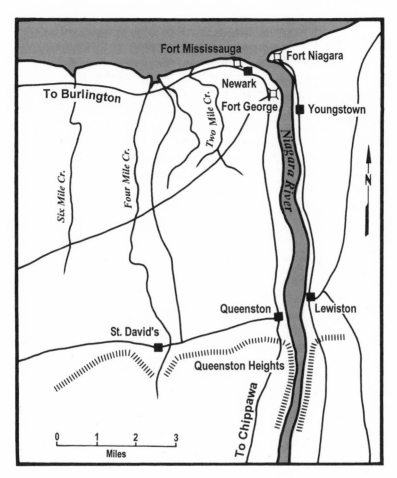

Niagara River

five men—was captured by Canadian militia. In his official report to Brown, Porter blamed his superior. "They are the victims," he wrote, "of your own generous policy of suffering the inhabitants who profess neutrality to remain unmolested." Porter was convinced that local women were passing information to their militia husbands and brothers who hid in the woods. Unlike in 1813, the Americans could no longer expect the willing support, open or otherwise, of a disaffected citizenry on the Niagara Peninsula.[73]

By mid-July, Riall had over 1,000 militiamen from the London and Lincoln Districts under arms on the Niagara Peninsula. This exceeded the number he could feed, and all but the most suitable were sent back to their homes. He was also concerned about their crops. The hay and corn were ripening, and eventually most of his militia would have to be released to harvest it. Riall sent some militiamen and Indians to raid Chippawa, expecting to capture American supplies there, but the raiders found nothing; the enemy supply line had already been moved east of the Niagara. Riall's maneuver force at Twenty Mile Creek was growing daily. On 15 July, Riall reported 1,436 regulars and eight guns in camp, with the Glengarries expected soon. Drummond had the Eighty-ninth Foot and De Watteville's walking to York; his transports, two brigs, were loaded with food and sailing to Riall. He ordered the next supply convoy of bateaux to bypass Kingston and to push on to the Niagara Peninsula. To make his supply operations more efficient, Drummond ordered the families of soldiers to move eastward to Kingston and the families of Indians to be put on half rations. Drummond was concentrating his forces to attack the Americans, and on 17 July, he departed Kingston to take command of the army in the field.[74]

Brown knew that time was on the side of the British. Chaffing at Chauncey's failure to appear, he digested Wood's appraisal of the defenses of Forts George and Mississauga and decided that his few heavy guns were insufficient to knock down their walls. "I am delayed here for the want of my battering guns," he wrote to Armstrong. "I expect them here by water from Sackett's Harbour." At the harbor, Gaines lost no time responding to Brown's request of 10 July for heavy guns. By the sixteenth, Gaines had five eighteen-pound guns and ammunition loaded in ten boats. Major Ludowick Morgan, with a crew of riflemen and a handful of Indians, embarked that evening but could not evade the Royal Navy vessels blockading the American naval base. Night after night they failed to elude the British naval patrols. Because courier service between Brown and Gaines was taking four or five days each way, Brown did not learn of Morgan's failure until it was too late.[75]

As British reinforcements arrived and Brown appeared settled in camp at Queenston, Riall became more confident. On 17 July, he moved his maneuver force from Twenty Mile Creek to Twelve Mile Creek. From that location he would be better able to support his militiamen and Indians who roamed the roads and woods, trying to thwart American forage parties and patrols. The Americans were quite active in these endeavors; Canadian Volunteers under Joseph Willcocks and Benajah Mallory guided Porter's men through the region to gather food and to intimidate the locals to stay out of the fight. In this last regard, they were unsuccessful; skirmishes every day attested to the Canadians' determination to resist the invaders. Major Daniel McFarland of the Twenty-third Infantry wrote to his wife, "The whole population is against us; not a foraging party but is fired on, and not infrequently returns with missing numbers." In this environment occurred an ugly incident reminiscent of the worst atrocities of 1813.[76]

The circumstances of the burning of the village of St. David's remain unclear. On 18 July, Porter sent New York militia Lieutenant Colonel Isaac W. Stone on a mission to clear the enemy from that village. St. David's was reputedly a loyalist stronghold and a militia headquarters. Stone led a small battalion composed of Boughton's mounted company and a company of infantry, about 215 altogether. Stone claimed that he accomplished his task without incident and while en route back to camp he saw St. David's in flames. At least eight structures were burned to the ground and livestock stolen. Brown had issued standing orders that the property of nonoffending civilians was to be respected. He handled this case as he had that of Captain Joseph Treat; immediately, and without adequate investigation, he dismissed Stone from the Left Division. The militia officer vehemently protested his innocence and maintained that he had seen regulars en route to St. David's. Although Brown's action served to reinforce his injunction against unnecessary destruction, it could not have improved relations between his regulars and his volunteers. The day after the burning of the village, Riall reported that his militia "seem actuated with the most determined spirit of hostility to the enemy." No matter who burned St. David's, the American cause suffered as a consequence.[77]

On 17 July, Brown ordered Hindman to emplace a company of artillery behind earthworks atop Queenston Heights. These guns protected the ferry site below, where supplies were crossed over from Lewiston. Sometime on 18 July, Brown decided to move on Fort George. By that time, he had likely received Gaines's warning that Chauncey would not appear off the Niagara Peninsula unless Yeo led him there. However, he probably had not learned that Major Morgan and the coveted heavy guns were still bottled up at Sacketts Harbor. No evidence exists that the commander of the Left Division knew the strength of British forces in the forts or in the field with Riall. Brown ordered the Left Division to march the following morning. At 7 A.M. on 19 July, the army struck tents and formed up, but at 11 A.M., Brown ordered the men to re-encamp. That evening, he issued orders to move out the following morning. His ten-day pause at Queenston was over. With or without the navy, Brown was going to force the issue.[78]

By marching toward Newark to threaten Forts George and Mississauga, Brown hoped to lure Riall from behind his defenses and offer open battle. There was the possibility that Morgan might arrive with some heavy guns. With these, Brown could open a formal siege of Fort George with, to his thinking, some prospect of success. Riall would be more tempted to try to raise the siege if he thought the forts were in imminent danger. By 20 July, Brown likely would have received Gaines's letter reporting that Morgan would depart on the 16 July and that Chauncey was ill but expected to sail in three or four days. Brown was likely disturbed to learn from Gaines that Armstrong had ordered the only regular infantry besides the riflemen at Sacketts Harbor, 300 soldiers of the Thirteenth

Infantry, to join the Right Division at Plattsburg. While Riall was receiving reinforcements daily, Brown, who was still responsible for the safety of Sacketts Harbor, was losing manpower. Nearly all of Red Jacket's native warriors had returned
to their homes. Certainly, Chauncey must have been even more reluctant to sail
too far from his base now that the army was sending away the Thirteenth
Infantry.[79]

The Left Division marched out of camp early on the twentieth, with Scott's
brigade in the lead, followed by Ripley and then Porter. Brown ordered the fortifications atop Queenston Heights destroyed. Scott arrived midday and set up
camp along the river and about a mile south of Fort George. He threw out pickets toward the fort. South of Fort George, the cleared field of fire extended about
one-half mile from the fort to where the woods began, cut by the river road and
other trails. Ripley encamped his brigade a little bit southwest of Scott. For the
next two days, British and American pickets skirmished between the fort and
the American camps, and both sides intermittently traded long-range artillery
fire. The British added Congreve rockets to the bombardment, but few were
injured on either side. West of the forts, the pace of skirmishing picked up as
Porter's mounted troops, including Harris's regulars, patrolled toward Riall's
field force. In spite of Brown's proclamation to the contrary, it seems that the
Americans arrested a handful of militiamen in their homes and sent them across
the river as prisoners. On 21 July, the British sent a schooner up the river to turn
Scott's flank, but the Americans responded by setting up a battery onshore that
countered the riverine threat. In the artillery duel at Fort George, Scott, always
leading from the front, had a horse shot out from under him by a nearby shell
burst. The British discovered the Americans setting up batteries opposite Fort
George in preparation for a siege. Riall sent a force of militiamen to Queenston,
but when they arrived, the Americans were already gone.[80]

Brown offered the British a chance to attack, but Riall refused to take the
bait; Riall believed that the American army was just too strong to attack with any
hope of success. Three deserters reported that Brown had 6,000 regulars and
1,400 volunteers and Indians, as well as six heavy guns to bombard the forts.
Riall accepted these accounts, as they confirmed his erroneous beliefs. Riall had
660 regulars and ten guns, three of which were heavies, in Fort George and 400
regulars and six heavy guns in Mississauga. He had at least 2,400 troops outside
the forts—nearly 3,500 in all. Riall ordered the commander of the two forts,
Lieutenant Colonel John G. P. Tucker, "to hold out to the last extremity." Tucker
expected to be attacked soon, and both he and Riall feared that the forts could
not survive a determined bombardment and assault. Riall was baffled as to what
to do, and he wrote of his concern to Drummond. "I am really in a very unpleasant predicament," he admitted. If he maneuvered his field force to challenge
Brown, part of Brown's force could move around him toward Burlington and

isolate Riall's division. Nor was Riall strong enough to move on Queenston to cut the American supply line. To Riall's mind, the answer lay in keeping his maneuver force out of contact and waiting for Drummond and reinforcements.[81]

From the American perspective, Riall had frustrated Brown's attempts to bring about a general battle. Although Riall believed his forts weak, Brown did not. He would not assault without a preliminary bombardment, and Brown believed his four eighteen-pound guns insufficient for the task. On 21 July, Brown ordered the army to march back to Queenston the following morning. Once there, where the road network gave him better opportunities to outflank Twelve Mile Creek, Brown could decide on his next move.[82]

Porter arrived at Queenston Heights first and captured a handful of Canadian militiamen. By midafternoon, the Left Division was encamped on the heights behind a screen of pickets and mounted patrols. Unaware that the Americans had departed their lines at Fort George, Riall sent Major Fitzgibbon, hero of Beaver Dams the previous year, to scout out the Americans. He reported the American withdrawal to Riall, who was now entirely puzzled by his adversary's activities.[83] In the skirmishing that day, an American patrol captured Captain William Johnson Kerr of the Indian Department. Kerr was Joseph Brant's son-in-law and had been implicated in the massacre and mutilation of a foraging party in 1813 during the American occupation of Fort George. Feelings against whites who led Indian warriors in ambushes ran deep among Americans, particularly when the action included scalpings, refusal to accept surrender, or the killing of prisoners. Captain Howard recorded in his journal his actions upon hearing that Captain Kerr was in American hands. "In the evening [I] waited on Gen[era]l Brown in company with Major Leavenworth and asked permission to *blow out Kerr's brains*, a very civil request truly, he having been the means of many murders during our previous campaign in that vicinity. But the general would not forgo the right of protection which was the prisoner's claim on him and the d——d villain escaped the fate he richly deserved."[84] The legacy of outrages in the war was unfortunately abundant. However, senior commanders exercised judgment and goodwill in controlling the base tendencies that dwelled just below the surface in their men.

On 23 July, Brown received bad news from Gaines. Morgan had been forced to return with the guns to Sacketts Harbor, and Chauncey's illness continued. No one knew when the fleet would sail. To Brown's way of thinking, a siege of the forts was out of the question, as was the hope of resupply along the shores of Lake Ontario. Brown's options were shrinking. With the basic assumption underlying his campaign plan—the cooperation of the Ontario squadron— shown to be incorrect, Brown might have hunkered down in a strong defensive position and waited for the British to try to eject him, or he might have returned to the American shore until Chauncey seized control of the lake. What happened next speaks to the drive and initiative of a new cadre of American officers whose quest to win the war would not so easily be denied. Brown met with his principal subordinates to discuss the situation. All concurred that the best way to restart the campaign was to bypass Riall and make a risky attack on Burlington Heights.[85]

Brown appeared unconcerned that he might lose the battle that he knew would follow his advance on Burlington. The risk, to his way of thinking, was largely logistical. He could hardly hope to protect a supply line strung out more than eighty-five kilometers from the Niagara River to Burlington Heights. After reporting his intentions to Armstrong, Brown gave the order to fall back to Chippawa. Divesting himself of all excess tentage and camp equipment and carrying as much food as he could, he was willing to gamble that the British would not refuse to fight once they discovered an American army threatening their land supply line. Brown won his gamble easily, although not in the manner he foresaw. Within forty-eight hours, Brown's and Drummond's armies were locked in mortal combat on a low crest along Lundy's Lane. The British had seized the initiative of the 1814 campaign.[86]

Brown did not hesitate to lay the blame for his failure to clear the British from the Niagara Peninsula in July squarely at Chauncey's feet. To reassure Brown, Armstrong professed that Madison himself understood that Chauncey would depart port on 1 July and that the president "was anxious to prevent any want of cooperation between the two arms from ignorance of each other's movements." He added that Brown had done his duty, "whatever may be the consequences." William Jones, secretary of the navy, was aghast to discover that the fleet had not departed Sacketts Harbor as he had understood it would. On 24 July, Jones implored Chauncey to sail "for the ultimate safety of the army." When Jones learned of Chauncey's illness, he ordered Stephen Decatur, then in New York, to go to Sacketts Harbor and assume command of the squadron if Chauncey was still sick. By the time Decatur received this order, Chauncey had recovered. On 1 August, the fleet left harbor and sailed to the mouth of the Niagara, where it forced a Royal Navy crew to destroy their brig rather than allow it to be captured. After leaving three vessels to watch the Niagara, Chauncey took the rest of the fleet to blockade Kingston. Chauncey controlled Lake Ontario until 21 September, when Yeo launched the *St. Lawrence*. With 112 guns, the *St. Lawrence* was the most powerful ship on the Great Lakes. However, the arms race continued as Chauncey's shipwrights pressed on with the construction of the *New Orleans*. The war ended before it was launched, and no decisive battle was fought.[87]

Chauncey took pains to explain his position. To Jones, he wrote that although he had hoped to sail on 15 July, the *Mohawk* needed ironwork and was not ready to sail until nine days later. Although he was still sick, he sailed on 1 August.

Chauncey explained his reluctance to cruise to the mouth of the Niagara by reminding Jones that there were only 700 regulars to defend Sacketts Harbor in his absence. In an unmistakable reproach of his superior, Chauncey added: "I cannot forbear expressing my regret that so much sensation has been excited in the public mind because this squadron did not sail so soon as the wise-heads that conduct our newspapers have presumed to think I ought." Stating that he had never promised to meet Brown, Chauncey went on to claim that his fleet "could be of no more service to General Brown and his army than it could to an army in Tennessee." Since Brown got no closer to the lake than Queenston, "the only service he could have derived from the fleet would have been our preventing the supplies of the enemy from entering the Niagara River." In summary, Chauncey reminded Jones that his "fixed determination has always been to seek a meeting with the enemy the moment the fleet was ready, and to deprive him of any apology for not meeting me."[88]

Chauncey's letter to Brown was caustic. Rebuking Brown for suggesting to Armstrong that Chauncey had pledged to meet the army at the head of the lake, he denied that he could have been of much assistance to the land force. Indignantly, Chauncey wrote: "That you might find the fleet somewhat of a convenience in the transportation of provisions and stores for the use of the army, and an agreeable appendage to attend its marches and countermarches, I am ready to believe, but, sir, the Secretary of the Navy has honored us with a higher destiny—we are intended to seek and to fight the enemy's fleet. This is the great purpose of the government in creating this fleet, and I shall not be diverted in my efforts to effectuate it by any sinister attempt to render us subordinate to or an appendage of the army."[89]

No less an authority than the disciple of the decisive naval battle himself, Alfred Thayer Mahan, picked apart Chauncey's rebuttal. He did not accept Chauncey's disingenuous argument that even had he sailed he could not have assisted Brown. Pointing out Riall's total dependence on resupply by water, Mahan contended that Chauncey could have easily prevented food or reinforcements from reaching him. Mahan was unrelenting in his critique. "It is indeed hard to believe that an army so little numerous as that of Brown could have accomplished the ambitious designs confided to it," he wrote, "but that does not affect the clear duty of affording it the utmost assistance that ingenuity could devise and energy effect."[90]

Chauncey had confused the ways, means, and ends of the war. Although control of Lake Ontario was a prerequisite for the seizure of Canada, such control might have been won in a number of ways. For example, permanently cutting the St. Lawrence or destroying the Kingston boatyards would likely have given the United States control of the lakes. Thus, the destruction of Yeo's fleet was a means to an end, not an end in itself. His fixation on winning both the arms race and a decisive battle, and his needless anxiety for the safety of his base, limited Chauncey's strategic vision. He became constitutionally unable to consider other options that might have yielded control of the lakes. Cooperation with Brown that threatened the destruction of Riall's division might very well have prompted Drummond to order Yeo out onto the lake, giving Chauncey his chance to replicate Perry's victory. But Chauncey was no Perry, and with that the British began a counteroffensive that ended at the gates of Fort Erie.

While the Left Division was striking America's last offensive blow of the war against an enemy growing in power, the Right Division was inactive, its general uninformed of his role in the strategic plan. George Izard commanded about 3,500 regulars along Lake Champlain. Under Izard's direction, his officers drilled the men seven hours each day using Steuben's *Blue Book*. Believing that he was outnumbered along the Richelieu-Champlain corridor, Izard's intention was to prepare his army to defend U.S. territory. As he readied his three brigades, Izard moved two of them north—one to the village of Champlain just south of the border, a second to Chazy, twelve kilometers farther south. The last he kept at Plattsburg, about twenty kilometers south of Chazy. On 22 June, eleven days before Brown invaded Canada, Izard received the campaign plan— or, rather, part of it—from Armstrong. The secretary of war, writing on 11 June, four days after the strategy session with the president, ordered the commander of the Right Division to establish and garrison a post on the south bank of the St. Lawrence River with about 1,500 men. This force would support armed galleys that were to operate on the river for the purpose of cutting the British line of communication. Armstrong did not tell Izard that his second mission was to make a demonstration toward Montreal to divert Prevost's attention from the attack across the Niagara.[91]

Izard must have privately questioned Armstrong's judgment: the secretary was telling Izard to divide his division in the face of a larger enemy. A diversion of 1,500 men to the St. Lawrence would leave too few to defend the traditional invasion route into the heart of the American North. Taking several days to ponder his reply, Izard wrote that the British had 5,500 troops and thirty guns within ten miles of the border poised for imminent attack. When the recruits ordered to Plattsburg arrived, Izard would battle the invaders near Chazy.[92] Certainly Armstrong was unaware of the condition of the Right Division, that most of the men were not veterans but had only recently joined the division. Izard wrote: "Raw officers have charge of raw recruits; and if they were not alarming to the safety of the country and the honor of our arms, the exhibitions in even old regiments, which not infrequently meet the eye, would excite ridicule as much as disgust."[93] Izard complained that recruits were deserting even before they joined the division. Even the regulars were leaving, some defecting to the enemy. Disciplinary problems kept the guardhouse full. "I do not however complain of the troops; with better officers, especially of the lower grades, in a few weeks they would be equal to the finest corps in any foreign service."[94] Izard, the South Carolinian, also complained about the blacks recruited into the New England regiments, "to the great annoyance of the officers and soldiers here."[95] Izard removed the black recruits from their units and formed them into "a sort of pioneer corps," which probably resembled a labor company more than the elite pioneer detachments of Scott's brigade.

Izard did not formally ignore Armstrong's order to fortify a post on the St. Lawrence, although he dallied so long as to subvert his superior's intent. On 1 July, Izard dispatched the talented engineer Major Joseph Totten to search for a suitable location. Ten days later, Totten found an ideal site about sixteen miles east of Ogdensburg where the river was only 500 yards wide and the topography well suited for firing batteries and defensive positions. The proposed spot, however, was nearly 150 miles from Plattsburg. Izard sent Totten's report to Armstrong, but there is no evidence that Izard took any further action to implement the secretary's orders.[96]

After learning of Brown's victory at Chippawa, Izard wrote again to Armstrong in an attempt to get his superior to change his orders. Izard intended to march 5,000 men toward the border in early August, a force, in his estimation, "entirely inadequate to the conquest of any important part of the country with the intention of retaining it."[97] He also voiced his concern for the Left Division and asked Armstrong if the Right Division should march on Kingston "should any accident" befall the Left Division. Armstrong, unsure of what to tell his commander at Plattsburg, referred the question to Madison, whose answer must have perplexed the cautious Izard. "It ought certainly be at the discretion of Izard," wrote Madison, "to accommodate his movements to those of the Enemy, and to his information from other commanders."[98] Madison, it seems, was coming around to understand that once the campaign began, it was not going to be coordinated from Washington but would depend on the cooperation of the commanders, both land and sea, in the theater of operations. Other than a small raid into Lower Canada in the last days of July that netted nine prisoners, Izard remained south of the border until the end of August. There is no evidence that the threat he and his 4,500 troops presented in any way diverted Prevost from amply supporting Drummond on the Niagara Peninsula.[99]

In mid-July, Prevost received word that the ministry was planning a strategic offensive. Prevost was given authority to conduct a number of local offenses that would secure Canada well into the future. Prevost was to destroy Sacketts Harbor and the American naval establishments on Lakes Erie and Champlain. Bathurst suggested attacks on Detroit and Maine. Even as Prevost read his instructions, nearly twenty battalions of infantry, provisions for six months, and £200,000 in specie were en route. Prevost was skeptical about the feasibility of a direct attack on Sacketts Harbor, but he was already contemplating the destruction of American power on Lake Champlain and the threat this posed to Montreal.[100] Assured of large reinforcements, Prevost transferred several battalions to Upper Canada, which, in turn, allowed Drummond the freedom of dispatching more troops to the Niagara Peninsula.

Shortly after receiving Bathurst's instructions, Prevost learned that the invasion of eastern Maine had begun. Vice Admiral Alexander Cochrane, in command of a joint army-navy force, seized Eastport on Passamaquoddy Bay on 11 July. Only the actual loss of territory forced Governor Caleb Strong of Massachusetts to allow his militia to come under federal control. This measure was insufficient to protect the District of Maine, because coastal fortifications were few and Strong refused to call out militiamen in the numbers needed to defend the coast. On 30 July, Prevost reported the destruction of both St. David's and Queenston by the Americans, and he encouraged the compliant Cochrane to retaliate. The seizure of eastern Maine was just the beginning of a series of naval raids that ended below the guns of Fort McHenry in Baltimore Bay.[101]

In Washington, apprehension about the impending shift of the strategic initiative to the British diverted Madison and his cabinet from the struggles of the valiant Left Division. Throughout June, Madison received reports of British intentions to attack along the Atlantic coast. He heard rumors that Admiral Cockburn was forming escaped slaves into military units for use in these attacks. At a cabinet meeting on 1 July, he declared that Washington itself would be an object of attack and that preparations for its defense must be made. His cabinet did not concur with the president's prediction—least of all Armstrong. Madison proposed building a force of 10,000, including 1,000 regulars, to defend the capital. Armstrong and Jones insisted that there were already more than that in the local militia who could be called up as needed.[102]

When Madison cited evidence of feverish shipbuilding activity north of Lake Champlain as cause to beef up McDonough's squadron, Secretary of the Navy Jones demurred, citing the expense involved. Fortunately, Madison insisted that Jones make every effort to improve the Lake Champlain flotilla. On Independence Day, Madison sent a letter to the state governors that called up 93,500 militiamen. He declared that "the late pacification in Europe offers to the enemy a large disposable force, both naval and military, and with it, the means of giving to the war here, a character of new and increased activity and extent."[103] America would soon pay the bill for years of unpreparedness. The irony of the situation was glaring. Hardly able to pay, uniform, feed, and shelter 2,500 militiamen and Indians making the major offensive of the war, the federal government was forced now to maintain thirty-seven times that number to defend its coastline.

Madison was also distracted by his growing distrust of Armstrong. In June, Madison directed his secretary of war to furnish all his correspondence with Generals Jackson, Harrison, Izard, Brown, and Gaines. Studying these, Madison discovered that Armstrong was using his position to secure the goodwill of these officers at Madison's expense. Furthermore, it was apparent that Brown and Izard were not corresponding with each other but were sending all information to Armstrong. It seemed to the president that Izard did not understand what Brown was trying to do or how he might best support the major effort of the war. On 27 July, Madison rebuked Armstrong for not directing his generals to share information and to cooperate more closely.[104] Perhaps Armstrong reexamined his decision not to place a single commander in charge of the Ninth Military District.

At the time when Brown most needed the attention of the president and the resources of the nation, these were denied him by the overriding imperative of the federal government to protect the coast from the hammer blows that were sure to follow Britain's triumph in Europe. In the last week of July, as Brown withdrew to Chippawa to resupply before advancing yet again, Sir Gordon Drummond arrived on the Niagara Peninsula determined once and for all to eject the American invaders. Fortunately for American honor, the courage of the men and the talents of the officers of the Left Division were up to the challenge.

CHAPTER EIGHT

Lundy's Lane

The Enemy's efforts to carry the hill were continued until about midnight, when he had suffered so severely from the superior steadiness and discipline of His Majesty's troops that he gave up the contest and retreated with great precipitation to his camp beyond the Chippawa.

—Drummond's Official Report, 27 July 1814

They were met by us near the Falls of Niagara, where a most severe conflict ensued; the enemy disputed the ground with resolution, yet were driven from every position they attempted to hold.

—Brown's Official Report, 29 July 1814

Hurrying from Kingston, Lieutenant General Sir Gordon Drummond arrived at York on 22 July. He brought with him reinforcements desperately needed to stop the American invasion: the Eighty-ninth Foot under the talented Lieutenant Colonel Joseph Morrison, and the flank companies of the 104th Foot. Awaiting Drummond was a letter from Major General Phineas Riall. His beleaguered commander on the Niagara Peninsula reported that the Americans were building gun positions at Youngstown for the purpose of bombarding Fort George. In response, Drummond conceived a plan to eliminate the threat to this essential fort. In doing so, he set into motion a train of events that led directly to Lundy's Lane, a turning point in the Niagara campaign.[1]

In a letter to Riall the following day, Drummond spelled out his analysis of the current situation and how he planned to regain the initiative. Drummond believed that the American fleet, which was still in Sacketts Harbor, could not arrive at the head of the lake for seven or eight days after sailing. This circumstance, reasoned Drummond, opened a window of opportunity to deal with the Americans without interference. Drummond ordered Lieutenant Colonel John

G. P. Tucker to attack from Fort Niagara on the twenty-fifth, with the mission of capturing the guns at Youngstown, and to seize or destroy all the boats he might come across. He wrote that "destruction of their boats . . . is an object of the greatest possible importance." Without river craft north of the Niagara Gorge, supplies for the American Left Division could come only from south of the falls.[2]

To keep Major General Jacob Brown, then at Queenston, from interfering with the operation on the eastern shore of the Niagara, Drummond ordered Riall to advance on Brown, going so far as to drive in the American pickets. Should Brown move to attack him, Riall was to withdraw. But if he must fight, Drummond directed Riall to "depend upon the superior discipline of the troops under your command for success over an undisciplined though confident and numerous enemy." Drummond wrote that he himself would arrive at Fort Niagara on the evening of the twenty-fourth and, after seeing off Tucker's movement, would join Riall on the twenty-fifth. If Tucker were successful, then Drummond would consider an all-out attack to defeat Brown's division and throw the Americans back across the river.[3]

Drummond also set forth his plans in a letter to Prevost that disclosed the risk he was taking. He reminded Sir George that despite the diversion to York of two brigades of bateaux from the Montreal to Kingston run, supplies were still "very far from sufficient" on the Niagara. He also told his senior that he had decided to release the York militiamen who had been guarding the provincial capital, because their crops were "in the greatest danger of being lost" if not harvested soon.[4] Remarkably, Prevost was also contemplating offensive action on the Niagara Frontier. On 25 July, before receiving Drummond's letter, Prevost suggested that Drummond strike out from Fort Niagara against Lewiston. He closed by stating his hope that Brown's army would "not escape without a severe retribution for the evils it has inflicted."[5] Neither Drummond nor Prevost fully understood yet that they were facing a particularly dangerous foe, unlike the irresolute opponents at Crysler's Farm or Chateauguay.

Across the lines, Brown too was planning offensive action. On 23 July, he received word from Brigadier General Edmund P. Gaines that the Americans still could not penetrate the Royal Navy blockade of Sacketts Harbor. Furthermore, Commodore Isaac Chauncey was quite ill, and there were no indications when the American fleet might sail. These circumstances meant that Brown would not have the heavy guns he believed were required to batter down the walls of Fort George, nor would he have ready access to supplies carried by the navy. It also meant that Commodore Sir James Yeo was free to deliver supplies and reinforcements to the Niagara. Brown remained determined to bring Riall to battle with or without the assistance of the Lake Ontario squadron. To do so, he resolved to march on Burlington Heights. This threat to the British supply line might just tempt Riall to leave the security of the forts and meet the Americans in the open. Before putting this plan into effect, Brown decided to divest his division of heavy baggage and to draw all the rations his men could carry with them. He even ordered the regimental surgeons to keep only one "hospital matron" with the regiment and to send the remainder of the nurses to the rear. Finally, Brown decided to fall back behind the security of the Chippawa River while preparing for this next move. By evening, the rumor of the imminent withdrawal and its purpose spread through the American ranks. So too swirled the rumor that Drummond himself was on his way with reinforcements.[6]

The day did not pass without skirmishing. Major Daniel McFarland took the Twenty-third Infantry out toward St. David's to "cut off the enemy." He marched his men through swamps and thick woods in a vain attempt to approach the British unseen. The enemy refused to stay and fight, and McFarland returned to camp only to report two of his men killed and no prisoners taken.[7]

At 10 A.M. on 24 July, the Left Division withdrew from its position at Queenston and rapidly marched upriver to the Chippawa battlefield, where the men set up camp. Scott recalled that the division "assumed a panic" in its movement. The First Brigade was positioned along the Chippawa River. Brigadier General Eleazar Ripley's Second Brigade and Brigadier General Peter B. Porter's Third Brigade camped south of the First Brigade and along the Niagara. Brown told Scott to prepare to march on 26 July back toward Queenston and try to draw Riall out for battle. Scott countered with a request to attack Burlington Heights directly with the First Brigade. Brown, fearful of dividing his forces in the face of the enemy, refused. If Scott got in trouble at Queenston, Brown could reinforce him handily. It would not be so easy to help Scott at Burlington, some sixty-five miles away from the American camp.[8]

As the Second and Third Brigades settled in for what they expected to be a few days of rest and preparation, the men of Scott's brigade were busy cooking and packing food into haversacks. Brown sent Captain Azariah Odell's company of the Twenty-third Infantry to establish a picket along the Portage Road a short distance north of the American camp. Scott posted the Ninth Infantry on the north side of the Chippawa to guard the bridge. Their commander, the dependable Henry Leavenworth, had been disgruntled since the battle nineteen days earlier. He took the opportunity to complain to Scott that Brown's official report of the battle had slighted the contribution of both Leavenworth and his men. Stating that he had lost confidence in the division commander, Leavenworth tendered his resignation. Scott himself persuaded Leavenworth to reconsider; this was no time for one of the army's finest battalion commanders to leave the service.[9]

Meanwhile, reinforcements in dribs and drabs were moving to join the Left Division. On 20 July, about 100 soldiers of the Twenty-second Infantry embarked at Erie heading for Buffalo. They marched on to Chippawa and joined their regiment under Colonel Hugh Brady. On 21 July, three companies of the First Infantry led by Lieutenant Colonel Robert C. Nicholas departed Erie in schooners. Nicholas, a Kentuckian, had entered the army as a captain in 1808 and since August 1812 had been the regimental lieutenant colonel. The First Infantry had been authorized by Congress in 1784 and recruited its men from the northeastern states. It had served continuously in the West, and when the war began, it lost one company at the Fort Dearborn Massacre and another at the surrender of Detroit. The companies with Nicholas had successfully defended Fort Madison near St. Louis in September 1812 and had remained there until the spring of 1814, when Secretary of War Armstrong ordered them eastward. This battalion of the First Infantry would reach the Left Division in time to fight at Lundy's Lane. The last regulars Armstrong dispatched from the West to join Brown were two companies of the Nineteenth Infantry. They remained at Cleveland during the battle but joined the army at Fort Erie in August.[10]

Other than placing the Ninth Infantry north of the river, Brown took no other steps to maintain contact with Riall. Unlike his usual practice, he failed to dispatch mounted patrols to keep an eye on enemy activities. Brown paid for this oversight the following day when Riall moved his division undetected to within a few miles of the American camp. Riall responded to Drummond's orders by notifying Lieutenant Colonels Thomas Pearson and Parry L. Parry to move their brigades, then at Twelve Mile Creek, toward the Americans.

Pearson commanded the bulk of Riall's light troops: the Glengarry Light Infantry Fencibles, the Volunteer Battalion of Incorporated Militia, the Nineteenth Light Dragoons, the Provincial Dragoons, and a company of three guns. Except for the Nineteenth and the artillery, this was a brigade of Canadians trained to the standard of regulars. The Glengarries, commanded by Lieutenant Colonel Francis Battersby, were battle-hardened and skillful forest fighters. The separate companies of the Incorporated Militia had fought several battles, but it was not until March 1814 that they were consolidated at York for training as a battalion. They were commanded by William Robinson, a thoroughly competent captain of the Eighth Foot who held the rank of provincial lieutenant colonel while with the Canadian battalion. Robinson was credited with turning his volunteers into well-trained soldiers. Drummond himself noted that the volunteer militiamen had "attained a highly respectable degree of discipline."[11]

Lieutenant Colonel Parry commanded the First Militia Brigade, a small unit of about 300 militiamen composed of detachments from the First, Second, Fourth, and Fifth Lincoln Militia and the Second York Militia. The Lincoln militiamen were locals, as were those of the Second York, which was raised from the loyal citizens around Burlington Bay. Many of these militiamen were experienced, having seen battle at Queenston and Fort George and any number of

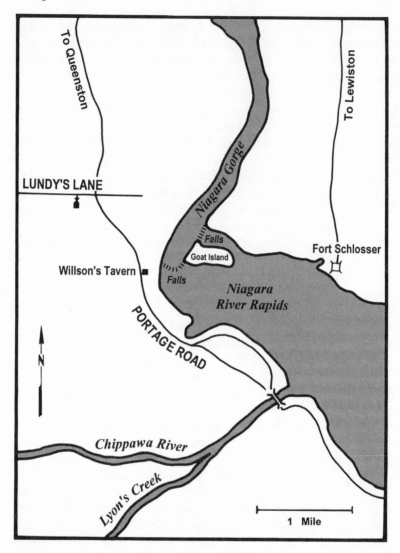

To Queenston

To Lewiston

Niagara Gorge

LUNDY'S LANE

Falls

Fort Schlosser

Willson's Tavern

Goat Island

Falls

Niagara River Rapids

PORTAGE ROAD

N

Chippawa River

Lyon's Creek

1 Mile

Niagara Falls and Vicinity

small actions. The Second Lincolns had fought most recently at Chippawa under Lieutenant Colonel Thomas Dickson, losing 47 of the 110 of them in the forest fight. Although not trained to the standard of regulars, they were nonetheless combat veterans and determined to defend their homes.[12]

Between them, Pearson and Parry commanded about 1,100 men. In the early hours of 25 July, the two brigades started the long march toward the junction of

Lundy's Lane and the Portage Road, which they reached at about 7 A.M. There, Pearson and Parry were joined by John Norton. Norton and a small band of his Grand River Indians, accompanied by some dragoons, set off south to locate the Americans and before long spotted Odell's picket. At midmorning, the alert Americans also spotted some of Norton's party at Willson's Tavern, a local landmark nearly overlooking Niagara Falls. Odell informed Leavenworth, who passed the report to Brown, who directed Lieutenant David Riddle to take 100 men of the Nineteenth Infantry to drive off the British. Late in the morning, Riddle crossed the bridge and moved into the woods, taking a long, indirect route toward Willson's Tavern.[13] While Brown was dealing with enemy patrols, a much more dangerous threat appeared on the other side of the Niagara. Drummond had arrived at Fort Niagara at dawn to learn that Riall, consistent with his orders, had started forces moving toward the Americans. Drummond ordered Lieutenant Colonel Morrison at Fort George to take his Eighty-ninth as well as detachments of the Royal Scots and the Eighth Foot and move south to reinforce Riall near Lundy's Lane. Moving parallel to Morrison on the eastern shore, Lieutenant Colonel Tucker led about 500 soldiers of the Eighth and Forty-first Foot, plus a handful of Indians and sailors, to push the Americans out of Youngstown and Lewiston. The twin columns started their movement at midmorning. Drummond chose to accompany Morrison.[14]

Pushing south, Tucker enjoyed mixed success. Although Lieutenant Colonel Philetus Swift's New York militia chose not to dispute either town, Tucker found neither guns nor boats. At noon, Drummond ordered Tucker and some of his men across the river to reinforce Fort George and the remainder to return to Fort Niagara. Satisfied that the forts in his rear were secure, Drummond continued on toward Queenston with Morrison's troops. However, the American militiamen had broken contact with Tucker and did not know that he had withdrawn. Expecting an imminent attack, the militia guarding a large cache of supplies at Fort Schlosser worked frantically to defend themselves. Swift sent urgent reports to Brown, reports that would send the First Brigade to disaster.[15]

Early in the afternoon, Brown read two of these reports. One stated that the British were in "considerable" force at Queenston (Morrison's column). The second stated that the British were "landing at Lewiston" (Tucker). Immediately recognizing that his plan to move on Burlington would be foiled if the supplies at Schlosser fell into enemy hands, Brown hurried an aide to Lewiston to assess the situation.[16] At midafternoon, Leavenworth spied a company of dragoons and two of infantry at Willson's Tavern. He sent this information to Brown and added the surmise that these troops were an indication of a much larger force nearby. Brown, however, dismissed Leavenworth's deduction. His intuition told him that since the greatest threat to his plans was the enemy's move on Schlosser, this must be the actual British intention. Presumably, the troops at Willson's Tavern were there to distract Brown from the main effort, an attack on Schlosser.[17]

While Brown was analyzing the British movement, Drummond was meeting with Riall at Queenston. Pleased with the ease with which Tucker had cleared the eastern shore, Drummond decided that the time was right to drive off the invaders. He ordered a concentration of forces at Lundy's Lane. From there he could block Brown's drive on Burlington or Queenston. Riall sent orders back to Colonel Hercules Scott at Twelve Mile Creek to bring all the regulars and the Second Militia Brigade to Lundy's Lane. Drummond hurried Morrison's column south to reinforce Pearson and Parry, already in defensive positions at Lundy's Lane.[18]

Late in the afternoon, Riall's orders arrived at Twelve Mile Creek, and Colonel Hercules Scott lost no time putting his troops in motion. Scott commanded the 103d Foot, a unit with a record of poor discipline and little battle experience. The other regular units were Lieutenant Colonel John Gordon's Royal Scots and Major Thomas Evans's Eighth Foot, both veterans of Chippawa. Scott's brigade was rounded out by the two flank companies of the 104th Foot, both composed of inexperienced troops.

Also moving with Colonel Scott was the Second Militia Brigade commanded by Lieutenant Colonel Christopher Hamilton. This brigade of about 250 men was composed of detachments from the Western and London Districts of Upper Canada: the First and Second Norfolk, the First Essex, the First Middlesex, and Caldwell's Western Rangers. Some members of the brigade likely had participated in the skirmishes common to western Upper Canada. By 1814, these small militia regiments had been successfully purged of persons sympathetic to the Americans. Altogether, Scott marched about 1,700 men and three guns toward Lundy's Lane.[19]

While a reinforced British army was converging on Lundy's Lane, Brown grew impatient at the lack of fresh news from the eastern shore. Earlier that day, Winfield Scott had repeated his offer to march his brigade to Burlington Heights. Now Brown hatched a plan that might aid the defenders of Fort Schlosser. No boats were immediately available to move troops across the river to reinforce Schlosser. However, a strong push toward Queenston on the western side of the Niagara might cause the British to recoil from pressing their advantage on the eastern side of the gorge. Brown gave the mission to Scott. Reinforced with Nathan Towson's company of artillery and Samuel Harris's dragoons, Scott "was particularly instructed to report in case the enemy should appear." Brown was convinced that not many British were between him and Fort George. For his part, the ever-pugnacious Scott believed that he had been ordered to find and fight the enemy.[20]

In short order, the First Brigade, the heroes of Chippawa, led by dragoons and supported by Towson's guns, departed camp heading north. The brigade had about 1,100 infantrymen in four regiments: Leavenworth's Ninth, John McNeil's Eleventh, Brady's Twenty-second, and Thomas Jesup's Twenty-fifth. Scott reported that "only two inhabitants had been seen in the march, and these, from ignorance or loyalty, said nothing that did not mislead. The population was hostile to Americans."[21] Scott received an accurate picture of his opposition from Mrs. Willson, who was American-born, when he stopped briefly at her tavern. Willson readily told Scott that Riall had with him 800 regulars (Pearson's brigade), 300 militia (Parry's brigade), some Indians (Norton), and two guns. Riall's division was located on the ridge crested by Lundy's Lane, which was on the other side of a band of woods about one-half-mile deep and pierced by the Portage Road. Believing that his force probably outnumbered that of Riall, Scott decided to attack. He sent a young engineer, Lieutenant David Douglass, back to Brown with the message that Scott was about to engage this body of the enemy. Scott then drew together his principal officers and there, within sight and sound of the thundering Niagara Falls, issued orders for an immediate advance. He ordered Harris out front and Leavenworth's Ninth Infantry to guard the left as the brigade advanced along the road.[22] Certainly Scott knew that it would take an hour or longer for Brown to receive Douglass's report and to get help on the way. Perhaps Scott expected to win another quick victory before Brown arrived. In any event, his rash decision to attack without personally viewing the enemy position resulted in an unnecessary drubbing of his well-trained, veteran brigade.

Harris's dragoons passed through the woods and saw the British drawn up in line of battle along the crest of a low ridge. Scott received their report as the infantry was entering the wood line. Scott recalled Leavenworth from the left flank to rejoin the march column on the road.[23] In a demonstration of confidence, he sent Jesup and the Twenty-fifth Infantry to the far right between the road and the river "to pass through the woods and be governed by circumstances."[24] As Scott emerged from the woods, he was surprised that the enemy force was larger than reported by Mrs. Willson. In his memoirs, Scott recalled that at that moment he could not "suppress his indignation at the blundering, stupid report made by the militia colonel to his confiding friend Major General Brown."[25] With this unkind thought, and without reconsidering his decision to attack, Scott ordered his three battalions to deploy in line and to advance. He had lost sight of Jesup's battalion still in the woods to the east.

The Americans, emerging from the woods, saw ahead a patchwork of cultivated fields edged by trails and rail fences. The open area was roughly 700 yards across and extended 600 yards from the wood line to Lundy's Lane, which ran northwest from its intersection with the Portage Road. Lundy's Lane itself was a tree-lined sunken road atop the dominant terrain feature, a low, long ridge.

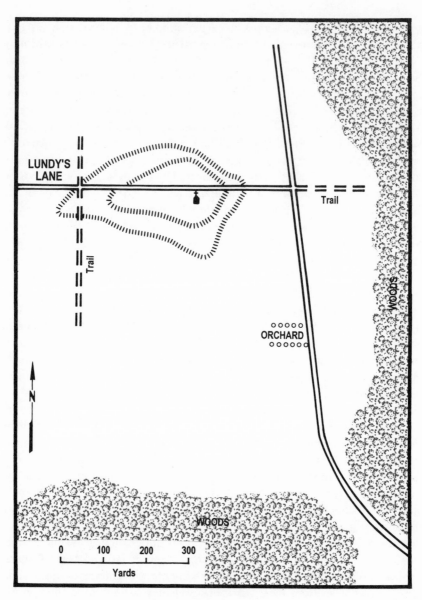

LUNDY'S LANE

Trail

Trail

ORCHARD

WOODS

WOODS

N

| 0 | 100 | 200 | 300 |

Yards

Lundy's Lane Battlefield

This ridgeline was about a mile long and fifty feet above the surrounding plain. The ridge was gently sloped on its southern and western faces and more steeply raked from the north and east. On the highest point of the ridge stood a log meetinghouse and a small cemetery. Near the cemetery were positioned five guns of the Royal Artillery. Southeast of the ridge was an orchard bounded on the east by the Portage Road.[26]

Winfield Scott might not have cursed that militia officer if Riall had had his way. When Riall received reports that a large force of Americans was approaching, he assumed that he was about to be attacked by Brown's entire army. With only Pearson's and Parry's brigades present, and Morrison still not in sight, Riall gave the order to abandon the ridge and fall back on Queenston. He sent a messenger to find Hercules Scott to tell him to change direction and to head for Queenston also. It was between 6:00 and 6:30 P.M. when Drummond, with Morrison in tow, approached Lundy's Lane to find Pearson's men heading north. Drummond, determined to fight, ordered them turned around. After meeting up with Riall, the two generals plotted out the distribution of troops on the ground. Discovering that Riall had ordered Hercules Scott's column away, Drummond sent a messenger to countermand that order. Drummond was pleased with the position Riall had chosen. The Americans would have to attack uphill, and the British guns would enjoy a significant range advantage over any American guns below. The ridgeline would shelter his troops from American fire if he chose to move them to the reverse slope. It was good ground to give battle against a superior force. The British, Canadians, and Indians had just assumed their battle positions as Scott's men boiled out of the wood line.[27]

Several long minutes were given over to the First Brigade's changing formation from march column to a firing line of three battalions. While forming, the Americans were constantly under fire from Captain James Maclachlane's five guns at the crest of the ridge. Scott sent the Ninth Infantry to the left of the road. The Twenty-second passed behind it and formed on its left. The Eleventh, moving behind both regiments, formed a line on the extreme left of the brigade. Drummer-boy Hanks, with the Eleventh Infantry, reported that he was still one-half mile from the battlefield when the firing began, and soon dragoon casualties, on their way back to the American camp, passed the Eleventh. Hanks remembered climbing over a fence separating the woods from an open field. "The cannon balls, grape shot, and musket balls flew like hailstones, and yet we were not firing a gun."[28]

Scott posted Towson's guns, two six-pounders and a howitzer, on the road as they emerged from the woods, and soon they were returning the British fire. Since Towson's targets were higher than his guns, he had to fire at a steep angle in order to reach out to the British guns. This meant that the American fire plunged on the Royal Artillery guns rather than striking at a glancing angle, which caused it to be less effective than the British fire. Low-angle fire was more efficient, since the cannonballs tended to bounce in low hops, carrying them deeper into the target. High-angle fire tended to bury itself in the dirt on impact. Major Jacob Hindman, Brown's artillery commander, had accompanied Scott. When he saw the large body of British and the advantage enjoyed by their cannon, he hurried back to Chippawa to bring up the companies of Captains Ritchie and Biddle.

The battle action at Lundy's Lane falls neatly into three phases. The first encompassed the fight of the First Brigade before the arrival of the rest of the Left Division. Within this phase occurred two separate yet simultaneous engagements: Scott's firefight below the ridgeline, and Jesup's battle to the east. The second phase began in the dark with the arrival of Ripley's and Porter's brigades on the battlefield and the successful attack on the British artillery. The last phase consisted of three unsuccessful British counterattacks launched by Drummond to drive the Americans off the crest of the ridge.

British artillery had been firing for some time before Scott managed to deploy his troops several hundred yards south of the British holding the ridgeline. In the face of solid cannonballs bounding through their ranks, many Americans wavered or fell back before their officers could bring them under control. Scott recalled that his order to return fire was followed by "a tremendous fire of all arms."[29] In fact, the Americans were too far away from the enemy atop the ridge to inflict many casualties. Early in the fight, McNeil was wounded and carried to the rear. Leavenworth recalled that the Americans fired their muskets for about an hour. The Glengarry Light Infantry Fencibles and some Royal Scots, militia, and Indians moved down off the ridge and took up positions behind cover, firing directly into the left flank of the Eleventh Infantry, which responded by refusing its left. Fortunately for the Americans, who were standing out in the open, the British and Canadians were about 200 yards distant, and casualties in the exchange were low.[30]

Soon, however, the Eleventh ran out of ammunition and was being shot to pieces by the continuous artillery fire. All the company commanders were killed or wounded. As Americans were wounded, they walked or were carried to the rear by their comrades, who might or might not return to the firing line. As this fine regiment melted away, some of the officers and men rallied to the colors of the Ninth. Then the Twenty-second also depleted its ammunition. Colonel Brady himself was severely wounded but refused to leave his men. The remnants of that proud corps folded in on the Ninth. Harris's dragoons were taking casualties and not contributing in any useful way to the fight. Harris withdrew them behind the woods and returned himself to the battle. Scott should have followed the example of his cavalry commander.[31]

In later years, Scott wrote that "the brigade was, from the first, under a heavy fire, and could not be withdrawn without a hot pursuit. Being but half seasoned

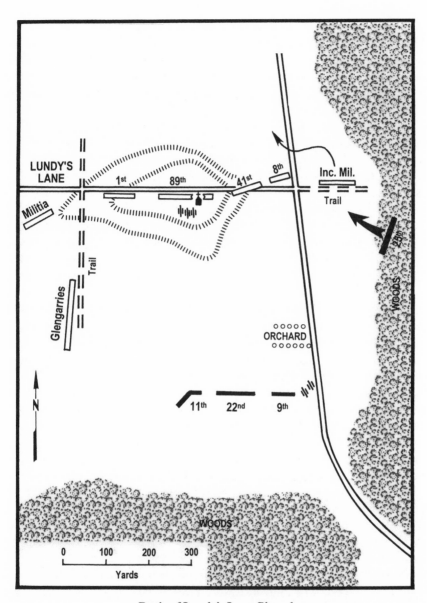

Battle of Lundy's Lane, Phase 1

to war, some danger of confusion in its ranks, with a certainty of throwing the whole reserve (coming up) into a panic, were to be apprehended; for an extravagant opinion generally prevailed throughout the army in respect to the prowess—nay, invincibility of Scott's brigade."[32] Besides reflecting the monumental ego of its author, this statement also speaks to Scott's unwillingness to consider other courses of action. It should have been clear to Scott that his musket fire, delivered at an extended range, was largely ineffective. A long wood line extended immediately to the rear of the brigade, where many of the wounded had sought shelter. It would have been a simple matter to withdraw the brigade, still in line, to the cover of the woods while awaiting the rest of the division. But as he watched his outnumbered troops fall about him, Scott could conceive only one alternative. He ordered an attack.[33]

Scott instructed Leavenworth, his only unwounded battalion commander, to form the men for the charge. Obediently, the proud soldiers of the ill-used brigade went to carry arms and stepped off. Before they had moved more than 100 yards, Scott saw how few soldiers were still on their feet, and he ordered the men to halt and resume firing. John Norton, watching from the west, appreciated Scott's dilemma. "Dread seemed to forbid his advance," he wrote, "and shame to restrain his flight."[34] Losing sight of Scott, Leavenworth sent Harris, still on horseback, to find the brigade commander and to recommend withdrawal. Scott soon reappeared and ordered Leavenworth to maintain his position as Brown was even then approaching. It was about 9 P.M.[35]

While the victor of Chippawa was losing his brigade minute by minute, Jesup and the Twenty-fifth Infantry were enjoying considerable success east of the Portage Road. Well suited to independent command, Jesup brought his men northward slowly and with stealth. Spotting the Volunteer Battalion of Incorporated Militia across their front, the Twenty-fifth charged out of a wood line. Surprised by the suddenness of the attack, the volunteer militiamen broke. Their commander, Lieutenant Colonel Robinson, was struck down by an American bullet and carried rearward. The Twenty-fifth continued its advance northward through the woods and brush and cleared the British from east of the Portage Road. The Incorporated Militia quickly recovered and re-formed west of the road, facing east.

As the light was failing, Jesup returned southward and sent a company to watch the junction of Lundy's Lane and the Portage Road. As many as 200 British soldiers, unaware that the road was now in American hands, were caught, disarmed, and escorted southward. In the dark, many managed to escape their captors but, deprived of their weapons, were effectively out of the fight. One who did not get away was Major General Riall himself, who had been wounded and was heading toward the rear to seek medical attention. The first physician

Riall met was American. Jesup, however, was unaware of the desperate situation of the rest of his brigade.[36]

Phase two of the battle began as the rest of the Left Division entered the fray. When Scott departed the American camp, neither of the other two brigades was in position to come to his aid if that proved necessary. Ripley was unaware of Scott's mission and presumed that he was drilling his men somewhere north of the Chippawa. As many as 200 of Ripley's men were outside the American camp washing their clothing or assigned to other duties. Porter's strength was even more degraded. Swift had about 250 militiamen with him on the eastern shore, and four other companies of the Third Brigade were guarding supplies between Chippawa and Buffalo. So confident that the British were not present in large numbers, Brown had not warned his subordinates to prepare for possible combat.[37]

When the sound of gunfire reached their ears, the American generals sprang to action. Porter and Ripley started to round up their men and prepare to march. Brown sent orders to Ripley to take his brigade as well as the artillery and march to Scott's assistance. He ordered Porter to prepare the Third Brigade for movement and to await orders. The Second Brigade was already forming when these orders arrived. Brown, his aides, and his engineer, Lieutenant Colonel William McRee, mounted their horses and rode north. Within minutes, the Second Brigade was on the move with about 750 infantry. Marching into camp at about this time was Lieutenant Colonel Nicholas and two companies of the First Infantry. Without waiting for orders, the Kentuckian marched his command of about 150 soldiers across the Chippawa bridge and toward the sound of the guns.[38]

On his way, Brown met up with Lieutenant Douglass and received a summary of what had transpired. Sensing from the sound of the cannon fire that the battle was larger than that suggested by the numbers Douglass had reported, Brown sent orders to Porter to bring the Third Brigade forward. As the small party approached the battlefield, McRee galloped forward to reconnoiter. As he broke out of the wood line, Brown saw the remnants of Scott's brigade facing a larger number of the enemy well situated atop a commanding ridge. He saw how severely the soldiers of First Brigade had suffered in the unequal contest. He saw numerous dead, wounded, and stragglers. He also saw opportunity. After baiting Riall for weeks, he now had him out of his forts and in the open. Brown sought out Scott and impatiently waited for Ripley's infantry and Hindman's guns.[39]

When he was within one-half mile of the battlefield, Ripley sent his aide, Captain William McDonald, ahead to receive Brown's orders. It was dusk, and Ripley knew that he would be deploying his men in the rapidly fading light. The

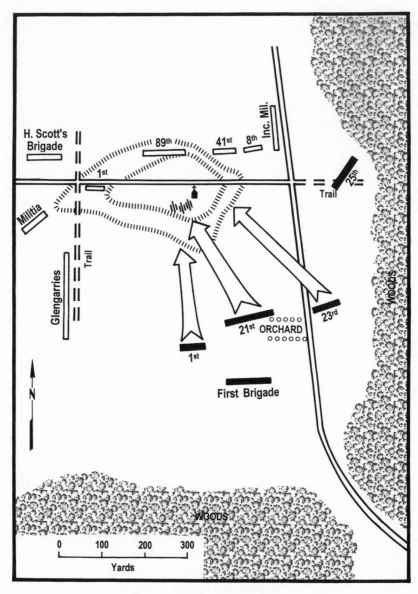

Battle of Lundy's Lane, Phase 2

First Brigade had ceased firing, but British artillery continued to fire intermittently into its ranks. Brown's orders arrived as the Second Brigade came upon the battlefield. Obediently, Ripley sent his troops forward, between Scott's depleted ranks and the ridge. Ripley formed his battalions on line with Miller's Twenty-first on the left and McFarland's Twenty-third on the right. Scott ordered the First Brigade to go into reserve. Leavenworth reorganized the shattered brigade into a single battalion. Colonel Brady, although wounded, took command. As the Second Brigade prepared to take up the fight, Drummond also received reinforcements. Hercules Scott was marching his weary troops onto the battlefield.[40]

Scott had brought his column of 1,800 men and three guns to within three miles of Lundy's Lane when he received Riall's order to move, instead, to Queenston. He had changed direction and marched another four miles when he received Drummond's order to return as quickly as possible to Lundy's Lane. He complied. When the men heard the sound of battle, they pushed on even faster. The contingent arrived at 9 P.M., and Drummond sent Scott to the far right of the line.[41]

As Hercules Scott was bringing his men into position, the Americans were delivering the decisive attack of the battle. McRee completed his quick reconnaissance and found Brown. He reported that the artillery position on the crest of the ridge was the key to the battle; if it were taken, the integrity of the British line would be seriously damaged. Agreeing, Brown ordered Colonel James Miller to attack the guns. Being informed of the presence of the First Infantry, Brown sent orders to Nicholas to form on the left of the Twenty-first and to protect their attack. Ripley found McFarland's Twenty-third Infantry and formed them up to protect the right flank of Miller's advance. With columns forming in the dark, out of sight of the adjacent regiments, and no signal agreed on to begin the crucial advance, there was every reason to believe that the attack would miscarry.[42]

And miscarry it nearly did. On the left, Nicholas apparently misunderstood his orders, because he led his small battalion directly toward the British guns. In doing so, he attracted intense fire that stopped his men cold. Nicholas ordered his command to withdraw back down the hill, out of effective musket range. The retreat was disorderly, and the officers of the First Infantry spent valuable time rallying and re-forming their men.[43]

On the right flank, the Twenty-third Infantry suffered a similar reversal. Ripley and McFarland had brought the battalion to within about 150 yards when the British opened fire. The column recoiled and fell back. Ripley, McFarland, and the other officers got the men back into attack column and tried again. This time, they marched to within twenty yards of the British line before opening fire. Now it was the turn of the British infantry to fall back down the slope, but not before their fire had killed Daniel McFarland.[44]

While the regiments on his flanks were withdrawing down the slope, James Miller was moving his men stealthily forward directly toward the British guns, aided by intense darkness. Apparently, the defenders were sufficiently distracted by the attacks of the First and Twenty-third Infantry that they did not see the Twenty-first until that body delivered a murderous volley directly into the artillery position from very short range. Immediately attacking with bayonets, the Twenty-first killed, captured, or drove off the gunners. No sooner had Miller re-formed his men atop the crest when the Eighty-ninth Foot rolled forward in a determined counterattack.[45]

Drummond was nearby when he saw his artillery fall into enemy hands. Riding up to Lieutenant Colonel Joseph Morrison, he ordered the Eighty-ninth to recapture the guns. Neither Miller nor Morrison was aware at the time that their regiments had faced each other at Crysler's Farm. On that battlefield, the Twenty-first had advanced and the Eighty-ninth defended. Now it was the British turn to attack. The Eighty-ninth marched forward in the dark to within a few yards of the Twenty-first, and the two sides opened fire at point-blank range, aiming their weapons at the muzzle flashes of their enemies. At some points, the fighting was hand to hand. In the face of intense fire, the British withdrew down the steep slope. Drummond reinforced his attack with other nearby troops, and Morrison led his men forward again and again, with the same result. This time, Joseph Morrison was wounded and carried to the rear. Drummond, urging on the assault, had his horse shot out from under him.

Refusing to accept the loss of the guns, Drummond ordered the Eighty-ninth to try a third time. It was during this third attack that Drummond was struck in the neck by an American ball. Blood gushed, and Drummond tied handkerchiefs around the wound to stop the flow. The assault was thrown back, with grievous losses to both battalions. The determined Drummond understood that only a heavy counterattack, one delivered by the bulk of his forces, could restore the situation. He could not allow the Americans to retain possession of his guns; without them, he could not meet the enemy in open battle. Without bothering to get his wound attended to by a physician, Sir Gordon Drummond prepared to show his foe what disciplined, steadfast British infantry could accomplish.[46]

In the lull that followed, the Americans struggled to consolidate their hold on the crest of the ridge. After the Twenty-first Infantry had repelled three determined counterattacks by the Eighty-ninth Foot, Ripley brought the Twenty-third onto the ridge to the right of the depleted ranks of Miller's battalion. At about the same time, Nicholas brought the First Infantry up and on Miller's left flank. These three regiments were roughly along Lundy's Lane and on the highest part of the ridge. Hindman brought three companies of artillery onto the hill and dispersed them across the American front.[47]

Within minutes, Porter appeared with his diminished brigade, about 300 men, and marched them to the far left of the American line, south of Lundy's Lane. He placed them at an oblique angle to the Second Brigade to protect the flank. Porter placed Lieutenant Colonel Dobbins's New York battalion on the left, the Fifth Pennsylvania Volunteers under Major Thomas Wood in the center, and Lieutenant Colonel Joseph Willcocks's Canadian Volunteers on the right alongside the First Infantry. Soon after, Jesup appeared on the right of the Twenty-third Infantry. Brown had found Jesup and the Twenty-fifth Infantry still on the right of the Portage Road and directed him to rejoin the rest of the Left Division. Jesup formed his battle line north of Lundy's Lane. Brown also brought Scott's brigade, now a single battalion, to the center and rear of the American position. Brady was too weak to continue to command, and that responsibility fell to the able Henry Leavenworth. It was 10:30 now, and the moon, which had weakly illuminated the battlefield, had set. The Americans were ready for a British counterattack, which was certain to follow.[48]

Drummond assembled the attacking force in a long line about 200 or 300 yards north of and roughly parallel to Lundy's Lane. He called back the Glengarries from their advance position on the western flank of the Americans. He anchored his left on the Portage Road. From east to west, his battle line consisted of the Incorporated Militia, part of the Royal Scots, the Eighth Foot, the battered Eighty-ninth, a detachment of the Forty-first, and the 103d. On the far right of Drummond's line were fragments of several regiments and the Glengarries. In all, Drummond had about 3,000 troops ready to assault.[49]

General Brown and his aide, Captain Ambrose Spencer, rode into the darkness forward of the American position. Perceiving troop movement in front of them, Spencer called out, "What regiment is that?" A voice replied, "The Royal Scots." The pair quickly returned to the American lines. The third and final phase of the battle was about to begin.[50]

Drummond's line tramped forward until they were within forty yards of the Americans. It is uncertain which side fired first, but for twenty minutes, controlled volleys crashed into the formed ranks. The infantry fired at musket flashes. At times, the lines were so close that soldiers reported seeing the buttons on their enemies' coats. Many American artillerists were cut down, leaving too few to serve the guns. Ripley coolly rode behind his men, issuing orders and reassuring them. Sergeant Commins of the Eighth Foot had only one explanation for the determination of the American Infantry. "The Yankees was loth to quit their position," he recalled, "and being well fortified with whiskey made them stand longer than ever they did."[51] If Brown had feared that the First and Twenty-third might break again, their performance reassured him. Later he

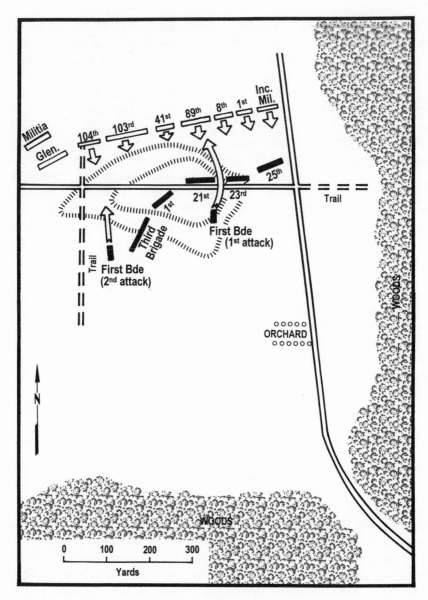

Battle of Lundy's Lane, Phase 3

reported that these two regiments had "assumed a new character. They could not again be shaken or dismayed."[52] Drummond ordered a withdrawal to regroup his men for another try.[53]

Between twenty and thirty minutes after they had pulled back, the stalwart British infantry surged forward again. This time, they halted further back from the American line than they had during their first counterattack. Once again the sides traded volleys of deadly musket fire. Seeing his lines thinning with every volley, Ripley urged Brown to bring Scott into action. Brown gave Scott the order, and he in turn told Leavenworth to form the men into an attack column and to bring them toward the right of the Second Brigade.[54] The ever-impetuous Scott later wrote that he "resolved to try an experiment."[55] He led the column of about 250 men forward. Before impacting on the British line, the enemy in front of him recoiled. Scott apparently turned the column toward the left, and as they passed in front of Ripley's men, they came under fire from both sides. Eventually, Scott and Leavenworth brought the splintered battalion back into the friendly lines on the left of the Third Brigade, the experiment a failure.[56]

Brown arrived in the midst of the Third Brigade to find them wavering. Porter and his officers urged the men to stand and fight, and they did so. Fortunately for these militia volunteers, the firefight was over in about twenty minutes. The British pulled back once again, and once again Drummond issued orders for another try.[57]

The thirsty, exhausted Americans prepared as best they could in the forty-five minutes between the second and third counterattacks. The American line, which had been fairly straight before the first attack, was now bent back into a horseshoe. Too many officers were wounded or dead. The men removed cartridges from the fallen. The Twenty-fifth Infantry was so badly depleted that Jesup was forced to array his men in a single rank in order to cover his front. Scott once again re-formed the remnants of his proud brigade into a column of fewer than 200 men. There was no mistaking that the Americans had been badly battered and might not survive another strong push. For his part, Drummond made no noticeable changes in his attack plan. When the men re-formed at about 11:30, he ordered them forward once again.[58]

The British line surged forward. Fighting was desperate. Winfield Scott, on his own initiative, launched another attack toward what he believed to be the right flank of the British attack. Out in front on foot, Scott led the column forward, but it drew intense fire from both the front and the left. The attack column fractured in two. The rear fell back, and the front inclined to the right and came in front of Porter's men. The proud soldiers of Scott's brigade had repeatedly demonstrated their willingness to follow their young brigadier into intense danger, but this time there was no going forward. Mortally wounded in this last attack was Captain Abraham Hull, son of the disgraced General William Hull who had abjectly surrendered Detroit two years earlier. Scott brought his men for a final time back to friendly lines. Then he moved to the far right of the line to see his other regiment, the orphaned Twenty-fifth. While speaking with Jesup, both officers were hit. It was Jesup's third wound, but he fought on. Scott was not so fortunate. A bullet caught him in the shoulder and knocked him to the ground. Winfield Scott was out of action and out of the war.[59]

On the crest of the hill, the fighting was most dire. The Royal Scots and the Eighty-ninth Foot fought hand to hand with the First and Twenty-first Infantry. Ripley was everywhere, urging his men to hold on. His horse had been killed beneath him, and two musket balls had pierced his hat, but Ripley was otherwise unharmed. Brown was not so lucky. A bullet passed through his thigh, and another missile struck his side soundly but did not penetrate. Then the British fell back down the slope and into the darkness. Amazingly, the outnumbered Americans had held onto the hill and the British guns. The wounded Drummond sought to reestablish control over his battered army.[60]

There was no apprehension of another attack; the Americans knew that they had won a hard-fought battle. The immediate needs of the army were to evacuate the wounded, re-form the units, and distribute water. Brown was weak from loss of blood, and he had decided to turn over command to Scott. Learning that Scott had already been removed from the battlefield, Brown resolved to continue in command himself rather than turn authority over to the suspect Ripley. Before departing the battlefield, Brown issued orders to remove the wounded. Once the wounded were on their way south, the brigade commanders should march their men back to camp. Once Brown was gone, Ripley, as senior officer present, was in charge of the troops still on the battlefield.[61]

During this postbattle phase, the seeds of an enduring controversy were planted. Due to miscommunication as well as a lack of rope and horses, the Americans failed to bring off the captured guns. Also, Ripley refused to obey what appeared to him to be an impossible order. As a result of these two events, the British reoccupied the crest of Lundy's Lane at dawn and repossessed their artillery. This gave them tangible evidence that they had vanquished the invaders. Whereas the matter of the guns can be attributed simply to carelessness, Ripley's alleged insubordination merits investigation.

The British did not interfere while the Americans left the battlefield. Wagons had been sent forward for the removal of the wounded. When this was accomplished, the ravaged brigades trudged back to camp. Sometime after 2 A.M., Brown sent for Ripley. He had heard rumors that the cannon had been left at the battlefield. Once he had ensured that the troops had gotten water, Ripley was to gather up the entire division and be back on the battlefield at dawn, "there to meet and beat the enemy if he again appeared."[62] Ripley did not protest, but neither did he pass Brown's order on to Porter or Leavenworth. For the most part, the exhausted troops collapsed and got what rest they could.

As dawn approached, it became obvious to Brown that no preparations were being made to comply with his orders. He sent his staff to visit every commander and convey Brown's order to immediately prepare to march. Sometime before 9 A.M. on 26 July, Ripley led about 1,500 troops north toward Lundy's Lane. In his ranks were hundreds who had missed the battle the day before because they had been on guard or work details and, in the confusion of battle, no one had fetched them from camp.

As Ripley drew closer, his scouts reported that thousands of British were in line of battle ready to take up where they had left off at midnight. Clearly, it would be an unequal fight. Porter, Leavenworth, and others were apprehensive that an attack could not succeed. Ripley returned to Brown's tent and, given the new circumstances, requested permission to return to camp behind the security of the Chippawa. Brown was indignant and refused. When told that Porter was also opposed to the attack, Brown angrily dismissed Ripley, saying, "Sir, you will do as you please." Brown was about to be evacuated to the hospital in Williamsville, where he had been preceded by both Scott and Riall. Before going, however, he sent a message to Edmund Gaines at Sacketts Harbor to assume command of the forces on the Niagara Frontier.[63]

Brown's intuition served him well, for if Ripley had been on the ridge at dawn, he might have been able to retrieve the guns.[64] At about dawn, Drummond sent John Norton to scout out the Americans, and that intrepid fighter reported that they were in their camp. Drummond, therefore, started moving his men back onto the battlefield sometime after 7 A.M. There they recovered their guns, evacuated the wounded, and went about the grisly but necessary task of disposing of the human remains. There were too many bodies to bury, and the British soldiers collected trees and rails from fences and began to burn the bodies. Shadrach Byfield of the Forty-first Foot recounted a gruesome tale. An Indian persisted in trying to throw a wounded American onto one of the fires, although repeatedly prevented from doing so by some of Byfield's comrades. Losing patience with the obstinate native, the British soldiers shot him and threw his body onto the fire.[65] In any event, when Ripley approached, Drummond and his troops were ready for action. Later that day, Drummond sought out a surgeon, who removed a bullet from the back of his neck.[66] Distracted by his wound and the state of his division, Drummond failed to take advantage of an unanticipated opportunity to destroy the Americans.

Inexplicably, Ripley not only refused to obey Brown's explicit order to continue the battle but also voluntarily gave up the strong defensive position behind the Chippawa River. With Brown on his way to Williamsville, Ripley was in command and knew that he would be held responsible for the fate of the Left Division. Ripley believed that his mauled army, now fewer than 2,000 effectives, was in danger of destruction by Drummond's obviously superior force. Despite the objections of Porter and McRee, Ripley ordered a withdrawal to the Black Rock ferry landing just below Fort Erie.[67]

Ripley's order—to abandon the line of the Chippawa River—struck Jesup as a grave blunder. Jesup believed that the main bridge could have been defended by as few as 300 men and that the potential bridge site at the juncture of the Chippawa and Lyon's Creek was likewise defensible. Jesup later judged that Ripley's "flight from Chippawa had shaken the confidence of all the principal officers of the army in his capacity to command in chief."[68]

Though the move to the ferry site was rapid, it was also orderly. Lieutenant Douglass recalled many years later: "There was no pursuit—no hanging upon our flanks or rear—no enemy visible, in any quarter. The march was as quiet as if it had passed through a portion of our own territory. It was . . . performed without the slightest disorder of any kind."[69] Leavenworth reported that "the march was in good order and nothing of use was left for the British."[70]

Ripley brought the Left Division to the ferry site, and the men were soon asleep "where and how they could."[71] Soon, however, his intention to cross the army over to the New York shore became known to the senior officers. Porter, McRee, Wood, Towson, and other officers protested vehemently. Withdrawal across the river was tantamount to declaring the campaign at an end. Had the Left Division not defeated the British, possession of the guns notwithstanding? On the morning of 27 July, Ripley sought out Brown on the American shore and requested permission to withdraw the army from Upper Canada. Exasperated with the seeming timidity of his subordinate, Brown rebuffed him. When Ripley disclaimed responsibility for the fate of the Left Division if it remained in Canada, Brown gave him a written order to defend Fort Erie. With this note in hand, Ripley returned to the army. Now, on 27 July, the Left Division was back where it had started on 3 July. The initiative was passing to the British, and much hard fighting remained.[72]

The battle of Lundy's Lane was the largest and hardest fought of the war until that time. After nearly 200 years, two major questions remain. First, who won? Second, why did the battle unfold as it did? Even today, adherents on both sides claim victory, as did the opposing commanders immediately following the battle. Drummond's official report to Prevost refused to recognize that the Americans retained firm possession of the crest of the ridge for several hours or had driven back repeated counterattacks. Brown reported to Armstrong that the British, "vastly superior" in numbers, had been "completely defeated." A year later, when some question of the outcome reached Brown's attention, he wrote to Porter and Miller. "Not a doubt resting on my mind," wrote Brown, "but that the enemy were defeated and driven from the field of battle." When asked their opinion by Brown, the two generals replied in a joint statement that there was "clear and unequivocal evidence that it [the battle] resulted in a decisive victory on the part of the American Army."[73]

By traditional measurements, a claim to victory can be made by both sides. These criteria are comparative casualties and retention of tangible evidence of victory, such as the ground or captured guns and colors. The following casualties were reported:

	Killed	*Wounded*	*Missing / Prisoners*	*Total*
Drummond	84	559	235	878
Left Division	173	571	117	860

Although the Americans lost a higher percentage of the troops engaged, this casualty count fails to distinguish clearly between winner and loser.[74]

When the last shot was fired, the Americans indisputably held the crest of the ridge and the captured guns and had repelled numerous attempts to retake them. The Americans voluntarily retired from the field in good order and without being pursued. The evidence is also clear that by midmorning the British had repossessed both the ridge and the guns and that the Americans chose not to renew the contest. In these circumstances, traditional methods of determining victor and vanquished are unsatisfactory.

If the victor is deemed to be the side that has gained the most from the battle, the side that has better advanced its campaign, then the results are easier to sort out. On 26 July, Brown's plan to advance on Burlington Heights was irretrievably shattered. Brown had had his chance to destroy a British army in the open, and he had failed. Worse yet, the new commander in the field, Ripley, had voluntarily relinquished the defensive line of the Chippawa River and had surrendered control of the western shore of the Niagara Valley all the way to Fort Erie. Drummond's army was badly injured, but by no means was it shattered. Drummond had secured the forts at the northern end of the Niagara, and he had blunted an American advance. Although there was still a lot of fight in both forces, the balance of combat power on the Niagara Peninsula had swung from the invaders to the defenders. Given these results, the conclusion is inescapable that the British won the battle of Lundy's Lane.

What circumstances, what decisions led to this result? An investigation of the naval situation and the comparative competence of the armies, as well as a look at the key commanders, provides some insights. The absence of an American fleet on Lake Ontario was a prerequisite of Drummond's plan. It is doubtful that he would have gone on the offensive had he been unable to move 400 troops and additional provisions to the mouth of the Niagara. Chauncey's claim to Brown "that the fleet could not have rendered you the least service during your late invasion upon Upper Canada" rings false.[75] Brown replied, "could the army have been supplied with provisions from the depots provided on the shores of Lake Ontario, we should not have doubted our ability (without reinforcements or additional guns) to carry the [Burlington] Heights; when we could have returned upon Forts George and Niagara or advanced upon Kingston."[76] Brown has only half the picture. Chauncey's cooperation would have assisted Brown's offensive, but equally important, it would have impeded Drummond's ability to stop him at Lundy's Lane. Referring to the boats that moved supplies and troops from York to Fort Niagara, Mahan concluded: "The employment of Dobb's four vessels, permitted by Chauncey's inaction, thus had direct effect upon the occurrence and the result of the desperately contested engagement which ensued, upon the heights overlooking the lower torrent of the Niagara."[77] Brown had refrained from assaulting Fort George because the Royal Navy had kept American siege guns bottled up in Sacketts Harbor. Now the Left Division was back at Fort Erie, in part because Drummond had decided, in the absence of Chauncey's opposition, to challenge Brown on the Niagara.

The nature of the armies at Lundy's Lane also suggests why the battle lasted as long as it did and why the casualties were relatively equal. The quality of the American army—regulars, volunteers, and militiamen; officers and soldiers— had improved considerably since 1812, to the point where it was the tactical equal of its British and Canadian counterpart. Fortescue judges that Lundy's Lane "was the best contested fight of the whole war."[78] The men of these two armies stood nearly toe-to-toe and exchanged deadly volleys of musket and artillery fire in the dark repeatedly, until one general decided to stop. The Eighty-ninth Foot charged the Twenty-first Infantry six times in a matter of hours, which speaks volumes about both corps. The soldierly skill, the valor, and the dogged determination of the common soldier on both sides inspire both awe and admiration. Drummond's instructions to Riall before the battle had suggested boldness against an "undisciplined" enemy. Even after the battle, Drummond persisted in the belief that his soldiers were more steadfast and skilled than the Americans. The British Right Division would pay a heavy price for Drummond's error of judgment.[79]

Another circumstance that perhaps in some small way affected the results of the battle was the quelling of disaffection on the Niagara Peninsula. In previous campaigns, an American commander could expect intelligence from local sympathizers. This time, only American-born Mrs. Willson provided information on the day of battle. At Lundy's Lane, the Canadian militiamen chose to stand and fight rather than slip away in the darkness. Even the American victory at

Chippawa failed to excite pro-American behavior among the locals. There were unmistakable signs that even in western Upper Canada, where disaffection had been most intense, sympathy for the American cause was waning. On 25 July, a small party of Americans landed at Long Point and raided the village of Char-lotteville. They had hardly entered the town when an alarm gun sounded. The Americans left immediately, and before they were half a mile offshore, nearly 300 of the local citizenry had gathered to repel the raid.[80]

Perhaps pro-American sympathies had been silenced by the executions on 20 July at nearby Ancaster of eight persons for treason. On the day of the bat-tle, Drummond's proclamation concerning the executions was released. In it, he stated that his goal was to put down rebellion and to suppress disaffection.[81] It appears that he met his objective; never again during the campaign would the local populous provide meaningful assistance to the American invaders, now hemmed into a very small parcel of Upper Canada.

The Left Division ended up at Fort Erie largely because of decisions made by four key players: Drummond, Brown, Scott, and Ripley. Assessment of these generals is worthwhile in understanding how the campaign took this decisive turn. The battle would not have taken place had Drummond not been astute enough to recognize a window of opportunity and had he not possessed the strength of character to take advantage of it. Drummond took a calculated risk. He fed troops and supplies westward as opportunities arose, knowing full well that once the American navy was loose on the lake, his troops west of York would be in peril. Perhaps he would not have been so quick to act had he seen the steadiness and discipline of the First Brigade at Chippawa.

Once on the peninsula, Drummond acted resolutely. He managed to con-centrate a large force, all those not necessary to defend the forts, on a suitable battlefield in time to fight. Only after three determined counterattacks failed to dislodge the Americans from the crest did he decide not to continue. Yet it is also clear that he did not handle the troops on the battlefield as skillfully as he might have done. With the First Brigade vulnerable and dying only a few hundred yards away, Drummond never ordered an attack to destroy it. Apparently, he thought he was facing the entire Left Division, or perhaps he was satisfied with killing them slowly. Also, he did not commit all his forces to the three counter-attacks; the troops on the far right of the line were not brought into play after sunset. Perhaps Drummond's greatest failure was in not pursuing the Left Divi-sion once it abandoned its position behind the Chippawa. The Americans were vulnerable as they marched and at their camp at the Black Rock ferry site. The British would pay the price for this blunder at the walls of Fort Erie.

Like Drummond, Brown had operational vision and was a risk taker. His plan to attack Burlington Heights was sound because it likely would have brought Riall out to battle. He accepted the heavy risk of moving without an adequate supply line. Brown's unfortunate omission was failing to maintain contact with Riall's field force at Twelve Mile Creek. Riall brought two brigades to Lundy's Lane unnoticed. This error led Brown to misread entirely the British plan. Perhaps Brown could not imagine Riall coming out from behind fixed defenses when he had assiduously avoided combat since his drubbing at Chippawa. It is possible that Brown did not consider that Riall would become more aggressive once he was reinforced. In any event, Brown was surprised, as he had been at Chippawa. Writing of this embarrassment to Governor Tompkins, Porter stated that "so far as depended on any previous arrangements or knowledge of the commanding officer, both engagements were wholly accidental and unexpected."[82] This is serious criticism for one charged with campaigning in enemy territory.

Brown was exceedingly careless not to tell Porter and Ripley what was happening at Lewiston or why Scott had left camp. Had he done so, his subordinates might have called in their work parties or made other preparations for combat. On the battlefield, Brown acquitted himself competently. He quickly arrayed his forces and determined the location of the decisive attack. He did not coordinate the attack well, however; each of the three columns acted independently. Once in possession of the crest, Brown deployed his forces and hung on. It might be argued that Brown was more determined than Drummond to win, that Brown's will was stronger than that of his opponent. Evidence of his indomitable spirit is found in his insistence the following day that Ripley continue the battle.

Brown and Scott were a winning combination. They were also a losing combination. Brown's operational judgment could not quite balance Scott's rashness. Scott committed his troops before his report could have reached Brown. Scott attacked without personally assessing the situation. He deployed his troops without an idea of how he might win. He kept no reserve. He continued an unequal contest while the best-trained brigade in the U.S. Army slowly died.[83] These are serious charges indeed. However, Brown reported to Armstrong that the First Brigade had "most skillfully and gallantly maintained the conflict."[84] Jesup addressed the issue directly in his memoirs and came down in Scott's favor. "His brigade had before beaten Riall in the field. Every officer and soldier of the brigade believed, and knew, that the thousand men led by Scott were able to beat double their number of British troops; to have hesitated a moment would have depressed their morale, and elevated that of the enemy."[85] Jesup, however, was not a target of the Royal Artillery; he was off on the right flank performing brilliantly and successfully. His peers—Brady, Leavenworth, and O'Neil—remained silent on the subject, and the nation embraced Winfield Scott as a hero.

Finally, one has to consider the unfortunate Ripley, blamed by Brown for throwing away victory.[86] Clearly, Ripley contributed much to the American effort. He kept the Twenty-third Infantry in the fight after McFarland's death. He encouraged his men throughout the fighting. He also disobeyed orders on the following morning. He did not tell Leavenworth and Porter to prepare their brigades to move before dawn. He departed camp several hours late. He refused to attack Drummond when explicitly ordered to do so. Ripley had forfeited Brown's confidence earlier in the campaign, and it is likely that their personal friction prompted Brown to rebuff Ripley's request not to fight again on the following day. Was Ripley justified in refusing battle? Certainly to attack a larger number of the enemy, well situated and supported by artillery, was risky. Repulse or defeat would likely have led to disaster had Drummond pursued. Even Scott, the previous evening, had drawn back from assaulting Drummond's inherently strong position. Ripley was wrong to disobey, but there is reason to believe that his disobedience saved the Left Division.

Another knotty point, however, is Ripley's abject failure to maintain the strong defensive line on the Chippawa. In giving up this position, he signaled American weakness to the enemy. In retreating, he put his army at grievous risk of destruction had Drummond moved quickly. It would have been nearly impossible to ferry the division back to New York had the British offered opposition. Fortunately for the American cause, Ripley listened to his fellow officers and decided to contact Brown for permission to withdraw the army from Upper Canada, rather than do so on his own authority. Brown's resolution to defend Fort Erie kept the campaign alive in its darkest hour.

Now, on 27 July, the remnants of the Left Division huddled around a tiny fort where the waters of Lake Erie flowed into the Niagara. The British, in overwhelming numbers, might appear at any moment. Gone were the determined Brown, the bold Scott, and a host of fine officers. If the Left Division were to survive, much less prosper, it would need to draw as never before on unknown reserves of strength and talent.

CHAPTER NINE

The Siege of Fort Erie

I shall be able to compel the force shut up in Fort Erie to surrender or attempt a sortie which can only terminate in his defeat.
—Lieutenant General Gordon Drummond to Sir George Prevost,
4 August 1814

On 27 July, commanding from a hospital bed in Williamsville, Jacob Brown gave his reluctant subordinate, Eleazar Ripley, a positive order to defend Fort Erie. Brown's brave decision breathed life into a faltering campaign. It also resulted in a six-week siege of the chief American camp on the Niagara Frontier and eventual transfer of the initiative from the British back to the Americans.

Grudgingly, and with no confidence of success, Ripley returned to the Canadian shore and set about the task given him. Unsure that his order would be obeyed, Brown directed his talented engineers, William McRee and Eleazar Wood, to place the fort in condition to withstand a British attack.[1] There was much to be done. The fort itself could hardly contain more than a small battalion of men, perhaps 200. Lieutenant McDonough, who commanded the garrison left there after the fort's capture on the first day of the invasion, had supervised a general improvement of the fort's defenses. Work parties had deepened the ditches, raised the fort's two bastions, and erected a redoubt that protected the bastions. However, McDonough had no inkling that the entire army would return one day and require the protection of the fort's walls.[2]

McRee and Wood began on 28 July to lay out the perimeter of a fortified camp large enough to enclose the Left Division. The engineers decided to build an earthen wall fronted by a ditch. The wall, or breastwork, would be anchored at one end by Fort Erie and at the other by an artillery battery atop Snake Hill, about 750 yards to the southwest. Between the fort and Lake Erie were the ruins

234

of a limekiln. This stone building would become another battery, and the gaps between it and the fort and lake would be closed by earthen breastworks. The rear of the camp was defined by the shoreline: supply boats could land directly at the camp. Orders assigned units to positions along the perimeter. Commanders put their men to work erecting the fortifications fronting their positions. The men worked quickly, for at any moment the British might appear in force.[3]

Inexplicably, Drummond did not move on the fort but kept his army well north near Lundy's Lane. Not until 30 July did the Americans report seeing any enemy at all near their camp, and that was a patrol of dragoons near the ferry site. Believing the horsemen to be the harbingers of a British attack, the Americans redoubled their efforts. Worried that Ripley might yet quit Canada, Brown sent him another explicit order. Ripley was not to consider surrendering either his army or Fort Erie. "If he [the British] attacks your position, I expect you to ruin him," Brown added.[4]

Little by little, the Left Division transformed an unremarkable plain south of Fort Erie into a substantial fieldwork defense. The long breastworks were six to seven feet high and five to sixteen feet wide at the base. The ditch surrounding the camp was six to ten feet wide and three to four feet deep. As the breastworks were being completed, work parties cut down small trees, sharpened the limbs, and piled them in front of and in the ditch or stuck the trunks into the exterior walls of the breastworks.[5] The Americans enhanced this abatis by interweaving the limbs with thorny vines. Lieutenant David Douglass recalled, "One night a deserter from the enemy became somehow entangled in it and remained several hours without the power to extricate himself; and when, after calling piteously for release, he was, at last, taken out, with the assistance of some of our men, his clothes were, for the most part, triumphantly retained by the relentless thorns and briars of the abatis."[6]

Inside the breastworks and set at right angles to them, the men raised earthen walls called traverses. The traverses were intended to stop solid shot that would otherwise continue its destruction as it careened through the camp. As time permitted, other traverses were thrown up throughout the camp. Some of the American cannon went into the bastions of Fort Erie. Other batteries were constructed at opportune locations. The limekiln was renamed Douglass battery after the young engineer commanding the two guns there. These guns were mounted and ready for action on 3 August. Snake Hill, a mound of sand about twenty-five feet high, became known as Towson's battery and held six cannon. These guns were in operation by 10 August. The thirty-seven-yard gap between Towson's battery and the lake was unfortified except for an abatis. To protect the northern approaches to the fortified camp, the Americans began construction of a hidden battery of four guns at Black Rock. Rounding out the defenses were

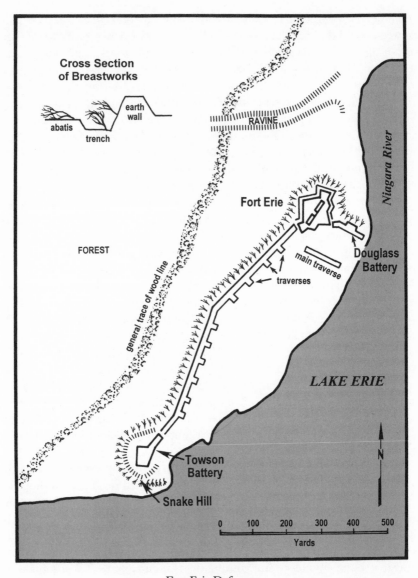

**Cross Section
of Breastworks**

abatis

trench

earth
wall

FOREST

general trace of wood line

RAVINE

Niagara River

Fort Erie

main traverse

traverses

Douglass
Battery

LAKE ERIE

Towson
Battery

Snake Hill

N

| 0 | 100 | 200 | 300 | 400 | 500 |

Yards

Fort Erie Defenses

the schooners *Ohio, Somers,* and *Porcupine* on station in Lake Erie, guarding the southern end of the camp.[7]

As Ripley oversaw what he believed to be a futile effort, Brown received discouraging information. Gaines, who had not yet received orders to take command at Fort Erie, sent word from Sacketts Harbor that between 19 and 22 July, 2,000 British troops had passed Ogdensburg marching west. They were driving 300 beef cattle with them. Commodore Chauncey, he continued, was still bedridden and complaining that his base would be left defenseless if he sailed to the Niagara. Thus, nothing was being done to stop the British from reinforcing Drummond.[8]

It appeared to Brown that he must build up his army quickly. He asked New York militia Major General Amos Hall to call up 1,000 militiamen. Hall issued an immediate draft for the required numbers. Brown sent word to his friend and political ally Governor Daniel Tompkins to call up between 3,000 and 4,000 more. "This state has suffered in reputation in this war; its militia have done nothing or but little, and that, too, after the state has been for a long time invaded," the former militia brigadier confided. "I find the inhabitants of this frontier more disposed to skulk from the danger that threatens them, than to arise in defense of their country and her rights," he continued. Brown's lowly estimation proved correct; eighteen days later, only 300 New Yorkers had responded to Hall's draft.[9]

Brown requested that the governor place all militia on the Niagara Frontier under Brigadier General Peter B. Porter. "I have found his mind cool and collected, and his judgment to be relied upon," remarked Brown.[10] When Tompkins read Brown's letter, he also had before him a letter from the disgruntled Porter. "But it is certain that no militia general is to gain any fame while united to a regular force and commanded by their officers," Porter complained. He was perturbed by Brown's order to attack at dawn on the day following Lundy's Lane, as well as by Ripley's "precipitate retreat" to Fort Erie. With Brown and the unbearable Scott both away, Porter was now second in command of the Left Division. But his hopes of ever commanding the division were crushed when he learned that Brown had sent for Gaines to replace Ripley. "In short," Porter grumbled, "I have been brigadiered till I am quite satisfied." His offer to resign his commission and the command of his "ragged, unprovided, and undisciplined" brigade was ignored by Governor Tompkins.[11]

Meanwhile, in Buffalo, an incident occurred that shed light on the state of native affairs. Having reached an agreement with the Grand River Indians to mutually withdraw from active warfare, the Seneca living near Buffalo were dismayed to discover a Canadian Indian spying on the Americans. Confronting this covert agent on the streets of the town, a group of Seneca surrounded him while one of their elders, Farmer's Brother, summarily executed him with a pistol shot.

They then carried the corpse from the city. When told the circumstances of the murder, town officials chose to ignore the incident. The New York Iroquois had not entirely abandoned their American allies.[12]

While the Americans were working frantically to secure their toehold in Canada, their adversaries were comparatively inactive. Drummond spent six critical days after the battle preparing his army to fight what he erroneously believed to be a much more numerous enemy. Procrastination cost him his best chance to defeat the invaders. Drummond's problems were twofold: he had to replace his lost regulars, and he had to feed and supply his army. Preoccupied with those challenges, he gave little thought to finding the Americans and discovering their designs.

Drummond had the service of two brigs, two schooners, and a number of bateaux to move troops and supplies on Lake Ontario. He ordered up De Watteville's regiment, then under command of Lieutenant Colonel Victor Fischer. In the absence of interference from the American fleet, this battalion was on the Niagara Peninsula on 1 August. With the manpower shortage satisfied for the time being, Drummond worked to ease his supply problem. Drummond released his sedentary militia with his recognition of their "zeal, bravery, and alacrity."[13] By this action, he decreased the number of people he had to feed. He also placed his weakest battalions—the Forty-first, the 100th, and now the Eighty-ninth—in the forts at the northern mouth of the Niagara. This put them closer to the source of supplies, the ships and bateaux shuttling between York and the Right Division. The men were put to work improving the defenses. An officer of the 100th, supervising work parties at Fort George, reported to the Marquis of Tweeddale, "were we four times the present strength, we could not finish this fort by Xmas." He added, "much can not be expected from the reg[imen]t, particularly as most of the officers are very young."[14]

Drummond made some tentative efforts to locate the Americans. On 27 July, Norton took a band of his warriors as far south as the falls but found no signs of the enemy. At dawn on the following day, Norton's party rafted across the Chippawa and began to scout southward along the Niagara. A detachment of the Nineteenth Light Dragoons paralleled Norton but kept to the back roads west of the Niagara. On 29 July, still several miles away from Fort Erie, Norton halted. He was joined by a party of Glengarries. This composite unit remained inactive through 31 July. On 30 July, the dragoons made a brief appearance at the western landing of the Black Rock ferry. It was this sighting that spurred the Left Division to redouble its efforts. Not until 3 August did Norton's natives and the Glengarries come within sight of Fort Erie.[15]

The British Right Division, meanwhile, had remained near Niagara Falls. On 31 July, after he had learned that the Americans were south of the ferry site, Drummond decided to resume his stalled offensive. He wrote to Prevost that his "sole attention" was focused on defeating the Americans near Fort Erie and that he was confident that he would be able to do so. Drummond revealed that although he was leaving the three forts in some jeopardy, the risk was worth the opportunity to defeat Brown's army.[16]

On 1 August, the Right Division began its movement toward Fort Erie. In a general order that day, Drummond revealed to his troops his intention to fight the more numerous Americans immediately if they could be "induced" to leave their fortifications. In any event, they were marching to defeat the enemy. Drummond relied on the superior training and steadiness of his troops for victory. He cautioned his men to show no signs of poor discipline. "Loose or irregular formations, disorder, or wavering in the ranks—noise or inattention to the word of command, as they tend to produce confusion," he warned, "also tend to reduce us to the level of our opponents and take from us all our advantages as disciplined troops."[17]

The enterprising Drummond, however, did not depend solely on a major battle to defeat the Americans. In a bold and inspired stratagem, Drummond planned to cut the flow of supplies into the enemy camp. On 2 August, he issued orders for a raiding party of 600 soldiers under Lieutenant Colonel John G. P. Tucker to cross the Niagara north of Black Rock and to move south to Buffalo, destroying supplies and capturing boats and guns. With their supplies gone, Drummond told Prevost, the Left Division would have no choice but to fight or surrender.[18] From the American standpoint, a providential event stymied Tucker's raid. Chauncey finally sailed on 1 August and brought with him to the Niagara Frontier a battalion of the First Rifle Regiment under the gifted tactician Ludowick Morgan. Morgan marched his green-coated riflemen directly to Buffalo. He placed his men at various positions from which they could secure the military supplies and facilities throughout the Buffalo and Black Rock area. Late in the day on 2 August, Morgan spied suspicious movements on the western shores of the Niagara. Surmising the enemy's intentions, Morgan gathered a force of about 240 riflemen and volunteers and placed them along the southern side of Conjocta Creek (modern name, Scajaquada), which flowed into the Niagara north of Black Rock. His men removed the planking from the center span of the sole bridge across the creek. Then they settled down behind timber breastworks to await events.[19]

At 2 A.M. on 3 August, Tucker crossed the Niagara with a formidable raiding party consisting of six companies of the Forty-first Foot and a composite battalion consisting of both flank companies of the 104th and the light companies of the Eighty-ninth and the 100th Foot. Two hours later, Tucker's men reached the Conjocta Creek Bridge and became aware that it was defended by an indeterminate number of the enemy. The British rushed the bridge in the dark, only to encounter a fusillade of accurate rifle fire and to discover that the

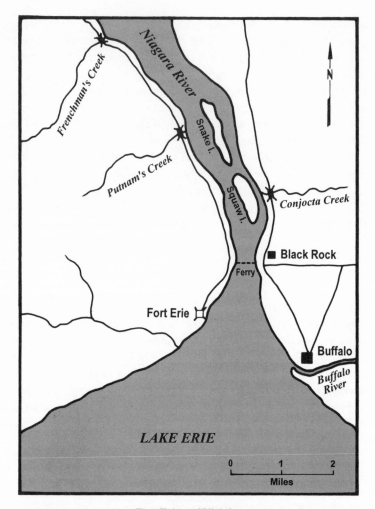

Fort Erie and Vicinity

planking was missing. The British withdrew and collected material to repair the bridge. Their next assault was again repulsed. Tucker sent a detachment farther east to look for a place to ford the creek and outflank the defenders. Anticipating this eventuality, Morgan dispatched sixty men to guard his right. Tucker's attempt to work his way around the Americans failed in the face of superior firepower. After two and a half hours, Tucker broke off the engagement and returned to the Canadian shore.[20]

In his official report, Tucker placed the blame on his troops and the broken bridge. According to Tucker, the soldiers demonstrated "an unpardonable degree of unsteadiness without possessing one solitary excuse to justify their want of discipline." Tucker convinced Drummond that the officers had performed their duties well and had succeeded in re-forming one group of panicking men. The casualties suggest a different conclusion. Tucker reported thirty-three casualties, none of whom were officers. Morgan's force suffered ten casualties, including three officers. Considering the difference in accuracy between the British musket and the American rifle, it is likely that if British officers had been leading from the front, then American fire would have hit some of them.[21]

Drummond learned of the failure of Tucker's raid while he was conducting a careful reconnaissance of Fort Erie. He saw the extensive breastworks connecting Fort Erie to the naturally strong position on Snake Hill and judged the defenses too strong to assault. He also learned of the three schooners patrolling the waters offshore. Despite these obstacles, Drummond decided to open a siege. He sent to Fort George for heavy guns to batter down the American defenses. "I shall be able to compel the force shut up in Fort Erie to surrender or attempt a sortie which can only terminate in his defeat," he wrote confidently to Prevost.[22]

The short engagement on Conjocta Creek was perhaps the most decisive skirmish of the campaign. Failing to cut off the American camp at Fort Erie from its base of supplies in Buffalo, Drummond faced three tough options. He could risk an assault, he could accept the American presence and fall back to a defensible position, or he could open a formal siege. Drummond chose the last. Never before had the British attempted to keep so many troops supplied for so long and so far from Kingston. The American supply line was fairly secure in the interior of New York, whereas Drummond's supply line was extensive and vulnerable to American naval attack. With Chauncey loose on Lake Ontario, Drummond was taking a considerable gamble. To his great credit, Drummond nearly made it work.

Drummond's decision to conduct a risky siege at the end of a long, frail supply line was consistent with the emerging shift in British strategy from defending Canada to taking the war to the United States. As thousands of experienced British troops disembarked at Quebec, Prevost pushed troops in Lower Canada westward to reinforce Drummond. Prevost was careful to maintain enough troops in the Champlain-Richelieu corridor to block Izard. As the troops poured in, Prevost designed an offensive campaign to take advantage of them. He envisioned a double offensive aimed at both Sacketts Harbor and Plattsburg. He would concentrate the newly arrived forces at Montreal by the end of August and strike in mid-September. Prerequisites for this major offensive were the Lake Ontario and Champlain squadrons. He wrote to Lord Bathurst that "without their aid and protection nothing could be undertaken affording a reasonable hope of substantial advantage." Since Vermonters were providing his forces with beef cattle, Prevost decided to limit his advance to the New York side of Lake Champlain.[23]

The long-anticipated buildup of British forces was witnessed by American spies. Izard reported to Armstrong that over 4,000 troops had arrived in Quebec between 20 July and 2 August. Between 30 July and 3 August, as many as 1,200 British troops were counted in boats moving westward on the St. Lawrence.[24] All this activity, as well as the ominous threat of British invasion from the sea, made Governor Tompkins exceedingly nervous. New York was vulnerable on four fronts: Plattsburg, Sacketts Harbor, the Niagara Frontier, and New York City. Tompkins believed that the British would attempt again their failed strategy of 1777—simultaneous thrusts up the Hudson and down Lake Champlain. Success would sever Federalist New England from the rest of the country and perhaps lead to a breakaway state there. Tompkins turned his attention to the fortifications protecting New York City and the Hudson River and called up 3,000 militiamen for their defense.[25] Facing multiple threats, Tompkins could not afford to be generous about assisting Brown on a thinly populated and distant frontier.

On 4 August, Brigadier General Edmund Gaines arrived on the Niagara Frontier and assumed command of the Left Division in Fort Erie. Brown, still recuperating, retained overall command of all U.S. forces in the Ninth Military District from Sacketts Harbor westward. Brown and many of his officers were elated that the ever-pessimistic Ripley was relegated once again to brigade command. Lieutenant Varnum wrote to his senator father that "since Gen[era]l Gaines has taken command, a new life and spirit appears to have been infused into our army."[26] Brown wrote to Armstrong that "under *his* command, this army will not permit the fair fame it has acquired to be sullied." He went on to warn his superior: "Should any officer arrive senior to Gaines but junior to me, I shall order him away, unless otherwise directed by you."[27]

Gaines wasted no time in taking charge. He inspected the men and found them healthy and in good spirits. He satisfied himself that his supply line to Buffalo, a small flotilla of bateaux and larger craft, was adequate to bring in provisions and to evacuate the wounded.[28] Then, in a bold decision, Gaines ordered an offensive. Gaines believed that he was opposed by about 4,000 troops, whereas he commanded fewer than 3,000. Nonetheless, on 6 August, he offered battle. Gaines drew up the Left Division in battle line on the plain outside his fortified camp. To lure the British to battle, Gaines sent Morgan and his riflemen into the woods toward the British camp. Morgan's orders were to drive in the British pickets but slowly retire when the British main body emerged to regain lost ground. This would present Drummond with an unmistakable invitation to battle.[29]

Morgan executed his part of the scheme according to plan. His men cleared the woods of Indians and picket guards and continued firing at the British defensive works for about two hours. Drummond sent the Glengarries and a small reserve to combat the Americans. Morgan dutifully withdrew, but Drummond withheld his troops from pursuing. The British never reached the edge of the woods facing Fort Erie and never saw the American battle line. Gaines's invitation to Drummond had not been refused; it had not been delivered.[30]

Drummond had more to worry about than a lapse of protocol. On 4 August, Chauncey's Lake Ontario squadron appeared at the mouth of the Niagara River. Once there, Chauncey spied the four Royal Navy vessels supporting Drummond's army. Three escaped into the mouth of the river and the protection of the guns of the three forts. The fourth vessel, a brig, ran aground. Its crew set fire to the ship rather than let it fall into American hands; then they escaped to the Canadian shore. Chauncey, believing that he had done all for the army that duty required of him, left three brigs to keep watch over the enemy craft in the river and took the rest of the squadron to Kingston to offer battle to Sir James Yeo.[31] With Chauncey on the lake, reinforcements for Drummond would have to march from Kingston, a trip taking anywhere from fifteen to twenty days. The flow of provisions from York and Kingston was cut off, and the British Right Division would have to subsist on stores already in the area. Fortunately for Drummond, he had enough food and equipment to begin a siege. His problem was to conclude the battle before food and supplies ran out.

British siege doctrine was fairly well developed by 1814. When a commander decided to besiege an enemy position, he turned over the technical aspects of the operation to his chief engineer. The engineer drew up the plans, which located batteries, defensive works, and connecting trenches. He tried to isolate the enemy from its source of supply and reinforcements. Often this meant encircling the enemy with guns and troops. The engineer sequenced the work and organized and directed the work parties. Most digging occurred at night to minimize the enemy's ability to bring fire on the diggers. The besieger's goal was to create a breach in the walls of the enemy's fortification before the enemy could repair it or create a new defensive work behind the one being battered down. This all had to be completed before a relief force arrived or before the besiegers ran out of food and ammunition. A siege required specialized materials: large guns, quantities of ammunition, timber for gun platforms and to hold up earthen walls, shovels, axes, and other tools.[32] Siegecraft was a very specialized military skill requiring particular competence. Unfortunately for Drummond, his chief engineer was not up to the task.

Lieutenant George Phillpotts was young and inexperienced, and he confronted a special situation. Because the American camp lay along the lakeshore, Phillpotts could not easily cut its supply line by the judicious placement of batteries. On the north and west side of the enemy camp lay a forest separated from the camp by a flat, open field. If handled correctly, this presented the British with a decided advantage. By locating a battery in the woods, the British could work on it day and night with little threat from American artillery in Fort Erie. When the battery was ready for action, the British could cut down the trees between the battery and the fort and open fire. Phillpotts appreciated the potential. He also appreciated that the American camp was long and narrow. By aligning their guns with the long axis of the camp, the British could cause considerably more damage, because there would be more targets to strike as the solid balls bounced through. Although the British battery would be in range of American guns located on the New York shore, its location in the forest would conceal it from direct observation.[33]

Drummond supported his engineer by establishing a line of pickets in the forest between the battery and the American camp. He also maintained a ready reserve to respond to any American attempt to interfere with the work parties. On 5 August, work began. Two days later, at dawn, the first British gun fired at the fort. To Drummond's distress, the battery was located at such a great distance that the solid shot inflicted little apparent damage. "I very much doubt," one Canadian observer recalled, "if one shot in ten reached the rampart at all, and the fortunate exceptions that struck the stone building at which they were aimed, rebounded from its sides as innocuous as tennis balls."[34] Phillpotts returned to his drafting table and recalculated a better firing position.

Although his guns were firing at Fort Erie, Drummond was convinced that the weak point in the American lines was between Snake Hill and the lake. Determined to crush the Americans as quickly as possible, Drummond hoped to conduct a short but heavy bombardment of Fort Erie and to deliver the main attack at the south end of the camp. In light of the large number of enemy he believed to be in the American camp, he considered the venture to be hazardous. Therefore, Drummond sent for every soldier on the Niagara Peninsula, except for those necessary to the defense of the three forts, to march to his siege camp.[35]

Activity in the American camp kept up with that of the British. Towson's battery on Snake Hill was ready for action on 10 August, and the Americans closed the gap between it and the lake with a line of abatis that was dense enough to slow down an attack but low enough to be fired over by infantry.[36] Some work parties thickened the abatis surrounding the camp, and others threw up tall traverses perpendicular to the line of British fire. Gaines hatched a plot to send a raiding party downriver at night to attack Drummond's headquarters but canceled the plan because there were insufficient boats to carry the number of soldiers necessary for the venture.[37]

The Americans expected an attack at any time, but morale in camp picked up on 9 August with the arrival of orders brevetting McNeil, Leavenworth, and Jesup to lieutenant colonel and Towson, Crooker, and Harrison to major for their gallantry on 4 and 5 July.[38] Two of Gaines's key subordinates, however, were disheartened. Porter wrote to Tompkins that the American position was

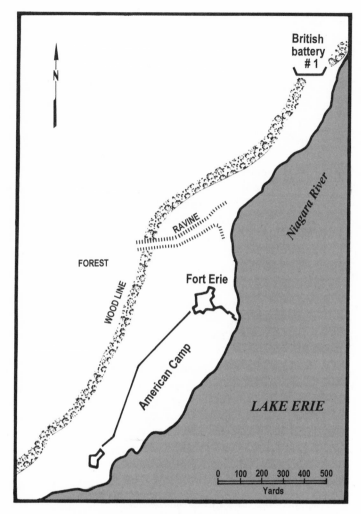

Fort Erie and British Battery 1

"wretched." Ripley apparently believed that he had little to contribute and asked Gaines for a two-month furlough. Gaines had no authority to grant leave to a general officer and referred the request to Brown.[39]

On the other side of the Niagara, American forces did their best to support their comrades holed up in Fort Erie. The two guns in the battery at Black Rock opened fire on the British battery and camp on 12 August, inflicting a few casualties. The quartermasters moved supplies deeper inland to avoid their destruction by British raiders. They also built boats to move supplies and, if necessary, to evacuate the Left Division. Brown was convinced that he could not withdraw the army. This activity would be noticed by the British, who would surely interfere. Brown concluded that the Left Division was safer where it was.[40]

Gaines, disappointed at not carrying out his plan to capture Drummond in his headquarters, contented himself by ordering frequent skirmishes in the forest to slow the British siege effort. Morgan's First Rifles were augmented by Captain Benjamin Birdsall's two companies of the Fourth Rifle Regiment, a new formation recruited in New York and Pennsylvania. Birdsall (a young graduate of West Point) and his men were a welcome addition to the besieged army. Gaines ordered his riflemen into the woods on 6, 10, and 12 August.

They faced light troops organized for forest fighting. Besides the handful of Indian warriors still with the army, Drummond had the service of the Glengarries and the Volunteer Battalion of Incorporated Militia. For the most part, casualties were few on both sides, and it is not clear to what degree this activity slowed down construction of the siege batteries. However, the cost to the Americans escalated on 12 August with the death of Ludowick Morgan. The Americans mourned the passing of this gallant soldier.[41] Within hours, however, their attention was diverted by a serious setback offshore.

The American Lake Erie squadron maintained three schooners in the waters around the American camp. The *Ohio, Somers,* and *Porcupine* were under the command of naval Lieutenant Augustus Conklin. When the four Royal Navy vessels supporting the Right Division were forced up the Niagara by Chauncey, their chief, Commander Alexander Dobbs, hatched a plot to redress the balance of naval power. He and seventy seamen and Royal Marines moved six small craft overland from Queenston to the shores of Lake Erie. His intention was to capture the three American schooners. Word of Dobbs's enterprise leaked to the Americans by way of a deserter. Lieutenant Colonel George McFeely in Buffalo tried to warn Conklin but was brushed off. On the evening of 12 August, the British vessels approached the anchored American vessels. In minutes, the raiders swarmed over the sides and seized *Somers* and *Ohio.* The *Porcupine* managed to evade capture. Losses were light on both sides, but Conklin and seventy of his men marched off into captivity. Now the American supply vessels ferrying back and forth across the Niagara were largely unprotected.[42]

The capture of the American schooners raised spirits in the British camp. Although the three remaining Royal Navy vessels were riding uselessly at anchor in the Niagara River, Drummond appreciated the service they and their crews had provided to the campaign. He wrote to Prevost that "without their valuable aid in the transport of troops and stores I certainly should not have been able to have attempted offensive operations so soon after my arrival."[43] The British enjoyed closer cooperation between the services than did their opponents. However, like Brown, Drummond was having problems with some of his subordinates.

He reassigned Lieutenant Phillpotts because he had erred in positioning the battery and because work was progressing so slowly. Drummond and Colonel Hercules Scott, one of his brigade commanders, had a mutual falling out. Scott requested to be relieved of brigade command and to return to command of his regiment, the 103d Foot. He had lost confidence in Drummond after watching his performance at Lundy's Lane. "I am sorry to say I could not then [at Lundy's Lane] or now observe the smallest appearance of generalship," he wrote to his brother. For his part, Drummond, when informing Prevost of Scott's request, concluded that he could "derive no assistance from that officer."[44] Hercules Scott got his wish and would be at the head of his regiment in the coming assault.

The British placed four guns in their battery, and at dawn on 13 August, the bombardment began in earnest. It continued until sunset and recommenced the next morning. Although set back so far that the guns did little damage to the fortifications, round shot that passed over the walls was deadly. Gaines reported forty-nine casualties in the two-day bombardment. The traverses were effective in limiting the damage, but they could not provide complete protection. The British artillerists fired their weapons at high angles, dropping the rounds between the traverses. At times, the solid iron balls would strike a traverse and ricochet along its length, taking down rows of tents and their occupants. An incident was reported of a sergeant who was being shaved under the protection of a traverse losing his head to an iron shot, the barber losing a hand. For their part, the British could only guess at the extent of damage being inflicted in the camp's interior. On the afternoon of 14 August, a mortar round struck an American powder magazine, resulting in a loud explosion but otherwise causing no harm. To Drummond and his men, however, the sound of the blast was evidence of serious damage and confirmation that the time was right to assault the American stronghold.[45]

Drummond planned a three-pronged assault of the American camp. Shortly before 2 A.M. on 15 August, a small body of Indians and light troops would make a demonstration against the center of the long breastwork connecting Fort Erie to Snake Hill. This would draw the enemy's attention to that part of the line. Then, at two o'clock, Lieutenant Colonel Fischer of De Watteville's regiment would lead the main assault, a bayonet attack by 1,000 men, through the gap between Snake Hill and the lake. Drummond was unaware that this gap had been closed with an abatis. Since it was important that the Americans not observe the assault force until it was too late to respond, Drummond "most strongly" recommended that the troops remove the flints from their weapons. Thus, no careless firing en route to the objective would alert the American sentries. Drummond reminded Fischer that an attack without firing would conceal from the enemy the number of attackers. The Americans, he continued, would expose themselves by their fire and also by their white trousers. The British regulars

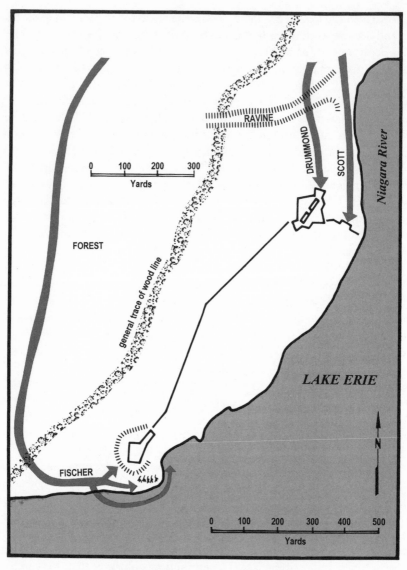

Fort Erie: Night Attack, 15 August 1814

wore gray trousers. Fischer was to "use the bayonet with the effect which that valuable weapon has been ever found to possess in the hands of British soldiers."[46] Drummond's decision to remove the flints from the weapons of his soldiers making the main attack was to have disastrous results. Perhaps he was trying to replicate the successful attack on Fort Niagara nearly nine months earlier. That attack had been delivered against a careless and unsuspecting enemy; this one was not.

Once Drummond perceived that Fischer was into the American camp, the second prong of the assault would spring forward. Hercules Scott would lead 700 men of his own regiment against the wall connecting Fort Erie to the lake. Once that attack was under way, Lieutenant Colonel William Drummond would charge directly against Fort Erie at the head of a column of 360 soldiers, sailors, and marines. These two assaults—led by Scott and Drummond—would keep the defenders on the walls, unable to respond to Fischer's silent bayonets cutting deep into the camp. Lieutenant General Gordon Drummond would retain a reserve of light troops under Lieutenant Colonel Tucker in the wood line opposite the northern face of the American camp.

To succeed, the British main attack (Fischer's column), had to penetrate the enemy camp before Gaines could respond with strong forces. Drummond needed to catch the Americans unprepared. This prerequisite would not be met. Since he had taken command, Gaines had been apprehensive of a British attack during hours of darkness. He had therefore directed that one-third of the garrison be on duty throughout the night while the remainder slept fully clothed with their weapons by their sides. On the afternoon of 14 August, when Gaines heard the British cheer the sound of the explosion of the powder magazine, intuition told him that attack was imminent. Gaines passed this assessment to his key officers. That evening found the Americans particularly vigilant.[47]

Gaines had positioned the units of the division so that regulars and militiamen were interspersed. Starting at the southern end of the camp and moving clockwise around the perimeter, he placed Ripley's Second Brigade, Porter's Third Brigade, and the First Brigade now commanded by Lieutenant Colonel Thomas Aspinwall. From the Second Brigade, the Twenty-first Infantry was responsible for the gap between Lake Erie and Snake Hill. Towson's artillerists defended their battery on the hill, and the Twenty-third Infantry defended a short line of the breastworks to the right of Towson's battery. The majority of the long breastworks was manned by Porter's brigade, reinforced by the First and Fourth Rifles. Inside Fort Erie, artillery Captain Alexander J. Williams commanded sixty gunners and six cannon. Major William A. Trimble led two companies of recruits of his regiment, the Nineteenth Infantry, which reinforced the artillerists. From Fort Erie to the shore was the First Brigade, reinforced by two companies of volunteer militia from Porter's brigade. In the middle of the First

Brigade was Douglass's battery, manned by the bombardiers from West Point. Gaines stationed his versatile engineers, McRee and Wood, along the northern and southern defenses, respectively. McRee commanded a cannon, and Wood led four companies of the Twenty-first Infantry. Pickets were put out in the woods to give early warning of attack. Gaines himself walked the entire perimeter, encouraging the men and passing instructions to senior officers. Altogether, Gaines had about 2,600 men, mostly veterans, awaiting the British onslaught.[48]

Fischer's column departed the British camp at 4 P.M. and moved undetected several miles through the forest to a waiting area west of Snake Hill. There the men rested into the evening hours, the officers ensuring that none deserted the ranks. At about 1 A.M. the British cannonade stopped. Gaines departed his quarters to walk the lines once more. His officers woke the men and put them in position to receive an attack. Fischer formed his attack column in the concealment of the forest. The advance guard, a "forlorn hope," was composed of parts of the light companies of the Eighth Foot and De Watteville's regiment. Behind them was the main body consisting of De Watteville's with the Eighth Foot in reserve. According to Drummond's plan, just before two o'clock, some soldiers and Indian warriors moved into the clearing opposite the center of the American breastworks and began firing.[49]

This was Fischer's signal to move out. As his men pushed forward toward the edge of the woods, they were fired on by American pickets from the Twenty-third Infantry. The sentinels did their job, giving warning to the men inside the camp. The British came on quickly. As the Americans withdrew through a narrow lane in the abatis, their leader, Lieutenant Belknap, bringing up the rear, received a bayonet wound. The fierce fight was on. As soon as Wood saw the attackers across the abatis, he ordered his men to fire. The musketry was too much for the advance guard and the De Wattevilles who were to their rear. Unable to return the fire, and unable to go forward, the attackers recoiled. But they came on again. The "forlorn hope" and some of the main body waded out into the lake and tried to outflank the low wall of abatis. Ripley, seeing their movement, sent two companies to the beach to oppose them. In the face of the withering fire, and unable to return it, the British surrendered or were cut down.[50]

Meanwhile, Towson's battery was firing furiously into the British main body and reserve. Gaines arrived at the scene of the struggle and was satisfied by Ripley and Wood that the situation was under control. Fischer's officers repeatedly formed the men in the darkness and led them forward against the abatis and Snake Hill. Some parties of British penetrated the abatis in front of Snake Hill. They threw up ladders, but these proved too short to surmount the sandy redoubt. Ripley counted a total of six attacks before the British finally withdrew. Some of De Watteville's regiment broke and ran back through companies of the Eighth Foot, throwing them into confusion. Ripley sent a detachment out of the camp to collect prisoners; a total of 147 were taken, including many who had waded around the abatis. The British main effort had failed.[51]

Fischer reported later that the attack had been stopped because the gap between Snake Hill and the lake "was found impenetrable." He then blamed the advance guard, which had retreated through the rest of the column, throwing them "into such confusion." The remainder of the column was thus stalled and, "exposed to a most galling fire," could not regain its momentum.[52] This report does scant justice to brave soldiers carrying out an attack that was flawed from its inception. Drummond believed the gap to be open, and because the abatis was low, even scouts, had they been sent, might not have detected its presence. The key to failure was Drummond's order to remove the flints. Unable to force their way through the abatis and unable to return fire, even the bravest troops might turn back. John Norton reached this same conclusion. "On the right the want of success was attributed to the flints, having been taken out of the muskets of the De Wattevilles by order of their commanding officer to prevent them from firing, which it effectually did, but at the same time by daunting the men, it might have had no less effect in checking their advance against the fire of the enemy."[53]

As the remnants of Fischer's broken column receded into the forest, the next prong of Drummond's attack moved forward. Colonel Hercules Scott led his regiment forward, easily pushing back the American pickets. As had those in the woods at the south end of camp, these American sentinels did their job well. They fired at the attackers, giving ample warning to the men at the walls, and fell back rapidly to avoid the friendly fire soon to follow. The defenders could hear Scott's officers issuing orders to their men to close ranks and prepare to charge. Not waiting, however, for the British to come into view, the American cannon and muskets opened up a horrendous firing that smashed Scott's assault before it fairly began. Scott was mortally wounded early in the fight by a single bullet penetrating his forehead. His major and fourteen other officers were felled. Without leadership, and in the confusion of a plan gone bad, the men broke into small groups. Some sought the protection of the wood line, but others moved to their right to join the attack starting against the nearest bastions of Fort Erie.[54]

Of the three prongs of the British attack, this one against Fort Erie proper enjoyed the most success. Lieutenant Colonel William Drummond's column made it to the ditch below the bastion with few casualties. His men threw up ladders and scrambled up and over the walls but were thrown back. Again and again they came on. Finally success came. In a desperate hand-to-hand fight in which no quarter was granted, two American artillery officers, Captain Williams and Lieutenant McDonough, died defending their guns. The surviving artillerists fled to a stone barracks, and the bastion fell to Drummond's men. However, they could not push the attack further into the interior of the fort against

Trimble's men firing from the security of the barracks. Lieutenant Colonel Drummond had not ordered his men to remove their flints; thus, they not only returned the American fire but also handily defeated the two or three counter-attacks sent to dislodge them.[55]

Gaines sent for reinforcements, and both Ripley and Porter responded, feeding men into the growing brawl in and around the bastion. Lieutenant Douglass turned the guns of his battery to the left and swept the approaches to the bastion, thus discouraging any reinforcements from aiding Drummond's beleaguered men. As the minutes accumulated into an hour, the stalemate continued. Then the fates interceded and tipped the balance decisively in favor of the Americans. Lieutenant Douglass later described what happened next:

> But suddenly, every sound was hushed by the sense of an unnatural tremor, beneath our feet, the first heave of an earthquake; and, almost at the same instant, the center of the bastion burst up, with a terrific explosion and a jet of flame, mingled with fragments of timber, earth, stone, and bodies of men rose, to the height of one or two hundred feet, in the air, and fell, in a shower of ruins, to a great distance, all around.[56]

Over the years, there was much debate over the cause of the explosion. Was it entirely accidental, a flame touching off the gunpowder magazine within the bastion? Or had an American donned a captured uniform coat and slipped into the British ranks to ignite the blast in a heroic suicidal gesture?[57] What is known for certain is that the British force in the bastion was all but annihilated, with Lieutenant Colonel William Drummond among the dead. Dazed survivors who could do so tried to withdraw to the wood line aided by Norton's warriors, who had worked their way toward the fort. The Americans quickly repossessed the bastion and fired on the retiring British.[58]

Gordon Drummond recognized defeat. He deployed his reserve to cover the withdrawal of the survivors of Scott's and Drummond's columns. Gaines sent some parties out of the fort to claim prisoners from among the wounded, but he did not sortie to drive off the besiegers. Both sides began the difficult task of finding and attending to the wounded. As dawn broke, Lieutenant Douglass toured the bastion. "The whole bastion," he recalled, "and its immediate neighborhood were heaped with dead and desperately wounded; while bodies and fragments of bodies were scattered on the ground in every direction. More than a hundred bodies were removed from the ruin."[59] Back in their camp, the British conducted roll calls to ascertain their losses. Drummond reported a total of 905 casualties in a battle lasting less than three hours.[60]

American casualties, in contrast, were light. Gaines reported only two officers and fifteen soldiers killed among a total of seventy-four casualties. The defense of Fort Erie made Edmund Pendleton Gaines's reputation. One month later he was brevetted to major general, and in November, Congress voted him its thanks. The states of New York, Virginia, and Tennessee presented Gaines with swords.[61] Brown's decision to call Gaines from Sacketts Harbor to replace Ripley was fully vindicated.

While the Americans took justifiable pride in their one-sided victory, Gordon Drummond had to deal with defeat. Yet another regiment, the 103d Foot, had been shattered. Drummond sent the 103d to garrison Fort Niagara, and he brought the Eighty-ninth, not yet recovered from its action at Lundy's Lane, forward to the siege camp. Drummond justified his assault to Prevost by noting that his bombardment had sufficiently softened up the defenders. He had chosen a surprise night attack to increase the chances of success. Drummond blamed the failure on the "disgraceful" conduct of De Watteville's regiment. He did not mention that Fischer's men had attacked without their flints. Prevost, in turn, gently criticized his subordinate for attacking in the dark because in such conditions, "chance and not skill too frequently decide the contest."[62]

Drummond wanted to resolve the siege quickly, because Chauncey's presence on Lake Ontario had effectively cut his supply line. All he could count on was the food and supplies then on the Niagara Peninsula. His decision to assault was justified, given what he understood of the situation: that there was an assailable gap in the defenses, that a night attack would catch his opponents unprepared, and that the Americans would crumble before a disciplined assault with cold steel. The American army of 1813 had demonstrated these shortfalls, but Drummond steadfastly refused to recognize the foe's dramatic improvement. As it turned out, Drummond's assumptions proved false, and the British Right Division suffered devastating consequences. Yet Gordon Drummond was as tenacious as a bulldog. To his credit, he refused to back off from the siege as long as he could keep his army fed and supplied with ammunition. The drama would continue for another month.

While the Left Division was struggling to retain a precarious hold in Canada, George Izard's Right Division was immobile on New York's northern frontier, transfixed by a sizable British force just across the border. In late June, Izard had received Armstrong's guidance to move a large contingent westward to cut the British line of communication along the St. Lawrence River. Izard selected a potential location near Ogdensburg from which he might accomplish that mission, but he warned Armstrong that he would be leaving Plattsburg and the Lake Champlain area vulnerable if he moved. He informed Armstrong that treasonous trade between Vermonters and the enemy was increasing scandalously. "On the eastern side of Lake Champlain," he wrote, "the high roads are found insufficient for the supplies of cattle which are pouring into Canada; like herds of buffalo, they press through the forest making paths for themselves." Without American beef, Izard concluded, British forces would starve. Izard also complained that his troops were behind in their pay and that some of the officers were resigning as they learned that the division might soon be in combat.[63] Izard continued to train his men in earnest and awaited further guidance from the secretary of war.

Armstrong sent no instructions to Izard until 27 July, the day of Madison's stinging rebuke for his secretary's handling of the campaign thus far. At Madison's prompting to use Izard to provide some measure of relief for the Left Division, Armstrong fired off a series of letters to his commander at Plattsburg between 27 July and 12 August. He outlined several options for the employment of the Right Division. Finally, Armstrong settled on ordering Izard to take 4,000 troops and either attack Kingston or move directly to the Niagara Peninsula to operate there against Drummond.[64] On 16 August, Armstrong wrote to Brown, telling him that help was on the way. Armstrong hinted to Brown that Izard's fears for Plattsburg derived from an overestimation of British strength. He also predicted that the enemy would make no move down Lake Champlain when Kingston was at risk. "Prevost understands his trade too well to hazard the loss of any principal post on the westward line of defence for the benefit of scattering firebrands and death among such villages as Plattsburg and Burlington."[65] Armstrong's strategic sense was failing both him and the nation.

Izard warned Armstrong in the strongest terms of the grave risk they were taking. "I will make the movement you direct if possible; but I shall do it with the apprehension of risking the force under my command and with the certainty that every thing in this vicinity but the lately constructed works at Plattsburg and at Cumberland Head will in less than three days after my departure, be in the possession of the enemy." He hinted that Armstrong was keeping him in the dark. "I knew of the proceedings at the westward," he wrote, referring to the Niagara campaign, "no more than you had communicated in the plan of campaign . . . and then I saw in the newspapers the Second [Left] Division was advancing." Finally, he demonstrated lack of confidence about his ability to accomplish his task. "Although I anticipate disappointment," he penned, "I will guard myself against disgrace." Izard later wrote that Armstrong should not expect him to march westward before 25 August. Again expressing his fears for the safety of the territory he was leaving, he cautioned Armstrong: "I must not be [held] responsible for the consequences of abandoning any present strong position."[66]

Izard gathered information in preparation for this lengthy move. He sent scouts to conduct a detailed reconnaissance of the routes west. He told them to report on the trafficability of the roads for men, artillery, and wagons, as well as the availability of food and forage. He wrote to Commodore Chauncey, asking what support he might expect to receive from the navy. Izard also negotiated an agreement with Major General Sir Thomas M. Brisbane, commander of the British advance guard in Lower Canada. The two generals forbade their respective pickets to fire on one another. However, a serious omission in his preparations was Izard's failure to inform Governor Tompkins that he would soon depart the northern frontier for Sacketts Harbor. In view of Izard's professed fears for the safety of the area, this oversight is bewildering. It was not until 23 August that Izard had militia Major General Benjamin Mooers call out a regiment of infantry and a company of dragoons to serve near the border. This was a scant force to replace 4,000 regulars.[67]

The most serious question in Izard's mind was the selection of a route westward. Izard had two choices. The northern route passed north of the Adirondacks to Malone and then along the St. Lawrence to Sacketts Harbor, a distance of about 200 miles. The southern route proceeded from Plattsburg south to Schenectady, west along the Mohawk River to Rome, and northwest to Sacketts Harbor. This route was considerably longer at about 300 miles. The northern route, however, penetrated the wilderness on roads of extremely poor quality. Encumbered by a wagon train, the slow-moving column would be vulnerable to ambush by Britain's Indian allies. The southern route enjoyed roads of relatively better quality, progressed through more settled land, and was secure from attack.[68] On 23 August, Izard directed Brigadier General Alexander Macomb to gather the principal officers to discuss the question of routes and to advise Izard. The group duly met, and Macomb reported to Izard that the body unanimously selected the southern route. Izard concurred and issued the order to move.[69]

Izard reorganized the Right Division into two brigades under Brigadier Generals Thomas A. Smith and Daniel Bissell. The division consisted of 4,000 infantrymen and dragoons, but no guns. The column would travel faster without cannon, and Izard expected to pick up artillerists and guns at Sacketts Harbor. Izard left Macomb in charge of 1,500 troops, as well as a large contingent of sick and convalescing soldiers. Macomb's mission was to defend Plattsburg, and events would show that Izard made an admirable choice. When he finally had sufficient wagons, Izard departed the Lake Champlain area with the Right Division and headed toward Schenectady. It was 29 August.

The Right Division averaged more than fifteen miles each day, with a few days thrown in for rest. Izard understood that speed was important, but he wanted to ensure that he did not wear out his troops on the long march. He wrote to Chauncey that he hoped to embark the division "on the moment of my arrival." Nineteen days later, on 16 September, the Right Division reached its goal, the naval base at Sacketts Harbor. Within days, Izard's men

Two Routes to Sacketts Harbor

were seaborne and on their way to the Niagara Peninsula and the last phase of the campaign.

In Washington, the president continued his examination of War Department correspondence, which had resulted in his stern admonition to Armstrong on 27 July. On 12 and 13 August, Madison wrote two lengthy letters to his secretary of war, chastising him not only for mishandling the campaign in the North but also for usurping presidential prerogatives. He belabored the point he had made earlier of the folly of trying to coordinate the activities of Izard and Brown from Washington. He asked a series of questions that penetrated to the heart of the campaign's design. Was it too late for Izard to cut the flow of the enemy's reinforcements on the St. Lawrence? If Izard were moving to the Niagara region, shouldn't Armstrong discuss this with the Navy Department? In light of Izard's departure, what arrangements had been made with Vermont and New York for the use of their militias to secure the bases on Lake Champlain?[70]

Shifting gears, Madison recounted instances in which Armstrong had assumed powers that Madison insisted were his alone. The president had learned that Armstrong had consolidated regiments by reading of it in the newspaper. Likewise, he learned after the fact that Armstrong had outlawed dueling on pain of summary dismissal from the service. Madison had not forgotten Armstrong's shady role in William Henry Harrison's resignation and Andrew Jackson's promotion. Each of these issues involved the making and breaking of officers—an important political matter, and one that Madison thought should pass across his desk for approval. The president then provided his secretary of war with a list of instances that required presidential endorsement prior to promulgation. In addition to the cases mentioned above, Madison added the court-martial of general officers, the requisition of militia into federal service, and operational instructions to the commanders of military districts. It was clear that Madison's faith in Armstrong was continuing on a slow decline.[71]

As a result of these biting reprimands, and perhaps to share responsibility should things go awry, Armstrong sought Madison's involvement in directing the campaign. Specifically, Armstrong asked the president whether Gaines might, on his own authority, retreat from Canada. Madison replied that such a decision, particularly in light of the number of British reinforcements moving westward, was within Gaines's discretionary authority. Madison continued that he preferred that Izard be used to stop the flow of enemy troops along the St. Lawrence. However, if that proved impractical, Madison suggested that Izard send 2,000 reinforcements to Gaines and retain the remainder at Sacketts Harbor. Madison revealed no qualms about Izard's taking the bulk of his forces away from the Champlain region.[72] Armstrong was satisfied to learn that the presidential advice was consistent with instructions he had been transmitting to his commanders in the field. Having launched Izard westward, Armstrong found that his attention and that of the president were soon captured by menacing events in other theaters of operation.

On Lake Ontario, Commodore Chauncey was unable to instigate the decisive naval battle for which he had painstakingly built his superb fleet. Reluctantly he had departed Sacketts Harbor on 1 August and rendered the Left Division a most valuable service by bringing Morgan's battalion of the First Rifles to the Niagara. He had also slowed the flow of reinforcements and supplies to Drummond's Right Division, an act that contributed directly to the end of the siege of Fort Erie. But the objective of Chauncey's protracted arms race, the destruction of Yeo's squadron, eluded him. By 9 August, Chauncey was loosely blockading Kingston, and he would remain there until late September, when Yeo emerged with the *St. Lawrence*. Rated at 110 guns, this was the most powerful warship to sail the Great Lakes during the war. Chauncey's largest ship, the *Superior,* had only sixty-two guns. With the preponderance of combat power now decidedly with the Royal Navy, it was Chauncey's turn to withdraw to the safety of his base, where two vessels, each as powerful as the *St. Lawrence,* were under construction. The decisive naval battle that both naval commanders professed to seek would never occur, and the campaign in the Central Theater of Operations dragged on.[73]

In the Western Theater, Madison's plan to recapture the strategic island of Michilimackinac collapsed. Lieutenant Colonel George Croghan, a competent and enterprising officer with experience in independent command, led a force of 750 regulars and militiamen to destroy British power on the upper Great Lakes.[74] Commodore Arthur Sinclair, commander of the Lake Erie squadron, moved Croghan's men from Detroit into Lake Huron. After burning the British trading posts on St. Joseph Island and at Sault St. Marie, Groghan and Sinclair arrived off Michilimackinac Island on 26 July. Unable to elevate their ships' cannon sufficiently to hit the timber stockade fort, Sinclair landed Croghan and his men on the opposite side of the island. As they were moving through the thick woods, Croghan's men were confronted by Lieutenant Colonel Robert McDouall of the Royal Newfoundland regiment. McDouall commanded a mixed body of regulars, militiamen, native warriors, and coureurs de bois, altogether not more than 450 men. In the confused fight that followed, Croghan was unable to move past the defenders and, despairing of taking the fort, called off the expedition.[75]

Sinclair brought Croghan's troops back to Detroit but left two schooners to maintain a blockade of Michilimackinac. In two separate attacks, on 3 and 6 September, British raiders seized both the *Tigress* and the *Scorpion*. With these two vessels converted to their use, the British maintained a firm hold on the strategic confluence of Lakes Huron, Michigan, and Superior until the end of the war.

The failure to reclaim the upper Great Lakes was of little significance compared to the humiliating hammer blows soon to fall on the Atlantic coast. Transported by the fleets at Halifax and Bermuda, thousands of British troops released from the war in Europe could land without warning virtually anywhere along America's Gulf and Atlantic coastline. Foreseeing this possibility, Madison, on 4 July, called on the state governors to prepare 93,500 militiamen for federal service.[76] The states complied in various degrees. Foremost in zeal was New York's governor Daniel Tompkins.

On 2 August, Tompkins ordered the mobilization of 3,000 militiamen to defend New York. Subsequently, he received Brown's request for more militia to come to the aid of the Left Division on the Niagara Frontier. Tompkins believed, not unreasonably, that it was more important to defend New York City than Buffalo, Sacketts Harbor, or even Plattsburg. Nonetheless, he was unwilling to leave Brown out on a limb. When he received Brown's entreaty, he had already resolved to go personally to New York City to oversee preparations there. Therefore, he dispatched an aide, Lieutenant Colonel John B. Yates, to Brown with full authority to act in the governor's name. Yates met with Brown at Canandaigua on 20 August. As a result of this meeting, Yates ordered the immediate mobilization of 4,000 militiamen from western New York to rendezvous at Williamsville on 1 September. Porter departed Fort Erie and arranged for the arming and equipping of this force. He also sought to prepare these militiamen for the request that they cross over into Canada to help the Left Division break Drummond's siege.[77]

Having sent help to Brown, Tompkins now focused attention on the danger to New York City. The City Council, on 9 August, had already formed a Committee of Defense, whose charter was to coordinate the defensive preparations. This body ordered the mobilization of the city's militiamen to repair forts guarding the land and sea approaches to the city. Within days, thousands of militiamen and other volunteers—men, women, and children, black and white—were busy digging trenches and throwing up earthen fortifications on Manhattan, Brooklyn, and the harbor islets. Social organizations, craft guilds, and churches mobilized their members to dig; the outpouring of effort bolstered Tompkins's confidence. Stephen Decatur commanded the naval forces in the harbor, and Morgan Lewis the land forces. Tompkins requisitioned steamboats on the Hudson to move militiamen to the city. On 31 August, New Yorkers held a grand review of their military forces; over 6,000 men were armed and in position to repel attack. Tompkins had put 14,000 other militiamen on notice to respond immediately to a call-up should the enemy appear. Fortunately for that city, the British chose to attack elsewhere.[78]

In Massachusetts, Federalist governor Caleb Strong, who had steadfastly refused to prosecute the war, slowly began to understand that Massachusetts and the District of Maine were not invulnerable to British retaliation. On 8 July, Henry Dearborn, commanding the First Military District headquartered at Boston, called for 1,100 militiamen for the immediate defense of that port. These citizen-soldiers balked at taking orders from regular army officers and complained to Strong. Within days, however, word that the British had seized Eastport, Maine, reached the governor's ears. On 9 August, a British squadron bombarded Stonington, Connecticut. Three days later, that state called up its quota of 3,000 troops. Strong was forced to act. On 6 September, he issued a general order calling up the entire militia artillery force and ordering an inspection of the remainder of his militia organization. Every man was to have a serviceable weapon, knapsack, and blanket. Strong ordered all deficiencies to be corrected by the "delinquent individual or by the town to which he may belong." Finally, Governor Strong ordered up two brigades of infantry and sent them to Boston.[79] Boston, like New York, was spared from British attack. The British chose to seize territory closer to home instead.

In June, Lord Bathurst, the British secretary for war, ordered Lieutenant General Sir John Sherbrooke, the military commander in Nova Scotia, to seize and retain eastern Maine. Bathurst's objective was to redraw the international boundary southward in order to shorten the land route between Quebec and the maritime provinces.[80] In accordance with these instructions, Admiral Sir Thomas Hardy led an expedition that captured Eastport. About half the citizens of that town swore allegiance to George III. Between 1 and 11 September, the British captured and occupied all of Maine east of the Penobscot River. A handful of American regulars and militiamen were easily dispersed. This expedition added 100 miles of coastline and 26,000 people to New Brunswick. Governor Strong, whose duty it was to defend the people of Maine, chose not to act but to protect Boston instead. The territory was returned to American control by the terms of the Treaty of Ghent, and the British departed in April 1815.[81]

As humiliating as it was to lose a portion of the rocky coast and thick forests of Maine, the loss of the nation's capital was mortifying. The seeds of the plan to burn Washington were planted in Upper Canada when Colonel John B. Campbell burned the port of Dover on 15 May before marching to join Scott at Buffalo. On 1 July, Prevost directed Drummond to notify the Americans that retaliation would follow. He sent word to Vice Admiral Sir Alexander Cochrane (commanding the Royal Navy in North American waters) to retaliate. Cochrane transmitted this order to his officers maintaining the blockade of the American coastline. "You are hereby required and directed," he wrote, "to destroy and lay waste such towns and districts as you may find assailable."[82] When men of the Left Division burned St. David's on 18 July, Prevost called on Cochrane once again "to inflict a severe retribution."[83] Cochrane had been ordered by London to assist Sherbrooke in seizing eastern Maine and also to operate against Washington and Baltimore. In early August, he set sail for the Chesapeake.

As early as 1 July, before the Left Division had departed American shores, the president informed the cabinet of his fears for the safety of Washington. On 2 July, he directed the creation of the Tenth Military District, under Brigadier General William H. Winder, with responsibility to defend Maryland, Washington, and northern Virginia. On 4 July, Madison issued a call-up of 93,500 citizen-soldiers. Armstrong refused to take seriously Madison's concerns. He did not assign a military staff to the Tenth District, so Winder was forced to do much of the administrative work himself. A militia general reported that in conversations with the secretary of war, Armstrong "expressed an opinion that the enemy would not come, or even seriously attempt to come, to this District."[84] Armstrong discouraged Winder from calling out the militia until an enemy attack appeared imminent. For his part, Winder, caught up in the minutiae of administration, failed to plan for an integrated defense of Washington and Baltimore or to gather the arms and equipment that would be required when the militia responded to an order to assemble.[85]

Winder had only a few weeks to prepare before the British arrived. On 20 August, Cochrane landed about 4,000 troops under Major General Robert Ross at Benedict, Maryland. By this stratagem, the British avoided the forts guarding the Potomac and confused the Americans as to their objective—Washington or Baltimore. At this time, Winder had only 1,700 troops—soldiers, sailors, marines, and militiamen—under his control. He sounded the alarm for the militia to rendezvous. Once it became apparent to Winder that Ross was heading for the capital, he gathered troops, numbering about 6,000, at Bladensburg to dispute the road to Washington. Madison, Monroe, and Armstrong all joined Winder on the battlefield to help as they might. It was not enough. On 24 August, the British regulars cut through Winder's larger force. Operating without artillery or cavalry, the British brushed aside the militia. The only serious opposition was offered by a small contingent of sailors and marines that held on until overrun.[86]

Casualties were low on both sides—71 Americans and 249 British. Despite these minor losses, the American force evaporated. James Madison and his cabinet officials fled the capital, as did most of the citizenry. The commander of the Washington Naval Yard burned that facility and all its stores. That night, the British occupied Washington and burned most of the public buildings and several private ones. Considering their standing orders to retaliate for Dover and St. David's, they demonstrated impressive restraint. Then Ross marched his men away from the American capital and reembarked on Royal Navy vessels. They disappeared over the horizon, and the Americans were entirely unsure of where they would strike next.[87]

Madison returned to Washington to survey the damage and to prepare for another attack. He had had enough of Armstrong's political machinations and military failures. On the evening of 29 August, he met one last time with his secretary of war. Armstrong blamed the cowardice of the militia for the loss of the capital. The president stated that Armstrong had lost the confidence of the citizens of Washington as well as of the militia officers, who had stated publicly that they would no longer obey Armstrong's orders. When Madison criticized him for neglecting the defenses of the capital, Armstrong offered to resign. Madison did not accept this offer immediately, but when it was repeated a few days later, he agreed to release Armstrong. The president appointed James Monroe as acting secretary of war, and within weeks, the Senate confirmed the appointment.[88]

Peace negotiations opened in Ghent on 8 August. If Madison expected relief as a result of these talks, he was to be disappointed. The British negotiators, a trio of lightweights, were bound by explicit instructions from Lord Castlereagh, the foreign secretary. Because of their proximity to London, the British diplomats could expect further guidance as events unfolded. The Americans—Henry Clay, Albert Gallatin, Jonathan Russell, John Quincy Adams, and James Bayard—were an impressive team. They had to be, since they were negotiating so far from Washington. Their instructions were to resolve any irritants with Britain: trade, Indian relations, boundaries, and general security. However, from the first, the two sides were miles apart.[89]

Britain's strategic offensive was accompanied by harsh demands. The British required that an international boundary be established between the United States and Indian territory. This territory would serve as a permanent buffer between the United States and British North America, and neither side could purchase land from the Indians. This proposal resembled Tecumseh's dream of an independent Indian confederacy. The British also demanded, as the price of peace, that the United States remove its fleet and forts from the Great Lakes, while the British could retain theirs. They further demanded cession of parts of Maine and other boundary adjustments in their favor. The U.S. commissioners concluded in their report to James Monroe "that there is not, at present, any hope of peace."[90] Still, the negotiators kept the process alive, hoping that military events might lead to a breakthrough. With negotiations deadlocked and the likelihood that the British would soon reappear on the Atlantic coast, Madison's and Monroe's attention was entirely distracted from the fate of the Left Division in Fort Erie.

CHAPTER TEN

The Siege Ends

My command must find relief in some way before many days.
—Major General Jacob Brown to Major General George Izard,
11 September 1814

*In the meantime I have strong grounds for thinking that the enemy will risque an
attack, an event which . . . I shall have to meet under every possible disadvantage, yet I
am very much disposed to hope may be the most fortunate circumstance that can
happen, as it will bring us into contact with the enemy at a far cheaper rate than if
we were to be the assailants, and may at the same time, I trust, bring to a happy crisis
a campaign which has been marked by a series of unlucky circumstances.*
—Lieutenant General Sir Gordon Drummond to Sir George Prevost,
14 September 1814

While the attention of the nation was drawn to the Atlantic coast and the fate of
the nation's capital, far to the north, the siege of Fort Erie ground on to its conclusion. After the Americans successfully repelled a determined British assault
on 15 August, morale in their camp improved. Engineer Lieutenant Douglass
recalled that "the troops who had really been somewhat dispirited, were immediately restored to cheerfulness and confidence; nor were these feelings again
subdued, during all the labors and privations of the subsequent siege."[1] Douglass exaggerated. The rain continued day after day, as did the hard labor. Gaines
had his men rebuild the northeast bastion of the fort, which had been all but
destroyed in the explosion. They built two more bastions on the western side of
Fort Erie and constructed a timber blockhouse between them. Work parties
threw up additional traverses inside camp and thickened the lines of abatis outside the walls until they encircled the entire camp. When planking was available,
the troops put floorboards in their tents so that they could sleep out of the mud

that was everywhere. All the while, British cannon threw round shot into the camp and took a steady toll of the defenders.[2]

Life in the British siege camp was nearly as wretched. American artillery inflicted few casualties because the camp was concealed from the view of the gunners in Fort Erie and Black Rock. However, the British soldiers had few tents, because every wagon and boat was dedicated to moving food and ammunition. The men built huts from boughs and timbers, but this offered little protection from the rain that fell nearly every day. Soon, the siege camp was like a swamp. Like the Americans, the British spent their days and nights on guard duty or constructing defensive works. It was a time of hard work and miserable living conditions punctuated by the excitement and danger of skirmish warfare.[3]

Drummond sent his engineers into the forest to locate and construct a second battery much closer to Fort Erie. Gaines's scouts reported this activity, and the American commander refused to allow this work to continue unchallenged. On 20 August, Gaines sent a large body of riflemen and infantry into the forest to interrupt the British work. They were met by John Norton and a band of warriors, who forced the Americans back into their camp with twelve casualties, at a cost of two natives wounded. Five days later, Major George Brooke and his Twenty-third Infantry surprised the British pickets, who fled leaving thirty muskets on the forest floor.[4] Canadian surgeon William Dunlop recalled that "during the whole time we lay before Fort Erie, bush-skirmishing was an every day's occurrence, and though the numbers lost in each of these affairs may seem trifling, yet the aggregate of men put *hors de combat* in a force so small as ours became very serious in the long run."[5] As a by-product of the skirmishes came another type of casualty—the deserter. Scores of war-weary American and British soldiers took the opportunity presented by the confusion of skirmish warfare to seek the relative safety of prisoner camp. Drummond and Gaines interrogated such deserters, and this proved their best source of information about what was occurring in the respective camps.[6]

Skirmishes slowed work on the second British battery but did not stop it. On 28 August, the British had four new guns in place only 750 yards from Fort Erie. Work parties began felling the trees between their second battery and the fort, only to find that there was a gentle rise in the forest floor that concealed the fort from the view of the British gunners. Thus, neither the American nor the British artillerists could see the strike of their rounds well enough to adjust fire accurately.[7] However, even inaccurate fire proved deadly. On some days, as many as 500 rounds fell into the American camp, inflicting, on average, about a dozen casualties daily.[8] The frequent skirmishes and daily bombardment eroded the numbers and morale of both sides. Relief came to both camps in similar forms.

Militia Major General Amos Hall's call in early August for 1,000 New Yorkers produced only 300 militiamen. There were problems paying and equipping even this small number. When Lieutenant Colonel John B. Yates called for 4,000 more on 20 August, Brown and Porter knew that much would have to be done to make a force of this size a reality. Brown wanted this militia body in federal service as early as 1 September. Porter left Fort Erie and met with militia officers throughout western New York to find the wherewithal necessary to equip the force. State arsenals, which had been depleted by two years of war, were levied again for weapons, flints, ammunition, cartridge boxes, canteens, knapsacks, and blankets. Even captured equipment was pressed into service. Slowly the material needs of the militia appeared at Batavia and Buffalo. The troops appeared too, in large numbers. Militia officers at their head, companies marched westward in response to the call. By the end of the first week of September, about 3,000 men were mustered into federal service and gathered on the Niagara Frontier. Brown, Gaines, and Porter all wondered whether they would volunteer to cross into Canada.[9]

Drummond too was being reinforced and, on balance, had nearly all the advantages. His men could not cite constitutional law to avoid fighting. They were well equipped and trained, and perhaps most important, they were peninsular veterans familiar with victory. In keeping with his operational plan to keep Drummond in the fight while attacking both Sacketts Harbor and Plattsburg, Prevost apportioned his new troops accordingly. He pushed the bulk of his heavy reinforcements, about 11,000 men, toward Odelltown for the move on Plattsburg. He sent a brigade under Major General Sir James Kempt to Kingston for the attack on Sacketts Harbor. By reinforcing Kingston, he thus released four more battalions, nearly 2,400 men, for Drummond's use on the Niagara Peninsula. The Eighty-second Foot arrived in Drummond's siege camp on 29 August, followed by the Sixth Foot on 2 September. On 30 August, Major General Richard Stovin, in command at Kingston, sent the Ninetieth Foot marching to the Niagara. Stovin retained the Ninety-seventh Foot in Kingston until Drummond sent for it. Drummond would have enough troops to maintain the siege.[10]

In the days following the disastrous night attack of 15 August, Drummond reevaluated his position. Reinforcements then en route would easily replace his losses. The construction of a second battery, and a third if necessary, closer to Fort Erie would maximize the effect of his heavy guns. He was not particularly concerned that the Americans were being reinforced by untrained, inexperienced militia. Yet all was not well for the British. On 18 August, Drummond's commissary officer reported that earlier projections of food resources were inaccurate. Instead of a six- to seven-week supply of food, rations would run out in just four weeks. Drummond's problem was to drive back the invaders before his food ran out. The only other alternative was to break off the siege and move his troops to the three forts or Burlington, where they could be fed more easily.[11] Drummond was too stubborn to accept defeat. He sent an urgent message to Prevost outlining his intention to attack as soon as reinforced and opportunity presented itself. He also requested emergency assistance from his superior. Drummond needed more artillerists and ammunition. He wanted a company of sappers and miners. He needed camp stoves, as the weather was turning colder. He needed food. Most of all, however, he needed Yeo's squadron to carry these resources westward. He urged Prevost to impress upon Yeo that the Right Division depended "almost entirely on his prompt and vigorous exertions for its relief, nay perhaps even for its safety." That same day he wrote to Yeo that the army's requirements for resupply "have become so alarmingly great and urgent that nothing but the assistance of the whole of H.M. squadron on Lake Ontario can enable it to continue its operations against the enemy or even retain its present position on this frontier." Drummond was desperate. Three days later, he again wrote to Prevost to "urge the Commodore to use all possible expedition in preparing the squadron for that service, which is certainly far more important than any other on which it can be employed, as on its rapid and successful performance depends the fate of this division."[12]

Drummond was asking something extraordinary of the navy. He knew that Chauncey was blockading Kingston and that Yeo would not sail before the 102-gun *St. Lawrence* was ready. In the best of circumstances, the *St. Lawrence* would frighten Chauncey back to Sacketts Harbor and keep him there while Yeo resupplied Drummond. The other scenario, a decisive naval battle, was equally likely and infinitely more risky. If Chauncey won, the fight for Upper Canada west of Kingston would be lost. Prevost pondered the alternatives. His supply officer confirmed Drummond's plight. Over half of the Right Division's rations were going to the western Indians who had remained hovering about the army since Procter's and Tecumseh's defeat nearly a year earlier. Prevost felt a moral obligation not to abandon them. Although there was plenty of American-supplied fresh beef in Lower Canada, there was not enough salt to prepare it for shipment westward, even if Yeo had been free to take it there. It was not yet harvest-time, and American raiders had been quite successful in destroying mills in Upper Canada. The key issue was the availability of the *St. Lawrence,* and Yeo reported that he would be ready to sail on or about 1 October. There it was then. Prevost boldly decided to risk the fleet to resupply Drummond as soon as Yeo was ready. Drummond would have to decide whether he could win quickly or maintain the siege for six more weeks.[13]

Lieutenant General Drummond decided to stick it out as long as he could. The intrepid and enterprising Captain Dobbs dispatched small craft to evade the American war ships watching the western end of Lake Ontario and make supply runs to York. Militia officers went into the countryside to encourage the farmers to harvest their wheat as soon as possible and to sell their surplus to the army. Drummond took as many artillerists as possible out of the three forts to man the guns in his siege batteries. Drummond maintained his siege army at the far end of an exceedingly frail tether. Something had to happen soon.[14]

What happened can only be described as the fates of war taking the decision out of human hands. On 28 August, a British shell came through the roof of Edmund Gaines's headquarters in Fort Erie, wounding the general severely. There was no question that Gaines would have to turn over command to one of the two brigadiers in camp. Ripley claimed illness and yielded seniority to the newly brevetted James Miller, hero of Lundy's Lane. Brown, still recovering from his own wounds in Batavia, departed for Buffalo as soon as he learned of Gaines's injuries. He was determined to take charge of the fight personally. Once again, as at Lundy's Lane, Brown and Drummond would match wills. However, hardly anyone was watching the unfolding drama on the Niagara. Attention was drawn to two other locations where the full might of British retribution was about to land: Plattsburg and Baltimore.[15]

John Armstrong failed his country when he refused to take seriously the president's concerns for the safety of Washington. His weak support for General Winder contributed directly to the defeat at Bladensburg and the subsequent burning of Washington. This error of judgment was compounded in the Northern Theater, where, in spite of repeated strident warnings from George Izard, Armstrong sent 4,000 of the best American troops marching toward Sacketts Harbor and Buffalo just days before 10,000 experienced British soldiers advanced on Plattsburg.

On 29 August, Izard and the Right Division set off toward Sacketts Harbor by way of Schenectady. He left behind Brigadier General Alexander Macomb with 1,500 troops and Captain Thomas McDonough's Lake Champlain squadron. Over the next week, militia Major General Benjamin Mooer managed to gather together about 1,500 militiamen, including a small battalion of Vermonters. There might have been more militia, but Izard's march took Governor Tompkins completely by surprise. Tompkins had already ordered 5,000 militiamen to Buffalo, perhaps another 2,000 to Sacketts Harbor, and 20,000 to New York City or awaiting orders to march there. The arsenals were virtually empty, and the best militiamen were already committed elsewhere.[16] While Armstrong's strategic myopia set up the conditions for a desperate struggle, Izard's penchant for secrecy considerably reduced the chance for success.

Sir George Prevost himself led Wellington's veterans southward across the border on 3 September. Prevost had engineered a successful strategic defense of British North America for two years, but now he was reverting to field command of a large offensive force. His goal was the complete destruction of American power on Lake Champlain. Such a result would support the negotiators' demands in Ghent to shift the border southward and to prohibit an American military presence on the lake. Prevost knew that naval power was ultimately the key to a successful campaign. His large force could be sustained only by resupply by water. Prevost's supply line extended southward from the St. Lawrence River along the Richelieu River and into Lake Champlain. This meant that his naval squadron would have to prevail over that of Captain McDonough.

Prevost's naval contingent was based at St. Jean on the Richelieu and was led by Captain George Downie. Downie worked feverishly to get the squadron ready, and it took Prevost's pointed gibes to get him to sail. Downie's largest vessel, the *Confiance*, carried thirty-eight guns. Altogether, his flotilla carried ninety-three guns. McDonough's flagship, the *Saratoga*, sported twenty-six guns, and the entire American squadron mounted eighty-six guns. Although the two fleets had a similar number of weapons, the British guns had an advantage at long range, and McDonough's larger number of carronades gave him the advantage in a short-range duel.[17]

Prevost's column moved southward, brushing aside an American security force of riflemen and militia, and on 6 September, 8,200 British soldiers occupied the abandoned city of Plattsburg. South of the city, the unfordable Saranac River lay between the British and American armies. Macomb occupied three earthen forts that overlooked the Saranac. To the east lay Plattsburg Bay and McDonough's squadron drawn up for battle. Prevost sent his men against two bridges across the Saranac, but the American regulars and militia threw back all attempts. Prevost decided to await Downie before pressing his attack.[18]

Finally, on 11 September, Downie's squadron rounded Cumberland Head and entered Plattsburg Bay. With no room for maneuver, Downie ordered his vessels to close in on their American counterparts, thus yielding the advantage of long-range superiority. The two-hour Battle of Plattsburg Bay was a slugfest. Downie brought *Confiance* to anchor opposite *Saratoga*, and the two flagships gave and received broadsides. The smaller vessels followed this example as best they could. Downie was killed early in the fight. Finally McDonough won by an unexpected maneuver. The wily commander had sprung his four largest vessels, a technique that allows a stationary ship to rotate 180 degrees one time. When every gun on *Saratoga*'s starboard was out of action, McDonough wound the ship around and presented *Confiance* with a fresh broadside. It was too much for *Confiance*, which struck its colors. The other British vessels followed suit.[19]

The naval battle, which started at 9 A.M., was supposed to be coordinated with a ground assault across the Saranac. Prevost did not give the order for his brigades to attack until 10 A.M. One British column managed to cross the Saranac, but two others were repulsed. Then, when he saw that Downie's

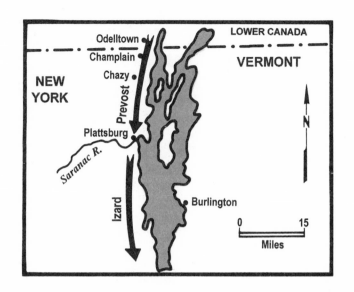

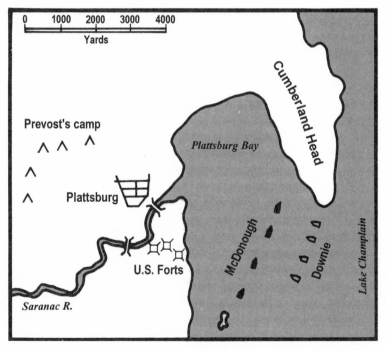

Prevost's Invasion

squadron was lost, Prevost sent word to his brigades to withdraw. Wellington's former officers were furious; victory was only an attack away. Amid the loud protests of his generals, Prevost brought his humiliated army back into Lower Canada. Along the way, over 200 British soldiers deserted. The American position on Lake Champlain was saved by determined sailors and soldiers and their resolute officers, as well as by the timidity of the commander in chief of British North America.[20]

Prevost can be criticized both for his handling of the battle and for his decision to withdraw. Had the ground attack preceded the naval engagement, it would have been possible to capture the American forts and thus force McDonough's flotilla out of the protection of Plattsburg Bay and into the lake. This would have given Downie a better opportunity to maneuver to keep the Americans at long range. Prevost's decision to withdraw without taking Plattsburg drew the most fire from his critics and eventually led to court-martial charges against him. Prevost believed that taking the base without destroying McDonough's fleet would have been pointless, because he could not maintain his army for long with a hostile fleet attacking his supply boats. Destruction of the naval base would have been an illusory victory, as the Americans could have moved their base of operations elsewhere. Prevost might have been heeding Bathurst's guidance, which discouraged any advance that placed his force at risk.[21] Prevost's decision, however, caused him to miss a grand opportunity. Had his ground force destroyed Macomb's army, the effect on the peace negotiations would have been immense, even if he later decided to withdraw. This is not a far-fetched scenario, given the strength and quality of his army. Macomb's men were certainly vulnerable to a siege, bottled up as they would have been in the small triangle formed on two sides by the Saranac and Plattsburg Bay. As it was, the last British soldiers crossed the border into Lower Canada on 25 September.

A month before, the British had departed Washington for parts unknown. James Monroe, the acting secretary of war, expected Richmond, Norfolk, or Baltimore to be the next target. The ease with which the British had seized the capital struck dread into the populace. The civic leaders of Baltimore, a city of 40,000, were determined to defend it. Every white male between sixteen and fifty was called up and armed. Federalist Senator Samuel Smith, a Revolutionary War veteran and a militia major general, was offered command by the city fathers. Accepting the command, Smith refused to subordinate himself to Major General William Winder, the district commander. Smith took full responsibility and full control. He put the citizenry to work digging earthworks east of the city. The militiamen, including many who had run at Bladensburg, were posted on the approaches to the city. In Fort McHenry, which guarded Baltimore Harbor, Lieutenant Colonel George Armistead prepared his force of 1,000 regulars for battle.[22]

Admiral Alexander Cochrane disembarked Major General Robert Ross's splendid infantry (nearly 5,000 strong) on 12 September about fourteen miles from the city. The redcoats had marched about halfway to Baltimore when they came upon 3,000 militiamen drawn up for battle across a narrow approach. While reconnoitering the American lines, Ross was felled by a sharpshooter. Command devolved upon Colonel Arthur Brooke. Unlike at Bladensburg, the militia fought hard and held out for several hours before falling back to the breastworks in front of the city. Brooke brought his men forward and prepared to attack the earthen fortifications. Cochrane moved his fleet as close to the city as he could in order to support the ground attack. He had to get past Fort McHenry if his naval guns were to be brought to bear on the American lines.

Cochrane opened the bombardment of Fort McHenry at dawn on 13 September and continued firing until 7 A.M. the following day. The bombardment was singularly unsuccessful; Armistead and his men simply refused to give up. With the failure of the Royal Navy to subdue the fort, Brooke was unwilling to risk an assault against superior numbers protected by earthworks. No doubt he was persuaded by the fine showing of the militia the day before. Brooke withdrew his men to the ships. All told, except for Armistead's regulars, the federal government had provided scant help to the defense of Baltimore. Its citizens, Samuel Smith, and the Maryland militia deserved most of the credit.

Cochrane sailed away, and by mid-October, most of the Royal Navy was in Halifax or Jamaica for the winter. Unaware of British intentions, as late as 2 October, Monroe expressed fears of renewed attacks on the East Coast. Rumor had reached Washington that Lord Hill, one of Wellington's most able subordinates, had arrived in Bermuda with "powerful reinforcements."[23] Monroe requested that the governor of Virginia call up 4,000 militiamen and send them to the national capital. However, the threat to America's Atlantic coast was over for the remainder of the year. While Madison and Monroe wondered whether Admiral Cochrane had truly departed, Jacob Brown was plotting an end to the siege of Fort Erie.

Major General Brown arrived at Fort Erie on 2 September and put Ripley in charge of the garrison, then numbering 2,246 effectives.[24] Brown believed that the force in the American camp was too small to last much longer in the face of a larger adversary. He also understood that evacuation of the fort would be extremely risky. Brown needed the militia gathering in Buffalo to volunteer to cross the river and reinforce the garrison.[25] He returned to Buffalo and turned his attention to feeding, arming, and training the thousands of New York militiamen arriving at Buffalo and persuading them to cross into Canada. Brown's intention was to coordinate the activities on the Niagara Frontier, leaving Ripley to focus on the defense of Fort Erie. At Buffalo, Brown was visited by newly brevetted Lieutenant Colonel Eleazar Wood. Wood persuaded Brown to move his headquarters to Fort Erie, arguing that the garrison would lose its "moral efficiency" under Ripley, who could not be trusted to defend the American camp with determination.[26] Brown returned to Fort Erie and left Porter in charge of readying the militia.

In the British camp, Drummond pushed forward preparations for another assault. Major General A. L. C. De Watteville arrived in camp on 1 September, sent by Prevost to assist Drummond. The following day, the Sixth Foot marched into camp. Work began immediately on a third battery, only 400 yards from Fort Erie and situated to fire directly on the stone barracks that had proved so troublesome to the attack three weeks earlier. Drummond gave the order to move some of the guns from batteries one and two into the third battery. The British continued to fire nearly 300 rounds each day into the American camp: solid shot, explosive shells, and Congreve rockets.[27]

Brown continued to send skirmishers into the forest to interfere with British work parties. On 5 September, a detachment of forty soldiers of the Twenty-first Infantry reinforced a picket from the Eleventh Infantry. Together they pushed back a British picket guard. Both sides threw in reinforcements. Lieutenant Colonel Joseph Willcocks, who commanded the Third Brigade while Porter was away, led 100 New York volunteers into the fray. The fight lasted about six hours, until a heavy rainfall persuaded both sides to break contact. Willcocks and Lieutenant Thomas Roosevelt of the New York Volunteers were killed in action. The news that the renegade Willcocks was dead boosted morale in the British camp and sounded the death knell for the Canadian Volunteers. The unpopular Benajah Mallory assumed command of the Volunteers, and from this point, the battalion dissolved as men deserted or chose to fight with other units. The Canadian Volunteers marked the extreme of dissent in Upper Canada, and it was fitting that the unit melted away, as did the disaffection that had spawned it.[28]

Drummond strained every resource at his command to keep the siege alive. He ordered the artillerists to slacken their fire so that they would have enough ammunition to support another assault. Drummond ordered every artillery round at Fort George brought forward except for 200 rounds per gun, the bare minimum to defend that fort. He sent three vessels to York to pick up supplies and the Ninety-seventh Foot, which was marching from Kingston. Drummond hoped to attack when the Ninety-seventh arrived in camp. Unfortunately for his plans, U.S. ships reappeared off York before the Ninety-seventh could be embarked, and that formation was forced to continue its tiring march to the Niagara Peninsula on roads reduced to mud pits.[29]

Drummond learned from deserters that several thousand New York militiamen were gathering at Buffalo and that as many as 2,500 had crossed on 10 September to join the garrison at Fort Erie. He ordered his artillery to cease firing to conserve ammunition in case of an American attack. "Every preparation has been made to give the enemy a warm reception," he wrote to Prevost.[30] Drummond began to see that he could no longer maintain the siege. The garrison inside Fort Erie was now as large as or larger than his siege force, and the Ninety-seventh would not arrive for several days. All forage within ten miles of the camp had already been consumed, and roads were all but impassable. The rain continued, the temperature was dropping, and the sick list grew accordingly. His men were without tents and stoves. "Should the rainy weather continue only for a few days," he wrote to Prevost, "I dread the effect it must have on the men in their present situation."[31]

As circumstances in the British camp deteriorated, that of the Americans improved. The New York militia had responded to the call-up with some enthusiasm, no doubt influenced by the expectation that they would be led by Brown and Porter, brave men and competent generals. Brigadier General Daniel Davis ordered out his entire brigade of Genesee County militia and marched them to Buffalo. Porter had tried to enlist Seneca warriors, but they maintained their neutrality. He had better luck persuading the militia officers that they and their men were needed at Fort Erie to save the remnants of the heroic Left Division.[32]

The moment of truth arrived on 9 September. Porter assembled more than 3,000 militiamen on the streets of Buffalo. A band played martial music in the pouring rain. Porter asked for volunteers to cross that evening into Canada. Captain Richardson's company from Cayuga County volunteered to a man. Others joined them. Porter marched this group around the block and across the front of those who held back. The volunteers cheered and cajoled the others. Slowly the ranks of the volunteers grew until they outnumbered those who steadfastly refused to leave New York. When Porter had gathered all who would cross, he marched them off to the boats. One volunteer, a lawyer, changed his mind and called out that it was unconstitutional to be sent out of the country. Porter sent officers to arrest him and take him back to Buffalo under guard. With order restored, the column embarked and crossed over in the darkness. Brown positioned the New York volunteers, about 2,200 in all, southwest of Snake Hill and far from the strike of British artillery. There the men threw up an earthwork wall to protect themselves. The militiamen who remained in Buffalo were put to work guarding supplies and drilling.[33]

With the arrival of the New Yorkers, Brown had the wherewithal to break the deadlock, a move he had contemplated ever since his return to Fort Erie. Brown's decision to sortie evolved over several days. One factor was the Right Division. Brown's understanding of Izard's mission came from Armstrong. According to the then secretary of war, Izard would bring the powerful Right Division to Sacketts Harbor. There, Izard and Chauncey would decide whether to attempt to take Kingston. If they decided not to attack the British naval base, Izard would move to the Niagara Frontier with 2,000 to 3,000 men. If Izard would soon be near, the possibility loomed of not only breaking the siege but also destroying Drummond's army between the two American divisions. However, if Izard and Chauncey launched an assault on Kingston, Brown would be on his own. Izard was Brown's superior, and Brown believed himself obligated to conform with any campaign plan Izard might propose. Brown wrote to Izard and Chauncey repeatedly to ascertain their intentions. However, he lost no time in devising his own plans to deal with Drummond.[34]

On 9 September, Brown gathered several of his senior officers together in an informal meeting to sound them out on what course of action should be followed. Brown himself did not offer an opinion or comment on those put forward, fearing that any loose words might find their way to the British camp. Already persuaded of the necessity of breaking the deadlock, Brown was disappointed that his trusted officers were in agreement to wait out the siege. After the meeting, Brown took Colonel Jesup into his confidence. "We must keep our own counsel," Jesup recalled his chief saying, "the impression must be made that we are done with the affair, but as sure as there is a God in heaven, the enemy shall be attacked in his works, and beaten too, soon as all the volunteers shall have passed over."[35]

Brown acquired his knowledge of the enemy largely from deserters; his skirmishers never got close enough to the British lines to bring back useful information. He personally interrogated every deserter brought into the camp. From them he learned that the British siege camp was two miles behind the siege batteries and entrenchments and that only one-third of Drummond's force was on duty in the siege lines at any time. He learned of the miserable living conditions of the enemy and that food was always in short supply. Lastly he learned that Drummond was constructing a third battery closer than the other two. Brown knew that his force, now largely untrained militiamen, could probably not beat British regulars in a stand-up battle like Lundy's Lane. He analyzed the facts and arrived at a plan. Brown resolved to sortie from the fort and make a surprise attack on the siege batteries for the purpose of destroying as many guns as possible. If the men could do this quickly enough, they could return to the safety of Fort Erie before Drummond's reserve at the siege camp could respond. With fewer guns, the bombardment would prove less costly to the Americans. Drummond might remain in place, but this would set him up for defeat if Izard arrived or if Chauncey returned in force.[36]

Once his mind was made up, Brown kept his secret and took measures that would deceive both his own army and Drummond. He ordered lumber planking to be sent over from Buffalo and put his troops to work improving the flooring of their tents, a sure sign that he was resolved to withstand a long siege. Knowing that Drummond interrogated American deserters, Brown sent over "deserters" with the story that the Americans were confident in their ability to outlast their besiegers. These double agents were to relate that Brown had called up the militia to guard provisions in Buffalo. Brown then ordered the militia in Buffalo to drill within sight of the Niagara in order to support his cover story.[37]

After the militia arrived in camp, Brown took Porter, McRee, and Wood into his confidence and directed them to draw up a detailed plan for his approval. These three met on several evenings. and Brown accepted their plan. On 16 September, Porter sent his aide, Major Donald Fraser, out into the forest with an odd mission. Fraser, without being told the purpose of his efforts, directed a large party of axmen to blaze two parallel trails from Snake Hill all the way to within 150 yards of battery number three. That they were undiscovered can only be attributed to the noise of the bombardment and the steady rainfall.[38]

That evening, Brown called together the officers who would lead the attack. He did not invite Ripley to this secret meeting. Brown issued his attack order and was pleased that the officers received it with enthusiasm. Brown directed a two-pronged attack. Porter would lead one force through the forest and fall on battery number three. Meanwhile, Miller would lead a second force into the ravine between Fort Erie and the forest. Once the sound of Porter's attack was heard, Miller would attack battery number two. Once the guns were destroyed, the two forces would withdraw. After this meeting, Brown sent a final "deserter" into the British camp with the story that all was calm in Fort Erie. At eight o'clock the following morning, Brown sent for Ripley and briefed him on the operation that was to begin in a few hours. Ripley expressed his fears that British scouts, who peered into the American camp from treetops, would see the attack columns leave the fort. Given this advance warning, Drummond would send his reserves into the entrenchments before the Americans arrived. As an afterthought, Brown offered command of the reserve to Ripley, who accepted. Ripley's mission was to support the withdrawal of Porter's and Miller's men back into the fort.[39]

That morning, 17 September, Brown finally received word from Izard. Brown learned that Izard would not attack Kingston but instead would come to the Niagara region and land somewhere "in the rear of the British." Izard expected his men to march into Sacketts Harbor on 15 or 16 September and to depart on Chauncey's fleet soon thereafter. Brown was pleased. It was possible that Izard's trained and experienced Right Division would be available very soon. It was still possible to destroy Drummond's force or at least to force them off of the Niagara Peninsula.⁴⁰ But Brown and Izard would have to hurry. The day before, 16 September, Drummond had decided to end the siege, and he had quietly issued orders to begin moving the siege guns rearward, back to Fort George. There were so few draft animals, however, that it would be several days before the guns were out of the three siege batteries.⁴¹

Porter started forming his men southwest of Snake Hill in midmorning and gave a stirring speech in which he presented his plan of attack. He divided his men into two columns preceded by an advance guard. Colonel James Gibson, a West Pointer, led the advance guard composed of 200 riflemen of the First and Fourth Rifles and a handful of Indians. Porter's right column was under command of the versatile engineer Eleazar Wood, also a West Pointer. Wood led Major George Brooke's combined battalion of the First and Twenty-third Infantry Regiments, about 400 men. Behind Brooke marched a small brigade of 500 New York volunteers and militiamen under Lieutenant Colonels James McBurney and George Fleming and Major Shearman Lee. Lee commanded the remnants of Swift's regiment that had joined the Left Division shortly after Chippawa. Porter's left column was commanded by Brigadier General Daniel Davis and consisted of another small battalion, about 500 militiamen, under Lieutenant Colonels Caleb Hopkins, William Churchill, and Isaac Crosby. Wood's column was to attack batteries three and two in order, while Davis's column was to protect them from interference. Since most of the New Yorkers were in civilian clothing, Porter had them tie red scarves around their heads. At about noon, Porter's force departed camp in a drizzle and picked up the marked trail leading to battery number three.⁴²

Soon thereafter, General James Miller infiltrated his men out of Fort Erie and into the ravine, where they lay down to conceal themselves. Miller's force consisted of two units. Colonel Moody Bedel commanded the Eleventh Infantry, and Lieutenant Colonel Thomas Aspinwall led a combined battalion of the Ninth and Nineteenth Infantry Regiments. When they were in position, Miller informed his men of the victory at Plattsburg, news of which had just arrived. General Ripley formed the reserve just outside the walls of Fort Erie in the concealed area between the two new western bastions of the fort. The reserve consisted of the Twenty-first Infantry and two companies of the Seventeenth Infantry. Lieutenant Colonel Thomas Jesup, his arm still in a sling from wounds received at Lundy's Lane, commanded the Twenty-fifth Infantry inside Fort Erie. Brown watched the deployment of Miller's and Ripley's commands from the walls of Fort Erie, and then he joined Miller in the ravine to wait for Porter's attack to begin.⁴³

In the entrenchments guarding the siege batteries, Colonel Fischer's duty brigade consisting of De Watteville's regiment and the Eighth Foot stood in the rain. They were taken by surprise at about 2:30 when Wood's and Davis's

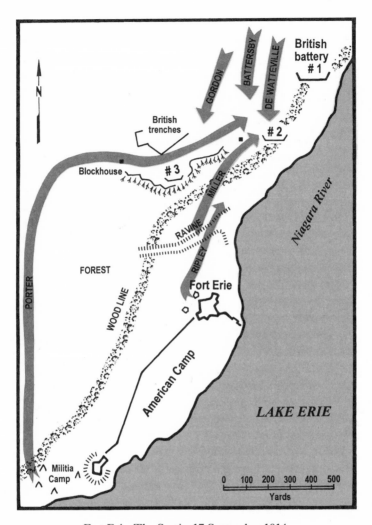

Fort Erie: The Sortie, 17 September 1814

columns appeared out of a light fog. The Americans overran battery number three and its protecting blockhouse, the defenders fleeing or surrendering. Porter's men knocked the trunnions off the siege guns with sledgehammers and smashed the carriages as best they could. They exploded the gunpowder before moving on to battery number two. When Brown heard the sound of the attack, he launched Miller into the gap between batteries two and three. Miller's command linked up with Porter's, and the converged columns thundered into battery number two. The British were waiting for them, but numbers told. Lieutenant

Barstow died while rallying a group of De Watteville's to defend their post. Within minutes, the Americans held undisputed possession of two batteries and the connecting trenches.[44]

When the noise of the battle at battery three reached the British camp, the men sprang into formation without orders. Major General De Watteville came on the scene first and organized the Royal Scots and the Eighty-ninth Foot. He sent them, under command of Lieutenant Colonel John Gordon, to counterattack battery number three. Drummond arrived as the noise moved toward battery number two. Drummond ordered De Watteville to counterattack toward that battery with the Sixth and Eighty-second Foot. Drummond formed up the Glengarries and sent them forward under their commander, Lieutenant Colonel Francis Battersby. The Americans stayed too long. Their units became increasingly confused and separated in the rain and darkness of the forest. As they moved on battery number one, they were met by the British reserves. Fighting was hand to hand, fierce, and bloody in the extreme.[45]

By all reports, the New Yorkers fought like regulars. Many of the rain-soaked muskets would not fire, and the men resorted to cold steel or using their weapons as clubs. General Davis died at the head of his brigade near battery number one. Porter received a sword cut to his hand and was momentarily captured, but a small party led by a sergeant rescued him. The accomplished engineer Eleazar Wood fell nearby. He died later that night, mourned by the entire army. His fellow West Pointer, Colonel Gibson, was killed in action at the head of his riflemen. Brown sent in Ripley and the reserve to extricate the others. Not twenty yards from the British, Ripley was struck in the neck by a musket ball. The bullet passed completely through his neck, and the general fell to the ground, momentarily unconscious. Command of the reserve devolved upon Lieutenant Colonel Timothy Upham. A bullet wound cost Aspinwall his arm. Ever so slowly, Miller and Porter, aided by Upham, pulled their men out of the maze of entrenchments and abatis and returned to the wood line. The British pushed them forward. Lieutenant Colonels Fischer, Gordon, and Pearson were all seriously wounded. Surgeon Dunlop, with the Eighty-ninth Foot, recalled that as the Americans withdrew, the western Indians fighting with the British "bounded forward with a horrible yell, threw themselves on the retreating enemy with their tomahawks, and were soon out of sight; but as we advanced, we saw they left their trace behind them in sundry cleft skulls." Once to the wood line, the British allowed the Americans to withdraw into Fort Erie unmolested. Nearly two hours had elapsed since the fighting began.[46]

In terms of casualties, the Americans had somewhat the better result. Brown reported a total of 511 casualties: 79 killed, 216 wounded, and 216 missing. Drummond reported capturing about 200, which accounts for those Brown reported as missing. Drummond reported 719 casualties: 115 killed, 178 wounded, and 426 missing. Most of the missing were prisoners, as Brown stated that he captured about 400 of the enemy. De Watteville's regiment, which had been in the trenches at the beginning of the attack, suffered the heaviest casualties: 62 killed, 36 wounded, and 166 missing.[47]

In spite of the heavy casualties, Brown was very pleased with the results of the sortie. He was effusive in his praise of engineers McRee and Wood. "No two officers of their grade could have contributed more to the safety and honor of this army," he wrote. As for Wood, Brown continued that he "died as he had lived, without a feeling but for the honor of his country and the glory of her arms."[48] Brown was gratified by the contribution of his fellow New Yorkers. "The militia of New York have redeemed their character; they behaved gallantly," he reported to the governor. Indeed they had. Porter's attack force included about 1,000 New Yorkers—200 volunteers and the rest militiamen. These militiamen, unlike those at Queenston, agreed to cross into Canada. When formed for the attack, they did not balk. In the forest, they more than held their own for two hours against battle-hardened regulars. When their powder was wet and their weapons failed to fire, they fought on. In spite of the death of General Davis and the capture of General Porter, they did not panic but obeyed their officers and maintained their ranks. Their conduct stands in stark contrast to the common understanding of the militia's reputation for craven behavior during the War of 1812.[49]

The sortie of 17 September may have confirmed Drummond's decision to break off the siege, but it probably did not speed up the withdrawal of the British Right Division. Drummond cited the increasingly bad weather and his men's complete lack of tentage and camp equipment as his reasons for leaving. Sergeant Commins recalled that the soldiers of his regiment, the Eighth Foot, were "chiefly sick, some with ague and so dispirited that it was found necessary to send us to some settled quarters." John Norton remembered that the British camp was inundated and that the "chilling blasts of Autumn began to be felt." Drummond reported that he had been attacked by 5,000 Americans, but he did not give this apparent disparity of numbers as justification for the withdrawal. His battle losses were made up in two days when the Ninety-seventh Foot arrived. The British buried the dead in the trenches and continued to pull back the cannon—fewer, now that several had been wrecked by Porter's men. On the evening of 21 September, the British left their campfires burning. Officers led the regimental columns northward across Frenchman's Creek. The pickets were the last to depart. That evening, the men bedded down in yet another downpour.[50]

Drummond continued the withdrawal, bringing most of the division north of the Chippawa River and leaving De Watteville in command of the rear guard between Frenchman's Creek and the Chippawa. Brown discovered that the siege was over on 22 September. He sent a body of light troops forward, and the next day they found the British evacuating supplies from some buildings beyond

Frenchman's Creek. When the British sighted the Americans, they burned the buildings. Brown was content to allow Drummond to escape rather than pursue him. "I do not intend to move the body of this army before I hear from you," he wrote to Izard.[51] With the siege of Fort Erie over, the campaign on the Niagara River began its last phase—Izard's offensive.

Analysis of the eight weeks between Lundy's Lane and the withdrawal of the British Right Division from the siege lines demonstrates a slow swinging of the balance of power from the British to the Americans. Drummond lost his best chance of defeating the Left Division when he failed to maintain close contact with the Americans after Lundy's Lane. By doing so, he might have found opportunities to strike at the foe while they were strung out marching back to the Black Rock ferry or while they were bivouacking in the open. The Americans were caught with their backs to the Niagara and insufficient boats to extract themselves. Perhaps Drummond's neck wound cooled his otherwise aggressive attitude. More likely, he had discovered that the Americans were not as brittle as he once believed, his subsequent statements on the subject notwithstanding. In any event, Drummond was somewhat more cautious in his dealings with the Left Division.

Was Drummond wise to begin the siege? He could not easily surround the American camp and cut off outside sources of supply. He stretched his own supply line to the breaking point. Drummond took a risk, but the potential pay-off was commensurate with that risk. Victory would eliminate the threat to the Niagara Peninsula for another year and perhaps influence the negotiations in Ghent. Activity at Fort Erie also distracted Washington from Prevost's impending invasion. Coupled with victories on the Atlantic coast, the British might have forced the Americans to sue for peace in 1814. Also, by isolating the largest American force in one spot, Drummond had a freer hand elsewhere. His raid toward Black Rock on 3 August to destroy American supplies was inspired, in spite of the results.

What of Drummond's decision to assault on 15 August? Drummond needed to win quickly before supplies ran out. With the bombardment ineffective, assault was his only recourse. The decision to assault was correct; its execution was fatally flawed. His plan depended on gaining access to the enemy camp through the gap between Snake Hill and Lake Erie. Given the crucial nature of this feature, it is inexcusable that Drummond failed to ascertain that the gap was not blocked by obstacles. His insistence on depriving the assault force of flints compounded the error. Although he received reinforcements, Drummond was discouraged from attempting another assault, probably by the arrival of militia reinforcements into the American camp. Despairing of success, Drummond wisely chose to break off the siege.

Was Brown wise to sortie? At the cost of heavy casualties, he destroyed some siege cannon—a poor trade indeed. However, even though Drummond had already decided to leave, the timing of the sortie gave the appearance that the American attack had broken the siege. Clearly, Brown's sortie was a much-needed moral victory. Now that the Left Division was free to maneuver, the campaign was open to new possibilities. However, just as Izard's Right Division was committed to the campaign, Drummond's army was no longer fixed in a vulnerable location.

What effect did the siege have on the campaign? Both sides were reinforced—Drummond by veteran troops, the Americans by untrained militia. What Drummond could not have anticipated was the impending arrival of Izard and 4,000 trained regulars. Likewise, the weeks of siege severely taxed the British supply situation. Drummond would have very little food or ammunition until Yeo arrived with supplies from Kingston, and that event was not anticipated before October. Drummond could no longer contemplate destroying the Left Division. He would be hard-pressed to avoid destruction himself by a numerically superior force of regulars when the American Right Division arrived on the Niagara Peninsula.

CHAPTER ELEVEN

Izard's Offensive

There is no doubt resting on my mind but that with three or four thousand regulars added to the remains of my division, and the volunteers that can be induced to join, that Drummond will be compelled to surrender to you, or retire.
—Major General Jacob Brown to Major General George Izard,
20 September 1814

Jacob Brown's optimistic letter was written after the sortie of 17 September. When George Izard arrived at Sacketts Harbor on 13 September, the situation was less hopeful. Izard had expected to find Commodore Isaac Chauncey at his base, his fleet prepared to move the Right Division, as he had been led to believe would be the case.[1] Instead, the American naval commander and the Lake Ontario squadron were blockading Kingston. Izard had a few days to ponder a critical question: where could his 4,000 trained regulars operate to advance the American situation in the Central Theater? Izard's last instructions from Washington had been written two weeks before the British burned Washington. Secretary of War Armstrong suggested to Izard that he first consider attacking Kingston. However, if the British naval base was too heavily defended, Armstrong urged Izard to consider uniting with the Left Division. Together, Izard and Brown could destroy Drummond's army and seize Forts Niagara and George.[2]

Waiting for Izard at Sacketts Harbor was an urgent letter from Brown, which seconded Armstrong's guidance. "I consider the fate of this army very doubtful unless speedy relief is afforded," wrote Brown from Fort Erie. According to Brown, the "wisest course" was for Izard to bring the Right Division to Buffalo. "Our united forces would, I have no doubt, be competent to drive Drummond from the field and perhaps capture him."[3] The next day, however, Brown appeared to equivocate. "If . . . you can succeed in carrying Kingston," he wrote to his superior, "you will accomplish a much more important object." If Izard chose to move to the Niagara region instead, Brown suggested that he consider landing near Fort George. "It would perhaps be the shortest cut to your object, the capture of Drummond and his army. He cannot escape," added Brown, "provided you can promptly form a junction with my present command."[4] Izard had not yet decided whether to attack Kingston or to bring his army to the Niagara Peninsula. However, if the Right Division was going to act "promptly," it needed naval assistance and favorable winds.

While still en route to Sacketts Harbor, Izard had written to Chauncey of his hope to embark the division as soon as it arrived. On 11 September, Chauncey replied that the fleet would be ready. As soon as Izard set foot in Chauncey's base, he sent a message to the commodore that the troops would arrive no earlier than 15 September and that he wanted to begin embarkation twenty-four hours later. On 15 September, Chauncey invited Izard to meet on the sixteenth at the squadron anchorage about eight miles from Sacketts Harbor. Izard declined to meet at that time because the first contingent of troops was marching into Sacketts Harbor. Izard asked Chauncey if the fleet could move 4,000 troops at sunrise on 18 September and take them to the mouth of the Genesee River. Izard had unilaterally decided to forgo attacking Kingston. Instead, he would move to rescue the Left Division. He wrote to Chauncey that it had become his "duty to hasten to his [Brown's] assistance and to proceed with the least possible delay to Buffalo." Chauncey replied that his transports could carry 1,500 to 2,000 troops and that he was "prepared to afford every assistance in his power." Chauncey had changed his tune since July, when he had refused to sail to assist Brown.[5]

As the Left Division marched into Sacketts Harbor, Chauncey broke off his blockade of Kingston. Commodore Sir James Yeo's ship of the line, *St. Lawrence,* was nearly ready to sail, and when it did, Chauncey knew that his squadron would be unlikely to win a decisive naval battle. In departing his station off Kingston, Chauncey was effectively yielding control of Lake Ontario to the Royal Navy. It would be best if he moved the army troops quickly in order to return to Sacketts Harbor before Yeo appeared with his stronger fleet. It was with this thought in mind that Chauncey conferred with Izard on 17 September. Chauncey apparently concurred with Izard's decision to move west, although he was concerned that the army leave a sufficient body of troops to defend Sacketts Harbor.

No evidence suggests that either commander pushed for an attack on Kingston. A successful attack at that point would have been the decisive stroke on Lake Ontario, and its effects would have been felt from Michilimackinac to Ghent and perhaps as far east as Vienna, where the statesmen of Europe were trying to gauge accurately one another's power. There was no need to occupy Kingston. If the Americans landed in force east of the British naval base, thus cutting the supply line into the city while Chauncey blockaded the harbor, Yeo might have been provoked into battle before *St. Lawrence* was ready. If the Americans took Kingston, they could destroy the base facilities even if Yeo remained at anchor. Once the shipyard and warehouses full of provisions for Drummond were destroyed, British power in Upper Canada would be demolished. The risk was that Chauncey would lose the naval battle, thus leaving the troops stranded in Canada without naval support and a chastised American fleet in its base licking its wounds. Brown, Winfield Scott, Oliver Hazard Perry, or Andrew Jackson would not have hesitated.

Izard and Chauncey agreed to begin embarkation on the following morning, 18 September. Chauncey would take on as much of the Right Division as he could, and the remainder would march westward. Izard put Lieutenant Colonel George Mitchell, who had saved the naval guns from capture at Oswego earlier that year, in charge of army forces at Sacketts Harbor and gave him two infantry battalions and a small contingent of artillerists. Chauncey would not commit himself to a destination for the Right Division. If the winds were favorable, he agreed to attempt to land Izard west of Fort George. However, if the winds were contrary, he would sail only as far as the mouth of the Genesee, and Izard would march the division the remaining distance. Chauncey wanted to be done with the army as soon as possible, in the hope that he might be able to take up the blockade of Kingston before the *St. Lawrence* sailed.[6]

That evening, a torrential rainfall began that continued through 18 September. If the storm did not abate soon, Izard would have to put his entire division on the road west. "I have in prospect two most important objects," he wrote to James Monroe, "the relief of a brave and valuable band of tried warriors and possible discomfiture of the enemy who besieges them."[7] The rain let up on 19 September, and that evening, Izard's infantry, more than 2,500 men, began loading onto Chauncey's transports. An adverse wind kept the ships in harbor, but Izard ordered his dragoons and artillerists to begin the long march westward. On 21 September, the Lake Ontario squadron departed. Finally, the Right Division continued its movement begun at Plattsburg on 29 August. Left behind were about 1,000 regulars and an equal number of militiamen to guard the naval base.[8]

The following day, the fleet arrived off the mouth of the Genesee River, and Chauncey disembarked Izard and his infantry. There is no evidence that the winds were contrary, and it is likely that Chauncey persuaded Izard to allow the fleet to return as quickly as possible to Sacketts Harbor. The army spent the next day gathering wagons, teams, and drivers. There were so few available that Izard was forced to leave some tentage and camp equipment. On 24 September, the Right Division picked up the march toward Batavia. Izard rode ahead of the troops and arrived the next day. Learning that Brown's sortie had lifted the siege,

Izard wrote to Brown proposing that the Right Division lay siege to Fort Niagara rather than marching on Buffalo. He requested that Brown come to Batavia to confer with him. Batavia was a decision point, because two roads departed that village leading west—one directly to Buffalo, and the other to Lewiston and closer to Fort Niagara.[9]

Brown received Izard's note and immediately set off for Batavia, arriving the next day. Izard's infantry had reached Batavia when the two generals met. Brown reported that he believed that Drummond had his main force behind the Chippawa River. He surmised that Drummond had no more than 3,000 regulars with him, not including the garrison at Burlington. Given these figures, a siege of Fort Niagara appeared feasible. Brown would pin down Drummond along the Chippawa while Izard opened the siege. Izard's skillful engineer and William McRee's West Point classmate, Major Joseph Totten, was brought into the planning conference. He would be a key player in conducting the operation. The only drawback was artillery, or the lack of it. Izard had brought none with him, and Brown had but one twenty-four-pound gun and a few eighteen-pounders. For the siege to begin, Brown would have to move artillery to Izard outside of Fort Niagara.[10]

Brown returned to Fort Erie and the Left Division. The Right Division rested at Batavia for several days. Izard thought further about his plan to besiege Fort Niagara. He wrote to Brown on 28 September, directing him to send three eighteen-pound guns immediately. Izard added that "although the artillery we can command is inadequate to a siege, we may indulge the hope that the ardor and skill of our troops will surmount the difficulties which will oppose us."[11] He knew that neither the recapture of Fort Niagara nor the destruction of Drummond's army was a decisive blow; the war would continue in Upper Canada as long as Kingston was in British hands. He also had second thoughts about accomplishing both those goals—destroying Drummond and recapturing Niagara—before the campaign season ended. Izard wanted the combined army, both his and Brown's divisions, to be in good shape when spring arrived. Izard began to think about establishing winter quarters in western New York. He wrote to Monroe that any requests for furlough from any of his or Brown's officers should be refused, "except under very urgent circumstances." He proposed continuing training the troops throughout the winter so that "early in the spring, before the enemy can receive reinforcements from Europe, the most important blows may be struck."[12]

On 1 October, as the Right Division picked up the line of march toward Lewiston, Izard abandoned his plan to besiege Fort Niagara. Perhaps he believed that the available artillery was insufficient, or perhaps Brown had left him with doubts when they met on the twenty-seventh. He wrote to Brown asking explicitly if, in Brown's judgment, the best course of action would be to unite the two divisions in Canada. If Brown answered affirmatively, then Izard proposed crossing the Niagara River near Fort Schlosser and landing just south of the Chippawa. At about the same time, Brown sent a note to Izard articulating his concerns. Brown warned his superior that the plan agreed on at Batavia would necessarily divide the command. He also advised Izard that the Left Division would have to be reinforced if Brown was to operate against Drummond behind the Chippawa. Finally, Brown suggested that the two American divisions join forces and operate directly against Drummond. Noting that the British were short of provisions, Brown suspected that if pressed, Drummond would retreat toward York rather than seek shelter in the three forts over the winter. Later, when Brown received Izard's note, he answered unequivocally: "I believe that the concentration of all your force, which of course includes that under my immediate command, on the western side of the Niagara River as the most advisable measure you can adopt under existing circumstances."[13]

On the morning of 5 October, Izard's division arrived at Lewiston. Izard could find no boats anywhere. What he did find was a letter from the secretary of war. Monroe gave Izard command of the Ninth Military District. Correcting one of John Armstrong's most self-defeating policies, Monroe stated that "military operations there must be combined and directed to one result, which can only be done by being placed in the hands of one commander."[14] Monroe also informed Izard that 1,000 troops in Detroit had been ordered to report to Izard. The balance of power had clearly swung toward the Americans.

Izard now commanded the largest force of regulars ever assembled west of Sacketts Harbor. Izard referred to this force as the Northern Army. His division became the Right Wing or the First Division, and Brown's was referred to as the Left Wing or Second Division in Izard's correspondence. The First Division was composed of two infantry brigades, a large contingent of dismounted and mounted dragoons, and numerous artillerists, most serving as infantry. Izard's strength was in his infantry, and a description of the two brigades illustrates the quality of this force.

The First Brigade was commanded by Brigadier General Thomas A. Smith. The thirty-three-year-old Smith started the war as the lieutenant colonel of the Rifle Regiment but was promoted almost immediately to colonel and commander of the regiment. He served in Georgia, and for a few weeks in 1812 he commanded a small force laying siege to St. Augustine in Spanish East Florida. Later he served in the Army of the Northwest under Harrison. Smith commanded the riflemen in Wilkinson's failed attempt to seize Montreal. His service record justified promotion to brigadier general in January 1814, and in March he commanded a brigade at La Colle Mill.

Smith's brigade consisted of the Fourth, Tenth, and Twelfth Infantry Regiments. The Fourth and Tenth Infantry operated together under Colonel Robert

Purdy. The Fourth was raised in 1808 in New England and fought at Tippecanoe under Harrison. Under then Lieutenant Colonel James Miller, the Fourth Infantry won an engagement at Maguaga before being surrendered by Hull at Detroit. When they were exchanged in November 1812, the veterans of Detroit formed the nucleus of the regiment that was then assigned to the Lake Champlain region. The Fourth fought tolerably well at Chateauguay under Purdy.

The Tenth Infantry was authorized by Congress in January 1812 and began recruiting in North Carolina and adjacent counties of Virginia. By September 1813, only a small battalion of about 200 had been raised, and these were sent to Plattsburg. The Tenth fought at Chateauguay as part of Izard's brigade. By June 1814, the battalion had 254 effectives when it was consolidated with the Fourth. Five hundred men recruited into the Tenth in 1814 were not sent to New York but were assembled in Washington to defend the nation's capital.

The Twelfth Infantry, a Virginia regiment, was authorized in January 1812, and the first three companies formed were marched to Buffalo, where they participated in Smyth's attempted invasion of Upper Canada. This small detachment remained on the Niagara Frontier until it was shipped east to join Wilkinson's expedition toward Montreal. The regiment fought at Crysler's Farm and survived the winter at French Mills. Now, under its major, Willoughby Morgan, the regiment had nearly 500 effectives. Like the Tenth, new recruits for the regiment were retained for the defense of the Atlantic coast, and about 150 soldiers of the Twelfth defended Fort McHenry in Baltimore Harbor.

Daniel Bissell of Connecticut commanded the Second Brigade. Bissell had come up through the ranks. In 1788, at the age of nineteen, Bissell enlisted in the First Infantry. Three years later, he was discharged as a sergeant and soon after was commissioned as an ensign. Bissell fought in the Indian wars in the Old Northwest and earned his promotion to colonel and command of the Fifth Infantry in August 1812. Bissell fought in Brown's advance guard during the Crysler's Farm campaign and at the age of forty-five was promoted to brigadier general in March 1814. Like Smith, Bissell commanded a brigade at La Colle Mill.[15]

The Second Brigade was composed of the Fifth, Fourteenth, Fifteenth, and Sixteenth Infantry Regiments. The Fifth Infantry was authorized by Congress in 1808 and recruited in Pennsylvania. Early in the war, a few companies were sent to the Niagara Frontier to serve in Smyth's division of the Army of the Center; the rest were dispatched to Greenbush to join Dearborn's Northern Army. The Fifth Infantry fought well at Stoney Creek, and its colonel, Daniel Bissell, led them during the Crysler's Farm campaign, in which they fought in Jacob Brown's advance guard. The Fifth spent a bitter winter at Chateauguay, New York, guarding the supply line to the army at French Mills. Like many of the regiments that wintered in the frozen reaches of New York State, most of the soldiers of the Fifth who could do so left the army when their enlistments were up. Fewer than 300 men of the Fifth Infantry were with their commander, Colonel Ninian Pinkney, when he marched into Lewiston in October.

Congress authorized the Fourteenth Infantry in January 1812, and recruiting started immediately in Virginia, Maryland, Delaware, and Pennsylvania. The first three companies marched to Buffalo in time for Smyth's attempts to invade Canada. Two hundred men of the Fourteenth, under their commander Lieutenant Colonel Charles Boerstler, raided across the Niagara River as a prelude to the invasion that never happened. The following summer, Boerstler surrendered a portion of the regiment at Beaver Dams. In July, Winfield Scott raided York and freed most of the captives taken at Beaver Dams and incarcerated there. The Fourteenth fought at Crysler's Farm and wintered at French Mills. The regiment was also present at La Colle Mill in March 1814. With Boerstler currently paroled, the Fourteenth Infantry was now commanded by Major Isaac D. Barnard.

The Fifteenth Infantry was authorized in January 1812 and recruited in the New York City area. Its first commander was Zebulon Pike, and he led the Fifteenth during Dearborn's short invasion of Lower Canada. Sickness struck the Fifteenth at its winter quarters on Lake Champlain, and over 100 soldiers were lost to disease. In 1813, the regiment fought at the battle for Fort George and at Crysler's Farm. The Fifteenth was present at La Colle Mill but did not fight. Major Henry Grindage would command the regiment for the upcoming campaign.

The last regiment in Bissell's brigade was the Sixteenth Infantry, which was authorized in January 1812 and recruited in eastern Pennsylvania. The Sixteenth was fortunate to serve in all major engagements under its regimental colonel, Cromwell Pearce. Pearce led the Sixteenth in Dearborn's invasion, during the raid on York, at the capture of Fort George, and at Stoney Creek, Crysler's Farm, and La Colle Mill. Pearce would lead the Sixteenth during its last campaign also.

A final regiment was soon to join the Northern Army. Secretary of War James Monroe, taking what steps he could to relieve the beleaguered Left Division, ordered Brigadier General Duncan McArthur in Detroit to send 1,000 men eastward. McArthur sent about 500 men of the hard-fighting Seventeenth Infantry. The Seventeenth was recruited in Kentucky and Ohio and was the mainstay of Harrison's Army of the Northwest. Detachments of the Seventeenth were at the River Raisin, the defense of Forts Meigs and Stephenson, and the Battle of the Thames, as well as numerous forest skirmishes. The Seventeenth had been called east in 1813 and garrisoned Sacketts Harbor during the Crysler's Farm campaign. Lieutenant Chunn's company fought at Lundy's Lane and the defense of Fort Erie as part of the Twenty-first Infantry. For its last campaign, the Seventeenth was led by Colonel John Miller. As Izard's division arrived at Lewiston, the Seventeenth Infantry was disembarking at Fort Erie.

As American strength in the Niagara region grew, Lieutenant General Gordon Drummond prepared his command for the inevitable attack. Drummond established his main defensive line along the Chippawa, but he placed a very strong advance guard under Major General De Watteville well forward of the Chippawa. De Watteville's mission was to give warning of American movements and to slow down their advance from Fort Erie. His first line was on Frenchman's Creek only four miles north of Brown's troops in Fort Erie. Here De Watteville placed some of Drummond's most effective soldiers—the Glengarry Light Infantry Fencibles and the Volunteer Battalion of Incorporated Militia supported by the Nineteenth Light Dragoons. Five miles behind them and positioned along Black Creek was the newly arrived Ninety-seventh Regiment of Foot, a veteran unit of the war on the Iberian Peninsula. De Watteville placed his fourth battalion, the Royal Scots, along Street's Creek. With his forces arrayed in this manner, De Watteville could effectively slow down an advance down the river as well as guard against Americans trying to cross the Niagara. Drummond kept direct control over three battalions: the Sixth Foot on the Chippawa, the Eighty-second Foot at Lundy's Lane, and the Eighty-ninth Foot at Queenston. Fearful that Fort Niagara might yet be attacked, Drummond gave command of the three forts—Niagara, George, and Mississauga—to Major General Richard Stovin. Stovin had the hard-used remnants of four battalions: the Eighth, Forty-first, 100th, and De Watteville's regiment. Finally, the 103d Foot was stationed at Burlington Heights to protect the provisions there. Drummond's positioning was flexible, allowing him to respond to attacks from Brown or from the New York shore.[16]

Drummond's weak point, as it had been since the siege began, was supply. In addition to rations and ammunition, he needed stoves, tools, and timber in order to put his army into winter quarters. Drummond, like Izard, knew that surviving the present campaign was not enough. The army that emerged in the spring better fit to fight would enjoy a decided advantage. Drummond pressed Prevost to send the fleet as soon as possible to deliver provisions and to move his most dilapidated battalions to York or Kingston to winter over. However, Yeo would not sail before the *St. Lawrence* was fully operational. When Chauncey lifted the blockade of Kingston long enough to move Izard, Drummond's supply officers at Kingston diverted another bateaux convoy from the Montreal-to-Kingston run and sent it on to York. This was dangerous business. The precious bateaux and crews were not only subject to capture while operating on Lake

Ontario but also unavailable to bring in rations that were piling up in Montreal. Drummond was so desperate to feed his army that he sent the Battalion of Incorporated Militia into the countryside to help the local farmers thresh their wheat. This necessary act weakened De Watteville's advance guard watching Brown in Fort Erie.[17]

On 2 October, Drummond learned that Izard was marching toward the Niagara Frontier with 2,500 troops. The British situation was now seriously threatened. A window of opportunity existed for the Americans until Yeo emerged from Kingston to lay claim to Lake Ontario. Drummond knew Izard's options. The Americans could lay siege to Fort Niagara, Izard could cross the Niagara River between Queenston and Fort George, or he could unite with Brown and try to penetrate the defensive line on the Chippawa River.

Drummond responded by further concentrating his force. He pulled everyone north of the Chippawa River except for a much-reduced advance guard on Black Creek consisting of a composite battalion of light infantry, the Glengarries, and some dragoons. Drummond's situation was becoming increasingly desperate.[18]

On 5 October, Brown and his commander of volunteers and militia, Brigadier General Peter B. Porter, met with Izard at Lewiston to hammer out a tactical plan. Brown and Porter persuaded Izard not to consider reducing Fort Niagara until Drummond had been dealt with. Izard decided to cross the Niagara near Fort Schlosser and unite with Brown's division south of the British defenses on the Chippawa. Brown's task was to position sufficient boats at a suitable crossing site. With this understanding, Brown and Porter returned to Fort Erie. The following day, Izard received alarming news from Sacketts Harbor. Rumors were rampant that the British had 5,000 troops at Kingston ready to attack Chauncey's base. In addition to the 1,000 regulars Izard had left there, 2,000 New York militiamen had responded to a general call–up. Too far away to assist Chauncey, Izard concentrated on the problems at hand.[19]

Brown wrote to Izard on 7 October informing his superior that boats were positioned near Fort Schlosser. The following day, he reassured Izard that his division would march in coordination with Izard's so that the entire force would appear together in front of the British at Chippawa. Brown doubted that Drummond would interfere with the American movement, but if he did, Brown stated that he "should be much pleased to meet him on the way."[20] Brown's confidence was offset by a serious error that undermined Izard's confidence in him.

Izard's division arrived at the mouth of Cayuga Creek near Schlosser on the morning of 8 October. There they found only thirty boats, sufficient to carry 750 troops at a time. Izard refused to cross his men over in four waves, and right-

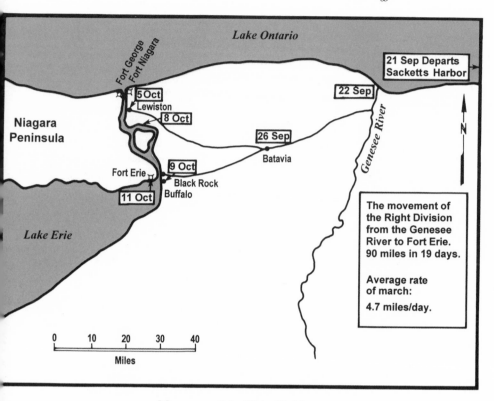

Movement of the Right Division

fully so. The first to land would be vulnerable to attack while awaiting the remainder of the division. Frustrated that Brown had not informed him about the insufficiency of boats, there was no alternative but to march to Black Rock, where Brown could protect Izard's men as they shuttled across the Niagara.[21]

Drummond watched Izard's movement southward with growing concern. He had received reports that Brown had been reinforced by the Seventeenth Infantry, as well as exaggerated reports that 2,000 militiamen had rallied at Buffalo. Drummond was convinced that Izard and Brown were preparing for a major attack. "I have undoubted intelligence," he wrote to Prevost, "that a great effort is about to be made by the enemy to capture or to force this division back from this frontier."[22] As the threat from the Americans grew larger and closer, the suspicion grew in Drummond's mind that Izard would try to pin him down along the Chippawa while Brown moved westward on Lake Erie and landed at Long Point or at the Grand River. From there, Brown could make a wide envelopment of Drummond's line and march on Burlington Heights, trapping the

British. Drummond countered by pulling nearly all his troops back behind Street's Creek and pushing militia units to watch crossing sites on the Chippawa as far west as Brown's Bridge, twenty-five miles from the main British camp at the mouth of the river.

Izard had nothing so elegant in mind. Izard's strength was in organizing and training; he was not a risk taker. Nor did he possess the intuition that marks brilliant commanders. He had brought a well-trained army west, and it arrived in excellent shape. The failure to press Chauncey to land him near Burlington exasperated Brown. Brown confided in his friend Armstrong that Izard's decision to land at the mouth of the Genesee was "mysterious." He complained of the slowness of Izard's movement. "The march from Genesee River to Black Rock had nearly exhausted my stock of faith and patience," he wrote.[23] In fact, during that movement, Izard's division averaged less than five miles per day.

In their outward dealings, both commanders were studiously correct. It was clear to both, however, that they approached warfare from different angles. Izard's military schooling steered him toward caution, whereas Brown was quite willing to join battle and depend on the superior fighting capability of his men. While the two Americans tried to accomplish something before the weather brought the campaign to a close, events in Ghent were moving in a direction that made the campaign critical to any final settlement.

In August, American negotiators had rejected harsh British demands for a separate Indian state, disarmament of the American side of the Great Lakes, and boundary adjustments in Britain's favor. Congress released news of Britain's price to end the war. Coming as it did only weeks after the burning of Washington, the public reaction was immediate and unanimous. Even Federalist newspapers called for energetic prosecution of the war. The deadlock in Ghent continued until mid-September.

The impetus for breaking the deadlock came from London. Lord Liverpool, the British prime minister, understood correctly that continued insistence on a native state was likely to bolster the American war effort. Prevost had pledged to his native allies that they would not be forgotten in the negotiations. However, Liverpool overruled the governor-general, and on 19 September, the British dropped an independent Indian state as a sine qua non. Instead, a few weeks later, the British formally proposed the principle of *uti possidetis* as a basis of boundary adjustments.[24]

By this principle, each side could retain the territory it won by force of arms. In the workings of diplomacy, however, pieces of land became the medium of exchange. The Americans held Fort Malden opposite Detroit, as well as Fort Erie. The British occupied eastern Maine, Fort Niagara, and Mackinac Island.

In the exchange, the burning of Washington had no value, because the charred remains of the White House remained in the hands of the United States. However, powerful British naval and land forces at Bermuda and Halifax and a large army at Montreal suggested that New Orleans, New York, and Plattsburg were potential targets for 1815. If the United States was forced to accept *uti possidetis*, then possession of the Niagara Peninsula, including Forts George and Mississauga, would be a valuable bargaining chip.

Monroe, however, instructed his negotiating team to resist *uti possidetis* in favor of status quo antebellum. While Izard's division was wending its way toward Black Rock, Monroe sent word to Ghent not to give up any territory or fishing rights. He understood that the British would not recognize the American view of neutral shipping rights or impressment, but the end of the war in Europe had rendered these issues irrelevant. Inexplicably, Monroe did not keep Izard abreast of the negotiations, nor did he send instructions that coordinated military and diplomatic activity. If the United States were going to be forced to accept *uti possidetis*, Monroe should have sent guidance to Izard, his only commander postured to capture enemy territory, to seize as much as he could as quickly as possible so that the negotiators would have additional trading material. If Izard recaptured Fort Niagara, Britain's claim on eastern Maine would have been weakened.

Analysis of Izard's activities over the next three weeks demonstrates no particular drive to influence events in Ghent. On 10 and 11 October, Izard crossed the First Division into Canada, encamping on the heights opposite Black Rock. Izard was pleased to see the Seventeenth Infantry, until inspection showed that three-quarters of their muskets were unserviceable. He attached the Seventeenth to Smith's brigade of his division. Izard left Major Hindman in charge of the garrison at Fort Erie. The First Division numbered 3,500 effectives. Brown's Second Division totaled 2,000 regulars and 800 militia volunteers. Brown's brigade commanders were Colonel Hugh Brady of the First Brigade, Brigadier General James Miller of the Second, and General Porter of the Third or Volunteer Brigade. On the morning of 13 October, Izard led both divisions northward. That evening, the Americans bivouacked on Black Creek.[25]

When Drummond learned that Izard was across the Niagara, he estimated that he would be confronted by 8,000 to 10,000 troops. Nonetheless, he was determined to halt the invaders on the Chippawa. He sent orders for the militia to muster, and he sent word to John Norton to bring his Grand River warriors as quickly as possible. He confided to Prevost that he did not expect many militiamen or natives to respond. Drummond set up signal cannon at Lundy's Lane and at Queenston so that he could quickly transmit orders to concentrate at

Chippawa. He ordered Stovin at Fort George to prepare a battalion of men to replace those at Queenston when the signal cannon was fired. Drummond was fortunate to regain the services of the Marquis of Tweeddale. His Achilles tendon had been severed at the Battle of Chippawa, and the commander of the 100th Foot was anxious to return to duty. Although he still required crutches whenever he dismounted his horse, Tweeddale was a welcome addition to Drummond's army, and Drummond rewarded him with command of the small brigade at Queenston. Drummond pushed his men to complete a series of redoubts behind the Chippawa and at the confluence of Lyon's Creek and that river. Then he waited.[26]

On the morning of 14 October, the Americans crossed Black Creek. Izard was slowed down because he rebuilt bridges as he went so that his artillery and wagons could cross the many streams emptying into the Niagara. Throwing up a bridge over Street's Creek, the Americans crossed the following day. The Glengarries maintained a picket line south of the Chippawa but withdrew at the approach of the foe. Once more, the Left Division stood on the ground where it had won its victory three months earlier. Izard positioned his two divisions from the edge of the Niagara westward to the point where Lyon's Creek entered the Chippawa. Then he brought forward his artillery.

In order to discover the number and location of Drummond's guns, Izard put a single cannon on the river road and fired at the blockhouses in the British camp. The Royal Artillery did not immediately return fire, and Izard noticed wagons and men departing camp. Hoping that the British were abandoning their positions, Izard ordered up the remainder of his artillery, and all six of his guns opened fire. The British returned fire with more and heavier pieces, but the Americans more than held their own. Izard reported silencing one gun, and Drummond admitted that several British pieces were struck. At dusk, Izard stopped the dueling and withdrew his small contingent of artillery.[27]

That night the ground was wet and the air very cold. Brown went to Izard to discuss ways of bringing the British to battle. Brown proposed to repeat a tactic he had used in July to force Riall out of his position. Izard agreed, and Brown returned to his headquarters to issue the necessary orders. The next day, 200 axmen went into the woods west of the Chippawa plain and began to improve the old log trail that led from Street's Creek to the point where Lyon's Creek joins the Chippawa. If his flank were seriously threatened, Drummond would either fight on less favorable ground or withdraw northward. Either event would break the potential stalemate on the Chippawa.[28]

Faced with an enemy at least twice as strong as his own force, Drummond was angered by Yeo's refusal to bring reinforcements and provisions. In his report to Prevost, he wrote "I cannot refrain from observing that if I had the 90th and one other strong and effective regiment (which can so well be spared) I am fully of the opinion that I should have it now in my power to strike a blow which would not only give immediate tranquillity to this province but go far towards finishing the war in Upper Canada."[29] Drummond added acidly, "should any disaster happen to this division . . . His Majesty's Naval Commander will in my opinion have much to answer for." Both army commanders, it seems, believed themselves abandoned by their naval counterparts.

On 16 October, Izard learned that Chauncey had returned to Sacketts Harbor eight days earlier. Sorely disappointed, Izard reasoned that any course of action he pursued would ultimately be fruitless. Even if he managed to force Drummond to fall back from the Chippawa, following him would be dangerous. "Every step I take in pursuit exposes me to be cut off by the large reinforcements it is in the power of the enemy to throw in twenty-four hours upon my flank or rear," he complained to Monroe.[30] Since in all probability he could not destroy Drummond, what was the point in continuing? He had already accomplished one of his stated goals—he had relieved the Second Division. "I confess, sir," he admitted to Monroe, "that I am greatly embarrassed. At the head of the most efficient army which the United States have possessed during this war, much must be expected from me, and yet I can discern no object which can be achieved at this point, worthy of the risk which will attend its attempt."[31] Izard had surrendered whatever advantage he might have had by the slowness of his movement from the Genesee River. He decided that he would spend the next few days looking for an opportunity to defeat Drummond, but failing that, he would put the army in winter quarters.

That day, Izard positioned his army just out of range of the British artillery in the hope that Drummond would come out from behind his defenses and accept battle. When Brown received orders to form his division behind the First Division, he took that as a sign that Izard was no longer interested in pursuing his plan to outflank the British. "When I beheld the display of force that was made before the works of Chippawa," Brown wrote to Armstrong, "I nearly lost all patience."[32] It was clear to Brown that Izard did not want his ideas, and Brown was uncomfortable in the role of subordinate after having been in charge for so long. Jacob Brown had been the driving force behind this campaign, and obeisance to military seniority was depriving him of that role.

Drummond refused to come out of his strong defensive position and give battle, as Riall had impetuously done in July. On 17 October, Izard ordered the army to break up camp and return behind Black Creek. He hoped that if he gave Drummond enough room to maneuver he might yet come out and fight. Drummond merely ordered out some infantry and dragoons to keep an eye on the Americans. Yeo appeared off the mouth of the Niagara on the morning of the eighteenth. He had sailed on the fifteenth from Kingston with the powerful *St. Lawrence.* It appeared to Drummond that there was now cause for guarded optimism and no good reason to risk a battle on Izard's terms.[33]

Izard had learned that a large quantity of flour was stored at Cook's Mill on Lyon's Creek about twenty miles' march from the American camp. Knowing that Drummond was having trouble finding enough food to feed his division, Izard saw an opportunity to make his enemy's plight more difficult. He ordered Brigadier General Bissell to seize the flour and either return with it or destroy it. Perhaps the loss of these stores would provoke Drummond to fight or withdraw closer to his source of supplies. Bissell departed camp on the morning of 18 October to fight the last battle of the Niagara campaign.[34]

Bissell took with him the four infantry battalions of his brigade, augmented by a company of riflemen and a troop of dragoons, about 900 men in all. The brigade picked up a road that paralleled Black Creek heading west, and near the source of the creek it turned north on another road leading directly to the mill. According to Bissell, the march took them "by very bad roads, and creeks, the bridges over which were broken down."[35] At the mill, Bissell's troops drove off a guard of about twenty soldiers. They then built a bridge over Lyon's Creek. Bissell camped on the southern shore but threw a security force across the river. This body was a composite battalion consisting of the rifle company and the light companies of the Fifth and Sixteenth Infantry Regiments.[36]

Drummond learned of an American force heading west within a few hours of Bissell's departure. Believing that this might be an attempt to outflank his position, Drummond sent his deputy quartermaster general, Colonel Christopher Myers, to see what the Americans were up to. Myers took with him the Glengarries and seven companies of the Eighty-second Foot. Drummond also sent a party to destroy Brown's Bridge, the last remaining bridge across the Chippawa. As Brown suspected, Drummond knew that he was vulnerable to being outflanked. Late in the afternoon, Drummond received reports that the American force had crossed Lyon's Creek, but it was fewer than 2,000 strong. Drummond sent Lieutenant Colonel Tweeddale with the 100th Foot, the remaining three companies of the Eighty-second, the two flank companies of the 104th, a six-pound gun, and a Congreve rocket launcher to augment Myers. Drummond told Tweeddale to get an accurate estimate of the size of the American force but to take no unnecessary risks. If it was less than 2,000, Drummond intended to send the Sixth Foot the next day and order Myers to attack the Americans. Late that evening, the Glengarries skirmished for a short time with Bissell's security force, but casualties were light.

On the morning of 19 October, Colonel Myers formed his troops on the north side of Lyon's Creek almost a mile east of the mill. His mission was to learn the American strength, not to become decisively engaged. He ordered

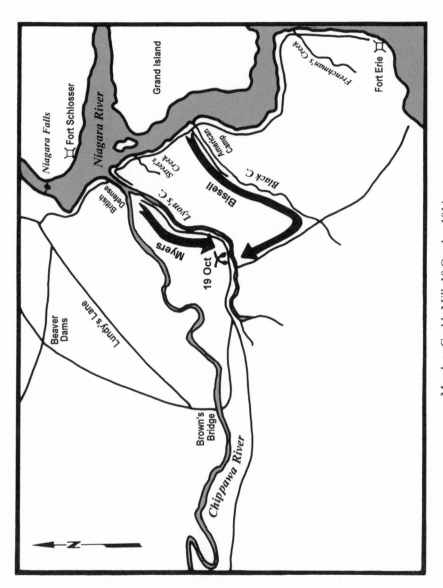

March to Cook's Mill, 18 October 1814

Lieutenant Colonel Battersby of the Glengarries to form his regiment into an extended line perpendicular to Lyon's Creek and to advance on the American light troops. Myers ordered Tweeddale to form the remainder of the brigade in a line behind the Glengarries and parallel to them. To the front of the Glengarries was a long but shallow ravine leading south into the creek. Beyond the ravine stood a small woods. The Americans were in these woods facing east. The Glengarries, expert and experienced forest fighters, moved across the ravine, slowly driving the outnumbered Americans out of the woods and back toward the bridge. The Glengarries followed but did not pursue. Tweeddale and the remainder of the British force were at least 1,000 yards behind the Glengarries, with the woods between the two.[37]

Upon hearing the gunfire, Bissell sprang into action, ordering the Fifth and Fourteenth Regiments across the bridge to support the light companies. He ordered Colonel Pearce of the Sixteenth and Major Grindage of the Fifteenth to "act as circumstances might require."[38] Colonel Pinkney of the Fifth and Major Barnard of the Fourteenth formed their men on a line facing east, with Pinkney on the left. The trained troops deployed quickly. Bissell ordered Barnard to advance directly toward the American light troops and to continue through them against the Glengarries in front of the woods. He ordered Pinkney to attack around the north of the woods, outflanking the Glengarries. Not to be left out of the fight, Pearce started bringing his men across the bridge, and Grindage led his troops along the southern shore of Lyon's Creek toward the sound of the fighting.

Now the Glengarries were outnumbered. Myers understood his mission well. Rather than sending Tweeddale forward in the attack, he pulled the Glengarries rearward the way they had advanced. As the Americans moved forward, the Glengarries passed back through the woods and over the ravine, taking a position adjacent to the main British battle line several hundred yards east of the ravine. It appeared to Bissell that his men were driving the enemy backward. He advanced his brigade as far as the western edge of the ravine and opened an intense musket fire at long range. The Sixteenth Infantry drew up to the Fourteenth along the eastern edge of the woods, and Grindage, still south of Lyon's Creek, fired toward the British line from across the water. Myers returned the Americans' fire with his cannon and rockets and prepared for the enemy to attack across the ravine. When Bissell would not budge from the wood line, Myers withdrew back up the road toward the main British camp about three miles. He left scouts forward to keep watch over the Americans. Bissell, believing that he had driven off the British, buried the dead, destroyed 200 bushels of grain, and returned to his camp south of the creek.

The Battle of Cook's Mill, or Lyon's Creek, was neither large nor decisive. The Americans reported sixty-seven casualties, and the British thirty-six. The commanders executed their orders well, and their troops maneuvered and fired

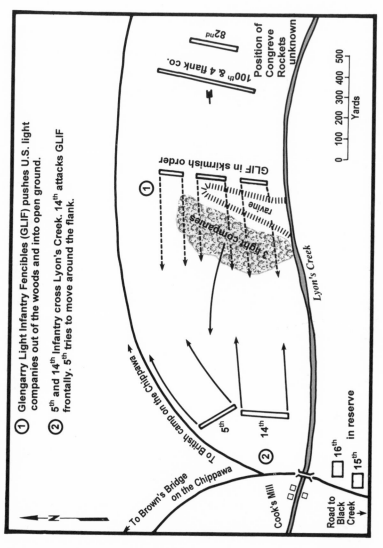

① Glengarry Light Infantry Fencibles (GLIF) pushes U.S. light companies out of the woods and into open ground.

② 5th and 14th Infantry cross Lyon's Creek. 14th attacks GLIF frontally. 5th tries to move around the flank.

82nd

100th & 4 flank co.

Position of Congreve Rockets unknown

0   100 200 300 400 500
Yards

GLIF in skirmish order

①

ravine

3 light companies

Lyon's Creek

To British camp on the Chippawa

5th

14th

②

To Brown's Bridge on the Chippawa

Cook's Mill

16th

15th in reserve

Road to Black Creek

N

Battle of Cook's Mill, Phase 1

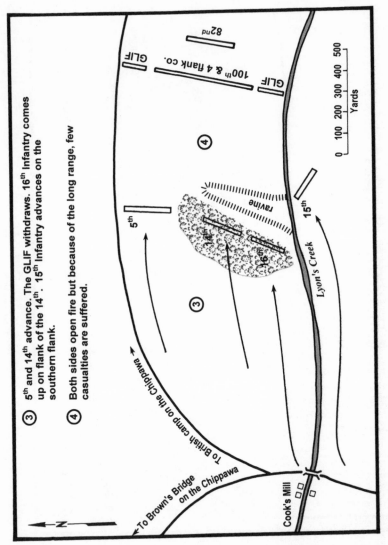

3. 5th and 14th advance. The GLIF withdraws. 16th Infantry comes up on flank of the 14th. 15th Infantry advances on the southern flank.

4. Both sides open fire but because of the long range, few casualties are suffered.

Battle of Cook's Mill, Phase 2

like the trained regulars they were. The two battle lines probably never drew closer than 300 yards. Bissell's men were very pleased with themselves. Up until this time, whatever glory had been won in the Central Theater belonged to Brown's Second Division or Macomb's brigade at Plattsburg.

Although Myers reported Bissell's strength at between 1,500 and 2,000, Drummond decided not to attack. Believing that Bissell was looking for a route around the British flank, Drummond surmised that Bissell had withdrawn because the roads were too poor to support artillery or wagons. Bissell, however, was merely depriving the British of grain and did not destroy the mill, although it was a legitimate military target. Drummond noted that since Izard had started north from Fort Erie, there had been no breaches of conduct. In his report to Prevost, he noted of his enemy that "he has been studiously cautious in abstaining from his burning and plundering system—probably admonished by the retaliation inflicted at Washington and on the coast."[39] It is more likely, however, that Izard's European military training led him to a more refined view of warfare, one that eschewed sentries sniping at one another or the unnecessary destruction of civilian property.

While Bissell and Myers exchanged long-range fire along Lyon's Creek, matters came to a head in the American headquarters. Brown had had enough, and when Izard suggested that he take his division to Sacketts Harbor, Brown jumped at the opportunity. Both generals were careful to make Brown's departure appear to be a response to reports of British intentions to seize the naval base. In his order to Brown, Izard stated that "it is of importance that the troops at Sackett's Harbor should be commanded by a general officer of the regular service and many circumstances point you out as the most proper person for that purpose."[40] Brown departed immediately, and Izard promised to send the Second Division on in a few days under newly arrived Brigadier General William Winder, that hard-luck officer who had been replaced as commander of the Tenth Military District.[41]

Izard tried one last time to coax Drummond to come out from his defenses and fight. On 21 October, Izard formed up the troops on Chippawa plain. Now that Yeo was off Fort Niagara, perhaps Drummond had been reinforced and would be willing, at last, to do battle. At noon, when Drummond had given no sign of willingness to fight, Izard ordered the troops to withdraw to the heights opposite Black Rock. The weather was cold and damp. Izard noted to Monroe that "the dysentery has already commenced its revenge among all ranks and our sick list is daily increasing."[42] He decided to leave a garrison at Fort Erie and put the rest of his troops in winter quarters on the New York side of the Niagara. Izard ended the Niagara campaign.

When Izard departed from his front, Drummond knew that the threat was over. Bissell's march had demonstrated the impracticality of using the road system to support an American attempt to outflank him. Drummond turned his attention to getting provisions to his men and putting them in warm quarters for the winter. His intention was to send his spent battalions to Kingston or York and replace them with fresh units. Although Yeo had been in the area for a few days, the winds had been such that he could send no boats to shore to communicate with Drummond. Drummond decided to meet with Yeo himself to arrange the movement of troops. Drummond was furious to learn that the squadron had brought only half of the Ninetieth Foot westward. Yeo wrote to Prevost that "the disappointment I experienced at finding that half the 90th Regiment had been left to struggle through the dreadful roads betwixt Kingston and York at such a season, and at such a crisis, was greater than I can express."[43] Drummond impressed Yeo that the squadron needed to make at least two more trips between Kingston and the Niagara region, and when Yeo departed on 22 October, he brought off the worn-out Eighth Foot and the flank companies of the 104th. These units had earned a rest, as had all the veterans of the Right Division.

Izard, like Drummond, was breaking up his army. On 22 October, he ordered Porter to take what was left of his brigade to Batavia and muster his volunteers out of federal service. On 25 October, the Third Brigade of the Second Division crossed the Niagara, and by 8 November, the men were on their way to their homes. On 24 October, Izard sent Winder and the remaining regulars of the Second Division on the muddy road to Sacketts Harbor. The veterans of Chippawa, Lundy's Lane, and the siege of Fort Erie departed Buffalo on 28 October. Marching through rain and sleet, with temperatures dropping to below freezing in the evenings, the men retraced the steps they had taken in the spring when they marched west from Sacketts Harbor to Scott's training camp at Buffalo. They arrived at their destination on 13 November, seventeen days after their long trek began.[44]

On 25 October, Izard gave the order to begin evacuation of that part of the First Division that was not tasked with garrisoning Fort Erie. Smith's brigade crossed first. The water was choppy, and the operation dragged on until 1 November. As soon as his men were safely in New York, Smith requested leave to see his family in Tennessee. Bissell, complaining of ill health, also asked permission to leave for the winter. The river crossing was watched closely by the Glengarries and Norton and a handful of his warriors. Norton was of the opinion that the Americans were leaving in toto.[45] His intuition proved correct.

On 30 October, Izard received guidance from Monroe to consider assuming a defensive posture and preparing for the next campaign in the spring. Although the destruction of Drummond's army would "be a happy event," with effects felt all the way to Europe, Monroe cautioned Izard not to take great risks to do so.[46] He noted that "the preservation of the troops we now have is important, not only for the protection of our frontier through the winter, but as a school of instruction and a model for the much greater army which it is contemplated to raise." Monroe had learned of the threat to Sacketts Harbor and urged Izard to either send Brown there or go himself. He also passed on the president's desire to send the Seventeenth Infantry back to Detroit.

These instructions confirmed Izard's actions thus far. They also guided him in his last major decision of the war: abandonment of Fort Erie. The difficulty of crossing the Niagara in winter highlighted the problem of keeping the garrison fed or helping them from Buffalo if they should be attacked. In a letter to Monroe, Izard wrote that these problems "induced me to examine maturely the advantages, and inconveniences of retaining Fort Erie under the American flag. I can find not one of the former, (except it being a trophy) which in any point of view would justify my exposing in a weak, ill-planned, and hastily repaired redoubt (it scarcely deserves even that humble designation) some hundreds of valuable officers and men."[47] Izard also noted that the battalion designated to garrison the post was experiencing "daily and numerous" desertions.[48] Izard polled three of his most trusted officers—Brigadier Generals Swartwout and Bissell and his engineer, Major Totten. Each agreed with Izard's inclination to abandon the post. Based on these circumstances, Izard decided that Fort Erie was to be "dismantled, evacuated, and destroyed." He put Hindman in charge of work parties ostensibly digging huts in the sides of the fortification, which would later be filled with gunpowder to destroy the fort.[49]

As early as 23 October, Drummond had become convinced that the Americans had "abandoned all idea of offensive operations."[50] Telling this to Prevost, he also confided that his medical condition was causing "great uneasiness and alarm and from which I continually suffer great distress." Drummond asked his superior to allow him to return to England as soon as possible. Like Brock before him, Drummond had successfully defended Upper Canada. Now it was time to go home. Before he left, however, he had to organize the army for the winter. He divided his force into two divisions: the Right Division under Stovin, and the Center Division commanded by De Watteville. Drummond decided to keep four battalions on the Niagara Peninsula—three in the forts and along the river, and one in Burlington. He planned to winter three more battalions at York, and five of his spent regiments (the Royal Scots; Forty-first, 100th, and 103d Foot; and De Watteville's) would join the Eighth and 104th at Kingston.

Surgeon Dunlop drew a remarkable portrait of one of Drummond's hard-used battalions. "My own regiment was wretchedly reduced; little more than three months before it had gone into the Battle of the Falls, five hundred strong, with a full complement of officers. Now we retired about sixty rank and file, commanded by a captain, two of the senior lieutenants carrying the colours, and myself marching in rear—voila, His Majesty's 89th Regiment of Foot!"[51] Reluctantly, Yeo sent transports to move the troops before weather shut down navigation on the lake. When he learned that Brown's division was leaving the area, Drummond briefly contemplated raiding into New York, but Yeo refused to assist him in that venture. On 7 November, his work completed, Sir Gordon Drummond departed the Niagara Peninsula for Kingston.[52]

No telling of the 1814 campaign on the Niagara Peninsula is complete without mention of McArthur's raid through western Upper Canada. In early August, Armstrong sent instructions to Brigadier General Duncan McArthur commanding in Detroit to begin operations against the Indians in the Michigan Territory. McArthur dutifully raised a regiment, 700 strong, of Kentucky and Ohio mounted volunteers. On 9 October, and on his own responsibility, McArthur decided to ride east toward Burlington Heights to relieve the pressure on the Left Division. Averaging nearly twenty miles each day, the Americans destroyed numerous mills and captured and paroled over 100 militiamen. They seized horses as they needed them. On 5 November, McArthur reached the Grand River, where he was opposed, from the opposite shore, by Grand River Iroquois, Canadian militia, and a handful of the Forty-first Foot. Unable to force a crossing and learning that Izard was moving his army back into New York, McArthur decided to return to Detroit. He continued destroying mills on his return, opposed unsuccessfully by small bodies of militia. The mounted volunteers returned to Detroit on 17 November. The human cost of the raid was one American life.[53]

McArthur's expedition had no effect on the ongoing campaign. Izard and Drummond heard only rumors of McArthur's activities, and there is no evidence that either commander made any decisions on that basis. As the first reports of the raid were contradictory, Drummond was unconcerned. "I doubt not it will prove that the parties in question are a small number of plunderers whom the armed settlers of the country ought to repel," he wrote to Prevost on 26 October.[54] On 30 October, he dismissed the raid as a "false alarm."[55] Only on 6 November, after McArthur had pulled back from the Grand River, did Drummond send De Watteville and a single battalion to respond to the reported raid.[56]

John Norton evaluated the raid in purely economic terms. "The only object however effectually accomplished by this dashing enterprize, was the destruction of four mills by 1000 men who had rode from Kentucky, a distance of 500 miles, and had been employed about two months, at the rate of a dollar per day to each man. We were able to rebuild the mills in less time, and at much less expense."[57] On another level, however, McArthur's raid speaks to the changing political environment and the difficulties of forming a sound operational plan. In 1812, when Hull arrived in western Upper Canada, pro-American sympathies were strong. The following year, Harrison could still receive assistance from the settlers. When the Americans departed, the pro-American Canadians were left to live with their loyalist neighbors. Months of civil conflict in the western counties had made the populace war weary. The destruction of mills and plundering of livestock by American raiding parties meant only suffering through the long, cold winter. By November 1814, pro-American sympathy had nearly vanished.

McArthur intended to relieve pressure on Brown's division. Had Brown or Izard known the strength of McArthur's column and his route, they might have coordinated their efforts with his. Brown's intention, and Drummond's fear, was to outflank the Chippawa position. Had he pushed across the Grand River and made a move on Burlington, McArthur might have caused Drummond to evacuate the Chippawa or at least prompted him to send a force to deal with the threat. These possibilities were lost because McArthur and Izard did not know each other's situation, nor did they coordinate their activities.

While McArthur was approaching the Grand River, Hindman and Totten were preparing Fort Erie for destruction. Hindman dispatched the cannon, more than twenty-five pieces, over to Buffalo. Totten supervised work parties digging shafts into the ramparts. He complained that water was entering the compartments where he intended to pack the gunpowder, a legacy of the long rainy season. On the morning of 5 November, Hindman and Totten directed the long fuses to be lit. The work parties boarded their boats and pushed off from shore. As they crossed the Niagara heading for Buffalo, the mines erupted one after another. Captain FitzGibbon of the Glengarries rode into the ruins, the first British soldier to do so other than deserters or prisoners since 3 July. He found burned buildings and collapsed ramparts. The stone barracks were reduced to piles of rock. Snake Hill was once again a mere mound of sand. The only provisions he discovered were a few barrels of damaged musket cartridges.[58]

The decision to abandon Fort Erie was shortsighted, and Izard's argument that its garrison could not be supported from Buffalo was disingenuous. After all, in similar circumstances, the British had maintained Fort Niagara in American territory for eleven months. While the British negotiators in Ghent were insisting on *uti possidetis*, it seemed odd that the government would condone Izard's voluntary surrender of a fortification in enemy territory. But that is what happened. On 9 November, Monroe wrote to Izard that the president approved of Izard's plan to relinquish Fort Erie. Monroe added that he saw "no essential advantage in holding the post of Erie."[59] Apparently, it did not occur to either Monroe or Madison that Fort Erie might be exchanged for Niagara in the final settlement.

Izard continued the dispersal of his army into winter quarters. Colonel John Miller marched the Seventeenth Infantry and the companies of the Nineteenth

Infantry, nearly 900 soldiers in all, to Erie. Captain Sinclair, commanding the fleet on the upper Great Lakes, could not get his vessels over the sandbar at Erie and could not, therefore, bring Miller's men to Detroit. The riflemen were posted on Conjocta Creek, the site of Morgan's brilliant victory. The infantry began building huts at Buffalo and Black Rock. The mounted dragoons were sent to the Genesee River Valley, where forage was readily found. The dismounted dragoons marched to Batavia to guard the stores there, and a battalion of artillerists was stationed near the hospital in Williamsville. Izard took steps to clear out the hospital. There were nearly 2,000 sick, wounded, or convalescing soldiers on the Niagara Frontier. As many as possible were sent to Greenbush.[60]

Izard complained to Monroe that many of the troops had not been paid since April, and many recruits had not yet received their enlistment bounties. "The situation of the officers," he continued, "who have now particularly need of money to make their arrangements for the winter, is extremely unpleasant."[61] For the most part, "arrangements for winter" meant leave to return to their homes. Cromwell Pearce, colonel of the Sixteenth Infantry, described the situation in the American camp: "As generals and subalterns obtained leave of absence before a hut was constructed to protect the soldiers from the inclemency of the winter, in a short time scarcely a general or field officer was to be found in camp."[62]

Izard himself had had enough. No sooner had the dust from the explosions settled back down on the ruins of Fort Erie than Izard wrote to Monroe asking permission to leave the Niagara Frontier. Citing failing health, Izard wanted to escape the notoriously cold Buffalo winter. He suggested that he spend the winter with his family in Philadelphia, where he could better prepare for the upcoming campaign by overseeing the flow of supplies and equipment into the Ninth Military District. Less than two weeks later, Izard recommended that Monroe replace him as commander of the district and appoint Brown in his stead. "General Brown is certainly a brave, intelligent and active officer," he argued. Not receiving a reply from the War Department, Izard offered to resign his commission. "I am fully aware," he wrote to Monroe, "that attempts have been made to lessen the confidence of the government . . . in my ability to execute the important duties entrusted to me." He hoped that his voluntary retirement would "relieve the department of war from some embarrassment."[63] When the War Department replied, it was to reassure Izard of the president's trust and to invite him to come to Washington to discuss the issues. Izard departed the Niagara Frontier on 25 January.

Cromwell Pearce, as senior colonel, assumed command of the First Division. Pay had not arrived, but winter clothing had—just in time for a brutal winter. Lake Erie froze over, and it was possible to walk from Buffalo to the ruins of Fort Erie. The War Department sent orders to move troops eastward to reinforce Macomb at Plattsburg. Eleven hundred infantry, dismounted dragoons, and artillerists made a winter march from western New York to the Champlain Valley. Pearce was left with a brigade of infantry and a battalion each of riflemen and artillerists around Buffalo. Upon inspection, Pearce discovered that there were no musket cartridges in the brigade except those in the men's cartridge boxes. The nearest were in Batavia. Contractors had difficulty getting meat to the army. Pearce's response was to order the daily ration of whiskey and bread doubled. "These measures," he recalled, "gave general satisfaction, and reconciled all difficulties."[64] The troops waited for spring and another campaign.

Madison and Monroe were already preparing for the next bout. In mid-October, Monroe reported to the Senate that the British could be expected to continue their attacks on the coast and that New York City and New Orleans were at particular risk. The administration understood, finally, that only regulars could be depended on. Monroe urged the Senate to raise the authorization of the regular army from 62,000 to 100,000 troops. Madison was prepared to ask Congress to make up recruiting shortfalls with drafts from the militia, those conscripted to serve two years. Many of the newly raised regiments would be used to protect the coast, but the administration had not forgotten about Canada. Monroe argued that defense alone could not bring the war to an honorable conclusion. Seizing Canada would provide "a safe pledge for an honorable peace."[65] John C. Calhoun followed the administration's lead. In a statement that succinctly summarized the course of the war so far, Calhoun told Congress that the enemy "relies not so much on his own strength as our weakness and disunion."[66] He urged Congress to man the coastal fortifications with regulars and place 50,000 additional regulars on the border to invade Canada as soon as the next campaign season opened.

While Congress debated the issue of expanding the regular army, the War Department struggled to develop a strategic plan. Monroe had learned from the mistakes of his predecessors. As early as 26 November, he consulted Izard. "I shall be glad to receive your opinion of the propriety of retaining our force at Buffalo, or on the strait. It appears to me that there is little to defend there, and that our future operations cannot well commence there with a view to any important effect."[67] Monroe determined that Montreal was the key to Canada, and he sent for a general who could deliver that island city. On 22 January 1815, Jacob Brown arrived in Washington to plan the next invasion of Canada.

While the American government was gearing up for another year of war, the deadlock in Ghent was unexpectedly broken. As late as November, the Liverpool ministry was committed to prosecuting a war of punishment and asked the Duke of Wellington to consider taking overall command in British North America. Wellington's reply was unexpected and harsh.

You have not been able to carry it [the war] into the enemy's territory notwithstanding your military success and now undoubted military superiority, and have
not even cleared your own territory on the point of attack. You cannot on any principle of equality in negotiation claim a cession of territory excepting in exchange
for other advantages which you have in your power. . . . Why stipulate for *uti possidetis?* You can get no territory; indeed, the state of your military operations, however creditable, does not entitle you to demand any.

Neither Liverpool nor Wellington knew at the time that Izard had abandoned
Erie. Nonetheless, the duke's advice carried great weight. The negotiations in
Vienna were going poorly, and the national debt after twenty years of war was
staggering. Liverpool's cabinet decided to put off a punitive war in America in
favor of preparing for another major European war. The negotiators in Ghent
received new instructions, and on 27 November, they dropped the demand for
uti possidetis. After that, negotiations moved quickly to a settlement acceptable
to both sides. Neither party lost territory. Neither party gave in on any principle. The troublesome issues were deferred to settlement by commission. On
Christmas Eve, the negotiators signed a treaty and sent it to their respective governments for ratification. In the end, the issue of whose flag flew over the ruins
of Fort Erie was entirely irrelevant.[68]

The British made their long-awaited attack on the American Gulf coast while
negotiations were concluding. America held its breath for three weeks as a powerful British army faced a mixed force of regulars, militia, volunteers, Indians,
and smugglers at New Orleans. On 22 January 1815, word of Jackson's spectac-
ular victory reached a thankful capital. News of the Treaty of Ghent arrived
three weeks later, and the Senate quickly ratified the welcomed document. London received the bitter news of the fate of the British army on the Mississippi
on 8 March. The British wasted little time in mourning; Napoleon entered Paris
on 20 March, and Britain steeled itself for yet another round in a long war. Veterans of Plattsburg, Baltimore, and New Orleans found themselves on an open
field in Belgium in June 1815, where they won more than enough glory to wipe
away the unpleasant memories of the war in North America.

CHAPTER TWELVE

Conclusion

Nobody expects an interminable war. After a conflict of three or four years, and perhaps sooner, a treaty of peace would be agreed on; nor is it certain, nor indeed very likely, that its terms would be more favorable to the interests of the United States, than the terms of the treaty made by Monroe and Pinkney, and scornfully rejected by Mr. Jefferson.

—*Connecticut Courant,* 6 November 1811

The last American invasion of Canada was a failure. Why did it fail, or, conversely, why did the British and Canadians succeed in retaining their territory? The reasons reside on several levels and run the gamut of wise and poor decisions, glaring omissions, the strengths and weaknesses of personalities and polities, and luck.

At the strategic level, the outcome of the campaign was influenced by three factors: the inability of the American government to harness and focus its extensive resources, American strategic confusion, and a flexible and efficient British strategy.

The United States enjoyed the advantages of sufficient population and agricultural and armaments production to support the war effort. The government could usually feed and arm its troops. However, throughout the war, there were never enough regulars to meet American needs. Despite an adult male population in excess of 700,000, the regular army never had more than 40,000 in the ranks. The recruiting effort barely brought in half of the numbers authorized by Congress. Neither Congress nor the administration could devise suitable inducements, and the government could not raise sufficient funds to pay the troops regularly. Volunteer corps often met their recruiting goals, but these soldiers were available for only six months at a time—hardly long enough to bring them up to the standards necessary to defeat British regulars in the open field. For too long, Republican ideology insisted that militiamen could be depended on to defend the nation. Not until the burning of Washington did Madison conclude that this principle was spurious. One result of a failed recruiting effort was that Jacob Brown struck the major blow of the government's strategy, the invasion of Canada, with fewer than 3,000 regulars. The absurdity of the American predicament was revealed by the War Department's attempts to reinforce Brown from distant garrisons at St. Louis and Detroit.

Nor could the administration harmonize a strategy in perpetual disarray. Madison never resolved the fundamental issue of the fate of Canada. Would he bring Upper and Lower Canada into the Union, or would he trade them for neutral rights and a repudiation of impressment? Reflecting this central ambiguity was the conduct of American commanders, at one time promising protection and citizenship and at another destroying private homes and property. Their waffling quickly squandered the considerable sympathy among many Canadians for the American cause. As American armies were repeatedly turned back at the frontier, Canadians who might have welcomed the protection of the American flag were cowed into neutrality. When American forces managed to remain in Canada for any length of time, their tactic of destroying mills, and thus the food supply of civilians and soldiers alike, was counterproductive. By 1814, Brown received little assistance from the populace.

Fundamental to American strategic difficulties was a failure to coordinate the efforts of the land and naval forces in a theater of operations. Only one person, the president, could exercise command over both the army and the navy. Madison presumed that his secretaries of war and navy would coordinate the efforts of their subordinates and that military commanders, mindful of the common cause, would cooperate in their operations. Such trust was misplaced, not because the commanders on the spot were unable or unwilling to cooperate but because their instructions from Washington, as well as the logic of their form of warfare, drove them apart as often as they brought them together. In the case of the Central Theater, the logic of the naval arms race on Lake Ontario and the consequent search for the decisive naval battle argued forcefully against mutual cooperation in 1814. As a corollary, the requirement to defend Sacketts Harbor was a continual distraction to Brown and later to Izard.

Most perplexing among the administration's long list of errors was the refusal to aim the invasions at a vulnerable spot. The capture and retention of either Montreal or Quebec City would have led to victory. The momentary capture of Kingston (long enough to destroy the shipyard and warehouses) or a stranglehold on a portion of the St. Lawrence River might well have resulted in the fall of Upper Canada. Yet Armstrong allowed Brown to operate on the Niagara Peninsula, and Madison did nothing to stop him. By attempting the more feasible rather than the most decisive, the Americans surrendered any real hope of strategic success.

Secretary of War Armstrong's failure to appoint a single commander for the Ninth Military District defies rational explanation. A military superior in Albany would be closer to the front and to the government of New York. Supervising a central staff, he could have coordinated and resourced all ground forces: regulars, volunteers, and militia. Armstrong, in Washington, failed to keep up with the evolving situation. The time wasted as information traveled from Plattsburg or Buffalo to the capital prevented any possibility of exploiting those narrow windows of opportunity that presented themselves from time to time. By retaining personal control of both the Left and Right Divisions, Armstrong introduced unnecessary friction that limited the potential for either force to contribute to its full potential. To his credit, Monroe corrected the situation, but too late to help the American cause.

Madison cannot escape responsibility for a flawed and untimely strategy for 1814. Waiting until June to issue a unified plan for the Western and Central Theaters, Madison insisted on retaking Michilimackinac Island. The expedition sent on this task deprived Brown of both vessels and men and thereby limited his options. Without adequate numbers of boats, Brown could not land his army on the Upper Canada side of Lake Erie, the most expeditious means of advancing on Burlington Heights. Instead, he was forced to cross the Niagara, seize Fort Erie, and find a way to cross the easily defended Chippawa River. From an operational point of view, Madison's focus on this western island is bewildering. Once Burlington and Fort George were in American hands, everything westward would fall as supplies ran out. Armstrong argued against Madison's proposal, but the president prevailed.

Had Madison promulgated his strategy earlier in the year, the Americans might have enjoyed greater success. The campaign season on the Great Lakes opened in April, while the ice along the St. Lawrence interfered with the movement of British troops and supplies for a few more weeks. Had the commanders in the field received guidance in March or even earlier, they would have had time to position troops and supplies to be ready to move as soon as weather conditions permitted. Likewise, state governors would have had time to raise and equip volunteers and militia and send them to camps for training. Madison's failure to hammer out a strategy before June is even more puzzling in view of his apprehension of the large number of British regulars released by the end of the war in Europe.

As it turned out, the release of Wellington's veterans for service in North America shifted the strategic initiative from the Americans to their adversaries. With the luxury of an immense navy and thousands of experienced regulars, and the will and skill to use them, the British were in the driver's seat. Unable to seize Canada in two years of fighting while Britain was preoccupied in a European war, America now had to defend a lengthy coast while trying one more time to invade Canada. Unable to get 2,500 militia volunteers trained and equipped in time to cross the Niagara River with Brown on 3 July, the administration now called for 93,500 militiamen to defend its coastal cities. To be sure, the various governors were more motivated to protect their cities than to invade Canada, yet the ill-proportioned effort highlights the inability of a weak national government to focus its power.

The administration was inept at coordinating military and diplomatic efforts. There is no evidence that Armstrong linked the guidance he issued to his field commanders to the aims of negotiations in Ghent. He failed to tell Brown and Izard the status of negotiations or how their efforts might move diplomacy in a favorable direction. The most glaring evidence of this failure was Madison's and Armstrong's willingness to allow Izard to give up Fort Erie and evacuate Canada on his own authority, even as the British insisted on *uti possidetis* as a basis of settlement. As late as November, a real possibility existed that the United States would emerge from the war without eastern Maine or New Orleans unless Izard retained a significant portion of Upper Canada to exchange for them.

A final piece of evidence that the Madison administration could not maintain a coherent strategy was the failure of its primary strategist, John Armstrong, to understand his foe once the British went on the offensive. He was guilty of trying to divine British intentions rather than examining their capabilities. Two failures stand out in particular. First, Armstrong refused to believe that Prevost would move to destroy American power on Lake Champlain. In spite of warnings from Izard and Governor Tompkins, Armstrong blithely ordered Izard's 4,000 soldiers to Sacketts Harbor, even as Prevost was readying 10,000 troops for the march on Plattsburg. Only a naval victory in Plattsburg Bay and Prevost's excessive caution saved the American base. Second, Armstrong could not fathom that the British would attempt to take their enemy's capital when other objectives beckoned. He failed to support Winder, his military commander, or to participate in any meaningful way to improve the city's defenses. In this instance, Armstrong's error was unredeemed by valor, and he was rightfully sacked.

In contrast, Prevost's defensive strategy embraced both the ground and the naval effort and was a judicious balance of ways, means, and ends. Understanding that his was a sideshow of a much wider conflict, Prevost was careful to protect Quebec and Montreal, his centers of gravity. While directing a defensive strategy, Prevost was not unwilling to sanction offensive action when the risks were small and the payoffs large. He allocated his limited resources commensurate with his objectives. He ensured that, for the most part, the naval and land efforts were coordinated. In this he was well served by two very capable subordinates, Yeo and Drummond, who understood the overall strategy and their part in it.

As the strategic balance shifted in favor of the British, Prevost was quick to make use of additional resources. He willingly fed reinforcements westward, confident that Drummond would use them well to retain Upper Canada and to carry the war southward if the opportunity arose. Prevost's undoing was the disastrous Plattsburg campaign. A competent defensive strategist, Prevost was less adept as a field commander. Unwilling to spend lives for trivial and temporary gains, he recoiled from assaulting the American defenses once the naval battle was lost. Perhaps he was so used to conserving his limited troop strength that he could not bring himself to change his ways when he was rich in soldiers. His subordinate commanders, accustomed to victory under Wellington, could not appreciate Prevost's reservations. In any event, Prevost's substantial contribution to the survival of British North America was overshadowed by his order to retreat from Plattsburg.

Fundamental to military success was the sustained logistical effort that fed Canadian and British soldiers and sailors and their Indian allies throughout the arduous campaign. The unsung heroes of 1814, and indeed the entire war, were the hundreds of militiamen of Lower Canada who moved troops, supplies, and equipment up the St. Lawrence to Kingston and beyond. Without solid logistical underpinning, Drummond could not have contemplated a defense of the Niagara Peninsula. Only in September, as temperatures dropped and Chauncey was out of port, was Drummond compelled to make a military decision based on anticipated logistical failure. He broke off the siege of Fort Erie rather than put his forces at undue risk. Nonetheless, supplies were sufficient to maintain the defensive line of the Chippawa until the end of the campaign season.

Coincident with military operations was the painstaking civil effort to suppress sympathy for the invaders among the American-born population. Starting with Brock, each lieutenant governor of Upper Canada used his civil authority to identify traitors and to punish them or force them out of the province. That they did so without provoking a sympathetic backlash is a credit to their judicious methods and regard for legal process. It is less remarkable that a handful were hung, drawn, and quartered than it is that hundreds were not. The military effect was consequential; Brown operated in a hostile environment. He could not attract Canadians to his side or gain useful information. On the contrary, the Canadian militia remained a potent if small auxiliary to Drummond's regulars.

Strategic issues alone cannot entirely explain the results of the campaign, although they weighed in heavily against the Americans. For the British, strategic advantages were somewhat balanced by a shift in the tactical balance in favor of the Americans.

From the very beginning, Britain's cause was aided immensely by the psychological impact of its Indian allies. The presence of a handful of Norton's warriors struck fear in the American ranks on Queenston Heights in 1812 and contributed to the collapse of the defense. The following year, the American commander at Stoney Creek decided to retreat rather than risk massacre. Weeks later, at Beaver Dams, an entire column surrendered when it was surrounded by a smaller body of natives. However, by 1814, the "scare value" was virtually nil. The Left Division, which included its own Indian warriors, was undaunted by Britain's native allies. Even the untrained Pennsylvania Volunteers more than held their own against those Indians in the forest fight at Chippawa.

A more extensive change was demonstrated in the character of the American militia. In 1812, thousands refused to cross into Canada. In 1814, the majority of militiamen not only agreed to cross but also fought hard and well. At Chippawa and Lundy's Lane, the militia volunteers did all that was asked of them, which included close-range combat. At the sortie from Fort Erie, their performance far exceeded any expectation. Certainly credit is due to their leaders: Generals Peter B. Porter, John Swift, and Daniel Davis, who led from the front. But inspirational leadership alone cannot explain this profound metamorphosis. Perhaps the explanation could be found in the ashes of Buffalo and the perception that homes in New York and Pennsylvania were at risk as long as the British remained in power in Upper Canada.

The change that largely redressed British strategic advantages was the transformation of the American regular army in the field. After two years of training, marching, and fighting, the quality of many American regiments was now equal to that of their enemy. The quality of the American recruit was not appreciably different in 1814 than in 1812. What had changed were the combat experience of the soldier and the quality of the officers and noncommissioned officers. Soldiers who had battle experience, even if it was defeat, are more hardened to future experiences. Additionally, officers and noncommissioned officers had learned their trade. Weak officers left the regiments. The most competent officers earned promotions—men like James Miller, Henry Leavenworth, Thomas Jesup, and Eleazer Wood. Illustrative of this transformation was Scott's training regimen at Buffalo; however, similar results were obtained at Plattsburg and elsewhere.

Unfortunately for the British, they persisted in the misplaced hope that the regiments of the Left Division were as brittle as those that had marched under James Wilkinson or Wade Hampton. Indeed, Drummond founded his operational plans on this assumption. The Battle of Chippawa should have served as warning that the current batch of American regulars was well trained, resilient, and not afraid to cross bayonets with the foe. Drummond maintained to the end the notion of the qualitative superiority of his regulars, as did Brown and

Scott for theirs. The truth is that man for man, officer for officer, the American regulars—infantry, artillery, and dragoon—were the equal of the British in the open field or the forest, day or night.

The shift toward tactical equilibrium partially addressed the worst deficiencies at the strategic level for the Americans. However, a full explanation of the American defeat can be derived only by an investigation of the quality of the decisions made by the respective commanders and the results on the battlefield. Without close cooperation between the army and navy, Brown's campaign plan could not yield strategic success. Battlefield victory, no matter how one-sided, could not gain for the Americans more than the Niagara Peninsula and, by default, western Upper Canada. Brown's land supply lines would not allow the Left Division to operate in force much beyond Burlington Heights. Brown well understood these limitations, and he depended on Chauncey to supply him once he reached Lake Ontario. Given this understanding, Brown's plan was entirely adequate to move the Left Division from Buffalo to the vicinity of Fort George. With Chauncey's assistance, he might seize Forts George and Mississauga. From there, Brown could then lay siege to Fort Niagara or, assisted by the Lake Ontario squadron, attack either Burlington Heights or York or perhaps Kingston itself.

Brown's invasion started well as Fort Erie fell on the first day at minimal cost in life to either side. Major Thomas Buck's decision to surrender the fort rather than attempt to defend it cost General Riall at least a full day of preparation time behind the Chippawa River. Had Riall moved to relieve Buck, the Left Division would have been fighting in two directions with a river at its back—not a promising situation. But Buck gave up Fort Erie, and Brown brought the entire Left Division unmolested to the shores of the Chippawa.

Riall's decision to attack forward of his defenses on the Chippawa was based on his false understanding of both Buck's situation and the supposed brittleness of American battalions. However, he escaped with his army intact because Brown and Scott were not prompt in pursuing Riall's broken division as it scrambled back over the river and into its defenses. Brown skillfully maneuvered Riall out of the line of the Chippawa, and their subsequent movement northward brought both armies closer to potential support—Riall from Drummond, and Brown from Chauncey.

The next few days, while Brown waited at Queenston for the American fleet to appear, were critical. Brown believed that he had gone about as far as he could without the siege guns and supplies he expected to arrive with Chauncey. With supplies carried by boat, Brown could move on Burlington Heights. With heavy guns, he could batter down the timber stockade walls of Fort George. He had neither. His only hope was to catch Riall's division one more time in the open and this time destroy it. To this end, he postured in front of Fort George, hoping to induce Riall to come out. Certain that he was greatly outnumbered, Riall never gave Brown the opportunity he craved. Unwilling to leave port before he was completely ready, and focused on a naval battle for supremacy of the lake, Chauncey left Brown unsupported. The American campaign was seriously injured by Chauncey's inactivity in July. Had he broken Yeo's blockade and sent even a few fighting ships to prowl the lake, Chauncey might have prevented Drummond from sending reinforcements to Riall. Had Major Ludowick Morgan escaped Sacketts Harbor with the siege guns Brown thought he needed, the campaign might have gone in another direction.

There was one opportunity, however, that Brown let slip. Brown could have gambled on a siege and assault of Fort George. He had a few heavy guns, and Riall's engineers had pronounced the walls of Fort George woefully inadequate. Assault might have proved costly and, if successful, could have led in only one direction: a subsequent siege of Fort Niagara. However, with Fort George in American hands, its guns preventing British supply boats from using the anchorage at the mouth of the Niagara, the eventual fall of Fort Niagara would be all but assured. This would certainly not equate to strategic victory, but the negotiations in Ghent might have proceeded more quickly once it was known that the Niagara River Valley was firmly in American hands.

Brown believed that Fort George was too strong to assault, and this led to the conclusion that he had no choice but to fall back when Chauncey failed to appear. Drummond's decision to go to the Niagara Peninsula himself upped the ante. He was not afraid to fight Brown in the open. Drummond's defeat would have opened the road to Burlington Heights and perhaps all the way to York. As it turned out, Drummond's victory at Lundy's Lane was a major setback to the American effort.

Brown lost the battle because he was surprised. By failing to maintain contact with the enemy, Brown allowed Drummond the luxury of concentrating his division on a nearby piece of defensible terrain. Without knowing where the enemy was, Brown sent Scott's brigade in harm's way. Echoing the failing of his superior, Scott failed to scout out the battlefield. As a result, he marched his well-trained, battle-experienced brigade to destruction. The heroic efforts of Thomas Jesup's men in turning the British flank, or James Miller's regiment in storming the crest of the hill, or the entire Left Division in holding on through three determined counterattacks, could not redeem Brown's and Scott's initial errors.

Ripley's inadequate preparations during the few hours after the battle of Lundy's Lane forfeited for the Left Division any hope of maintaining a semblance of victory. It was inexcusable for him not to pass on to his subordinate commanders Brown's order to return to the battlefield at dawn. Ripley led his men out of camp too late the following morning to capitalize on the battlefield success earned at such a cost the evening prior. Ripley's decision to abandon the naturally strong defensive position along the Chippawa and to retreat back to the ferry landing opposite Black Rock compounded his error and nearly ended the campaign. The American effort was kept alive by Brown's determination to defend Fort Erie and Drummond's failure to pursue his crippled foe.

Drummond's inactivity during the week following Lundy's Lane can hardly be excused, as the British threw away their best chance to eject the invaders. When he finally moved, Drummond seemingly regained his daring as well as his resolution. His attempt to cut the American supply line from Buffalo was as inspired in conception as it was flawed in execution. Drummond's audacious decision to lay siege to Fort Erie was a calculated gamble. Victory would mean the utter destruction of the American Left Division, but even a stalemated siege would keep the American invaders too occupied to cause mischief elsewhere. Defeat of the siege, in contrast, might only cost the loss of Fort Erie itself.

Drummond's order to remove the flints from the weapons of the assault force and his inadequate reconnaissance of the American defenses were keys to defeat during the night attack of 15 August. However, even with their flints, the British would have had a very tough time. Edmund P. Gaines transfused his determination to his men, and they would not have yielded the fort easily. The explosion in the bastion ended the British attack, which had already stalled without hope of moving forward. The tremendous cost in British lives from this accidental detonation, however, meant that Drummond would not soon attempt another assault.

Drummond's decision to end the siege because of lack of supplies coincided with Brown's daring sortie of 17 September. To all outward appearances, the American attack broke the siege. Regardless of interpretation, the initiative had once more passed to the invaders; with the arrival of George Izard's powerful Right Division, the Americans had yet another chance to gain the Niagara Peninsula. Izard's inertia and timidity squelched this possibility. Moving slowly, unsure of his objective, devoid of a plan of operation, Izard managed to bring the formidable Northern Army to the Chippawa River, where he was opposed by a very apprehensive Drummond. And there Izard remained. Other than posturing before Drummond and ineptly offering battle on uninviting terms, Izard could come up with no promising ideas. He failed to take advantage of Brown's offer to force a crossing upstream. Even General Daniel Bissell's flank march to Cook's Mill had no greater objective than to destroy flour. Izard wanted victory but was unwilling to take calculated risks and was even more loath to pay the necessary price in human life. These twin characteristics raised Drummond and Brown to a level of generalship unapproached by Izard. Generalship is also marked by superior judgment—making the correct decision at the proper time—and by the courage to follow through.

The four months of fighting on the Niagara Peninsula were marked by hero-ism and sacrifice by the many thousands of participants: British, Canadian, and American regulars and militiamen and the native warriors representing both the Iroquois Nation and the remnants of Tecumseh's confederation. Both sides exhibited generally effective levels of military competence and leadership, start-ing with the soldier and proceeding up to brigade level. In the final analysis, the last American invasion of Canada failed for strategic and operational reasons. Foremost were strategic confusion, the inability to concentrate a larger number of regulars at Buffalo, Chauncey's failure to aid Brown in July, Brown's lapse of reconnaissance prior to Lundy's Lane, Ripley's loss of nerve afterward, and finally Izard's imperfect generalship. Jacob Brown assessed the campaign in a letter to the ex–secretary of war, John Armstrong. "It is fortunate for the army and this nation that a fair experiment has been made with a part of our land forces, that a few brave men have met the enemy and triumphed over a superior number of troops hitherto esteemed the best in the world. But the general exe-cution of the plan of campaign has been disgraceful."[1]

AFTERWORD

The birthplace of the regular army is not at Valley Forge, but along the Niagara in 1814.
—Donald E. Graves

Although the campaign on the Niagara had some impact on the speed of nego-tiations in Ghent and on the terms of that treaty, its effects on the professional-ization of the U.S. Army has been dealt with only generally. This afterword takes a preliminary step in advancing the Graves thesis. The success achieved on the Niagara suggested to James Monroe, acting secretary of war, what could be accomplished in 1815 with the leaders and soldiers from that campaign. When the war ended and Congress ordered a reduction in force, Madison disregarded the accepted usage of seniority in order to capture the talent from that campaign in the peace establishment. The fortuitous blending of leaders of the Niagara campaign with the obvious talents of Secretary of War John C. Calhoun led to a period of reform that professionalized the army and prepared it for the war with Mexico. Finally, a short biographical sketch of some of the veteran leaders of Niagara illustrates that Madison's trust was not misplaced.

Learning from the mistakes of Madison and John Armstrong, Monroe understood the imperative of deriving a campaign strategy early in the year. On 2 January 1815, he directed Jacob Brown to report to Washington to discuss "many subjects of high importance to the public, relating to future operations in the quarters in which you have commanded." Since George Izard had been granted permission to travel to Washington, Monroe placed Peter B. Porter in command on the Niagara Frontier, with authority to call out militia as neces-sary. However, even before Brown arrived in Washington, Monroe derived the general outline of the 1815 campaign plan and sent it to Governor Daniel Tomp-kins of New York. Monroe fully understood that the efforts made against Michilimackinac and the Niagara Peninsula in 1814 had been misdirected. To correct Madison's and Armstrong's strategic error, Monroe focused his efforts at breaking the British line of communication along the St. Lawrence.[1]

Monroe envisaged three concentrations of forces, one each at Sacketts Harbor and Plattsburg, potential jumping-off positions, and a third at Johnstown, New York. This later location, one easily supplied and accessible to the other two, would be the assembly point for a huge force that could move to either Sacketts Harbor or Plattsburg as the time for the invasion arrived. Thus, the British would be kept ignorant of the proposed invasion route until the last moment. From Sacketts Harbor, the Americans could focus on Kingston itself or move down the St. Lawrence, a repeat of James Wilkinson's 1813 campaign. Of course, this effort would require considerable cooperation from Commodore Isaac Chauncey, which was not likely, given the events of 1814. An invasion force departing Plattsburg would drive up the Richelieu Valley and threaten Montreal directly. It would capitalize on the destruction of the British naval forces achieved by Thomas McDonough's squadron the previous September.[2]

In the face of huge British reinforcements into Canada, Monroe understood that the current regular force was woefully inadequate. However, he anticipated imminent congressional approval for 60,000 more troops, a combination of volunteers and militia. Monroe intended to raise half of this number in New York and Vermont for use in the upcoming invasion. He transmitted to Tompkins his great determination. "I wish to convey to you, in confidence, as distinctly as I am able at this time, the measures which are contemplated by the government to secure a speedy and honorable peace. We can break the power of the enemy on this continent the next campaign, and we must do it." Tompkins's role was to raise the forces. His reward was the privilege of naming the officers. Monroe emphasized the selection of officers. "I need not remark that too much care and caution in making a judicious selection of officers for the command of these corps, and of all the subalterns in each, cannot be observed. A judicious selection will eminently contribute to success in raising the men; it will also contribute equally to success in the field against the enemy." He went on to state that Madison would give Porter a commission as major general in the regular army—certainly a mark of confidence in Porter, as well as a reward to New York for raising this large force.[3]

Shortly after Monroe made his plans known to Tompkins, he met with Brown. Apparently, Brown agreed with Monroe's strategy, and Monroe conferred upon him command of the entire invasion army. Monroe immediately sent Brown to visit with Tompkins and the governor of Vermont to speed up the raising of the invasion forces. Monroe rightly saw his role as providing Brown with troops, equipment, and supplies. He expected the British to bring no more than 30,000 troops to oppose the invasion and therefore estimated that Brown would need 40,000 to succeed. "If we fail to raise a force which will put the result beyond hazard, so far as certainty attainable, we ought not to make the attempt, but rest satisfied with making a defensive, inglorious war for the nation, however honorable it may be for the gallant officers who conduct and may be employed in it."[4]

As a rather telling mark of the confidence that Madison and Monroe had in Brown, Monroe instructed Brown to "fix on some highly meritorious character . . . and recommend [him] to the President for the rank of brigadier general." Brown was instructed to exercise care in selecting officers and was pointedly counseled "not to be governed in these appointments by party considerations, but to confide in, and associate in command, with those who have supported the government, any meritorious, honorable men, who, jealous of the rights and honor of this country, are willing to indicate them in the present controversy."[5]

Monroe's foray into developing a campaign strategy is remarkable on several issues and reflects a mature grasp of the operational considerations and an appreciation for his role. Monroe understood that time was imperative—time to decide, time to prepare. Madison had not blessed the strategic plans for 1814 until 7 June of that year. That left precious little time for Armstrong to deploy troops to Brown at Buffalo. Monroe knew that it would take time to raise and train a large volunteer force, so he set the wheels in motion as soon as he could. Monroe also had the determination to set the operational goal—cutting the St. Lawrence between Kingston and Montreal—for his commander in the field and to trust two key governors with this information. This was unlike Armstrong, who had dithered with Wilkinson as late as October as to the focus of the 1813 invasion. Monroe's operational plan was flexible, allowing the responsible commander to select the specific invasion route unhampered by troop concentrations that might limit his choice. Finally, the secretary of war understood that his primary role, once operational guidance was issued, was to provide resources for the effort. Monroe knew that he needed a very large force to be successful and that officer selection was key not only to fighting but also to raising the force. He was wise to eliminate party membership as a consideration, as this had been a limiting factor in raising regiments in New England in 1812. How he was going to raise such a large army in view of past recruiting failures and outright Federalist resistance to the war currently being demonstrated in Hartford was a separate issue and quickly became irrelevant. On 16 February, Monroe notified commanders of military districts that the Senate had ratified the Treaty of Ghent.

Within days, William Branch Giles, chairman of the Senate Military Affairs Committee, notified Monroe that Congress was anxious to reduce the army as soon as practical and invited the secretary of war to submit his views. Monroe was peeved that Giles expected a quick reply rather than a considered one. He wrote to Scott, "The passion is strong for general reduction. I hope it may be confined within proper limits."[6] Two days after receiving Giles's request, Monroe responded that the war had changed the nation. "By the war we have acquired a character and rank among other nations which we did not enjoy before. . . . We cannot go back. The spirit of the nation forbids it. The privations to which our citizens have been exposed, the losses which they have suffered with extraordinary patience and fortitude, and the blood which has been gallantly shed in defense of our rights, point out our future course of conduct, and impress on us new obligations to pursue it." Noting that Britain still had 35,000 troops in North America, Monroe suggested pacing the American reduction to that of its former enemy. He reminded Giles that there remained unresolved issues with Spain. Alluding to the several destructive British raids on the coast, Monroe noted a pressing need to maintain and man coastal fortifications. As for relations with the natives, Monroe stressed establishing forts "at such points as will secure to us, in future the friendship and exclusive commerce with the Indian tribes, within our limits." Monroe closed with a recommendation to maintain a peace establishment of 20,000 soldiers representing all corps: infantry, rifles, cavalry, and artillery. He further recommended maintaining the Corps of Engineers at its present strength. Perhaps sensing that Congress would not countenance paying for such numbers, Monroe asserted that such an authorization would typically result in 10,000 to 12,000 effectives. Left unstated was that the more expensive and potentially patronage-ridden officer complement would remain filled close to full strength.[7]

Congress was only partially persuaded by Monroe's logic. Rather than create an establishment that would presumably remain understrength, it directed that the authorization be fixed at 12,383 officers and men. Of these, 10,000 would be in the infantry, rifles, and artillery, and the dragoons were deleted as too expensive and less useful overall. The remainder would make up the Corps of Engineers and the technical and administrative staff corps. Reducing the number of enlisted men was fairly simple, as many enlistments expired with the peace. However, officers were an entirely different problem. The officer corps would shrink from 3,495 authorized positions to 656, or 19 percent of the wartime total. Who would stay, and who would go? What would the selection criteria be, and who would apply them? It is in the answers to these questions that the talented officers of the Niagara campaign came to enjoy far-ranging influence over the interwar army.

Congress directed that the number of general officers be reduced to two major generals and four brigadiers, as well as a quartermaster general and adjutant general. Madison disregarded seniority in his selection of the general officers to be retained, thus setting an example for further selections. Alexander J. Dallas, acting secretary of war when Monroe returned to the State Department, notified Andrew Jackson and Jacob Brown on 14 March of Madison's desire to retain them in their current ranks. The president, the confidential correspondence related, was "fully impressed" with their merit. The other major generals, notably George Izard, were eased out, probably by mutual consent. Clearly, Madison wished to preserve proven war-fighting talent. One week later, Gaines, Scott, and Macomb were also invited to remain as three of the four brigadier generals. The fourth selection for brigadier was delayed until 21 April. Eleazar Ripley had demanded a court of inquiry, which Madison ordered dissolved. Between that action and changes in leadership at the War Department, Ripley was notified late of his selection for retention but was mollified by brevet promotion to major general. Thus, of the six general officers of the line retained, five had won laurels in the Central Theater, four on the Niagara.[8]

Mindful of congressional desire to reduce the officer corps as rapidly as possible, Madison directed Brown, Scott, Macomb, and later Ripley to select officers for retention. Because of pressing military matters, including the turnover of Fort Bowyer, it was unlikely that Jackson and Gaines, who had been sent to New Orleans as Jackson's second in command, would travel to Washington to participate on the selection board, but the president afforded both generals the opportunity to submit recommendations for selection. Thus all four of the general officers who would nominate the leadership of the peace establishment had their experience in the Central Theater, and three during the Niagara campaign. Cognizant of the imbalance on the selection board, Dallas directed all regimental commanders to rate their subordinates and provide this information for board consideration. Dallas enjoined them to identify "officers of great merit, who intend to remain in service." This undoubtedly spurred a flood of correspondence from individual officers to the War Department requesting retention on active duty. Noticeable by its lack of representation among the general officers and the selection board was the West. The War Department extended to Brigadier General Duncan McArthur, commanding the Eighth Military District, a singular privilege. Among the brigadier generals who would not be retained, only McArthur was asked to provide input to the selection process. "As the officers of the regiments which are in service within your military district are probably not well known to those who are to select the officers for the peace establishment, a report from you of their respective merit would be desirable, particularly of the field officers."[9]

Madison provided the selection board with detailed guidance. Its charter included recommending an organization for the army and locations of units, as well as selecting officers for retention. As to the latter, Madison directed that field-grade strength (majors, lieutenant colonels, and colonels) be reduced from 216 to 39 and that company-grade officers (ensigns, lieutenants, and captains) decrease from 2,055 incumbents to 450. He was adamant that "those only should be recommended . . . who are competent to engage an enemy in the field of battle." The board was not to use selection as an opportunity to provide a livelihood to those crippled in battle; Congress would see to those unfortunates if it chose to. The board was directed to make selections based on "distinguished military merit" and "approved moral character." If the board had to choose among equal candidates, length of service, financial situation, and potential for civilian pursuits would serve as subordinate considerations. Madison even suggested that difficult decisions be referred "to the chance of a lottery." The president noted that the resultant list must be perceived as being derived from an impartial process and that the list eventually approved by Congress must withstand public scrutiny. To further assist the selection board, Madison directed Daniel Parker, the adjutant and inspector general, to provide applications for discharge and retention, as well as testimonials and input from regimental commanders. Finally, the board was directed to complete its work by 1 May.[10]

These instructions are remarkable for what were not included as selection criteria. Unlike with previous reductions in the army, the board was not enjoined to consider seniority or party affiliation. Nor was the board required to maintain a regional balance among the resultant officer corps or to confine itself to those regiments raised specifically for the war. Clearly, military merit and character were primary. These characteristics could be discerned from reputation or the reports of the regimental commanders. However, personal observations during the campaign served as a more trustworthy guide. On 10 May, Madison dismissed the board. In doing so, he stressed the impartiality of the resultant list and the unanimity of the board members.[11]

It is not surprising that officers who had served during the 1814 Niagara campaign enjoyed a higher rate of selection than those who had not, illustrated by the following statistical analysis. Of the twenty-eight officers who held general or field officer rank, including those holding these ranks by brevet, who can be positively identified as having served with the Left Division sometime during the campaign, twenty-three (82 percent) are found on the 1816 register of the army. By comparison, only 50 percent of the general and field-grade officers known to have been present with Izard's Right Division on the Niagara were officers in 1816. Yet even this result is favorable to the overall retention rate of 18 percent for officers of field grade. The conclusion is apparent: Brown, Scott, and Ripley retained those officers whose character and merit during active campaigning were known to them. It is reasonable to conclude that Macomb's influence ensured that other officers who served on Lake Champlain were represented among the chosen.[12]

The officers of the Left Division retained in service presumably were proud of their collective accomplishment on the Niagara. They enjoyed a national reputation, with the officers at New Orleans and Plattsburg, for having defeated the best the British could put in the field, and they basked in the warm glow of an honorable peace. The fierce combat during the hot summer and rainy fall of 1814 on the Niagara was a defining moment for many of them. Certainly they had been exposed to the worst of the War Department's mismanagement and ill-contrived policy, particularly in regard to tactical doctrine, supply, transportation, and subsistence. They also recognized, if they had not before, how proper training and confident, bold leadership could produce victory on the battlefield. These officers perhaps retained a skeptical view of the use of militia as the cornerstone of national defense. Presumably, they were appreciative of the general officers who had handpicked them for retention. All in all, they collectively appreciated that it was high time to enact some reforms, not the least of which was to build the foundation for a professional officer corps, one typified by shared values, military education, and long-term service. In this regard, they were blessed by a particularly skillful and successful secretary of war, John C. Calhoun.

Calhoun had been a war hawk, and in 1817 he typified the newfound sense of nationalism that resulted from the Treaty of Ghent and the Battle of New Orleans. A strong supporter of the Madison administration, the young and ambitious South Carolinian was proud to join Monroe's cabinet. He chose the equally ambitious Major Christian Vandeventer as chief clerk, a position better understood today as an assistant secretary. Calhoun's impact on reform within the army and professionalization of the officer corps was profound. He succeeded in achieving economy by increasing efficiency.[13]

His first task was reorganization of the staff departments. The secretary of war personally directed the two commanders of the military departments, Brown and Jackson, as well as the heads of the staff departments. Three of these departments—Engineers, Commissary General of Purchase, and Apothecary General—were not located in the national capital. Logistics functions (providing supplies, rations, and transportation) were handled haphazardly by chiefs and clerks with overlapping responsibilities and supported by a chaotic accounting system. Calhoun drafted a bill to create order from this bureaucratic jumble. Congress acceded to his wishes with few changes. In April 1818, congressional action created positions for a surgeon general, quartermaster general, and commissary general to join the army staff, which was consolidated in Washington. Thus, the various staff functions were finally organized under chiefs who reported directly to the secretary of war. Calhoun went further. He directed his chiefs to draw up internal policies and procedures for the operations of the new departments. He also devised and implemented strict procedures for accounting for funds that moved authority and responsibility downward to the officers on the spot who were obligating government money. These officers (such as paymasters and assistant quartermasters general) were then subject to regular accounting using standard procedures and forms.

Calhoun was also acutely aware that there were no comprehensive policies and regulations that governed how the army operated. What existed was a collage of policies that were contradictory, failed to address substantive issues, and did not command widespread adherence. In 1818, Scott offered to devise a set of regulations for the army. Calhoun accepted Scott's offer and passed his product with minor revision to Congress, which approved Scott's work in 1820.

Calhoun was also a proponent of internal improvements, using a loose construction of the Constitution to free the national government to build roads and canals as well as improve harbors and waterways for the general good of the country. Masking general improvements as necessary measures to improve the national defense, he sent the army to perform these tasks. The burning of Washington and the successful defense of Fort McHenry in Baltimore Harbor convinced many of the need to defend America's ports and coastal cities with masonry fortifications. The War Department recruited engineer Simon Bernard, a veteran of the Napoleonic Wars, to lead a board tasked to determine the best locations for an elaborate system of coastal fortifications. Joseph Swift and William McRee resigned in protest at this apparent insult to American engineers. Nonetheless, Bernard was given the brevet rank of brigadier general and went about his task. The board of engineers reported in 1821 that coastal defense depended on the navy, strong fortifications that were well situated, a robust coastal road network, and finally regular army units backed up by a well-trained militia. Congress agreed, and the Corps of Engineers set off on a long-term program of designing and administering the construction of a number of coastal forts. Inland roads were not neglected. Both the Corps of Engineers and the Quartermaster General Department oversaw the marking and clearing of hundreds of miles of roads to connect army posts in the West. Although much of the hard labor of road building was done by civilian employees, soldiers were often tasked with constructing these military roads when they were not otherwise occupied. The roads served the civilian sector more than the military, as traffic routes were no longer tied to rivers, and regional markets emerged or were enlarged.

A less dramatic reform, but one that proved essential to army operations on an ever-expanding frontier, was the shift in responsibility for feeding the army from contractors to a military staff department. Late in the war, Congress asked Monroe for his opinion on the subject. The acting secretary of war consulted with Scott, Gaines, and Colonel John Fenwick. Their recommendation was to bring the provision of rations under direct military control, for all the obvious reasons. With the end of the war, this initiative was shelved until the outbreak of the First Seminole War in 1817. The breakdown of the contractor system in supporting Jackson's army in Florida persuaded Congress to act on Monroe's earlier recommendation. Colonel George Gibson of Jackson's staff became the first commissary general in 1818.[14]

Calhoun was instrumental as well in nurturing the incipient professionalization of the officer corps. A profession demonstrates three characteristics: specialized skill, usually the result of focused education; a concept of service to society; and sense of corporateness.[15] Even before Calhoun took office, the War Department sent officers to Europe to investigate the latest developments in military science. William McRee, and Sylvanus Thayer enjoyed an extended visit to France and returned with large numbers of books that ended up at West Point. Calhoun protected the military academy from numerous assaults, and the appointment of Thayer as superintendent marked the academy's beginning as the very foundation of the American profession of arms.

After the economic panic of 1819, Congress took an ax to federal expenditures, and the army was a prominent candidate for cuts. Calhoun planned for the inevitable and proposed an expansible force, one that retained the current force structure but with reduced numbers of enlisted soldiers in the companies. Thus, the trained officers of the line and staff would be retained. In time of national emergency, the companies could quickly recruit up to full strength. However, Congress was pointedly aware that officers were the expensive commodity. Thus Congress chose to reduce the force structure to seven infantry and four artillery regiments. Manpower was slashed to three generals and 6,000 officers and men. As before, a board chose officers for retention. Jackson accepted the governorship of Florida; Macomb was pleased to receive command of the Engineer Corps, although it came with a demotion; and Ripley was discharged. Thus Brown was the surviving major general with the new title of commanding general, although his duties and prerogatives were ill defined.

When Calhoun left the War Department to become vice president in 1825, he left it organized for efficiency and staffed by competent officers and clerks. The army was smaller and spread thinly across the wide frontier and coast. However, it was a professional force of long-term officers who took their role in national security seriously. The army had grown used to the regulations put in place by Calhoun, and each year a new crop of officers, trained at West Point, joined their corps and regiments. Leading them were the veterans of the War of 1812, and prominent among these were the officers who had fought the long Niagara campaign. A review of the careers of a few of these soldiers points to their influence on the army's mission, reform within the army, and the professionalization of the officer corps.

Despite the residual effects of wounds received at Lundy's Lane, Jacob Brown was determined to continue on active duty at war's end. Selected along with Jackson as one of the army's two major generals, Brown was given command of the Northern Department. He made up for his lack of technical training in military science with his superb judgment and cool demeanor. Brown gave Calhoun unstinting loyalty and support, and he threw himself into the task of securing the northern and western frontiers. Chosen commanding general in 1821, Brown moved his headquarters to Washington. He used his political influence to support the army and its infant academy on the Hudson. Jacob Brown, whose force of will inspired the Left Division to victory and glory, died of a stroke in 1828.

Other than for short intervals, Edmund Pendleton Gaines served as a commissioned officer since 1799 and as a general officer from 1814. Still suffering from wounds received at Fort Erie, Gaines arrived at New Orleans just days after Jackson's stunning victory. Selected by Madison as one of four brigadiers retained in the postwar army, Gaines remained in the Southern Department under Jackson. There he was charged with keeping the peace along the border with Spanish Florida. Like Jackson, Gaines was vain and brash, prone to act precipitously rather than consider the possible outcomes of his actions. He forced the implementation of treaties with the Creeks, pursued raiding Seminoles across the international border, and dealt with rough-and-tumble frontiersmen who did not respect the niceties of international diplomacy. With the reorganization of the army in 1821, the president appointed Gaines to command the new Western Department. Gaines was effective on the frontier but sparked quarrels with his superiors and peers. His ongoing dispute with Scott over seniority was embarrassing to both himself and the army. Gaines was a proponent of use of the railroad for defense and economic development. Out of favor with Scott, now the commanding general, Gaines sat out the Mexican War. The defender of Fort Erie died of cholera in 1848.

The contributions of Winfield Scott to the development of the U.S. Army and the professionalization of the officer corps are extensive. Upon the ratification of the Treaty of Ghent, Scott was in command of the Tenth Military District. After participating on the board that selected officers for retention, Scott traveled to Europe to learn what he could of the advances made in military science during the Napoleonic Wars. Congress had been very interested in the lack of a uniform drill, and Scott was personally involved in the writing of several drill manuals prior to the war with Mexico. He commanded briefly in the Black Hawk War and the Second Seminole War and from time to time conducted diplomacy with the British. At the death of Macomb in 1841, Scott became the commanding general and took an active part in reforming army life. His campaign to take Mexico City electrified the nation and firmly established Scott as a giant among America's military commanders. His foray into politics ended with his defeat as a presidential candidate of the Whig Party in 1852. Undaunted and despite his advancing years, Scott laid out in bold strokes the war plan that, with some modification, won the Civil War for the Union. Winfield Scott passed away in 1866 at West Point.[16]

Eleazar Ripley suffered in comparison to Brown and Scott, the lions of the 1814 campaign. Even Porter and Gaines gathered more laurels. Ripley was personally very courageous. His calm demeanor, firm orders, and penchant for being in the thick of the fight inspired confidence on the battlefield. Nonetheless, his lack of dash and aggressiveness, when measured against the other general officers, was palpable. He forfeited their confidence, and despite his selection to continue as a brigadier general in the postwar army, his days were numbered. Resigning from active duty in 1820, Ripley moved to New Orleans and represented Louisiana in Congress for two terms. Santa Anna had Ripley's son, Henry, executed as part of Fannin's command at Goliad in 1836. Eleazar Wheelock Ripley died in 1839.

Perhaps second only to Scott among the veterans of the Niagara campaign, Thomas Jesup made an enduring contribution to the running of the U.S. Army. Surviving the reduction of the army as a major in the First Infantry Regiment, Jesup was appointed quartermaster general in 1818. Although he had made his reputation as a combat leader at Chippawa and Lundy's Lane, Jesup transitioned smoothly to administrative tasks. He gave life to his department and to logistics throughout the army. With a handful of trained officers, the Quartermaster Department managed the transportation and supply of a force that was thinly spread and constantly moving westward with the frontier. Whether building roads and storehouses or distributing supplies, Jesup insisted on strict accountability of funds. In spite of formidable obstacles, his department supported the force fighting the Indians and Mexicans. Placed in command of troops in the Second Seminole War, Jesup was strongly criticized for capturing Osceola by a questionable ruse. Thomas Sidney Jesup died in 1860 after serving as quartermaster general for forty-two years.

Other officers of the Left Division served the army well and gave it its distinctive character. Hugh Brady served for decades as a regimental commander and received a brevet promotion to major general in 1848. The disabled John McNeil also served as a regimental commander until his resignation in 1830, when he accepted the post of collector of the port of Boston. Henry Leavenworth was instrumental in founding three important frontier posts: Fort Snelling, Jefferson Barracks, and the post that carries his name to this day and is home to the army's famed Command and General Staff College, Fort Leavenworth. George Mercer Brooke, who won two brevets during the siege of Fort Erie, served long and well on the frontier and ended his career in 1851, a brevet major general. Nathan Towson, the artillery company commander, won three brevets during the war and served as the army's paymaster general from 1819 until his death in 1854. William Jenkins Worth, Scott's aide-de-camp, had a distinguished career leading troops in the Second Seminole War and the war with Mexico.

Other Left Division alumni made their mark outside the military service. James Miller left the service in 1819 to become governor of the Arkansas Territory. Despite losing an arm at Fort Erie, Thomas Aspinwall was selected for retention in the postwar army. However, President Madison had other ideas and appointed Aspinwall to serve as U.S. consul in London, a post he retained until 1856. The young engineer turned battery commander, David Bates Douglass, taught at the military academy until resigning in favor of a successful engineering career.

Clearly, the officers who distinguished themselves at Chippawa, Lundy's Lane, and the siege of Fort Erie were a remarkable group who left their deep imprint on the U.S. Army in the years following the War of 1812. President Madison's farsighted decision to retain officers based on merit and character rather than seniority and political influence was instrumental in professionalizing the service. Never again would the U.S. Army begin a war so utterly and completely unprepared as it had in 1812. In large measure, the nation owes this attainment to the leaders of the Left Division.

NOTES

Chapter 1. The Road to War

1. Harvey to Murray, 17 December 1813, in *The Documentary History of the Campaign upon the Niagara Frontier*, ed. E. A. Cruikshank, 9 vols. (Welland, Ontario: Lundy's Lane Historical Society, 1902–1908), 9:3–4; hereafter *DHCNF.*

2. Statement by Robert Lee (who was in the fort during the attack) in *American State Papers: Military Affairs*, 7 vols. (Washington, D.C.: Gales and Seaton, 1832–1861), 1:488; hereafter *ASP:MA.*

3. This short account of the destruction of the Niagara Frontier is derived from two sources: House Committee Report 386, "Property Lost or Destroyed (Niagara Frontier)," in *The New American State Papers: Military Affairs*, ed. Benjamin F. Cooling, 19 vols. (Wilmington, Del.: Scholarly Resources, 1979), 5:266–296 (hereafter *NASP:MA*); and William Dorsheimer, "The Village of Buffalo during the War of 1812," *Buffalo Historical Society Publications* 1 (1879): 185–209.

4. Cass to Armstrong, 12 January 1814, in *ASP:MA*, 1:487–88.

5. Tompkins to Armstrong, 2 January 1814, Madison Papers, reel 15, Library of Congress (hereafter LC), Washington, D.C.

6. This discussion of the maritime issues is largely a synthesis of two sources that, when taken together, are comprehensive and convincing. They are Reginald Horsman, *The Causes of the War of 1812* (Philadelphia: University of Pennsylvania Press, 1962), and Donald R. Hickey, *The War of 1812: A Forgotten Conflict* (Urbana: University of Illinois Press, 1989).

7. Speech of William A. Burwell, in *Annals of Congress: Debates and Proceedings in the Congress of the United States, 1789–1824*, 42 vols. (Washington, D.C.: n.p.,1834–1856), 10-2, p. 584; hereafter *AC* (10-1 refers to the Tenth Congress, first session; similar notations are used in subsequent citations).

8. Harrison to Secretary of War, February 1811, in *American State Papers: Indian Affairs*, 2 vols. (Washington, D.C.: Gales and Seaton, 1832–1834), 1:800; hereafter *ASP:IA.*

9. The newspapers are full of this notion. For a sampling, see the *Lexington (Ky.) Reporter*, 21 January, 24 March, and 30 May 1812; the *Circleville (Ohio) Fredonian*, 12 February, 18 March, 8 April, and 30 May 1812; and the *Kentucky Gazette*, 14 April and 26 May 1812.

10. *Quebec Gazette*, 19 December 1811.

11. James Madison: War Message, 1 June 1812, in *A Compilation of the Messages and Papers of the Presidents, 1789-1897*, ed. James D. Richardson, 10 vols. (Washington, D.C.: n.p., 1909), 1:499–505.

12. An Act Declaring War, in *AC*, 12-1, pp. 2322–23.

13. A candidate for the standard book-length account of the first American invasion northward is George F. G. Stanley's *Canada Invaded: 1775–1776*, Canadian War Museum Series, Historical Publications Number 8 (Toronto: Samuel Stevens Hakkert, 1977). The following account is drawn primarily from Stanley's narrative.

14. Washington to Landon Carter, 30 May 1778, in *The Writings of George Washington*, 39 vols. (Washington, D.C.: U.S. Government Printing Office, 1931–1940), 11:492–93.

15. Speech by Henry Clay, 10 February 1810, in *AC*, 11-1, pp. 579–80.

16. Clay to Thomas Bodley, in *The Papers of Henry Clay*, ed. James F. Hopkins and Mary W. M. Hargreaves, 5 vols. (Lexington: University of Kentucky Press, 1959–1973), 1:842.

17. Speech by Peter B. Porter, 6 December 1811, in *AC*, 12-1, pp. 50–51.

18. Speech by Richard M. Johnson, 9 December 1811, in ibid., p. 640.

19. Jefferson to Duane, 4 August 1812, Jefferson Papers, reel 46, LC.

20. Late in the war, Madison directed his treasury secretary, A. J. Dallas, to prepare a document titled "Exposition of the Causes and Character of the War," in *AC*, 13-3, pp. 1416 ff. An attempt to improve public relations, this document denied that the acquisition of Canada had ever been on the administration's agenda. The administration also denied that it had approved Hull's or Smyth's proclamations through its negotiating team at Ghent in a diplomatic note, "American to British Commissioners," dated 13 October 1814.

Chapter 2. The Disappointing War

1. A succinct analysis of Canadian agriculture is found in Glenn A. Steppler, "Logistics on the Canadian Frontier, 1812–1814," *Military Collector and Historian* 31 (spring 1979): 8–10.

2. "Output of Arsenals, Harpers Ferry and Springfield up to 1817," in *ASP:MA*, 1:679–80.

3. A scholarly discourse on Brock's contribution to the war effort is William K. Lamb's essay "Sir Isaac Brock: The Hero of Queenston Heights," in *After Tippecanoe: Some Aspects of the War of 1812*, ed. Philip P. Mason (East Lansing: Michigan State University Press, 1963). See also Ernest Cruikshank, "A Study of Disaffection," in *The Defended Border*, ed. Morris Zaslow (Toronto: Macmillan, 1964), p. 207.

4. Julius W. Pratt, *Expansionists of 1812* (Gloucester, Mass.: Peter Smith, 1957), p. 131.

5. James Ripley Jacobs and Glenn Tucker, *The War of 1812: A Compact History* (New York: Hawthorn Books, 1969), p. 43.

6. There are several scholarly analyses of strategic naval considerations. One useful work is C. P. Stacey's "Naval Power on the Lakes, 1812–1814," in Mason, *After Tippecanoe.*

7. The stories of the regular British regiments are fairly well told in numerous unit histories and well documented in the public record. The contribution of the Canadian militia has only recently been related. A comprehensive description of the militia of Lower Canada is Michelle Guitard's *The Militia of the Battle of Chateauguay: A Social History* (Ottawa: Parks Canada, 1983). Guitard outlines the chain of command and administration from the ministry in London through the civil and military hierarchy in British North America, down to the militia units. A summary that ably addresses the militia of both provinces is George F. G. Stanley's "The Contribution of the Canadian Militia during the War," in Mason, *After Tippecanoe.*

8. Stanley, "Contribution of the Canadian Militia," p. 30.

9. Brock to Prevost, 12 July 1812, in *Select British Documents of the Canadian War of 1812,* ed. William Wood, 3 vols. (Toronto: Champlain Society, 1920–1928), 1:352–55.

10. The War Department's best estimate of the strength of the regular army during the war is "House Executive Document #72: Number of Troops in the War of 1812," 4 March 1858, in *NASP:MA,* 5:337–41. The War Department offered Congress an incomplete return of the recruiting effort in "Executive Document: Military Force in June 1812," 9 June 1812, in *ASP:MA,* 1:319–20. This document also includes the location of all regular forces prior to the war.

11. William Duane, *The American Military Dictionary* (Philadelphia: William Duane, 1810).

12. "List of Militia Returns during the War," n.d., in *ASP:MA,* 1:679. The most comprehensive study of the contribution of the American militia is C. Edward Skeen, *Citizen Soldiers in the War of 1812* (Lexington: University Press of Kentucky, 1999).

13. These figures are derived from two sources: "Executive Document: Number of Militia Called into Service in the Years 1812, 1813, & 1814," 16 January 1821, in *ASP:MA,* 2:279–82; and "House Executive Document #72: Number of Troops in the War of 1812," 4 March 1858, in *NASP:MA,* 5:337–41.

14. "Number of Militia Called into Service," in *ASP:MA,* 2:282.

15. The constitutional basis of the militia and its poor showing in the war are examined by Robert L. Kerby in his study "The Militia System and the State Militias in the War of 1812," *Indiana Magazine of History* 73 (1977): 102–24. Kerby concludes that the responsibility for the militia's unpreparedness belongs to the states themselves, not the federal government.

16. "Executive Document: The Militia," 13 February 1813, in *ASP:MA,* 1:330–34. This report is a compilation of returns made by the states between 1809 and 1812 and is the best approximation of the posture of the militia at the start of the war.

17. Phillip R. Shriver, ed., "Broken Locks and Rusty Barrels: A New York Militia Company on the Eve of the War of 1812," *New York History* 67 (July 1986): 353–57.

18. There are a growing number of studies of native North Americans' participation in the War of 1812. Two complementary essays are Reginald Horsman's "The Role of the Indian in the War of 1812," in Mason, *After Tippecanoe,* and Carl Benn's "Iroquois

Warfare, 1812–1814," in *War along the Niagara: Essays on the War of 1812 and Its Legacy,* ed. R. Arthur Bowler (Youngstown, N.Y.: Old Fort Niagara Association, 1991).

19. Speech by John C. Calhoun, 6 May 1812, in *AC,* 12-1, p. 1397.

20. Eustis was openly criticized in Congress. See speech by Obadiah German, in ibid.

21. Two sources are particularly useful as overviews of logistics from the American perspective. The first is Marguerite McKee, "Service of Supply in the War of 1812," *Quartermaster Review* 6 (March–April 1927): 45–55. The second is Erna Risch, *Quartermaster Support of the Army: A History of the Corps, 1775–1939* (Washington, D.C.: U.S. Government Printing Office, 1962), chap. 5.

22. J. Mackay Hitsman, *The Incredible War of 1812: A Military History* (Toronto: University of Toronto Press, 1965), pp. 246–47.

23. An assessment of the governor-general's strategy is found in J. Mackay Hitsman, "Sir George Prevost's Conduct of the Canadian War of 1812," *Report of the Annual Meeting of the Canadian Historical Association* (1962): 34–43.

24. A. L. Burt, *The United States, Great Britain and British North America: From the Revolution to the Establishment of Peace after the War of 1812* (1940; reprint, New York: Russell and Russell, 1961), pp. 321–22.

25. Brock to Prevost, December 1811, in *DHCNF,* 3:22.

26. Eustis to Congress, 5 December 1811, in *NASP:MA,* vol. 1, item 19.

27. "Report on Fortifications," 3 December 1811, in *ASP:MA,* 1:87–91.

28. Speech by Peter B. Porter, reprinted in *National Intelligencer,* 25 February 1812.

29. Henry Adams, *History of the United States during the Administrations of Jefferson and Madison,* 9 vols. (New York: Charles Scribner's Sons, 1931), 6:297.

30. Speech by Obadiah German, 13 June 1812, in *AC,* 12-1, pp. 271–83.

31. Madison to Jefferson, 17 August 1812, in *James Madison Papers* (Washington, D.C.: Library of Congress, 1965), 8:211.

32. Jefferson to Duane, 4 August 1812, Jefferson Papers, reel 46, LC.

33. Dearborn to Eustis, 8 August 1812, quoted in Benson Lossing, *The Pictorial Fieldbook of the War of 1812* (New York: Harper and Brothers, 1868; reprint, Somersworth, N.H.: New Hampshire Publishing Company, 1976), p. 381.

34. The standard work covering the war in this theater of operations is Alec R. Gilpin's *The War of 1812 in the Old Northwest* (East Lansing: Michigan State University Press, 1958).

35. Prevost to Brock, 10 July 1812, quoted in J. Mackay Hitsman, *Safeguarding Canada, 1763–1871* (Toronto: University of Toronto Press, 1968), p. 90; Hull's Proclamation, 13 July 1812, in Wood, *British Documents,* 1:355–57.

36. Brock's Proclamation, 22 July 1812, as printed in the *Kingston Gazette,* 28 July 1812.

37. Madison to Dearborn, 7 October 1812, Madison Papers, reel 14, LC.

38. Dearborn to Eustis, 7 August 1812, Dearborn Papers, LC.

39. The naval operations and underlying strategies of the war, on both the high seas and the inland lakes, are extensively covered in the scholarly literature. The longtime standard work is Captain Alfred Thayer Mahan, *Sea Power and Its Relations to the War of 1812,* 2 vols. (Boston: Little, Brown, 1905). A fresh look is provided by Robert Malcomson, *Lords of the Lake: The Naval War on Lake Ontario, 1812–1814* (Annapolis, Md.: Naval Institute Press, 1998).

40. The standard biography of this secretary of war is C. Edward Skeen, *John Armstrong, Jr. 1758–1843: A Biography* (Syracuse, N.Y.: Syracuse University Press, 1981). Armstrong had a personal connection with the abortive 1775 attempt to take Quebec. Killed in the assault was his brother-in-law, General Richard Montgomery.

41. There are numerous popular accounts of the Battle of Lake Erie. A few are worthy of special attention. Captain W. W. Dobbins, son of Perry's sailing master, wrote *History of the Battle of Lake Erie*, 2d ed. (Erie, Pa.: Ashby, 1913). Although he emphasizes the disadvantages of the American squadron compared with the British, Dobbins is even-handed in his treatment of the Perry-Elliott conflict. Two more recent accounts are Richard Dillon, *We Have Met the Enemy* (New York: McGraw-Hill, 1978), and Robert and Thomas Malcomson's well-documented *HMS* Detroit: *The Battle for Lake Erie* (St. Catherines, Ontario: Vanwell, 1990). Written from American and Canadian perspectives, respectively, the Malcomsons' account is both more comprehensive and more analytical than Dillon's. Finally, a scholarly study is Gerry T. Altoff's "Oliver Hazard Perry and the Battle of Lake Erie," delivered at the War on the Great Lakes symposium in 1987 and published in *Michigan Historical Review* 14 (fall 1988): 25–57. Altoff colaborated with David C. Skaggs to produce the fine study *A Signal Victory: The Lake Erie Campaign, 1812–1813* (Annapolis, Md.: Naval Institute Press, 1997).

42. Perhaps the most comprehensive analysis of the British-Indian alliance in the West and the campaigns that resulted in the military defeat of that alliance is John Sugden, *Tecumseh's Last Stand* (Norman: University of Oklahoma Press, 1985).

43. Armstrong's note to the Cabinet, 8 February 1813, in the U.S. Executive Department Document, "Causes of the Failure of the Army on the Northern Frontier," in *ASP:MA*, 1:439.

44. A serious question that has defied satisfactory solution is why the secretary of war continued to endorse offenses west of the St. Lawrence when cutting that river promised more decisive results. Burt, in his diplomatic history *The United States, Great Britain and British North America*, offers a novel answer. He suggests that for many Americans, the invasion of Canada was not so much conquest as "a triumphal progress of liberation." Upper Canada, settled largely by Americans, was more amenable to liberation than Lower Canada, peopled by francophones who had no love for American republicanism and Protestantism.

45. Speech by Morris Miller, 14 January 1814, in *AC*, 13-2, pp. 956, 972.

46. Maryland Memorial, February 1814, in ibid., p. 1204.

47. Monroe to Commissioners, 23 June 1813, in *American State Papers: Foreign Relations*, 6 vols. (Washington, D.C.: Gales and Seaton, 1833–1859), 3:700–701; hereafter *ASP:FR*.

48. J. W. Fortescue, *A History of the British Army*, 10 vols. (London: Macmillan, 1920), 10:105–6.

49. A scholarly analysis of British designs on Maine is Barry J. Lohnes, "A New Look at the Invasion of Eastern Maine, 1814," *Maine Historical Society Quarterly* 15 (summer 1975): 4–29.

50. Tompkins to Armstrong, 2 January 1814, and Tompkins to Madison, 3 January 1814, Madison Papers, reel 15, LC.

Chapter 3. The Central Theater of Operations

1. The single source that clarifies the confusing system of districts, divisions, and departments of the U.S. Army is Raphael P. Thian's *Notes Illustrating the Military Geography of the United States, 1813–1880* (Washington, D.C.: U.S. Government Printing Office, 1881; reprint, Austin: University of Texas Press, 1979). The Tenth Military District was created in 1814 in response to the growing threat of invasion along the eastern seaboard.

2. New York City was the center of the Third Military District, which included New Jersey as well as the New York Highlands and Long Island. It was generally understood that New York was threatened more by seaborne raid or invasion rather than by attack down the Champlain-Hudson corridor. To ease the embarrassment of Dearborn's dismissal, he was given command of the Third Military District and therefore responsibility for the defense of New York City.

3. Useful material on waterborne logistics can be found in Frederick C. Drake's essay "The Niagara Peninsula and Naval Aspects of the War of 1812," in *The Military in the Niagara Peninsula*, ed. Wesley B. Turner (St. Catherines, Ontario: Vanwell Publishing, 1990), p. 5.

4. A solid analysis of the British line of communication through the Western and Central Theaters is C. P. Stacey's "Another Look at the Battle of Lake Erie," *Canadian Historical Review* 34 (March 1958): 41–51. Stacey argues that the American line of communication to Lake Erie enjoyed several advantages over that of the British, which gave Perry a decided edge in contesting the lake with Barclay.

5. Lossing, *Pictorial Fieldbook*, p. 601.

6. A useful discussion on the state of transportation on the American side of the Central Theater is found in Harry F. Landon, *Bugles on the Border: The Story of the War of 1812 in Northern New York* (Watertown, N.Y.: *Watertown Daily Times*, 1954), pp. 7–9.

7. Stacey, "Another Look," p. 46; Landon, *Bugles*, pp. 7–8.

8. There are a few good analyses of the effects of terrain on military operations throughout the Central Theater. Already mentioned is Stacey's "Another Look." An even more comprehensive treatment is Glenn A. Steppler, "A Duty Troublesome beyond Measure" (master's thesis, McGill University, 1974). A brief summary of Steppler's thesis was published as "Logistics on the Canadian Frontier 1812–1814," *Military Collector and Historian* 31 (spring 1979): 8–10.

9. Drake, "Niagara Peninsula," p. 26.

10. Armstrong presented these facts to the cabinet in a note dated 8 February 1813 in "Executive Document: Causes of the Failure of the Army on the Northern Frontier," 2 February 1814, in *ASP:MA*, 1:439.

11. For wartime demographics of Lower Canada, see Guitard, *Militia of Chateauguay*, pp. 20–21.

12. Benn, "Iroquois Warfare," p. 61.

13. Stanley, *Canada Invaded*, pp. 12–13.

14. Fred Landon, *Western Ontario and the American Frontier* (Toronto: Ryerson Press, 1941), pp. 1–3, 13–22.

15. There is no consensus as to the demographic makeup of Upper Canada at the beginning of the war. Estimates of the number of white residents vary from 70,000 to 90,000. I have rendered a middle position synthesized from Stanley and F. Landon, as well as from the following secondary sources: Ernest A. Cruikshank, *The Battle of Fort George* (1896; reprint, Niagara-on-the-Lake, Ontario: Niagara Historical Society, 1990), p. 12; Stanley, "Contribution of the Canadian Militia," in Mason, *After Tippecanoe*, pp. 31–32; R. Arthur Bowler, "Propaganda in Upper Canada in the War of 1812," in *War along the Niagara*, p. 78; and Wesley B. Turner, *The War of 1812: The War that Both Sides Won* (Toronto and Oxford: Dundurn Press, 1990), p. 26. A firsthand account of the settlements of western Upper Canada is Michael Smith, *A Geographical View of the Province of Upper Canada and Promiscuous Remarks upon the Government* (Hartford, Conn.: n.p., 1813). In the three years following initial publication, this popular volume was edited and reprinted five times.

16. Wartime York has been the subject of numerous studies, yet there is no agreement as to its peacetime or wartime populations. Part of the problem was the transient nature of the citizenry, perhaps living in town only temporarily while waiting to purchase land elsewhere. In wartime, many of the disaffected left the towns to escape persecution or jail. Loyalists in outlying areas moved into the towns for protection against marauders, particularly if the husband was off on military duty. Benson Lossing cites York's population in 1812 at 900. Louis Babcock claims 800 inhabitants in 1813, and Carl Benn figures that there were 625 citizens in York in 1813. There are no reliable numbers for Kingston's population. See Lossing, *Pictorial Fieldbook*, p. 586; Louis L. Babcock, *The War of 1812 on the Niagara Frontier* (Buffalo, N.Y.: Buffalo Historical Society, 1927), p. 78; Carl Benn, *The Battle of York* (Belleville, Ontario: Mika Publishing, 1984), p. 9.

17. Cruikshank, *Battle of Fort George*, p. 12; Landon, *Western Ontario*, pp. 13–22.

18. Information on the early years of the Niagara District comes from William Kirby, *Annals of Niagara*, 2d ed. (Toronto: Macmillan of Canada, 1927), p. 216. Kirby, a staunch loyalist, was born in England in 1817. He lived in Cincinnati for seven years before immigrating to Canada. The first edition of this popular history was published in 1896, publication information unknown.

19. Babcock, *Niagara Frontier*, p. 16.

20. Brian Leigh Dunnigan, *A History and Guide to Old Fort Niagara* (Youngstown, N.Y.: Old Fort Niagara Association, 1985), p. 18.

21. David A. Owen, *Fort Erie (1764–1823): An Historical Guide* (Niagara Falls, Ontario: Niagara Parks Commission, 1986), pp. 42–49.

22. See Benn, "Iroquois Warfare," p. 61, and Daniel J. Glenney, "An Ethnohistory of the Grand River Iroquois and the War of 1812" (master's thesis, University of Guelph, 1973), p. 4.

23. Landon, *Bugles*, pp. 5–9.

24. Babcock, *Niagara Frontier*, p. 138.

25. Ibid., pp. 16–27; Lossing, *Pictorial Fieldbook*, p. 379.

26. Brian Leigh Dunnigan chronicled the architectural and military history of the fort in two works: his *History and Guide* previously cited, and *Forts within a Fort: Niagara's Redoubts* (Youngstown, N.Y.: Old Fort Niagara Association, 1989).

27. Cruikshank, *Battle of Fort George,* p. 30; Landon, *Western Ontario,* p. 40.

28. Landon, *Bugles,* p. 10. Oswego's economy was based on the salt trade, with nearly $1 million worth of salt shipped annually from Oswego to customers up and down Lake Ontario. See also Landon, *Western Ontario,* p. 40.

29. See Petition to the Prince Regent by representatives of the Commons of Lower Canada Provincial Parliament, March 1814, in Public Archives of Canada, C.O. 42/156, pp. 225–26; hereafter PAC.

30. This discussion on the bateaux service is drawn from Steppler, "Logistics on the Canadian Frontier," pp. 8–9.

31. Landon, *Bugles,* pp. 7–11; Pratt, *Expansionists of 1812,* pp. 174–75.

32. Landon, *Bugles,* pp. 10–12.

33. Cruikshank, *Battle of Fort George,* p. 29; Landon, *Western Ontario,* p. 39.

34. Guitard, *Militia of Chateauguay,* pp. 16–18, 29–30.

35. Kirby, *Annals of Niagara,* p. 163.

36. Brock to Prevost, 12 July 1812, in Wood, *British Documents,* 1:352–55.

37. A worthy study of the political climate in Upper Canada is Bowler's "Propaganda in Upper Canada," in his *War along the Niagara,* pp. 77–92.

38. Glenney, "Ethnohistory," p. 9.

39. Ibid., pp. 51–55; Donald J. Goodspeed, "The Role of the Indians in the War of 1812," in Turner, *The Military in the Niagara Peninsula,* p. 134.

40. See Lossing, *Pictorial Fieldbook,* pp. 374–75; and Guitard, *Militia of Chateauguay,* p. 34.

41. John Norton, *The Journal of Major John Norton* (1816), ed. Carl F. Klinck and James J. Talman (Toronto: Champlain Society, 1970), pp. 287–89. Norton's journal is the most comprehensive primary source written by an Indian to come out of the war years.

42. Ibid.; Glenney, "Ethnohistory," pp. 61–66.

43. Dorsheimer, "Buffalo during the War," p.188.

44. Fragmentary accounts of this September council appear in newsprint. Jasper Parrish, Granger's assistant, made a report dated 14 September 1812 that was originally printed in the *Ontario Repository* and reprinted in *Niles' Register* on 17 September 1812. Other accounts were printed in *Niles' Register* on 26 September and 3 October 1812. An interesting overview touching on diplomacy and the organization of Iroquois fighting units is Arthur C. Parker, "The Senecas in the War of 1812," *New York State Historical Association Proceedings* 15 (1916): 78–90. Parker, himself descended from a Seneca veteran of the war, provides insights on Seneca motivation in backing the American cause, as well as lists of both male and female native warriors.

45. Norton, *Journal,* p. 294.

46. Norman C. Lord, ed., "The War on the Canadian Frontier, 1812–14: Letters Written by Sergeant James Commins, Eighth Foot," *Journal of the Society for Army Historical Research* 18 (winter 1939): 200.

47. Benn, "Iroquois Warfare," p. 61.

48. Glenney, "Ethnohistory," pp. 29–30.

49. Horsman, "The Role of the Indian in the War," p. 68.

50. No recent historian disputes the contribution of the natives to British success on several battlefields. Taking an extreme position, Goodspeed in "Role of the Indian"

argues persuasively that without their Indian allies, the British would almost certainly have been defeated in 1812. However, few historians have assessed whether Indian customs, such as the killing of prisoners, were decisive in extending the American public's willingness to support a flagging war effort on a national level. Certainly Kentucky provided its sons unsparingly to revenge early "atrocities."

Chapter 4. Startling Victories, Unexpected Defeats

1. Cruikshank, "Disaffection in Upper Canada," in Zaslow, *The Defended Border,* pp. 210–12. Cruikshank cites the *Buffalo Gazette* on 21 July and 11 August 1812, which describes several accounts of fugitives from Canada, the result of efforts by Canadian authorities to remove the disloyal element prior to the inevitable clash of arms.

2. This letter is quoted in Babcock, *Niagara Frontier,* pp. 32–33.

3. Risch, *Quartermaster Support,* p. 165.

4. Ibid., pp.168–69.

5. Boyd commanded in New Hampshire, Massachusetts, Rhode Island, and Connecticut and was subordinate to Dearborn. Boyd was a career soldier, having commanded large numbers of troops on the Indian subcontinent as a mercenary before returning to the United States to command the Fourth Infantry at Tippecanoe.

6. Lossing, *Pictorial Fieldbook,* p. 381.

7. Babcock, *Niagara Frontier,* pp. 37–46.

8. There are many accounts of Chauncey's first months at Sacketts Harbor and the beginning of the naval arms race on Lake Ontario. A particularly detailed yet succinct analysis is C. Winton-Clare, "A Shipbuilder's War," in Zaslow, *The Defended Border,* pp. 165–73. Accounts of the sailors moving to Sacketts Harbor appear in *Niles' Register,* 3 and 24 October 1812.

9. C. P. Stacey, who served as director of the Canadian Army Historical Section from 1945 to 1959, wrote a concise yet comprehensive treatment of Isaac Brock's classic campaign. In "The Defence of Upper Canada, 1812" (in Zaslow, *The Defended Border,* pp. 11–20), Stacey analyzes Brock's activities through the prism of the principles of war and finds them to "serve as an object lesson to every officer who would learn the arts of command." The role of the Grand River Indians in the days prior to the battle is found in Norton, *Journal,* pp. 302–3.

10. Dearborn to Van Rensselaer, 26 September 1812, quoted in Lossing, *Pictorial Fieldbook,* p. 384.

11. There is no regiment-by-regiment analysis of the regular army during the War of 1812. There are no regimental histories written by members of the regiments. Only a few unit accounts have been written in the twentieth century, and these are sketchy, since official records are incomplete and personal journals and correspondence scarce. For this short analysis of the regulars fighting under Van Rensselaer and several like it that follow, I drew data from dozens of primary and secondary sources, most of which are fragmentary, none of which are comprehensive. I built the body of data on a framework provided by Francis B. Heitman, *Historical Register and Dictionary of the U.S. Army 1789–1903,* 2 vols. (Washington, D.C.: U.S. Government Printing Office, 1903). Heitman has preserved

the official organization of each type of regiment (2:572–79), the names of the field-grade officers and capsule histories of regular regiments (1:50–141), and a chronological list of battles and units known to have participated in them (2:391–94).

12. An excellent, if short, scholarly analysis of Queenston is Theodore J. Crackel's chapter "The Battle of Queenston Heights," in *America's First Battles*, ed. Charles E. Heller and William A. Stofft (Lawrence: University Press of Kansas, 1986). Crackel's discourse on doctrinal confusion is quite valuable in understanding the serious impediments to adequate performance of the U.S. Army.

13. Two secondary studies that expand on Norton's account of the decisive role of the Grand River Indians at Queenston are Glenney, "Ethnohistory," pp. 75–76, and Goodspeed, "The Role of the Indians," p. 140.

14. Anonymous letter dated 17 October 1812 and published in *Niles' Register* on 7 November 1812.

15. Winton-Clare, "Shipbuilder's War," p. 167; Landon, *Bugles*, p. 21. Chauncey's account of the engagement with the *Royal George* is his report, Chauncey to Hamilton, 13 November 1812, in William S. Dudley and Michael J. Crawford, eds., *The Naval War of 1812, Documentary History* (Washington, D.C.: U.S. Government Printing Office, 1985), 1:344–46.

16. Prevost's proclamation was published in the *Montreal Courant* on 19 September 1812 and reprinted in *Niles' Register* on 12 December 1812.

17. A short account of the execution appeared in *Niles' Register* on 31 October 1812.

18. A comprehensive history of the Voltigeurs, whose formal name was the Provincial Corps of Light Infantry, is found in Guitard, *Militia of Chateauguay*. An informative account of their intrepid commander is J. Patrick Wohler, *Charles de Salaberry* (Toronto: Dundurn Press, 1984).

19. There is no detailed account of Dearborn's abortive invasion. I have synthesized this narrative from several sources, but primarily from Lossing, *Pictorial Fieldbook*, p. 639, and Turner, *The War that Both Sides Won*, p. 56.

20. Smyth to Eustis, 20 October 1812, as quoted in Frank H. Severance, "The Case of Alexander Smyth," *Buffalo Historical Society Publications* 18 (1914): 220.

21. Smyth to Dearborn, 24 October 1812, quoted in Severance, "Alexander Smyth," p. 221.

22. Most of the documentary evidence of Smyth's abortive invasion was provided by Smyth himself to the House of Representatives on 8 February 1814. Smyth submitted sixty-one documents, which the House collectively titled "On the Manner in which the War Has Been Conducted," in *ASP:MA*, 1:490–510; Dearborn's letter to Smyth, dated 21 October 1812, is document no. 12, pp. 493–94. Dearborn wrote, "You should, if possible, be prepared for crossing with three thousand men, with artillery, at once." In the same letter, Dearborn twice suggested that Smyth consult with his principal officers before making critical decisions. However, the overall tone of the letter does not suggest that Dearborn would perfunctorily disapprove of any decisions made by the commander at the scene. Dearborn's detailed advice to his subordinate is perhaps indicative of a commander, untried himself, working at a distance with an inexperienced subordinate and attempting to restore a situation following an unmitigated disaster.

23. Severance, "Alexander Smyth," p. 224.

24. "On the Manner in which the War Has Been Conducted"; Captain King's reports on the Twelfth and Fourteenth Infantry Regiments are documents nos. 3 and 4, in *ASP:MA*, 1:491–92.

25. Ibid., document no. 22, p. 496.

26. Ibid., document no. 27, p. 497.

27. Babcock, *Niagara Frontier*, pp. 68–69.

28. Alexander Smyth to "a committee of patriotic citizens of the western counties of New York," 3 December 1812, reprinted in *Niles' Register*, 26 December 1812.

29. Peter B. Porter in a report published in the *Buffalo Gazette*, 14 December 1812, and reprinted in *Niles' Register*, 2 January 1813.

30. Anonymous letter of an officer at Buffalo written on 29 November 1812 and reprinted in *Niles' Register*, 19 December 1812. Circumstantial evidence suggests that the writer was an officer of volunteers in McClure's regiment.

31. "On the Manner in which the War Has Been Conducted," document no. 35, pp. 500–501. This report by Major David Campbell to Smyth on 27 November 1812 indicates widespread sickness. Campbell closes his report by noting that he "begs leave to assure the General that he has no view of paralyzing the operations of the army, by making this report at this important period."

32. Smyth to "a committee of patriotic citizens."

33. Porter to the *Buffalo Gazette*, 8 and 14 December 1812, reprinted in *Niles' Register*, 26 December 1812 and 2 January 1813, respectively.

34. *Ontario Messenger* (Canandaigua, N.Y.), reprinted in *Niles' Register*, 19 December 1812.

35. "On the Manner in which the War Has Been Conducted," document no. 31, p. 499, and document no. 53, p. 507.

36. Smyth to Dearborn, 4 December 1812, reprinted in *Niles' Register*, 26 December 1812.

37. Both of these regiments saw extensive combat in the war, and both acquired reputations for competence and bravery. Unfortunately, no unit history has been written on either regiment. Some material is available in John R. Elting, ed., *Military Uniforms in America*, 3 vols. (San Rafael, Calif.: Presidio Press, 1977), 2:40–41, 74–75. This series is produced by the Company of Military Historians and is unexcelled in its description of many of the physical aspects of the armies of the War of 1812.

38. There are few accounts of the raid on Ogdensburg. Readers might consult Landon, *Bugles*, p. 31; Lossing, *Pictorial Fieldbook*, pp. 577–81; or the U.S. Executive Department Document, "Causes of the Failure of the Army on the Northern Frontier," in *ASP:MA*, 1:440–41.

39. Landon, *Bugles*, pp. 31–36.

40. "Causes of the Failure of the Army on the Northern Frontier," in *ASP:MA*, 1:439–88; Armstrong's proposal is found in his note to the cabinet dated 8 February 1813, p. 439.

41. Armstrong to Dearborn, 10 February 1813, in ibid., p. 439, and Dearborn to Armstrong, 18 February 1813, in ibid., p. 440.

42. Dearborn to Armstrong, 3 and 9 March 1813, in ibid., p. 441.

43. Dearborn to Armstrong, undated, in ibid., p. 442.

44. Armstrong to Dearborn, 29 March 1813, in ibid.

45. Armstrong to Dearborn, 19 April 1813, in ibid., p. 443.

46. A short, popular work that makes extensive use of primary source material is Benn, *The Battle of York.* Benn's evenhanded treatment reaches sound conclusions as to the significance of the raid on York to operations in the Central Theater.

47. Part of the mythology of the War of 1812 is that the British burned Washington in just retaliation for the burning of York. The evidence of the American occupation of the capital of Upper Canada is presented and analyzed by W. B. Kerr in "The Occupation of York (Toronto), 1813," *Canadian Historical Review* 5 (1924): 9–21. Kerr finds that the evidence reveals widespread looting but does not support conclusively the intentional burning of Parliament by the Americans. Kerr also sees much to blame in Dearborn's failure to control his soldiers.

48. Dearborn to Armstrong, 28 April 1813, in *ASP:MA*, 1:443.

49. Stanley, "Contribution of the Canadian Militia," in Mason, *After Tippecanoe*, p. 38; Cruikshank, "A Study of Disaffection," pp. 212–15.

50. Hitsman, "Prevost's Conduct of the War," p. 39.

51. Vincent's comments are quoted in Cruikshank, *Battle of Fort George,* p. 34.

52. The account of the Battle of Fort George is synthesized from several sources: Cruikshank, *Battle of Fort George;* George F. G. Stanley, *The War of 1812: Land Operations* (Toronto: Macmillan of Canada, 1983), pp. 179–87; and Babcock, *Niagara Frontier,* p. 83.

53. There are several personal accounts of the attack on Fort George. One such is found in a letter from James Miller to his wife, Ruth, written on 28 May 1813. Miller commanded the Sixth Infantry in the assault landing and supported Scott's advance party. He remarked on the "astounding torrent of shot" that greeted the landing boats when they were still 150 yards from shore. Papers of John McNeil, LC.

54. Dearborn to Armstrong, 27 May 1813, in *ASP:MA*, 1:444.

55. John C. Fredriksen, ed., "Chronicle of Valor: The Journal of a Pennsylvania Officer in the War of 1812," *Western Pennsylvania Historical Magazine* 67 (July 1984): 265.

56. Altoff, "Perry and the Battle of Lake Erie," p. 33.

57. Dearborn to Armstrong, 27 May 1813, in *ASP:MA*, 1:444.

58. Frederick C. Drake, "The Niagara Peninsula and Naval Aspects of the War of 1812," in Turner, *The Military in the Niagara Peninsula,* p. 16. Drake assesses the amphibious landing at Fort George as "the high point of American military-naval cooperation on Lake Ontario to subjugate the Canadas."

59. John Coker to Yeo, 19 March 1813, Admiralty Out-Letters, ADM 2/1376, pp. 249–52, Public Records Office (hereafter PRO), London.

60. A popular biography that captures many of the important issues, although dealing with them simplistically, is Frank B. Latham, *Jacob Brown and the War of 1812* (New York: Cowles, 1971). See also Fletcher Pratt, "Sword of the Border," *Infantry Journal* 44 (September–October 1937): 387–93.

61. Lynn Montross ("America's Most Imitated Battle," *American Heritage* 7 [April 1956]: 37–101) has gone so far as to suggest that Brown's inspiration for the use of the militia at the defense of Sacketts Harbor was Daniel Morgan's victory at Cowpens. Montross argues that Brown, like Morgan before him, knew how much reliance he might put

on his militia and designed his battle plan around this limitation. Montross probably makes too much of superficial similarities.

62. Brown to Tompkins, 1 June 1813, quoted in *Journal of the Military Service Institution* 32 (January–June 1903): 408–13.

63. Drake, "Naval Aspects," p. 27.

64. Turner, The *War that Both Sides Won*, p. 66.

65. Narratives of Stoney Creek are found in virtually all the literature that addresses major land operations. A quality piece from the Canadian perspective is George F. G. Stanley's short contribution to the Canadian Battle Series, *Battle in the Dark: Stoney Creek, June 6, 1813* (Toronto: Balmuir, 1991). A firsthand account from the American perspective comes from Ephram Shaler, a junior officer in the Twenty-fifth Infantry. Shaler disputes the notion that the Americans were unprepared. See John C. Fredriksen, ed., "Memoirs of Captain Efraim Shaler: A Connecticut Yankee in the War of 1812," *New England Quarterly* 57 (1984): 411–20.

66. Dearborn to Armstrong, 6 June 1813, in *ASP:MA*, 1:443.

67. There is no adequate monograph, scholarly or popular, on the action at Beaver Dams. This account is synthesized from Babcock, *Niagara Frontier,* pp. 95–99; Stanley, *War of 1812,* pp. 192–200; Turner, *The War that Both Sides Won,* p. 75; Glenney, "Ethnohistory," pp. 109–10; and Norton, *Journal,* p. 332.

68. FitzGibbon to Kerr, 30 March 1818, in *DHCNF,* 6:120–21.

69. Armstrong to Boyd, 30 July 1813, in *ASP:MA*, 1:450.

70. Armstrong to Dearborn, 1 July 1813, in ibid., 1:449.

71. Boyd to Armstrong, 31 July 1813, in ibid., 1:450; Lossing, *Pictorial Fieldbook,* pp. 626–27.

72. Bisshop's raid and the Seneca declaration of war appear in Babcock, *Niagara Frontier,* pp. 105–8.

73. Norton, *Journal,* p. 338.

74. Scott to Boyd, 3 August 1813, in *ASP:MA*, 1:450.

75. For some thoughts on the logic of the naval arms race, see Winton-Clare, "A Shipbuilder's War," pp. 168–69.

76. Expositions on the nature of the arms race on Lake Erie are Altoff, "Perry and the Battle of Lake Erie," pp. 29–41; Stacey, "Another Look," pp. 47–51; and Turner, *The War that Both Sides Won,* pp. 65–66.

77. Armstrong to Harrison, 22 September 1813, in *ASP:MA*, 1:463–64.

78. Armstrong to Wilkinson, 23 July and 8 August 1813, in ibid.

79. The evolution of the plan, a confusing and convoluted process, is presented, along with the Battles of Chateauguay and Crysler's Farm, in several secondary sources. For a fuller treatment, I recommend Stanley, *War of 1812,* pp. 225–70; and John K. Mahon, *The War of 1812* (Gainesville: University Presses of Florida, 1972), pp. 202–16. Hampton had repeatedly warned Armstrong of problems—sickness, insufficient ammunition, and the poor level of training of his regulars. See Hampton to Armstrong, 7, 22, and 25 September 1813, in *ASP:MA*, 1:458–59.

80. Hampton's report is in Hampton to Armstrong, 1 November 1813, in *ASP:MA*, 1:461.

81. Hampton to Wilkinson, 8 and 12 November 1813, in ibid., 1:462. The Battle of Chateauguay is the source of the myth that 300 French Canadian militiamen threw back an overwhelming American force of 7,900, thus saving Montreal and indeed all Canada. Guitard in *Militia of Chateauguay* dispels some of the myth. She estimates that 3,000 Americans and 1,700 Canadians were present in the battle area and that approximately 2,000 Americans faced 300 Canadians in the actual fighting. A worthy popular narrative of the defeat of Hampton's force is Victor Suthren, *Defend and Hold: The Battle of Chateauguay*, Canadian Battle Series (Ottawa: Balmuir, n.d.). The latest biography of the Canadian commander is Wohler, *Charles de Salaberry*.

82. The British, in designing medals to commemorate the battle, called it Chrystler's Farm, although the owner spelled his name Crysler. Although purists use the original spelling, a majority of historians have designated this the Battle of Chrysler's Farm or sometimes Chrysler's Field.

83. The single best study of this battle is Donald E. Graves, *Fields of Glory: The Battle of Crysler's Farm, 1813* (Toronto: Robin Brass Studio, 1999). Two other accounts of the battle are Ronald L. Way, *The Day of Crysler's Farm* (n.p.: Ontario–St. Lawrence Development Commission, n.d.); and Charles W. Elliott, "The Indispensable Conquest," *Infantry Journal* 45 (July–August 1938): 334–42. A biographical sketch of Joseph Morrison is William J. Patterson, "A Forgotten Hero in a Forgotten War," *Journal of the Society for Army Historical Research* 68 (spring 1990): 7–21.

84. Harrison Ellery, ed., *The Memoirs of General Joseph Gardner Swift* (Worcester, Mass.: F. S. Blanchard, 1890), p. 121. Swift, the first graduate of West Point, also recorded that Wilkinson was using opium to treat his stomach ailment while on campaign and that he was not discreet about his displeasure at Armstrong's presence at Sacketts Harbor or his intense dislike of Hampton.

85. Wilkinson to Hampton, 12 November 1813, in *ASP:MA*, 1:463.

86. Armstrong to Wilkinson, 18 November 1813, in ibid., 1:480.

87. Donald E. Graves, "I Have a Handsome Little Army . . . ," in Bowler, *War along the Niagara*, p. 46.

88. Armstrong's biographer, C. Edward Skeen, makes a similar assessment in *John Armstrong*, p. 166.

89. Wilkinson to Armstrong, 2 October 1813, and Scott to Wilkinson, 11 October 1813, in *ASP:MA*, 1:470, 482.

90. McClure to Armstrong, 17 November 1813, Armstrong to McClure, 25 November 1813, and McClure to Armstrong, 10 December 1813, in ibid., 1:484–86; McClure to Tompkins, 10 December 1813, in *DHCNF*, 8:264.

91. Murray to Vincent, 13 December 1813, in Wood, *British Documents*, 2:482–83.

92. Armstrong to McClure, 4 October 1813, in *ASP:MA*, 1:484.

93. McClure to Armstrong, 13 December 1813, in ibid., 1:486. For a fuller treatment of these events, see Babcock, *Niagara Frontier*, p. 120.

94. Drummond to Prevost, 20 and 22 December 1813, in Wood, *British Documents*, 2:490–92, 500–505.

95. District General Order, 28 December 1813. Harvey to Riall, 29 December 1813. and Drummond to Prevost, 30 December 1813, in ibid., 2:507–12.

96. Cass to Armstrong, 12 January 1814, in *ASP:MA*, 1:487–88.

Chapter 5. Polarizing Attitudes, Stagnating Strategies

1. "On the Manner in Which the War Has Been Conducted," pp. 339–60; Lossing, *Pictorial Fieldbook*, p. 788.

2. John N. Crombie, ed., "The Papers of Major Daniel McFarland," *Western Pennsylvania Historical Magazine* 51 (April 1968): 101–25; emphasis in original.

3. There are several sources that document the punitive nature of the raids into western Upper Canada. One of these is Edward Ermatinger, *Life of Colonel Talbot and the Talbot Settlement* (St. Thomas, Ontario: A. McLachlin's Home Journal Office, 1859; reprint, Belleville, Ontario: Mika Silk Screening, 1972). Talbot, a militia officer who participated in the Battle of Lundy's Lane and the siege of Fort Erie, was one of those local leaders sought by American and renegade Canadian raiders.

4. For a fuller description of some of the excesses in the Western and Central Theaters, see Turner, *The War that Both Sides Won*, p. 86; Stanley, *War of 1812*, p. 193; testimony of Robert Lee, "Causes of the Failure of the Army on the Northern Frontier," in *ASP:MA*, 1:488; and Babcock, *Niagara Frontier*, pp. 127–29.

5. Babcock, *Niagara Frontier*, pp. 108, 137. Prevost's General Order, 22 February 1814, in Wood, *British Documents*, 2:516–17.

6. The standard works on the disloyal residents of Upper Canada are both by Ernest A. Cruikshank. I refer readers to "A Study of Disaffection," previously cited, and "The County of Norfolk in the War of 1812," *Ontario Historical Society Papers and Records* 20 (1923): 9–40. However, neither Cruikshank nor any other scholar has been able to estimate the number of pro-Americans who fled Upper Canada during the war.

7. Cruikshank, "A Study of Disaffection," pp. 213–20; Drummond to Bathurst, 20 March 1814, *Ontario Historical Society Papers and Records* 19 (1922): 39.

8. For a fuller treatment of British propaganda, see Bowler, "Propaganda in Upper Canada." The collaboration of Canadian and American ideological allies is explored by Jane Errington and George Rawlyk, "The Loyalist-Federalist Alliance of Upper Canada," *American Review of Canadian Studies* 14 (summer 1984): 157–76. Strachan, an Anglican priest, was appointed first bishop of Toronto and became leader of the Family Compact, the alliance of political and social elite of the province.

9. The archival material on the Canadian Volunteers has been extensively searched, and several scholarly articles deal comprehensively with the corps and its leaders. I recommend that interested readers begin with Cruikshank's "A Study of Disaffection." Donald E. Graves reconstructs the operational history in "The Canadian Volunteers, 1813–1815," *Military Collector and Historian* 31 (fall 1979): 113–17. Also useful is A. H. U. Colquhoun, "The Career of Joseph Willcocks," *Canadian Historical Review* 7 (December 1926): 287–93. The total number that served with the Canadian Volunteers is unknown, but after the war, 268 former members of this corps or their survivors were awarded over 74,000 acres of land for their services. See *ASP:MA*, 2:577, item 247; *NASP:MA*, 5:300.

10. Landon, *Bugles*, pp. 6, 36; Turner, *The War that Both Sides Won*, p. 72.

11. Glenney, "Ethnohistory," pp. 122–24; George F. G. Stanley, "The Significance of the Six Nations Participation in the War of 1812," *Ontario History* 55 (1963): 227.

12. Glenney, "Ethnohistory," p. 131; Kirby, *Annals of Niagara*, pp. 234–35. The report

of the murder in Buffalo comes from two sources. The first is an eyewitness account by a white man, Asa Warren; see Frank H. Severance, ed., "Two Dramatic Incidents," *Buffalo Historical Society Publications* 5 (1902): 62. The second is Seneca tradition; see Parker, "Senecas in the War of 1812."

13. Norton, *Journal*, p. 293; Glenney, "Ethnohistory," pp. 112–15.

14. Cruikshank reports the harassment by natives in *Battle of Fort George*, p. 29. He quotes Michael Smith, a U.S. citizen living in Upper Canada, from a small volume Smith wrote titled *A Geographical View of the Peninsula of Upper Canada*, published in 1813.

15. Stanley, *War of 1812*, p. 226.

16. Chauncey to Jones, 4 July 1813, in *ASP:MA*, 1:382.

17. *ASP:MA*, 4:281, item 435. The issue of espionage in the War of 1812 has been virtually untouched by scholars. Documentation is understandably scarce, as commanders would be loath to keep sensitive information in copybooks or journals. Kilbourn's story came to light as a result of his petition to Congress for compensation for his wartime losses.

18. There are several scholarly investigations of the naval arms race on Lake Ontario in 1814. One is Winton-Clare, "A Shipbuilders War"; Winton-Clare is the nom de plume of British naval historian R. C. Anderson. Ernest A. Cruikshank's "The Contest for the Command on Lake Ontario in 1814," *Ontario Historical Society Papers and Records* 21 (1924): 99–159, is virtually fundamental to an understanding of naval operations during the campaign on the Niagara. A succinct analysis of the American failure on the Great Lakes is Drake's "The Niagara Peninsula and Naval Aspects of the War of 1812," in Turner, *The Military in the Niagara Peninsula*. Joseph M. Thatcher's short piece "A Fleet in the Wilderness," in Bowler, *War along the Niagara*, enhances our understanding of what was going on in the shipbuilding operations at Sacketts Harbor. Finally, there is the recent comprehensive study by Malcolmson, *Lords of the Lake*, which will be recognized as the standard.

19. Yeo to Prevost, 8 October 1813, in Wood, *British Documents*, 1:26–27.

20. Yeo to Prevost, 29 September 1813, quoted in Landon, *Bugles*, p. 5.

21. The observation of asymmetries in the opposing fleets was made by Drake, "The Niagara Peninsula and Naval Aspects of the War of 1812," pp. 28–31.

22. Landon, *Bugles*, pp. 3, 23–24, 30. See also Yeo to Prevost, 25 October 1813, in Wood, *British Documents*, 1:28–29.

23. Fortescue, *History of the British Army*, 10:101; Fredriksen, "Chronicle of Valor," pp. 272–73. This journal was compiled by Lieutenant Colonel George McFeely of the Twenty-second Infantry, an eyewitness to the events at La Colle Mill. See also D. C. L. Gosling, "The Battle at La Colle Mill, 1814," *Journal of the Society for Army Historical Research* 47 (1969): 169–74. The British battle report is found in Williams to Vincent, 31 March 1814, in Wood, *British Documents*, 1:14–16.

24. Kirby, *Annals of Niagara*, p. 228; Cruikshank, *Battle of Fort George*, p. 14; Drummond to Prevost, 15 April 1814, in Wood, *British Documents*, 1:46; Drummond to Prevost, 10 March 1814, in ibid., 3:93–94.

25. Irving Brant, *James Madison: Commander in Chief, 1812–1836* (Indianapolis: Bobbs-Merrill, 1961), p. 253. This is the sixth and final volume of Brant's biography of Madison.

26. U.S. Executive Department Document, "Bounties and Premiums for Recruits," in *ASP:MA*, 1:511; and the debates titled "Additional Rifle Corps," in *AC*, 13-2, p. 1264.

27. "Additional Rifle Corps," in *AC*, 13-2, pp.1256, 1260.

28. Drummond to Prevost, 22 December 1813, in Wood, *British Documents*, 2:500–505; Drummond to Prevost, 21 January 1814, PAC RG8, C.682.

29. Drummond to Prevost, 9 January 1814, in Wood, *British Documents*, 2:513–14.

30. Harvey to Riall, 23 March 1814, in ibid., 3:98–105; Drummond to Prevost, 7 April 1814, in *Documentary History of the Campaign on the Niagara Frontier in 1814*, pt. 1, ed. Ernest A. Cruikshank (Welland, Ontario: Lundy's Lane Historical Society, 1896), p. 7. Note that this is different from the nine-volume series with a similar title published between 1902 and 1908 and previously cited as *DHCNF;* Cruikshank's 1896 version is hereafter referred to as *DHCNF* (1896).

31. The discussion among Prevost, Drummond, and Yeo concerning the proposed attack on Sacketts Harbor is contained in several letters, some of which most probably crossed in transit. See Prevost to Drummond, 23 April 1814, and Drummond to Prevost, 28 April 1814, quoted in Cruikshank, "Contest for Lake Ontario," pp. 114–15. See also Nichol to Drummond, 22 April 1814, deposition of Constant Bacon, 2 April 1814, and Drummond to Prevost, 25 April 1814, in Cruikshank, *DHCNF* (1896), pp. 9–12. Finally, refer to Prevost to Drummond, 30 April 1814, in Wood, *British Documents*, 3:49–50.

32. Tompkins to Armstrong, 2, 9, and 16 January 1814, and Tompkins to Madison, 3 January 1814, Madison Papers, reel 15, LC.

33. Armstrong to Brown, 28 February 1814, two letters marked nos. 1 and 16, Papers of Jacob Brown and Winfield Scott, Buffalo and Erie County Historical Society (hereafter Brown and Scott Papers, BECHS).

34. Ibid.

35. An eyewitness account of the march has been preserved in John C. Fredriksen, ed., "The War of 1812 in Northern New York: The Observations of Captain Rufus McIntire," *New York History* 68 (July 1987): 309–10.

36. Armstrong to Brown, 20 March 1814, Brown and Scott Papers, BECHS.

37. Izard to Armstrong, 7 May 1814, and Armstrong to Izard, 18 May 1814, in George Izard, *Official Correspondence with the Department of War* (Philadelphia: Thomas Dobson, 1816), pp. 2–4, 20–21.

38. Brown to Armstrong, 17 April 1814, in Jacob Brown's Orderly Book, undated, Buffalo and Erie County Historical Society Manuscript Collection; hereafter Brown's Orderly Book.

39. Chauncey to Jones, 11 April 1814, quoted in Cruikshank, "Contest for Lake Ontario," p. 117. Gaines to Brown, 14 April 1814, Brown to Gaines and Brown to Chauncey, 18 April 1814, and Brown to Armstrong, 20 April 1814, Brown's Orderly Book.

40. Brown to Scott, 20 April 1814, Brown's Orderly Book; Brown to Scott, 22 April 1814, in Brown Collection, Clements Library, University of Michigan, Ann Arbor; Brown to Armstrong, 25 April 1814, Brown's Orderly Book; Armstrong to Madison, War Department/Letters Sent to the President (RG 107), National Archives (NA). A full treatment of the evolving strategy is found in Jeffrey Kimball, "Strategy on the Northern Frontier: 1814" (Ph.D. diss., Louisiana State University, 1969), pp. 159–69.

Chapter 6. Final Preparations

1. Winfield Scott was perhaps the most accomplished American general between Washington and Grant. The Scott legend got a boost from his first biographer, Edward D. Mansfield, *The Life of General Winfield Scott* (New York: A. S. Barnes, 1848). Scott himself misled historians of the War of 1812 in his *Memoirs of Lieutenant General Scott*, 2 vols. (New York: Sheldon, 1864). The venerable old man made claims about his influence that have been challenged only in the last several years. Another biography, like Mansfield's a source of anecdotes, is Marcus J. Wright, *General Scott* (New York: D. Appleton, 1894). Other biographies are Arthur D. H. Smith, *Old Fuss and Feathers* (New York: Greystone Press, 1937), and Charles Winslow Elliott, *Winfield Scott: The Soldier and the Man* (New York: Macmillan, 1937). A short sketch is found in Roger J. Spiller, ed., *Dictionary of American Military Biography* (Westport, Conn.: Greenwood Press, 1984), 3:972–75; hereafter *DAMB*. A newer biography, written for a popular audience, is John S. D. Eisenhower, *Agent of Destiny: The Life and Times of General Winfield Scott* (New York: Free Press, 1997). Finally, a superb biography is Timothy D. Johnson, *Winfield Scott: The Quest for Military Glory* (Lawrence: University Press of Kansas, 1998).

2. Gaines's single biography is James W. Silver, *Edmund Pendleton Gaines: Frontier General* (New Orleans: Louisiana State University Press, 1949). See also *DAMB*, 1:363–66.

3. Ripley was one of the few officers whose careers did not profit from participation in the 1814 Niagara campaign. His book-length biography, written by his nephew, is uncritical; see Nicholas Baylies, *Eleazar Wheelock Ripley* (Des Moines, Iowa: Brewster, 1890). Another similarly uncritical sketch is Charles R. Corning, "General Eleazar Wheelock Ripley," *Granite Monthly* 17 (July 1894): 1–13. A balanced and generally sympathetic essay is J. Michael Quill's entry in *DAMB*, 3:916–19. Ripley's request for a political appointment is found in Ripley to Madison, 29 March 1814, Madison Papers, reel 16, LC. Brown's and Scott's initial impressions of Ripley are found in Brown to Armstrong, 8 May 1814, Brown's Orderly Book; and Scott to Brown, 23 May 1814, Brown and Scott Papers, microfilm collection, reel M65-27, BECHS.

4. Brown to Armstrong, 17 April 1814, Brown's Orderly Book.

5. U.S. Executive Department Document, "A Report of the Army, Its Strength and Distribution," in *ASP:MA*, 1:535; U.S. Executive Department Document, Army Paymaster to the House, "Bounties and Premiums for Recruits," in ibid., 1:511; U.S. Executive Department Document, Secretary of War to the Senate, "Return of Enlistments," in ibid., 1:519–20; and "New Rules for Recruiting the Army," prepared by John R. Bell, Inspector General, 4 June 1814, Madison Papers, reel 16, LC.

6. Brown to Armstrong, 19 June 1814, Brown's Orderly Book.

7. Like most American regiments of this war, a comprehensive regimental history of the Ninth Infantry does not exist. This short history is synthesized from numerous primary and secondary sources, as are the histories of the other units of the Left Division. A useful collection of biographical sketches of the principal officers of Brown's division is John C. Fredriksen, *Officers of the War of 1812* (Lewiston, N.Y.: Edwin Mellen Press, 1989); Aspinwall's biography appears on pp. 53–55, and Leavenworth's on pp. 61–63. Leavenworth's biography also appears in *DAMB*, 1:599–602.

8. For a short biography of McNeil, see Fredriksen, *Officers*, pp. 65–67. See also Daniel Doan, "The Enigmatic Moody Bedel," *Historical New Hampshire* 25 (fall 1970): 27–36.

9. See Fredriksen, *Officers*, pp. 89–91, for notes on Miller's service during the war.

10. Some of the material on the Twenty-fifth Infantry is found in the diary of George Howard, Manuscript Collection, BECHS. Captain Howard commanded a company of the Twenty-fifth and was well regarded by Scott. The biographies of Gardner and Jesup are found in Fredriksen, *Officers*, pp. 33–35, 73–75. See also Chester L. Kieffer, *Maligned General: The Biography of Thomas Sidney Jesup* (San Rafael, Calif.: Presidio, 1979). An uncritical biography is Fred E. Hagen, "Thomas Sidney Jesup," *Quartermaster Review* 11 (September–October 1931): 44–47. Jesup's command appointment appears in Scott's General Order of 16 May 1814.

11. McFarland's letters are an interesting source of the details of army life during this war; see Crombie, "Papers of Major Daniel McFarland," For Brooke's biography, see Fredriksen, *Officers*, pp. 93–95.

12. Biographical information on Morgan and Appling appear in Lossing, *Pictorial Fieldbook*, pp. 848, 800.

13. For a detailed account of this young cavalryman's exploits, see Frank H. Severance, ed., "Service of Capt. Samuel D. Harris," *Publications of the Buffalo Historical Society* 24 (1920): 327–42.

14. Hindman and Towson are treated in Fredriksen, *Officers*, pp. 117–19, 125–27.

15. Brown's officers trained and fought superbly during the campaign of 1814. In this regard, they were probably atypical of the officer corps in general. It is probably fair to judge that the officer corps, though it displayed many professional traits, could not yet be characterized as a professional corps. Agreeing with this view is William B. Skelton, whose study *An American Profession of Arms: The Army Officer Corps, 1784–1861* (Lawrence: University Press of Kansas, 1992), is a wide-ranging investigation of the roots of a professional army. Skelton concludes that although the seeds of professionalism were planted during the last war with Britain, a professional officer corps grew from the post-war reforms.

16. Tompkins to Armstrong, 2 January 1814, Madison Papers, reel 15, LC.

17. Tompkins' General Order, 13 March 1814, in *Public Papers of Daniel D. Tompkins: 1807–1817 (Military)*, 3 vols. (New York: Wynkoop, Hollenbeck, Crawford, 1898), 2:478; hereafter *Tompkins Papers*. Tompkins had great faith in Porter's military abilities and had proposed to James Wilkinson that Porter command any contingent of militia associated with Wilkinson's operations; see *Tompkins Papers*, 2:380.

18. Biographical sketches of Red Jacket and Farmer's Brother are found in Lossing, *Pictorial Fieldbook*, pp. 802, 848.

19. Cruikshank, "A Study of Disaffection," p. 220; Graves, "The Canadian Volunteers," p. 115; Joseph A. Whitehorne, *While Washington Burned: The Battle for Fort Erie, 1814* (Baltimore: Nautical and Aviation Publishing Company of America, 1992), pp. 137–42.

20. Brown's General Order, 7 April 1814, Izard's Order Book, Manuscript Collection, BECHS.

21. Scott's Brigade Order, 7 April 1814, Izard's Order Book.

22. Brown to Armstrong, 17 April 1814, Brown's Orderly Book; Hall's General Order, 10 April 1814, Izard's Order Book.

23. Scott's Brigade Orders, 14 and 18 April 1814, and Scott to Leavenworth, 14 April 1814, Izard's Orderly Book; Lester W. Smith, ed., "A Drummer Boy in the War of 1812: Memoirs of Jarvis Frary Hanks," *Niagara Frontier* 7 (summer 1960): 53–62.

24. Brown to Scott, 20 April 1814, Brown's Orderly Book; Brown's General Order, 21 April 1814, Izard's Order Book.

25. Fredriksen, "War of 1812 in Northern New York," p. 311.

26. Scott to Brown, 17, 22, and 23 May 1814, Brown and Scott Papers, BECHS. A discussion of uniform procurement in general is found in McKee, "Service of Supply." A more focused investigation of the clothing shortage is Rene Chartrand, "The U.S. Army's Uniform Supply 'Crisis' during the War of 1812," *Military Collector and Historian* 40 (summer 1988): 63–65.

27. See Scott's General Orders of 23 and 26 April 1814 and 24 and 29 May 1814 and his Brigade Order on 23 June 1814, Izard's Order Book.

28. Scott, *Memoirs*, p. 119.

29. Scott's General Orders of 22 and 28 April 1814, Izard's Order Book.

30. There are two particularly illuminating essays on American tactical doctrine. The first is Theodore J. Crackel's chapter on the Battle of Queenston Heights in Heller and Stofft, *America's First Battles.* Crackel concludes that the U.S. Army entered the war with no standard drill manual nor a consensus of opinion as to which of several drill manuals was best suited for America's needs. The second scholarly work is Donald E. Graves, "Dry Books of Tactics: U.S. Infantry Manuals of the War of 1812 and After," *Military Collector and Historian* 38 (summer 1986): 51–61 and (winter 1986): 173–77. Graves concludes that the U.S. Army began the conflict with two official drill manuals: Von Steuben's *Blue Book* for the militia, and Alexander Smyth's *Regulations for the Field Exercises, Manoeuvres and Conduct of the Infantry* for the regulars. However, in March 1813, William Duane's *Handbook for Infantry* replaced Smyth's as the official manual.

31. Graves, "Dry Books of Tactics," p. 58.

32. Scott, *Memoirs*, p. 120.

33. Donald E. Graves, who has investigated the 1814 campaign at length and with success, doubts that Scott formed officer squads. As evidence, he cites a lack of reference to officer training in orders, no corroboration by any of his officers, and that his officers should have been familiar with Smyth's drill manual, which was very close to the French system. See Graves, "I Have a Handsome Little Army . . . A Re-examination of Winfield Scott's Camp at Buffalo in 1814," in Bowler, *War along the Niagara*, pp. 43–52.

34. Scott's General Order, 22 April 1814, Izard's Order Book.

35. Scott's General Orders of 1 and 7 May 1814, Izard's Order Book; Howard to wife Sarah, 22 May 1814, George Howard Papers, microfilm collection, roll M86-10, BECHS.

36. The characteristics and limitations of black powder weapons largely defined tactics of the day. The reader is referred to two worthwhile sources: James E. Hicks, "United States Military Shoulder Arms, 1795–1935, Part 1: The Smoothbore Flintlock as a Military Arm." *Journal of the American Military History Foundation* 1 (spring 1937): 22–33; and Peter Hofschroer, "Flintlocks in Battle," *Military Illustrated: Past and Present* 1 (June–July 1986): 30–35.

37. Scott, *Memoirs*, p. 119; Scott to Brown, 30 April 1814, Brown and Scott Papers, BECHS.

38. Scott to Brown, 23 May 1814, Brown and Scott Papers, BECHS.

39. Scott to Winder, 16 May 1814, quoted in Elliott, *Winfield Scott*, p. 148.

40. Scott's General Order, 29 May 1814, Izard's Order Book.

41. Scott's General Order, 25 May 1814, and his Brigade Orders of 17 and 23 June 1814, Izard's Order Book.

42. A full treatment of the subject is John S. Hare, "Military Punishments in the War of 1812," *Journal of the American Military Institute* 4 (1940): 225–39. To put executions into perspective, during the war, 206 soldiers were sentenced to death, and 205 were executed.

43. U.S. Congressional Document, "Resignation of Lieutenant John Clarke," in *ASP:MA*, 4:687.

44. Mansfield, *Life of Scott*, p. 101.

45. Scott's Brigade Order, 15 April 1814, Izard's Order Book; Scott to Brown, 4 May 1814, Brown and Scott Papers, BECHS.

46. Scott's General Order, 31 May 1814, Izard's Order Book.

47. Scott's General Orders, 3 and 4 June 1814, Izard's Order Book. Eyewitness accounts of the executions at Buffalo are found in Howard to wife Sarah, 8 June 1814, George Howard Papers, and in Smith, "Drummer Boy," p. 55. The account of the court-martial at Sacketts Harbor is found in Crombie, "Papers of Major Daniel McFarland," p. 113.

48. Brown to Bomford, 11 May 1814, Brown and Scott Papers, BECHS.

49. Scott to Brown, 30 April and 23 May 1814, ibid.

50. Brown to Simmons, 18 June 1814, ibid; Scott's remarks, U.S. Executive Document, "Subsisting the Army," in *ASP:MA*, 1:600.

51. Scott's General Order, 24 May 1814, Izard's Order Book; Scott to Brown, 23 May 1814, Brown and Scott Papers, BECHS.

52. Scott to Brown, 30 April and 4 May 1814, Brown and Scott Papers, BECHS; Cruikshank, "A Study of Disaffection," p. 220.

53. Orne's Intelligence Report no. 1, 2 May 1814; Scott to Brown, 4 May 1814, Brown and Scott Papers, BECHS.

54. Scott's comments are reported in Babcock, *Niagara Frontier*, p. 110. Scott's opinion of the militia was somewhat tempered by age and experience. In his memoirs, he wrote that volunteers and militia were "oftener an element of weakness than of strength" (*Memoirs*, p. 115).

55. Porter to Tompkins, 8 April 1814, in *DHCNF* (1896), pp. 7–8.

56. Tompkins's General Order, in *Tompkins Papers*, 2:478–79.

57. Porter to Tompkins, 3 May 1814, in *DHCNF* (1896), pp. 13–14; Brown to Armstrong, 30 May 1814, Brown's Orderly Book; Brown to Porter, 19 May 1814, and Porter to Brown, 25 May 1814, Brown and Scott Papers, BECHS.

58. Porter to Brown, 8 June 1814 (two letters), Brown and Scott Papers, BECHS; Armstrong to Brown, 9 June 1814, and Brown to Porter, 11 June 1814, Brown's Orderly Book.

59. Scott to Brown, 23 May 1814, and Brown to Porter, 23 June 1814, Brown and Scott Papers, BECHS; Porter to Tompkins, 3 July 1814, quoted in Babcock, *Niagara Frontier*, p. 147.

60. Porter to Tompkins, 3 May 1814, in *DHCNF* (1896), pp. 13–14; Scott to Brown, 23 May 1814, Brown Collection, Clements Library; Brown to Armstrong, 3 June 1814,

Brown's Orderly Book; Glenney, "Ethnohistory," pp. 132–33; Parker, "Senecas in the War of 1812," pp. 89–90; Carl Benn, "Iroquois Warfare, 1812–1814," in Bowler, *War along the Niagara*, p. 63.

61. Scott to Brown, 23 May 1814, Brown Collection, Clements Library.

62. Fenton to Scott, 3 May 1814, Brown and Scott Papers, BECHS; Brown's General Order, 13 June 1814, Izard's Order Book. See also Whitehorne, *While Washington Burned*, pp. 23–25, 102. Although regular regiments have not had their stories recorded, the tale of the Pennsylvania militia regiment that joined Brown's invasion is told in two memoirs. The first is by the commander himself; see James Fenton, *Journal of the Military Tour by the Pennsylvania Troops and Militia under the Command of Col. James Fenton, to the Frontiers of Pennsylvania and New York* (Carlisle, Pa.: George Kline, 1814). The other is by a captain in Fenton's regiment; see Samuel White, *History of the American Troops during the Late War, under Command of Colonels Fenton and Campbell* (Baltimore: B. Edes, 1830). The mutiny among Fenton's men is recorded in White, *American Troops*, pp. 8–11. There are two accounts by enlisted men; see Joseph E. Walker, ed., "A Soldier's Diary for 1814," *Pennsylvania History* 12 (October 1945): 292–303, and "The Narrative of Alexander McMullen, a Private Soldier," in *Soldiers of 1814: American Enlisted Men's Memoirs of the Niagara Campaign*, ed. Donald E. Graves (Youngstown, N.Y.: Old Fort Niagara Association, 1995).

63. Prevost to Drummond, 26 March 1814, in *DHCNF*, 9:261–62.

64. Harvey to Riall, 23 March 1814, in *DHCNF* (1896), pp. 3–6.

65. Deposition of Constant Bacon, 2 April 1814, and Nichol to Drummond, 2 April 1814, in *DHCNF* (1896), pp. 9–10.

66. In compiling the historical sketches of British and Canadian military units, I synthesized numerous primary and secondary sources. Two texts are mainstays. The first is Charles H. Stewart, *The Service of British Regiments in Canada and North America*, 2d ed. (Ottawa: Department of National Defence Library, 1964). This document is the single most comprehensive examination of the subject and was compiled largely from regimental histories. The second source is L. Homfray Irving, *Officers of the British Forces in Canada during the War of 1812–15* (Welland, Ontario: Welland Tribune Print, 1908). This publication was sponsored by the Canadian Military Institute and includes a wealth of data on regulars, fencibles, militia, and officers in the Indian Department.

67. Riall to Drummond, 15 March 1814, in Wood, *British Documents*, 3:97–98.

68. Prevost's General Order, 19 March 1814, in ibid., 3:13–14; see also Pierre Berton, *Flames across the Border* (Boston: Little, Brown, 1981), p. 279.

69. Norton, *Journal*, p. 348; Drummond to Prevost, 10 April 1814, in *DHCNF* (1896), pp. 8–9. The symbol of the Prophet's claim to Tecumseh's special favor with the British was the presentation to him of a sword and pistols in the name of the prince regent.

70. Drummond to Prevost, 10 March 1814, in Wood, *British Documents*, 3:93–94; Drummond to Prevost, 25 April 1814, in *DHCNF* (1896), pp. 11–12; Drummond to Prevost, 26 April 1814, PAC, RG 8 C683, p. 53.

71. Drummond to Bathurst, 3 July 1814, in *DHCNF* (1896), p. 24; Steppler, "A Duty Troublesome beyond Measure," pp. 157–72.

72. The story of the treason trials is most completely told by William R. Riddell, "The Ancaster 'Bloody Assize' of 1814," *Ontario Historical Society Papers and Records* 20

(1923): 107–25. Riddell was a justice of the Supreme Court of Ontario. Included is a short history of the legalities of the charge of high treason and a description of the grisly means of execution.

73. Drummond to Prevost, 19 May, 4 and 7 June 1814, and Yeo to Drummond, 3 June 1814, in Wood, *British Documents*, 3:71, 77–78, 92–93, 75–76.

74. For Brown's orders, see John Armstrong, *Notices of the War of 1812*, 2 vols. (New York: Wiley and Putnam, 1840), 2:72. Rufus McIntire, a company commander under Mitchell, recorded his firsthand impression; see Fredriksen, "War of 1812 in Northern New York," p. 312.

75. Fischer to Harvey, 7 May 1814, Drummond to Prevost, 7 May 1814, and Yeo to Croker, 9 May 1814, in Wood, *British Documents*, 3:57–60, 52–57, 61–66; Brown to Armstrong, 8 May 1814, Brown's Orderly Book. See also Cruikshank, "Contest for Lake Ontario," pp. 118–22.

76. Brown to Scott, 28 April 1814, Brown and Scott Papers, BECHS.

77. Brown to Armstrong, 29 April 1814, Brown's Orderly Book.

78. Armstrong to Madison, 30 April 1814, Brown and Scott Papers, BECHS; Armstrong to Brown, 7 May 1814, Brown's Orderly Book; Madison to Jones, 4 May 1814, Madison Papers, reel 27, LC; Brant, *James Madison*, p. 256.

79. Brown to Scott, 4, 11, and 16 May 1814, Brown and Scott Papers, BECHS.

80. Sinclair to Scott, 3 and 5 May 1814, and Scott to Brown, 4 May 1814, ibid.

81. Brown to Armstrong, 21 May 1814, Brown's Orderly Book; Brown to Mitchell, 21 May 1814, Brown to Gaines and Brown to Hindman, 25 May 1814, Brown and Scott Papers, BECHS; Crombie, "Papers of Major Daniel McFarland," pp. 113–14.

82. Scott, *Memoirs*, p. 121; Brown to Armstrong, 25 and 29 April, 19 May, and 3 June 1814, Brown's Orderly Book; Brown to Scott, 16 May 1814, and Scott to Brown, 17 May 1814, Brown and Scott Papers, BECHS.

83. Armstrong to Brown, 25 May 1814, and Armstrong to Scott, 25 and 28 May 1814, Brown and Scott Papers, BECHS.

84. Brown to Armstrong, 15 and 19 June 1814, Brown's Orderly Book.

85. Cabinet Notes, 7 June 1814, Madison Papers, reel 27, LC. A fuller treatment of this pivotal meeting appears in Brant, *James Madison*, pp. 262–63.

86. Armstrong to Brown, 9 June 1814, and Brown to Armstrong, 17 June 1814, Brown's Orderly Book (note: Brown penned three letters to the secretary of war on 17 June); Brown to Jenkins, 21 June 1814, Brown and Scott Papers, BECHS.

87. Jones to Madison, 6 June 1814, Madison Papers, reel 16, LC; Fortescue, *History of the British Army*, 10:104–5.

88. Brown to Chauncey, 18 April 1814, and Brown to Armstrong, 7 June 1814, Brown's Orderly Book.

89. Brown to Gaines, 21 June 1814, Brown and Scott Papers, BECHS.

90. Gaines to Brown, 6 June 1814, Armstrong to Brown, 20 June 1814, Brown and Scott Papers, BECHS; Armstrong, *Notices*, 2:83; Brown to Chauncey, 21 June 1814, Brown's Orderly Book. Brown's estimate of the comparative strength of the fleets is found in an undated document in Brown's Orderly Book.

91. Chauncey to Brown, 25 June 1814, Brown's Orderly Book.

92. Brown to Sinclair, 18 June 1814, Kennedy to Brown, 20 June 1814, and Jones to

the Commander at Erie, 20 June 1814, Brown and Scott Papers, BECHS; Brown to Armstrong, 19 June 1814, Brown's Orderly Book.

93. Brown to Gaines, 7 June 1814, Brown and Scott Papers, BECHS; Brown to Armstrong, 12, 19, and 26 June 1814, Brown's Orderly Book; Brown's General Orders of 6, 13, 19, 24, and 25 June 1814, Izard's Orderly Book.

94. Brown to Armstrong, 12 and 26 June 1814, Brown's Orderly Book; Brown to the Officer Commanding Detroit, 22 and 23 June 1814, Brown and Scott Papers, BECHS.

95. War Department Document, "A Report of the Army, Its Strength and Distribution, Previous to the 1st of July, 1814," in *ASP:MA*, 1:535.

96. Gaines to Brown, 25 June 1814, Brown and Scott Papers, BECHS.

97. There are few regimental histories of U.S. regiments in the War of 1812. A notable exception is the Twenty-second Infantry, which boasts two short histories that appeared in a journal of local history: William Y. Brady, "The 22nd Regiment in the War of 1812," *Western Pennsylvania Historical Magazine* 32 (March–June 1949): 56–60, and John Newell Crombie, "The Twenty-second U.S. Infantry," *Western Pennsylvania Historical Magazine* 60 (1967): 133–47 (part 1) and 221–36 (part 2). These accounts are richly supplemented by the diary of one of the regiment's senior officers, Lieutenant Colonel George McFeely. A well-edited version of the McFeely diary is Fredriksen, "Chronicle of Valor."

98. Crombie, "Papers of Major Daniel McFarland," p. 119; Brown's General Order, 29 June 1814, and Scott's Brigade Order, 30 June 1814, Izard's Order Book.

99. Talbot to Riall, 16 May 1814, in Wood, *British Documents*, 3:88–90; "Opinion of the Court of Enquiry on the Conduct of Colonel Campbell," Riall to Drummond, 19 May 1814, Drummond to Prevost, 27 and 31 May 1814, including a statement by Mathias Steele, in *DHCNF* (1896), pp. 8, 14–17; Armstrong to Brown, 2 June 1814, Brown and Scott Papers, BECHS; Brown to Armstrong, 17 June 1814, Brown's Orderly Book; Brown's General Order, 30 June 1814, Izard's Order Book.

100. Drummond to Prevost, 14 May 1814, in Wood, *British Documents*, 3:67–70; Appling to Gaines, 30 May 1814, Brown and Scott Papers, BECHS. An expanded treatment of the skirmish at Sandy Creek and its significance for the naval balance of power on Lake Ontario is found in Mahan, *Sea Power*, 2:285–90.

101. Chauncey to Jones, 30 May 1814, Madison Papers, reel 16, LC; Brown to Armstrong, 7 June 1814, Brown's Orderly Book.

102. Historians have generally ignored Izard. A short biography is G. E. Maurigault, "The Military Career of General George Izard," *Magazine of American History* 19 (June 1888): 463–78; Izard's letter to Armstrong, dated 7 May 1814, is found on pp. 471–72. A more satisfying study is John C. Fredriksen, "A Tempered Sword, Untested: The Military Career of General George Izard," *Journal of America's Military Past* 25 (winter 1999): 5–16.

103. Armstrong to Izard, 14 May 1814, quoted in Maurigault, "Military Career of George Izard," p. 471.

104. Armstrong to Izard, 25 May 1814, and Izard to Armstrong, 12 July 1814, in Armstrong, *Notices*, 2:119–20.

105. Armstrong to Madison, 20 May 1814, and Madison to Armstrong, 15 June 1814, Madison Papers, reel 16, LC; Brant, *James Madison*, pp. 267–68.

106. The gray uniforms of Scott's regulars became a part of America's military lore, coupled as they are with the Battles of Chippawa and Lundy's Lane. Two works are indispensable in sorting out fact from folktale: David H. Schneider, "Gray Uniforms on the Niagara: Winfield Scott's Infantry Brigade, 1814," *Military Collector and Historian* 33 (winter 1981): 170–72, and Chartrand, "Uniform Supply Crisis."

Chapter 7. The Opening Battles

1. Memoranda of Occurrences etc. Connected with the Campaign of Niagara, Manuscript Collection, BECHS; hereafter Memoranda of Occurrences. This narrative document, not in Brown's handwriting, is purportedly a copy of his journal and may later have been recopied and edited by another. Although its origin is uncertain, it appears to accurately capture Brown's actions and intentions. Another document that corroborates the events of the campaign is a twenty-one-page letter written by Porter in 1840; hereafter Porter's 1840 letter. Though it was written many years after the fact, some aspects of Porter's account are developed to a high level of detail. This letter is found in the Peter B. Porter Papers, BECHS.

2. Scott, *Memoirs*, p. 12.; Thomas J. Jesup, *Memoirs of the Campaign on the Niagara*, Manuscript Collection, BECHS; Severance, "Service of Samuel Harris," pp. 327–34.

3. Memoranda of Occurrences.

4. Ibid.

5. Ibid.; Porter's 1840 letter.

6. Memoranda of Occurrences; George Howard, *Diary of George Howard*, Manuscript Collection, Connecticut Historical Society; W. H. Merritt, "Journal of Events Principally on the Detroit and Niagara Frontiers," in Wood, *British Documents*, 3:642. Howard was a captain in Jesup's battalion and an eyewitness to the initial part of the campaign, although he missed Lundy's Lane. Merritt was a militia captain and served in the Niagara Light Dragoons, a volunteer unit on active status. At the time of Chippawa, Merritt commanded the Troop of Provincial Dragoons, the successor to the Niagara Light Dragoons. He was in the very thick of the fighting on the Niagara Peninsula throughout the war, and his journal is a valuable record of the many skirmishes fought there.

7. Memoranda of Occurrences; Howard, *Diary;* Merritt, "Journal," 3:642; Inspector General report, Left Division, in *DHCNF* (1896), p. 42; Owen, *Fort Erie*, p. 49.

8. Memoranda of Occurrences; Brown to Armstrong, 7 July 1814, in *DHCNF* (1896), pp. 38–43; Porter to Tompkins, 3 July 1814, in ibid., pp. 26–27.

9. Riall to Drummond, 6 July 1814, in *DHCNF* (1896), pp. 31–33; Norton, *Journal*, p. 348.

10. Ernest Green, *Lincoln at Bay: A Sketch of 1814* (Welland, Ontario: Tribune-Telegraph Press, 1923), p. 40; Scott to Adjutant General, 15 July 1814, in *DHCNF* (1896), pp. 44–47.

11. Green, *Lincoln at Bay*, p. 40; Howard, *Diary;* John C. Fredriksen, "Niagara, 1814: The United States Army Quest for Tactical Parity in the War of 1812 and Its Legacy" (Ph.D. diss., Providence College, 1993), p. 82.

12. Memoranda of Occurrences; Norton, *Journal*, p. 349.

13. Austin to Gaines, 4 July 1814, Brown's Orderly Book; Brown to Gaines, 6 July 1814, Brown and Scott Papers, BECHS; Porter's 1840 letter; Walker, "A Soldier's Diary for 1814." This last item is the diary of Private John Witherow of Fenton's regiment.

14. Merritt, "Journal," 3:644; Green, *Lincoln at Bay;* Scott's Memorandum, erroneously dated 4 June 1814, in *DHCNF* (1896), pp. 27–28.

15. Accounts of the existence and size of the tongue of woods vary. Lossing, who visited Chippawa fifty years after the battle, saw no hint of this important feature and omitted it from his map (see *Pictorial Fieldbook*, p. 810). Jeffrey Kimball's scholarly study follows Lossing ("Battle of Chippawa: Infantry Tactics in the War of 1812," *Military Affairs* 32 [winter 1967–1968]: 180). Yet eyewitnesses remark on this feature and note that the view between the two tributaries was blocked by woods, a fact otherwise unaccountable. I have chosen Porter's description of the irregular wood line, since he lived on the Niagara Frontier for many years and had opportunities after the war to take a more leisurely look at his battlefield. The *tête-de-pont* battery remains a mystery as to its size and exact position. The only visual clues are a sketch by Lossing of what appears to be portions of a triple line of tall earthworks south of the river. The purpose of a *tête-de-pont* is to physically protect a bridge from direct enemy fire; thus it is placed on the enemy's side of the bridge. Yet eyewitness accounts are ambiguous, and it is possible that this fortification was on the north side of the Chippawa.

16. Fortescue wrote: "Either the post should not have been held at all, or its commander Major Buck of the Eighth, should have defended it to the last; and it is clear that Buck did not do his duty" (*History of the British Army*, 10:107).

17. Brown to Armstrong, 6 and 7 July 1814, Brown's Orderly Book.

18. James Hall, "Biographical Sketch of Major Thomas Biddle," *Illinois Monthly Magazine* 2 (September 1831): 554; Green, *Lincoln at Bay;* Brown's General Order, 5 July 1814, Izard's Order Book.

19. Brown to Armstrong, 7 July 1814, Brown's Orderly Book. Brown had no authority to dismiss officers from the service without due process. Armstrong backed his subordinate commander, but after the war, a board of inquiry cleared Treat of Brown's unjust charges and revoked his summary punishment.

20. Riall to Drummond, 6 July 1814, in *DHCNF* (1896), pp. 31–33; Drummond to Prevost, 11 July 1814, in Wood, *British Documents*, 3:123–25.

21. Memoranda of Occurrences; Porter's 1840 letter.

22. Scott, *Memoirs*, pp. 13–14.

23. Porter's 1840 letter.

24. Porter's forest fight is reported in several accounts, many of which are contradictory. Each eyewitness saw only pieces of the action and in the heat of combat can be excused for inferring a general flow of events from limited knowledge. I have reconstructed this account from several sources, among which are Memoranda of Occurrences; Porter's 1840 Letter; Scott, *Memoirs;* White, *American Troops;* Norton, *Journal;* Merritt, "Journal"; the official reports of the principals involved; and Green, *Lincoln at Bay.*

25. Riall to Drummond, 6 July 1814, in Wood, *British Documents*, 3:115–20. Riall sent Norton on a wide envelopment, and he saw little action. However, Norton's secondhand account of the battle appears in his journal on pp. 349–52.

26. Mansfield, *Life of Scott,* p. 105; Memoranda of Occurrences; Brown to Armstrong, 7 July 1814, Brown's Orderly Book; Smith, "Drummer Boy," p. 56.

27. Porter's 1840 letter; White, *American Troops,* pp. 15–16; anonymous captain of Fenton's regiment, in *DHCNF* (1896), p. 49.

28. Merritt, "Journal"; Inspector General report, 9 July 1814, in *DHCNF* (1896), p. 42; Green, *Lincoln at Bay,* p. 12.

29. Riall to Drummond, 6 July 1814, in Wood, *British Documents,* 3:115–20.

30. Scott to Adjutant General, 15 July 1814, in *DHCNF* (1896), pp. 44–47; Jesup, *Memoirs;* Lossing, *Pictorial Fieldbook,* p. 809; Smith, *Old Fuss and Feathers,* p. 114; Kimball, "Battle of Chippawa," p. 182.

31. Hindman to Adjutant General, 13 July 1814, in *DHCNF* (1896) p. 44; Scott to Adjutant General, 15 July 1814, in ibid., pp. 44–47; Mackonochie to Major General Glasgow, 19 August 1814, in ibid., p. 49; anonymous letter printed in *Baltimore Federal Gazette,* 25 July 1814, reprinted in ibid., pp. 49–50. See also "Obituary of Jacob Schmuck," *Army and Navy Chronicle* 1 (May 1835): 159. Lieutenant Schmuck commanded one of Towson's guns and lost ten of his eleven crewmen at Chippawa.

32. Brown to Armstrong, 7 July 1814, Brown's Orderly Book; Scott to Adjutant General, 15 July 1814; Hindman to Adjutant General, 13 July 1814; Memoranda of Occurrences.

33. Jesup, *Memoirs;* Howard, *Diary;* Porter's 1840 letter; George Hay, "Recollections of the War of 1812," *American Historical Review* 32 (1927): 73.

34. Riall to Drummond, 6 July 1814, in Wood, *British Documents,* 3:115–20; Lossing, *Pictorial Fieldbook,* pp. 810–11; Fortescue, *History of the British Army,* 10:109.

35. Porter's 1840 letter; Brown to Armstrong, 5 and 6 July 1814; Memoranda of Occurrences. Sergeant Commins of the Eighth Foot remembered that the men of the Right Division "retreated deliberately to our own ground" (Lord, "War on the Canadian Frontier," p. 208). Another indication that the British withdrawal was not a rout was that numerous wounded were brought off the field. Merritt, who arrived just after the battle, reported that every house in Chippawa was "filled with wounded" (Merritt, "Journal," p. 615).

36. Porter's 1840 letter; Memoranda of Occurrences; Hindman to Adjutant General, 13 July 1814; Brown to Armstrong, 7 July 1814, Brown's Orderly Book; Severance, "Service of Samuel Harris," pp. 334–35.

37. Adams, *History of the United States,* 2:45.

38. Fortescue, *History of the British Army,* 10:110.

39. Riall overestimated the size of Brown's division. After the battle, Riall personally interrogated a captured officer of Fenton's regiment. When that unfortunate officer told his captor that the army strength was about 5,000, Riall replied: "That is not true sir, you know it is not, you have more than double that number" (White, *American Troops,* p. 23).

40. For the differing views of the timing of Brown's order to Ripley, see Memoranda of Occurrences and an extract from *Niles' Register* reprinted in *DHCNF* (1896), pp. 47–48.

41. Brown to Armstrong, 7 July 1814, Brown's Orderly Book.

42. Porter to Tompkins, 29 July 1814, in *DHCNF* (1896), pp. 101–3.

43. Brown to Armstrong, 7 July 1814, Brown's Orderly Book. For an example of the perception of the regulars concerning the forest fight, Major McFarland of the Twenty-

third Infantry recorded in his diary on 6 July that "our Indians and Pa. Militia fought well" (Crombie, "Papers of Major Daniel McFarland," p. 120).

44. Brown's response was reported by Pennsylvanian Samuel White (*American Troops,* p. 25), who overheard the remark on 6 July in the British camp where he was being held captive. The story is repeated in Smith, *Old Fuss and Feathers,* p. 119.

45. Casualty figures are found in Riall's official report of 6 July 1814. Tweeddale probably remembers wrongly that only one officer was well enough to assume command. Still, his regiment suffered twelve officer casualties, including two killed in action. See Hay, "Recollections of the War of 1812," p. 73.

46. Merritt, "Journal," p. 615; Green, *Lincoln at Bay,* p. 12.

47. Brown's General Order, morning, 6 July 1814, Izard's Order Book; Porter's 1840 letter.

48. Brown to Armstrong, 6 July 1814, Brown's Orderly Book.

49. Memoranda of Occurrences.

50. Jesup, *Memoirs;* Lossing, *Pictorial Fieldbook,* pp. 813–14.

51. Memoranda of Occurrences; Brown to Armstrong, 11 July 1814, Brown's Orderly Book; Crombie, "Papers of Major Daniel McFarland," p. 121; Drummond to Prevost, 13 July 1814, in *DHCNF* (1896), p. 56.

52. Brown to Armstrong, 11 July, 1814, Brown's Orderly Book; Merritt, "Journal," pp. 615–16; Severance, "Service of Samuel Harris," p. 336.

53. Drummond to Prevost, 9 July 1814, in Wood, *British Documents,* 3:112–14; Drummond to Prevost, 10 July 1814, in *DHCNF* (1896), pp. 35–37.

54. Glenney, "Ethnohistory," pp. 133–35; Norton, *Journal,* pp. 349–52; Porter's 1840 letter; Babcock, *Niagara Frontier,* p. 156.

55. Ibid.

56. Brown to Gaines, 10 July 1814, Brown's Orderly Book.

57. Brown's General Order, 9 July 1814, Izard's Order Book; Brown to Armstrong, 11 July 1814, Brown's Orderly Book.

58. Memoranda of Occurrences; Brown to Gaines, 10 July, 1814, Brown's Orderly Book; Riall to Drummond, 9 July 1814, in *DHCNF* (1896), p. 54.

59. Brown's General Order, 10 July 1814, Izard's Order Book; David B. Douglass, "Reminiscences of the Campaign of 1814 on the Niagara Frontier," *Historical Magazine* 2 (July 1873): 11, 69. Douglass delivered these four sequential lectures in 1840, and *Historical Magazine* published them thirty-three years later in issues 1 through 4, July through October 1873.

60. Jesup, *Memoirs;* Memoranda of Occurrences; Brown to Gaines, 10 July 1814, Brown's Orderly Book.

61. Drummond to Prevost, 10 and 13 July 1814, in *DHCNF* (1896), pp. 35–37, 127–30.

62. Correspondence between Brown and Scott, 10 July 1814, Papers of Brown and Scott, BECHS. The brave and inspiring Lieutenant William Jenkins Worth went on to command a division under Scott in Mexico. Fort Worth, Texas, commemorates his name.

63. Brown to Armstrong, 10 July 1814, Brown's Orderly Book; Gardner to McNeil, 9 August 1814, John McNeil Papers, LC.

64. Brown's General Order, 10 July 1814, Izard's Order Book; Brown to Armstrong, 11 July 1814, Brown's Orderly Book; Severance, "Service of Samuel Harris," p. 337.

65. Drummond to Prevost, 11 July 1814, in *DHCNF* (1896), pp. 54–55. At least one Canadian militiaman doubted the reliability of his peers at Kingston. Escaping militia duty by sailing to Sacketts Harbor, he reportedly told Gaines "that more than two-thirds of the militia would throw down their arms" if the Americans attacked Kingston. See Gaines to Brown, 14 July 1814, Brown and Scott Papers, BECHS.

66. Chauncey to Brown, 8 July 1814, and Gaines to Brown, 3 and 12 July 1814, Brown's Orderly Book.

67. Riall to Drummond, 12 July 1814, in Wood, *British Documents*, 3:133–37.

68. Evans to Riall and Porter's Brigade Order, 13 July 1814, in *DHCNF* (1896), pp. 62–63.

69. Secret memorandum (undated) signed by Deputy Adjutant General Lieutenant Colonel John Harvey, in *DHCNF* (1896), p. 57; Merritt, "Journal," p. 616.

70. Brown's General Order, 13 July 1814, Izard's Order Book. A company of Fenton's Pennsylvanians was sent back across the Niagara to guard the new supply point at Lewiston. John Witherow, a member of that company, recorded in his diary on 14 July his assessment of some of his fellow militiamen. "This day," he penned, "some of the cowards that wouldn't cross the river came down from Buffalo and joined our company again" (Walker, "A Soldier's Diary for 1814").

71. Brown to Chauncey, 13 July 1814, Brown's Orderly Book.

72. Ibid.

73. Tucker to Riall, 15 July 1814, and Porter to Brown, 16 July 1814, in *DHCNF* (1896), pp. 66–69. An examination of these two official reports illustrates how differently the opposing commanders perceived the fairly simple sequence of events.

74. Riall to Drummond and Drummond to Prevost, 15 July 1814, and Riall to Drummond, 17 July 1814, in *DHCNF* (1896), pp. 65, 59, 69–72; Drummond to Prevost, 16 July 1814, in Wood, *British Documents*, 3:132–37.

75. Gaines to Brown, 15 July 1814, Brown and Scott Papers, BECHS; Gaines to Morgan and Gaines to Brown, 16 July; Brown to Armstrong, 17 July; and Gaines to Brown, 20 July 1814, Brown's Orderly Book.

76. Riall to Drummond, 16 and 17 July 1814, and McFarland to wife, undated, in *DHCNF* (1896), pp. 66–67, 69–72, 73.

77. Brown's General Order, 19 July 1814, Izard's Order Book; Stone to Tompkins, 25 July 1814, and Secord's statement to the Assembly, undated, in *DHCNF* (1896), pp. 72–74; Riall to Drummond, 19 July 1814, in Wood, *British Documents*, 3:138–39.

78. Brown's General Order, 17 July 1814, Izard's Order Book; Douglass, "Reminiscences," p. 69.

79. Brown to Armstrong, 22 July 1814, in *DHCNF* (1896), pp. 86–87; Gaines to Brown, 15 July 1814, Brown and Scott Papers, BECHS.

80. Memoranda of Occurrences; J. B. Varnum Jr. to J. B. Varnum Sr., 24 July 1814, Manuscript Collection, BECHS; Merritt, "Journal," pp. 642–43; Douglass, "Reminiscences," pp. 69–70; Riall to Drummond, 21 and 22 July 1814, in *DHCNF* (1896), pp. 78–81.

81. Riall to Drummond, 17 and 20 July 1814, in *DHCNF* (1896), pp. 69–72, 75–76; Riall to Drummond, 10:30 P.M. 20 July 1814, in Wood, *British Documents*, 3:139–40.

82. Brown's General Order, 21 July 1814, Izard's Order Book; Brown to Gaines, 23 July 1814, Brown's Orderly Book.

83. Brown to Armstrong, 22 July 1814, Brown's Orderly Book; Riall to Drummond, 22 July 1814, in *DHCNF* (1896), p. 81; Douglass, "Reminiscences," p. 70.

84. Howard, *Diary.*

85. Gaines to Brown, 20 July 1814, Brown and Scott Papers, BECHS; Memoranda of Occurrences.

86. Brown's General Order, 23 July 1814, Izard's Order Book; Brown to Gaines, 23 July 1814, Brown and Scott Papers, BECHS; Memoranda of Occurrences; Brown to Armstrong, 25 July 1814, in *DHCNF* (1896), p. 87.

87. Armstrong to Brown, 22 July 1814, Memoranda of Occurrences; Jones to Chauncey, 24 July 1814, William Jones Papers, Historical Society of Pennsylvania; Winton-Clare, "A Shipbuilder's War," pp. 171–73.

88. Chauncey to Jones, 10 August 1814 (two letters), in *DHCNF* (1896), pp. 126–29.

89. Chauncey to Brown, 11 August 1814, in ibid., pp. 129–30.

90. Mahan, *Sea Power,* 2:301–2. A revisionist perspective is provided by William S. Dudley in his essay "Commodore Isaac Chauncey and U.S. Joint Operations on Lake Ontario" in *New Interpretations in Naval History,* ed. William B. Cogar (Annapolis, Md.: Naval Institute Press, 1989), pp. 139–55. Dudley proposes that Chauncey could not leave Yeo in his rear to attack Sacketts Harbor while he was delivering guns and supplies to Brown. Dudley's argument is weakened by two points. First, Brown did not need Chauncey's fleet. A few transports could have delivered guns and supplies as long as Yeo was blockaded in Kingston. Second, the fortifications at Sacketts Harbor had been considerably improved since the previous year, a fact not lost on Yeo and Drummond.

91. Izard to Armstrong, 10 June 1814, and Armstrong to Izard, 11 June 1814, in Izard, *Official Correspondence,* pp. 26–30, 33–34.

92. Izard to Armstrong, 25 June 1814, in ibid., pp. 35–40.

93. Ibid.

94. Izard to Armstrong, 19 July 1814, Secretary of War Letters Received (M221), roll 62, NA.

95. Izard to Armstrong, 3 July 1814, in Izard, *Official Correspondence,* pp. 45–47.

96. Totten to Izard, 11 July 1814, Secretary of War Letters Received (M221), roll 62, NA.

97. Izard to Armstrong, 19 July 1814, ibid.

98. Madison to Armstrong, Madison Papers, reel 27, LC.

99. Izard to Armstrong, 31 July 1814, Secretary of War Letters Received (M221), roll 62, NA; Izard to Armstrong, 7 August 1814, in Izard, *Official Correspondence,* pp. 60–61.

100. Bathurst to Prevost, 3 June 1814, in Hitsman, *Incredible War of 1812,* pp. 249–51; Prevost to Bathurst, 12 July 1814, in Hitsman, "Prevost's Conduct of the War," p. 41.

101. Lohnes, "A New Look at the Invasion of Eastern Maine," pp. 9–12; Prevost to Cochrane, 30 July 1814, in *DHCNF* (1896), pp. 176–77.

102. Brant, *James Madison,* pp. 270–71.

103. Ibid.; War Department Document, "Detail for the Militia Service under Requisition of July 4, 1814," in *ASP:MA,* 1:550.

104. Madison's notes on correspondence, 27 July 1814, Madison Papers, reel 27, LC; Brant, *James Madison,* pp. 264–66, 277–78.

Chapter 8. Lundy's Lane

1. Fortescue, *History of the British Army,* 10:111.

2. Harvey for Drummond to Riall, 23 July 1814, in *DHCNF* (1896), pp. 82–84.

3. Ibid.; Harvey for Drummond to Tucker, 23 July 1814, in ibid., pp. 84–85.

4. Drummond to Prevost, 23 July 1814, in ibid., pp. 85–86.

5. Prevost to Drummond, 25 July 1814, in ibid., pp. 170–71.

6. Brown to Gaines, 23 July 1814, Brown's Orderly Book; Gaines to Brown, 20 July 1814, Brown and Scott Papers, BECHS; Brown's General Order, 23 July 1814, and Brown's Morning Orders, 24 July 1814, Izard's Order Book; J. B. Varnum Jr. to J. B. Varnum Sr., 24 July 1814, Manuscript Collection, BECHS; Douglass, "Reminiscences," p. 71.

7. Crombie, "Papers of Major Daniel McFarland," p. 121.

8. Douglass, "Reminiscences," p. 71; Scott, *Memoirs,* p. 136; Memoranda of Occurrences.

9. Jesup, *Memoirs;* Leavenworth to Scott, 24 July 1814, Jesup Papers, LC.

10. Extract from *Niles' Register* reprinted in *DHCNF* (1896), pp. 74–75; Nicholas's biography appears in Lossing, *Pictorial Fieldbook,* p. 820.

11. Drummond to Prevost, 27 July 1814, in *DHCNF* (1896), pp. 87–92.

12. Donald E. Graves, *The Battle of Lundy's Lane* (Baltimore: Nautical and Aviation Publishing, 1993), p. 228. The second and revised edition of Graves's work is published under the title *Where Right and Glory Lead: The Battle of Lundy's Lane, 1814* (Toronto: Robin Brass Studio, 1997). Graves has not only made sense of the many conflicting reports of battle action at Lundy's Lane but also ferreted out details of organization and weaponry that eluded prior scholars. This study is indebted to his efforts.

13. Fortescue, *History of the British Army,* 10:112; Graves, *Lundy's Lane,* pp. 90–93.

14. Drummond to Prevost, 27 July 1814, in *DHCNF* (1896), pp. 87–92; Fortescue, *History of the British Army,* 10:111.

15. Drummond to Prevost, 27 July 1814, in *DHCNF* (1896), pp. 87–92; Graves, *Lundy's Lane,* pp. 90–91.

16. Brown to Armstrong, 7 August 1814, Brown's Orderly Book.

17. Jesup, *Memoirs.*

18. Fortescue, *History of the British Army,* 10:112; Graves, *Lundy's Lane,* p. 91.

19. Graves, *Lundy's Lane,* p. 228.

20. Memoranda of Occurrences; Brown to Armstrong, 7 August 1814, Brown's Orderly Book; Graves, *Lundy's Lane,* p. 95.

21. Scott, *Memoirs,* p. 138.

22. Douglass, "Reminiscences," pp. 71–72; Leavenworth's statement of the events of 25 July 1814, Manuscript Collection, BECHS.

23. Severance, "Service of Samuel Harris," p. 339; Douglass, "Reminiscences," p. 72.

24. Jesup, *Memoirs.*

25. Scott, *Memoirs,* p. 140.

26. Although Lossing and Babcock both provide descriptions of the battlefield at Lundy's Lane, the most complete depiction is found in Graves, *Lundy's Lane,* chaps. 6 and 7.

27. Norton, *Journal,* p. 359; Drummond to Prevost, 27 July 1814, in *DHCNF* (1896), pp. 87–92; Graves, *Lundy's Lane,* pp. 99–101.

28. Smith, "Drummer Boy," p. 57.

29. Scott, *Memoirs*, p. 140.

30. Leavenworth's statement, BECHS; Norton, *Journal*, p. 357; Graves, *Lundy's Lane,* pp. 112–13.

31. Leavenworth's statement, BECHS.

32. Scott, *Memoirs*, p. 141.

33. Ibid.

34. Norton, *Journal*, p. 357.

35. Leavenworth's statement, BECHS.

36. Jesup, *Memoirs.*

37. Baylies, *Ripley*, pp. 35–45; Miller to anon., 28 July 1814, and Porter to Tompkins, 29 July 1814, in *DHCNF* (1896), pp.105–6, 101–3.

38. Memoranda of Occurrences; Graves, *Lundy's Lane*, p. 121.

39. Memoranda of Occurrences; Douglass, "Reminiscences," pp. 72–73.

40. Brown to Armstrong, 7 August 1814, Brown's Orderly Book; Baylies, *Ripley*, p. 38; Graves, *Lundy's Lane*, pp. 125–27; Leavenworth's statement, BECHS.

41. Babcock, *Niagara Frontier*, p. 163; Graves, *Lundy's Lane*, p. 123.

42. Miller's memoir, in Armstrong, *Notices*, 2:222; McDonald's testimony, in Baylies, *Ripley*, p. 38; Graves, *Lundy's Lane*, p. 126.

43. Graves, *Lundy's Lane*, pp. 128–29.

44. Brown to Armstrong, 7 August 1814, Brown's Orderly Book; McDonald to Jesup, 18 March 1817, Jesup Papers, Manuscript Collection, Military History Institute; Baylies, *Ripley*, p. 38.

45. Miller's memoir, in Armstrong, *Notices*, 2:222; Miller to Brown, 20 November 1818, Memoranda of Occurrences; Douglass, "Reminiscences," p. 73.

46. Miller's memoir, in Armstrong, *Notices*, 2:222; Miller to wife, 28 July 1814, in Robert J. Holden, "General James Ripley: Collector of the Port of Salem Massachusetts," *Essex Institute Collections* 104 (October 1968): 283–302; Graves, *Lundy's Lane,* p. 131.

47. Graves, *Lundy's Lane*, pp. 134–35.

48. Douglass, "Reminiscences," p. 73; Memoranda of Occurrences; Jesup, *Memoirs;* Leavenworth's statement, BECHS; Graves, *Lundy's Lane*, p. 118.

49. For the organization of Drummond's force and a description of the three counterattacks, this study is indebted to the superb detective work and scholarship of Donald Graves.

50. Memoranda of Occurrences.

51. Lord, "War on the Canadian Frontier," p. 209.

52. Brown to Armstrong, 7 August 1814, Brown's Orderly Book.

53. Jesup, *Memoirs;* McDonald's testimony, in Baylies, *Ripley*, p. 38; Graves, *Lundy's Lane*, pp. 144–50.

54. Memoranda of Occurrences; Leavenworth's statement, BECHS.

55. Scott, *Memoirs*, p. 143.

56. Leavenworth's statement, BECHS; Scott, *Memoirs*, p. 143; Graves, *Lundy's Lane,* p. 151.

57. Memoranda of Occurrences; Jesup, *Memoirs*.

58. Jesup, *Memoirs;* McDonald's testimony, in Baylies, *Ripley*, p. 38; Graves, *Lundy's Lane*, pp. 153–54.

59. Brown to Armstrong, 7 August 1814, Brown's Orderly Book; Memoranda of Occurrences; Babcock, *Niagara Frontier*, p. 171.

60. Jesup, *Memoirs;* Memoranda of Occurrences.

61. Memoranda of Occurrences; Porter and Miller to Brown, 29 July 1815, Memoranda of Occurrences; Jesup, *Memoirs;* Brown to Armstrong, 7 August 1814, Brown's Orderly Book.

62. Brown to Armstrong, 7 August 1814, Brown's Orderly Book; Memoranda of Occurrences.

63. Memoranda of Occurrences; Leavenworth's statement, BECHS; Babcock, *Niagara Frontier*, p. 169.

64. An American regimental surgeon, Dr. Bull, rode to the battlefield at daybreak and saw no sign of the British. "I went forward more than a mile beyond this point [the battlefield] and saw no enemy" (Bull's statement, 31 July 1814, in *DHCNF* [1896], p. 104).

65. Byfield's observations are found in John Gellner, ed., *Recollections of the War of 1812: Three Eyewitness Accounts* (Toronto: Baxter, 1964), p. 38. Sergeant Commins also recalled that the bodies were burned rather than buried and stated that "although it may appear inhuman was absolutely necessary and consequently justifiable."

66. Fredriksen, "Niagara, 1814," p. 157.

67. Douglass, "Reminiscences," p. 127.

68. Jesup, *Memoirs*.

69. Douglass, "Reminiscences," p. 128.

70. Leavenworth's statement, BECHS.

71. Douglass, "Reminiscences," p. 127.

72. Lossing, *Pictorial Fieldbook*, p. 829.

73. Drummond to Prevost, 27 July 1814, in Wood, *British Documents*, 3:144–51; Austin for Brown to Armstrong, 29 July 1814, Brown's Orderly Book; Brown to Porter and Miller, and Porter and Miller to Brown, 29 July 1815, Memoranda of Occurrences.

74. The most thorough analysis of battle casualties is found in Graves, *Lundy's Lane*, pp. 173–86. It would be difficult to challenge or to improve on Graves's findings.

75. Chauncey to Brown, 10 August 1814, Brown's Orderly Book.

76. Brown to Chauncey, 4 September 1814, Brown's Orderly Book.

77. Mahan, *Sea Power*, 2:308.

78. Fortescue, *History of the British Army*, 10:116.

79. Drummond's General Order, 1 August 1814, cautions his soldiers that instances of ill discipline "reduce us to the level of our opponents—and take from us all our advantages as disciplined troops."

80. McDonald to Kennedy, 27 July 1814, in *DHCNF* (1896), p. 114.

81. Drummond's Proclamation, *York Gazette*, 25 July 1814.

82. Porter to Tompkins, 29 July 1814, in *DHCNF* (1896), pp. 101–3.

83. Graves estimates that the First Brigade suffered 60 percent casualties in the first phase of the battle. See Graves, *Lundy's Lane*, p. 113.

84. Brown to Armstrong, 7 August 1814, in *DHCNF* (1896), pp. 97–101.

85. Jesup, *Memoirs*.

86. Brown to Armstrong, 7 August 1814, in *DHCNF* (1896), pp. 97–101.

Chapter 9.   The Siege of Fort Erie

1. Memoranda of Occurrences.

2. Douglass, "Reminiscences," p. 128; Owen, *Fort Erie*, p. 49.

3. Douglass, "Reminiscences," p. 129.

4. Brown to Ripley, 31 July 1814, Memoranda of Occurrences.

5. Smith, "Drummer Boy," p. 60.

6. Douglass, "Reminiscences," p. 138.

7. Ibid., p. 129; Silver, *Edmund Pendleton Gaines*, pp. 40–41; Fredriksen, "Niagara 1814," p. 179.

8. Gaines to Brown, 27 July 1814, Brown and Scott Papers, BECHS.

9. Brown to Tompkins, 1 and 19 August 1814, Brown's Orderly Book; extract from *Niles' Register*, 13 August 1814, reprinted in *DHCNF* (1896), p. 110.

10. Brown to Tompkins, 1 August 1814, Brown's Orderly Book.

11. Porter to Tompkins, 29 July 1814, in *DHCNF* (1896), pp. 101–3.

12. Asa Warren, "Two Dramatic Incidents," *Buffalo Historical Society Publications* 5 (1902): 61–62.

13. General Order, 26 July 1814, in Wood, *British Documents*, 3:151–57.

14. Martin to Tweeddale, 2 August 1814, Papers of George Hay, National Library of Scotland.

15. Norton, *Journal*, p. 359; Douglass, "Reminiscences," p. 129.

16. Drummond to Prevost, 31 July 1814, in *DHCNF* (1896), pp. 115–16.

17. General Orders, 1 August 1814, in Wood, *British Documents*, 3:171–74.

18. Harvey to Conran, 2 August 1814, and Drummond to Prevost, 4 August 1814, in ibid., 3:174–76, 167–70.

19. Morgan to Brown, 5 August 1814, in *DHCNF* (1896), pp. 121–22.

20. Morgan to Brown, 5 August 1814, in ibid.; Babcock, *Niagara Frontier*, pp. 184–88.

21. Tucker to Conran, 4 August 1814, in Wood, *British Documents*, 3:177–78; Morgan to Brown, 5 August 1814, in *DHCNF* (1896), pp.121–22.

22. Drummond to Prevost, 4 August 1814, in Wood, *British Documents*, 3:167–70.

23. Prevost to Bathurst, 5 August 1814, nos. 183 and 184, in *DHCNF* (1896), pp. 172–73.

24. Izard to Secretary of War, 11 August 1814, Secretary of War Letters Received (M221), roll 62, NA; Arnold Smith to Samuel Brown, 4 August 1814, Scott and Brown Papers, BECHS.

25. Tompkins to Major General Lewis, 2 August 1814, and Tompkins's address to the Legislature, 27 September 1814, in *Tompkins Papers*, vol. 3.

26. J. B. Varnum Jr. to J. B. Varnum Sr., 11 August 1814, Manuscript Collection, BECHS.

27. Brown to Armstrong, 5 August 1814, Brown's Orderly Book.

28. Whitehorne, *While Washington Burned,* pp. 48–49.

29. Gaines to Brown, 7 August 1814, Brown's Orderly Book.

30. Ibid.; Drummond to Prevost, 8 August 1814, in *DHCNF* (1896), pp. 124–26.

31. Chauncey to Brown, 7 August 1814, Brown's Memoranda, LC.

32. B. P. Hughes, "Siege Artillery in the 19th Century," *Journal of the Society for Army Historical Research* 60 (autumn 1982): 130.

33. Whitehorne, *While Washington Burned,* pp. 56–57.

34. William Dunlop, *Recollections of the War of 1812,* 2d ed. (Toronto: Historical Publishing Company, 1908), pp. 62–63.

35. Drummond to Prevost, 8 August 1814, in *DHCNF* (1896), pp. 124–26.

36. Douglass, "Reminiscences," p. 131.

37. Gaines to Brown, 10 August 1814, Brown's Orderly Book.

38. Gardner to McNeil, 9 August 1814, John McNeil Papers, LC; Gardner to Jesup, 9 August 1814, Jesup Papers, LC. These two orders carry the names of all six recipients of brevets. Lieutenant Varnum wrote that the garrison was "hourly in expectation of a spirited attack" (Varnum to Varnum, 10 August 1814, Manuscript Collection, BECHS).

39. Porter to Tompkins, 9 August 1814, in *DHCNF,* 2:431; Gaines to Brown, 10 August 1814, Brown's Orderly Book.

40. Varnum to Varnum, 11 August 1814, Manuscript Collection, BECHS; Drummond to Prevost, 12 August 1814, in *DHCNF* (1896), pp.132–34; Brown to Armstrong, 10 August 1814, Brown's Orderly Book.

41. Gaines to Brown, 10 August 1814, Brown and Scott Papers, BECHS; Gaines to Secretary of War, 11 and 13 August 1814, in *DHCNF* (1896), pp. 137–38; Drummond to Prevost, 12 August 1814, in *DHCNF* (1896), pp. 132–34.

42. Dobbs to Yeo and Drummond to Prevost, 13 August 1814, and Conklin to Kennedy, 16 August 1814, in *DHCNF* (1896), pp. 134–37; Fredriksen, "Chronicle of Valor," p. 284.

43. Drummond to Prevost, 12 August 1814, in *DHCNF* (1896), pp.132–34.

44. Scott to his brother, 12 August 1814, and Drummond to Prevost, 12 August 1814, in *DHCNF* (1896), pp. 130–34.

45. Drummond to Prevost, 13 August 1814, in ibid., p. 134; Report of Killed and Wounded, undated, in ibid., p. 137; Silver, *Edmund Pendleton Gaines,* p. 42. The story of the barbershop decapitation is found in Babcock, *Niagara Frontier,* p. 191, and Whitehorne, *While Washington Burned,* p. 61.

46. Harvey to Fischer, 14 August 1814, in Wood, *British Documents,* 3:185–87.

47. Douglass, "Reminiscences," p. 131. Although several descriptions of Fort Erie survive, none gives a "snapshot" of the defensive works at the time of the 15 August assault. The Public Archives of Canada possesses three maps of the American camp, two drawn from the British perspective (i.e., from the outside looking in), and a third drawn in November after the Americans vacated the fort and blew up the walls. A fourth map and description come to us from Lieutenant David Douglass of the company of bombardiers, sappers, and miners. Douglass's documents are found in the William Trimble Papers at the Ohio Historical Society.

48. The precise arrangement of the defenders cannot be found in a single primary source. The most useful sources are Gaines to Secretary of War, 23 August 1814, in

DHCNF (1896), pp. 151–52; Douglass, "Reminiscences," pp. 131–33; Babcock, *Niagara Frontier,* p. 193; Lossing, *Pictorial Fieldbook,* p. 834; Fredriksen, "Niagara, 1814," pp. 200–203; and Silver, *Edmund Pendleton Gaines,* p. 43. Biographical information for Major William Allen Trimble is found in Fredriksen, *Officers,* pp. 85–87.

49. Drummond to Prevost, 15 August 1814, in Wood, *British Documents,* 3:178–84; Silver, *Edmund Pendleton Gaines,* p. 46.

50. Ripley to Gaines, 17 August 1814, in *DHCNF* (1896), pp. 156–58.

51. Ripley to Gaines, 17 August 1814, and Gaines to the Secretary of War, 23 August 1814, in *DHCNF* (1896), pp. 156–58, 151–52.

52. Fischer to Harvey, 15 August 1814, in ibid., pp. 144–45.

53. Norton, *Journal,* p. 363.

54. Douglass, "Reminiscences," p. 132; Ernest A. Cruikshank, "Drummond's Night Assault upon Fort Erie, August 15–16, 1814," in Zaslow, *The Defended Border,* p. 159.

55. Ripley to Gaines, 17 August 1814, and Gaines to the Secretary of War, 23 August 1814, in *DHCNF* (1896), pp. 156–58, 152–56; Cruikshank, "Drummond's Night Assault," p. 159; Whitehorne, *While Washington Burned,* p. 63.

56. Douglass, "Reminiscences," p. 133.

57. There were several theories on the cause of the explosion, usually addressing the issue of whether it was caused intentionally or accidentally. A most interesting exchange of letters was published in various newspapers in western New York in 1853. These letters were republished in *Historical Magazine* 2 (October 1873): 216–24.

58. J. LeCouteur to his brother, 29 July 1869, in *DHCNF* (1896), pp. 168–69; William Dunlop, *Recollections of the War of 1812* (Toronto: Historical Publishing Company, 1908), pp. 84–85.

59. Douglass, "Reminiscences," p. 134.

60. Return of Killed, Wounded, and Missing, in *DHCNF* (1896), pp. 148–49.

61. Lossing, *Pictorial Fieldbook,* p. 835.

62. Drummond to Prevost, 15 and 16 August 1814, in Wood, *British Documents,* 3:178–84, 189–94; Prevost to Drummond, 26 August 1814, in *DHCNF* (1896), pp. 174–75.

63. Izard to Secretary of War, 31 July 1814, Secretary of War Letters Received (M221), roll 62, NA.

64. Izard to Secretary of War, 7 August 1814, ibid.; Brant, *James Madison,* p. 281; Fredriksen, "Niagara, 1814," p. 174; Izard, *Official Correspondence,* pp. 61–63.

65. Armstrong to Brown, 16 August 1814, Brown's Orderly Book.

66. Izard to Secretary of War, 11 and 20 August 1814, Secretary of War Letters Received (M221), roll 62, NA.

67. Izard to Secretary of War, 11 and 23 August 1814, and Cumming to Izard, 14 August 1814, ibid.

68. Maurigault, "Military Career of George Izard," p. 473.

69. Izard to Macomb, 23 August 1814, Secretary of War Letters Received (M221), roll 62, NA.

70. Madison to Armstrong, 12 August 1814, Madison Papers, reel 27, LC.

71. Madison to Armstrong, 13 August 1814, ibid.

72. Madison to Armstrong, 14 August 1814, ibid.

73. When he arrived off Kingston, Chauncey wrote to Secretary of the Navy Jones: "My fixed determination has always been to seek a meeting with the enemy the moment the fleet was ready, and to deprive him of any apology for not meeting me" (Chauncey to Jones, 10 August 1814, in *DHCNF* [1896], pp. 128–29).

74. Croghan was the nephew of George Rogers Clark and had successfully commanded Fort Stephenson during its long siege. Croghan's reputation did not suffer from his failure at Michilimackinac, and he died a brevet brigadier general.

75. This summary of the campaign against Michilimackinac is derived from several sources. Chief among them are Hitsman, *Incredible War of 1812*, pp. 204–5; Stanley, *War of 1812*, pp. 293–95; and Lossing, *Pictorial Fieldbook*, p. 850.

76. Executive Document, Secretary of War to State Governors, 4 July 1814, in *ASP:MA*, 1:550.

77. Memoranda of Occurrences; Tompkins to Brown and Tompkins to Lewis, 13 August 1814, Brown and Scott Papers, BECHS; Tompkins to Yates, 13 August 1814, in *Tompkins Papers*, 3:495–96; Brown to Gaines, 20 August 1814, and Brown to Tompkins, 21 August 1814, Brown's Orderly Book.

78. This account of the defensive efforts in New York City is taken from Lossing, *Pictorial Fieldbook*, pp. 969–77. The regular army engineer charged with designing the defenses was Colonel Joseph G. Swift, the first graduate of West Point. A summary of the defensive preparations is found in Ellery, *Memoirs of General Joseph Gardner Swift*, pp. 133–45.

79. Congressional Document: Services of the Militia of Massachusetts, 23 February 1824, in *ASP:MA*, 3:8–31.

80. Bathurst to Sherbrooke, 6 June 1814, Public Archives of Nova Scotia.

81. George F.G. Stanley, "British Operations on the Penobscot in 1814," *Journal of the Society for Army Historical Research* 19 (1940): 168–78; Lohnes, "A New Look at the Invasion of Eastern Maine."

82. Quoted in Babcock, *Niagara Frontier*, pp. 140–43.

83. Prevost to Cochrane, 30 July 1814, in *DHCNF* (1896), pp. 176–77.

84. Van Ness to Richard M. Johnson, 23 November 1814, in *ASP:MA*, 1:580–82.

85. Brant, *James Madison*, pp. 284–87.

86. Mahon, *War of 1812*, pp. 289–305.

87. Brant, *James Madison*, p. 304.

88. Madison recorded this meeting in an undated memorandum, Madison Papers, reel 27, LC.

89. A short, useful analysis of the negotiations to end the war can be found in chapter 15 of Burt's *The United States, Great Britain and British North America*.

90. Commissioners to Secretary of State, 12 and 19 August 1814, in *ASP:FA*, 3:705–10.

Chapter 10. The Siege Ends

1. Douglass, "Reminiscences," p. 135.

2. Owen, *Fort Erie*, p. 50; Fredriksen, "Niagara 1814," p. 228.

3. Lord, "War on the Canadian Frontier," p. 211; Dunlop, *Recollections,* pp. 58–59.

4. McMahon to Jarvis, 22 August 1814, and Gaines to Secretary of War, 23 August 1814, in *DHCNF* (1896), pp. 166–68, 151–52.

5. Dunlop, *Recollections,* p. 67.

6. Drummond to Prevost, 21 and 27 August 1814, and Gaines to Secretary of War, 23 August 1814, in *DHCNF* (1896), pp. 183–86, 188–89, 166–68; Douglass, "Reminiscences," p. 136.

7. Drummond to Prevost, 27 August 1814, in *DHCNF* (1896), pp. 188–89; Douglass, "Reminiscences," p. 136; Fredriksen, "Niagara, 1814," p. 229.

8. Douglass, "Reminiscences," p. 136.

9. Brown to Armstrong, 19 and 25 August 1814, Brown's Orderly Book; Brown to Gaines, 20 August 1814, Brown and Scott Papers, BECHS.

10. Drummond to Prevost, 16 August 1814, in Wood, *British Documents,* 3:189–94; Baynes to anonymous (probably Drummond), 26 August 1814, Dickson to Meyers, 28 August 1814, and Stovin to Drummond, 28 August 1814, Brown and Scott Papers, BECHS; Prevost to Drummond, 26 August 1814, in *DHCNF* (1896), pp. 174–75.

11. Drummond to Prevost, 18 August 1814, in Wood, *British Documents,* 3:194–95.

12. Ibid.; Drummond to Yeo, 18 August 1814, and Drummond to Prevost, 21 August 1814, in *DHCNF* (1896), pp. 182–86.

13. Prevost to Bathurst and Robinson to Prevost, 27 August 1814, in *DHCNF* (1896), pp. 179–82.

14. Drummond to Prevost, 24 August 1814, and Militia General Order, 25 August 1814, in *DHCNF* (1896), pp. 186–87.

15. Memoranda of Occurrences; Brown to Armstrong, 31 August 1814, Brown's Orderly Book. On 9 October 1814, Major General Gaines, then sufficiently recovered from his wounds, assumed command of the Fourth Military District, which encompassed eastern Pennsylvania, Delaware, and New Jersey.

16. Tompkins to Davis, 10 September 1814, Tompkins to Lewis, 15 September 1814, and Tompkins to Monroe, 29 September 1814, in *Tompkins Papers,* 3:528–29, 555.

17. A satisfactory account of the British campaign against the American base at Plattsburg is found in Allan S. Everest, *The War of 1812 in the Champlain Valley* (Syracuse, N.Y.: Syracuse University Press, 1981), pp. 164–92. See also Edward P. Hamilton, "The Battle of Plattsburg," *Vermont History* 31 (1963): 94–105, and James A. Carr, "Climax at Lake Champlain," *National Defense* (November–December 1978): 59–92.

18. Macomb's report appears in Macomb to Williams, published in *Journal of the Military Service Institution* 12 (1891): 76–79. Plattsburg's defensive works were designed by Macomb's three West Point–educated officers: Joseph G. Totten, Rene DeRussy, and George Trescott.

19. Everest, *War in the Champlain Valley,* pp. 179–87.

20. Ibid., pp. 185–90.

21. Bathurst to Prevost, 3 June 1814, quoted in Hitsman, "Prevost's Conduct of the War," p. 41.

22. This account of the battle for Baltimore is taken largely from Mahon, *War of 1812,* pp. 305–16, and Jacobs and Tucker, *War of 1812,* pp. 151–52.

23. Monroe to Barbour, 2 October 1814, in *ASP:MA,* 1:524.

24. Strength report dated 31 August 1814, in Babcock, *Niagara Frontier,* p. 216.

25. Brown to Chauncey, 4 September 1814, Brown's Orderly Book.

26. Memoranda of Occurrences.

27. Drummond to Prevost, 2 September 1814, in *DHCNF* (1896), pp. 190–91.

28. Ripley's General Order, 6 September 1814, in ibid., pp. 194–95; Graves, "Canadian Volunteers," pp. 115–16.

29. Drummond to Prevost, 8 September 1814, in *DHCNF* (1896), pp. 195–97; Steppler, "A Duty Troublesome beyond Measure," p. 190.

30. Drummond to Prevost, 11 September 1814, in *DHCNF* (1896), pp. 198–99.

31. Drummond to Prevost, 11 and 14 September 1814, in ibid., pp. 198–201.

32. Yates to Tompkins, 3 September 1814, in ibid., p. 192; Fredriksen, "Niagara, 1814," p. 236.

33. Brown to Tompkins, 26 September 1814, Brown's Orderly Book; Babcock, *Niagara Frontier,* p. 215; Dorsheimer, "Buffalo during the War," p. 206; Elijah D. Efner, "The Adventures and Enterprises of Elijah D. Efner," *Buffalo Historical Society Publications* 4 (1896): 41; Douglass, "Reminiscences," p. 139.

34. Brown to Chauncey, 4 September 1814, and Brown to Izard, 9, 15, and 18 September 1814, Brown's Orderly Book.

35. Memoranda of Occurrences; Jesup, *Memoirs;* Lossing, *Pictorial Fieldbook,* p. 837.

36. Memoranda of Occurrences; Brown to Izard, 11 September 1814, and Brown to Monroe, 29 September 1814, Brown's Orderly Book; Brown to Tompkins, 29 September 1814, in *DHCNF* (1896), pp. 211–15.

37. Memoranda of Occurrences.

38. Porter to Brown, 23 September 1814, in *DHCNF* (1896), pp. 208–11; William A. Bird, "The Sortie from Fort Erie," *Buffalo Historical Society Publications* 5 (1902): 95–98. See also Douglass, "Reminiscences," p. 140. Fraser was a lieutenant in the Fifteenth Infantry and a militia major while on duty with General Porter. Jesup disputes any significant involvement by Porter before the attack. He stated in his memoirs that he "was in a situation to know that the conception, plan and execution, were all his [Brown's] alone."

39. Memoranda of Occurrences.

40. Izard to Brown, 13 September 1814, and Brown to Izard, 17 September 1814, Brown's Orderly Book.

41. Whitehorne, *While Washington Burned,* p. 76; Fredriksen, "Niagara, 1814," p. 237; Steppler, "A Duty Troublesome beyond Measure," p. 192.

42. Porter to Brown, 23 September 1814, in *DHCNF* (1896), pp. 208–11; Brown to Monroe, 29 September 1814, Brown's Orderly Book; Babcock, *Niagara Frontier,* p. 226.

43. Brown to Monroe, 29 September 1814, Brown's Orderly Book; Efner, "Adventures," p. 53; Lord, "War on the Canadian Frontier," p. 210; Memoranda of Occurrences.

44. Brown to Monroe, 29 September 1814, Brown's Orderly Book; Porter to Brown, 23 September 1814, in *DHCNF* (1896), pp. 208–11; Efner, "Adventures," p. 53.

45. Drummond's General Order, 18 September 1814, and Drummond to Prevost, 19 September 1814, in *DHCNF* (1896), pp. 202–6; Dunlop, *Recollections,* pp. 74–75.

46. Brown to Monroe, 29 September 1814, Brown's Orderly Book; Jesse Perse Harmon, "War of 1812: Experiences of Jesse Perse Harmon," *Vermont Quarterly* 21 (Janu-

ary, 1953): 50–51; Baylies, *Ripley,* pp. 70–71; Miller to wife Ruth, McNeil Papers, LC; Dunlop, *Recollections,* pp. 74–75.

47. Brown to Secretary of War, 29 September 1814, in *DHCNF* (1896), pp. 211–15; De Watteville to Drummond, 19 September 1814, in Wood, *British Documents,* 3:195–99.

48. Brown to Monroe, 29 September 1814, Brown's Orderly Book.

49. Brown to Monroe, 29 September1814, and Brown to Tompkins, 20 September 1814, Brown's Orderly Book.

50. Drummond to Prevost, 21 September 1814, quoted in Hitsman, *Incredible War of 1812,* p. 83; Harvey's Memorandum, 21 September 1814, in Wood, *British Documents,* 3:201–2; Lord, "War on the Canadian Frontier," p. 211; Norton, *Journal,* pp. 363–65.

51. Brown to Izard, 23 September 1814, and Brown to Monroe, 29 September 1814, Brown's Orderly Book

Chapter 11. Izard's Offensive

1. Chauncey to Izard, 11 September 1814, in Izard, *Official Correspondence,* p. 79. Chauncey wrote that "the fleet under my command shall be in a state of preparation to receive the troops as soon as they arrive."

2. Armstrong to Izard, 12 August 1814, in Izard, *Official Correspondence,* pp. 69–71.

3. Brown to Izard, 10 September 1814, in ibid., p. 86.

4. Brown to Izard, 11 September 1814, in ibid., pp. 87–88.

5. "Minutes of Correspondence between General Izard and Commodore Chauncey," Secretary of War Letters Received (M221), roll 62, NA; Izard to Chauncey, 16 September 1814, in Izard, *Official Correspondence,* pp. 80–81.

6. Izard to Armstrong, 17 September 1814, in Izard, *Official Correspondence,* p. 90.

7. Izard to Monroe, 18 September 1814, Monroe Papers, reel 5, LC.

8. Izard to Monroe, 20 September 1814, Secretary of War Letters Received (M221), roll 62, NA.

9. Izard to Monroe, 28 September 1814, in Izard, *Official Correspondence,* pp. 92–95.

10. Izard to Brown, 25 September 1814, and Brown to Izard, 26 September 1814, Brown's Orderly Book; Izard to Monroe, 28 September 1814, in Izard, *Official Correspondence,* pp. 92–95.

11. Izard to Brown, 28 September 1814, Brown's Orderly Book.

12. Izard to Monroe, 28 September 1814, in Izard, *Official Correspondence,* pp. 92–95.

13. Izard to Brown, 1 October 1814, and Brown to Izard, 2 and 5 October 1814, Brown's Orderly Book.

14. Monroe to Izard, 27 September 1814, and Izard to Monroe, 7 October 1814, in Izard, *Official Correspondence,* pp. 95–96.

15. A short biography of Bissell is Harold W. Ryan, "Daniel Bissell—His Story," *Missouri Historical Society Review* 12 (October 1955): 32–44.

16. Drummond to Prevost, 24 September 1814, in Wood, *British Documents,* 3:199–201.

17. Drummond to Prevost, 28 September 1814, PAC, RG8, C685, pp. 293–94; Prevost to Bathurst, 11 October 1814, in *DHCNF* (1896), p. 245.

18. Drummond to Prevost, 2 October 1814, in Wood, *British Documents*, 3:204–6.

19. Izard to Monroe, 7 October 1814, in Izard, *Official Correspondence*, pp. 97–99; Izard to Brown, 6 October 1814, Brown's Orderly Book.

20. Brown to Izard, 7 and 8 October 1814, Brown's Orderly Book.

21. Izard to Brown, 9 October 1814, Brown's Orderly Book; Izard to Monroe, 16 October 1814, in Izard, *Official Correspondence*, pp. 100–104.

22. Drummond to Prevost, 10 October 1814, in Wood, *British Documents*, 3:208–10.

23. Brown to Armstrong, 2 November 1814, Brown and Scott Papers, BECHS.

24. Frank A. Updyke, *The Diplomacy of the War of 1812* (Baltimore: Johns Hopkins University Press, 1915); Burt, *The United States, Great Britain and British North America*, pp. 357–61.

25. Izard to Monroe, 16 October 1814, in Izard, *Official Correspondence*, pp. 100–104.

26. Drummond to Prevost and Harvey to Stovin and Tweeddale, 11 October 1814, in Wood, *British Documents*, pp. 211–17; Hay, "Recollections," p. 74.

27. Izard to Monroe, 16 October 1814, in Izard, *Official Correspondence*, pp. 100–104. A soldier of the Seventeenth Infantry wrote home that "our first cannonading silenced theirs. Ours played some time and theirs was still" (Sprague to Haydon, 27 October 1814, Manuscript Collection, BECHS).

28. Brown to Armstrong, 2 November 1814, Brown and Scott Papers, BECHS.

29. Drummond to Prevost, 15 October 1814, in Wood, *British Documents*, pp. 217–18.

30. Izard to Monroe, 16 October 1814, in Izard, *Official Correspondence*, pp. 100–104.

31. Ibid.

32. Brown to Armstrong, 2 November 1814, Brown and Scott Papers, BECHS.

33. Drummond to Prevost, 18 October 1814, in Wood, *British Documents*, pp. 219–21; Izard to Monroe, 23 October 1814, in Izard, *Official Correspondence*, pp. 104–6.

34. Izard to Monroe, 23 October 1814, in Izard, *Official Correspondence*, pp. 104–6.

35. Bissell to Izard, 22 October 1814, in John C. Fredriksen, ed., "A Poor but Honest Sodger: Colonel Cromwell Pearce 16th U.S. Infantry and the War of 1812," *Pennsylvania History* 52 (July 1985): 150.

36. No one has successfully reconstructed the battle action at Lyon's Creek. The reports are incomplete and confusing. The following tactical description appears to reconcile most of the primary sources, which are Bissell to Izard, 22 October 1814, and Pearce's account, in Fredriksen, "A Poor but Honest Sodger, " p. 150; Drummond to Prevost, 18 October 1814, and Myers to Drummond, 19 October 1814, in Wood, *British Documents*, 3:219–26; and Hay, "Recollections," p. 75.

37. Myers to Drummond, 19 October 1814, in Wood, *British Documents*, 3:221–26; Bissell to Izard, 22 October 1814.

38. Bissell to Izard, 22 October 1814.

39. Drummond to Prevost, 20 October 1814, in Wood, *British Documents*, 3:221–26.

40. Izard to Brown, 20 October 1814, Brown's Orderly Book.

41. Mitchell, in command of army troops at Sacketts Harbor, sent three messages to Izard reporting on Chauncey's fear for the safety of his base. See Mitchell to Izard, 10, 15, and 25 October 1814, in Izard, *Official Correspondence*, p. 145. Brown was concerned that his division be put on the road quickly. In his note to Izard agreeing to take command of Sacketts Harbor, he requested that Winder follow him "as soon as possible with

the troops" (Brown to Izard, 19 October 1814, Brown's Orderly Book). Izard was careful to explain to the secretary of war that sending Brown away was a mutual decision of the two division commanders (Izard to Monroe, 23 October 1814, in Izard, *Official Correspondence,* pp. 104–6).

42. Izard to Monroe, 23 October 1814, Secretary of War Letters Received (M221), roll 62, NA.

43. Drummond to Prevost, 20 October 1814, in Wood, *British Documents,* 3:221–26.

44. Whitehorne, *While Washington Burned,* pp. 88–89.

45. Norton, *Journal,* p. 366; Izard to Monroe, 17 November 1814, in Izard, *Official Correspondence,* pp. 118–19.

46. Monroe to Izard, 24 October 1814, in Izard, *Official Correspondence,* pp. 107–9.

47. Izard to Monroe, 2 November 1814, in ibid., pp. 110–13.

48. A British officer recorded that "deserters are coming in from them every day in great numbers, young boys without a shoe to their feet complaining they have no pay for this twelvemonths" (Captain William Sleigh to his parents, 24 October 1814, George Hay Papers, National Library of Scotland).

49. Izard to Monroe, 2 November 1814, in Izard, *Official Correspondence,* pp. 110–13.

50. Drummond to Prevost, 23 October 1814, in Wood, *British Documents,* 3:226–31.

51. Dunlop, *Recollections,* p. 87.

52. Drummond to Prevost, 26 and 30 October and 5 and 9 November 1814, and Drummond to Yeo, 4 November 1814, in Wood, *British Documents,* pp. 232–49.

53. This short account of McArthur's expedition is derived from several sources. See Robert B. McAfee, *History of the Late War in the Western Country* (1816; reprint, Bowling Green, Ohio: Historical Publishing Company, 1919), pp. 479–89; Norton, *Journal,* pp. 369–70; Cruikshank, "County of Norfolk"; Stanley, "Contribution of the Canadian Militia," in Mason, *After Tippecanoe,* pp. 43–44.

54. Drummond to Prevost, 26 October 1814, in Wood, *British Documents,* 3:232–33.

55. Drummond to Prevost, 30 October 1814, in ibid., 3:234–36.

56. Drummond to Prevost, 30 October 1814, in ibid., 3:245–49.

57. Norton, *Journal,* pp. 369–70.

58. Totten to Izard, 1 November 1814, and Izard to Monroe, 8 November 1814, in Izard, *Official Correspondence,* pp. 150–51, 114–16; Drummond to Prevost, 5 November 1814, in Wood, *British Documents,* 3:239–44; Harmon, "Experiences of Jesse Perse Harmon."

59. Monroe to Izard, 9 November 1814, in Izard, *Official Correspondence,* pp. 117–18.

60. Izard to Monroe, 8 and 26 November 1814, in ibid., pp. 114–16, 121–22; Sinclair to Izard, 16 November 1814, and Izard to Miller, 21 November 1814, Secretary of War Letters Received (M221), roll 62, NA.

61. Izard to Monroe, 26 November 1814, in Izard, *Official Correspondence,* pp. 121–22.

62. Fredriksen, "A Poor but Honest Sodger," p. 151.

63. Izard to Monroe, 8 and 20 November and 18 December 1814, in Izard, *Official Correspondence,* pp. 114–16, 119–20, 130–31.

64. Monroe to Izard, 26 November 1814 and 12 January 1815, and Izard to Monroe, 1 and 15 January 1815, in Izard, *Official Correspondence,* pp. 124–25, 135, 131–33; Fredriksen, "A Poor but Honest Sodger," p. 151.

65. Monroe to Senate, 17 October 1814, in *ASP:MA*, 1:514–15; Brant, *James Madison*, p. 337.

66. Speech by John C. Calhoun, 25 October 1814, in *AC*, 13-3:465–70.

67. Monroe to Izard, 26 November 1814, in Izard, *Official Correspondence*, pp. 124–25.

68. As late as 26 October, the American negotiators warned Monroe that Britain would seize New Orleans and retain it by virtue of *uti possidetis* as the basis of a settlement. See Russell to Monroe, 26 October 1814, Monroe Papers, reel 5, LC. Two articles analyze the reasons why Britain gave up the demand for *uti possidetis*. The reader is referred to Dudley Mills, "The Duke of Wellington and the Peace Negotiations at Ghent in 1814," *Canadian Historical Review* 2 (March 1921): 19–32; and Wilbur D. Jones, ed., "A British View of the War of 1812 and the Peace Negotiations," *Mississippi Valley Historical Review* 45 (1958): 481–87.

Chapter 12. Conclusion

1. Brown to Armstrong, 2 November 1814, Brown and Scott Papers, BECHS.

Afterword

1. Monroe to Brown, 2 January 1815, and Monroe to Porter, 16 January 1815, Secretary of War Letters Sent (M6), NA. An interesting analysis of Monroe's efforts is C. P. Stacey, "An American Plan for a Canadian Campaign," *American Historical Review* 46 (January 1941): 348–57. Stacey is mildly critical of Monroe's handling of planning details but is generally approving of his strategic sense.

2. Monroe to Tompkins, 4 February 1815, Secretary of War Confidential Letters Sent (M7), NA.

3. Ibid.

4. Monroe to Brown, 10 February 1815, Secretary of War Confidential Letters Sent (M7), NA.

5. Ibid.; Monroe to Macomb, 10 February 1815, ibid.

6. Monroe to Scott, 21 February 1815, ibid.

7. Monroe to Giles, 22 February 1815, Secretary of War Reports to Congress (M220), NA.

8. Dallas to Jackson and Brown, 14 March 1815; Graham to Gaines, Scott, and Macomb, 21 March 1815; and Dallas to Ripley, 21 April 1815, Secretary of War Confidential Letters Sent (M7), NA.

9. Graham to Brown, Scott, and Macomb, 21 March 1815; Graham to Jackson, 27 March 1815; Graham to Gaines, 27 March 1815; Dallas to Commanding Officers of the Army, 14 March 1815, Secretary of War Confidential Letters Sent (M7), NA. Graham to McArthur, 3 April 1815, Secretary of War Letters Sent (M6), NA.

10. Dallas to Brown, Macomb, and Scott, 8 and 17 April 1815, Secretary of War Confidential Letters Sent (M7), NA; Dallas to Parker, 10 April 1815, and Dallas to Brown, Scott, Macomb, and Ripley, 18 April 1815, Secretary of War Letters Sent (M6), NA.

11. Dallas to Brown, Scott, Macomb, and Ripley, 10 May 1815, Secretary of War Letters Sent (M6), NA.

12. The results of the selection board have not survived, and there is no record of any adjustments made by Madison prior to their being sent to the Senate. It is interesting to note that two brigadier generals were retained as colonels, as well as a handful of majors retained as captains. They kept their wartime ranks as brevets.

13. The Calhoun reforms are addressed in several sources. I depended heavily on two: Roger J. Spiller, "John C. Calhoun as Secretary of War, 1817–1825" (Ph.D. diss., Louisiana State University, 1977), and Skelton, *American Profession of Arms.*

14. Secretary of War to House Military Committee, 23 December 1814, Secretary of War Reports to Congress (M220), NA.

15. There are many definitions of professionalism. This comes from Allan R. Millett and Peter Maslowski, *For the Common Defense* (New York: Free Press, 1984), p. 126.

16. Scott was an ideal choice to represent the U.S. Army in Europe. See Dallas to Scott 16 and 19 June 1815, Secretary of War Confidential Letters Sent (M7), NA. For congressional concern with tactical doctrine, see Secretary of War to House of Representatives, 22 November 1814, Secretary of War Reports to Congress (M220), NA.

BIBLIOGRAPHY

Primary Sources

MANUSCRIPT COLLECTIONS

Public Archives of Canada
  Manuscript Group 24

Archives of Ontario
  Niagara Historical Society Papers

National Library of Scotland
  George Hay Papers

Buffalo and Erie County Historical Society
  Brown and Scott Papers
  Goodyear Collection
  George Howard Papers
  Peter B. Porter Papers

Library of Congress
  Jacob Brown Papers
  Henry Dearborn Papers
  Thomas Jefferson Papers
  Thomas S. Jesup Papers
  James Madison Papers
  John McNeil Papers
  James Monroe Papers
  Winfield Scott Papers

Clements Library, University of Michigan
Collection of Jacob Brown and Winfield Scott

National Archives
M6   Secretary of War Letters Sent
M7   Secretary of War Confidential and Unofficial Letters Sent
M41   Peter B. Porter Papers
M127   Secretary of War Letters Sent to the President
M220   Secretary of War Reports to Congress
M221   Secretary of War Letters Received, Registered Series
M565   Adjutant General Letters Sent
M566   Adjutant General Letters Received
M711   Adjutant General Register of Letters Sent

DOCUMENTARY SOURCES

American State Papers: Foreign Relations. 6 vols. Washington, D.C.: Gales and Seaton, 1833–1859.

American State Papers: Indian Affairs. 2 vols. Washington, D.C.: Gales and Seaton, 1832–1834.

American State Papers: Military Affairs. 7 vols. Washington, D.C.: Gales and Seaton, 1832–1861.

Annals of Congress: Debates and Proceedings in the Congress of the United States, 1789–1824. 42 vols. Washington, D.C.: n.p., 1834–1856.

Armstrong, John. *Notices of the War of 1812.* 2 vols. New York: Wiley and Putnam, 1840.

Cooling, Benjamin F., ed. *The New American State Papers: Military Affairs.* 19 vols. Wilmington, Del.: Scholarly Resources, 1979.

Cruikshank, Ernest A., ed. *Documentary History of the Campaign on the Niagara Frontier.* Welland, Ontario: Lundy's Lane Historical Society, 1896.

———. The Documentary History of the Campaign upon the Niagara Frontier. 9 vols. Welland, Ontario: Lundy's Lane Historical Society, 1902–1908.

Dudley, William S., and Michael J. Crawford, eds. *The Naval War of 1812, Documentary History.* Washington, D.C.: U.S. Government Printing Office, 1985.

Izard, George. *Official Correspondence with the Department of War.* Philadelphia: Thomas Dobson, 1816.

Public Papers of Daniel D. Tompkins: 1807–1817 (Military). 3 vols. New York: Wynkoop, Hollenbeck, Crawford, 1898.

Supplementary Despatches, Correspondence and Memoranda of Field Marshal Arthur, Duke of Wellington. 15 vols. London: John Murray, 1862.

Wood, William, ed. *Select British Documents of the Canadian War of 1812.* 3 vols. Toronto: Champlain Society, 1920–1928.

BOOKS

Dunlop, William. *Recollections of the War of 1812.* Toronto: Historical Publishing Company, 1908.

Ellery, Harrison, ed. *The Memoirs of General Joseph Gardner Swift.* Worcester, Mass.: F. S. Blanchard, 1890.

Fenton, James. *Journal of the Military Tour by the Pennsylvania Troops and Militia under the Command of Colonel James Fenton, to the Frontiers of Pennsylvania and New York.* Carlisle, Pa.: George Kline, 1814.

Gellner, John, ed. *Recollections of the War of 1812: Three Eyewitness Accounts.* Toronto: Baxter, 1964.

Graves, Donald E., ed. *Merry Hearts Make Light Days: The War of 1812 Journal of Lieutenant John LeCouteur, 104th Foot.* Ottawa: Carleton University Press, 1993.

————. *Soldiers of 1814: American Enlisted Men's Memoirs of the Niagara Campaign.* Youngstown, N.Y.: Old Fort Niagara Association, 1995.

Hopkins, James F., and Mary W. M. Hargreaves, eds. *The Papers of Henry Clay.* 5 vols. Lexington: University of Kentucky Press, 1959–1973.

Norton, John. *The Journal of Major John Norton.* Edited by Carl F. Klinck and James J. Talman. Toronto: Champlain Society, 1970.

Richardson, James D., ed. *A Compilation of the Messages and Papers of the Presidents, 1789–1897.* 10 vols. Washington, D.C.: U.S. Government Printing Office, 1909.

Scott, Winfield. *Memoirs of Lieutenant General Scott.* 2 vols. New York: Sheldon, 1864.

Smith, Michael. *A Geographical View of the Peninsula of Upper Canada and Promiscuous Remarks upon the Government.* Hartford, Conn.: n.p., 1813.

White, Samuel. *History of the American Troops during the Late War, under the Command of Colonels Fenton and Campbell.* Baltimore: B. Edes, 1830.

The Writings of George Washington. 39 vols. Washington, D.C.: U.S. Government Printing Office, 1931–1940.

ARTICLES

Archer, Mary R., ed. "The Journal of Major Isaac Roach." *Pennsylvania Magazine of History and Biography* 17 (1893): 129–58, 281–315.

Brady, Hugh. "A Biographical Sketch of General Hugh Brady by Himself." *Pioneer Society of Michigan* 3 (1903): 84–92.

Crombie, John N., ed. "The Papers of Major Daniel McFarland." *Western Pennsylvania Historical Magazine* 51 (April 1968): 101–25.

Douglass, David B. "Reminiscences of the Campaign of 1814 on the Niagara Frontier." *Historical Magazine* 1–4 (July–October 1873).

Efner, Elijah D. "The Adventures and Enterprises of Elijah D. Efner." *Buffalo Historical Society Publications* 4 (1896): 34–54.

Fredriksen, John C., ed. "Chronicle of Valor: The Journal of a Pennsylvania Officer in the War of 1812." *Western Pennsylvania Historical Magazine* 67 (July 1984): 243–84.

————. "Memoirs of Captain Ephraim Shaler: A Connecticut Yankee in the War of 1812." *New England Quarterly* 57 (1984): 411–20.

————. "A Poor but Honest Sodger: Colonel Cromwell Pearce 16th U.S. Infantry and the War of 1812." *Pennsylvania History* 52 (July 1985): 131–61.

————. "The War of 1812 in Northern New York: The Observations of Captain Rufus McIntire." *New York History* 68 (July 1987): 297–324.

Hall, Amos. "Militia Service of 1813–1814." *Buffalo Historical Society Publications* 5 (1902): 26–62.

Harmon, Jesse Perse. "War of 1812: Experiences of Jesse Perse Harmon." *Vermont Quarterly* 21 (January 1953): 48–51.

Harris, Samuel D. "Services of Captain Samuel D. Harris." *Buffalo Historical Society Publications* 24 (1920): 327–42.

Hay, George. "Recollections of the War of 1812." *American Historical Review* 32 (1927): 69–78.

Howard, Florence, and Mary Howard, eds. "Letters of John Patterson, 1812–1813." *Western Pennsylvania Historical Magazine* 23 (June 1940): 99–101.

Howe, Eber D. "Recollections of a Pioneer Printer." *Buffalo Historical Society Publications* 9 (1906): 377–406.

Jesup, Thomas. "Who Captured General Riall?" *Historical Magazine* 8 (July 1870): 54–55.

Lord, Norman C., ed. "The War on the Canadian Frontier, 1812–1814: Letters Written by Sergeant James Commins, Eighth Foot." *Journal of the Society for Army Historical Research* 18 (winter 1939): 199–211.

Parker, Wilmond W., ed. "Letters of the War of 1812 in the Champlain Valley." *Vermont Quarterly* 12 (April 1944): 104–24.

Ryan, Harold W. "Daniel Bissell—His Story." *Missouri Historical Society Review* 12 (October 1955): 32–44.

Shriver, Phillip R., ed. "Broken Locks and Rusty Barrels: A New York Militia Company on the Eve of the War of 1812" [Memoirs of Henry Leavitt Elsworth]. *New York History* 67 (July 1986): 353–57.

Smith, Charles C., ed. "Memoirs of Thomas Aspinwall." *Proceedings of the Massachusetts Historical Society* 7 (November 1891): 30–38.

Smith, Lester W., ed. "A Drummer Boy in the War of 1812: Memoirs of Jarvis Frary Hanks." *Niagara Frontier* 7 (summer 1960): 53–62.

Walker, Joseph E., ed. "A Soldier's Diary for 1814." *Pennsylvania History* 12 (October 1945): 292–303.

Warren, Asa. "Two Dramatic Incidents." *Buffalo Historical Society Publications* 5 (1902): 61–62.

NEWSPAPERS

Buffalo Gazette
Connecticut Courant (Hartford)
Kingston Gazette (Upper Canada)
Niles' Register (Baltimore)
Montreal Courant
Montreal Gazette
Ontario Messenger (Canandaigua, N.Y.)
Quebec Gazette
The Reporter (Lexington, Ky.)

Secondary Sources

BOOKS

Adams, Henry. *History of the United States during the Administrations of Jefferson and Madison.* 9 vols. New York: Charles Scribner's Sons, 1931.
Altoff, Gerard T. *Deep Water Sailors and Shallow Water Soldiers.* Put-in-Bay, Ohio: Perry Group, 1993.
Babcock, Louis L. *The War of 1812 on the Niagara Frontier.* Buffalo, N.Y.: Buffalo Historical Society, 1927.
Baylies, Nicholas. *Eleazar Wheelock Ripley.* Des Moines, Iowa: Brewster, 1890.
Beirne, Francis F. *The War of 1812.* New York: E. P. Dutton, 1949.
Benn, Carl. *The Battle of York.* Belleville, Ontario: Mika Publishing, 1984.
Berton, Pierre. *Flames across the Border.* Boston: Little, Brown, 1981.
———. *The Invasion of Canada, 1812–1813.* Boston: Little, Brown, 1980.
Bowler, R. Arthur, ed. *War along the Niagara: Essays on the War of 1812 and Its Legacy.* Youngstown, N.Y.: Old Fort Niagara Association, 1991.
Brant, Irving. *James Madison Commander in Chief, 1812–1836.* Indianapolis: Bobbs-Merrill, 1961.
Burt, A. L. *The United States, Great Britain and British North America: From the Revolution to the Establishment of Peace after the War of 1812.* 1940. Reprint, New York: Russell and Russell, 1961.
Chartrand, Rene. *Uniforms and Equipment of the United States Forces in the War of 1812.* Youngstown, N.Y.: Old Fort Niagara Association, 1992.
Clary, David A., and Joseph W. A. Whitehorne. *The Inspectors General of the United States Army, 1770–1903.* Washington, D.C.: Center for Military History, 1987.
Cogar, William B., ed. *New Interpretations in Naval History.* Annapolis, Md.: Naval Institute Press, 1989.
Cruikshank, Ernest A. *The Battle of Fort George.* 1896. Reprint, Niagara-on-the-Lake, Ontario: Niagara Historical Society, 1990.
Dillon, Richard. *We Have Met the Enemy.* New York: McGraw-Hill, 1978.
Dobbins, W. W. *History of the Battle of Lake Erie.* 2d ed. Erie, Pa.: Ashby, 1913.
Duane, William. *The American Military Dictionary.* Philadelphia: William Duane, 1810.
Dunnigan, Brian Leigh. *The British Army at Mackinac, 1812–1815.* Mackinac Island State Park Commission, 1980.
———. *Forts within a Fort: Niagara's Redoubts.* Youngstown, N.Y.: Old Fort Niagara Association, 1989.
———. *A History and Guide to Old Fort Niagara.* Youngstown, N.Y.: Old Fort Niagara Association, 1985.
Eisenhower, John S. D. *Agent of Destiny: The Life and Times of General Winfield Scott.* New York: Free Press, 1997.
Elliott, Charles Winslow. *Winfield Scott: The Soldier and the Man.* New York: Macmillan, 1937.
Elting, John R., ed. *Military Uniforms in America.* 3 vols. San Rafael, Calif.: Presidio Press, 1977.

Ermatinger, Edward. *Life of Colonel Talbot and the Talbot Settlement.* St. Thomas, Ontario: A. McLachlin's Home Journal Office, 1859. Reprint, Belleville, Ontario: Mika Silk Screening, 1972.

Everest, Allan S. *The War of 1812 in the Champlain Valley.* Syracuse, N.Y.: Syracuse University Press, 1981.

Fitzgibbon, Mary Agnes. *A Veteran of 1812: The Life of James Fitzgibbon.* Toronto: William Briggs, 1894.

Fortescue, J. W. *A History of the British Army.* 10 vols. London: Macmillan, 1920.

Fredriksen, John C. *Officers of the War of 1812.* Lewiston, N.Y.: Edwin Mellen Press, 1989.

Fryer, Mary Beacock. *Battlefields of Canada.* Toronto: Dundurn Press, 1986.

Gilpin, Alec R. *The War of 1812 in the Old Northwest.* East Lansing: Michigan State University Press, 1958.

Graves, Donald E. *The Battle of Lundy's Lane.* Baltimore: Nautical and Aviation Publishing, 1993.

———. *Fields of Glory: The Battle of Crysler's Farm, 1813.* Toronto: Robin Brass Studio, 1999.

———. *Red Coats and Grey Jackets: The Battle of Chippawa.* Toronto: Dundurn Press, 1994.

———. *Where Right and Glory Lead: The Battle of Lundy's Lane, 1814.* Toronto: Robin Brass Studio, 1997.

Green, Ernest. *Lincoln at Bay: A Sketch of 1814.* Welland, Ontario: Tribune-Telegraph Press, 1923.

Guitard, Michelle. *The Militia of the Battle of the Chateauguay: A Social History.* Ottawa: Parks Canada, 1983.

Hannay, James. *History of the War of 1812.* Toronto: Morang, 1905.

Heitman, Francis B. *Historical Register and Dictionary of the U.S. Army, 1789–1903.* 2 vols. Washington, D.C.: U.S. Government Printing Office, 1903.

Heller, Charles E., and William A. Stofft, eds. *America's First Battles.* Lawrence: University Press of Kansas, 1986.

Hickey, Donald R. *The War of 1812: A Forgotten Conflict.* Urbana: University of Illinois Press, 1989.

Historical Collections: Collections and Researches Made by the Michigan Pioneer and Historical Society. Lansing, Mich.: Wyncoop, Hallenbeck, Crawford, 1909.

Hitsman, J. Mackay. *The Incredible War of 1812: A Military History.* Toronto: University of Toronto Press, 1965.

———. *Safeguarding Canada, 1763–1871.* Toronto: University of Toronto Press, 1968.

Horsman, Reginald. *The Causes of the War of 1812.* Philadelphia: University of Pennsylvania Press, 1962.

Howard, Robert West. *Thundergate: The Forts of Niagara.* Englewood Cliffs, N.J.: Prentice-Hall, 1968.

Irving, L. Homfray. *Officers of the British Forces in Canada during the War of 1812–15.* Welland, Ontario: Welland Tribune Print, 1908.

Jacobs, James Ripley, and Glenn Tucker. *The War of 1812: A Compact History.* New York: Hawthorn Books, 1969.

Johnson, Crisfield. *History of Erie County, New York.* Buffalo, N.Y.: Matthews and Warren, 1876.

Johnson, Timothy D. *Winfield Scott: The Quest for Military Glory.* Lawrence: University Press of Kansas, 1998.

Kieffer, Chester L. *Maligned General: The Biography of Thomas Sidney Jesup.* San Rafael, Calif.: Presidio, 1979.

Kirby, William. *Annals of Niagara.* 2d ed. Toronto: Macmillan of Canada, 1927.

Landon, Fred. *Western Ontario and the American Frontier.* Toronto: Ryerson Press, 1941.

Landon, Harry F. *Bugles on the Border: The Story of the War of 1812 in Northern New York.* Watertown, N.Y.: *Watertown Daily Times,* 1954.

Latham, Frank B. *Jacob Brown and the War of 1812.* New York: Cowles, 1971.

Litt, Paul, Ronald F. Williamson, and Joseph A. Whitehorne. *Death at Snake Hill: Secrets from a War of 1812 Cemetery.* Toronto: Dundurn Press, 1993.

Lossing, Benson. *The Pictorial Fieldbook of the War of 1812.* New York: Harper and Brothers, 1868. Reprint, Somersworth, N.H.: New Hampshire Publishing Company, 1976.

Mahan, Alfred T. *Sea Power and Its Relations to the War of 1812.* 2 vols. Boston: Little, Brown, 1905.

Mahon, John K. *The War of 1812.* Gainesville: University Presses of Florida, 1972.

Malcomson, Robert. *Lords of the Lake: The Naval War on Lake Ontario, 1812–1814.* Annapolis, Md.: Naval Institute Press, 1998.

Malcomson, Robert, and Thomas Malcomson. *HMS Detroit: The Battle for Lake Erie.* St. Catherines, Ontario: Vanwell, 1990.

Mansfield, Edward D. *The Life of General Winfield Scott.* New York: A. S. Barnes, 1848.

Mason, Philip P., ed. *After Tippecanoe: Some Aspects of the War of 1812.* East Lansing: Michigan State University Press, 1963.

McAfee, Robert B. *History of the Late War in the Western Country.* 1816. Reprint, Bowling Green, Ohio: Historical Publishing Company, 1919.

Millett, Allan R., and Peter Maslowski. *For the Common Defense.* New York: Free Press, 1984.

Owen, David A. *Fort Erie (1764–1823): An Historical Guide.* Niagara Falls, Ontario: Niagara Parks Commission, 1986.

Powell, E. Alexander. *Gentlemen Rovers.* New York: Charles Scribner's Sons, 1913.

Pratt, Julius W. *Expansionists of 1812.* Gloucester, Mass.: Peter Smith, 1957.

Quimby, Robert S. *The U.S. Army in the War of 1812: An Operational and Command Study.* East Lansing: Michigan State Press, 1997.

Risch, Erna. *Quartermaster Support of the Army: A History of the Corps, 1775–1939.* Washington, D.C.: U.S. Government Printing Office, 1962.

Rogers, Robert Louis. *History of the Lincoln and Welland Regiment.* Ottawa: privately printed, 1954.

Sapio, Victor. *Pennsylvania and the War of 1812.* Lexington: University Press of Kentucky, 1970.

Silver, James W. *Edmund Pendleton Gaines: Frontier General.* New Orleans: Louisiana State University Press, 1949.

Skaggs, David C., and Gerard T. Altoff. *A Signal Victory: The Lake Erie Campaign, 1812–1813.* Annapolis, Md.: Naval Institute Press, 1997.

Skeen, C. Edward. *Citizen Soldiers in the War of 1812.* Lexington: University Press of Kentucky, 1999.

———. *John Armstrong, Jr. 1758–1843: A Biography.* Syracuse, N.Y.: Syracuse University Press, 1981.

Skelton, William B. *An American Profession of Arms: The Army Officer Corps, 1784–1861.* Lawrence: University Press of Kansas, 1992.

Smith, Arthur D. Howden. *Old Fuss and Feathers.* New York: Greystone Press, 1937.

Spiller, Roger J., ed. *Dictionary of American Military Biography.* Westport, Conn.: Greenwood Press, 1984.

Stagg, J. C. A. *Mr. Madison's War.* Princeton, N.J.: Princeton University Press, 1983.

Stanley, George F. G. *Battle in the Dark: Stoney Creek, June 6, 1813.* Toronto: Balmuir, 1991.

———. *Canada Invaded: 1775–1776.* Canadian War Museum Series, Historical Publications Number 8. Toronto: Samuel Stevens Hakkert, 1977.

———. *The War of 1812: Land Operations.* Toronto: Macmillan of Canada, 1983.

Sugden, John. *Tecumseh's Last Stand.* Norman: University of Oklahoma Press, 1985.

Suthren, Victor. *Defend and Hold: The Battle of Chateauguay.* Canadian Battle Series. Ottawa: Balmuir, n.d.

Thian, Raphael P. *Notes Illustrating the Military Geography of the United States.* Washington, D.C.: U.S. Government Printing Office, 1881. Reprint, Austin: University of Texas Press, 1979.

Turner, Wesley B. *British Generals in the War of 1812: High Command in the Canadas.* Montreal and Kingston: McGill-Queens University Press, 1999.

———. *The Military in the Niagara Peninsula.* St. Catherines, Ontario: Vanwell Publishing, 1990.

———. *The War of 1812: The War that Both Sides Won.* Toronto and Oxford: Dundurn Press, 1990.

Updyke, Frank A. *The Diplomacy of the War of 1812.* Baltimore: Johns Hopkins University Press, 1915.

Way, Ronald L. *The Day of Crysler's Farm.* N.p.: Ontario–St. Lawrence Development Commission, n.d.

Welsh, William J., and David C. Skaggs, eds. *War on the Great Lakes: Essays Commemorating the 175th Anniversary of the Battle of Lake Erie.* Kent, Ohio: Kent State University Press, 1991.

White, Patrick C. T. *A Nation on Trial: America and the War of 1812.* New York: John Wiley and Sons, 1965.

Whitehorne, Joseph A. *While Washington Burned: The Battle for Fort Erie, 1814.* Baltimore: Nautical and Aviation Publishing Company of America, 1992.

Wohler, J. Patrick. *Charles de Salaberry.* Toronto: Dundurn Press, 1984.

Wright, Marcus J. *General Scott.* New York: D. Appleton, 1894.

Zaslow, Morris, ed. *The Defended Border.* Toronto: Macmillan, 1964.

ARTICLES

Altoff, Gerry T. "Oliver Hazard Perry and the Battle of Lake Erie." *Michigan Historical Review* 14 (fall 1988): 25–57.

Archer, George W. "George Edward Mitchell, Physician and Soldier." *Military Surgeon* 88 (June 1941): 670–73.

Atkinson, C. T. "Foreign Regiments in the British Army, 1793–1802." *Journal of the Society for Army Historical Research* 22 (1943–1944): 265–66.

Bird, William A. "The Sortie from Fort Erie." *Buffalo Historical Society Publications* 5 (1902): 95–98.

Brady, William Y. "The 22nd Regiment in the War of 1812." *Western Pennsylvania Historical Magazine* 32 (March–June 1949): 56–60.

Carr, James A. "Climax at Lake Champlain." *National Defense* (November–December 1978): 59–92.

Chartrand, Rene. "The U.S. Army's Uniform Supply 'Crisis' during the War of 1812." *Military Collector and Historian* 40 (summer 1988): 63–65.

Colquhoun, A. H. U. "The Career of Joseph Willcocks." *Canadian Historical Review* 7 (December 1926): 287–93.

Corning, Charles R. "General Eleazar Wheelock Ripley." *Granite Monthly* 17 (July 1894): 1–13.

Crombie, John Newell. "The Twenty-second U.S. Infantry." *Western Pennsylvania Historical Magazine* 60 (1967): 133–47, 221–36.

Cruikshank, Ernest A. "The Contest for the Command of Lake Ontario in 1814." *Ontario Historical Society Papers and Records* 21 (1924): 99–159.

———. "The County of Norfolk in the War of 1812." *Ontario Historical Society Papers and Records* 20 (1923): 9–40.

Doan, Daniel. "The Enigmatic Moody Bedel." *Historical New Hampshire* 25 (fall 1970): 27–36.

Dorsheimer, William. "The Village of Buffalo during the War of 1812." *Buffalo Historical Society Publications* 1 (1879): 185–209.

Douglas, R. Alan. "Weapons of the War of 1812." *Michigan History* 47 (1963): 321–26.

Dudley, William S. "Naval Historians and the War of 1812." *Naval History* 4 (spring 1990): 52–57.

Egan, Clifford L. "The Origins of the War of 1812: Three Decades of Historical Writing." *Military Affairs* (April 1974): 72–75.

Elliott, Charles W. "The Indispensable Conquest." *Infantry Journal* 45 (July–August 1938): 334–42.

Errington, Jane, and George Rawlyk. "The Loyalist-Federalist Alliance of Upper Canada." *American Review of Canadian Studies* 14 (summer 1984): 157–76.

Fredriksen, John C. "A Tempered Sword, Untested: The Military Career of General George Izard." *Journal of America's Military Past* 25 (winter 1999): 5–16.

Gero, Anthony. "American Deserter Notices in the Northern Theater, 1813–1815." *Military Collector and Historian* 38 (summer 1986): 72–73.

———. "Some Notes on New York's Black Regiments, 1814 to 1815." *Military Collector and Historian* 31 (spring 1979): 36.

Goodman, Warren H. "The War of 1812: A Survey of Changing Interpretations." *Mississippi Valley Historical Review* 28 (September 1941): 171–86.

Gosling, D. C. L. "The Battle at La Colle Mill, 1814." *Journal of the Society for Army Historical Research* 47 (1969): 169–74.

Graves, Donald E. "The Canadian Volunteers." *Military Collector and Historian* 31 (fall 1979): 113–17.

———. "Dry Books of Tactics: U.S. Infantry Manuals of the War of 1812 and After." *Military Collector and Historian* 38 (summer 1986): 50–61 and (winter 1986): 173–77.

———. "William Drumond and the Battle for Fort Erie." *Canadian Military History* 1 (1992): 25–43.

Hacker, Louis M. "Western Land Hunger and the War of 1812." *Mississippi Valley Historical Review* 10 (March 1924): 365–95.

Hagen, Fred E. "Thomas Sydney Jesup." *Quartermaster Review* 11 (September–October 1931): 44–47.

Hall, James. "Biographical Sketch of Major Thomas Biddle." *Illinois Monthly Magazine* 2 (September 1831): 549–61.

Hallahan, John M. "No Doubt Blamable: The Transformation of Captain Winfield Scott." *Virginia Cavalcade* 40 (spring 1991): 160–71.

Hamilton, Edward P. "The Battle of Plattsburg." *Vermont History* 31 (1963): 94–105.

Hare, John S. "Military Punishments in the War of 1812." *Journal of the American Military Institute* 4 (1940): 225–39.

Heller, Charles E. "Those Are Regulars by God." *Army* (January 1987): 52–54.

Henderson, Robert. "His Majesty's Canadian Regiment of Fencible Infantry, 1803–16." *Military Illustrated Past and Present* 38 (July 1991): 27–33.

Hicks, James E. "United States Military Shoulder Arms, 1795–1935." *Journal of the American Military History Foundation* 1 (spring 1937): 22–33.

Hitsman, J. Mackay. "Glengarry Light Infantry Fencibles." *Journal of the Society for Army Historical Research* 34 (1956): 139.

———. "Sir George Prevost's Conduct of the Canadian War of 1812." *Report of the Annual Meeting of the Canadian Historical Association* (1962): 34–43.

Hofschroer, Peter. "Flintlocks in Battle." *Military Illustrated: Past and Present* (June–July 1986): 30–35.

Holden, Robert J. "General James Miller: Collector of the Port of Salem, Massachusetts." *Essex Institute Collections* 104 (October 1968): 283–302.

Hollon, W. E. "Zebulon Montgomery Pike and the York Campaign, 1813." *New York History* 30 (July 1949): 259–75.

Horsman, Reginald. "On to Canada: Manifest Destiny and the United States Strategy in the War of 1812." *Michigan Historical Review* 13 (fall 1987): 12–18, 21–22.

———. "The Paradox of Dartmoor Prison." *American Heritage* 26 (February 1975): 13–85.

Hughes, B. P. "Siege Artillery in the 19th Century." *Journal of the Society for Army Historical Research* 60 (autumn 1982): 129–49.

Johnson, Timothy D. "Lundy's Lane: Winfield Scott's Blunder to Glory." *Military History Quarterly* 8 (autumn 1995): 78–87.

Jones, Wilbur D., ed. "A British View of the War of 1812 and Peace Negotiations." *Mississippi Valley Historical Review* 45 (1958): 481–87.

Kerby, Robert L. "The Militia System and the State Militias in the War of 1812." *Indiana Magazine of History* 73 (1977): 102–24.

Kerr, W. B. "The Occupation of York (Toronto), 1813." *Canadian Historical Review* 5 (1924): 9–21.

Kimball, Jeffrey. "The Battle of Chippawa: Infantry Tactics in the War of 1812." *Military Affairs* 32 (winter 1967–1968): 169–86.

Leslie, J. H. "Chrysler's Farm." *Journal of the Royal Artillery* 63 (July 1936): 189–99.

Lewis, Howard T. "A Re-analysis of the Causes of the War of 1812." *Americana* 6 (1911): 506–16, 577–85.

Lohnes, Barry J. "A New Look at the Invasion of Eastern Maine, 1814." *Maine Historical Society Quarterly* 15 (summer 1975): 4–29.

MacLeod, Malcolm. "Fortress Ontario or Forlorn Hope? Simcoe and the Defence of Upper Canada." *Canadian Historical Review* 53 (June 1972): 149–78.

Martin, John D. P. "The Regiment De Watteville: Its Settlement and Service in Upper Canada." *Ontario History* 52 (March 1960): 17–30.

Maurigault, G. E. "General George Izard's Military Career: A Reply to Mr. Henry Adams." *Magazine of American History* 26 (December 1891): 457–62.

———. "The Military Career of General George Izard." *Magazine of American History* 19 (June 1888): 463–78.

McKee, Marguerite. "Service of Supply in the War of 1812." *Quartermaster Review* 6 (March–April 1927): 45–55.

Mills, Dudley. "The Duke of Wellington and the Peace Negotiations at Ghent in 1814." *Canadian Historical Review* 2 (March 1921): 19–32.

Montross, Lynn. "America's Most Imitated Battle." *American Heritage* 7 (April 1956): 37–101.

"Obituary of Jacob Schmuck." *Army and Navy Chronicle* 1 (May 1835): 159.

Parker, Arthur C. "The Senecas in the War of 1812." *New York State Historical Association Proceedings* 15 (1916): 78–90.

Patterson, William J. "A Forgotten Hero in a Forgotten War." *Journal of the Society for Army Historical Research* 68 (spring 1990): 7–21.

Pratt, Fletcher. "Sword of the Border." *Infantry Journal* 44 (September–October 1937): 387–93.

Riddell, William R. "The Ancaster 'Bloody Assize' of 1814." *Ontario Historical Society Papers and Records* 20 (1923): 107–25.

Schneider, David H. "Grey Uniforms of the Niagara: Winfield Scott's Infantry Brigade, 1814." *Military Collector and Historian* 33 (winter 1981): 170–72.

Severance, Frank H. "The Case of Alexander Smyth." *Buffalo Historical Society Publications* 18 (1914): 214–55.

———. "Service of Captain Samuel D. Harris." *Buffalo Historical Society Publications* 24 (1920): 327–42.

Sheppard, George. "Deeds Speak: Militiamen, Medals, and the Invented Traditions." *Ontario History* 83 (September 1990): 207–32.

"Siege of Fort Erie, August 1814." *U.S. Military Magazine* 2 (March 1841): 65–72.

Skelton, William B. "High Army Leadership in the Era of the War of 1812: The Making and Remaking of the Officer Corps." *William and Mary Quarterly* 51 (April 1994): 253–74.

Smith, Derek. "Frontier Armageddon at Bloody Fort Mims." *Army* 40 (January 1990): 44–50.

Stacey, C. P. "An American Plan for a Canadian Campaign." *American Historical Review* 46 (January 1941): 348–57.

———. "Another Look at the Battle of Lake Erie." *Canadian Historical Review* 34 (March 1958): 41–51.

Stagg, J. C. A. "Enlisted Men in the United States Army, 1812–1815." *William and Mary Quarterly* 43 (October 1986): 615–45.

———. "James Madison and the 'Malcontents': The Political Origins of the War of 1812." *William and Mary Quarterly* 33 (October 1976): 557–85.

Stanley, George F. G. "British Operations in the American North-West, 1812–15." *Journal of the Society for Army Historical Research* 22 (1943–1944): 91–106.

———. "British Operations on the Penobscot in 1814." *Journal of the Society for Army Historical Research* 19 (1940): 168–78.

———. "The Canadian Militia during the Colonial Period." *Journal of the Society for Army Historical Research* 24 (1946): 30–41.

———. "The New Brunswick Fencibles." *Canadian Defence Quarterly* 16 (October 1938): 39–53.

———. "The Significance of the Six Nations Participation in the War of 1812." *Ontario History* 55 (1963): 215–31.

Steppler, Glenn A. "British Military Artificers in Canada, 1760–1815." *Journal of the Society for Army Historical Research* 60 (autumn 1982): 150–63.

———. "Logistics on the Canadian Frontier, 1812–1814." *Military Collector and Historian* 31 (spring 1979): 8–10.

Talbot, George F. "General John Chandler of Monmouth Maine." *Collections of the Maine Historical Society* 9 (1887): 169–205.

UNPUBLISHED WORKS

Fredriksen, John C. "Niagara, 1814: The United States Army Quest for Tactical Parity in the War of 1812 and its Legacy." Ph.D. diss., Providence College, 1993.

Glenney, Daniel J. "An Ethnohistory of the Grand River Iroquois and the War of 1812." Master's thesis, University of Guelph, 1973.

Kimball, Jeffrey. "Strategy on the Northern Frontier: 1814." Ph.D. diss., Louisiana State University, 1969.

Spiller, Roger J. "John C. Calhoun as Secretary of War, 1817–1825." Ph.D. diss., Louisiana State University, 1977.

Steppler, Glenn A. "A Duty Troublesome beyond Measure." Master's thesis, McGill University, 1974.

Stewart, Charles H. *The Service of British Regiments in Canada and North America.* 2d ed. Ottawa: Department of Defence Library, 1964.

INDEX

Wilkinson, James, *continued*
  Ninth Military District and, 81
  Northern Army of, 33
  offensive by, 34, 104
  relief of, 111
  at Sacketts Harbor, 86
  at St. Lawrence, 109
Willcocks, Joseph, 98, 121, 122, 143, 191, 196
  Canadian Volunteers and, 52, 97
  at Fort Erie, 272
  at Lundy's Lane, 223
Williams, Alexander J.
  death of, 251
  at Fort Erie, 249, 251
Willson, Mrs., 213, 230
Willson's Tavern, 211, 212
Winder, William H., 66, 67, 68, 78, 79, 130, 159, 160
  Armstrong and, 261
  Baltimore defense and, 270
  at Bladensburg, 267
  capture of, 83
  Izard and, 302
Wood, Eleazar, 154, 172, 194, 196, 234, 250, 276, 279, 314
  British defenses and, 164
  at Chippawa, 178
  death of, 278
  at Fort Erie, 272, 275
  scouting by, 184
Wood, Thomas, 223, 228

Wool, John E., 61, 63
Woolsey, Melancthon, 158
Worth, William Jenkins, 190, 329, 358n62

Yates, John B., 259
  militia and, 265
Yeo, Sir James Lucas, 32, 33, 79, 101, 102, 112, 114
  arms race and, 144
  Barclay and, 104
  blockade by, 258, 316
  at Burlington Bay, 84
  Chauncey and, 84, 85, 108, 146, 152, 153, 191, 243, 258
  command for, 77
  Drummond and, 194, 302
  at Fort Niagara, 301
  at Kingston, 145
  at Niagara River, 295–96
  at Sacketts Harbor, 76–77, 78, 145, 347n31, 360n90
  short-range fighting and, 103
  St. Lawrence and, 200, 283, 289
  strategy and, 146, 312
York, 47, 48, 141
  attacking, 72, 73–75, 82–83, 92, 94, 96, 101, 116, 151
  fall of, 99
  harbor at, 41
  population of, 337n16
Young King, wounding of, 82